DEBT OF HONOUR

DEBT OF HONOUR
Winchester City's First World War Dead

incorporating notes and appendices, including a reprint of the
Winchester War Service Register
of those from the city who served

JEN BEST

edited, with an Introduction by

TOM BEAUMONT JAMES

HOBNOB PRESS
2018

First published in the United Kingdom in 2018

by The Hobnob Press,
8 Lock Warehouse, Severn Road, Gloucester GL1 2GA
www.hobnobpress.co.uk

© Jen Best and Tom Beaumont James, 2018

The Authors hereby assert their moral rights to be identified as the Authors of the Work.

All rights reserved. No part of this publication may be reproduced, stored in a retrieval system, or transmitted in any form or by any means, electronic, mechanical, photocopying, recording or otherwise, without the prior permission of the publisher and copyright holder.

British Library Cataloguing in Publication Data
A catalogue record for this book is available from the British Library

ISBN   978-1-906978-65-5 (paperback)
       978-1-906978-66-2 (hardback)

Typeset in Doves Type, Bookman Old Style and Adobe Caslon.
Typesetting and origination by John Chandler

Printed by Lightning Source

Illustrations
Cover: Sergeant Charles Russell of the Hampshire Regiment. Died 17 November 1918. (See Appendix 3). Source: Private Collection.

Back Cover: Winchester Fallen engraved on the west face of The Hampshire Regiment Memorial Cross, The Close. Photograph: Barry Best.

Frontispiece: Contemporary postcard photograph of The Hampshire Regiment Memorial Cross west of the cathedral. By C. E. S. Beloe. By courtesy of Alan Bungey. Private Collection.

CONTENTS

Dedication	vi
Acknowledgements	vii
Introduction	ix
Abbreviations	lv
The Fallen	1
Appendices	225

1	A. Cecil Piper (ed), *Winchester War Service Register. A Record of the Service of Winchester Men in the Great War 1914-1918* (Winchester: Warren and Co. 1921) (*WWSR*)	225
2	The structure of The Hampshire Regiment during the First World War (The Royal Hampshire Regiment Museum)	391
3	Six men in addition to 'Winchester's 459' (Alan Bungey)	394
4	Deaths by Street	397
5	Casualties by Rank etc	402

Select Bibliography	405
The Authors	407

Note: Maps of Winchester will be found on pages 398-400

DEDICATED TO ALL THOSE WHO SUPPORTED
WINCHESTER MEN FROM THE HOME FRONT.

IN PARTICULAR
MRS F. J . BOWKER,
HON. SECRETARY,
HAMPSHIRE PRISONERS OF WAR FUND

ACKNOWLEDGEMENTS

This project arose partly from an undergraduate dissertation by Claire Atkins submitted in 1999 entitled 'A study of military monuments and service in First World War Winchester'.[1]

Since 2009 it has been carried forward by Jen Best who has researched the biographies of the fallen largely on her own giving the project many, many hours in the course of which she has assembled an impressive archive. Naval and army data was checked by Gavin Edgerley-Harris (GJEH), who has saved us from errors, and provided very many invaluable insights into military history of the First World War. At The Hampshire Regiment Museum and Archive, Colin Bulleid and Rachel Holmes checked the data we provided on those from The Hampshire Regiment who gave their lives. Some 200 men, – some 43% of all the deaths from the city - had served in the regiment in some capacity, alhough some 8% were serving with other units when they died. Rachel Holmes's researches are more detailed on the fallen than we have reproduced in this volume, and may be followed up via the Regimental Museum at Serle's House, Southgate Street, Winchester. Likewise Major (Retd) Ken Gray kindly looked through the records of Rifle Regiments for us and supplied additional data. Ian Maine at The Royal Marines Museum at Southsea checked the entries for Marines. Ross Wilson at the University of Chichester kindly read and made very useful comments on a partial draft. Tom Beaumont James has coordinated the project and has contributed to the Introduction and helped check the final text. Any remaining errors are, of course, the responsibility of the authors. Among many others who helped Mark Allen always generously shared his expertise on modern military and Winchester history, and was always a staunch supporter at the University of Winchester and also as Editor of the Winchester Series at the University of Winchester Press. Caroline Scott and her colleagues in the St Bartholomew's, Hyde First World War project

---

[1] Submitted as a final year dissertation for a BA degree in Archaeology and Computing, King Alfred's College, Winchester.

kindly answered queries and provided data on those men they have studied. Chris Grover shared her knowledge of suburban houses. For the fallen of the Diocesan Training College (from 1928 King Alfred's Diocesan Training College, now the University of Winchester) we have drawn on the detailed researches of John Hartley of the Winton Club. A project coordinated by Peter Lidgitt relating to men from the Training College who fell, is now available on line at https://wtcfallen.com. We are most grateful to Steve Jarvis for data on memorials in Winchester, and for many other insights and observations and these are acknowledged in the notes below. We are also grateful for inspiration to press on to the late Christopher Wallace as coordinator of the 1914-2014 projects in Winchester, to the staff of the Hampshire Archive and Local Studies centre, especially Gill Rushton and to Suzanne Foster at the Winchester College Archive.

Our families have been hugely supportive in technical as well as more traditional supportive roles during what has been at times a difficult journey. Publication was set for July 2016 the centenary of the first day of the battle of the Somme, but due to illness from Autumn 2015 the project was unavoidably suspended. It was agreed therefore to limit further research and proceed in late 2018 with the work we had carried out to ensure prompt publication. We apologise for any lacunae arising from this unexpected interruption of the project and hope that what we have achieved finds favour. We are therefore especially grateful to John Chandler who very generously at short notice stepped forward to typeset our work and take production forward.

The preliminaries and introduction are set, appropriately, in Doves Type, a fine Arts & Crafts typeface created by Emery Walker before 1900. Following a dispute with his printer and publisher Walker destroyed the type and its matrices between 1913 and 1917 by throwing them into the River Thames from Hammersmith Bridge. The modern face has been recreated for typesetting from examples of books published using it.

We are grateful to Alan Bungey for the digitised version of the *Winchester War Service Register*.

JB/TBJ
October 2018

INTRODUCTION

THIS VOLUME FOCUSES on the men of the city of Winchester who gave their lives in the First World War. It is not in any sense a history of Winchester during the First World War, although, for example, its contents could be used to reconstruct an overview of where city men gave their lives and died, and from Appendix 1 where they served. It cannot be a history of the First World War in all its theatres. An introduction to this may be found for example in Hew Strachan, *The First World War* (rp. 2014). Neither is it a history of the two main regiments with depots in the city during the war – the Hampshires and the Rifle Brigade. Men with Winchester addresses enlisted and or served in every branch of the services, as the biographies below demonstrate. The nine or so who were killed on the first day of the Somme, 1 July 1916, came from a variety of different units as shown below. Some with Winchester addresses came from overseas. We cannot know their motivations in most cases, though it is reasonable to surmise that the requirements of naval and military deployment, family connections, friendships, personal skills and a desire to get into action were strong early in the war, while conscription drew in more mature family men, for example, later on. In essence it is a work of commemoration.

WHY WINCHESTER?

AS A COMMUNITY Winchester is unusual, but not unique, in that no monument was erected to the city's war dead on which their names were engraved as a group.[1] Reasons for this and a narrative of how that came about is found below. The fallen from the city of Winchester and their lives,

---

[1] Four members of Winchester College, G.M. Bell (30), A.B.K. Cook (99), H.C.H. Gould (172) and L.C. B. Russell (358), were staff and/or boys at Winchester College, included in the *WWSR* as they had Winchester city addresses beyond the College. Their names are carved in the War Cloister at the College. We are grateful to Suzanne Foster for this detail.

war service and sacrifice have descended into obscurity over the century since the outbreak of hostilities in August 1914. There has for some years now been some interest in them. This began with an undergraduate dissertation in 1999 by Claire Atkins at King Alfred's College, now the University of Winchester. Since 2009 it has been carried forward by Jen Best who has compiled a catalogue of the fallen marked as such in the *Winchester War Service Register* (*WWSR*) and has researched the individual dead whose names are marked with a cross in that list, the alphabetical biographical material which is the core of this book. The memorial *WWSR* for the city published in 1921 is, as it turned out, the only place in which the names of these men are recorded as a group. The *WWSR* therefore provides a monument to both those who served and a memorial those who died.[1] Research for this project is concerned only with the latter group: those who are recorded there as having died.

POPULATION, RELIGION AND MILITARY HERITAGE BEFORE THE GREAT WAR

BEFORE THE NORMAN Conquest, Winchester's population is reckoned to have been some 8,000. In 1148 Winchester had 57 parish churches besides monasteries – such as the cathedral priory - and a nunnery. By then royal status was migrating to London, with Winchester becoming an ecclesiastical centre for its wealthy diocese. None the less by around 1300 population is estimated to have been some 11,625. The plague of 1348-50 devastated the city and thereafter the population declined. In 1524 it was only some 3,000, a recovery from previous lows. In the post-medieval period the city encountered religious reorganisation and resulting loss of income, continuing plagues and the abandonment of Wolvesey Palace the residence of the bishop at Winchester by the bishops probably soon after 1700 when they moved to Farnham Castle in Surrey, contributed to a further lowering of the profile of the city. Thus the population remained comparatively low both in terms of its previous population and in terms of wider demographic developments. It was some 4,000 in 1725, but rose later in the century to some 6,000 when census data begins in 1801. It did not recover to overtake the pre-

---

[1] A. Cecil Piper (ed), *Winchester War Service Register. A Record of the Service of Winchester Men in the Great War 1914-1918* (Winchester: Warren and Co. 1921) (*WWSR*). Reprinted here as Appendix 1.

1350 population computed as 11,625 in c 1300 until between 1841 and 1851.¹ These totals were low, and growth slow, compared with general population increase in Britain at that time. In 1901 the population was reckoned at 21,702: in 1911 Winchester had a population of 23,378.

In the early twentieth century there was only a handful of churches and chapels within the historic walled area and a number in the suburbs where the population was expanding. It was in these, and other places of worship, that the names of those from the city who gave their lives are generally to be found although their names were not engraved into stone. Locally within the city many, though not all, were recorded in churches and chapels and on some secular memorials. Anglican churches included St Lawrence north-west of the cathedral, St Maurice in the High Street largely rebuilt in the nineteenth century, and two nineteenth century new churches Holy Trinity (1851-4) and St Thomas's (1857). Beyond the line of the walls some ancient churches survived: St John the Baptist and St Peter Chesil in the eastern suburb; St Michael to the south and St Cross Hospital (substituted for the parish church of St Faith demolished in 1507). St Bartholomew's, Hyde, lay to the north, St Matthew's in Weeke, and Winnal was a village church north-east of the city. In the growing suburbs new churches had been provided: Christ Church to the south, All Saints at Highcliffe and St Paul's.

These Anglican town churches were supplemented, and in some cases preceded, by the eighteenth-century Catholic Milner Chapel in St Peter Street. St Peter's Catholic Church dates from 1926. No memorial is found either in the Roman Catholic Milner Hall (Chapel) or its adjacent successor St Peter's, nor does any such list survive in the church's archive. It is believed that some fifteen members of the Roman Catholic congregation gave their lives.² Nonconformist places of worship with memorials included the United

---

1   These population figures and those below assembled in T.B.James 'The Population of Winchester over 2,000 Years: a survey' *Hampshire Field Club and Archaeological Society, Section Newsletters*, New Series, No. 9 Spring 1988, pp. 1-3.
2   John Thornhill the St Peter's Archivist kindly supplied the following information. A list of dead entitled 'Names below' is no longer extant there. An embryonic list of subscribers towards a remembrance cross for the fallen is headed 'Mrs Smith 2, Westgate Lane – 5s –' but no other names are appended. Serjeant Robert W. Smith (385) of the Rifle Brigade was entered in the *WWSR* as of 2, Westgate Lane and noted as having given his life (see below and also TNA WO 372/18/169314). No cross seems to have been erected. The issue of religious ownership of memorialisation is not a major theme of our work:

Reformed Church in Jewry Street, the Wesleyan Methodist Chapel in St Peter's Street, Primitive Methodist Chapel in Parchment Street, and the Baptist Chapel in City Road.

Winchester has a long association with armies as well as the church. Thus today we find the major memorials to those who died in the World Wars placed near the west end of the mighty cathedral.. Preceded by Iron-Age camps at St Catharine's Hill south east of the city and Erdbury (Oram's Arbour) north west adjacent to, and overlapping with, the city, superseded perhaps by a Roman camp and then Roman defences, Winchester was a Burghal Hidage military centre c 900 CE. The Normans refurbished the defences and built a castle complex which served as a military base for long periods thereafter until the end of the twentieth century. From this barrack city many soldiers proceeded *en route* to embarkation at Southampton and elsewhere for various campaigns, including the French wars of the eighteenth and early nineteenth centuries, the Crimean War in the 1850s and the South African War of c 1900. These traditions culminated in the forces which set sail for all the war zones of the First and Second World Wars. In addition to barracks during the Great War (a term used interchangeably with First World War especially before 1945) and a dedicated railway siding for the barracks, there was a military camp and prisoner of war facility on Morn Hill to the east of the city on the site of the former medieval hospital there.[1]

MEMORIALISATION AND COMMEMORATION OF THE FIRST WORLD WAR DEAD OF WINCHESTER
The making of the Winchester War Service Register (reprinted as Appendix 1 below)

FOLLOWING THE END of the Great War the population of Winchester in 1921 was 23,791, some 400 more than in 1911. The *WWSR* published in 1921 identified 459 men who died out of 3,454 listed in the *Register*, both figures debated for reasons discussed below, a mortality rate of just over

---

    we cite anecdotal evidence only. However, the great majority of those who gave their lives would have been in a cultural sense, Church of England. John Thornhill also discovered a list of 'Boys of St Peter's School who have joined up' and a list of 'Children whose relations are serving this Country'. Both lists have furnished additional material to the biographies which follow.

1 Discussed by Philip Marter in the 'Archaeology and Memory' Conference (University of Winchester 2014).

13.25% of those who served, or 1.93% of the city's population as counted in 1921.[1] However, as the amended memorial lists for Winchester and other data show these figures derived from the *WWSR* are by no means precise, merely indicative. In the brief Introduction to the *WWSR* no sources are given but 'the thanks of the compilers are due to those who have helped them by collecting and furnishing information, and there have been many who have given time and trouble that their fellow-citizens who have served should be amongst those who have left a name behind them'. It is most likely that the method, as used elsewhere, was to issue a form which was filled in and returned. This might explain why, for example, Charles Russell (see Appendix 3 and front cover) who died six days after the Armistice 1918, a prisoner of Turks taken at Kut is not noted as a casualty or having died. The news of his death may not have reached Winchester at the time the form was filled in with such details as were known about his service were passed to the War Service Register compilers, and were not later corrected the news of his death as the prisoners returned. As shown below entries on the *WWSR* were originally intended to be deaths only up to the 11 November 1918, although some later deaths were included from 1919.[2]

The *WWSR* is clear about the Committee's initial aims in compiling the register: those marked with a cross as Killed in Action, Died of Wounds, died of illness, drowned etc having served 'from the Declaration of War to the Signing of the Armistice', provide an insight, if not a universally observed one, into why some names are included but others were not:

'The names are arranged in strict alphabetical order of surnames, the address being given under each name. Where no address is found, it has either been impossible to obtain it, or the person has since left Winchester. The rank in the next column is the highest rank attained. Then follow the name of the unit first joined and the date and rank on joining; units to which transferred; theatres of war in which served; honours gained; nature of any casualties with dates. Names with a cross prefixed signify those who were killed or died during the War.'[3]

---

1 Calculated on 458, see below re Marshall/Moore.
2 We are grateful to Alan Bungey for the information on Russell (see Appendix 3). Reasons for his omission as a death from the *WWSR* remain the authors' speculation. Arthur Allen (8) wounded at Kut in 1916, but who 'as a result of wounds' died in March 1919 is included in the *WWSR*.
3 Not strictly followed as Gerald Cassidy who Died of Wounds in March 1919 and fifteen others who also died in 1919 are found in the *WWSR*.

These dates are on the whole reliable, but on occasion either due to a misprint by the typesetter, or because of faulty information from informants, discrepancies in dates occur, for example in the case of Lance-Serjeant Tom Rickman (348) who appears in the *WWSR* as wounded 'Oct 1915' with a date of death as 'Sept 1916' when, in the War Office records, his death is dated to 27 September 1915 – before, in the *WWSR* chronology, he was wounded.[1] Discrepancies also occur with regard to cause of death: Walter Steele (402) was recorded in the *WWSR* as 'Killed in Action' while his Medal Index Card records 'Died'.[2] John Pack (309) of HMS Opal is recorded on the *WWSR* as 'Killed in Action.' His naval record distinguishes his death – drowned – from accident, disease or as the result of enemy action.[3] There are various discrepancies between his *WWSR* entry and Naval Records, a not uncommon occurrence. Different sources record Killed in Action or Died of Wounds, and we note certain of these discrepancies in footnotes.

The *WWSR* did not claim, and nor does our website (https://debtofhonourwinchester.weebly.com/) or this book arising from current research, to furnish comprehensive detail of men's service careers, let alone their lives. The compilers of the *WWSR* conceded that 'while in many cases more details of individual service could undoubtedly have been obtained, in many others this was impossible; their memorial has perished with them and it has been thought better to confine the details to what could be given on a uniform basis than to risk the disparagement of those who have rendered equal service, but whose record it has not been possible to obtain.'

There was no less grief among families and friends of those whose lives and deaths were little documented, than among those whose lives and deaths were well documented. For this reason the current project is intended as a balanced account of all those from the city of Winchester recorded with a cross in the *WWSR* as having died, broadly following the dictum of the *WWSR*, but with refined and to a limited extent expanded information. The well-attested reticence of men to talk about their war experiences when at home is obviously exacerbated in the cases of those who died. Thus not surprisingly details of ranks, service, dates and locations of death differ in the *WWSR* compiled often some years after they fell. In the case of Jack

---

1   Numbers in brackets in the Introduction are the numbers assigned to each individual in the biographical text below, i.e. Tom Rickman is number (348) etc. WO 372/16/229035.
2   WO 372/19/32107.
3   ADM 188/327/191353.

Sippetts (374), recorded in the *WWSR* as a Private, other sources record him as a Serjeant. In the heat of war designations might, and sometimes evidently did, change rapidly maybe well ahead of the bureaucracy? No date of death or place is given in the *WWSR* for Sippetts, although further research has revealed that he died in Mesopotamia in October 1918. It remains obscure why this information was unavailable to the compilers of the *WWSR* assembling data a year or so later. He may, for example, have been a temporary resident in Winchester when he was working at Sherriff and Ward's shop at 12, High Street.[1] In some cases it can be shown that deaths, for example in Mesopotamia in 1916, were not confirmed until the following year, on occasion over a year after the death of the soldier. See for example Charles Avery (15) who was killed on 21 January 1916, but his death was not confirmed until December 1917; William White (447), also of The Hampshire Regiment died as a prisoner of Turks on 22 July 1916 but his death was not confirmed until the next year.

Feelings were still very raw between 1918 and 1921. The editor of the *WWSR* apologised for the delay in publication, due to lack of funding, as seen in the discussion of the War Memorial Committee minutes below, the data having been collected 'immediately after the signature of Peace'. Publication became possible because of funding from the Winchester War Memorial Committee, which in 1921 was still debating the form of the proposed city war memorial. The Committee were aware that Winchester College was commissioning its War Cloister, and there were some anxieties that the city should not be seen to do less for its sons than the less venerable institution on College Street.[2] The *WWSR* was one memorial which could be agreed on and it provided a specific number of deaths which could be engraved on the memorial west of the cathedral, although this never happened. There are many reasons why the data in the *WWSR* contain errors and are self-contradictory, which are discussed in detail below.

Inevitably as so many had died, and where there was considerable doubt and uncertainty about the fate of so many others, the *WWSR* and other memorial lists do not tally. Examination of the wider group of Winchester memorials beyond the *WWSR* led to the conclusion that there was a significant underestimate in the *WWSR* of the numbers who gave their lives. In addition to those at churches and chapels, there are

---

1   See notes on Balls (20) and Sippetts.
2   https://www.winchestercollegeatwar.com/war-cloister provides a ready guide to the basics.

nominal memorials in educational establishments and at other institutions for example at Winchester College, Peter Symonds College, St Thomas's School, Hampshire County Council Offices and elsewhere, also at the now University of Winchester, formerly the Diocesan Training College for male teachers (Winton Chapel and Memorial Room). The DTC was closed during the war and was not involved in official memorialisation discussions in Winchester. Among decorations awarded to its members was a VC for a former student, and an MC for a serving member of staff and other decorations. V. S. Manley, a student at the DTC, left a rich personal archive of the war, now in the Hampshire Record Office, including lists of those who gave their lives. His life was blighted by his experiences.[1] A memorial to the thirty-seven former pupils of West Downs School on Romsey Road (now the West Downs Campus of the University of Winchester) was sited in public view on the Corner of Queen's Road and Romsey Road, west of the city. A private memorial existed within the school grounds, now relocated to the Slimbridge Wildfowl and Wetlands Trust, Gloucestershire. Peter Scott, whose mother sculpted the memorial, was the founder of Slimbridge and an old boy of the school. After the school was closed and the area across the road was developed, the public memorial was moved twice in the course of which the plinth containing the names was lost, although memorial boards are found in the former chapel of the school.[2]

Across the city, individuals are recorded in various stained glass windows, by the occasional memorial doorway and by returned battlefield crosses. Memorials where they have survived in Winchester churches, chapels of different denominatons and and other institutions have been examined and a database compiled by Steve Jarvis. Jarvis's wider database thus comes close to providing the list of those who fell both in Winchester and other Hampshire communities, whether carved in stone or recorded in other media.[3] He reckons

[1] See Tom Beaumont James, *The University of Winchester: 175 years of values-driven Higher Education* (Third Millennium, London 2015), especially pp 54-61.

[2] Mark Hichens, *West Downs: a portrait of and English Prep* School (Pentland Press 1992); A4 information sheet by JEA/RNA 11 November 2012.

[3] Steve Jarvis pers. comm. CD-ROM *War Memorials of Hampshire 1914-1918, 1939-1945* by Steve and Jennny Jarvis. Where he has recorded a Winchester memorial or memorials these are included here: where he has not recorded a memorial this is noted as 'Winchester memorial not found'. The Jarvises' long-term project on memorialisation in Hampshire including Winchester and on other aspects of the First World War has further revealed that some listed as

that there are an additional 108 names of Winchester men who fell on surviving city memorials than are found in the *WWSR*.[1] Alan Bungey, as shown in Appendix 3 has discovered and researched a further six men who gave their lives in addition to the 458/459 we have identified.[2] A notable loss of a church war memorial was that from St Maurice, south of High Street where a parish was formed to include areas such as that of the former, previously demolished, churches of St Mary Kalendar (which lay north of High Street) and the long-lost church of St Peter Colebrook in the south east of the city. Thus people who died, such as Leonard Arthur Balls (20) and Jack Sippetts (374) both of 12 High Street (i.e. Sherriff and Ward's department store where they served as draper's assistants) and about a dozen men with Colebrook addresses are likely to have appeared on the lost St Maurice memorial together with men who had addresses in parts of High Street and The Square. By contrast Arthur Cook (99)[3], whose parents had a Colebrook address had Winchester College connections and is memorialised in the War Cloister there. A group of some eighty people noted in the *WWSR* as having given their life, has been identified as having no known Winchester memorial. Others, however, were not memorialised in the *WWSR*, perhaps because they died away from theatres of war, for example after Discharge (e.g. Andrew Bellinger (32), of exposure at Gravesend, Kent, Reginald Pritchard (339), Edward Smart (376) of tuberculosis at Kings Somborne etc). Some may have lost faith in religious

    survivors died after they were Discharged from the army and so were not included, although some who were Discharged were memorialised in the city churches. In the case of Thomas Paget Bosworth, the *WWSR* records that he had survived, when he appears among the fallen on the memorial at St Bartholomew's, Hyde.

1. Steve Jarvis pers. comm. St Maurice church, apart from the tower was demolished in the 1960 and its war memorial plaque, now lost, entrusted to the City Council. Jarvis gives a total of 567, but as shown here the total in the *WWSR* was in fact 458/459.
2. Alan Bungey's researches are reported here in Appendix 3. Because these casualties were not noted in the *WWSR* we have not included them in the body of the biographical text, sticking to the names published in the *WWSR*. One of his men, Harry Edmonds, shared a fate, drowning, with George Flux (143) who did find a place in the *WWSR*. There is clearly scope for further research into many aspects of Winchester and the First World War of which casualties is one. We are very grateful to Mr Bungey for making us aware of his researches and sharing them with us.
3. See https://www.winchestercollegeatwar.com/archive/arthur-basil-kemball-cook/

commemoration of their loved ones. Some, as at Southampton, may have been Jewish or of other faiths or denominations unrepresented by memorials in places of worship at Winchester.[1]

Information taken from Jarvis's database of city memorials is included under individuals' names below.[2] This reveals that some individuals were commemorated in more than one place in the city in addition to their war grave or panel reference elsewhere in Britain and overseas. Many of the dead including sailors who went down with their ships, men who fought Turks at Gallipoli, or Germans on the Somme, at Cambrai and elsewhere – such as William Hayward (193) – have no known grave and are listed on various memorials, Portsmouth Naval Memorial, Menin Gate, Helles Memorial, Turkey etc. The Helles Memorial includes two men from HMT Royal Edward, Harry Edmonds (see Appendix 3) and George Flux (143) both Serjeants, former reservists in The Hampshire Regiment en route to Gallipoli (Dardanelles).

William Wright (456) appears both inside and outside the church on memorials at Easton as well as in St John the Baptist church in the eastern suburb. Robert Gudgeon (179) also commemorated at St John the Baptist, is further memorialised at the Anglican Church of St Swithun's, Hither Green, Kent. Hugh Elgee (128), by contrast, is listed on a memorial in All Saints church in Winchester and also on a plaque in Otterbourne church where his father was sometime an incumbent, although he does not appear on the Otterbourne general memorial outside that church. William Powney (332), son of Salisbury parents, is commemorated in the Salisbury Book of Remembrance in St Thomas's, Salisbury and also at St Matthew's and St Paul's in Winchester.[3] Lionel Penson (319) exemplifies those who are commemorated beyond Winchester, on the South Leigh, Oxfordshire, memorial but does not have a church memorial in Winchester. The Stacey brothers both served and lost their lives in the War, they fought in different regiments and whereas Frederick (396) has a memorial at St Thomas's,

---

1 The war memorial for the deconsecrated St Peter Chesil church, formerly located beside the north door of that church, has been copied and removed. The record of the war dead for St Peter Chesil is now found at All Saints, Highcliffe, the active church for he area. Steve Jarvis pers.comm. Entries below for those from St Peter Chesil are entered as 'St Peter Chesil (All Saints)'.
2 Taken, with thanks, from the list compiled by Steve Jarvis. For the Hampshire War Memorials see www.warmemorials.hampshire.org.uk
3 www.scribd.com; www.wiltshire-opc.org.uk South Leigh Oxfordshire.

Winchester no Winchester memorial has been located for his brother Frank (395).[1]

Occasionally a wooden cross from a war burial, a tangible link to a casualty, is to be found in a place of worship in the city, for example that of Leonard Russell (358) (Killed in Action 7 October 1916) at St Cross, perhaps recovered when replaced by a durable grave marker by the then Imperial War Graves Commission. Who collected this relic is not known to us, but is likely to have been a family member or friend. His father was a military man resident at St Cross Mede and his mother a daughter of a former Warden of Winchester College. The family no doubt negotiated an agreement, perhaps with The Master of St Cross, whose son was also killed two years on in 1918. Apart from correspondence and meetings with families during home leave there was little or no contact between those at home and those serving. Very few parents had the opportunity or the means to visit their sons while they were serving. A glimpse of such a meeting could therefore be newsworthy. Thus the *Hampshire Chronicle* reported that Canon Braithwaite, who lived at 9, The Close near the cathedral, met his son Philip in Paris in November 1915 having not seen him since he had left for service in India 'some time ago.' Philip Braithwaite (46) was killed in September 1918.[2]

For the population of the city of Winchester the losses in the First World War represent the greatest single loss of the lives of adult men in the city since the plague in the fourteenth century. That the pestilence was a disaster for the city is not in doubt. At the time of that plague there was no tradition of recording names in public places. Indeed so comprehensive was the chaos of the plague that any recording of names would have been extraordinary even in a literate society. We know that not everyone died, but they could not have known then that this would not happen and the attested figure of over 60%,

---

[1] Charles Reeve of The London Regiment who died on 23 August 1914 is buried in the city, but not found in the *WWSR*. Commemorated on the CWGC his early death was before as Kate Tiller puts it '...repatriation of the dead was forbidden from an early stage of the First World War....' *Remembrance and Community*, p. 7.

[2] In August 1916 the Rev. J.L.B. James, then a curate also in the Winchester Diocese at St Peter's, Bournemouth, completed the Introduction to his *Story of France 1814-1914* (London: Nelson 1916) in the Rue de Seine, whence the volume was distributed among the forces to contribute to understanding of why the English were, following the Entente Cordiale of 1904, fighting alongside the French, a traditional enemy for centuries.

and higher on some of the Bishop of Winchester's estates in Hampshire must have appeared to presage doom for the whole population.[1]

By 1918 things had changed: memorialisation by listing of names was becoming standard practice among military units nationally and locally, as seen in the cathedral and at Winchester College and elsewhere in the city at the time of the Boer War of 1899-1902. So it is surprising at first sight in this respect that the memorial inscription to the Winchester men does not list their names as was becoming customary.

THE WINCHESTER CITY MEMORIAL AND A WIDER PICTURE

WINCHESTER AS A community is unusual in that no monument was erected to the city's war dead on which their names were engraved as a group. Andover (214), Basingstoke (233), Petersfield (100), however, all have carved lists of names on town memorials. Southampton's war memorial has 1,996 and Portsmouth also erected a memorial listing all those who died in order of seniority of the forces, starting with the Senior Service, the Royal Navy, then listing Army dead.[2] In all these places names of those who died were engraved. Memorialisation in communities by name-carving arose in time because, from 1915, repatriation of bodies was forbidden by governments on a number of grounds including hygiene, the scale of the mortality and consequent effects on morale, and because repatriation as an option had only been possible for those with the means to achieve it for their loved ones. The decision contributed to a sense of social equality of sacrifice.

---

1   Ole J. Benedictow *The Black Death 1346-1353. The Complete History.* Woodbridge: The Boydell Press, 2004, p 377 where it is argued that the overall mortality for England was 'of the order of magnitude of 62.5%' and Paula Arthur, 'The Impact of the Black Death on Seventeen Units of Account of the Bishopric of Winchester' PhD University of Southampton, 2005), 2 vols. See citation in Ole J. Benedictow, *What Disease was Plague? On the controversy over the Microbiological Identity of Plague Epidemics in the Past,* Leiden: Brill, 2010, p 482.
2   http://www.dailyecho.co.uk/news/9178685.Andover_War_Memorial_listed_by_English_Heritage; http://www.victoriacountyhistory.ac.uk/explore/items/basingstoke-war-memorial; http://www.roll-of-honour.com/Hampshire/Petersfield.html; http://www.southampton.gov.uk/libraries-museums/local-family-history/cenotaph.aspx; http://www.roll-of-honour.com/Hampshire/Portsmouth.html

Rolls of honour, followed by carving of names, provided places where those without the means to travel abroad to scattered cemeteries might have a place to visit to mourn. But collection of names and carving of names was not universal, and as shown below, to an extent actively discouraged by authorities. Bournemouth, for example, erected a memorial but did not carve names on it: these were entered post-war in a book following enquiries among church groups and public requests for information. This yielded 650 names of 'Men and Women', entered in the book to be kept in the Hall of Memory in the town.[1] Some numbers, at Petersfield (100), Winchester (460) and Bournemouth (650) were probably rounded up.

Recording the names in stone was inevitably controversial, and has continued to be so. At Basingstoke disagreements followed the selecting of the names, with a recent estimate suggesting that almost three times as many from the community gave their lives as were recorded on the memorial. At Southampton controversy forced the town authorities shortly to add a further 203 names to the 1,793 carved on the memorial in 1922, while dispute has continued there about the lack of inclusion of Jewish names on the Christian monument: only one Jew was listed, when community historians estimate that one in ten of Jewish men in the town gave their lives. At Andover another issue beset the war memorial: the subsequent re-siting of the First World War Memorial from outside the Guildhall met with a continuing protest.[2]

MEMORIALISATION AND COMMEMORATION OF THE FIRST WORLD WAR DEAD OF WINCHESTER
Choosing and funding a monument

THE MEMORIAL TO the Winchester dead found on the west face of the county regiment memorial west of the cathedral, gives a number of 460 dead. This memorial, after lengthy discussion, was a product of the Winchester War Memorial and Peace Committee, for which minutes survive from the meeting of 7 January 1919, when the initial meeting was chaired by Mayor Alderman Edmeades, with aldermen Stopher and Dyer and councillors Shenton and Mathews present.[3] It was decided at that meeting

1 M. A. Edgington, *Bournemouth and the First World. The Evergreen Valley 1914-1919* (Bournemouth Local Studies Publications no 675, 1985).
2 In the course of refashioning the Southampton War memorial in recent years, more names have been added. There are now 2,368.
3 Memorial Committee HALS HRO W/B5/40/1.

that 'there should be a definite War Memorial to mark in some manner the great sacrifice made by so many of the city's sons in the war, but they [i.e. the Committee] have not felt it their duty to suggest what form the memorial should take.' It was therefore decided to convene a public meeting. This was convened about a month later on 3 February at noon. Here it was resolved that a memorial to 'those citizens who have fallen in the Great War' should be 'erected by public subscription'. It was noted that soundings had been taken with the county, which had established a parallel Hampshire and Isle of Wight War Memorial Committee, for a 'larger and bolder scheme' to be created by combining together with the city. It was further noted that representation on a committee to be appointed to consider various proposals was to be as follows: Town Council (5),[1] High Steward, MP, Cathedral, College, Rifle Depot, Hampshire Regiment Depot, Friendly Societies (3), Trades and Labour Committee, Women's Citizens Association (2), Parochial Clergy, Roman Catholic.

This Committee of nineteen, compares with a much more broadly based body at Colchester, also a garrison town, but with a population of some 43,000 in 1911 and 1921, and therefore twice the size of Winchester. At Colchester the committee, including representatives of Discharged Soldiers and Sailors, nonconformists, nurses, schools and others amounted to forty-four to which may be added single representatives from thirteen specified businesses and one each from the Corporation, Post Office, Railway and Gas Company to make a total of 61.[2]

The meeting of 21 February in Winchester noted that the War Memorial Committee was to be separate from the Peace Committee and initial schemes were mooted. The mayor read a list of suggestions ranging through a Temple of Honour to the creation of a roadway, to be called the 'Sacred Way' or '*Via Sacra*' from the west end of the cathedral to Southgate Street, and it was noted that Alderman Stopher was a leading advocate of this scheme, supported by the Dean (the representative of the cathedral) and Lord Selborne (prominent on the county committee, and closely associated with Winchester College, of which he became Warden in 1920, and the city of which he became High Steward in 1929. His second son, Robert, had

[1] One representative each unless otherwise stated.
[2] Kate Tiller, 2014, *Remembrance and Community: War Memorials and Local History*, (British Association for Local History, 2013) p. 31.

been killed in 1916). Mention was made of Herbert Baker, the architect, as the designer of the monument and associated scheme. The group moved to 'interviewing' representatives of various proposed schemes, which included The Temple of Honour proposed to be sited on St Giles's Hill to the east of the city; an Art Gallery and Memorial Hall; clubs for young men and girls; two cottage schemes (unnecessary); old people's accommodation (cost prohibitive); baths and canteens for the poor (not a lasting memorial); improvement to the gateway of Hyde Abbey (not a major monument); a market cross (not unique in the city); structural addition to the county hospital (not unique and lasting, finance already at hospital); a granite cross at the North Walls, City Road, Jewry Street junction; a subvention of £50 or £100 to building a church in an outlying part of Canada (not fitting, not in the city); a statue representative of Winchester (form of such a statue queried by the committee); a Victory Arch and Gateway Entrance to the cathedral by way of Market Street (from an artistic point of view a most unsuitable site for a memorial, the committee declared, but this was the site favoured by townspeople who entered the cathedral grounds there, as explained below, rather than through a hole in the vestigial Close wall which originated at the time of the Black Death to the west of the cathedral, as part of the Sacred Way scheme); establishment of a local industry with provision for children of those who had lost family (not a permanent memorial); belfry tower south of the cathedral (cathedral had sufficient bells); improvement of High Street by widening of Jewry Street and Southgate Street etc (cost impractical and unsuitable memorial). Most of these were ruled out for the reasons quoted or summarised here in brackets.

It was resolved to cooperate with the County Memorial in the opening up of the road from Southgate Street to Great Minster Street 'with suitable buildings' and within their 'definition of a suitable memorial', towards the west end of the cathedral, the Sacred Way. Beyond that select schemes would be taken to the public meeting – the Temple of Honour on St Giles's Hill; the Art Gallery and Memorial Hall; the Boys' and Girls' club. Beyond these proposals £50 would be allocated for a gun emplacement on St Giles's Hill, and £50 towards the printing of the *Winchester War Service Register*.

It became apparent that the county memorial would 'almost certainly' be built in the city, and that the County was prepared to withdraw their scheme for a Memorial Gateway to the west end of the cathedral in favour of the Sacred Way. So the city Committee unanimously declared themselves in favour of joining with the County in this memorial on condition that a 'definite place in the scheme is reserved for a commemoration of Winchester Men' who have 'made the Great Sacrifice".

From this point onwards debates were about details of the Sacred Way (for example the opening of discussions regarding purchase of the necessary buildings west of the Close, and then objections to the demolition of historic buildings there, for example), and discussions about which of the other schemes might be preferred to be implemented, with emphasis on issues such as the pursuance of the gun emplacement (with flagstaff) on St Giles's Hill, or other suitable site.

Finance began to loom. Herbert Baker's plans for the scheme were costed at £21,770. By the early December meeting, funds available from the County were £6,213 12s, while the city had amassed £1,292 15s 11d. It was noted that Southampton had completed their memorial, and had £100 in hand. Thereafter scaling down was the order of the day: on 21 March 1921 it was noted that there were insufficient funds to realise the scheme on a large scale, but on the plus side the Dean and Chapter had sanctioned the proposal of a cross. It was acknowledged that the Sacred Way road scheme in its entirety should be abandoned. Without reciting every detail, the discussions swayed this way and that. The proposal for an arch containing the names of the deceased was noted as abandoned on 1 April 1921, and the names were to be inscribed in a book to be deposited in the cathedral. Alderman Stopher moved that the city should withdraw from the joint venture and go it alone, but was defeated by a single vote. It was resolved that the joint project should proceed on the key condition that £250 be given towards the publication of the *WWSR*. It was by that time more than two years since discussions had opened and thirty months since the armistice, fund raising was proving increasingly difficult. Hopes of raising funds from the towns in the county proved false: Bournemouth proffered no money, Portsmouth and Southampton offered a 'small amount', but all three already had their memorials funded, varied though they were. The remaining achievable objectives within the funding available were for the memorial cross and suitable inscription (£3,500 from the County and £1,000 from the city), to which would be added memorial volumes to be placed within the cathedral. Herbert Baker was instructed to simplify his plans for the cross.[1] On 30 May 1921 the Committee agreed that

---

[1] Herbert Baker's fees had already amounted to £106 17s 6d by September 1919, when the city agreed to pay half and the county the other half. HALS HRO W/B5/40/1.

detail of the plain or decorated nature of the top of the cross was to be left to the architect and the tender for the memorial, steps, court, seating, removal of trees and levelling of the ground came in at £3,750 with £391 for the alteration of the path,[1] totalling £4,141. Messrs Holloway Bros's estimate was accepted with the work to be carried out in three months.

The contractors were reliable, enabling the unveiling of the memorial on Monday 31 October 1921 to the 'countless host' of 'Hampshire's sons' who had been killed in the Great War.[2] An emotional piece from the *Hampshire Observer*, reprinted in *The Hampshire Regimental Journal* reported the fine contribution of the men of Hampshire to the war effort, and the appropriateness of Winchester, 'the ancient capital of the realm' as the 'universally accepted' place for a 'shrine'. It was further noted that 'after larger schemes had been found impossible, Mr Herbert Baker, F.R.I.B.A. has designed a worthy memorial cross and court to the memory for the glorious dead' as a 'noble monument to the corporate contribution of the County and the City to the national sacrifice'.

THE MEMORIAL

THE WAR MEMORIAL to the west of Winchester Cathedral unveiled on the last day of October 1921 thus commemorates on its east face those men of Hampshire and the Isle of Wight and, on the west face, those of Winchester city who gave their lives.

Below the stem of the cross a legend runs round the whole monument from east to west which reads:[3]

HE SHALL DELIVER THEIR SOULS FROM FALSEHOOD AND WRONG: AND DEAR SHALL THEIR BLOOD BE IN HIS SIGHT.

---

1 The path in question, today paved, leads west from the memorial towards Great Minster Street. There were problems over two great lime trees and the postion of the Jackson tomb, which would have affected the straight course of the proposed path.

2 For an account of the ceremony and those present see *The Hampshire Regiment Journal*, November 1921 pp.177ff.

3 The inscriptions are rendered here in capitals following the form on the monument but are not set out using the same distribution of words by line. Punctuation is slightly amended. One Winchester man, William Rowell (354), lost his life serving on HMS Hampshire.

In the centre on the west face, between two Hampshire roses, the dates 1914-1919 are carved.

Below there are panels to the south and the north either side of a central panel. The central panel reads:

TO THE GLORY OF GOD AND IN PROUD AND GRATEFUL MEMORY
OF THE UNCOUNTED HOST FROM HAMPSHIRE AND THE ISLE OF
WIGHT WHO DIED FOR ENGLAND IN THE GREAT WAR WHEN SERVING
IN THE NAVY THE MERCANTILE MARINE, THE ARMY AND THE
AIR FORCE BE MINDFUL OF THEM, O LORD AND GRANT TO THEIR
CHILDREN THE SAME FAITHFULNESS

1914 - 1919
TO SEVEN THOUSAND FIVE HUNDRED AND FORTY ONE OF THE
REGULAR, MILITIA, TERRITORIAL & SERVICE BATTALIONS OF THE
HAMPSHIRE REGIMENT WHO DIED IN FLANDERS, FRANCE, ITALY,
RUSSIA, MACEDONIA, PALESTINE, EGYPT, MESOPOTAMIA, PERSIA,
INDIA AND SIBERIA OR BY THE DARDANELLES OR WERE LOST AT SEA
IN THE MEDITERRANEAN

The side panels read:

TO SEVENTY FOUR
OF THE HAMPSHIRE
YEOMANRY CARABINIERS

TO THREE HUNDRED
AND EIGHTY SIX OF THE ROYAL ENGINEERS
AND THE HAMPSHIRE
ROYAL ARTILLERY

TO FORTY EIGHT
OF THE ROYAL ARMY MEDICAL CORPS AND THE HAMPSHIRE ROYAL
ARMY SERVICE CORPS

TO SEVEN HUNDRED
AND THIRTY SEVEN OF
H.M.S. HAMPSHIRE SUNK BY A MINE OFF THE ORKNEY ISLANDS JUNE
5TH 1916

Those members of the 'vast concourse' of people who attended on that October day and who were located behind the monument as shown in the *Hampshire Observer* photograph of the scene would have seen the following inscription memorial to the men of Winchester city:[1]

> TO THE GLORY OF GOD AND IN
> PROUD AND GRATEFUL MEMORY
> OF FOUR HUNDRED AND SIXTY
> CITIZENS OF WINCHESTER
> WHO UPHELD UNDER KING
> GEORGE V THE TRADITIONS
> OF SERVICE AND SACRIFICE
> HANDED DOWN FROM THE
> DAYS OF KING ALFRED
>
> *IN THE SIGHT OF THE UNWISE*
> *THEY SEEMED TO DIE....*
> *YET IS THEIR HOPE FULL OF*
> *IMMORTALITY.*

The greatest single group of men from the city of Winchester who gave their lives, around 200, served in the Hampshire Regiment and associated units.

The Rifle Brigade (The Prince Consort's Own) and The King's Royal Rifle Corps Rolls of Honour within the cathedral list 30,000 dead also commemorated by a separate substantial memorial north-west of the cathedral's west front. There were many Riflemen who served from the City some two dozen of whom appear among the fallen the *WWSR*. The memorial to the King's Royal Rifle Brigade, was unveiled to the north-west of the cathedral on 24 May, Empire Day, 1922 together with the Roll of Honour set between nave pillars in front of a large crowd of dignitaries, clergy and families associated with the regiment. It was recorded at that time that 12,824 members of the Rifle Corps had given their lives: 567 Officers, 74

---

[1] The part of the county memorial at the west end of the cathedral which refers to the men of Winchester city does not appear in the Imperial War Museum database http://www.iwm.org.uk/memorials/search. Apparently those recording looked only at he east face and not behind at the west face of the memorial.

Warrant Officers, 2,174 NCOs, 23 Buglers and 9,986 Riflemen. In addition there had been 'not less than' 145,000 casualties in total among the Riflemen.

Winchester College, which had lost some 500 boys, old boys and staff (G. M. Bell (30) appears in the *WWSR*, staff, one of a few found there) – the equivalent of an entire generation at that date, began a well-supported War Memorial fund. As with the city, the first achievement was the publication, at the College on a grand scale, of four volumes including biographies, pictures, some letters and other materials organised under the dates at which each person entered the College. These came out in 1921.[1] This provided a basis on which to plan and execute the Winchester College War Cloister with its roll-call of names, like the county and city memorial by Herbert Baker. This extraordinary achievement between 1922 and 1924 created, according to the College's war cloister website the 'largest private war memorial in Europe'. It cost £65,000. This was envisaged as a grand scheme of cloister memorial, with carved names, regimental badges and representation of the four corners of the Empire in stone, and a hall. Sufficient funds were forthcoming in addition for refurbishments in the chapel, and bursaries for boys affected by the war. Despite there being £10,000 left over, the 'New Hall' was not built until the late 1950s, following a further appeal to commemorate Wykehamists killed in the Second World War.

THE COMMITTEES' DEBATES AND CORRESPONDENCE REPORTED IN THE *HAMPSHIRE CHRONICLE*

OFFICIAL SOURCES, MINUTES and material monuments tell one side of the story. However they do not give oxygen to wider public opinion, which was necessarily cursorily recorded in brief minutes as the discussion proceeded. Correspondence and reports in the *Hampshire Chronicle*[2] provide a valuable further perspective including personal interventions from correspondents, including the Bishop, Edward Talbot, an anonymous Wykehamist, former service people, bereaved parents and some whose schemes of remembrance had been rejected. The paper also recorded in some detail discussions at meetings both of the Hampshire and Isle of Wight County Memorial Committee and the tensions between the county and the

1   M. J. Rendall (ed.), *Wykehamists who Died in the Great War*, four volumes, (Winchester 1921).
2   This discussion based on material from the *Hampshire Chronicle* and other local newspapers and the records of the Committee cited above.

Winchester War Memorial Committee. In the end, as ever, it came down to money as shown above.

From the beginning of the reporting on memorials wider issues appear. For example an early objection to the War Graves' Commission refusing relatives the right to select a 'stone of their own choosing' for a grave marker.[1] At the same period the debate ensued over the offer from the Ministry of a tank to the city in recognition of 'services rendered by the city to the military during the war'. This offer was initially rejected, Alderman Stopher stating the city 'should not accept this hideous thing'. After reflection however the tank was accepted, as a symbol specific to the recent war as opposed to a gun which could represent any war. Further debate this way and that led to the siting of the tank at the recreation field, and so less prominent, a decision hotly challenged in the community.[2]

Senior Church of England clergy were prominent in the reporting of progress and discussions. Bishop Talbot, whose son Gilbert[3] was killed at Hooge in 1915, took an early lead in a letter to the paper in which he urged collective memorialisation of what he referred to as 'men of all kinds' was preferable to individual memorials. All names, he proposed should be recorded on vellum and placed among parish records, multiplication of tablets and brasses he concluded would be 'undesirable' but a communal memorial of a 'high level of workmanship' should recall the fallen of the Great War.[4] The Dean meanwhile, at that early stage, reportedly reassured city and county families with a vision of the gated *Via Sacra* west of the cathedral in which he imagined a 'panel for each village in Hampshire with Winchester at the centre', presumably the panels bearing the names of the fallen. This persuaded the city at first to agree to go in with the county.[5] Thus it appeared that in the early summer 1919 all was going smoothly forward for a joint city and county memorial. A joint sub-committee of the county and city committees was entrusted with carrying the matter forward.

However, round the corner at Winchester College all was not plain

---

1 *HC* 15.2.19
2 *HC* 1 and 8.3.1919
3 Gilbert Talbot's memorial was the foundation of Talbot House (TocH) a Christian centre initially at Poperinghe in the war zone, but later in London and elsewhere. Having dispensed with paid staff it survives today as a voluntary organisation.
4 *HC* 15.3.1919
5 *HC* 15.3.1919

sailing. An angry 'Old Wykehamist' had contacted *Country Life* to object in the strongest terms to the College's memorial plans and his objections were repeated in the *Hampshire Chronicle*. The College committee's proposals he declared amounted to 'iconoclasm', 'destroying the charm of the old school'. In being wedded to one architect and one plan they were creating 'too much an advertisement for the living and too little of a memory of the dead'. He went further to claim that 'recalcitrant members' had been 'discarded' from the committee which had decided by 'a modest majority' to 'carry out their grandiose scheme'.[1]

Through the summer of 1919 debates continued both within the city community and between the city and the county memorial groups but the early consensus clearly broke own. For the county, led by an occasionally very frustrated Lord Selborne, the issue was clear enough, that the county memorial would focus on the county regiment which included many from the city. On 2 August, for example, it was reported that the 'immense' delays were already nine months since the armistice, and that the county should proceed without the city. For the city fathers it was more difficult and here they swithered to and fro between being part of the county scheme, having a separate monument adjacent to it, or making their own arrangements. As shown above the scheme for a westerly gated Sacred Way was soon abandoned and with it the idea of a panels of community names. Individuals' voices and representations from local interest groups flesh out what can be learnt from committee minutes. The proposal for an arched structure, with names, to the north, near the Morley College almshouses towards the High Street, was favoured in the city at large as it was from there that the residents, who largely lived north of the cathedral and High Street, entered the cathedral grounds. This can bee seen in the casualties by street in Appendix 4, people from the Brooks area and Hyde, north of High Street and from the eastern suburb, for example Wales Street were the largest groups of casualties. This change of plan was supported by the Dean who had previously endorsed the westerly Sacred Way.[2]

Surprisingly the voices of those who served and survived only occur

[1] HC 29.3.1919. It was subsequently reported that some scaling down of the proposed Winchester College scheme was under consideration: that '22-14 Kingsgate Street 'cannot be saved' but 9, 10, 15 and 16 may be reprieved. Whether in reponse to objections such as that outlined here is obscure.
[2] HC 2.8.1919. The Dean, William Furneaux was replaced by Holden Hutton during 1919 which may have affected this decision.

late in the debates about memorialisation. Thus on rare occasions through the discussions that summer other voices are heard. Those who had fought were apparently not so enthusiastic about large, stone erections. For example in May a 'Soldier who fought in France' wrote in support of those who had proposed practical schemes urging for proper homes and education not 'marble columns' etc, schemes he thought would raise 'boys who may honour their country' not 'Bolshevists and Strikers'. In September, late in the day, we hear the views of Mr J. H. Burden representing demobilised and discharged men to the committee said he had been asked to say that his people were not in favour of these memorial schemes but urged that 'something more useful and substantial' be instituted. He further observed that the discharged men would like to see a cross with all the names, pointing out with good reason that other towns had full plaques of names of the fallen.[1] On the same September day it was recorded that the committee agreed that all the names should be recorded, but that that motion should be put to the citizens before any final decision was made. Thus, as late as September 1919 because of these wrangles, arrangements had not been set in place by the committees for subscriptions to a war memorial fund, nearly a year after the end of hostilities. The failure to get agreement resulted in Winchester falling behind the rest of the county in establishing its war memorial, and more crucially in obtaining funds for architect Baker's scheme which was still in August to cost £13,000 with a £2,000 contingency. When funds were sought round the county for this central county and city memorial responses received indicated that other communities had proceeded with selection of their war memorials, mostly including names, and that they were unable to commit funds to the central scheme.

OUTCOMES OF THE WAR MEMORIAL COMMITTEES AND MEMORIALISATION

COMMEMORATION OF THE men lost from Winchester city during the First World War was a difficult, contested and ultimately somewhat minimalist achievement compared to the efforts on behalf of the county regiment, whose memorial was shared with the city, likewise the Rifle Brigade and soon afterwards Winchester College's Memorial Cloister. That about half of those from the city gave their lives serving in the Hampshire

---

[1] *HC* 3.5.1919 and 20.8. 1919

Regiment, and another two dozen or so in the Rifle regiments meant that at both unveiling ceremonies there were wreaths laid on behalf of the Winchester city dead. In the case of the county/city memorial on 31 October 1921 among many tributes to county and city 'a beautiful chaplet of palm leaves and exquisite flowers inscribed: 'In very grateful memory of Winchester's sons who laid down their lives in the Great War in the cause of Honour, Justice and Freedom.' The Mayor then laid a wreath 'of extraordinary beauty' from the Women of Winchester 'in proud and ever loving memory of our Sons, Husbands and Brothers, who made the supreme sacrifice in the Great War 1914-1919. From the Women of Winchester.'

> They pass beyond our touch, beyond our sight,
> > Never, thanks God, beyond our love and prayers,
> And, even as out of darkest night,
> > Dawn stealeth unawares,
> So, from our night of sorrow and distress,
> > We, who are left in loneliness below,
> May catch some vision of blessed ness
> > Which our beloved know.
> > "Their souls are in the hand of God."

A Naval tribute of orchids, liliums and carnations was inscribed:

> 'From the Royal Navy. In honoured memory of the officers and men of the County of Hampshire and City of Winchester who lost their lives in the Great War, 1914-1918.'

There were other wreaths and tributes laid, including one from ex-Mayor of Winchester and ex-Mayoress Edmeades.

At the unveiling of the Rifle Brigade memorial on 24 May 1922, Empire Day, a ceremony which was recorded in the KRRC *Chronicle* as being unsurpassed in being 'impressive and dignified or touched with such noble grandeur.' Again, among wreaths laid by royalty among many others, a wreath inscribed 'To the Glorious memory of our brave Riflemen from the city of Winchester, Stanley Clifton, Mayor.' The fewer than half a dozen Winchester College men who appear in the *WWSR* are commemorated in Winchester College's War Cloister with their names carved there. Otherwise memorials in places of worship, schools, outside and inside West Downs school etc record those who died, some over and above the record found in the *WWSR*, but nowhere as a group. So far as memorials at the cathedral and in the Close are concerned, over half the Winchester men who died are not commemorated in the main city memorials by name in the Hampshire Regiment and Rifle Brigade Rolls of Honour. So far as can be determined the *WWSR* was neither deposited in the cathedral nor - as at Exeter another county and regiment barrack town, as well as being a hospital focus for wounded from the continent [1]– in the base of the city war memorial.

A variety of reasons may be forwarded as to why no carved roll of honour for those from Winchester city who died was created. First, Winchester was settled as the memorial site for the 'countless numbers' of dead from the county of Hampshire and the Isle of Wight and funds were not available to carve up the names of those of the county regiment who gave their lives, let alone those of the city. It is now reckoned that over 8,000 from the Hampshire Regiment and associated units gave their lives.[2] Second the Rifle Depot's presence in the city with its memorial and roll of honour like that for the Hampshire Regiment, installed in the cathedral demanded, in view of the large numbers of casualties from that branch of the army, some special recognition, but given the large numbers without individual carved names. Third, the outpouring of funds for the sons of Winchester College engendered plans far beyond the reach of city and county alike, although they shared the same architect. Elsewhere, for example at Basingstoke, as Colchester and at Exeter, wealthy individual donors contributed funds and/or sites and for monuments which were partly or completely separate from the ecclesiastical establishment:[3] no

---

[1] For Exeter see 'The changing Memories and Meanings of the First World War Expressed through Commemorations in Exeter, Devon' by Samuel Walls, in *Historical Archaeologies of Cognition* Ed James Symonds, Anna Badcock and Jeff Oliver (Equinox, Sheffield, 2013), pp. 176-190.

[2] Colin Bulleid pers. comm.

[3] Kate Tiller, *Remembrance and Community*, cover and pp. 30-33 for Colchester; for Exeter see Wall, 2013, pp 176-190. Such memorials were in certain respects less constrained, with less religious symbolism – featuring winged Victory and St George representation as at Colchester where the High Steward had contributed £23,000 to buy the castle and to contribute to the memorial site, its railings etc. At the Northernhay Gardens at Exeter where the monument included sculptures which showed, unusually a prisoner, and a female figure in the form of a VAD nurse. The Exeter memorials used locally quarried stone, not an option in Winchester, but providing in Devon a further local link in remembrance.

such donors were forthcoming at Winchester. Fourth the decision to join with the county, as one suspects concerned Alderman Stopher, meant that with the funds available the city was contributing only one quarter of the funds for the whole county/city project, depending on contributions from often poorer people. By not erecting a nominal roll for the city as a whole, Winchester city avoided some of the problems which beset other towns in Hampshire. Throughout the lengthy, and ultimately fruitless debates about recording of names through the summer of 1919 those who attended the city meetings, whether the War Memorial Committee, or citizens' open meetings, there was always strong support, indicated by recurrent loud applause as recorded in the press, for the recording of all the names. On 20 September, late in the day, Canon Braithwaite, whose son had been killed, was urging for the recording of names and the suggestion that there should be a separate city memorial to that for the county was welcomed with 'loud applause'. This solicited a suggestion from a city councillor that there should be a north porch added to the cathedral where all the names would be recorded. But this was not to be.

It is striking that the leaders of the committees, such as Lord Selborne, and other interested community leaders such as Bishop Talbot, had lost sons in the war, as had Canon Braithwaite and members of the city council. Winchester was a predominantly Church of England cathedral city and the choice of a cross in the cathedral Close might seem inevitable, if exclusively Church of England, facing the True Christian architecture of the cathedral's west end. The memorial to the Hampshire Regiment referred solely to the men fighting for 'England'. However, Herbert Baker's other Winchester memorial, the War Cloister at Winchester College, was if not 'early Christian' arguably 'pagan' in its Romanesque arcades, and not at all in keeping with the fourteenth century Gothic of the buildings of the College itself and the west end of the cathedral – maybe something in the back of the mind of the angry Wykehamist who complained to *Country Life* and in the *Hampshire Chronicle* about 'iconoclasm'? As noted elsewhere the Roman Catholic response was apparently muted, not least because of the Irish situation by 1918, but from comparing the *WWSR*, and research into burial of the individuals listed there, with correspondence in the *Hampshire Chronicle* an indication of intention from one family becomes apparent. Lieutenant

Athol Gudgeon (178), son of George and Hilda Gudgeon died in 1917 of wounds after the torpedoing of HMS Ettrick. He is buried in the St James's Catholic cemetery on West Hill. His father wrote a letter to the *Hampshire Chronicle* arguing for a 'massive' bronze cross crucifix to be erected on St Giles's Hill, not far from the family home on the north-western side of that hill at St John's Mead. Although not explicit, this letter and the support for the St Giles's Hill crucifix as an 'emblem of Christianity', stated as the 'focus of those who fought'[1] this plea might be interpreted as an effort to prise the war memorial from the sole hands of the county and city Church of England hierarchy, and place it beyond the confines of the cathedral Close. For Athol Gudgeon's parents such a memorial, with its catholic iconography, would rise above the city and its sight line might connect directly with their son's personal war memorial on the West Hill opposite? However, his brother Robert (179) is commemorated at the Anglican St John's Church near the family home, and in the Anglican Church at Hither Green. A third brother was a chaplain to the forces (see Appendix 1). Therefore it would be unwise to read too much into Athol Gudgeon's family's Catholicism.

Was the failure to have the *WWSR* deposited in the cathedral a missed opportunity, or maybe an acknowledgement of the religiously pluralistic backgrounds of those who fought? Although now rarely found in its printed form, the *WWSR* did achieve its aim of providing, funded from war memorial committee monies, a list of those who served and those who gave their lives, in a form which could be obtained by ordinary people whose loved ones had fought and died. The project, printed here, to rediscover brief lives and service records of the men from the city of Winchester who gave their lives in the Great War may, it is hoped, redress the lacunae of a century ago. On another positive note the yew walk, promised in 1921, but prevented by the existence of mighty lime trees, grave markers and so on was achieved by the end of the decade as circumstances changed, as is shown on a sheet of notes inserted at that date in the War Memorial Committee minute book. Today, therefore, approaching from the west through the dignified yew avenue, the visitor is first confronted by the statement of Winchester's 460 dead, and the accompanying text on the tradition they represented in the city. However, this memorial to the city's First World War dead is not in the prominent northern position favoured by residents in the discussions which followed the Armistice, but is out of sight behind the county memorial,

1 *HC* 13.9.1919

perhaps explaining why it was overlooked by the compilers of the Imperial War Museum memorials database? This research reveals the tip of an iceberg in research which it hoped others may follow up.

THIS EDITION OF THE FALLEN FROM THE CITY OF WINCHESTER RECORDED IN THE *WWSR*

THE BIOGRAPHICAL TEXT here is an extract from the *WWSR* of the entries for the fallen, those marked with a cross as having been Killed in Action, Died of Wounds or died of illness etc having served 'from the Declaration of War to the Signing of the Armistice'. This basic source has been collated with information on the Commonwealth War Graves Commission (CWGC) website to give Grave References (GR) and Panel References (PR) for memorials. The CWGC online source amalgamates previous records under a Commonwealth head and provided the basis for the First World War National Roll of Honour. The CWGC is a valuable source, but contains occasional slips: Ernest Harold Alexander (6) for example appears as 'Harrold'. Some of these errors and inconsistencies no doubt resulted from the transfer of the data into the online version by the use of OCR (Optical Character Recognition), a mechanised process in which certain characters may be misread. For example the vessel on which James Wedge (441) was serving when he died was Dover Patrol M21. OCR online version records this as HMS May, but in the printed Register the ship is correctly cited as M21.[1] It is not always clear why certain casualties were apparently not buried but recorded on a panel when a grave might have been expected. Frank Steel (401) Died of Wounds on 27 August 1918 but no grave is cited, he is commemorated on Panel 7 of the Vis-en-Artois Memorial.

There are many reasons why the data in the *WWSR* contains errors and is self-contradictory. For example the question of age. Age at death and next of kin are often found in the CWGC or elsewhere. Fortunately we can attempt to check ages using other sources such as the census, notably 1911 the most recent available under the 100 years rule which preserves anonymity in public records for a century. But successive censuses do not always agree. Most

---

[1] Steve Jarvis kindly furnished this example. Comparison with printed registers has not been systematically carried out.

people involved in the First World War were young men born since 1880, so additional information is available in the decennial censuses of 1881, 1891 and 1901. Other sources yielding age and date of birth include naval records and the attestation papers of soldiers from Canada. Records from the Regimental Archive of The Hampshire Regiment contain ages given by close family. On the whole there is general agreement within a year over dates of birth in the different records, with the censuses taken earlier in an individual's life tending to be more accurate. Deaths occurred far from home in the heat of battle, or where communications were poor. Information relayed to Britain could be deficient and by the end of the war, memory might have become erroneous. Neither was the typesetting of the *WWSR* consistent. Thus, for example, the phrase 'Missing (believed Killed)' is variously set, often as 'Missing, believed Killed' and with varied capitalisation. Sometimes the less final term 'Missing' is used on its own. Elsewhere 'Wounded and Missing (believed Killed)' appears. Records, for example, WO 372/ Medal Index Cards, can fill in some of the missing men's fates, for example Ernest Judd (220) in the *WWSR* is recorded as 'Missing (believed Killed)', but in his army records he is recorded as 'Killed in Action.' The reverse is the case with John Meacher (278) who was recorded in the *WWSR* as 'Killed in Action', but in the central record as 'Missing, assumed dead'. These nuanced entries do not change the sense of what happened to individuals, but do illuminate aspects of information gathering, record keeping and commemoration, especially where individuals' fates were not known during the conflict. There is a fine line between Killed in Action and Died of Wounds and in many cases they are almost indistinguishable: to die in an ambulance en route to a casualty station is scarcely different to being Killed in Action and the terms are often used apparently interchangeably in reportage for the *WWSR*. Thus John Worsam (455) exemplifies those reported in the *WWSR* as Killed in Action, but who is recorded elsewhere, for example in the CWGC as Died of Wounds. In certain official records, for example those compiled into SDGW, Died of Wounds is preferred to the *WWSR*'s Killed in Action. It may be argued that those who died of wounds may have suffered longer than those Killed in Action. The suffering of the individual cannot be measured. Families may have been reassured by letters of condolence from the front stating that their boy had been shot through the head and had died instantly, as for example, Pioneer Harry Mitchell (287).[1]

1 R Hamps Notes. RH. How men died was significant to the bereaved. A classic account is found in Vera Brittain's *Testamant of Youth* (1933), in which she details her protracted and strenuous efforts by interviewing witnesses to

At first it was expected that the war would be short and of limited scope: no arrangements were envisaged for mass burials of those who died, or that men's places of death would not be known. The wide geographical range of combat, for example in Africa, Mesopotamia and the Balkans (which included Turkey as a theatre of war and therefore Gallipoli) losses of prisoners of war etc in these far off places were not envisaged. The Winchester evidence provides a mini-snapshot of this process. Thus the first Winchester dead, on 26 August 1914 were buried in a Communal Cemetery at Fontaine-au-Pire (Douglas Cowan (102)) and the Porte de Paris Cemetery at Cambrai (John Ball (19)) while Alfred Bell (29) and Archibald Chalk (80) were later recorded on the La Ferté-Sous-Jouarre Memorial.

Thomas Drake (119), killed in the Longido Hills in East Africa on 3 November 1914 was at first 'buried where he fell and a stone erected' but later as burial became more systematised his remains were moved to the Dar es Salaam War Cemetery. In Britain there was a greater likelihood of death in one location, for example Gravesend in Kent, where William Facey (136) died in 1916, was followed by his remains being moved nearer home. Thus Facey was buried at the Winchester St Giles's Hill Cemetery, not far from his Winchester address in Eastgate Street.[1] Athol Gudgeon (see above), who died at Haslar Hospital, Portsmouth after suffering wounds when his ship was torpedoed in 1917, was buried at the St James's Catholic Cemetery, the only Winchester war grave recorded in that location. Not all who died in Britain were returned to Winchester, thus Bertie Marsh (264), son of the Marshes of 8, Little Minster Street, who Died of Wounds in June 1918 was buried at Cardiff (Cathays), Cemetery in Wales. Harold Forster (149) exemplifies a case of a soldier who was noted as Missing (believed Killed) on 29 May 1918 as recorded in the *WWSR*, but whose remains were recovered and buried later in a British cemetery. Forster was the most decorated soldier from the city, and also one of the most decorated county cricketers in the War: he played county cricket for Hampshire. George Freemantle (153), who died at Ypres in August 1917, exemplifies a case in which the body was not recovered. Edward Jupe (223), on the other hand, who died of sunstroke at Simla in India in 1918 might have been expected to have a grave, but none is recorded and he is commemorated on a Panel in Delhi. In other cases

reassure herself that her brother Edward had indeed been shot through the head as she had been informed.
1 See also Sidney Hawkins (Leeds, buried Sparsholt, Hants) (191); George Hewlett (202) place of death NK, buried St Giles's Hill Cemetery.

cemeteries for example in Peshawar and in Southern Russia can no longer be maintained and those buried there are commemorated on appropriate memorials, for example in Delhi and Turkey.

Despite the intention to record only service up to the Armistice in November 1918 and the collection of data immediately after the signature of the peace, sixteen men who died in 1919 are listed in the *WWSR*, ten of whom died in January to March of that year. Harry Hedges (198) died of influenza in France on 14 February; Frederick Bishop (39), whose death occurred on 21 February is also noted as having died of influenza and is buried in the West Hill Cemetery in the city. That great epidemic then raging is likely to have carried off others also at that time, although not all. Gerald Cassidy (78), who died in March 1919 being recorded as having died of a disease 'of the nervous system.' Of the six who died from May onwards in that year, the latest in 1919 in the *WWSR* was Frederick Wake (430) who died on 29 August 1919. His Medal Index Card (MIC WO 372/) says nothing about his death. Perhaps he was among the many who died after they had been Discharged from the forces and therefore whose deaths were not recorded on their MIC. In general those who died after Discharge were not 'recognised' as War deaths in the CWGC. In this regard Edward Smart (376), below, who was Discharged in December 1914 as unfit for War service but who died of tuberculosis in March 1916 is unusual in being recognised by the CWGC.

Thus although 'The material was collected shortly after [the signature of Peace]' the costs of making 'the book within the reach of all' delayed publication until 1921 when the War Memorial Committee recognised the book as 'an integral part of that Memorial.'[1] Between the Armistice in November 1918 and publication of the *WWSR* in 1921 through the active agency of those involved in 'collecting and furnishing' information, the list was compiled. The apparently simple basis of domicile 'at the outbreak of the War' acted as the ground rule. We know, however, that some listed were not resident in Winchester at the outbreak of war in 1914. James Dennistoun (112) was running his parents' sheep station in New Zealand, although the parents had returned to England as war loomed. He joined them in England later.

This question of domicile is noteworthy. The *WWSR* says it contains, 'so far as it has been possible to ascertain, the names of all men domiciled in Winchester at the outbreak of the War who have served in any branch of

1   HALS HRO W/B5/40/1 for the minutes of the War Memorial Committee.

His Majesty's Forces from the Declaration of the War to the Signing of the Armistice.' It is not immediately clear why certain individuals, often from the Empire, are found in the Winchester list as no immediate relations or parents were at first apparent and, like Dennistoun (112), were probably not domiciled in Winchester at the outbreak of the War despite the claims of the compilers of the *WWSR*. However, some of these men can be shown to have been born in Winchester, for example Henry Bellinger (33) and Harry Brewer (50), both serving with Canadian forces.' The Everest brothers, Harold and Reginald (132, 133) served in the King's Royal Rifle Corps and the Canadian Light Infantry respectively. Both were sons of William and Eleanor Everest of 34, Hyde Close, they lost their lives ten days apart in the Autumn of 1916. Four Fulford brothers from 1, Queens Road, fought in the War, three in The Hampshire Regiment. Of the four, two died, Archibald (154) in 1916 as POW of Turks; his older brother Clarence (155) in August 1917 with the Canadian Infantry at Lens.

In the cases of five individuals a last address in Winchester is not given in the *WWSR*: here we have entered (No address given). Migrants who perceived (or whose relations perceived) them to be Winchester people illustrate how those in the Empire still held their origin/a place in England as their 'home' even if they had left many years earlier, or their Winchester address at the onset of the Great War proved impossible to find. Many of the Australians and Canadians who fought in the War were natives of Britain. Helpers were no doubt friends, relations, service contemporaries and others. Those who passed the 'Winchester' domicile test of residence 'at the outbreak of the War' were included. The War Memorial Committee, chaired by the mayor, Alderman A. R. Dyer whose son Capt. Dyer (124) of the Hampshire Yeomanry had been killed in East Africa in 1917, comprised Aldermen, service officers, representatives of the cathedral etc, who authorised the assembling of the data. The Committee, chaired by Alderman Dyer and included Mr W. R. Mathews whose son Lieut. William Mathews (272) gave his life at Flers with the King's Royal Rifle Corps in 1916, attended to the *WWSR*.

Any such work of assembling data will inevitably contain numbers of errors, inconsistencies between sources, and slips. Our efforts a hundred years on will also not meet with universal approval. We apologise for any

---

1 Records of Australians and Canadians are online and are especially full and helpful.

such errors. In the spelling of a surnames, Leonard Ball (20) in the *WWSR*, is entered as Balls in the Service Record; Jesse Jeffrey (215) appears as such in the *WWSR*, but as Jeffreys in the official record of service. Both spellings are given here as it is known that errors occur both in official records, such as those for soldiers, and in the *WWSR*. First names are more frequently reported differently in different sources, for example Charles H. Sticklan (also Sticklen) (404) appears in the *WWSR*, but as Herbert Charles in military records. James A. Cobb in the *WWSR* (93) appears elsewhere as Arthur James Cobb and so on.

HMS Faulknor is listed as HMS Faulkner in Henry Dowse's entry (118). Other errors and inconsistencies are exemplified by the entries relating to those who lost their lives when HMS Good Hope was lost with all hands at the battle of Coronel on 1 November 1914.[1] These details also provide an insight into the method of compilation and printing of the *WWSR*. Thomas Alexander's entry (7) in the *WWSR* says that he served on HMS Good Hope and was 'Killed in Action' at the 'Falkland Islands', George Groves (177) was 'Drowned' in the loss of the "Good Hope"[2] in 'Nov. 1914' while Bruce Jupe (222) was 'Killed in Action' November 1914 'Chilian Coast' on the same ship and in the same engagement, and appears in de Ruvigny's Roll as 'lost in action' in that engagement.[3] Their naval records confirm the date of 1 November, and that they were on the same ship. Thereafter confusion reigns: the location where HMS Good Hope was lost – the Falkland Islands and the Chilian Coast being on the east and west respectively of the continent of South America with the loss attested to have been off Chile. Such discrepancies and uncertainties suggest that the *WWSR* was typeset from a collection of individual records, or record cards, compiled and handed to the printers but which were not compared with one another for consistency and no editorial intervention occurred. Access to surviving central records today makes a more full account possible than in 1921, but cannot be free of error.

1   David Hepper, *British Warship Losses in the Ironclad Era 1860-1919* (London: Chatham Publishing, 2006) p. 28. Thomas Alexander (7), George Groves (177), Bruce Jupe (222), William Lansley (231), Cecil Patterson (314), Albert Smith (377) (just states '1914').
2   In the *WWSR* ships' names are normally given in italics without inverted commas, occasionally as in Groves's entry, though not elsewhere for the Good Hope. Inverted commas are used elsewhere, e.g. for the "Prince Edward".
3   See reference to losses on HMS Queen Mary, below.

This work provides an edition of the records of the Winchester city fallen extracted from the *WWSR*, amplified by addition of further data which has been collected. It is not a history of all from Winchester who served in the First World War, but provides a fuller account of the shortened lives of those who died than is to be found in the *WWSR*. Thus starting with the fallen in the *WWSR* the text has been enhanced by checking and adding additional materials where possible.[1] Thus if the individual was a sailor his abbreviated Service Papers have been examined (for Ratings ADM 188/). These records can be very detailed showing service on many ships and shore establishments, details of physical characteristics, height etc. All this detail has not been transcribed here although reference is given for interested parties to follow up. In the case of George Dawkins whose brother Frank (110) was killed, the entry in the *WWSR* referring only to HMS Constance has been entered below, rather than a full account of his Naval Service Record, for which see Appendix1.

For army personnel Medal Index Cards show details of name, rank, number, regiment, medals awarded and, sometimes, entry into theatre of war. Occasionally Service Papers for soldiers survive (WO 339/ as for Edgar Fielder (138) and William Mathews(272)).[2] Finding records of individuals in online sources is hit and miss according to the vagaries of record-keeping and indexing of sources and the relative ease or otherwise of access to sources in that medium. Thus Private Alfred Scaddan (360) in the *WWSR* appears in the CWGC as 'Scuddan' and in the WO 372/ as 'Scaddon'. Albert Single's records (373) in both those sources were not found. His late death in 1919 after the end of the War might be partly responsible for the lack of entry on the CWGC, (although some who died later than he are recorded there) again probably due to his Discharge before his death. William Trimble (419) in the *WWSR* proved very elusive as he is entered in official records as Tremble.

From time to time relics relating to the Winchester fallen are sold, medals of Charles (159) and Frederick (160) Gardner and Tom Rickman (348), for example, and a bronze memorial plaque relating to Cecil Shefferd (166). Charles Summerbell's medals (407) were sold in 2012: his service papers show him as 'Discharged'; therefore he does not appear on the CWGC. He died after Discharge on 7 June 1917 from tuberculosis. No date of death is given in the *WWSR*. Another case of a Discharged man whose death is included

---

1 See Bibliography.
2 Mathews variously recorded as Mathews or Matthews.

is Harold White (444), who was Discharged 'sick' in August 1915, his death recorded in the *WWSR*, but not in his army records. Ranks occasionally differ between the *WWSR* and 'official' sources. Frederick Adams (2) is referred to on the CWGC as 'Sergeant' in the *WWSR* as 'Sergeant Major'. Ernest Wyatt (459) is listed in the *WWSR* as CSM, but his MIC record refers to him as a Private. Elsewhere discrepancies are less distinct: the occasional Lance-Corporal recorded on the *WWSR* as Corporal; or a Private as a Lance-Corporal.[1] During the cut and thrust of campaign it is possible that men were promoted (and some demoted and raised in rank again later), and that these changes never made their way in their entirety into the vast bureaucracy which underpinned the war effort – or like the names - were mis-recorded.

Other repositories than The National Archives have been found to contain records, for example the Imperial War Museum Private Papers Collection which contains two Flying Log Books for Captain Alexander Mayo (275). Where access to regimental diaries has been possible (see Abraham, for example) some additional detail has been added, but it is by no means certain in every case that an individual was engaged in the actions described, or lost their life there. Where evidence indicates that a person gave their life in particular circumstances in a specific action, for example in the cases of Edward Bligh (41) and Gawain Bell (30), such data is included in their brief biography. Where evidence exists of their unit being engaged more generally in a particular action, as in the case of Arthur Abraham (1), gassed in September 1918, information is footnoted. Battalion diaries, accounts of the loss of ships and similar records provide insights into the experiences of both officers and other ranks. Citations for gallantry, such as those for Harold Forster set down below, take us further into the precise circumstances and the horror and terror which must have surrounded those men while Harold Forster managed, despite everything to show not only exceptional courage and resourcefulness, but also was reported as remaining 'perfectly cheerful' throughout one of the several actions in which he displayed his conspicuous gallantry while fellow officers and men around him fell.

Time has been given to looking at the various decennial censuses to gather further information on family background, parents and siblings (at those snapshot dates 1891, 1901 and 1911), occupations places of birth etc.

---

1   SJ suggests that as Lance-Corporal was an appointment, those of that rank would return to being a Private at death.

Except in the case, for example of Canadian nationals who gave their place of birth as Winchester, where the place of birth was other than Winchester was recorded in the census, such other places have been entered. Otherwise places of birth, if known, were Winchester and have not been repetitively entered. This information has only been included where there is in our view reasonable evidence which identifies individuals sharing the same name. Such evidence contributes to a clearer picture of relationships, if any, between pre-war and wartime work. For example Edward Smart (d. 1916) (376), a Groom in 1911, became a Driver in the Royal Horse Artillery, an appropriate role for his skills and knowledge. The majority of soldiers and sailors, especially those in the Service battalions however experienced a military existence in all respects far removed from their previous experience and lives. Occupations added into the biographies below are given a capital letter at the beginning, as Groom, above.

The 1911 census questionnaire asked couples to state how many completed years they had been married, marriage dates derived from that source entered below will therefore be approximate within one year. Some material has been gleaned from websites such as Ancestry, Findmypast (the BMD information from Findmypast.co.uk, as they give the maiden names of wives). http://www.freebmd.org.uk/ - allows free access to view the indexes. [Mark Allen writes: It's not quite complete, I think, but fairly much so (Findmypast is complete, but subscription is required). As they are indexes, they tell you who is listed as getting married on each page of the register. There are two weddings per page, so when you do a search you'll get four names. As long as you know the Christian name of the wife, and the other wife on the page doesn't have the same Christian name, you will be able to tell what the maiden name is.]

Winchester College men who died in the Great War are not generally included here as they have their own extensive record and publication already referred to.[1] However, a very few are included from that college with Winchester addresses and who appear in the *WWSR* among the fallen. Those from the men's Diocesan Training College for the dioceses of Winchester and Salisbury (later King Alfred's Diocesan Training College, and now the University of Winchester) who died other than those who already appear in the *WWSR*[2] have their names carved into the panelling

1 *Wykehamists who Died in the War 1914-1918*, 4 vols. (Winchester, 1921)
2 John Hartley researched the service of those from the Diocesan Training College and his findings are now found in the Hampshire Record Office and at

of the University of Winchester, King Alfred's College Old Chapel (Winton Memorial Room).

NOTE ON TERMINOLOGY

REGIMENTAL NOMENCLATURE IS taken from *The Monthly Army List September 1918* and succeeding sources which address changes in regimental names, and is entered throughout.

In the cases of Rifle Regiments, KRRC, 1/8th Bn The Hampshire Regiment etc we have used the term 'Private' although some are entered in the *WWSR* as 'Rfn' (Ball (19), Bell (29), Brewer (49)). This term was current during the War but as Major Gray writes 'After years of struggle the use of the rank of Rifleman in place of Private was officially recognised by Army Order 222 1923, dated June 1923.'[1] We have preferred the term Private to Rifleman, although Rifleman may also be mentioned.

The addition of the prefix 'Royal' to certain units which occurred after that date of service enlistment, for example the Army Service Corps in which William Harvey (189) served became the Royal Army Service Corps in 1918. Harvey's *WWSR* record gives 'R.A.S.C.' but so far no precise date of death from tuberculosis has been found for him. However by the time the *WWSR* was finally published in 1921, some regimental titles had been updated for the *WWSR*, others not. Thus while some entries include 'Royal', for example in the case of Harry Maton (273), RASC who would have enlisted in 1910 in the Army Service Corps, which would still have been the ASC when he was killed and would likely have been the nomenclature known for Canteen assistant Tom Stainer who died in December 1918, others in the ASC and neither of those who served in the Army Pay Corps (APC) had 'Royal' added to the title of their regiment for the *WWSR*. Service in the Army Service Corps in the edited entries below is referred to without the 'Royal' addition to the title.[2]

---

the University of Winchester.
1 Major (Retd) Ken Gray, pers. comm. See also *Rifle Brigade Chronicle*, 1923, p. 194.
2 Thus H. C. Hall (183) appears as no 1396 in that List, but was killed on 4 September 1918.: *WWSR* entry merely reads 'Killed in Action, 1918'. The Army Pay Corps, Royal from 19118/19. See Bertram Middleton (281) who enlisted in the APC in 1914 but left to join the Argyll and Sutherland Highlanders with whom he was serving when he lost his life. No R was added to the APC in the

Regimental and battalion detail may be used to distinguish those who were regulars, and those who were conscripts. 'Service' battalions were formed to serve overseas and were not reservists, for example William Gardiner (158) of the 6th (Service) Bn The Wiltshire Regiment who enlisted in January 1916 and was killed the same year.

Where the *WWSR* says 'Belgium', 'Flanders' or 'France' and CWGC gives 'France and Flanders' as theatres of action for an individual we have used on occasion the term 'Western Front' which stretched through what is now Belgium and northern France, and includes both 'France' and 'Flanders'. Henry Lees (237), for example, is recorded in the *WWSR* as having served in 'France'. However, when he was Killed in Action he was commemorated on the Tyne Cot memorial in Belgium.

While there are various indicators of locations some consistency has been attempted. Thus Gallipoli appears in the Service Records of some in the *WWSR*, others who took part in the same actions are noted as 'Dardanelles': we have put therefore 'Gallipoli (Dardanelles)' in all cases, including sailors. Technically these Turkish actions were in the 'Balkans' Theatre of War, see for example the WO 372/ for Charles Flux (142) of The Hampshire Regiment. For a location well known in Britain and Ireland in one form (e.g. Ypres) that better known form is preferred, rather than the name as recorded today (Ieper) and found on the CWGC. It is hoped that confusion has been avoided by using the combination Ypres (Ieper).

Place name forms and spellings follow the *WWSR*, with explanations noted as necessary. Historic names which appear in the *WWSR*, for example Constantinople for modern Istanbul, are preferred for consistency. Salonica, as in *WWSR*, for Salonika, etc. Accents have been added where they are used in the *WWSR* – e.g. for Armentières. However no check has been done on all other French forms such as Etaples etc. Locally the spelling Chilcomb, as used in the *WWSR*, is used throughout, rather than the alternative Chilcombe. It is reckoned that a reference to 'Neenes' Road was Nuns Road etc. (4)

Care has been taken to refer to regiments and branches of the Services correctly, expanding the detail in the *WWSR*. Thus in the first entry, for Abraham, his regiment The Queen's (Royal West Surrey Regiment) is set down in full in the caption line, but such full titles may be shortened in the text which follows. Douglas Alexander (5) would have joined The Royal

---

WWSR in his case.

Flying Corps as a cadet, but by the time he lost his life on 8 October 1918, the Royal Air Force had been established on 1 April of that year. Guy Bartlett (26) was commissioned in the RAF on 1 April 1918 and was killed on 6 April. For military ranks and promotions not every detail is given here. Men, for example, who progressed from the ranks to commissions, are entered here at the rank which they achieved at their death and/or as printed in the *WWSR*. The term 'Serjeant' as opposed to 'Sergeant' is preferred here as that was the usual form during the First World War. Nonetheless, the CWGC for example uses 'Sergeant Major' on occasion.

EDITORIAL METHOD.

IN PREPARING THIS text we have copied from the *WWSR* the individual entry for each man who lost his life, including the Winchester address where given, as noted above, the baseline for the compilers 1918-21. Each man is given a number which is referred to where mention is made in the Introduction.

For example:

305 WINKWORTH, William, Private, 9432, [**Medal Index Card WO 372/**][1] 4th Bn The Rifle Brigade (The Prince Consort's Own), [**1918 Army List**] d. 10 May 1915 aged 31 [*WWSR*/**CWGC**].

Son of Thomas Winkworth of 6, Bank Street, Ashford, Kent [**CWGC?**]. Born Winchester 1884 [**Census/SDGW**]. Living in Water Lane aged 7, 1891 [**Census**]. Husband of Bessie Winkworth of 5, Nutley Lane, Reigate, Surrey.[**CWGC/?BMD**] In 1911 a Journeyman Baker living with Bessie and Ernest Winter Arnold at 2, Holly Cottages, Smelthy Lane, Lower Kingswood, Reigate.[**Census**] [2] Enlisted in 1903 [*WWSR*, **SDGW**] at Winchester [**SDGW**]. Served in France [*WWSR*]. Wounded in 1914. [*WWSR*] Killed in Action 10 May 1915 [*WWSR*/**WO372/**]. Commemorated on Ypres (Menin Gate) Memorial, Ypres (Ieper), West-Vlaanderen, Belgium (PR Panels 46-48, 50). [**CWGC**] [3]

Thus each entry is compiled from a variety of sources, many of which

[1] WO 372/22/22864.
[2] 20, Parchment Street address in *WWSR* possibly an address given to the CWGC when they were informed of the death.
[3] CWGC.

agree in repeating the same information (e.g. date of death), but where there is disagreement, for example on date of death, we note that. Generally, but not always, military and CWGC records are more accurate than the *WWSR*. The compilation is derived from the Commonwealth War Graves Commission, and Soldiers Who Died in the Great War (SDGW) databases, Medal Index Cards (WO 372/) and for Naval Ratings (ADM 188/) from The National Archive (TNA) as outlined above to provide basic material on each man: name(s) as given in these additional records, number as appropriate, rank etc. The highest rank an individual attained known to the compilers of the *WWSR* appears in the second column of the *WWSR* set between two sets of dots. In some cases the compilers made no entry in this column and we have inserted [BLANK]. In the final column other service details are given. Here, as in the *WWSR* 'Then follow the name of the unit first joined and the date and rank of joining; units to which transferred; theatres of war in which served; honours gained; nature of any casualties with dates.' Chronological data is not always clear, as for example in the service joining dates of some Canadians, when compared to data in the *WWSR*. Information collected is entered more or less in this order, however in some cases honours gained are entered after the record of death. In John R. Adams's (3) case in the second column he is entered as 'L.S.' (Leading Seaman) and in the final column as 'O.S.' (i.e. Ordinary Seaman), however in his service papers it appears that he entered a 'Boy 2nd class'. Such additional information is added in the second, numbered, section here. Because these details are available in sources elsewhere, such as service papers and partially available on the *WWSR* itself, we have not entered promotions but have used the convention of highest rank at death.

 Evidence for those serving with Australian and Canadian forces is found online and is in certain respects more detailed than its British counterparts. For Australians such as Frank Fraser (151), whose neat signature is found on his papers – he was formerly a Clerk - we are reminded of the six weeks sea-journey to reach England, before service could begin. Edwin Covey's (100) online record contains his letter to next of kin in the event of his death and the possessions returned to his kin which are listed – ID disk, whistle, knife, photos, letters etc.[1] Frederick Fitt's (141) records from Australia include much detail including an apparent reference to a request for,

---

[1] On the CWGC he is entered as Edwin Haney Covey. His Australian record suggests the more likely name of Harvey.

and despatch of, a photo in 1918 to a Mrs H. E. ҁHooper, of 21, St Thomas Street, Winchester, the address given in the *WWSR*. Canadian records, as noted above, can provide explanations as to why apparently Canadian men appear on the *WWSR* who can be shown to be natives of Winchester and who migrated. Records in New Zealand show James Dennistoun (112) photographed there during his involvement with Captain Scott's expedition to the South Pole in 1912.[1]

To avoid overloading the text with footnotes we have not footnoted all sources in every case. Thus the *WWSR* entry at the top of the entry for each man copies that in the 1921 printed version. In the material below material is taken in each case from the records of the Commonwealth War Graves Commission (CWGC), which contain some details of service and age at death, which we have used here, commemoration and grave data, and may contain information on family/next of kin. Soldiers Died in the Great War (SDGW) data has also been incorporated and is often indicated by a phrase opening 'Enlisted...' places of enlistment are from SDGW. Data from the Medal Index Cards provides further data, on other ranks' numbers, regimental details, date of death etc. Inevitably sources conflict – for example in the death of a submariner J. R. Adams (3) three dates are given: no one saw the craft strike a mine and date of death is therefore uncertain. Such discrepancies are impossible to resolve and are therefore merely noted. Searches have been made of decennial censuses up to 1911, and are not footnoted in all cases to save space. Citations: always from *The London Gazette*, WO 372 (see V. Bennett) but do not always survive tho' listed in *LG*.

WINCHESTER SERVICEMEN WHO FELL IN THE FIRST WORLD WAR.

A S EXPLAINED ABOVE, in 1911 Winchester had a population of 23,328, and was some 400 more in 1921. The War Service Register gives a list of some 3,500 who served giving a mortality rate of some 13%. As a former barrack town until the end of the twentieth century Winchester has a long military pedigree.

To write a full and detailed account of all engagements and circumstances in which men from the city of Winchester gave their lives would

---

[1] See below entry for Dennistoun and associated footnote.

involve writing a complete history of the Great War. That is clearly out of the question. In most cases it is impossible to tell how and in what capacity particularly infantrymen gave their lives. Two examples of the uncertainties and pitfalls of trying to match individuals to specific engagements illustrate this point.

It is possible to illustrate the kinds of specific actions in which the casualties gave their lives but the detail of which company they were in is beyond the scope of this study. For example in the case of Private William Baird (17) and others, the Battalion diary shows the following for the days before he was killed on 10 August 1915: on the 8 and 9 August 1915 10th Hampshires left bivouac about 9.30. They proceeded north up the Chailac Dere. They reached their destination, after many delays caused by blockages of other troops, at 04.00 on the 9 August. They were deployed at 05.30. At 08.00 'A' and 'B' company attacked contour 270 but only reached within 800 yards of the ridge. They entrenched for the night, taking many casualties because of shrapnel fire. On 10 August 1915 a general Turkish counter attack developed about 04.30. 10th Hampshires were sent to reinforce 'A' and 'D' company positions below the crest of the Chunuk (or Chanuk) Bair ridge. It is probable this is when Baird, and others, were killed. They retired after being cut off from the regiments to their right to Green Hill where they remained for the rest of the day.[1]

Evidence from Battalion diaries may refer to an individual such Pte Arthur Abraham (1), but does not necessarily prove that he was killed in the action cited. According to the Battalion diary for The Queen's (Royal West Surrey Regiment), in the days leading up to his death on 21 September the Battalion undertook routine training. On the evening of 16 September 1918 they moved up to the Saulcourt area, near the village of Lieramont. The villages and surrounding roads were heavily bombed and machine gunned by aircraft during the night. On 17 September there was a conference of Battalion commanders at Brigade Headquarters, and on 18, 19 and 20 September the Battalion, under heavy shell fire, machine gun fire and gas, were engaged in what later became known as the Battle of Epehy. Private Abraham was gassed on 20 September and died the following day. While it is highly likely this location and engagement is correct, we cannot ultimately be certain. For this reason we have not attempted to reconstruct the theatres

---

1   C.T.Atkinson (ed) *The Royal Hampshire Regiment 1914-18*. Vol 2 (Glasgow: Glasgow University Press 1952) p. 97.

of death of soldiers in detail although undoubtedly such evidence could provide colour to the bald statements of their deaths.

Citizens signed up into all three services as the roll of the fallen shows below. They fought and died in a wide variety of theatres which may be broadly defined from their records as on the High Seas (Mediterranean, North Sea, Pacific etc) and below the waves in submarine warfare; South and East Africa, Egypt, Palestine and Mesopotamia and India; the Balkans (which included Gallipoli (Dardanelles)); and the Western Front (France and Flanders), others are referred to as having served just in 'France' and that is reproduced here. Soldiers from Winchester fought and died in engagements both in France and Flanders and beyond, in defence of the Empire and at sea. Some died of disease, some were captured and died at prisoners of war.

The total of dead, 458/459 is consistent with our researches, one discrepancy from 460 on the stone memorial being Albert Moore of the Rifle Brigade who fought with distinction first under the name Moore (265/289), but who subsequently it seems because he was excluded from service by age,[1] reenlisted under his mother's name, Marshall, and who Died of Wounds on 12 May 1915 and is entered twice in the *WWSR*.[2]

By far the largest group of those who gave their lives were from, or as some time associated with The Hampshire Regiment and its associated units as set down above from the Regimental memorial. Nearly 200 of those 458/459 who died fall into this category.

Winchester men gave their lives throughout the war from August 1914. The first Winchester men who gave their lives on 26 August 1914 included John Ball (19) and Archibald Chalk (80). Both had enlisted earlier in the month and had been in France for only three days when they were killed. Hampshires died at Le Cateau and Riflemen in the retreat from Mons. As the war gathered momentum and spread Harry Winkworth, Chief Cook on HMS Hawke (450) was the first sailor from the city to die on 15 October when some 500 were drowned in the loss of the ship. Three days later the first officer from the city to lose his life was Major John Morrah (290) on 18

---

1 Derek Whitfield 'To what extent did voluntaryism characterise Winchester's response to the war in 1914 and 1915. Unversity of Birmingham MA dissertation, 2015. Available through the Western Front Association website. We are very grateful to Derek Whitfield for his support and insights during our work.
2 We are grateful to Gavin Edgerley-Harrris for solving this conundrum. See Marshall/Moore below.

October. Three Naval personnel, for example, from Winchester gave their lives at the Battle of Coronel, off Valparaiso, Chile on 1 November 1914;[1] On 3 November the first death of a Winchester city man in Africa occurred when Thomas Drake (119), Trooper in the East African Mounted Rifles gave his life in the Longido Hills in German East Africa.

Many soldiers from The Hampshire Regiment were lost at Gallipoli in 1915. At the Somme on 1 July 1916 some nine Winchester city soldiers from the Berkshires, the Hampshires, the KRRC and Thomas Cox (105)[2] of the 3rd Wessex Field Ambulance of the Royal Army Medical Corps were killed. Winchester men also engaged in war in the air, as members of the Royal Flying Corps and Royal Air Force. We find men from the city present throughout hostilities. At Jutland in 1916 men served both on HMS Queen Mary where, although nine men survived, over 1,600 lives were lost all entered in this list as 'Killed in Action' rather than as on other ships where the term 'Drowned' is used,[3] and HMS Ardent, from which there were 73 survivors, both ships being lost; on 10 November 1918, the day before armistice, Charles Gardner (159) was lost on HM Paddle Minesweeper Ascot, the last ship to be torpedoed in the War.[4] Several Winchester men, all associated with the Royal Field Artillery, were killed or taken prisoner on 21 March 1918, the first day of the German Spring Offensive: Albert Aslett (13), Captain Robert Gudgeon (179) and Percy Norgate (302) (the latter two both wounded and taken prisoner and who later died), Edward Smith, was also taken prisoner, but survived. His brother (379) of The Hampshire Regiment, had already been killed in 1915. This snapshot shows how Winchester men were engaged in the conflict from the beginning in August 1914 to the Armistice in November 1918 and beyond.

[1] James Dennistoun's brother George is reported to have been engaged in the battle on Lake Nyasa (Lake Malawi), reputedly the first naval engagement of the War.
[2] Thomas was the second of three Cox brothers to give their lives. His brother Frederick (104) had been killed on 31 May 1916, and his brother Frank (103) was to die on 7 August 1917. This family suffered the greatest loss of any recorded in the Great War in Winchester and has been researched by Alan Bungey to whom we are grateful for this information.
[3] A nuance to indicate, perhaps, the HMS Queen Mary blew up rather than sank with much loss of life? See Thomas Judd etc. Rowell, a Stoker on HMS Hampshire, was recorded as 'drowned' in the *WWSR* whereas Albert Smith (377), a Stoker on HMS Good Hope, was recorded as Killed in Action.
[4] Hepper, 2006, *passim*.

This account of the lives of these 'forgotten' men from the city of Winchester is intended to commemorate their service and lives a hundred years on. Neither of the compilers of this book have any memory of any individuals from this group, although through a public awareness effort we have been contacted by and have corresponded with some who have memories and/or knowledge of aspects of the lives of these men as relations or in other ways. The study contains the outline of a quantitative history of these men, but circumstances prevented completion of that aspect of our study. Commemoration is a separate issue from memory, and this book and associated materials while being commemorative of the individuals named is also intended a century on to provide a tangible memorial to a group of Winchester men who gave their lives but whose names were not memorialised in stone in their city.

TBJ/JB

DEBT OF HONOUR

ABBREVIATIONS

ADM	Admiralty Records
Bde	Brigade
Bdr	Brigadier/Bombardier
Bn	Battalion
Bty	Battery
CWGC	Commonwealth War Graves Commission
DOW	Died of Wounds
GR	Grave Reference
HC	*Hampshire Chronicle*
HMPMS	His Majesty's Paddle Minesweeper
HMS	His Majesty's Ship
IWM	Imperial War Museum
KIA	Killed in Action
L.-Corpl.	Lance-Corporal[1]
LG	*The London Gazette*
Lt.-Col.	Lieutenant-Colonel
MIC	Medal Index Card (army personnel – TNA WO 372/)
NK	Not Known
POW	Prisoner of War
PR	Panel(s) Reference
PRO	Public Record Office, Kew
Rd	Road
Sqdn	Squadron
St	Street (or Saint according to context)
TNA	The National Archive, Kew (Incorporating the Public Record Office (PRO))
WO	War Office record. Found at the The National Archive (TNA)
WWSR	A Cecil Parker (ed) *Winchester War Service Register. A Record of the Service of Winchester Men in the Great War 1914-1918* (Winchester: Warren and Co. 1921)

1 We have followed the *WWSR* in hyphenating ranks.

THE FALLEN

✠ABRAHAM, J. ... Pte. ... Lond. P.O. Rifles, Dec. 1917, Rfn. R.W.S. France. Gassed, Sept. 20, 1918. *Died, Sept. 21, 1918.* (89, Upper Brook Street)

1. ABRAHAM, Arthur John, Private, 30999,[1] 7th (Service) Bn The Queen's (Royal West Surrey Regiment), d. 21 September 1918 aged 18.

Son John and Emma Abraham of The Cemetery Lodge, St James's Lane. At school 1911, aged 11. Joined the London Post Office Rifles in December 1917, enlisting at Southampton, and served in France, later transferring to the Royal West Surrey Regiment.[2] During 20 September he was gassed and died the next day.[3] Buried in St Sever Cemetery Extension, Rouen, France (GR R. III. G. 10.).[4] Memorial at Holy Trinity.

✠ADAMS, FREDERICK ... R.S.M. ... Can. Cav., Sept. 1914, Pte. France. Wounded, 1915. *Killed in Action, Mch. 12, 1918.* (5, Maidstone Terrace)

2. ADAMS, Frederick, Regimental Serjeant Major,[5] 13714, 5th Bn Canadian Infantry (Western Cavalry), d. 12 March 1918 aged 37.[6]

---

1 John added from WO 372/1/7943. G/30999.
2 No reference to London PO Rifles on MIC or SDGW.
3 Evidence from Battalion Diaries may refer to an individual such as this, but does not necessarily prove that he was killed in the action cited. According to the Battalion diary for the Royal West Surrey Regiment, in the days leading up to his death the Battalion undertook routine training. On the evening of 16 September 1918 they moved up to the Saulcourt area, near the village of Lieramont. The villages and surrounding roads were heavily bombed and machine gunned by aircraft during the night. On 17 September there was a conference of Battalion commanders at Brigade Headquarters, and on 18, 19 and 20 September the Battalion, under heavy shell fire, machine gun fire and gas, were engaged in what later became known mas the Battle of Epehy.
4 CWGC.
5 CWGC states Sergeant. Standard form used here is Serjeant, see Introduction p.xlvii.
6 http://www.collectionscanada.gc.ca/databases/cef/index-e.html .

Son of Henry and Ellen Adams. Born 1881, living at 33, Hyde Street.[1] At school aged 10 in 1891, living at The Albert Inn, Kingsgate Street. Married Ellen Matilda Retallick in the Autumn of 1914 who was living at 107, Paulet Road, Camberwell, London at his death. His next of kin was his mother, Ellen, of 5, Culver Road, which is the same address as 5, Maidstone Terrace. Served in the South African Campaign and on 17 September 1914 joined the Canadian Cavalry. According to his Canadian attestation papers his trade was a Carpenter before re-enlisting. Served in France and was wounded in 1915. Killed in Action on 12 March 1918. Buried in Aix-Noulette Communal Cemetery Extension, Pas de Calais, France (GR II. B.19.).[2] Memorial at St Michael's.

✠ADAMS, JOHN R. ... L.S. ... R.N., 1910, O.S. North Sea. Despatches, 1917. *Killed in Action, Dec. 1, 1916.*
(Hill View, Bar End)

3. ADAMS, John Roderick,[3] Leading Seaman, 235273, HM Submarine E37. Royal Navy, d. 3 December[4] 1916 aged 27.

Born 27 August 1889 at Sutton, Surrey. Joined the Royal Navy in 1907.[5] HMS Bonaventura at Portsmouth, 1911 aged 21. Married Christine Cumming in 1915. Mentioned in Despatches 1917. Contemporaries believed the submarine struck a mine and sank in the North Sea.[6] The discrepancy in the dates of death of 30 November and 1 December and could relate to the day the submarine sailed and the following day when it struck a mine. The date of 3 December appears anomalous. Commemorated on the Portsmouth Naval Memorial (PR 12).[7] Memorials at All Saints and Chilcomb.

✠ALEXANDER, ARTHUR E. ... L.-Corpl ... R. Berks, May 1916, Pte. Dorset. India, Mesopotamia. *Died in Hospital,* 1918.
(44, Nuns Road)

4. ALEXANDER, Arthur Evelyn, Lance-Corporal, 26115,[8] 2nd Bn The Dorsetshire Regiment , d. 5 July 1918 aged 31.

Son of John and Harriet Mary Alexander. A Grocer's Assistant in 1911.

---

1   Canadian Attestation Papers.
2   CWGC.
3   John Rodway in ADM/417/235273 for his Service Record. There would normally be an ADM citation record also in the ADM 188s, but none was found in this case.
4   The Submarine Museum gives 30 November. Naval Casualty Records 1914-19 say 3 December.
5   TNA Online Royal Navy Ratings Service Records 1853-1923 states joined in 1907.
6   Hepper, 2006, p. 75 records E37 lost on 1 December.
7   CWGC.
8   WO 372/1/42817.

Married Autumn 1914 to Harriett Ada Waterman of Neenes (?Nuns) Rd, Winchester.¹ Enlisted in the Royal Berkshire Regiment in 1916 at Winchester. Died in hospital, 5 July 1918. Buried at Winchester (West Hill) Old Cemetery (GR 1962).² Memorial at St Bartholomew's.

✠ALEXANDER, DOUGLAS G. ... Cadet ... Hants Y., 1913, Tpr. R.F.C. France. Belgium, Egypt. *Killed in Egypt, Oct.* 8, 1918. (Lawn House, Eastgate Street)

5. ALEXANDER, Douglas Glencross, Flight Cadet, 204933,³ 20th Training Wing, Royal Air Force, d. 8 October 1918 aged 24.

Son of Robert and Edith Alexander, of Glencross, Morn Hill, Chilcomb. Family living at Lawn House, 28, Eastgate Street in 1901. Worked in Guildford, Surrey, as a Draper's Assistant in 1911. Enlisted in 1913 at Guildford and served as a Private in Royal West Surrey Regiment (1150).⁴ Corporal in the Hampshire Yeomanry (later 15th (Service) Bn (2nd Portsmouth) The Hampshire Regiment).⁵ A territorial soldier he entered theatre of war in France with 1/1st Hampshire Carabiniers Yeomanry sometime after the beginning of 1916.⁶ Served on the Western Front. Joined the RFC⁷ as a cadet and was based at Aboukir in Egypt, where the Royal Flying Corps (later RAF from 1 April 1918) had a training school. Killed here on 8 October 1918. Buried in Alexandria (Hadra) War Memorial Cemetery, Egypt.⁸ Memorial at St John the Baptist.

His brothers, Stuart and Sydney, served in the Royal Garrison Artillery, then in the Hampshire Yeomanry and survived the War.

✠ALEXANDER, ERNEST H. ... Pte. ... . Hants Y., June 1915, Tpr. Hants. France, Belgium. Wounded, Nov. 1917. *Killed in Action, Oct.* 14, 1918. (1, Wales Street)

1   Nuns Road in the *WWSR.* 'Neenes' on the CWGC.
2   CWGC.
3   WO 372/1/431171. RHamps Notes. RH gives this number as his new number when all territorials were renumbered early in 1917 when he was Cpl Alexander.
4   SDGW.
5   15th also known as (Hampshire Carabiniers) Bn The Hampshire Regiment amalgamated from 27 September 1917. See Appendix 2 for the structure of the Hampshire Regiment during the First World War. RH.
6   RHamps Notes. RH. No mention of RFC on Medal Roll.
7   RAF founded from RFC 1 April 1918. Enlisted in RFC, died in RAF. SDGW.
8   CWGC.

6. ALEXANDER, Ernest Harrold,[1] Private, 205557,[2] 15th (Hampshire Carabiniers) Bn The Hampshire Regiment, d. 14 October 1918 aged 22.

Fifth son of Frederick William and Mary Ann Alexander of 1, Wales Street.[3] He was a Page Boy at Northgate School, St Cross Road in 1911 aged 14. Enlisted at Winchester in 1915 in the Hampshire Carabiniers Yeomanry[4] and landed at Le Havre in 1916. 205557 was his number when renumbered with all territorials in early 1917.[5] Served on the Western Front from early 1917, was wounded in 1917 and Died of Wounds on 14 October 1918 shortly after being brought in to the 15th Cheshire Aid post.[6] Buried in Dadizeele New British Cemetery, Moorslede, West-Vlaanderen, Belgium (GR I. D. 25.).[7] Memorials at St John the Baptist.

His eldest brother Thomas, listed below, was Killed in Action on 1 November 1914. His younger brother Walter served in the Army Service Corps (Mechanical Transport) and survived the War.

⌘**ALEXANDER, THOMAS A. ... Blacksmith's Mate ... R.N., 1904. Stoker. H.M.S. *Good Hope*. Killed in Action, Nov. 1, 1914, *Falkland Islands*.**
   (1, Wales Street)

7. ALEXANDER, Thomas Alfred, Blacksmith's Mate, 7537,[8] HMS Good Hope, Royal Navy, d. 1 November 1914 aged 22.[9]

Son of Frederick William and Mary Ann Alexander, of 1, Wales Street, born 28 March 1892.[10] A Royal Navy Stoker in 1911 at Portsmouth, aged 19. Enlisted in 1911.[11] Killed in Action 1 November 1914 at the Battle of Coronel off

1 CWGC has Harrold. 3, Wales Street in 1911.
2 WO 372/1/43277, states Ernest H.
3 *The Hampshire Regimental Journal*, November 1918, p 244 for an obituary and a letter from the padre who buried him. Gives his age as 21.
4 See Appendix 2. RH. Became part of the 15th (Service) Bn The Hampshire Regiment in September 1917 which adopted the title 15th (Hampshire Carabiniers).
5 See Appendix 2.
6 RH notes KIA.
7 CWGC.
8 ADM 188/1033/7537. M/7537. This Service Record gives Thomas only as his forename. [Note states '?5982/MIC A + B].
9 HMS Good Hope was sunk at Coronel off Chile – see other entries in this record – this reference to the Falkland Islands, east of South America, is an error. However, informants of the WWSR may have heard that the Good Hope had called in at the Falklands for coal. There, Captain Cradock of the Good Hope quipped that he was leaving his medals, as he would not need them, but he did take his dog: the medals survived, Cradock and the dog were lost. (C. B. James, pers. comm.).
10 3, Wales Street in 1911. Birth from SDGW.
11 Service Records say 1911, when he signed up for 12 years. *WWSR* states 1904.

Valparaiso, Chile.¹ The reference to the Falkland Islands here must be an error. Commemorated on the Portsmouth Naval Memorial (PR 5.).² Memorial at St John the Baptist and Wesleyan Methodist Chapel, St Peter's Street.

His brother Ernest H., listed above, was Killed in Action on 14 October 1918. His brother Walter H. served in the Army Service Corps (Mechanical Transport) and survived the War.³

✠**ALLEN, ARTHUR H. ... Sergt. ... Hants, Sept. 1914, Pte. India, Mesopotamia. Wounded, July 29, 1915.** *Died, Mch. 2, 1919, as result of wounds.*
(17, Union Street)

8. ALLEN, Arthur Harold, Serjeant, 200724, 1/4th Bn The Hampshire Regiment, d. 2 March 1919 aged 27.

Son of Samuel and Mary Allen. Born at Alresford. A Milkman in 1911. Joined The Hampshire Regiment in September 1914 and served in India and Mesopotamia. Listed as formerly 4/2788. Wounded at the relief of Kut,⁴ 29 July 1915. Died on 2 March 1919 from wounds.⁵ Buried at St Cross (St Faith's) Burial Ground.⁶ Memorial at Wesleyan Methodist Chapel, St Peter's Street.

✠**ANDREWS, FRANK ... A.B. ... R.N., 1914. North Sea.** *Died, 1916.*
(63, Parchment Street.)

9. ANDREWS, Frank, Able Seaman, J/304271PO,⁷ HMS Canada. Royal Navy, d. 27 December 1916 aged 20.

Son of Lucy and stepson of William Moran, born 10 December 1896. Errand Boy in 1911 and an Electrician's Mate when he joined the Royal Navy 1914. Served on the North Sea. Died on 27 December 1916 from heart disease and chronic nephritis on HM Hospital Ship Soudan. Buried at the Lyness Royal

---

1 Hepper, 2006, p. 28.
2 CWGC.
3 *The Hampshire Regimental Journal*, November 1918, p. 244 refers to an older brother or Ernest Alexander, see above, also in The Hampshire Regiment and wounded in Yorkshire in November 1918..
4 An example of someone who survived captivity but died soon after the Armistice. Many who died post war were not included in *WWSR*..
5 WO 372/1/54973.
6 Unknown if he had been Discharged.
7 ADM 188/707/30427 provides his correct number. J/304271PO . 304271 is an error in the CWGC: perhaps J/30427/PO. The ADM 188s provide occupations prior to enlistment. SDGW.

Naval Cemetery, Island of Hoy, Orkneys (GR B. 68.).¹ Memorial at Holy Trinity.

✠**ANDREWS, JAMES C. W. ... Corpl. ... R.G.A., 1907, Gun. France. Wounded, Aug. 15, 1915.** *Killed in Action, Sept. 23, 1917, Vimy Ridge.*
 (1, Cross Keys Passage)

10. ANDREWS, James Charles William, Corporal, 26665,² 6th Siege Bty Royal Garrison Artillery d. 23 September 1917 aged 29.

Son of William E. and Emma Andrews, of 1, Cross Keys Passage. Born at Woodstone. Joined the Royal Garrison Artillery at Portsmouth in 1907. Based at Golden Hill Fort, Freshwater, Isle of Wight in 1911, aged 23. Served on the Western Front. Wounded on 15 August 1915 he was Killed in Action on 23 September 1917 at Vimy Ridge.³ Buried in Trois Arbres Cemetery, Steenwerck, Nord, France (GR I. Y. 36.).⁴ Memorial at St John the Baptist as William Andrews.

His brothers Arthur and Frederick served in the Royal Navy and survived the War.

✠**ANDREWS, WILLIAM ... Bdr. ... R.H.A., Aug. 1914, Gun. France.** *Killed in Action, Nov. 5, 1914.*
 (8, St. John's South)

11. ANDREWS, William, Bombardier, Bty⁵ Royal Horse Artillery, d. 5 November 1914 age unknown.⁶

Enlisted in August 1914. He served in France and was Killed in Action 5 November 1914.⁷

---

1 CWGC.
2 WO 372/1/94022.
3 NB Cemetery a distance away from Vimy Ridge. GJEH pers. comm.
4 CWGC. St John Baptist memorial reference SJ, pers. comm.
5 Bombardier Andrews remains difficult to identify. No record of him has been found in WO 372/ nor does he appear on the CWGC as a casualty in 1914. A William Andrews is found serving Overseas in 1911, at Dilkousha, Lucknow, India. SJ suggests this is an error for the previous or following entry. The previous entry died 1917 and the following entry in 1914.
6 NB A Corporal William Andrews of the Royal Garrison Artillery d 4 November 1918.
7 Not found on CWGC.

✠ANDREWS, WILLIAM J. ... Gun. ... R.F.A., Sept. 1914, Flanders, France. Wounded, Dec. 3, 1914. *Died of Wounds, Dec. 14 1914.*
(41, North Walls)

12. ANDREWS, William John, Gunner, 17921,¹ 106th Bty 12th Bde Royal Field Artillery, d. 4 December 1914 aged 45.

Son of John and Eliza Andrews. Married Mary Louise Woodmore in 1895 and they settled at 41, North Walls. In 1911 William and Mary had five children, one son and four daughters.² William John enlisted in the Royal Artillery in February 1888 aged 18. A Carman in 1911. In September 1914 he re-enlisted in the Royal Field Artillery at Winchester. Served on the Western Front as a Gunner. Wounded on 3 December 1914 he Died of Wounds the next day.³ Buried in Merville Communal Cemetery, Nord, France (GR I. K. 19.).⁴ Memorials at St John the Baptist and the Primitive Methodist Chapel in Parchment Street.

Their son William George served in the Royal Naval Air Service and Royal Air Force and survived the war.

✠ASLETT, ALBERT G. ... Corpl. ... R.G.A., Aug. 1914. France. Wounded, May 1915. *Killed in Action,* 1918.
(38, St. Catherine's Road)

13. ASLETT, Albert George, Corporal, 41318,⁵ 366th Siege Bty Royal Garrison Artillery, d. 21 March 1918 aged 21.

Son of Edwin and Amelia Aslett, of 38, St Catherine's Road. An Errand Boy for a local Chemist in 1911. Enlisted in August 1914 in the Royal Garrison Artillery at Winchester. Served on the Western Front, in France and Belgium. Wounded in May 1915 he was Killed in Action on 21 March 1918. Commemorated on the Arras Memorial, Pas de Calais, France (PR Bay 1).⁶ Memorial at All Saints and Chilcomb.

✠ATTWOOD, WILLIAM ... Pte. ... R. Sussex, Aug. 1914, Pte. France. *Killed in Action, Sept.* 1915.
(10 Staple Garden)

1 WO 372/1/95353.
2 Census 1911.
3 SDGW states KIA 4 December 1914.
4 CWGC.
5 WO 372/1/136316.
6 CWGC.

14. ATTWOOD, William Charles, Private, SR/1862,[1] 7th (Service) Bn The Royal Sussex Regiment, d. 11 September 1915 aged 21.[2]

Attwood was the son of Mr and Mrs C. Attwood, of 10, Staple Garden. In 1911 he was an Errand Boy, aged 17, one of six children. Enlisted in The Royal Sussex Regiment at Brighton in August 1914 and served in France with the British Expeditionary Force. The 7th Battalion was one of the first Service battalions of Lord Kitchener's New Army to be formed. The Battalion landed at Boulogne on 1 June 1915. Killed in Action on the 11 September 1915 just prior to the Battle of Loos. Buried at Houplines Communal Cemetery Extension, Nord, France (GR II. A. 15.).[3] Memorial at St Thomas's.

His brother Albert served in The HampshireRegimentand in India and Mesopotamia and Percy served in the Royal Navy, The Hampshire Regiment and Royal Engineers in Italy and survived the War.[4]

**AVERY, CHARLES W. ... Pte. ... Hants, Sept. 1914, Pte. Mesopotamia. *Killed in Action, Jan.* 21, 1916.
   (21, Canon Street)**

15. AVERY, Charles William, Private, 201062,[5] 1/4th Bn The Hampshire Regiment, d. 21 January 1916 aged 19.

Eldest son of Charles and Jessie Avery, of 21, Canon Street. In 1911 he was a Draper's Errand Boy aged 14. A territorial soldier, he enlisted at Winchester in The Hampshire Regiment, aged 18 in September 1914.[6] Served in Mesopotamia with the 1/4th Battalion and was Killed in Action at the Battle of Umm El Hanna on 21 January 1916. However his death was not confirmed until December 1917. Commemorated on Basra Memorial, Iraq (PR 21 and 63.).[7] Memorial at St Michael's.

1 WO 372/1/151509. SDGW.
2 The Long Long Trail www.1914-1918.net/sussex.htm. MIC states 23.11.15 entry to France: but if this man, he was dead by then.
3 CWGC.
4 Albert E. Attwood published a memoir *In the Running* (Ilfracombe, Devon: Stockwell, Ltd, 1977) in which he described service in the First World War in India at Quetta and mentioned Staple Gardens and his brother's death in France and its impact on him, also the loss of cousins (pp. 14-20). Albert Attwood had been a College servant at the Diocesan Training College before the War and would therefore have been acquainted with some students there who fought and died. (HRO 47M91WQ4/6/2 for Attwood's book and accompanying papers).
5 WO 372/1/157928. RHamps Notes. RH also records a number 3244, perhaps the number he received in 1914. As he was still missing and his death unconfirmed until December 1917 he was given a new number in the renumbering in 1917. Colin Bulleid, pers. comm.
6 SDGW states enlisted at Salisbury Plain, Wiltshire.
7 CWGC.

He had a younger brother, Percy Albert, who served in The Hampshire Regiment, won the Meritorious Service Medal, the Médaille Militaire and survived the War.

✠AXE, THOMAS A. ... P.O. ... R.N., 1902. Grand Fleet. *Killed in Action, June 1, 1916. Jutland.*
(23, Union Street)

16. AXE, Thomas Albert, Petty Officer, 216370,[1] HMS Ardent, Royal Navy, d. 1 June 1916 aged 29.

One of seven children of Henry John and Caroline Axe. Born 7 April 1886. In 1901 he was a Errand Boy aged 14. Enlisted in the Royal Navy in 1904 and served with the Grand Fleet on a variety of ships HMS Agincourt, Argonaut, Hindustan and Natal and Shore Establishments (Excellent, Tamar, Victory). In 1910 he married Harriet Cox in Brighton, Sussex. In 1911 he was aged 24 serving at Hong Kong. Passed Petty Officer training in the Spring of 1912 while serving on HMS Tamar. Killed in Action on 1 June 1916 during the Battle of Jutland, the largest naval battle of the War, while serving on HMS Ardent which was shelled by German ships and sunk by SMS Westfalen with the loss of 73 men.[2] Buried at Fredrikstad Military Cemetery, Norway, in the small war plot.[3] Memorial at Holy Trinity as Albert T. Axe.[4]

✠BAIRD, WILLIAM A. ... Pte. ... Hants, Aug. 1914, Dardanelles. *Killed in Action, Aug. 10, 1915.*
(4, Cossack Lane)

17. BAIRD, William Alexander, Private, 10439,[5] 10th (Service) Bn The Hampshire Regiment, d. 10 August 1915 aged 20.

Eldest of three children born to William and Florence v by 1911. His father had been in the The King's Royal Rifle Corps and died in 1911. He was an Errand Lad in 1911, aged 16. Enlisted at Winchester in August 1914. Served at Gallipoli (Dardanelles) with the 10th (Service) Battalion The Hampshire Regiment and was Arrived in the Gallipoli theatre of war 5 August 1915: Killed in Action on 10 August 1915, days after landing on the peninsula.[6]

1 ADM 188/379/216370.
2 Hepper, 2006, p. 63.
3 CWGC.
4 SJ pers. comm.
5 WO 372/1/187123.
6 The Battalion diary shows the following for the days before he was killed. On the 8 and 9 August 1915 10th Hampshires left bivouac about 9.30. They proceeded north up the Chailac Dere. They reached their destination, after many delays caused by blockages of other troops, at 04.00 on the 9 August. They were deployed at 05.30. At

Commemorated on The Helles Memorial, Turkey (PR 125-134 or 223-226 228-229 and 328).[1] Memorial at Holy Trinity.

✠BAKER, GEORGE C. ... Pte. ... T.R., Sept. 1917, Pte. Lond, att. R.B. France. *Killed in Action, June 2, 1918, Albert.* (56, Sussex Street)

18. BAKER, George Charles, Private, 38786,[2] The Rifle Brigade (The Prince Consort's Own) posted to 1st/17th (County of London) Bn (Poplar and Stepney Rifles) The London Regiment, d. 2 June 1918 aged 18.

Only son of George and Fanny L. Baker, of 56, Sussex Street. At school aged 11 in 1911. Enlisted in the Training Reserve in Winchester, September 1917 and is recorded as formerly 8/20782, 34th TR.[3] Landed at Calais on 3 April 1918. Attached to the 17th London Regiment on 5 April. Served on the Western Front and was Killed in Action at Albert, 2 June 1918.[4] Buried at Franvillers Communal Cemetery Extension, Somme, France (GR I. E. 7.).[5] Memorial at St Thomas's.

✠BALL, JOHN W. ... Rfn. ... R.B., Aug. 1914, Rfn. France. *Killed in Action, Aug. 26, 1914, in Retreat from Mons.* (6, Chester Road)

08.00 'A' and 'B' company attacked contour 270 but only reached within 800 yards of the ridge. They entrenched for the night, taking many casualties because of shrapnel fire. On 10 August 1915 a general Turkish counter attack developed about 04.30. 10th Hampshires were sent to reinforce 'A' and 'D' company positions below the crest of the Chunuk (or Chanuk) Bair ridge. It is probable this is when Baird , and others listed below, were killed. They retired after being cut off from the regiments to their right to Green Hill where they remained for the rest of the day. C. T. Atkinson (ed) *The Royal Hampshire Regiment 1914-18.* Vol 2 (Glasgow: Glasgow University Press 1952) p. 97. See J. C. Green etc who also died in this action. Also R Hamps Notes. RH.

1 CWGC. If KIA then why no graves for those who died here? Baird, Gillett, Garratt, Green etc. Hart?
2 WO 372/1/192417.
3 CWGC and SDGW agree he was serving with The Rifle Brigade when he was killed.
4 CWGC/SDGW. 34 TR a training reserve formerly 13th Hampshires, provided reinforcements to 32nd Division. The 8 prefix on his number is for the 8th Training Reserve Brigade. 20860 is a Somerset Light Infantry number. After he finished his training he was transferred to The Rifle Brigade and renumbered as S/38761 the S prefix is for one of The Rifle Brigade battalions.
5 CWGC.

19. BALL, John W.[1] Private, 9588,[2] 1st Bn The Rifle Brigade (The Prince Consort's Own), d. 26 August 1914 aged 44.

Born at 'Tedbury' (Tetbury), Gloucestershire in 1870.[3] Enlisted in The Rifle Brigade (The Prince Consort's Own) at Cardiff in August 1914, landed in France 23 August and served on the Western Front. Killed in Action, 26 August 1914 in the retreat from Mons. Buried at Porte de Paris Cemetery Cambrai, France (GR II. A. 27.).[4] Memorials at St Bartholomew's and St John the Baptist.

✠**BALL, LEONARD A. ... Pte. ... Hants, Sept. 1914, Pte. Mesopotamia. *Died, July* 11, 1916, *Amara.***
(12, High Street)

20. BALLS, Leonard Arthur,[5] Private, 2818, [6] 1/4th Bn The Hampshire Regiment, d. 11 July 1916 aged 27.

Son of Frederick and Susan Mercy Balls, of 75, Parchment Street. Born at Egham, Surrey. A Drapery Salesman in Winchester High Street in 1911.[7] Enlisted in The Hampshire Regiment at Hamilton Camp in September 1914 and served in Mesopotamia where he arrived in the theatre of war on 18 March 1915. Severely wounded on 29 July 1916. Died in Amara, 11 July 1916. Buried at Amara War Cemetery, Iraq (GR IX. G. 2.).[8] No Winchester Memorial found.[9]

✠**BARING, GUY V. ... Lt.-Col. ... Coldstream Gds., Aug. 6, 1914, Major. France. Despatches twice. *Killed in Action, Sept.* 15. 1916, *Somme.***
(60, Kingsgate Street)

21. BARING, The Hon. Guy Victor, Lieutenant-Colonel,[10] 1st Bn Coldstream Guards, d. 15 September 1916 aged 43.

1 Initial W. comes from *WWSR*, p. 8, CWGC and MIC both just say J. A fragment of additional local knowledge? See Reginald Giles. Some doubt whether the Bristol, see below, and Winchester John Ball was the same man, but the ages on the census and at death match. A John Ball, married to Mary Ball was living at 9A, Middle Brook Street in 1911.
2 WO 372/1/207625 WO 372/1/2077725.
3 SDGW says born 'Tedbury'. However, see following note.
4 CWGC. The John Ball noted here as buried in the Pas de Calais, was born in 1870 and is likely to be the married man living at Middle Brook Street in 1911.
5 SDGW has Arthur Leonard Balls.
6 WO 372/1/211989. Ball in *WWSR*.
7 See also Jack Sippetts of 12, High Street, (Sherriff and Ward's shop, Mark Allen pers. comm.) also a Draper's Assistant.
8 CWGC has Leonard Arthur Balls. Also R Hamps Journal. R Hamps Archive queries 'Died' date. RH.
9 ?St Maurice, lost.
10 WO 372/1/229523.

Eldest son of Alexander Hugh Baring, 4th Baron Ashburton and Lady Leonora Ashburton. Born at Piccadilly, London in 1873.[1] His father had died in 1889. Joined the Coldstream Guards in 1897 and saw service in the Boer War with the 2nd Bn Coldstream Guards. Promoted to Major during the War he fought at Belmont, Modder River, Dreifontein and Johannesburg. In 1901 he was seconded for service with the Foreign Office. He married Olive Althea Smith of Biddesden House, Andover, in 1903 and they had Simon Alexander Vivian born 1906 and Amyas Evelyn Giles born 1910. Guy Baring became Member of Parliament for Winchester in 1906. In 1911 recorded as Member of Parliament, aged 38. He rejoined his regiment on the 6 August 1914 two days after Britain declared war. Served on the Western Front, mainly in France. Mentioned in Despatches twice and was promoted to Lieutenant-Colonel on the 2 October 1915. Killed in Action 15 September 1916 on the Somme, while leading the first battalion attacking[2] German trenches SE of Ginchy. Buried at Citadel New Military Cemetery, Fricourt, France (GR II. A. 9.).[3] Memorial at Peter Symonds School, a plaque in Winchester Cathedral. Also commemorated at Northington and at Ludgershall, Wiltshire.

His brother also served in the Coldstream Guards during the Boer War.

✠**BARNEY, HAROLD G. ... Pte. ... Hants, Oct. 1916, Pte. France. Killed in Action, Oct. 10, 1917, Langemarck. (14, Hyde Abbey Road)**

22. BARNEY, Harold George, Private, 203399,[4] 2nd Bn The Hampshire Regiment, d. 10 October 1917 aged 19.

Only son of George Henry and Fanny Barney, 14, Hyde Abbey Road. At school in 1911 aged 13. A territorial soldier who enlisted in 1/4th Bn The Hampshire Regiment at Winchester, October 1916 and transferred to the 2nd Bn and served on the Western Front theatre of war arriving after the beginning of 1917. Killed in Action 10 October 1917 at Langemarck. Commemorated on the Tyne Cot Memorial, Zonnebeke, West-Vlaanderen, Belgium (PR 88 to 90 and 162.).[5] Memorial at St Bartholomew's.

---

1 Kelly's *Handbook* (1901), p. 116.
2 WO 95/1219. Battalion Diary.
3 CWGC. The findmypast Parish Records Collection refers to a grave at Ludgershall, Wiltshire. This is incorrect. His name appears on the War Memorial plaque in the parish church as his wife came from Biddesden Manor in the parish. We are grateful to the incumbent for opening the church to show the memorial.
4 WO 372/2/7439. R Hamps Notes. RH.
5 CWGC.

✠**BARRETT, EDGAR F. ... Pte. ... Hants, Feb. 3, 1918, Pte. Germany.** *Died, May* **7,** 1919, *Cologne.*
  (1, Ivy Terrace, Bar End)

23. BARRETT, Edgar F., Private, 03079,[1] 15th (Hampshire Carabiniers) Bn The Hampshire Regiment, d. 7 May 1919 aged 19.

Son of Frederick and Elizabeth Barrett of 1, Ivy Terrace, Bar End. At school in 1911 aged 11. Enlisted in The Hampshire Regiment, 3 February 1918 and served in Germany with the 15th (Hampshire Carabiniers) Bn in the Army of Occupation, but not apparently in a theatre of war.[2] Died 7 May 1919 at Cologne. Buried at Cologne Southern Cemetery, Cologne, Nordhein-Westfal, Germany (GR III. F. 20.).[3] Memorial at St Peter Chesil (All Saints) and the Primitive Methodist Chapel in Parchment Street.

He had two brothers who both served in the War and survived. Leonard V. was a Corporal in the Army Service Corps (Mechanical Transport) in France, Reginald F was an Officers' Cook in the Royal Navy and served and other ships.

✠**BARRINGTON, WILFRED ... Pte. ... Devon, Dec. 1917, Pte. France.** *Killed in Action, Aug.* **30,** 1918, *Beugny.*
  (Hillside Cottage, Sleeper's Hill)

24. BARRINGTON, Wilfred, Private, 31866 (formerly 8/11653),[4] 1st Bn The Devonshire Regiment, d. 30 August 1918 aged 18.

Son of John and Emily Barrington, of Hilcot Cottage,[5] Sleeper's Hill. Aged 11 in 1911. Enlisted 8/11653 in The Devonshire Regiment in Southampton, December 1917 and served on the Western Front. Killed in Action 30 August 1918 at Beugny. Commemorated on Vis-en-Artois Memorial, Pas de Calais, France (PR Panel 4). Memorials at Christ Church and St Cross Chapel.

✠**BARTLETT, ALLAN O. ... Lieut. and Q.M. ... Hants, Sept. 1914, Pte. Camel Corps. India, Palestine.** *Killed in Action, October,* **1918.**
  (72A, High Street)

1 No MIC found and not on Medal Roll. This number in the CWGC is incorrect. See Atkinson, 2, p. 436. Mrs F. Barrett of 1, Ivy Terrace alone mentioned on CWGC. See Appendix 2. R Hamps Notes. RH.
2 R Hamps Notes. RH.
3 CWGC.
4 WO 372/2/16951. 'formerly' reference SJ pers. comm.
5 CWGC has Hilcot Cottage.

25. BARTLETT, Allan Owen, Lieutenant[1] and Quartermaster, Army Service Corps, d. 15 October 1918 aged 30.

Eldest son of Jesse and Agnes Kate Bartlett. Born at Bedhampton. Aged 12 in 1901, not found in 1911 census. Having left the Diocesan Training College in 1909 in 1913 Bartlett married Marie Ernestine Vizetelly and they had one son, John, born in 1916.[2] Enlisted in The Hampshire Regiment in September 1914 and served in India and Palestine (3267 and territorial number 201082). He was commissioned into the Army Service Corps 12 June 1918. Entered a theatre of war after the beginning of 1916 and probably servied with the 2/4th Bn The Hampshire Regiment first.[3] Killed on 15 October 1918. Buried in Jerusalem War Cemetery, Israel and Palestine (including Gaza) (PR O. 26.).[4] Memorials at Peter Symonds School, St Thomas's Church and School and University of Winchester King Alfred's College Old Chapel (Winton Memorial Room).[5]

Had a younger brother, Alec, who served in The Hampshire Regiment in India and Mesopotamia.

✠**BARTLETT, GUY G. ... 2nd Lieut. ... R.E. (Motor Despatch Rider), Apl. 1916, Corpl. R.F.C. Flanders.** *Killed in Action, Mch.* **1918.**
  (26, Edgar Rd)

26. BARTLETT, Guy George, 2nd Lieutenant,[6] 48 Sqdn Royal Air Force, d. 6 April 1918 aged 21.

The only son of Samuel George and Catherine Ann Bartlett of Dawn House, Upper Headland Park Road, Preston, Paignton, Devon. At school aged 11 in 1911, living at 2, Ranelagh Road. Enlisted in April 1916 aged 18 and served in Flanders in the Royal Engineers as a Motor Dispatch Rider (161318). Commissioned 2nd Lieutenant into the RAF on 1 April 1918 and was Killed in Action five days later while serving as an observer.[7] Commemorated on the Arras Flying Services Memorial, Pas de Calais, France.[8] Memorials at Peter Symonds School and the United Church on Jewry Street.

1   WO 372/2/22315. CWGC 2nd Lieutenant.
2   She remarried and lived at Easton. SJ pers. comm. For this and other additional data for Bartlett.
3   R Hamps Notes. RH.
4   Noteworthy *WWSR* does not mention (R) ASC.
5   John Hartley, DCT.
6   WO 372/2/23044.
7   www.forumeerstewereldoorlog.nl/viewtopic.php?t=18627. Apparently the day the RFC became the RAF. SJ pers.comm. has commission dated 26 September 1917.
8   CWGC.

✠**BATES, ALAN ... L.-Corpl. ... Hants, Aug. 1914, Pte. Mesopotamia. Wounded twice. Taken Prisoner by Turks, Mch. 1917.** *Died, Nov. 12, 1917, Amara.*
  (Mill House, St. Cross)

27. BATES, Alan Gathorne, Private, 200931[1] 1/4th Bn The Hampshire Regiment, d. 12 November 1917 aged 23.

Second son of Henry George and Ada Mary Bates, of The Stores, Bell Street, Andover Road, Ludgershall, Wiltshire. Born at Alresford. He was a Moulder at an Iron Works in 1911 (the Winchester Motor and Dean's Engineering Company) aged 17 living with his parents at St Catherine's Cottage, St Cross. By the time of Alan Bates's death his father was working as a gardener for the Barings at Biddesden near Andover. Guy Baring MP also gave his life. See above.In August 1914 Bates enlisted in The Hampshire Regiment as a Private at Salisbury, Wiltshire (4/3035). Arrived in Mesopotamia theatre of war on 18 March 1915 with 1/4th Bn The Hampshire Regiment. Wounded twice and then in March 1917 he was taken prisoner by Turks.[2] Died a Lance-Corporal prisoner of war on 12 November 1917. Buried in Amara War Cemetery, Iraq (GR XIV. B. 22.).[3] Memorial at St Cross Chapel.

His younger brother Cyril Henry served in Mesopotamia as a Lance-Corporal in The Hampshire Regiment, was wounded in March 1917 and survived the War.

✠**BECKINGHAM, ALBERT ... C.Q.M.S. ... R.B., rejoined Aug. 1914, Rfn. France. Wounded once. M.M. 1916, Despatches 1916.** *Killed in Action, Apl. 16, 1917, Arras.*
  (7, Hedges Buildings)[4]

28. BECKINGHAM, Albert, Company Quartermaster Serjeant, B/53[5]. 7th (Service) Bn The Rifle Brigade (The Prince Consort's Own), d. 16 April 1917 aged 37.

Son of Charles and Lucy Beckingham, of Sandleheath, Salisbury. Born at Sandleheath. Married Alice Lucy Sherwood in 1908. They had Albert, born 1910, and Dorothy, born 1911. A General Labourer in 1911, aged 31. By 1914

1 WO 372/2/36139. MIC cataloguers have misread 931 as 431 as in the CWGC.
2 Details of his service, his wounds and the ailments from with he died are detailed in the Regimental Journals in an appreciation of his life on which this brief biography has drawn for some details. R Hamps Notes. RH.
3 CWGC Winchester.
4 Hedges Buildings described as 'Alresford Road' for Charles Morris, below, also given as 'Magdalen Hill.'
5 WO 372/24/4107.

he was a 'Time Expired Man': re-enlisted August 1914 and landed in France 19 May 1915 and served on the Western Front. Mentioned in Despatches in 1916 and was awarded the Military Medal on 27 October 1916. Died of Wounds, 16 April 1917 at Arras.[1] Buried in Duisans British Cemetery, Etrun, Pas de Calais, France (GR III. B. 7.).[2] Memorials at All Saints, Chilcomb and St John the Baptist.

London Gazette, Index, 1916, Vol. IV

War Office. 27 October 1916. His Majesty the King has been graciously pleased to award the military medal for bravery in the field to the undermentioned Non-Commissioned Officers and men:-

B/53 Sjt. A. Beckingham, Rif. Bgd.

✠BELL, ALFRED G. ... Rfn. ... R.B., 1908, Rfn. France. *Killed in Action, Aug. 26, 1914.*
(13, Water Lane)

29. BELL, Alfred George,[3] Private, 7796,[4] 1st Bn The Rifle Brigade (The Prince Consort's Own), d., 26 August 1914 aged 31.

Son of Alfred and Emily Bell of 42, Eastgate Street. Enlisted in The Rifle Brigade in Winchester, 1908. Married Alice Mary Prangle in 1910. In 1911 Kathleen Freeda was born. A General Labourer in 1911, aged 28 living at 23, Colson Road. Served in France under the name George Bell. The 1st Bn The Rifle Brigade was mobilized on 5 August and spent the next two weeks training at Colchester. They disembarked at Le Havre on 23 August 1914. in Action. Commemorated on La Ferté-Sous-Jouarre Memorial, Seine-et-Marne, France.[5] Memorial at St John the Baptist.

✠BELL, GAWAIN M. ... Major ... Hants, Oct. 1914, Capt. France. D.S.O. 1917. *Killed in Action, July 31, 1917, Ypres.*
(Culver's Close)

30. BELL, Gawain Murdoch, Major,[6] 11th (Service) Bn (Pioneers) The Hampshire Regiment, d. 31 July 1917 aged 40.

---

1 MIC states Died of Wounds. Also SDGW.
2 CWGC gives Morn Hill.
3 Alfred in *WWSR*.
4 WO 372/2/83786.
5 CWGC.
6 WO 372/24/4317.

Son of William Henry and Jane Westnay Bell, of York. Born at York. First class degree in Natural Science, Cambridge. 1901 appointed 2nd Lieutenant 2nd Volunteer Battalion The Hampshire Regiment. Chief Mathematical Master at Winchester College and Housemaster of Bramston's. Listed in 1911 as House Master and Assistant Master, Culver Close, Winchester, aged 33. Joined The Hampshire Regiment 1914. Entered a theatre of war (France) on 18 December 1915 with 11th Bn The Hampshire Regiment. Awarded the Distinguished Service Order in late 1916.[1] Killed in Action 31 July 1917 at Ypres while with a party making up roads for heavy guns to be moved up. His wounds proved fatal and 'he was greatly missed'.[2] Buried in Brandhoek New Military Cemetery, Ypres (Ieper), West-Vlaanderen, Belgium (GR I. E. 6.).[3] Memorial at St Michael's.

✠BELL, PERCY ... [BLANK] ... R.G.A., 1909. France. *Killed in Action, Mch. 10, 1915, Neuve Eglise.*
(89, Wales Street)

31. BELL, Percy, Gunner, 37328,[4] 115th Heavy Bty Royal Garrison Artillery, d. 10 March 1915 aged 22.

Son of Alfred and Emily Bell of 89, Wales Street. A Fishmonger in 1911, aged 18. Enlisted in Southampton, landed in France on 2 October 1914 and served on the Western Front. Killed in Action at Neuve Eglise on 10 March 1915.[5] Commemorated on Ypres (Menin Gate) Memorial, Ypres (Ieper), West-Vlaanderen, Belgium (PR Panel 9).[6] Memorials at St John the Baptist.

His older brother, Frederick, served in France and Salonica as a Corporal in the Royal Berkshire Regiment, and survived the War. One of his younger brothers, William, was in the Royal Marines, served in the North Sea on HMS Galatea and HMS Furious and survived the War.

✠BELLINGER, ANDREW E. ... Conductor ... R.A.O.C., 1896, Pte. Gallipoli, Palestine. Despatches twice. *Died of exposure.*
(42, Tower Street)

1 *LG* 12.07.1901 p. 4646 and 4.01.1917 p. 231.
2 Atkinson, 2, pp. 132, 206, 232, 449, 460.
3 CWGC. More information and photograph in *Wykehamists who Died in the War 1914-1918*, 4 vols. (Winchester, 1921) volume ii, p. 2 where burial place described as 'near Vlamertinghe' and in *The Wykehamist* October 19th (No 567). Additional detail in an appreciation in The Royal Hampshire Regiment Archive. R Hamps Notes. RH.
4 WO 372/2/87335.
5 MIC WO 372 as above.
6 CWGC.

32. BELLINGER, Andrew Ernest, Conductor, S/3575,[1] Army Ordnance Corps, d. 11 August 1919 aged 44.

Son of William Bellinger, a Serjeant in The Rifle Brigade, and Emelie Bellinger of 2, Victoria Road, Hyde in 1891.[2] Born at Aldershot. His mother Jessie died in 1881 and his father remarried in 1882. Andrew Bellinger was previously a Carriage Builder's apprentice: he enlisted in 1896, served in the Boer War as a Corporal in the Army Ordnance Corps and remained in the army as a Clerk, as recorded in 1911, aged 36. Married in 1910. Served at Gallipoli (Dardanelles) and Palestine from 27 July 1915. Mentioned in Despatches twice and received the Long Service and Good Conduct Medal. Died of exposure on 11 August 1919. Buried in Sheerness (Isle of Sheppey) Cemetery (GR A. 40).[3] No Winchester memorial found.

Four of his brothers joined up before 1914 and all four saw service in the First World War; three of them survived.[4]

⌘BELLINGER, HENRY G. ... Corpl. ... R.B., rejoined 1914, Rfn. P.P.C.L.I. France. *Killed in Action, Jan. 8, 1915, St. Eloi.* (42, Tower Street)

33. BELLINGER, Henry George, Lance-Corporal, 1264, Princess Patricia's Canadian Light Infantry (Eastern Ontario Regiment),[5] d. 8 January 1915 aged 39.

Son of William and Emelie Bellinger of 2, Victoria Road, Hyde in 1891. Born 20 June 1878. His mother Jessie died in 1881 and his father remarried in 1892. A Canadian National. Husband of Mary Ann Bellinger. He had three brothers, see below. Father of Mrs Mildred Pollock (formerly Bellinger) of 14, Devonshire Avenue, Brantford, Ontario. Apprenticed as a Tailor to a Mr Cooper for five years before joining the army in 1897. Served in the Boer War during the Relief at Ladysmith and other campaigns with the 1st Bn Rifle Brigade. Permitted to live in Canada from 1906 and enlisted in the Canadian Army in 1907. Re-enlisted in 1914 and served in France. Killed in Action 8 January 1915 at St Eloi. Buried in Voormezeele Enclosure No 3, Belgium (GR III. K. 3.).[6] No Winchester memorial found.

1 WO 372/24/4422; /24/4421 contains the MID reference LG 28.1.16 p. 1205; /2/91676.
2 1911 census son of stepmother Emily (Emelie) Bellinger (widow) of 42, Tower Street (SJ).
3 CWGC.
4 Henry below was his half brother, by the second wife.
5 Canadian papers suggest he was in 3rd Canadian Infantry, possibly a different regiment? http://www.veterans.gc.ca/eng/collections/virtualmem/Detail/456268.
6 CWGC.

Several brothers joined up before the War. His brother Jesse served in the Royal Naval Air Service. Brother Leonard served as a Private in The Rifle Brigade and brother Reginald served as a Staff Serjeant in the Army Ordnance Corps. All three survived the War. Is Andrew, listed above, was killed.

✠**BENDLE, WILLIAM J. ... Pte. ... Hants, Sept. 1914, Pte. Mesopotamia. Taken Prisoner by Turks, Apl. 1916.** *Died, May 5, 1916, Shanram.*
(12, King Alfred Terrace)

34. BENDLE, William Jesse, Private, 201103,[1] 1/4th Bn The Hampshire Regiment, d. 5 May 1916 aged 21.

Son of Ernest and Ruth Bendle, of 12, King Alfred Terrace. Born at Poole, Dorset. A Dental Mechanic in 1911, aged 17. A territorial soldier who enlisted in The Hampshire Regiment in Winchester, September 1914 (3296). Served in Mesopotamia. Taken prisoner by Turks in April 1916 and died 5 May 1916 at Shanram.[2] Commemorated on Basra Memorial, Iraq (PR Panel 21 and 63.).[3] Memorial at St Bartholomew's.[4]

✠**BENNETT, VICTOR ... Pte. ... Hants, Oct. 1915, Pte. India, Palestine, France.** *Killed in Action, Nov.* **4, 1918. M.M. 1918.**
(8, Culver Road)

35. BENNETT, Victor (Joss), Private, 201752,[5] 2/4th Bn The Hampshire Regiment, d. 4 November 1918 aged 21.

Youngest son of Frank Bennett and Emma Bennett of 8, Culver Road. In 1911 he was at school, aged 14, the youngest of four brothers, all of whom served in the First World War. Prior to enisting he served with Messrs Fielder and son, builders. Enlisted in 4th Bn The Hampshire Regiment at Winchester in October 1915.[6] Served in India, Egypt, Palestine and France, where he was awarded the Military Medal in 1918. Entered a theatre of war sometime after the beginning of 1917. Listed for this award in the June Supplement of *The London Gazette*.[7] Fatally wounded on 4 November 1918 he died. Buried in

1 WO 372/2/94998.
2 Modern spelling Shumran sometimes Shumran Bend. Atkinson, 2, p. 281. His father's advertisement for his missing son is recorded in the Journal. Other sources at The Royal Hampshire Regiment Archive record his death variously as at during the siege of Kut, at Baghdad and at 'Shurah'. Also records him as 2/4th attached 1/4th Bn. R Hamps Notes. RH.
3 CWGC.
4 Jesse W. Bendle on memorial. SJ pers. comm.
5 WO 372/2/10485
6 Additional information in this entry from R Hamps Notes, Journal. RH.
7 WO 372/23/79152. Supplement to the *London Gazette*, 17 June 1919. 7672. MM

Awoingt British Cemetery, Nord, France (GR III. C. 9.).¹ Memorials at St Michael's and St Thomas's School.

Alfred served at Gallipoli (Dardanelles) and France as a Private in The Rifle Brigade, Machine Gun Corps and His Majesty's Transport (Aragon). William served at Gallipoli (Dardanelles), Egypt and Palestine as a Corporal in the Army Service Corps. James served in France as a Company Quartermaster Serjeant in The Rifle Brigade, winning the Distinguished Conduct Medal in 1915. All three survived.

✠BERRY, FREDERICK J. ... Sergt. ... K.R.R.C., Jan. 1906, Rfn. France. *Killed in action, Feb.* 11, 1916, Givenchy.
(17, Clausentum Road)

36. BERRY, Frederick John, Serjeant, 6787,² 1st Bn The King's Royal Rifle Corps, d. 11 February 1916 aged 27.

Son of Henry and Harriet Berry of 17, Clausentum Road. Born at Kings Worthy: he was living with his parents at The Signal Box, Kings Worthy in 1891. Enlisted in The King's Royal Rifle Corps in Winchester, January 1906. Listed as a Bugler in the 1st Bn The King's Royal Rifle Corps in 1911, aged 22. Served on the Western Front. Killed in Action 11 February 1916 at Givenchy. Buried in Guards Cemetery, Windy Corner, Guinchy France (GR I. J. 8.). ³ Memorial at St Cross Chapel.

✠BIGNELL, JESSE ... Corpl. ... Essex, Dec. 1914, Pte. France. Wounded, Oct.10, 1915, and Aug. 2, 1917. *Killed in Action, Oct.* 8, 1917.
(34, Stockbridge Road)

37. BIGNELL, Jesse, Lance-Corporal, 16309,⁴ 10th (Service) Bn The Essex Regiment, d. 8 October 1917 aged 34.

Son of Thomas and Louisa Bignell of 17, Lower Stockbridge Road. A Grocer's Assistant in Abridge Essex in 1911, aged 28. Enlisted in The Essex Regiment in Warley, Essex, December 1914. Served on the Western Front and was wounded 2 August and 10 October 1915. Killed in Action 8 October 1917. Buried in Nine Elms British Cemetery, Poperinge, West-Vlaanderen, Belgium (GR IV.

---

    citations not published. In Journal but not found by RH. End of the war just before he was killed. RH. Siege began December, so an early casualty.
1 CWGC.
2 WO 372/2/116609.
3 CWGC.
4 WO 372/2/138891.

B. 6.).¹ Memorials at St Matthew's and St Paul's.

His brother, William served in India, Egypt and France as a Serjeant in The Hampshire Cyclists Battalion and survived the War.

✠**BINSTEAD, GEORGE A. ... Pte. ... . Hants (T.F.), 1913, Pte. India, Mesopotamia. Wounded once.** *Died of Wounds, Dec. 22, 1915, Kut.*
(23, Middle Brook Street)

38. BINSTEAD, George Alfred, Private, 1894,² 1/4th Bn The Hampshire Regiment, (Territorial Force), d. 22 December 1915 aged 21.

Son of William George and Annie Binstead of 23, Middle Brook Street. A Tailor's Errand Boy in 1911, aged 17. Enlisted in The Hampshire Regiment in Winchester, 1913 (4/1894). Entered a theatre of war with 1/4th Bn The Hampshire Regiment on 3 March 1915. Served in India, Mesopotamia. Died of Wounds, 22 December, 1915 at Kut. Buried in Kut War Cemetery, Iraq (GR Q. 17.).³ Memorial at Holy Trinity.

His brother, Charles F. served in France as a Corporal in The Hampshire Regiment. Wounded, July 1916 and October awarded the Military Medal 1918. His brother, William C. served in India, Mesopotamia as a Gunner⁴ in The Hampshire Regiment. Both survived the War.

✠**BISHOP, FREDERICK ... Staff Capt. ... Cheshire, Sept. 1914, Pte. France. M.C., Despatches.** *Died of influenza.*
(33, North Walls)

39. BISHOP, Frederick, Staff Captain, 5th Bn The Cheshire Regiment, d. 21 February 1919 aged 31.⁵

Son of Henry and Rosa Bishop of 33, Trinity Terrace, North Walls, where he was living in 1891. Trained as a teacher and left the Diocesan Training College in 1908. Enlisted in September 1914 and served in France. Later commissioned and was awarded the Military Cross and was Mentioned in Despatches.⁶ Died of influenza in 1919. Buried in Winchester (West Hill) Old Cemetery (GR

1   CWGC.
2   WO 372/2/146055.
3   CWGC.
4   WO 372 MIC states Machine Gun Corps. *WWSR* for William states Armd. Motor Car.
5   WO 372/2/158574.
6   *LG* citations not found.

2923).¹ Memorials at Peter Symonds School, St John the Baptist and University of Winchester, King Alfred's College Old Chapel (Winton Memorial Room) and at St Thomas;s School.²

His brother, Herbert William served as a Private in The Devonshire Regiment and then the Royal Flying Corps. His brother Charles served as a Wireless Telegraphist in the Royal Engineers in Palestine. Both survived the War.

✠**BLANDFORD, ARCHIE ... Sergt. ... Can. Rif., Feb. 1915, Rfn. France.** *Killed in Action, Apl.* **9, 1917,** *Vimy.*
   (14, St. John's North)

40. BLANDFORD, ARCHIE, Serjeant, 628010, 14th Bn Canadian Infantry (Quebec Regiment), d. 9 April 1917 age unknown.

Son of Eli Blandford. Born 28 August 1882 at Melbury Abbas, Dorset. In 1911 Eli and Emma Blandford were recorded at 73, Canon Street. According to his attestation papers he was a Baker prior to enlisting. Blandford was a Canadian national.³ Enlisted in The Hampshire Regiment in Winchester, February 1915 and served in France. Killed in Action on 9 April 1917 at Vimy Ridge. Buried in Nine Elms Military Cemetery, Pas de Calais, France (GR I. A. 28.).⁴ Memorial at St John the Baptist.

✠**BLIGH, EDWARD H. S. ... Lieut. ... R.N.D, Drake Bn., Oct. 1914. Sub-Lieut. Gallipoli. Despatches, Sept. 1915.** *Killed in Action, Sept.* **10, 1915,** *Dardanelles.*
   (Prior's Barton, Kingsgate Street)

41. BLIGH, Edward Henry Swinburne, Lieutenant, Drake Battalion. 63rd (Royal Naval Division) Royal Naval, Volunteer Reserve, d. 10 September 1915 aged 31.

Son of the Rev. the Hon. Henry Bligh and the Hon. Mrs Anne Bligh, of Priors Barton. Born at Hampton Hill, Middlesex. A Barrister at Law in 1911, aged 26. Commissioned as a Temporary Sub-Lieutenant in October 1914. Served at Gallipoli (Dardanelles). On 23 July 1915 he was promoted to Temporary Lieutenant. Mentioned in Despatches in September 1915.⁵ On 10 September

1   CWGC.
2   John Hartley.
3   http://www.collectionscanada .gc.ca/databases/cef/index.
4   CWGC.
5   Transcript found on the Royal Naval Division 1914-1919 entry on Findmypast website.

he was mortally wounded¹ while with digging parties at the front and died shortly afterwards at No 11 Casualty Clearing Station. 'Rev. BJ. Failes'. Buried in Lancashire Landing Cemetery, Turkey (GR A. 75.).² Memorials at St Cross Chapel and St Peter Chesil.

✠**BOGIE, ANDREW W. ... C.Q.M.S. ... Hants, 1914, Sergt. Mesopotamia. Despatches, M.S.M. Taken Prisoner by Turks at Kut.** *Died, Sept. 22, 1916, Yarbaschi.*
(22, St. Paul's Hill)

42. BOGIE, Andrew William, Colour Serjeant, 200023,³ 1/4th Bn The Hampshire Regiment, d. 22 September 1916 aged 32.

Eldest son of Peter Kerr Bogie and Katherine Bogie of 22, St Paul's Hill, Winchester. Born at St Andrew's, Catet, St Peter Port, Guernsey. In 1910 he married Florence Moss in Norfolk, they lived at 22, St Paul's Hill. Having left the Diocesan Training College in 1904 he was working as an Elementary Schoolmaster in 1911. They are listed in 1911 as living in 11, Highfield Villas, St Cross, when he was 29, and in 1913 they had a son Kenneth A. Bogie.⁴ A territorial since 1908 he enlisted in The Hampshire Regiment in Winchester, 1914. Served with the 1/4th Battalion in Mesopotamia, where he was Mentioned in Despatches and was awarded the Meritorious Service Medal.⁵ Taken prisoner by Turks at Kut he died after months in captivity on 22 September 1916 of dysentery at Yarbaschi. Buried in Baghdad (North Gate) War Cemetery, Iraq (GR XXI. R. 21.).⁶ Memorials at St Paul's, St Matthew's and University of Winchester, King Alfred's College Old Chapel (Winton Memorial Room) and at St Thomas's School where he was assistant master.

✠**BOSANQUET, EDWARD C. B. ... Capt. ... S.A. Imp. Light Horse, Sept. 1914, Corpl. Home.** *Drowned by enemy action, Sept. 12, 1918.*
(10, St. Cross Road)

43. BOSANQUET, Edward Claude Bernard, Captain, 555, 2nd South African

1 'GSW Head' i.e. GunShot Wound.
2 CWGC..
3 WO 372/2/197830.
4 BMD Vol. 2C p. 265 for 1913 birth. By the time of his death his wife was living at 1, St Paul's Terrace, Winchester.
5 No mention of MSM or MID in Regimental Journals, but reference to a Military Medal awarded on 3 June 1916 for service in the defence of Kut. This and other additional material in this biography from Regimental Journals etc. From the records of Mrs Bowker's support of the captive troops we learn he was 5'10" with size 9 shoes and his hat size was 6 ¾. R Hamps Notes. RH.
6 CWGC.

Imperial Light Horse,[1] d. 12 September 1918 age unknown.

Son of Laetitia Bosanquet aged 57 in 1911 of 10, St Cross Road with Dorothy, 22. Edward Bosanquet not found. Enlisted in September 1914 and was commissioned into the Royal Garrison Artillery but was invalided out with heart trouble. He and his wife were drowned returning to South Africa when the SS Galway Castle was torpedoed by enemy action, 12 September 1918. Some 744 people were drowned including 399 invalided South African Troops and 207 crew.[2] No Winchester memorial found.

✠**BOSWORTH, WILFRED J. ... C.Q.M.S. ... Hants, 1889, Pte. R. Innis. Fus. Aden.** *Missing.*
(32, Hyde Close)

44. BOSWORTH, Wilfred James, Company Quartermaster Serjeant,[3] The Hampshire Regiment, d. age unknown.

Son of Sarah Jane Bosworth. Husband of Wilhelmina. They had Beatrice Winifred. An Assurance Agent in 1911 aged 28 living with his mother at 32, Hyde Close. Served in Aden, and transferred from The Royal Inniskilling Fusiliers. Memorial at St Bartholomew's. Not found in the Archive of The Royal Hampshire Regiment.[4]

✠**BOYES, SYDNEY W. C. ... L.-Corpl. ... Hants, Aug. 1914, Pte. S.W.B. Mesopotamia, Salonica, France.** *Killed in Action, Nov. 24, 1917.*
(20, Middle Brook Street)

45. BOYES, Sydney W. C., Private, 40507,[5] 11th (Service) Bn (2nd Gwent) The South Wales Borderers, d. 24 November 1917 aged 30.

Son of Enos and Alice Louisa Boyes of 20, Middle Brook Street. Born 1887 the eldest of five children listed in 1911 when he was a Baker, aged 24. Enlisted in The Hampshire Regiment in August 1914 at Winchester. Entered a theatre of war as 3/2512 (Special Reservist) on 30 September 1915 apparently renumbered as 30783.[6] later being posted to The South Wales Borderers. Served in Mesopotamia, Salonica and France and was Killed in Action on 24 November

1   WO 372/2/220625. MIC states he died in The Royal Garrison Artillery.
2   Great War Forum. Refs for Galway Castle etc. No CWGC ref as he had been Discharged from the army.
3   WO 372 not found; not in SDGW.
4   Not on CWGC, no MIC. Thomas Paget Bosworth recorded in the *WWSR* as having survived is also on the memorial at St Bartholomew's.
5   WO 372/3/20802. Journal ref to birth of son 1915. RH
6   R Hamps Notes. RH.

1917.¹ Buried in Cite Bonjean Military Cemetery, Armentieres, France (GR II. B. 45.).² Memorial at Holy Trinity.

✠BRAITHWAITE, PHILIP P. ... Capt. ... Cav. (Ind. Army), Dec. 1914, 2nd Lieut. Jacob's Horse. India, France, Palestine. Wounded, Sept. 12, 1917. Despatches. *Killed in Action, Sept. 23, 1918.*
(9, The Close)

46. BRAITHWAITE, Philip Pipon, Captain,³ Cavalry (Indian Army), d. 23 September 1918 aged 38.

Son of Canon Philip Richard Pipon Braithwaite and his wife Jessie Beatrice Mackenzie Douglas of The Close. Philip was not found in 1911, probably in India, but his family were listed in The Close. Enlisted in December 1914, first command in December 1914, and served in India, France and Palestine. Indian Army Reserve of Officers attached to the 36th Jacob's Horse Regiment/ Indian Cavalry. In France in mid-November 1915 when his father met him in Paris, having not seen him since Captain Braithwaite had gone out to India 'some time ago.'⁴ Mentioned in Despatches.⁵ Wounded 12 September 1917 and was Killed in Action 23 September 1918.⁶ Buried in Haifa War Cemetery, Israel and Palestine (including Gaza) (GR A. 37.).⁷ No Winchester memorial found, memorial at Andover Mission Room.

✠BRAMBLE, WILFRED E. ... Pte. ... Hants, Dec. 1916, Pte. Mesopotamia. *Died*, 1919, *India*.
(37, Nuns Road)

47. BRAMBLE, Wilfred Edmund (or Edmond), Private, 201773,⁸ 1/4th Bn The Hampshire Regiment, d. 19 June 1919 aged 24.

Son of William and Edith Bramble of 37, Nuns Road. Born at Cheriton. A Farm Labourer in 1911, aged 16. Enlisted December 1916. Served in Mesopotamia and India. He was attached to the 1st Battalion The Royal Sussex Regiment. Died 1919 in India. Buried at Peshawar (GR B.C. XLV.55.)

1 SDGW and CWGC record 23 November.
2 CWGC. Also gives Sydney so other names not known.
3 No MIC found.
4 *Hampshire Chronicle*, Saturday 20 November, 1915. (Information researched by Peter Symonds College volunteer)
5 MiD citation not found. *LG* 1 July 1919 notice for creditors, will etc
6 Listed in *Quarterly Indian Army List*, January 1918.
7 CWGC.
8 WO 372/3/40843.

and commemorated on Delhi Memorial (India Gate), India (PR Face 23). [1] Memorial at St Bartholomew's.

♱BREADMORE, PERCY G. ... Pte. ... R. Berks, Nov. 1914, Pte. France, Wounded, Aug. 1916. *Killed in Action, Apl.* **28, 1917,** *Gouzeaucourt.*
   (188, Stockbridge Road)

48. BREADMORE, Percy George, Private, 37641, [2] 2nd Bn Princess Charlotte of Wales's (Royal Berkshire Regiment), d. 28 April 1917 aged 23.

Born at Stockbridge. In 1901, aged 7, a Boarder with John and Elizabeth Frowd of Owslebury. A Draper's Apprentice in 1911 aged 17 at 9/10, South Street, Chichester, Sussex. Enlisted in the Royal Berkshire Regiment in Reading, Berkshire, November 1914. Served on the Western Front. Wounded August 1916 he was Killed in Action 28 April 1917 at Gouzeaucourt. Buried in Villers-Guislain Communal Cemetery, Pas de Calais, France (GR B. 10.).[3] Memorials at St Matthew's and St Paul's.

♱BREWER, CHARLES W. ... Rfn. ... K.R.R.C., rejoined Aug. 1914, Rfn. France. *Killed in Action,* **Sept. 14, 1914,** *Aisne.*
   (4, Cross Street)

49. BREWER, Charles William, Private, 2374,[4] 2nd Bn The King's Royal Rifle Corps, d. 17 September 1914 aged 34.

Born at Birmingham. Married Henrietta Sillence in 1907.[5] In 1911, when he was 31, they had three children, Charles born 1909, Frank born 1910 and Florence born 1911. Living with father-in-law at 33, Upper Brook Street. A Bricklayer/Labourer according to the 1911 census. Enlisted in The King's Royal Rifle Corps in Birmingham and re-enlisted August 1914. Served in France and was Killed in Action 17 September 1914 at Aisne. Commemorated on La Ferté-Sous-Jouarre Memorial, Seine-et-Marne, France.[6] Memorial at St Thomas's.

♱BREWER, HARRY J. S. ... Gun. ... R.G.A., Oct. 1915, Gun. France. Belgium. *Killed in Action,* ***July*** **15, 1917,** *Nieuport.*
   (24, Hyde Abbey Rd)

1 CWGC. The grave at Peshawar can no longer be maintained.
2 WO 372/3/51151.
3 CWGC.
4 WO 372/3/58753.
5 CWGC states she married (Hutson) of 22, King's North Terrace, Bell's Lane, Hoo, Rochester, Kent.
6 CWGC.

50. BREWER, Harry John Stanley, Gunner, 128770,[1] 222nd Siege Bty Royal Garrison Artillery, d. 15 July 1917 aged 21.

Son of Edwin and Matilda Elizabeth Brewer, of Bradford, Ontario, Canada. Born in Winchester. Enlisted at Southampton, October 1915 and served in France and Belgium. He was formerly 1790, 2/2 Co., Hants RGA (TF). Killed in Action on 15 July 1917 at Nieuport. Buried in Coxyde Military Cemetery, Koksijde, West-Vlaanderen, Belgium (GR I. H. 43.).[2] Memorial at St Bartholomew's.

✠**BRIGGS, GEORGE L. C. ... Sub-Lieut. ... R.N., Sept. 1913, Mid. H.M.S.** *Princess Royal* **and** *Genista. Killed in Action,* **Oct. 23, 1916.**
(Qu'Appelle, Sleeper's Hill)

51. BRIGGS, George Leonard Clayton, Sub-Lieutenant,[3] HMS Genista. Royal Navy, d. 23 October 1916 aged 20.

Son of Col. W. E. Briggs, and Mrs M. G. Briggs, of Qu'Appelle, Sleeper's Hill. Born at Kings County, Parsonstown, 25 Jaunuary 1896. Entered service 15 January 1909. A Student Naval Cadet in 1911, aged 15. Enlisted in September 1913 and served on Princess Royal and HMS Genista, Royal Navy.[4] Promoted Sub-Lieutenant 15 August 1916. Killed in Action 23 October, 1916. Commemorated on Portsmouth Naval Memorial (PR 11.).[5] Memorials at Christ Church and St Thomas's.

✠**BRIGHT, ERNEST ... Corpl. ... Dorset, Pte. France.** *Killed in Action,* **1915,** *Hill* **60.**
(15, Canon Street)

52. BRIGHT, Ernest Arthur, Serjeant, 7937,[6] 1st Bn The Dorsetshire Regiment, d. 14 June 1915 aged 25.

Born 1888. Married Lavinia Lloyd in 1913, of Horsemens Bridge, Westbury-on-Severn, Gloucestershire, cited as Next of Kin.[7] Enlisted in The Dorsetshire Regiment in Winchester before the War; the 1911 census records him at Minden Barracks, Deepcut, Surrey, aged 23. Served on the Western Front.

1 WO 372/3/59180.
2 CWGC.
3 ADM 196/146/151; /118/95. Recorded that he had 'a fair knowledge of French. Very keen & hardworking'.
4 *Genista* torpedoed by a submarine, 23 October 1916. Hepper, 2006, p. 71.
5 CWGC.
6 WO 372/3/70611 states he died 17 June 1915 (SJ notes14 June as correct).
7 SJ for her address and kinship.

Killed in Action 14 June 1915 at Hill 60. Commemorated on Ypres (Menin Gate) Memorial, Ypres (Ieper), West-Vlaanderen, Belgium (PR Panel 37.).[1] No Winchester memorial found.

✠**BRIGHT, ERNEST G. ... Pte. ... R.M.L.I., Sept. 1914, Pte. Hants. Belgium, Egypt, Dardanelles, North Sea, France. Wounded, June 23, 1915.** *Killed in Action, Apl. 11, 1917, Arras.*
    (2, Southgate Street)

53. BRIGHT, Ernest George, Private, 25944,[2] 1st Bn The Hampshire Regiment, d. 11 April 1917 aged 18.

Son of the late Henry Bright and Maria Alice Bright of 2, Southgate Street, born 12 February 1898. At school in 1911, aged 13. Enlisted in The Royal Marine Light Infantry on 20 August 1914 aged 16.[3] Served in Belgium, Egypt, Gallipoli (Dardanelles), North Sea and France. Wounded 23 June 1915 and transferred from The Royal Marine Light Infantry (PO/17546) to The Hampshire Regiment. Killed in Action 11 April 1917 at Arras. Commemorated on the Arras Memorial, Pas de Calais, France (PR Bay 6.).[4] Memorials at St Thomas's Church and School, and at the Hampshire County Council.

His brother, Harry C., listed below, was Killed in Action 4 September, 1916 on the Somme.

✠**BRIGHT, HARRY C. ... L.-Corpl. ... Hants, June 1914, Pte. Devon. Dardanelles, France.** *Killed in Action, Sept.* **4 1916,** *Somme.*
    (2, Southgate Street)

54. BRIGHT, Harry Charles, Lance-Corporal, 33527,[5] 1st Bn The Devonshire Regiment, d. 4 September 1916 aged 19.

The eldest son of Henry Bright and Maria Alice Bright of 2, Southgate Street. His father died while Harry was still in his teens. An Office Boy in 1911, aged 14. Enlisted in The Hampshire Regiment in June 1914. Transferred from the 3rd (Reserve) Bn The Hampshire Regiment (formerly 9562)[6] entered a thatre oof war on 25 May 1915. Subsequently transferred to The Devonshire Regiment. Served at Gallipoli (Dardanelles) and France. Killed in Action on 4 September

1   CWGC.
2   WO 372/3/706/30
3   SJ gives his birth as 12 February 1896. Pers. comm.
4   CWGC.
5   WO 372/3/70839.
6   R Hamps Notes. RH. records this number as 9566.

1916 on the Somme.¹ Commemorated on the Thiepval Memorial, Somme, France (PR Pier and Face 1 C.).² Memorials at St Thomas's Church and School.

His brother Ernest, listed above, was killed in 1917 at Arras.

☦BRIGHT, WILLIAM A. ... A.-Sergt. ... R.G.A. (T.F.), 1912, Gun. France. *Killed in Action, July 20, 1917, Dickebusch.* (15, Colson Road)

55. BRIGHT, William Alfred, Serjeant, 352267,³ 15th (Hants) Heavy Bty Royal Garrison Artillery, d. 20 July 1917 aged 25.

Son of Mr James Henry and Mary Ann Bright of 15, Colson Road. Born at Hurstbourne Priors, Whitchurch, 1892.⁴ An Engine Cleaner in 1911, living at 51, Nuns Road, aged 19. and enlisted at Eastleigh. Served on the Western Front. Killed in Action 20 July 1917 at Dickebusch. Buried in Dickebusch New Military Cemetery Extension, Ypres (Ieper), West-Vlaanderen, Belgium (GR II. C. 1.).⁵ Memorial at St John the Baptist.

☦BROAD, CHARLES G. ... Pte. ... R. Warwick, Sept. 1918, Pte. Home. *Died, Oct. 14, 1918.* (12, Back Street, St. Cross)

56. BROAD, Charles George, Private, 59456,⁶ 5th⁷ Bn The Royal Warwickshire Regiment, d. 14 October 1918 aged 18.

Son of Ernest and Louisa Broad of 12, Back Street, St Cross. Born 1900. At school in 1911, aged 11. Enlisted in Southampton, September 1918. Died, 14 October 1918. Buried in St Cross (St Faith's) Burial Ground.⁸ Memorial at St Cross Chapel.

☦BROOKS, ALBERT E. ... Pte. ... Hants Cyc., Oct. 1915, Pte. Hants. France. *Killed in Action, Sept. 3, 1916, Somme.* (27, Trinity Terrace)

1 The Battalion War Diary for 3 and 4 September states that the 1st Battalion The Devonshire Regiment was attacking German positions at Wedge Wood and Leuze Wood, which became known as the Battle of Guillemont. SDGW.
2 CWGC.
3 WO 372/3/71264.
4 SDGW.
5 CWGC.
6 MIC not found, but see G. H. Vacher, below: possibly Service Papers at WO 339 (unexamined).
7 Could be 1/5th or 2/5th ?or 3/5th. When he died it would have been 1/5th and 2/5th, but possibly not known.
8 CWGC.

57. BROOKS, Albert Ernest, Private, 29472,[1] 14th (Service) Bn (1st Portsmouth) The Hampshire Regiment, d. 3 September 1916 aged 20.

Son of Richard and Laura Brooks of 3, Edgar Road. Living in 1911 at 27, North Walls.[2] Enlisted in The Hampshire Regiment in Southampton, October 1915 and served on the Western Front. Transferred from Hampshire Cyclists Battalion.[3] Killed in Action 3 September 1916 on the Somme. Commemorated on the Thiepval Memorial, Somme, France (PR Pier and Face 7 C and 7 B.).[4] Memorials at St Bartholomew's, St John the Baptist, Wesleyan Methodist Chapel, St Peter's Street and Peter Symonds School.

✠**BROWN, JOHN ... C.S.M. ... K.R.R.C., Sept. 1914, Sergt. York. France. Wounded, May 24, 1916.** *Killed in Action, Oct. 6, 1916.*
   (5, Freelands Buildings)

58. BROWN, John, Company Serjeant Major, 10826,[5] 21st Bn The King's Royal Rifle Corps, d. 10 October 1916 age uncertain.

Born 1886. In prison in Winchester in 1911: an ex-soldier.[6] Enlisted in September 1914.[7] Transferred from The Yorkshire Regiment and was wounded 24 May 1916. Killed in Action 10 October 1916. Commemorated on the Thiepval Memorial, Somme, France (PR Pier and Face 13 A and 13 B.).[8] Memorial at Holy Trinity.

✠**BROWN, OSBERT H. ... Major ... R.B., Sept. 1911, Rfn. France. Wounded, July 1916. D.S.O. 1916, M.C. 1916, Despatches 1917,** *Killed in Action, Nov. 1, 1916, Armentières.*
   (102, High Street)

59. BROWN, Osbert Harold, Major,[9] 11th (Service) Bn (Cambridgeshire) The Suffolk Regiment, d. 1 November 1916 aged 24.

Son of Alfred Robert and Annie Brown of 3, Geneva Road Kingston-on-Thames but born Winchester in 1893. In 1901 family living at 9, Southgate

1 WO 372/3/92979.
2 ie 27, Trinity Terrace, North Walls.
3 R Hamps Cyclists Bn see Appendix 2..
4 CWGC.
5 MIC not found.
6 A common name, difficult to follow up. SJ information re prison, pers. comm.
7 Date of enlistment not found in SDGW.
8 CWGC. R[ifleman]/10826.
9 WO 372/3/124454 and CWGC give his rank as Major (elsewhere Captain). *WWSR* his regiment as The Rifle Brigade.

Street. Educated at Peter Symonds, went up to Cambridge in 1910 and studied mathematics at Pembroke College.[1] Enlisted in The Rifle Brigade (The Prince Consort's Own) in September 1914. Served in France. Commissioned into The Suffolk Regiment he was wounded in July 1916. Awarded the Distinguished Service Order and the Military Cross in 1916. Mentioned in Despatches.[2] Killed in Action 1 November 1916 at Armentieres. Buried in Brewery Orchard Cemetery, Nord, France (GR I. B. 5.).[3] Memorials at St Lawrence's, St Thomas's and Peter Symonds School.

His brother, George R. Brown, served in France as a Lieutenant in the Royal Engineers and the Royal Garrison Artillery and survived the War.

✠**BROWNING, WILLIAM, J. ... Sergt. ... Warwick, June 1915, Pte. France.** *Killed in Action, Dec.* **5, 1917,** *Cambrai.*
   (42, North Walls)

60. BROWNING, William James, Serjeant, 202629,[4] 2nd/6th Bn Royal Warwickshire Regiment, d. 5 December 1917 aged 30.

Son of Frederick G. and Annie Browning of 42, North Walls. Born 1885, living at 48, West Street, Hereford as a Shop Assistant in 1911. Married Ida E. Tonsley of 19, York Road, Northampton in 1915 when cited as his next of kin.[5] A Shop Assistant in Hereford in 1911, aged 26. Enlisted in Birmingham, June 1915. Served on the Western Front. Killed in Action 5 December 1917 at Cambrai. Commemorated on the Cambrai Memorial, Louverval, Nord, France (PR Panel 3.).[6] Memorial at St John the Baptist.

His brother, Walter F. served in France and Egypt in the Hampshire Yeomanry and survived the War.

✠**BRYANT, RICHARD G. ... Pte. ... Hants, Jan. 1916, Pte. France.** *Killed in Action. Oct.* **1, 1917,** *Ypres.*
   (12, North Walls)

61. BRYANT, Richard George, Private, 22661,[7] 14th (Service) Bn (1st

1   http//:www.pem.cam.ak.uk/wp-content/uploads/2014/08/Pembroke-College/Cambridge-the-dead-of-the-war-of-1914-1918-2.pdf
2   *LG* references not found.
3   CWGC.
4   WO 372/3/137227.
5   BMD Vol. 3B p. 120.
6   CWGC.
7   WO 372/3/146544. Journal 1917. RH detail from journal and ?Moody's undertakers Basingstoke. NB 29 not 28.

Portsmouth) The Hampshire Regiment, d. 1 October 1917 aged 28.¹

Second son of William and Mary Bryant of 12, North Walls. Born 1889, a Carpenter in 1911, aged 22. Later a cabinet Maker with Messrs Moody of Basingstoke. Played with he Winchester Soldiers Home Band for eight years. Enlisted in Basingstoke, January 1916. Entered theatre of war with 1st Bn The Hampshire Regiment, subsequently transferred to 2nd nd then to the 14th (Service) Bn.² Served on the Western Front and was Killed in Action 1 October 1917 at Ypres. Buried in Westoutre British Cemetery, Heuvelland, West-Vlaanderen, Belgium (GR A. 11.).³ No Winchester memorial found.

His brother, Percy W. served in France as a Private in the Royal Berkshire Regiment, Tank Corps and Royal Air Force, was wounded in October 1917and survived the War.

✠BRYON, G. H. ... Pte. ... D.L.I., 1916, Pte. France, Belgium. *Killed in Action, Sept. 21, 1917.* (43, Parchment Street)

62. BRYON, George Henry, Private, 302519,⁴ 12th (Service) Bn The Durham Light Infantry, d. 21 September 1917 aged 36.

Son of Mrs Mary Ann Bryon of 13, Locking Road, Weston-super-Mare, Somerset. Born 1881 at Belfast, Antrim. A Stationer's Assistant in 1911, aged 30. Enlisted in The Durham Light Infantry in Winchester, 1916. Served in France and Belgium and was Killed in Action 21 September 1917. Buried in Hooge Crater Cemetery, Ypres (Ieper), West-Vlaanderen, Belgium (GR XIII. H. 4/5.).⁵ No Winchester memorial found.

✠BUCK, JAMES, H. ... Pte. ... Hants, 1915, Pte. India. *Died of Enteric, 1916, Quetta.* (17, Andover Road)

63. BUCK, James Henry, Private, 3854, 1/4th Bn The Hampshire Regiment, d. 13 July 1916 aged 24.⁶

Son of the late Tom Buck and Harriet Mundy (formerly Buck) of 17, Andover Road. Born at Gibraltar. Not found in 1911. Enlisted in Winchester in 1915.

1 R Hamps Notes. RH gives age as 29.
2 Additional material in this biography from Regimental Journals R Hamps Notes. RH.
3 CWGC.
4 WO 372/3/148468.
5 CWGC.
6 WO 372/3/151562. 3857 in R Hamps Notes. RH. Medal Roll says 2/4th.

Entered a theatre of war after the beginning of 1916 and served in India. Died of enteric fever, 13 July 1916 at Quetta. Buried at Karachi Cemetery (GR A/D.N.25) commemorated on Delhi Memorial (India Gate), India (PR Face 23.).[1] Memorial at St Matthew's and St Paul's.

✠BUCKLAND, CHARLES H. ... Pte. ... Glos., May 1916, Pte. M.G.C. France. Wounded once. *Killed in Action, Aug. 27, 1917.*
(23, St. Swithun Street)

64. BUCKLAND, Charles Henry, Private, 73318,[2] 183rd Coy. Machine Gun Corps (Infantry), d. 27 August 1917 aged 31.

Son of John and Mary A. Buckland of 23, St Swithun Street (1901 and 1911, 21, St Swithun Street, 1891). Born 1885. In 1911 an Assistant to Wine Merchants at 3/5, Popes Head Alley, London, EC aged 26. Enlisted in Winchester, May 1916. Served on the Western Front. Transferred from The Gloucestershire Regiment (formerly 5566) and was wounded once. Killed in Action 27 August 1917. Commemorated on the Tyne Cot Memorial, Zonnebeke, West-Vlaanderen, Belgium (PR Panel 154 to 159 and 163A.).[3] Memorial at St Thomas's Church and School.

✠BUGG, NOBLE G. ... Gun. ... R.G.A., July 1915, Gun. France. *Died of Pneumonia, Feb. 4, 1919.*
(7, Chesil Terrace)

65. BUGG, Noble George, Gunner, 371454,[4] 176th Anti-Aircraft Section. Royal Garrison Artillery, d. 4 February 1919 age uncertain.

Son of John and Rebecca Bugg of 7, Chesil Terrace.[5] Born 1882.[6] Not found in 1911. Bugg enlisted in July 1915 and served in France. Died of pneumonia, 4 February 1919. Commemorated in Wandsworth (Streatham) Cemetery (PR Screen Wall. D. 227.).[7] Memorial at St Peter Chesil (now at All Saints).

✠BULL, JOHN. ... Pte. ... Hants Y., June 1916, Tpr. Hants. France. *Killed in Action, Feb. 15, 1917.*
(54, Canon Street)

1 CWGC gives his age at death. The grave at Peshawar can no longer be maintained.
2 WO 372/3/153243.
3 CWGC.
4 WO 372/3/160540. MIC and CWGC both record 'George'.
5 Formerly 6, The Weirs.
6 SJ pers. comm.
7 CWGC.

66. BULL, John, Private, 33197,¹ 14th (Service) Bn (1st Portsmouth) The Hampshire Regiment, d. 15 February 1917 aged 44.

Son of Steve and Mary Bull. 1891 family at 59, Colebrook Street. Born 1877. Married Maud Harder in 1907, cited as Next of Kin at 12 Minster Street. Had Ethel, Charles and William in 1911, living at 33, Water Lane. A Carman in 1911, aged 34. Enlisted in Winchester, June 1916 and entred a theatre of war that year with 15th (Service) Bn, (2nd Portsmouth). Subsequentky transferred to 14th (Service) Bn (1st Portsmouth) and was attached to Royal Engineers' Tunnelling Company. Served on the Western Front and was Killed in Action 15 February 1917. Buried in Mendinghem Military Cemetery, Poperinge, (Ypres) Ieper, West-Vlaanderen, Belgium (GR II. A. 7.).² Memorial at St Michael's.

✠BUNBURY, WILFRED J. ... Capt. ... N. Fus., Aug. 1914, 2nd Lieut. France. Wounded, May 1915. *Killed in Action, April 15, 1917, Arras.*
(No address given)

67. BUNBURY, Wilfred Joseph, ³ 4th Bn The Northumberland Fusiliers,⁴ died 15 April 1917 aged 35.

Son of Col. C. T. Bunbury of Cotswold House, Winchester, late of The Rifle Brigade and Harriot Emily Bunbury, sister of Sir Lawrence Dundas, 3rd earl and first marquis of Zetland of 22, Ovington Gardens, Chelsea. Born 1882. Husband of the late Dorothy Beresford née Preston who he had married in 1908. Two daughters in 1909 and 1911. School at Beaumont College and then a Student in Ushaw College, Durham in 1901, aged 19. Not found in 1911. A Stockbroker in Newcastle. Enlisted 4 August 1914 as a private, commissioned 12 August; Lieutenant December 1914. Served with BEF. Wounded at St Julien (second Battle of Ypres) May 1915. Became a Brigade physical training expert and then to a depot in Co Cork, Ireland for convalescing soldiers. Returned to France 8 March 1917. Killed in Action 15 April 1917 while leading his men to take the Tower of Wancourt. Buried Wancourt British Cemetery, Special Memorial 72.⁵ No Winchester memorial found.

1 WO 372/3/163244; CWGC states attached Tunnelling Company: still a Hampshire so no new number RH.
2 CWGC.
3 From WO 372/3/168667; CWGC etc. A lengthy and detailed de Ruvigny entry (Findmypast website) contains further information. Also information from Ushaw College Archivist, *Hull Daily Mail* and censuses. Picture etc on http://www.4thbnnf.com/53_fusilierprofiles.html#bunbury
4 MIC states 6th Bn Territorial. Could be 1st /2nd or 3rd/6th.
5 CWGC.

✠**BURGESS, FRANK ... Sergt. ... K.R.R.C., Sept. 1914, Rfn. France.** *Believed Killed in Action, Mons.*
(10, Ashley Terrace)

68. BURGESS, Frank, Serjeant, 6505,[1] 1st Bn The King's Royal Rifle Corps, d. 28 October 1914 aged 26.

Son of William and Emmeline Burgess. In 1901 family at 26, Clifton Road. Not found in 1911. Married Ethel Burgess of Chale, 34, Henry Road, Chelmsford, Essex.[2] Enlisted in Winchester, September 1914 and served on the Western Front. It is possible that he Died of Wounds received at the Battle of Mons. Buried in Ypres Town Cemetery, Ypres (Ieper), West-Vlaanderen, Belgium (GR C. 1.).[3] Memorials at St Matthew's and St Paul's.

✠**BURNETT, HENRY ... Pte. ... Hants, Sept. 1914, Pte. Persian Gulf.** *Killed in Action, July* **5, 1915.**
(13, Boundary Street)

69. BURNETT, Henry, Private, 2816,[4] 1/4th Bn The Hampshire Regiment, d. 5 July 1915 aged 26.

Son of John and Charlotte Burnett of 88, Wales Street in 1911. Born 1889. A Bricklayer in 1911 aged 22. Enlisted at Hamilton Camp, September 1914. Served in the Persian Gulf and landed in Mesopotamia March 15 and entered a theatre of war on 18 March with 1/4th Bn. Killed in Action 5 July 1915. Buried in Basra War Cemetery, Iraq (GR II. R. 7.).[5] Memorial at Holy Trinity.

His brother John served at Gallipoli (Dardanelles) as a Private in The Hampshire Regiment, was wounded 12 August 1915 and survived the War.

✠**BURROWS, JOHN J. ... Gun. ... R.G.A., Nov. 1915, Gun. France. Wounded, Dec. 19, 1917.** *Died of Wounds, Dec.* **21, 1917,** *Rouen.*
(19, Colebrook Street)

70. BURROWS, John Joseph, Gunner, 136576,[6] 25th Heavy Bty Royal Garrison Artillery, d. 21 December 1917 aged 32.

Son of Tom and Mary Burrows of 31, Water Lane (1891, 1901, 1911). Born

1 WO 372/3/177734.
2 Address from SJ.
3 CWGC.
4 WO 372/3/187396. MIC states 5a Mesopotamia RH (1 Fr, 2b Gallipoli).
5 CWGC.
6 WO 372/3/197/155.

1885. Married Frances Marion Bauman in 1906 and they had two children by 1911, Doris Rose and Cecil William, at 9, St Swithun Street. A Tailor Maker in 1911, aged 26. Enlisted in Winchester, November 1915 and served on the Western Front. Wounded 19 December 1917 and Died of Wounds 21 December 1917 at Rouen. Buried in St Sever Cemetery Extension, Rouen, France (GR P. V. D. 7B.).[1] No Winchester memorial found.[2]

✠BURTON, ALBERT T. ... Stoker ... R.N., Nov. 1910, Stoker. North Sea; H.M.S. *Queen Mary*. *Killed in Action, May 31, 1916, Jutland.*
(4, Westgate Lane)

71. BURTON, Albert Thomas, Stoker 1st Class, K/17109,[3] HMS Queen Mary. Royal Navy, d. 31 May 1916 aged 22.

Son of Thomas and Elizabeth Burton of 4, Westgate Lane. Born 23 March 1894.[4] A Bottle Washer/Brewer in 1911, aged 18. Enlisted in December 1912. Served on The North Sea on HMS Queen Mary and was Killed in Action 31 May 1916 during the Battle of Jutland.[5] Commemorated on Portsmouth Naval Memorial (PR 17.).[6] Memorials at St Thomas's Church and School.

Three of his brothers served in the War. Ernest served in the North Sea as a Stoker in the Royal Navy, Henry served in Mesopotamia and India as a Lance-Corporal in the Hampshire Yeomanry and The Hampshire Regiment and William C. served in the North Sea, Baltic and Falkland Islands on HMS Princess Royal, Royalist, and Cornelia as a Stoker in the Royal Navy. All three survived the War.

✠BURTON, WILLIAM F. ... Rfn. ... R.B., Mch. 1915, Rfn. France, Belgium. Wounded, Aug. 8, 1917. Gassed, 1918. *Killed in Action, Oct. 2, 1918, Ypres.*
(22 Colebrook Street)

72. BURTON, William Frederick, Private, 47839,[7] 1st Bn The Royal Irish Rifles,[8] d. 2 October 1918 aged 34.

Son of Frederick and Elizabeth Burton of 3, Water Close, Colebrook Street

1 CWGC.
2 ? St Maurice, lost.
3 ADM 188/901/17109.
4 1911 Census states 1893. Birth date from SDGW.
5 Hepper, 2006, p. 60. HMS Queen Mary, a battle cruiser, blew up. Nine survivors.
6 CWGC.
7 WO 472/3/203984.
8 CWGC has 1st Bn Royal Irish Rifles. See rogerbutlerellis.com for obituary.

(cited as Next of Kin). Born 1886.[1] 1901 and 1911 William Burton was living at 24, Colebrook Street. A Shop Assistant in 1911, aged 25. Enlisted in Winchester, March 1915. Served in France and Belgium. Formerly 9151, The Rifle Brigade.[2] Wounded 8 August 1917 and gassed in 1918. Killed in Action 2 October 1918 at Ypres. Commemorated on the Tyne Cot Memorial, Zonnebeke, West-Vlaanderen, Belgium (PR Panel 138 to 140 and 162 to 162A and 163A.). No Winchester memorial found.[3]

✠**CALLEN, SIDNEY J. ... Pte. ... Hants, Sept. 1914, Pte. Egypt, Palestine.** *Killed in Action, Nov. 22, 1917.*
   (13, Egbert Road)

73. CALLEN, Sidney James, Private, 200976,[4] 2/4th Bn The Hampshire Regiment, d. 22 November 1917 aged 19.

Eldest son of the family of Sidney Ernest and Fanny Callen of 13, Egbert Road. Born at Botley in 1898. At school in 1911 aged 13. Prior to joining up was employed by Messrs W. Carter & Co. of Parchment Street. A territorial soldier who enlisted on Salisbury Plain, Wiltshire, September 1914 (3008).[5] Served in Egypt and Palestine, entered a theatre of war in 1916. Killed in Action 22 November 1917. Buried in Jerusalem War Cemetery, Israel and Palestine (including Gaza) (GR K. 77.).[6] Memorial at St Bartholomew's.[7]

✠**CANCELLOR, DESMOND B. ... Lieut. ... Hants, Apl. 1917, 2nd Lieut. France. Wounded, July 23 and Aug. 22, 1917. M.C. 1918.** *Killed in Action, Nov. 1918, near Préseau.*
   (23, Edgar Road)

74. CANCELLOR, Desmond[8] Bertram, Lieutenant, 3rd (Reserve) Bn attd 1st Bn The Hampshire Regiment, d. 1 November 1918 aged 20.

Only son of Bertram Douglas Cancellor and Marion Effie Cancellor (formerly of 16, Christchurch Road) of Queen Anne Chambers, High Street, Winchester. Born 1897. At school at Twyford in 1911, aged 12 and then at Radley College.[9] Enlisted in Winchester, April 1917. Served in France. Commissioned 26

1 Discrepancy over age at death.
2 SDGW.
3 ? St Maurice, lost.
4 WO 372/3/240368.
5 This biography extended from Regimental Journals etc. R Hamps Notes. RH.
6 CWGC.
7 Sydney on memorial.
8 WO 372/4/5652 listed there as 'Dumond'. RH Journal. Picture. Radley, NC Oxford 1918
9 Further details of his life, schooling, university plans and military career are found in the Regimental Journals. R Hamps Notes. RH.

April into The Hampshire Regiment. Wounded 23 July and 22 August 1917. Awarded the Military Cross. Killed in Action 1 November 1918 near Preseau. Buried in Denain Communal Cemetery, Nord, France (GR D. 7.).[1] Memorials at Holy Trinity and Twyford Preparatory School.

Military Cross citation from *The London Gazette*, 3 October 1919:[2]

'2nd/Lt. Desmond Bertram Cancellor, Hampshire. R., Spec. Res., attd 1st Bn. For most conspicuous gallantry and fearless leadership. On the 24th October, 1918, at Monchaux when the bridging party was trying to bridge the river under heavy fire, he swam the river alone, and rushed the nearest machine-gun post. This splendid example of dash led other men to follow him across, and a bridge-head was gained. He undoubtedly saved a very critical situation.'

✠**CARTER, ARTHUR F. ... L.-Corpl. ... Hants (T.F.), 1894, Pte. Hants. India. *Died, Feb. 15, 1916.***
(4, Penarth Place)

75. CARTER, Arthur Fred, Lance-Corporal, 102,[3] 1/4th Bn The Hampshire Regiment d. 15 February 1916 aged 48.

Son of Albert Carter of 4, Penarth Place, St Thomas Street. Born 1868. A Clerk in 1911 aged 43. Enlisted in Winchester 1894 and served in India. Awarded Territorial Efficiency Medal. Entered a theatre of war (Mesopotamia) on 18 March 1915 with 1/4th Bn. Died of Wounds on 15 February 1916. Buried in Quetta Government. Cemetery (GR 2305). Commemorated on Delhi Memorial (India Gate). (PR Face 23).[4] Memorial at St Thomas's Church.[5]

✠**CARTER, GEORGE ... Pte. ... Hants, June 1916, Pte. France. Wounded, July 31, 1917.   *Killed in Action, July* 31, 1917, *St. Julien.***
(46, North Walls)

76. CARTER, George, Private, 249936,[6] 14th (Service) Bn (1st Portsmouth) The Hampshire Regiment, d. 31 July 1917 age unknown.[7]

---

1 CWGC.
2 Issue 31583, p. 12276.
3 WO 372/4/32650. Additional material from R Hamps Notes. RH.
4 CWGC.
5 Recorded only as Frederick on memorial.
6 WO 372/4/35293.
7 Not found in census to check age. Journal entry lists him among wounded but actually wounded and killed at the same time. However, this is listed under September suggesting his demise was in that month, September 1917. RH.

Family at 46, North Walls in 1911, George not found. Enlisted in Winchester June 1916 and entered a theatre of war the same year with 1st Bn The Hampshire Regiment. He transferred to the 14th (Service) Bn and served on the Western Front. Wounded Killed in Action 31 July 1917 at St Julien. Buried in Ypres (Menin Gate) Memorial, Ypres (Ieper), West-Vlaanderen, Belgium (PR Panel 35.).[1] Memorials at Holy Trinity and St John the Baptist.

✠**CARTER, JOHN ... Sig. ... R.E., Sept. 1917, Sig. France. Killed.**
(1, Queensland Terrace)

77. CARTER, John, Sapper,[2] 325815, Corps of Royal Engineers, d. 2 May 1919 aged 41.[3]

Son of Thomas and Jane Carter. Born at Collingbourne Ducis, Wiltshire, in 1878. Married Margaret Kathleen Rolph in 1907 and by 1911 had Leslie John born 1909 in Marlborough, Wiltshire. Worked in the Civil Service, Post Office Sorting in 1911, aged 33 when living at 111, Owens Road. Served in France and died 2 May 1919. Buried in Winchester (West Hill) Old Cemetery (GR 41. 16628.).[4] No Winchester memorial found.

✠**CASSIDY, GERALD. ... Boy ... R.N., 1913, Boy. H.M.S.** *Powerful* **and** *Crescent.* **Died, Mch. 1919.**
(13, Eastgate Street)

78. CASSIDY, Gerald, Boy 1st Class, 25703, [5] HMS Victory, Powerful and Crescent. Royal Navy, d. March 1919 aged 20.

Son of John William and Jane Elizabeth Cassidy of 34, London Road, Southwark, London SE. Born at Southwark, London 27 April 1898. Aged 12 in 1911.[6] Enlisted in 1913 and died of a disease of the nervous system in March 1919.[7] Memorials at Holy Trinity and St John the Baptist.

His brother, John Alfred, served in France as a Private in the Royal Irish Rifles and survived the War.

---

1 CWGC.
2 WO 372/4/36993.
3 Late date of death for inclusion. Died of 'flu?
4 CWGC.
5 ADM 188/698/25703. J/25703
6 Census suggests birth as 1899.
7 Not found on CWGC.

✠**CAUSTON, JERVOISE P. ... Capt. ... Hants, 1914, 2nd Lieut. India, France.** *Killed in Action, Apl. 22, 1918, near Bethune.*
(Master's Lodge, St. Cross)

79. CAUSTON, Jervoise Purefoy,[1] Captain, 1st Bn The Hampshire Regiment, d. 22 April 1918 aged 24.[2]

Son of Francis Jervoise Causton (Master of St Cross) and Laura Georgina Causton, of The Master's Lodge, St Cross. Born at Petersfield in 1894. At Charterhouse School, Godalming, Surrey in 1911, aged 17 and the at University College, Oxford. Awarded Order of Merit there for Senior Scholarships in 1909. A recruit for the Rifle Corps Cadets in 1909 becoming a Lance-Serjeant in 1912.[3] Enlisted in 1914 and served in India and France. Served in 6th (Duke of Connaught's Own) Battalion (Territorial). Entered a theatre of war (France) on 29 May 1917. Killed in Action 22 April 1918 near Bethune serving with 1st Bn The Hampshire Regiment. Buried in Gonnehem British Cemetery, Pas de Calais, France (GR B. 8.).[4] Memorial at St Cross Chapel.

✠**CHALK, ARCHIBALD ... Rfn. ... R.B., Aug. 4, 1914, Rfn. France.** *Killed in Action, Aug. 26, 1914.*
(4, St. Clement Street)

80. CHALK, Archibald, Private, 9905,[5] 1st Bn The Rifle Brigade (The Prince Consort's Own), d. 26 August 1914 aged 30.

Son of Thomas and Mary Chalk in 1891 of 5, St James's Lane, later of 4, St Clement Street. Born at Aldershot in 1884. A Postman in 1911 aged 27. Enlisted in Winchester on 4 August 1914 and entered France on 23 August.[6] Served on the Western Front. Listed as formerly 5847, The Royal Sussex Regiment.[7] Killed in Action, 26 August 1914. Commemorated on La Ferté-Sous-Jouarre Memorial, Seine-et-Marne, France.[8] Memorial at St Bartholomew's.[9]

His brother Frank Albert served as a Corporal in the Royal Flying Corps and survived the War.

---

1 WO 472/4/57299. Atkinson, 2, pp. 342-3.Additional material found in the Regimental Journals. R Hamps Notes. RH.
2 CWGC 1st Bn, SDGW 6th Bn.
3 Charterhouse School Archive.
4 CWGC.
5 WO 372/4/65010.
6 Two weeks' training is unusual.
7 SDGW.
8 CWGC.
9 Chalke on memorial.

✠**CHALK, ARTHUR ... Pte. ... R.M.L.I., Dec. 1916, Pte. France.** *Killed in Action, Oct. 1917, Passchendaele.*
(75, Chesil Street)

81. CHALK, Arthur, Private, PLY/1789-S-,[1] 2nd RM Bn RN Div. Royal Marine Light Infantry, d. 26 October 1917 aged 37.

Son of George Chalk of Cheriton. Born 1 January 1880.[2] Not found in 1911. Enlisted 9 December 1915 and served on the Western Front. Temporarily posted to the Royal Berkshire Regiment 28 December 1916. Killed in Action 26 October 1917 at Passchendaele. Commemorated on the Tyne Cot Memorial, Zonnebeke, West-Vlaanderen, Belgium (PR Panel 1 and 162A.).[3] No Winchester memorial found.

✠**CHANDLER, ERNEST ... Rfn. ... R.B., 1888, Rfn. France.** *Killed in Action, Mch. 11, 1915, Neuve Chapelle.*
(7, Maidstone Terrace)

82. CHANDLER, Ernest C., Private, 7255,[4] 2nd Bn The Rifle Brigade (The Prince Consort's Own), d. 11 March 1915 aged 33.

Son of Mrs Harriet Chandler of 7, Maidstone Terrace, Culver Road. Born 1882. In 1911 serving at Fort William, Calcutta, India, aged 29. Enlisted in Winchester and served on the Western Front. Killed in Action 11 March 1915[5] at Neuve Chapelle, France. Commemorated on Le Touret Memorial, Pas de Calais, France (PR Panel 44.). Memorial at St Michael's.

He had two brothers who served in the War. Frank, listed below, was Killed in Action 19 December 1914. Herbert served in France as a Private in the Army Service Corps (Mechanical Transport) and survived the War.

✠**CHANDLER, FRANK ... Rfn. ... Hants, 1902, Pte. R.B. France.** *Killed in Action, Dec. 19, 1914, Armentières.*
(7, Maidstone Terrace)

83. CHANDLER, Frank S., Private, 3573,[6] 1st Bn The Rifle Brigade, d. 19 December 1914 aged 25.

1 ADM 159/178/1789.
2 Royal Marines' records.
3 CWGC. His next of kin recorded as 'Friend', Mrs Alice Norman of 75, Chesil Street. In 1911 an Alice Ellen Norman lived at 20, Clausentum Road, St Cross, on separation allowance.
4 WO 372/4/74908. No date of death.
5 CWGC notes 14 March.
6 WO 372/4/75020.

Son of Mrs Harriet Chandler of 7, Maidstone Terrace, Culver Road. Born 1889. In 1911 aged 22. Enlisted in Winchester and served on the Western Front. Transferred from The Hampshire Regiment, but did not serve with them in a theatre of war.[1] Killed in Action 19 December 1914 at Armentieres. Buried in Rifle House Cemetery, Comines-Warneton, Hainaut, Belgium (GR IV. G. 15.).[2] Memorial at St Michael's.

He had two brothers who served in the War. Ernest, listed above, was Killed in Action 11 March 1915 at Neuve Chapelle. Herbert served in France as a Private in the Army Service Corps (Mechanical Transport) and survived the War.

✠**CHAPMAN, FRANK J. ... Pte. ... Hants, Sept. 1914, Pte. India, Persian Gulf. Taken Prisoner by Turks, Apl. 29, 1916, Kut.** *Died of Enteric,* **Oct. 1916.**
   (4, Andover Road)

84. CHAPMAN, Frank James, Private, 201058,[3] 1/4th Bn The Hampshire Regiment, d. 15 October 1916 aged 22.

Son of James and Catherine A. Chapman of White House, St Cross 1911, later 3, Front Street, St Cross. Born at Rustington, Sussex in 1894. A Law Clerk in 1911, living at 3, Front Street aged 17. A territorial soldier, enlisted on Salisbury Plain, Wiltshire, September 1914 (3238). Served in India and the Persian Gulf. Entered a theatre of war with 1/4th Bn on 18 March 1915. Taken prisoner by Turks on 29 April 1916 at Kut and died of enteric fever, 15 October 1916. Commemorated on Basra Memorial, Iraq (PR Panel 21 and 63.).[4] Memorial at St Paul's.

✠**CHASTON, EDWARD A. ... L.-Corpl. ... Hants Y., Aug. 1914, Tpr. Hants. Italy, France,** *Killed in Action,* **Oct. 14, 1918, Menin.**
   (13, Edgar Road)

85. CHASTON, Edward Alfred, Lance-Corporal, 204734,[5] 15th (Service) Bn (2nd Portsmouth) The Hampshire Regiment.[6] d. 14 October 1918 aged 22.

---

1 Not on MIC. SDGW. Young age of joining up aged c. 13 in 1902 possibly correct. Additonal information from R Hamps Notes. RH.
2 CWGC.
3 WO 372/4/81223. R Hamps Notes. RH. Journal gives date of death as 15 October 1916. The Bowker papers in Regimental Archive give his height as 6' his shoe size as 9 and his hat size as 7. Also his place of death as 'Airan'.
4 CWGC.
5 WO 372/4/93300. RH notes. Wounded and died same day. *Journal* entry details much active service.
6 15th (Hampshire Carabiniers) Bn The Hampshire Regiment. See Appendix 2

Eldest son of Alfred Edward and Lucy Waters Chaston of Triscombe, 13, Edgar Road and 45, High Street. Born 1897. At Trafalgar House school, Winchester and, in 1911, at Dean Close, Cheltenham, aged 14. In 1914 pupil in the engineering works of the London and South-Western Railway at Eastleigh. A territorial soldier enlisted in Winchester, August 1914 (10820 and served in Italy and France for two and a half years before his death, 'a bright and lovable disposition'.[1] Entered a theatre of war after the beginning of 1916. Transferred from Hampshire Yeomanry. Wounded Summer 1918 in the right arm. Died of Wounds from further wounds, 14 October 1918 in an ambulance en route to hospital. Buried in Ypres Reservoir Cemetery, Ypres (Ieper), West-Vlaanderen, Belgium (GR II. C. 10.).[2] Memorials at Christ Church, two small brass plaques, same words on each, preacher and leader's pews.

His brother Richard D. enlisted on 26 September 1918 as a Private in The Royal Warwickshire Regiment and survived the War.

✠**CHATFIELD, WILLIAM L. ... Pte. ... Hants Y., Jan. 1915. Hants. France. Wounded, July 31, 1917.** *Killed in Action, Nov. 4, 1918, Beaudignies.*
(4, Ranelagh Road)

86. CHATFIELD, William Leslie, Private, 33124,[3] 2/4th Bn The Hampshire Regiment, d. 4 November 1918 aged 21.

Son of Frederick William and Matilda Maria Chatfield of Branksome, 4, Ranelagh Road. Born 1897. At school in 1911, living at 38, Upper High Street, aged 14. Enlisted in Winchester, January 1915 and served on the Western Front. Entered a theatre of war after beginning of 1916 with 14th (Service) Bn, (1st Portsmouth) The Hampshire Regiment and subsequently transferred from the Hampshire Yeomanry to 2/4th Bn on the Western Front. Wounded 31 July and in September 1917. Killed in Action 4 November 1918 at Beaudignies. Buried in Ruesnes Communal Cemetery, Nord, France (GR I. B. 23.).[4] Memorial at St Cross Chapel.

✠**CHURCHER, HENRY T. ... C.S.M. ... Hants, 1914, Pte. Egypt, France.** *Killed in Action, Sept. 19, 1918.* **M.M., 1918.**
(3, Avenue Road)

1 *The Hampshire Regimental Journal*, November 1918, p 244 for his death and an account of his life. R Hamps Notes. RH.
2 CWGC.
3 WO 372/4/93898. RH notes *Journal* records significant battle on 31 July: VC action at Tower Hamlets. See Atkinson, 2, Somme. Additional material from R Hamps Notes. RH.
4 CWGC.

87. CHURCHER, Henry Thomas, Company Serjeant Major, 201109,[1] 2nd/4th Bn The Hampshire Regiment, d. 19 September 1918 aged 28.[2]

Eldest son of Lot and Elizabeth Churcher of 3, Avenue Road. Born at Bemerton, Salisbury, Wiltshire in 1891. A Domestic Gardener in 1911 aged 20. Enlisted in Winchester in September 1914. Served in Egypt, France and Flanders. He entered a theatre of war with 2/4th Bn sometime after beginning of 1916. Awarded the Military Medal in 1918.[3] Died of Wounds, 19 September 1918. Buried in Terlincthun British Cemetery, Wimille, Pas de Calais, France (GR IV. B. 4.).[4] Memorials at St Matthew's and St Paul's.

He had two brothers who served in the War. Ernest C. served in France as a Lance-Corporal in the Army Service Corps and was wounded 5 October 1918. Harold J. served in Egypt, Palestine, France and Germany as a Corporal in The Hampshire Regiment, was wounded 1 December 1917. Both survived the War.

⛧**CLARK, GERALD M. ... Major ... O.T.C., 1900, Capt. Northants. France. Despatches 1916. *Killed in Action, July 14, 1916.***
(24, Ranelagh Road)

88. CLARK, Gerald Maitland, Major,[5] 6th (Service) Bn The Northamptonshire Regiment, d. 14 July 1916 aged 35.[6]

Son of the Rev. W. M. Clark and Mrs Annette L. Clark formerly of Kingsgate House (1891 and 1901 recorded at 51 and 52/1, Kingsgate Street). Born at Hampstead, Middlesex in 1880. A Schoolmaster in 1911 at St Andrews College (Workhouse and Workhouse Infirmary), Bradfield, Bucklebury, Reading, Berkshire, aged 31. Enlisted 1906 and transferred to The Northamptonshire Regiment from the Officer Training Corps.[7] Served in France. Mentioned in Despatches in 1916.[8] Killed in Action 14 July 1916. Commemorated on Thiepval Memorial, Somme, France (PR Pier and Face 11 A and 11 D.).[9] Memorials at St Cross Chapel and St Lawrence's.

1   WO 372/4/118443; /23/90487 (MM).
2   Atkinson, 2, p. 373 'missing'. R Hamps Notes. RH. give age as 27 etc.
3   *LG* 24.1.1919 no p. given. Citation not extant (RH).
4   CWGC.
5   WO 372/4/128939. MiD not found.
6   CWGC 6th Bn, SDGW 9th Bn.
7   '... old by Master'. Bradfield College website.
8   *LG* 15.06.1916. p. 5945.
9   CWGC.

✠**CLARK, HENRY P. ... Pte. ... A.V.C., Jan. 1916, Pte. Oxf. and Bucks L.I. France.** *Killed in Action, Dec. 22, 1917, Cambrai.*
(8, Mants Lane)

89. CLARKE, Henry P, Private, 27275,[1] 5th Bn The Oxford and Buckinghamshire Light Infantry, d. 22 December 1917 aged 23.

Son of the late Henry and Mary Clarke.[2] Born Birmingham. Not found in 1911. Enlisted in January 1916 at Winchester, served in France.[3] Transferred from the Army Veterinary Corps. Killed in Action 22 December 1917 at Cambrai. Commemorated on Tyne Cot Memorial, Zonnebeke, West-Vlaanderen, Belgium (PR Panel 96 to 98.).[4] No Winchester memorial found.

✠**CLARK, REGINALD J. ... Rfn. ... R.A.O.C., June 1916, Pte. R.B. France.** *Missing, Nov. 30, 1917.*
(40, Fairfield Road)

90. CLARK, Reginald James, Private, 33649,[5] 12th Bn The Rifle Brigade (The Prince Consort's Own), d. 30 November 1917 aged 32.

Son of Harry Clark of Salisbury. Born at Salisbury, Wiltshire in 1885. Husband of Millicent Clark of Rosebank, Easton, Winchester.[6] An Ironmonger's Clerk in 1911, boarding at 17, Eastgate Street, aged 26. Enlisted in June 1916. Served on the Western Front. Listed as Formerly 019593, AOC and transferred from Royal Army Ordnance Corps.[7] Killed in Action 30 November 1917. Commemorated on the Cambrai Memorial, Louverval, Nord, France (PR Panel 10 and 11.).[8] Memorials at St Matthew's, and St Paul's.

✠**CLARKE, WILLIAM J. ... Pte. ... Hants, Aug. 1914, Pte. Egypt, Mesopotamia.** *Drowned, Jan. 23, 1915.*
(85, Colebrook Street)

91. CLARKE, William John.[9] Private, 2409,[10] 1/4th Bn The Hampshire Regiment, d. 23 January 1916 ? aged 32.

---

1 WO 372/4/143339. Note variant Christian and surname. MIC also refers to Veterinary Corps as well as Oxford and Buckinghamshire.
2 Address not given.
3 SJ notes 'R[esident] or B[orn]? Winson Green, Warwicks' ie Birmingham.
4 CWGC.
5 WO 372/4/133980. Has him as S/33649. See also John Reeves S/9147.
6 GJEH checked Easton War Memorial 17.12.12. Clark not listed there.
7 SDGW.
8 CWGC.
9 Parents not known.
10 WO 372/4/151257. RH notes.

Born at St Michael's in 1883.¹ Not found in 1911. Enlisted in Winchester. Died on 23 January 1916.² Served in Mesopotamia. He entered a theatre of war with 1/4th Bn on 18 March 1915. Commemorated on the Basra Memorial, Iraq (PR 21 and 64).³ No Winchester memorial found.⁴

✠**CLOWES, CHARLES G. E. ... Lieut. ... K.R.R.C., 1912, 2nd Lieut. France, Belgium. Wounded, Oct. 8, 1914. *Killed in Action*, Feb. 15, 1915, *Ypres*.**
   (Milnthorpe, Airlie Road)

92. CLOWES, Charles George Edric, Lieutenant,⁵ 1st Bn attd 3rd Bn The King's Royal Rifle Corps, d. 18 February 1915 aged 22.⁶

Youngest son of Maj. Charles Edward Clowes (late 4th and 2nd Bns 60th Rifles, and 10th (Service) Bn The King's Royal Rifle Corps) and of Mrs Isa Clowes of Milnthorpe, Winchester. Born 28 February 1892. Husband of Isa. Educated at Eton. A Gentleman Cadet in 1911, at Sandhurst, Camberley, Surrey, aged 19. Enlisted in 1912. Went to the Front with 2nd Bn on Mobilization Served in France and Belgium. Wounded 8 October 1914 in the trenches, invalided home. Rejoined his Bn in December. Mortally wounded at St Eloi on 15 February 1915 and Died of Wounds 18 February 1915 'a most promising young officer, and much esteemed by his comrades.'⁷ Buried in Bailleul Communal Cemetery, Nord, France (GR F. 8.).⁸ Memorials at Christ Church, St Cross and Twyford Preparatory School.

His brother John L. served in France, Salonica, Belgium and Germany as a 2nd Lieutenant and Acting Major in The King's Royal Rifle Corps then transferred to the Machine Gun Corps. He was Mentioned in Despatches, won the Belgian Croix de Guerre and survived the War.

✠**COBB, JAMES A. ... Tpr. ... Hussars, Aug. 1914, Tpr. France, Belgium. *Killed in Action*, *May* 13, 1915, *Ypres*.**
   (3, Abbey Passage)

93. COBB, Arthur James,⁹ Private, 14479,¹⁰ 10th (Prince of Wales's Own Royal)

1   BMD.
2   SDGW, Armed Forces Registration Event (Death), CWGC all say 1916.
3   CWGC.
4   ? St Maurice, lost.
5   WO 372/ MIC not found.
6   Discrepancy in date of death.
7   Additional information and photographic image courtesy of K. Gray, pers. comm.
8   CWGC.
9   Note reversal of Christian names.
10 WO 372/4/177926. MIC states nothing about Household Cavalry. SDGW gives Household Cavalry.

Hussars. Household Cavalry and Cavalry of the Line, d. 13 May 1915 aged 27.

Son of James and Amelia Cobb of 3, Abbey Passage.¹ Born 1888. A Carman, Corn Merchant in 1911 aged 23. Enlisted in Household Cavalry in Southampton, August 1914. Served in France and Belgium. Killed in Action 13 May 1915 at Ypres. Commemorated on Ypres (Menin Gate) Memorial, Ypres (Ieper), West-Vlaanderen, Belgium (PR Panel 5.).² Memorial at St John the Baptist.

Two of his brothers served in the War. George served in the Hampshire Yeomanry. William P. served in France in the Hampshire Yeomanry, Border Regiment and East Lancashire Regiment and was promoted to Signaller. Both survived the War.

✠**COBERN, WESLEY V. ... Rfn. ... R.B., 1903, Rfn. France. *Killed in Action, Oct.* 18, 1914, *Armentières.***
  (72, Parchment Street)

94. COBERN, Wesley Vincent, Private, 8502,³ 3rd Bn The Rifle Brigade, d. 18 October 1914 aged 31.

Son of Thomas William and Agnes Eliza Cobern of 72, Parchment Street. Born 1884. A Military Clerk in 1911. Enlisted in Winchester, 1903. Entered France 10 September 1914. Served on the Western Front and was Killed in Action 18 October 1914 at Armentieres. Commemorated on Ploegsteert Memorial, Comines-Warneton, Hainaut, Belgium (PR Panel 10.).⁴ Memorials at Holy Trinity and Wesleyan Methodist Chapel, St Peter's Street.

His brother Wilfred G., listed below, was Killed in Action 15 June 1915 at Basra.

✠**COBERN, WILFRED G. ... Corpl. ... Hants (T.F.), Pte. Hants. India, Persian Gulf. *Killed in Action, June* 15, 1915, *Basra.***
  (72, Parchment Street)

95. COBERN, Wilfred George, Lance-Corporal, 2570,⁵ 1/4th Bn The Hampshire Regiment, d. 15 June 1915 aged 37.

Son of Thomas William and Agnes Eliza Cobern of 72, Parchment Street. Born 1879. A Photographer in 1911 aged 32. Enlisted in Winchester. Served in India and the Persian Gulf. Transferred from The Hampshire Regiment (Territorial

1   4, in 1911.
2   CWGC.
3   WO 372/4/179079. Both MIC and CWGC have Wesley. Vincent from SDGW.
4   CWGC.
5   WO 372/4/179081.

Force). He entered a theatre of war with 1/4th Bn on 18 March 1915. Killed in Action 15 June 1915 in Basra.¹ Buried in Basra War Cemetery, Iraq (GR V. B. 4.).² Memorials at Holy Trinity and Wesleyan Methodist Chapel, St Peter's Street.

His brother Wesley V., listed above, was Killed in Action 18 October 1914 at Armentieres.

✠**COLES, FRANK ... C.S.M. ... Hants (T.F.), Aug. 1914, Pte. India, Mesopotamia. Taken Prisoner by Turks, Apl. 29, 1916, Kut.** *Died of Dysentery, Sept. 18, 1916.*
(2, Andover Road)

96. COLES, Frank, Company Serjeant Major, 200011,³ A Coy. 1/4th Bn The Hampshire Regiment (Territorial Force), d. 18 September 1915 aged 31.

Only son of Charles and Elizabeth Coles of 2, Andover Road. Born at Alresford in 1885. A Printer's Composition (sic) in 1911, aged 26.⁴ A territorial soldier he enlisted in Winchester, August 1914. Served in India and Mesopotamia. He entered a theatre of war on 18 March 1915 with 1/4th Bn. Taken prisoner by Turks 29 April 1916 at Kut. Died of dysentery 18 September 1916. Buried in Baghdad (North Gate) War Cemetery, Iraq (GR XXI. K. 16.).⁵ Memorials at St Matthew's and St Paul's.

✠**COLES, SYDNEY J. ... Pte. ... Hants, Sept. 1914, Pte. India, Mesopotamia.** *Missing, believed killed, Jan. 21, 1916.*
(44, Western Road)

97. COLES, Sydney James, Private, 201057,⁶ 1/4th Bn The Hampshire Regiment, d. 21 January 1916 aged 21.

Son of the late Thomas Henry Coles and Rose Flitton (formerly Coles) of 9, Gladstone Street. Born at Portsferry, Co. Down, Ireland, 1895. Worked as a Coach Trimmer in 1911, living with his grandmother etc, at 68, Western Road, aged 16. Apprenticd with Messrs. Easther, Ltd., Jewry Street (now Mr. F. J. Matthews), and afterwards secured a 'good position' at Reading. Enlisted

1   R Hamps Notes. RH. Journal states he died of heat stroke, but in another place gives his death as of disease at Basra on 13 June 1915.
2   CWGC.
3   WO 372/4/199663. RH *Journal?* SJ writes 'Lance Sergeant'.
4   A mistranscription of Compositor?
5   CWGC. R Hamps Notes. RH. Journal states he died at 'Afrum Karra, Hissa.' Another soldier noted by the Bowker charity his details were recorded as height 5'11 ½ , size 9 shoe and hat size 7.
6   WO 372/4/201057.

on Salisbury Plain, Wiltshire, September 1914 (3237). Served in India and Mesopotamia. Entered a theatre of war with 1/4th Bn on 18 March 1915. Killed in Action at Shumran Bend 21 January 1916.[1] Commemorated on Basra Memorial, Iraq (PR Panel 21 and 63.).[2] Memorials at St Matthew's, St Paul's and St Thomas's School.

✠COLLINS, HERBERT F. ... Pte. ... Hants Y. Nov. 1914, Tpr. Hants. France. *Killed in Action, Mch. 1918, Cambrai.* (Park Road Nursery)

98. COLLINS, Herbert Frederick, Private, 33443,[3] 11th Bn The Hampshire Regiment (11th Reserve Cavalry subsequently 11th Bn (Pioneers)), d. 22 March 1918 aged 20.

Son of Edwin James Collins and Annie Collins of Park Road Nursery. Born at Winkfield, Berkshire in 1898. At school in 1911 aged 13. Enlisted in Winchester, November 1914 and served on the Western Front. Transferred from the Hampshire Yeomanry to the Pioneers 11 December 1916 with whom he served in a theatre of war. Killed in Action 22 March 1918 at Cambrai. Commemorated on Pozieres Memorial, Somme, France (PR Panel 48.).[4] Memorial at St Bartholomew's.

His brother Bernard W. served in India, Mesopotamia and Persia as a Private in The Hampshire Regiment, and survived the War.

✠COOK, ARTHUR B. K. ... 2nd Lieut. ... R.F., Feb. 1915, 2nd Lieut. France. *Killed in Action, July 7, 1916, Ovillers.* (6, The Close)

99. COOK, Arthur Basil Kemball,[5] 2nd Lieutenant, 9th Bn Royal Fusiliers, d. 7 July 1916 aged 30.

Son of Arthur Kemball Cook and the late Lucy Frances Cook of Colebrook House.[6] Born 1886. A Student Architect in 1911 living at 12, College Street

1   R Hamps Notes. RH. It is noted that he was recorded as 'missing' after an engagement in Mesopotamia according to his family for almost two years before his death was confirmed.
2   CWGC.
3   WO 372/4/211169. For Hampshire Yeomanry see Appendix 1. R Hamps Notes. RH. contributed additional material to this biography.
4   CWGC. GJEH notes: Pozières distant from Cambrai.
5   WO 372/4/236236. Entered as 'Kimball'.
6   A.B.K. Cook was teacher at Winchester College for just one term, Sep-Dec 1914. He was also a boy there, in College 1898-1904. 11 Edgar Road is a boarding house - called Du Boulays. His father was housemaster there 1893-1909. See https://www.winchestercollegeratwar.com/archive/arthur-basil-kemball-cook/. We are grateful

aged 25. Commissioned into the Regiment in Winchester, February 1915. Served in France. Killed in Action 7 July 1916 at Ovillers. Commemorated on Thiepval Memorial, Somme, France (PR Pier and Face 8 C 9 A and 16 A.).[1] No Winchester memorial found.[2]

⚔COVEY, EDWIN H. ... Pte. ... A.I.F., Oct. 1914, Pte. Gallipoli, France. *Killed in Action, July* 2, 1916, *Armentières*.
  (2, Westgate Lane)

100. COVEY, Edwin Harvey, Private, 1322,[3] 3rd Bn Australian Infantry, Australian Imperial Forces,[4] d. 2 July 1916 aged 25.

Son of Edwin Covey and Annie Covey of 3, Churchill Terrace, Crondall, Farnham, Surrey (sic).[5] Born at Chertsey, Surrey in 1893. An Errand Boy in 1911 aged 18. Family living at 2, Westgate Lane in 1911. Enlisted in October 1914. Served at Gallipoli (Dardanelles) and in France. Died of Wounds from a bomb 2 July 1916 at Armentieres. Buried in Sailly-sur-la-Lys Canadian Cemetery, Pas de Calais, France (GR I. A. 15.).[6] No Winchester memorial found.

His brother, Percy, listed below, was Killed in Action, 6 August 1915. His brother Albert E. served in India and Mesopotamia as a Private in The Hampshire Regiment and survived the War.

⚔COVEY, PERCY ... Pte. ... A.I.F., Oct. 1914, Pte. Gallipoli, France. *Killed in Action*, Aug. 6, 1915.
  (2, Westgate Lane)

101. COVEY, Percy, Private, 1486,[7] 4th Bn Australian Infantry, Australian Imperial Forces, d. 6 August[8] 1915 aged 21.

Son of Edwin and Annie Covey of 3, Churchill Terrace, Crondall, Farnham, Surrey (sic).[9] Born at Chertsey, Surrey in 1895. An Errand Boy in 1911 aged 16. Family living at 2, Westgate Street in 1911. Enlisted in October 1914. Served at Gallipoli (Dardanelles) and was Killed in Action 6 August 1915.

   to Suzanne Foster for this information..
1 CWGC 'Kemball'.
2 ? St Maurice, lost. His parents had a Colebrook Street address.
3 No MIC.
4 Check ref for Australian website. Entered as 'Harvey'. His records contain information not regularly preserved for British – letter to next of kin; returned possessions, listed – ID disk, whistle, knife, photos letters etc.' www.awm.gov.au.
5 Church St in CWGC
6 CWGC 'Haney' is an error.
7 No MIC. See notes on Edwin Covey above.
8 CWGC states between 6 and 9 August.
9 Church St in CWGC..

Commemorated at Lone Pine Cemetery, Anzac, Nr Gallipoli, Turkey (PR Sp. Mem. A. 4.).[1] No Winchester memorial found.

His brother Edwin H., listed above, served at Gallipoli (Dardanelles) and France and was Killed in Action 2 July 1916. His brother Albert E. served in India and Mesopotamia as a Private in The Hampshire Regiment and survived the War.

✠COWAN, DOUGLAS H. ... 2nd Lieut. ... Hants 1912, 2nd Lieut. France. *Killed in Action, Aug. 26, 1914. Cambrai.* (Little Meade, Cheriton Road)

102. COWAN, Douglas Henderson, 2nd Lieutenant,[2] 1st Bn The Hampshire Regiment, d. 26 August 1914 aged 23.

Son of David T. Cowan, MA (Director of Education, Hampshire, The Castle Winchester) of Little Meade, Cheriton Road. Born at Beccles, Suffolk 10 October 1890.[3] Listed as 2nd Lieutenant, 3rd Hampshires in 1911 living at 9, Clifton Road, aged 20. He was gazetted to The Hampshire Regiment 3rd Bn (Special Reserve) on 22 May 1912. Entered a theatre of war with 1st Bn on 23 August 1914. Killed in Action 26 August 1914 at Cambrai.[4] Buried in Fontaine-Au-Pire Communal Cemetery, Nord, France (GR I. B. 74.).[5] Memorial at Christ Church and Peter Symonds School.

✠COX, FRANK ... Pte. ... N. Fus., Sept. 25, 1914, Pte. France. *Killed in Action, Aug. 8, 1917, Nieuport.* (1 Culver Road)

103. COX, Frank, Private, 16/967,[6] 16th Bn The Northumberland Fusiliers, d. 9 August 1917 aged 24.

Son of George and Ellen Cox of 3, Bucklands Terrace, Leap Cross, Hailsham, Sussex. Born 1893. A Book Binder in 1911 living at St Swithuns Cottage, Maidstone Terrace, aged 18. His parents at 1, Culver Road in 1911.[7] Enlisted in Winchester 25 September 1914. Served on the Western Front. Killed in

---

1 CWGC.
2 WO 372/5/50298.
3 1911 Census suggests 1891.
4 Atkinson, 2, p. 13. 'one of nearly 200 Hampshires lost on 25-26 August at the Battle of Le Cateau'.
5 CWGC. Cemetery used by the Germans after Le Cateau. Some British buried there.
6 WO 372/5/59136.
7 Maidstone Terrace is in Culver Road. See Frederick Cox below for next of kin etc.

Action 9 August 1917 [1] at Nieupoort, near Albert. Buried in Ramscappelle Road Military Cemetery, Nieuport, West-Vlaanderen, Belgium (GR I. B. 20.).[2] Memorial at St Michael's.

He had three brothers who served in the War. Thomas, listed below, was Killed in Action on 1 July 1916. Frederick G., listed below, was Killed in Action on 31 May 1916. Walter served in India as a Private in The Hampshire Regiment and survived the War.

⚔**COX, FREDERICK G. ... Stoker ... R.N., 1904. H.M.S.** *Queen Mary. Killed in Action, May 31, 1916, Jutland.*
(1, Culver Road)

104. COX, Frederick George, Leading Stoker, 232313,[3] HMS Queen Mary. Royal Navy, d. 31 May 1916 aged 28.

Son of George and Ellen Cox of 3, Bucklands Terrace, Leap Cross, Hailsham, Sussex. Born at High Barnet, Hertfordshire, 22 April 1888 according to his Naval Records. Enlisted in 1904. Listed as a Stoker 1st Class on HMS Essex, Fourth Cruiser Sqdn, Palma Bay, Balearic Islands in 1911 aged 22. 1911 parents living at 1, Culver Road. Given as his next of kin in Naval records. Killed in Action 31 May 1916 at the Battle of Jutland.[4] Commemorated on Portsmouth Naval Memorial (PR 16.).[5] Memorial at St Michael's.

He had three brothers who served in the War. Frank, listed above, was Killed in Action on 9 August 1917 at Nieuport. Thomas, listed below, was Killed in Action on 1 July 1916 at Albert. Walter served in India as a Private in The Hampshire Regiment and survived the War.

⚔**COX, THOMAS ... Pte. ... R.A.M.C., Sept. 15, 1914, Pte. France.** *Killed in Action, July 1, 1916, Albert.*
(1, Culver Road)

105. COX, Thomas, Private, 2041,[6] 26th (3rd Wessex) Field Ambulance. Royal Army Medical Corps, d. 1 July 1916 aged 25.

Son of George and Ellen Cox of 3, Bucklands Terrace, Leap Cross, Hailsham,

---

1 SDGW.
2 CWGC.
3 ADM 188/411/232313. SDGW. The 3 Cox brothers were the largest family group to die in Winchester in the War..
4 Hepper, 2006, p. 60.
5 CWGC. See Frank Cox above for Culver Road.
6 WO 372/5/63708.

Sussex. Not found in 1911 but parents living at 1, Culver Road in 1911.[1] Enlisted in Winchester 15 September 1914 and served in France. Killed in Action[2] near Albert 1 July 1916 the first day of the Battle of the Somme. Buried in Albert Communal Cemetery Extension, Somme, France (GR I. H. 19.).[3] Memorial at St Michael's.

He had three brothers who served in the War. Frank, listed above, was Killed in Action 9 August 1917. Frederick G., listed above, was Killed in Action 31 May 1916 Walter served in India as a Private in The Hampshire Regiment and survived the War.

✠**CROSS, ERNEST ... Pte. ... Hants, Sept. 1914, Pte. India, Persian Gulf.** *Died, July* **28, 1916,** *Quetta.*
   (12, St. John's Street)

106. CROSS, Ernest, Private, 2820,[4] 1/4th Bn The Hampshire Regiment, d. 28 July 1916 aged 32.

Youngest son of George Cross of 12, St Johns Street. Born 1884. A Bricklayer in 1911 aged 27. Enlisted in The Hampshire Regiment at Hamilton Camp September 1914. Served in India and the Persian Gulf. Entered a theatre of war (Mesopotamia) with 1/4th Bn on 18 March 1915. Died 28 July 1916 at Quetta. Buried in Quetta Govt Cemetery (GR 2386). Commemorated on Delhi Memorial (India Gate) (PR Face 23.).[5] Memorial at St John the Baptist.

✠**CRUTE, WILLIAM H. ... Pte. ... Hants, Nov. 1914, Pte. Mesopotamia, France. Wounded, Jan. 21,1916.** *Killed in Action,* **1917.**
   (12, Lower Brook Street)

107. CRUTE, William Henry, Private, 32711,[6] 2nd Bn The Hampshire Regiment, d. 4 September 1918[7] aged 27.

Son of Emily Kate Punter (formerly Crute) of 79, Lower Brook Street. Born 1892. A Boot Shop Assistant in 1911, heading the household, aged 19, with his mother.[8] In 1901 living at same address with grandfather William M.

1   See Frank and Frederick Cox above.
2   SDGW states DOW. Albert CCE associated with DOW, i.e. Casualty Clearing Station. GJEH.
3   CWGC.
4   WO 372/5/102340. Regimental Journal says he died aged 34. R Hamps Notes. RH.
5   CWGC.
6   WO 372/5/117860.
7   Discrepancy 1917/18 date of death.
8   Apparently she was not married. SJ pers. comm.

Crute, there again in 1911. Enlisted in Winchester in November 1914. Initially served with 1/4th Bn under 3411. Wounded 21 January 1916 with 1/4th Bn. Re enlisted under 32711. He subsequently served with the 14th (Service) Bn, (1st Portsmouth) Hampshire Regiment and 2nd Bn. Reported as having 'pyrexia of unknown origin' and being at 3rd Rest Camp, fit, 4 November 1917. Killed in Action 4 September 1918.[1] Buried in Strand Military Cemetery, Comines-Warneton, Hainaut, Belgium (GR VIII. B. 10.).[2] No Winchester memorial found.

✠DAVIDGE, ERNEST ... L.-Corpl. ... Hants, July 1916, Pte. R. Berks. France. Wounded, Apl. 28, 1916. Taken Prisoner by Germans, Apl. 23, 1917. *Died, May* 6, 1917.
(81, Upper Brook Street)

108. DAVIDGE, Ernest, Lance-Corporal, 33281[3], 1st Bn Princess Charlotte of Wales's (Royal Berkshire Regiment), d. 6 May 1917 aged 31.

Son of Frederick and Isabella Davidge. Born 1885. Husband of Alice Maud Mary of Gracious Street, Selborne, Alton in 1909 and they had Mary (1911 census). A Carman in 1911, aged 26 at 81, Trinity Rectory, Upper Brook Street. Enlisted in The Hampshire Regiment in Winchester, July 1916 (211430. Served on the Western Front but not with The Hampshire Regiment.[4] Wounded 28 April 1916 and taken prisoner by Germans, 28 April 1917. Died 6 May 1917. Buried in Cologne Southern Cemetery, Cologne, Nordhein-Westfal, Germany (GR XVIII. B. 5.).[5] Memorial at Holy Trinity.

✠DAVIS, FRANCIS ... Pte. ... Wilts, 1906, Pte. France, Belgium. *Killed in Action, Nov. 1914, in Retreat from Mons.*
(46, Wales Street)

109. DAVIS, Francis, Private, 5951,[6] 1st Bn The Duke of Edinburgh's (Wiltshire Regiment), d. 31 October 1914 aged 34.

Son of George and Annie Davis of 46, Wales Street. Born at Warminster, Wiltshire.[7] Enlisted in 1906 at Pontypridd, Wales. Not found in 1911. Served in France and Belgium. Killed in Action 31 October 1914 in the retreat from

---

1 Atkinson, 2, pp. 367-8. Additional materil in this biography from R Hamps Notes. RH.
2 CWGC. Some information and photos for Crute but unconvinced it is the same man. JB.
3 WO 372/5/174926.
4 SDGW.
5 CWGC. R Hamps Notes. RH. state that he did not serve overseas with The Hampshire Regiment.
6 WO 372/5/204421.
7 SDGW.

Mons. Commemorated on Le Touret Memorial, Pas de Calais, France (PR Panel 33 and 34.).¹ Memorial at St John the Baptist.

✠DAWKINS, FRANK ... Pte. ... Devon Y., Mch. 1917, Tpr. Cheshire. *Killed in Action, Apl.* 29, 1918.
(8, Greenhill Terrace)

110. DAWKINS, Frank, Private, 72137,² 9th (Service) Bn The Cheshire Regiment, d. 29 April 1918 aged 19.

Son of George Dawkins and Emma Dawkins of 8, Greenhill Terrace. Born 1899. At school in 1911 aged 12. Enlisted in Winchester, March. 1917 and served on the Western Front. Listed as Formerly 3972, Devon Yeomanry.³ Killed in Action 29 April 1918. Buried in Klein-Vierstraat British Cemetery, Kemmel, Heuvelland, West-Vlaanderen, Belgium (GR V. D. 6.).⁴ Memorials at St Paul's, St Matthew's and St Thomas's School.

His brother George served on HMS Constance⁵ as a Stoker in the Royal Navy and survived the War.

✠DEAR, DOUGLAS G. ... Pte. ... Hants, Jan. 1914, Pte. India, Mesopotamia. *Killed in Action Jan.* 21, 1916, *Kut.*
(12, St. Leonard's Road)

111. DEAR, Douglas Gaunttett,⁶ Private, 200384,⁷ 1/4th Bn The Hampshire Regiment, d. 21 January 1916 aged 18.

Elder son of late William James Dear and Mary Ann Dear of 15, Sussex Street. Born 1898. In 1901 family at 16, St John's Street, in 1911 family at 1 and 2 Hedges Buildings. Aged 13 in 1911. Enlisted in Winchester, January 1914 and served in India and Mesopotamia. Entered a theatre of war with 1/4th Bn on 25 October 1915. Noted as a 'signaller'. Killed in Action 21 January 1916 at Kut (Um El Hanna), initially posted as 'missing'. Commemorated on Basra Memorial, Iraq (PR Panels 21 and 63.).⁸ Memorials at All Saints, St John the Baptist and Chilcomb.⁹

1 CWGC.
2 WO 372/5/215811. Mentions The Devonshire Regiment.
3 16th (Royal 1st Devon and North Devon,The Devonshire Yeomanry) The Devonshire Regiment.
4 CWGC.
5 *WWSR*. See Introduction for George Dawkins as an example of the use of the *WWSR* record with regard to service.
6 Gauntlett? Census 1911.
7 WO 372/5/234183. Formerly 2263. R Hamps Notes. RH, state this was a 'wrong' renumbering as 200384. Other additional material in this biography from the Notes.
8 CWGC.
9 SJ states DGD appears with photo in Warren's *WWSR* in HRO. SJ has his 'D Plaque

⊕**DENNISTOUN, JAMES R. ... Lieut. ... N. Irish Horse, 2nd Lieut. R.A.F. France. Wounded and taken Prisoner by Germans, June 26, 1916.** *Died of Wounds, Aug. 9,1916, at Ohrdruf.*
(The Lodge, Bereweeke Road)

112. DENNISTOUN, James Robert, Lieutenant,[1] North Irish Horse and 23 Sqdn The Royal Flying Corps, d. 9 August 1916 aged 33.

Son of George James and Emily Dennistoun (née Russell), of Peel Forest, Timaru, New Zealand who visited Britain in July 1914 and lived in Winchester, where they had been married in 1888 at St Bartholomew's, Hyde by Rev. Stephen Bridge, Emily's relative. Also had a Compton address. They died in Hampshire, buried in Torquay, Devon.[2] Malvern College 1898-1901, House 4, Modern wing (rather than Classical), house prefect. Noteworthy mountaineer in New Zealand; joined Captain Scott's Terra Nova expedition ship 1911-2. In the War left Wellington NZ c 28 February 1915: arrived England 14 April, stayed in Winchester. Considered the Argyll and Sutherland Highlanders, but they were not about to go to France. Enlisted 2 June at Antrim in the North Irish Horse; transferred to Hemel Hempstead, Herts., then to the cavalry school at Netheravon, Wiltshire, where also visited the flying school. Went to Ireland and enlisted at Antrim in The North Irish Horse on 2 June. Went to France January 1916 with The North Irish Horse. and wrote about his intention to join the RFC. Transferred to Royal Flying Corps (cousin Herbert Russell already a RFC pilot) c.8 June 1916. On 26 June was observer-gunner in aircraft flown by Herbert Russell. Shot down near Arras; Dennistoun (shot and seriously wounded) and Russell (wounded in crash) both taken prisoner. Died of Wounds, 9 August 1916 at Ohrdruf, Thuringia. Buried in Niederzwehren Cemetery, Kassel, Hesse, Germany (GR IV. H. 2.).[3] Memorials at St Matthew's and St Paul's ('Dennistown'), and in New Zealand.

His brother George H.[4] served on Lake Nyasa (Lake Malawi), Central Africa (the first naval engagement of the War) and previously in Samoa. A Commander

---

and Scroll.'
1 WO 372/6/4061. RFC records
2 http://muse.aucklandmuseum.com/satabases/cenotaph/33709.detail   Dennistoun was involved with Captain Scott's expedition in 1912, and was photographed in New Zealand. See Guy Mannering, *Peaks and Passes of J.R. D.* (Geraldine, NZ, 1999). I am grateful for this information and reference to Anne Strathie who is researching Scott's expeditionaries in the First World War, and who has also gathered material from many other sources including the Malvern College Archives. https://paperspast.natlib.govt.nz/newspapers/CHP19210510.2.70?query=George+dennistoun+obituary. Obituary of George Dennistoun: the father's obituary which validates much of the above.
3 CWGC for spellings of Kassel, Hesse etc.
4 *WWSR.*

in the Royal Navy, was awarded the Distinguished Service Order 1916 and survived the War.

☦DICKER, PERCY J. ... Pte. ... Middlesex, Aug. 1915, Pte. R.A.M.C. France. Wounded, Nov. 1916. *Killed in Action, Aug. 2, 1917.*
(9, Nelson Road)

113. DICKER, Percy John, Private, 65245,[1] 73rd Field Ambulance Royal Army Medical Corps, d. 2 August 1917 aged 23.

Son of John and Alice Dicker of 9, Nelson Road, Highcliffe Park, Winchester. Born at Ovington in 1895. A Domestic Groom in 1911, living at Rose Cottage, Ovington aged 16. Enlisted in Wood Green, August 1915 and served in France. Transferred from the Middlesex Regiment. Wounded November 1916 and Killed in Action 2 August 1917. Address given as Old Southgate, Middlesex.[2] Buried in Perth Cemetery (China Wall), Zillebeke, Ypres (Ieper), West-Vlaanderen, Belgium (GR I. G. 22.).[3] Memorials at All Saints and Chilcomb.

☦DICKINSON, E. ... 1st A.M. ... Hants V., 1914, Tpr. R.A.F. France, Belgium. *Died, Feb. 22, 1919, St. Omer.*
[No address given]

114. DICKINSON, Ephraim, 21630.[4] Mechanical Transport 1st Aircraft Depot Repair Park d. 22 February 1919 aged 33.[5]

Son of John and Naomi Dickinson of Wigan. Born at Orrell, Lancashire in 1886, aged 5 in 1891. A Bookseller an Stationer in 1911 aged 25 living in a boarding house at Penrith, Cumberland. Married Doris Irving of 13, Lowther Street, Penrith in 1917 in Cumberland.[6] Enlisted March 1916. Served with RFC/RAF in Flanders. Died 23 February 1919. Buried at Longuenesse (St Omer) Souvenir Cemetery, Pas de Calais, France. (GR V. F.36) . Memorial at United Church, Jewry Street.[7]

---

1 WO 372/6/21938.
2 Address from SDGW.
3 CWGC. See RAMC/WWI.com. Memorialised.
4 No MIC or RAF record found. JB has photo at time of his transfer from RFC or RNAS to RAF stating his enlistment date.
5 Still in France 1919 – died of influenza? See Harry Hedges.
6 BMD.
7 CWGC. Gives date of death as 23 February, 22 February on memorial.

✠**DOBSON, FRANCIS W. ... Tpr. ... Coldstream Guards, Aug. 1914, Tpr. France.** *Wounded and Missing, believed Killed,* **Dec. 22, 1914,** *Givenchy.*
   (County School for Girls, Cheriton Road)

115. DOBSON, Francis William, Private, 11114,¹ 1st Bn Coldstream Guards, d. 22 December 1914 aged 21.

Son of Jesse and Ellen Dobson, of Winterbourne, Cheriton Road. Born at Marlborough, Wiltshire.² Not found in 1911. Enlisted in London, August 1914 and served on the Western Front. Listed as Wounded and Missing, Believed Killed, 22 December 1914 at Givenchy. Commemorated on Le Touret Memorial, Pas de Calais, France (PR Panels 2 and 3.).³ Memorials at St Matthew's and St Paul's.

✠**DOUGLAS, CHARLES E. G. ... Pte. ... Hants, 1913, Pte. India, Persian Gulf.** *Died, June* **15, 1915,** *Basra.*
   (22, Cheriton Road)

116. DOUGLAS, Charles Edwin Gardiner, Private, 2147,⁴ 1/4th Bn The Hampshire Regiment d. 12 June 1915 aged 20.

Son of Charles Henry and Elizabeth Agnes Douglas of 22, Cheriton Road. Born 1896. In 1901 and 1911 family living at 36, Western Road. At school in 1911 aged 15. Enlisted in Winchester 1913 and served in India and the Persian Gulf with A Coy. Entered a theatre of war (Mesopotamia) with 1/4th Bn on 18 March 1915. Died 12 June 1915 at Basra. Buried in Basra War Cemetery, Iraq (GR VI. B. 3.).⁵ Memorials at St Matthew's and St Paul's, Hampshire County Council, Peter Symonds School and St Thomas's School.

✠**DOWSE, CLIFFORD T. ... Pte. ... Hants Y., Apl. 1916, Tpr. Hants. France.** *Killed in Action,* **Sept. 14, 1918.**
   (5, Andover Road)

117. DOWSE, Clifford T., Private, 204744,⁶ 15th (Service) Bn (2nd Portsmouth) The Hampshire Regiment⁷ d. 4 September 1918 age unknown.

Son of Mr and Mrs Douse (sic) of 26, Colson Road. Not found in 1911. Before

1 WO 372/6/44376.
2 SDGW.
3 CWGC. SDGW.
4 WO 372/6/71630.
5 CWGC. SDGW. R Hamps Notes. RH. state that he died of disease.
6 No MIC found.
7 For Hampshire Yeomanry see Appendix 2.

the war employed by Mr Elkinton, butcher. Married Miss Russell daughter of the cricket professional at of West Downs and left a son aged three. Enlisted in, April 1916 (2180) and served in France. Transferred from the Hampshire Carabiniers Yeomanry, 3/1st . subsequently 15th (Hampshire Carabiniers) Bn. Entered a theatre of war after the beginning of 1916.[1] Killed in Action 14 September 1918. Buried in Messines Ridge British Cemetery, West-Vlaanderen, Belgium (GR III. C. 7.).[2] Memorials at St Matthew's and St Paul's.

⌖DOWSE, HENRY A. ... Y. Sig. ... R.N., 1898, Boy. North Sea; H.M.S. *Faulkner. Died, May* 18, 1916, *Glasgow.*
(56-58, Colebrook Street)

118. DOWSE, Henry Alfred, Yeoman of Signals, 192186,[3] HMS Faulknor. Royal Navy, d. 18 May 1916 aged 34.

Son of James and Priscilla Dowse. Husband of Maud, 2, Roronto Road, ?Buckland, Portsmouth.[4] Born 1 October, 1881.[5] Previously a Labourer he enlisted in Royal Navy in 1898. Serving in the East Indies in 1911, aged 29. Served in North Sea aboard HMS Faulknor.[6] Died from disease at The Royal Infirmary, Glasgow 18 May 1916. Buried in Portsmouth (Kingston) Cemetery (GR Pink's. 9. 24.).[7] No Winchester memorial found.[8]

His brother William J. served in Mesopotamia as a Private in The Connaught Rangers then the Army Service Corps (Mechanical Transport), and survived the War.

⌖DRAKE, THOMAS H. ... Tpr. ... E.A. Mounted Rif., Aug. 1914, Tpr. E. Africa. *Killed in Action, Nov.* 3, 1914, *Longido.*
(Wyke Hill House, Weeke)

119. DRAKE, Thomas Harold, Trooper, 125,[9] The East African Mounted Rifles, d. 11 November 1914 aged 31.

Son of the late Arthur John Drake and Emily Drake of Wyke Hill House, Weeke. Born at Stratford, Essex 2 December 1883. Educated at Temple Grove,

1 This information and additional material in this biography see R Hamps Notes. RH. For the 15th Bn development see Appendix 2.
2 CWGC. SDGW not found. R Hamps Notes. RH. States 4 September as date of death.
3 ADM 188/329/192186.
4 SJ.
5 1911 Census suggests 1882.
6 H.M.S. Faulknor, error in *WWSR*. C.B. James, pers. comm.
7 CWGC.
8 ? St Maurice, lost.
9 WO 372/6/89035.

East Sheen then Marlborough College, Wiltshire. Not found in 1911: family at Wyke House. Emigrated to East Africa in 1906 as a settler and enlisted in The East Africa Mounted Rifles August 1914. Served in German East Africa. Killed in Action 3 November 1914 on the Longido Hills. Buried in Dar es Salaam War Cemetery, Tanzania (GR Coll. grave 8. E. 6-13.).[1] Memorials at St Matthew's and St Paul's.

'He was buried where he fell and a stone erected by his friends and that of seven others who fell on the same day'[2] However later his remains moved to Dar es Salaam.

✠DUFFIN, WILLIAM J. ... Pte. ... Hants, Aug. 1914, Pte. France. *Killed in Action, Apl. 1, 1915, France.*
   (8, Hedges Buildings)

120. DUFFIN, William J., Private, 4480,[3] 1st Bn The Hampshire Regiment, d. 1 April 1915 aged 38.

Son of William and Mary Ann Duffin of Kings Worthy. Born at Kings Worthy in 1877. Married Rose[4] of 8, Hedges Buildings, Magdalen Hill in 1905. They had twins, James Henry and John Gilbert, born 1907. A Gas Stoker in 1911 aged 34, when he also had a stepson William John Steele aged 17. Enlisted in Winchester, August 1914, a Special Reservist. Entered a theatre of war with 1st Bn on 13 December 1914. Served on the Western Front and was Killed in Action 1 April 1915. Buried in Lancashire Cottage Cemetery, Ploegsteert, Comines-Warneton, Hainaut, Belgium (GR I. F. 18.).[5] Memorials at All Saints, St John the Baptist, Chilcomb and Kings Worthy.

✠DUMMER, FREDERICK ... Pte. ... R. Berks, 1915, Pte. France. *Killed in Action, Oct. 23, 1916, France.*
   (11, Tower Street)

121. DUMMER, Frederick W., Private, 37222,[6] 2nd Bn Princess Charlotte of Wales's (Royal Berkshire Regiment), d. 28 October 1916 aged 27.

Son of Mrs Agnes Dummer of 11, Tower Street. Born 1889 recorded with parents Alfred and Agnes Dummer at 65, North Walls in 1891. A Tailor Maker in 1911 aged 22. Enlisted in Reading, Berkshire in 1915. Served on the Western

1 CWGC.
2 De Ruvigny, also gives date of birth (Findmypast website).
3 WO 372/6/105846. Additional material in this biography from R Hamps Notes. RH.
4 Pre-1912 records do not give maiden names.
5 CWGC.
6 WO 372/6/111346. SDGW.

Front. Killed in Action 23 October 1916[1] on the Somme. Commemorated on Thiepval Memorial, Somme, France (PR Pier and Face 11 D.).[2] Memorial at St Thomas's.

He had three brothers who served in the War. Alfred served in France as a Private in The Devonshire Regiment, and transferred to the Royal Engineers. Charles served in France as a Private in The Hampshire Regiment. Richard served in Egypt and India as a Private in The Hampshire Regiment, transferred to the Labour Corps and was wounded 9 April 1918. All three survived the War.

✠DUNMILL, JOHN B. ... Bdr. ... R.G.A., 1917, Gun. France. *Killed in Action, Feb. 2, 1918.*
   (St. Clement's, Hyde Street)

122. DUNMILL, John Barrow, Gunner, 163556,[3] 110th Siege Bty Royal Garrison Artillery, d. 2 February 1918 aged 32.

Son of Alfred Thomas and Mary Elizabeth Dunmill of Maidstone, Kent. Born at Maidstone.[4] Husband of Maggie of St Clement's, Hyde Street, Winchester[5] and worked as a Bank Official. Enlisted in Winchester, 1917 and served on the Western Front. Killed in Action[6] 2 February 1918. Buried in Tincourt New British Cemetery, Somme, France (GR IV. D. 24.).[7] Memorial at Holy Trinity.

✠DUNN, FRANK ... Pte. ... Lond., Feb. 1917, Pte. France. *Killed in Action.*
   (6, Arthur Road)

123. DUNN, Frank, Private, 535043,[8] 1st /15th (County of London) Bn The London Regiment (Prince of Wales's Own Civil Service Rifles), d. 26 September 1917 aged 40.

Son of John and Harriett Dunn of Sturry, Canterbury, Kent. Born at Sturry in 1879. Married Elizabeth E. Didby in 1905 and they had two children by 1911, Eugenie born 1907 and Sydney born 1910 living at 6, Arthur Road.[9] A

1   SJ states 28th.
2   CWGC.
3   WO 372/6/119639.
4   SDGW. Not found in 1911.
5   Pre-1912 marriage records do not routinely provide maiden names.
6   SJ notes Died of Wounds.
7   CWGC.
8   WO 372/6/120326.
9   His wife recorded at '34, Honeybrook Road, Clapham Park, London formerly of 6, Arthur Road (1911)' according to SJ. Ie address are of wife/widow/ /NOK at time of serviceman's death.

Bootmaker Dealer in 1911 aged 32.. Enlisted in Winchester in February 1917. Served on the Western Front. Posted to 2nd/12th (County of London) Battalion (The Rangers) The London Regiment. Killed in Action 26 September 1917. Buried in Tyne Cot. Commemorated on the Tyne Cot Memorial, Zonnebeke, West-Vlaanderen, Belgium (PR Panel 152.).[1] Memorial at St Bartholomew's.

✠**DYER, ARTHUR F. R. ... Capt. ... Hants Y. 1902, Tpr. Hants, K.A. Rif. E. Africa.** *Killed in Action, Sept. 30, 1917, Nitua.* **(6, Grafton Road)**

124. DYER, Arthur Francis Rayner, Captain,[2] attd as Adjt, 3rd /2nd Bn King's African Rifles, d. 30 September 1917 aged 34.

Eldest son of Alderman Arthur R. and Elizabeth Dyer of Palm Hall, Winchester. Born at Braintree, Essex in 1884, educated at Taunton College and Millhill School. Married Elsie M. Harrod in 1913. Noted at 6, Grafton Road.[3] Enlisted in The Hampshire Regiment at Winchester, 1902 serving as a territorial Corporal. Assisting in father's Provision Merchant business in 1911 aged 27. Served in East Africa. Commissioned from the Hampshire Carabiniers Yeomanry/The Hampshire Regiment on 6 February 1915. Killed in Action 30 September 1917 at Nitua.[4] Buried in Dar es Salaam War Cemetery, Tanzania (GR 6. G. 25.).[5] Memorials at Christ Church (listed only as Francis Dyer), St Lawrence, United Church, Jewry Street.

✠**EADE, CHARLES A. ... Drummer ... Hants, 1913, Drummer. India, Mesopotamia.** *Killed in Action, Jan. 21, 1916.* **(11A, Union Street)**

125. EADE, Charles A., Private, 1910,[6] 1/4th Bn The Hampshire Regiment, d. 21 January 1916 aged 21.

Son of Charles and Emily Justina Eade of 11A, Union Street. Born 1895. An Errand Boy in 1911 living at 5, Lawn Street aged 16. A territorial soldier he enlisted in Winchester, 1913. Served in India and Mesopotamia. Entered a theatre of war (Mesopotamia) with 1/4th Bn on 18 March 1915. Killed in

---

1 CWGC.
2 WO 372/134616.
3 R Hamps Notes. RH. contains much further information on his life and service record and an account of his memorial service organised by his Masonic Lodge at St Lawrence Church, with a list of attendees. The Notes suggest his widow moved to Palm Hall.
4 SJ.
5 CWGC.
6 WO 372/139460. Only Charles on MIC.

Action[1] at the Battle of Umm El Hanna 21 January 1916. Commemorated on Basra Memorial, Iraq (PR Panel 21 and 63.).[2] Memorials at Holy Trinity and St Thomas's School.

He had two brothers who served in the War. Edward A. served in North Sea and Russia as a Signaller in the Royal Navy. William C. served in France as a Private in The Hampshire Regiment, was wounded 1916 and 1917. Taken prisoner by Germans March 1918. Both survived the War.

✠**EADE, HARRY A. F. ... Pte. ... Hants, May 1914, Band Boy. France.** *Killed in Action, May* **1918,** *France.*
   (18. North View)

126. EADE, Harry Arthur Frederick, Private, 9593,[3] 2nd Bn The Hampshire Regiment, d. 9 May 1918[4] aged 19.

Son of William James and Mary Jane Eade of 18, North View (later of Cams Hall, Fareham). Born 1899. At school at Guston, near Dover, Kent in 1911. Enlisted in Winchester May 1914. Served on the Western Front. Entered a theatre of war (France) with 2nd Bn at some point after the beginning of 1916. Killed in Action 9 May 1918 France.[5] Buried in Pernes British Cemetery, Pas de Calais, France (GR II. B. 20.).[6] Memorial at Christ Church.

His father William J. rejoined in September 1914 and served at home as a Serjeant in The Hampshire Regiment. His brother William R. G. served in India, Palestine and France as a Private in The Hampshire Regiment. Both survived the War.

✠**EDWARDS, FREDERICK ... Pte. ... Hants, Mch. 1916, Pte. India, Egypt, Palestine. Wounded, Apl. 10, 1918. Taken Prisoner by Turks.** *Died of Wounds, May* **25, 1918,** *Jabez.*
   (1, Greenhill Road)

127. EDWARDS, Frederick, Private, 241826,[7] 2/5th Bn The Hampshire Regiment, d. 25 May 1918 aged 33.

1   SJ notes 'Died'.
2   CWGC.
3   WO 372/139552.
4   Atkinson, 2, p. 350. See note below. Nothing happening on 9 May: a 'week after 5 May 25 casualties.'
5   R Hamps Notes. RH. Regimental Journal says died of injuries received in action on 9 May 1918.
6   CWGC.
7   WO 372/6/166693. R Hamps notes. RH. Gives number as 241286.

Son of John (House Painter) and Clara Edwards of 1, Greenhill Road. Born at Handley, Dorset in 1886. A Bricklayer in 1911 aged 25. Enlisted March 1916. Served in India, Egypt and Palestine. Wounded 10 April 1918 and taken prisoner by Turks on the same day. Died of Wounds 25 May 1918 at Jabez. Buried in Ramleh War Cemetery, Israel and Palestine (including Gaza) (PR V. 28. Special Memorial).[1] Memorials at St Matthew's, St Paul's and St Thomas's School.

✠**ELGEE, HUGH ... Capt. ... S.W.B., 2nd Lieut. Egyptian Army. Dardanelles. *Killed in Action, July 6, 1915, Gallipoli*. (Chilcomb Manor)**

128. ELGEE, Hugh Francis, Captain,[2] South Wales Borderers attached Egyptian Army, d. 6 July 1915 aged 35.

Son of the Rev. Francis, sometime Vicar of Otterbourne, and Mrs Elgee. Not found in 1911 census, but relatives living at Chilcomb Manor. Served at Gallipoli (Dardanelles). Enlisted in The South Wales Borderers. His secondary regiment is listed as the Egyptian Army. Killed in Action 6 July 1915 at Gallipoli (Dardanelles). Buried in Twelve Tree Copse Cemetery, Turkey (PR Special Memorial C. 126.).[3] Memorial at All Saints and at Chilcomb, also a plaque in Otterbourne Church.[4]

His brother Cyril Hannond Elgee, Captain in the Bedfordshire Regiment, died in 1917.[5] His brother Ernest A. served as a Captain in the Remount Department and survived the War.

✠**ELKINS, FREDERICK ... Pte. ... Dorset, Sept. 1914, Pte. Dardanelles. *Killed in Action, Aug. 19, 1915*. (16, Granville Place)**

129. ELKINS, Frederick, Private, 11774,[6] 5th Bn The Dorsetshire Regiment, d. 19 August 1915 aged 25.

Son of Mrs Emma Elkins of 16, Granville Place, Wharf Hill. Born at Chilcomb in 1889. Not found in 1911. Enlisted in Winchester September 1914 and served at Gallipoli (Dardanelles). Killed in Action near Dead Man's House, Suvla 19

---

1 CWGC.
2 WO 372/6/182518.
3 CWGC. Note: 3360 identified, 2500 unidentified burials in the cemetery.
4 www.roll-of-honour.com/Hampshire/Otterbourne. Not on Otterbourne War Memorial but on plaque in church. GJEH pers. comm.
5 Plaque in Otterbourne Church.
6 WO 372/6/183381. SDGW.

August 1915.¹ Commemorated on The Helles Memorial, Turkey (PR Panel 136 to 139.).² Memorials St John the Baptist and St Peter Chesil (All Saints).

His brother Ernest H. served in Mesopotamia, Palestine and Syria as a Private in The Hampshire Regiment, transferred to The Leicestershire Regiment, and survived the War. His brother Herbert, listed below, Died 4 March 1916.

✠**ELKINS, FREDERICK A. ... Pte. ... Hants, Sept. 11, 1914, Pte. India. Mesopotamia. Taken Prisoner by Turks.** *Died, Aug. 7, 1916, Baghdad.*
(31, Eastgate Street)

130. ELKINS, Frederick Arthur, Private, 3246,³ 1/4th Bn The Hampshire Regiment, d. 7 August 1916 aged 25.

Son of Robert and Emily Elkins of 7, Percy Terrace, Water Lane. Born 1889. A Shop Porter in 1911, living in Water Lane, aged 22. Enlisted in Salisbury, Wiltshire 11 September 1914. Served in India and Mesopotamia. Entered a theatre of war with 1/4th Bn (Mesopotamia) on 18 March 1915. Taken prisoner by Turks at Kut and died 7 August 1916 in Baghdad. Buried in Baghdad (North Gate) War Cemetery, Iraq (GR XIV. A. 13.).⁴ Memorial at St John the Baptist.

✠**ELKINS, HERBERT J. ... Pte. ... Hants, Aug. 1914, Pte. Dardanelles, France. Wounded, Aug. 10, 1915.** *Died, Mch. 4, 1916, Rouen.*
(16, Granville Place)

131. ELKINS, Herbert James, Private, 9928,⁵ 1st Bn The Hampshire Regiment, d. 4 March 1916 age unknown.

Son of Mrs Emma Elkins of 16, Granville Place. Born at Chilcomb. Not found in 1911. Enlisted in Winchester August 1914 and served at Gallipoli (Dardanelles), France and Flanders. Entered a theatre of war (Gallipoli) with 10th Bn on 5 August 1915. Wounded 10 August 1915.⁶ Died 4 March 1916 at Rouen. Buried in St Sever Cemetery, Rouen, France (GR A. 18. 4.).⁷ Memorials

1   www.keepmilitarymuseum.org/gallipoli/
2   CWGC.
3   WO 372/183383. D. Coy. SDGW.
4   CWGC.
5   WO 372/6/183411. SDGW.
6   R Hamps Notes. RH. state he was wounded in action Gun Shot Wound (GSW) right shoulder. University War Hospital, Southampton, 5 September 1915. Subsequently transferred to 1st Bn in France.
7   CWGC.

at St Peter Chesil (All Saints) and St John the Baptist.

See Frederick Elkins his brother above.

✠**EVEREST, HAROLD R. ... Rfn. ... K.R.R.C., Sept. 1915, Rfn. France. Wounded, Sept. 18, 1916. *Died of Wounds*, Sept. 24, 1916, *Etaples*.**
   (34, Hyde Close)

132. EVEREST, Harold Robert, Private, 7129,[1] 18th (Service) Bn (Arts and Crafts) The King's Royal Rifle Corps, d. 24 September 1916 aged 31.

Son of William and Eleanor Everest of 34, Hyde Close where they were living in 1891, 1901 and in 1911 when Eleanor was a widow. Born 1886. An Assistant Teacher in 1911, boarding at Western Cross, Odiham, Hartley Wintney, aged 25. Enlisted in London, September 1915. Served on the Western Front. Wounded 18 September 1916 and Died of Wounds 24 September 1916 at Etaples. Buried in Etaples Military Cemetery, Pas de Calais, France (GR XI. A. 11A.).[2] Memorials at St Bartholomew's, Peter Symonds and St Thomas's schools.

His brother Reginald B., listed below, was Killed in Action, 4 October 1916.

✠**EVEREST, REGINALD B. ... Pte. ... P.P.C.L.I., Dec. 1915, Pte. France. *Killed in Action*, Oct. 4, 1916, *France*.**
   (34, Hyde Close)

133. EVEREST, Reginald Bertram, Private, 487499,[3] Princess Patricia's Canadian Light Infantry (Eastern Ontario Regiment), d. 4 October 1916 aged 33.

Son of the late William Everest and of Eleanor Everest of 34, Hyde Close. He was a Canadian National. A Broker according to his Attestation Papers. Enlisted in Montreal in December 1915 and served in France. Killed in Action 4 October 1916 near Courcelette in France. Commemorated on The Vimy Memorial, Pas de Calais, France.[4] Memorials at St Bartholomew's and St Thomas's School.

His brother Harold R., listed above, Died of Wounds.

1   WO 372/6/239270. C/7129.
2   CWGC.
3   www.canadiangreatwarproject.com/searches/soldierDetail.asp?1d=60847.
4   CWGC.

✠EYLES, ARTHUR E. ... Pte. ... Hants, Jan. 1915, Pte. Dardanelles. *Killed in Action, Aug. 6, 1915.*
(13, Bridge Street)

134. EYLES, Arthur Edward (Edward Arthur), Private, 15234,[1] 2nd Bn The Hampshire Regiment, d. 6 August 1915 aged 36.

Son of William and Mary J. Eyles of Front Street, St Cross. Born at St Cross 1879.[2] Married Lily Ruth Brown[3] in 1903 and they had three children by 1911: James Arthur William born 1904, Betsy Mary May born 1907, Daisy Lilian Elsie born 1910. A Bricklayer's Labourer in 1911 aged 32. Enlisted in Winchester, January 1915. Served at Gallipoli (Dardanelles). Entered a theatre of war (Gallipoli) as a reinforcement for the 2nd Bn on 15 June 1915. Killed in Action 6 August 1915.[4] Commemorated on The Helles Memorial, Turkey (PR Panel 125-134 or 223-226 228-229 and 328.).[5] Memorial at St Peter Chesil.

✠EYLES, WILLIAM J. ... Pte. ... Hants, rejoined Mch. 1915, Pte. Dardanelles. Wounded, Aug. 6, 1915. *Died of Wounds, Oct. 20, 1918.*
(10, Upper Brook Street)

135. EYLES, William J., Private, 15888,[6] 3rd (Reserve) Bn The Hampshire Regiment, died 20 October 1918 aged 46.

Son of William and Mary Jane Eyles of 8, Upper Brook Street in 1911.[7] Born 1872. In 1881 at St Cross, Upper Farm aged 7, his father a Carter.[8] Married Ruth Fletcher in 1898. In 1901 at 20, Upper Brook Street, William J. Eyles being a Private in The Hampshire Regiment. In 1911 at Hinton, Woodlands, Bramdean, Alresford.[9] They had six children by 1911: Dorothy born 1900, William born 1901, Alfreda born 1902, Albert born 1905, Reginald born 1907, Arthur born 1911. Served in the South African War. A Carter on a Farm in 1911 aged 39. Re-enlisted in Winchester 29 March 1915 and served at Gallipoli (Dardanelles). Entered a theatre of war on 17 July 1915 as a rienforcement for

1   WO 372/7/4193. MIC and CWGC say Edward Arthur, *WWSR* states Arthur E.
2   http://1914-1918.invisionzone.com/forums/index.php?showtopic= 139409.
3   Otherwise Pragnell (formerly Eyles).
4   R Hamps Notes. RH. From Regimental Journals: Reported missing at the Dardanelles on August 6th, 1915, now reported killed, Pte. A. Eyles, Hampshire Regt .....brother of Pte. W. J. Eyles, late of Bramdean, wounded same day. R Hamps hve him as Edward Arthur. Both brothers probably served in the South African War.
5   CWGC.
6   WO 372/7/4539. See also http://1914-1918.invisionzone.com/forums/index. Returned home wounded from 2nd Bn and died with 3rd (Reserve) Bn.
7   See notes to Edward Eyles, above.
8   Discrepancy in age/date of birth, but 1872 confirmed in later sources.
9   Census notes from SJ. Wife at 10, Upper Brook Street at his death? SJ note.

the 2nd Bn. Wounded 6 August 1915. He was discharged due to 'sickness' not wounds on 22 January 1916 according to Regimental records.[1] Died of Wounds, 20 October 1918. Buried in Winchester (Magdalen Hill) Cemetery, Chilcomb (GR W. 80.).[2] No Winchester memorial found.

✠**FACEY, WILLIAM H. ... Staff Sergt. ... R.E., 1900, Spr. Home. Died, Aug. 4, 1916, *Gravesend*.**
(25, Eastgate Street)

136. FACEY, William Henry, Forward Works Staff Serjeant, 5510,[3] Royal Engineers, d. 4 August 1916 aged 35.

Son of William George and Annie Louisa Facey 61, St John's Street. Born 1881. Husband of Mabel A. (25, Eastgate Steet).[4] Enlisted in Winchester in 1900. A Whitesmith at Kingston Barracks, Kingston on Thames, Surrey in 1911 aged 30. Died 4 August 1916 at Gravesend, Kent. Buried at Winchester (St Giles's Hill) Cemetery.[5] Memorial at St John the Baptist.[6]

✠**FARMER, JOSEPH V. L. ... Stoker ... R.N., 1913, Stoker. North Sea, Salonica, France; H.M.S. *Paragon*. Killed in Action, Mch. 18, 1917, *off Dover*.**
(42, Upper Brook Street)

137. FARMER, (Joe) Joseph Victor Lloyd, Stoker 1st Class, 19105,[7] HMS Paragon. Royal Navy, d. 18 March 1917 aged 25.

Son of the late William and Elizabeth Edwards (formerly Farmer) of 42, Upper Brook Street. Born 6 March 1893 at Andover. Aged 18, no occupation given in 1911. Formerly a Drayman when he enlisted in 1913. Served on the North Sea, the Salonica campaign and France aboard HMS Paragon. Killed in Action 18 March[8] 1917 off Dover when on the Dover Patrol a radio intercept led to the challenging of ships which turned out to be German destroyers. They sank the Paragon with depth charges. There were ten survivors.[9] Commemorated on Portsmouth Naval Memorial (PR 26.).[10] Memorial at Holy Trinity.

1   R Hamps Notes. RH. for this reference and other additional material in this biography.
2   CWGC..
3   No MIC found. SDGW
4   CWGC.
5   CWGC. No GR on CWGC database.
6   We are grateful to Peter Eagling for visiting St John's Church to research this.
7   ADM 188/19105. K/19105. Joe Victor Lloyd.
8   SDGW 18th CWGC 17th.
9   Hepper, 2006, p. 83.
10 CWGC.

✠**FIELDER, EDGAR J. ... Lieut. ... Hants, Sept. 1914, Pte. R. Lancs. France.** *Killed in Action, Apl.* **8, 1917,** *Arras.*
(39, Upper High Street)

138. FIELDER, Edgar John, 2nd Lieutenant,[1] 8th (Service) Bn The King's Own (Royal Lancaster Regiment), d. 8 April 1917 aged 28.

Son of John and Eliza Lavinia Fielder of Westgate, Winchester. Born 1889. Family at 39, Upper High Street 1901. A Builder's Assistant in 1911 aged 22. Enlisted in September 1914. Served as a Corporal with 4th Bn, The Hampshire Regiment but did not serve overseas with that Regiment. Commissioned as a Lieutenant in the King's Own (Royal Lancaster Regiment).[2] Entered a theatre of war (France) on 4 September 1916. Killed in Action 9 - 12 April 1917[3] at Arras. NOK sister, Elsie Fielder, Westgate, Winchester.[4] Buried in Faubourg D'Amiens Cemetery, Arras, Pas de Calais, France (GR III. P. 13.).[5] Memorial at St Thomas's Church.

His brother Frank, listed below, was Missing August 1915 at Suvla Bay.

✠**FIELDER, FRANK ... C.S.M. ... Hants, Aug. 1914, Pte. Gallipoli.** *Missing, Aug.* **1915,** *Suvla Bay.*
(39, Upper High Street)

139. FIELDER, Frank, Company Serjeant Major, 653,[6] 1/8th (Isle of Wight Rifles, Princess Beatrice's) Bn The Hampshire Regiment, d. 12 August 1915 aged 29.

Son of John and Eliza Lavinia Fielder of Westgate, Winchester.[7] Born 1886. A Bank Clerk in 1911 living at Ivy Cottage, 216, High Street, Slough, Buckinghamshire aged 25. Enlisted in East Cowes, Isle of Wight, August 1914. Entered a theatre of war Gallipoli (Dardanelles) on 10 August 1915, reported missing on 12 August 1915.[8] Killed in Action 12 August 1915 at Suvla Bay. Commemorated on The Helles Memorial, Turkey (PR Panel 125-134 or 223-226 228-229 and 328.).[9] Memorial at St Thomas's Church.

His brother Edgar J., listed above, was Killed in Action 8 April 1917.

1 WO 372/7/55938. WO 339/48606. Folder of Service Papers at TNA. Not examined.
2 SJ has Private (3209).
3 SDGW gives 12 April 1917.
4 SJ.
5 CWGC.
6 WO 372/7/55950.
7 See Edgar J. Fielder for other family details.
8 R Hamps Notes. RH. for this an other material relating to the Fielder brothers.
9 CWGC.

⋈**FIFIELD, JACK ... Pte. ... Hants, May, 1916, Pte. France.**
Killed in Action, Aug. 17. 1918, *Kemmel*.
(1, Elm Road)

140. FIFIELD, Basil (Jack), Private, 24686,[1] 15th (Hampshire Carabiniers) Bn The Hampshire Regiment, d. 16 August 1918 aged 20.

Only son of Ernest Walter and Charlotte Elizabeth Fifield of 'Winford' 1, Elm Road. Born 1898. At school in 1911 living at 3, St Paul's Terrace, Upper Stockbridge Road aged 13. Worked in the office of his father, the head accountant in the Carriage and Waggon Department of the London and South-Western Railway, Eastleigh. Enlisted in Winchester, May 1916 and served on the Western Front. Entered a theatre of war with 1st Bn after beginning of 1916. Subsequently transferred to the 14th (Service) Bn, (1st Portsmouth) The Hampshire Regiment and then to the 15th (Service) Bn The Hampshire Regiment as a Signaller. Killed in Action 17 August 1918 at Kemmel.[2] Buried in Lijssenthoek Military Cemetery, Poperinge, West-Vlaanderen, Belgium (GR XXV. E. 27A.).[3] Memorials at St Matthew's and St Paul's.

⋈**FITT, FREDERICK H. ... [BLANK] ... A.I.F., 1917, France.**
Killed in Action, Aug. 1918.
(21, St. Thomas Street)

141. FITT, Fred(erick) Harold, Private, 7243,[4] 1st Bn Australian Imperial Forces, d. 23 August 1918 aged 29.

Born either at Petersfield or Winchester.[5] Son of Fred Percival Fitt of Glen Mitchell, Bodangora, New South Wales and of Gertrude Alice Yeats (formerly Fitt in 1926) living at ?Duske Street, Tamworth, New South Wales, Australia in 1922. Mother listed as Next of Kin resident at South Grafton. Born at Petersfield. Formerly a Book Keeper. Not found in 1911. Enlisted in 1917 and served in France. Killed in Action 23 August 1918. Buried in Heath Cemetery, Harbonnieres, Somme, France (GR VII. A. 19.).[6] Memorials at Peter Symonds and St Thomas's schools.

1   WO 372/7/57933. For Hampshire Yeomanry see Appendix 2.
2   R Hamps Notes. RH. agree 16 August with *WWSR*. Additional material in this biography from R Hamps Archive.
3   CWGC.
4   http://mappingouranzacs.naa.gov.au/file-print.html?b=3909838&r=FITT Details of service, death, site of burial and notes of correspondence with Mrs H E ?Hooper of 21 St Thomas Street Winchester re dispatch of photo in 1918 etc etc.
5   SJ gives Petersfield.
6   CWGC gives Winchester as place of birth. SJ identifies a memorial to F W Fitt at Peter Symonds as relating to this man.

✠FLUX, CHARLES ... Pte. ... Hants, 1911, Pte. India, France, Mesopotamia, Dardanelles. Wounded three times. *Died from Pneumonia, Oct. 13, 1918, Mesopotamia.*
(49, Wharf Hill)

142. FLUX, Charles, Private, 8770,[1] 1/4th Bn The Hampshire Regiment, d. 13 October 1918 aged 29.

Youngest of six sons of the late James and Emily Flux of 49, Wharf Hill. Born 1891. Enlisted in Winchester in 1911 as a regular soldier and was at Wellington Lines, Aldershot aged 20. Served in India, France, Mesopotamia and Gallipoli (Dardanelles). Entered a theatre of war (Gallipoli) on 25 April 1915 and was wounded for he first of three times three ddays later.[2] He died from pneumonia 13 October 1918 in Mesopotamia. Buried in Tehran War Cemetery, Iran (GR IV. A. 10.).[3] Memorial at St Peter Chesil.

His brother George Henry, listed below, was drowned 13 August 1915.

✠FLUX, GEORGE H. ... Sergt. ... Hants, Aug. 1914, Pte. Mediterranean. *Drowned in H.M.S. "Royal Edward," Aug. 13, 1915.*[4]
(13, Upper Wolvesey Terrace)

143. FLUX, George Henry, Serjeant, 4515,[5] 2nd Bn The Hampshire Regiment, d. 13 August 1915 aged 41.

Son of James Henry and Emily Flux (née Hicks).[6] Born 1874. Married Eliza Alice in 1904 and by 1911 they had Elsie born 1906, Nellie born 1908[7] and Dorothy born 1910. A Stoker Sewage Destructor in 1911 living at 66, Canon Street aged 37. Wife Next of Kin at 13, Upper Wolvesey Terrace. Enlisted in Winchester, August 1914. He was a Secial Reservist, suggesting previous

---

1   WO 372/7/98455. Discrepancy in records over his number 5770/8770.
2   R Hamps Notes. RH. for additional material in this biography. There is an account of his service in the Royal Hampshire Regiment Archive.
3   CWGC.
4   Inverted commas round "Royal Edward" suggest this was typeset from a previous written source: mostly ships not entered in inverted commas. The Royal Edward's loss is not entered in Hepper, 2006. The website Navy List states it was HMT Royal Edward, ie a transport. Family tradition records that he died on the Alexandria, 'the first ship to be sunk in the War, en route to fight Johnny Turk.' Pers. comm. Vi Richards to whom we are most grateful. See also Appendix 3 for HMT Royal Edward.
5   WO 372/7/98483. 3/4515.
6   ie gives his parents' address at Wharf Hill. See also www.findagrave.com for further details.
7   Died 1996.

military service.¹ Served in the Mediterranean Expeditionary Force. Drowned aboard HMS Royal Edward 13 August 1915 en route to the Dardanelles. Commemorated on The Helles Memorial, Turkey (PR Panel 125-134 or 223-226 228-229 and 328.).² Memorials at All Saints and St Peter Chesil.

His brother Charles, listed above, died from pneumonia, 13 October 1918 in Mesopotamia.

✠FLYNN, WILLIAM ... Sergt. ... S.W.B., Aug. 1914, Corpl, Dardanelles, Mesopotamia. Wounded, Aug. 12, 1915. *Killed in Action, Apl. 9, 1916.*
(10, Freelands Buildings)

144. FLYNN, William, Serjeant, 12267,³ 4th (Service) Bn South Wales Borderers, d. 9 April 1916 age unknown.

Born at Briton Ferry, Glamorgan. Not found in 1911. Enlisted in Brecon, Breconshire August 1914 and served at Gallipoli (Dardanelles) and in Mesopotamia. Wounded on 12 August 1915. Killed in Action 9 April 1916.⁴ Commemorated on Basra Memorial, Iraq (PR Panel 16 and 62.).⁵ Memorial at Holy Trinity.

✠FORBES, JOHN ... Pte. ... Sea. H., June 1915, Pte. France. *Killed in Action, Aug. 19, 1916, France.*
(25, Sussex Street)

145. FORBES, John, Private, 9037,⁶ 8th (Service) Bn Seaforth Highlanders (Ross-shire Buffs, the Duke of Albany's), d. 19 August 1916 age unknown.

Born at Dalry, Midlothian. Married Ethel Mary native of Winchester in 1906 and they had Marjorie born 1907, according to the 1911 census when he was not found. Enlisted in Edinburgh, Midlothian June 1915. Served on the Western Front. Killed in Action 19 August 1916 in France. Commemorated on Thiepval Memorial, Somme, France (PR Pier and Face 15 C.).⁷ Memorials at St Matthew's and St Paul's.

---

1. R Hamps Notes. RH. for this and other additional detail in this biography.
2. CWGC.
3. WO 372/7/100156.
4. Winchester address at time of death. SDGW.
5. CWGC.
6. WO 372/7/106098. S/9037. His number is incomplete on TNA index 903. making searching more challenging.
7. CWGC.

✠**FORD, C. H. ... Pte. ... Hants (T.F.), 1914, Pte. India, Mesopotamia.** *Killed in Action, Jan. 21, 1916, Kut.*
(No address given)

146. FORD, Charles Henry (C.H.).,[1] Private, 200714,[2] 1/4th Bn The Hampshire Regiment, d. 21 January 1916 age unknown.

Enlisted at Hamilton Camp in 1914.[3] Served in Mesopotamia.[4] Killed in Action 21 January 1916 at Kut.[5] Commemorated on the Basra Memorial, Iraq. (PR Panel (21 and 63). Memorial at St Thomas's School.

✠**FORD, VICTOR W. ... Sergt. ... Hants, 1912, Pte. India, Mesopotamia. Taken Prisoner by Turks, Apl. 1916, Kut.** *Died, Sept. 21, 1916.*
(10, Colebrook Place)

147. FORD, Victor William, Serjeant (Trumpeter), 855314,[6] 1/5th Hants (Howitzer) Bty Royal Field Artillery, d. 21 September 1916 age unknown.

Born at Andover. Not found in 1911. Enlisted in Newport, Isle of Wight in 1912 and served in India and Mesopotamia.[7] Taken prisoner by Turks, April 1916 at Kut. He died 21 September 1916. Buried in Baghdad (North Gate) War Cemetery, Iraq (GR XXI. Q. 25.).[8] No Winchester memorial found.[9]

His brother Hubert W. served in the North Sea and the Mediterranean aboard HMS Commonwealth, Lord Nelson and Emperor of India as a Private in the Royal Marines and survived the War.

✠**FORDER, FRANCIS J. ... Pte. ... Hants, May, 1910, Pte. India, Mesopotamia. Taken Prisoner by Turks, Apl. 1916, Kut.** *Died, July 7, 1916, Baghdad.*
(75, Parchment Street)

1 NB A second Charles H Ford who survived listed in the *WWSR*.
2 WO 372/7/107715. SDGW.
3 In 1911 a Charles Henry Ford aged 16, a Bookseller's Assistant was boarding at 23 Tower Street, Winchester. Described as 'India Resident', born 1895, his mother Mignonette, b. in Singapore. SJ identifies him as his man. British India Office Birth Records give a date of birth as 14 June 1894.
4 Atkinson, 2, p. 163.
5 At the relief of Kut, the Battle of Umm El Hanna by the Tigris. 1/4th Hampshires lost 13 officers and 230 men, but were not the hardest hit.
6 WO 372/7/111275. Unit title correct GJEH. SDGW.
7 R Hamps Notes. RH. states not serve overseas with Hampshire Regiment. Probably pre-war Territorial.
8 CWGC.
9 ? St Maurice, lost.

148. FORDER, Francis James, Private, 1417,[1] 1/4th Bn The Hampshire Regiment, d. 7 July 1916 aged 23.

Son of Blanche Isabel Forder of 75, Parchment Street. Born at Eastleigh in 1893. A Plumber's Mate in 1911 living at 11, Andover Road aged 18. A territorial soldier he enlisted in Winchester, May 1910. Served in India and Mesopotamia. Entered a theatre of war (Mesopotamia) with 1/4th Bn on 22 October 1915. Taken prisoner by Turks April 1916 at Kut and died 7 July 1916 at Baghdad.[2] Buried in Baghdad (North Gate) War Cemetery, Iraq (GR VI. H. 8.).[3] Memorials at St Matthew's and St Paul's.

✠**FORSTER, HAROLD T. ... Major ... R. Berks, Pte. Northants. France, Belgium. Wounded, Oct. 1914. Wounded and *Missing (believed Killed)*, May 29, 1918. D.S.O. and Bar, M.C. and Bar. (14, Avenue Road)**

149. FORSTER, Harold Thomas, Major,[4] attd 2nd Bn Princess Charlotte of Wales's (Royal Berkshire Regiment), d. 29 May 1918 aged 39.[5]

Born 14 November 1878. Played cricket for Hampshire.[6] In 1911 at Fort Burgoyne, The Red Huts, Military Quarters at Castle Hill, Langdon Fort and Military Prison Governor's Quarters, Dover. Served in France, Belgium. The promotion to the rank of Lieutenant is dated 28 December 1915 in *The London Gazette*. Awarded the Distinguished Service Order and Bar and the Military Cross and Bar. Transferred from The Northamptonshire Regiment and was wounded October 1914. Died of Wounds 29 May 1918. Body recovered and buried in the newly opened Terlincthun British Cemetery, Wimille, Pas de Calais, France (GR VII. A. C. 12.). Memorials at St Paul's and St Thomas's School.

(First) MC published in *The London Gazette* 27 July 1916. 'For gallantry and devotion to duty. A very gallant warrant officer, he has maintained the same

1 WO 372/112525.
2 R Hamps Notes. RH. states 17 July and provides other detail. Bowker says he was in the 2/6th Bn.
3 CWGC.
4 WO 372/7/117810. Service Papers at WO 339/2100.
5 It is unususual in the *WWSR* to place the medals at the end. Added later? Because he was an officer? Exemplifies a 'Missing (believed Killed)' case where the remains were subsequently recovered and a burial place allocated.
6 See http://1914-1918.invisionzone.com/forums/index for information on his life, cricket average etc. Forster 'won more gallantry awards than any other man who played first-class cricket', according to Andrew Renshaw in *Wisden on The Great War: the Lives of Cricket's Fallen 1914-1918* (London: Wisden, 2014). Despite his cricketing prowess Wisden missed Forster but an obituary finally appeared in the Supplementary Obituaries in Wisden 2015 as a result of Renshaw's research for which we are very grateful..

standard in the performance of his duties.'

(First) DSO published in *The London Gazette* 26 September 1917. 'For conspicuous gallantry and devotion to duty. He took over command of his battalion when his colonel had become a casualty, and led them with great skill to their objective, twice changing direction in order to avoid hostile barrage. He then made a personal reconnaissance and ascertained the position of the enemy, after which he formed a defensive flank, and was able to re-establish his line when it had been driven back by determined hostile counter-attacks. He remained perfectly cheerful throughout, showing a fine example of fearlessness and contempt for danger.'[1]

(Second DSO) Supplement to *The London Gazette,* 9 January, 1918

Lt. Harold Thomas Forster, DSO, MC, Royal Berkshire Regiment

'For conspicuous gallantry and devotion to duty during an attack. He performed invaluable work as Adjutant throughout the day, rallying and controlling the men and showing great grasp of the situation. He set a fine example of courage and resource to all.'

(Second MC) Supplement to *The London Gazette,* 16 September, 1918

Lt. (A./Maj.) Harold Thomas Forster, DSO, MC, Royal Berkshire Regt, attd Northamptonshire Regt.

'For conspicuous gallantry and devotion to duty. He assumed command of his battalion when his Colonel was killed, and by his coolness and skill extricated it from a critical situation and formed a defensive flank of the utmost importance. For three days and nights, by his pluck and energy, he set an example to his men of inestimable value under adverse conditions of continuous and heavy shell fire.'

✠FRANCIS, ALBERT E. ... Corpl... . Hants Y., May 1916, Tpr. M.P. Home. *Killed in Action, Mch. 25, 1918, Arras.*
(11, Andover Road)

150. FRANCIS, Albert Edward, Private, 205506,[2] 15th (Service) Bn (2nd Portsmouth) The Hampshire Regiment d. 25 March 1918 aged 42.

Born at Putney, London in 1876. Married Mary in 1906 and by 1911 they had two children, Albert born 1907 and Winifred Mary born 1909. A Police

1   Cited from Renshaw's transcript.
2   WO 372/7/142479.

Constable in 1911 living at 35, Hyde Street aged 35. Enlisted in Winchester, May 1916 in the 15th (Hampshire Carabiniers) Bn The Hampshire Regiment. Entered a theatre of war (France) with Hampshire Carabiniers Yeomanry at some point after the beginning of 1916 but after their amalgamation the 15th (Service) Bn in 1917.[1] Served on the Western Front.[2] Killed in Action 25 March 1918 at Arras – the 'First Day of Spring' offensive. Buried in Achiet-le-Grand Communal Cemetery Extension, Somme, France (GR II. I. 1.).[3] Memorials at St Matthew's and St Paul's.

✠FRASER, FRANK A. ... Sig. ... A.I.F., May 1916, Sig. France. *Killed in Action*, Oct. 9, 1917, *France*.
   (Links Road)

151. FRASER, Frank Arthur, Signaller, 5795,[4] 18th Bn Australian Infantry, AIF, d. 9 October 1917 aged 35.

Son of Charles and Margaret Elizabeth Fraser of 37, Monks Road. Born at Notting Hill Gate, Middlesex in 1883. Served twelve years in the Royal Navy in the East Indies and Aden. Serving at Aden in the East Indies in 1911 aged 28. Formerly a Clerk when he enlisted in Winchester, May 1916 and served on the Western Front. At time of enlistment was living at Arcadia, 207, Victoria Street, ?Darlinghurst, New South Wales.[5] Killed in Action 9 October 1917 in France. Buried in Dochy Farm New British Cemetery, Zonnebeke, West-Vlaanderen, Belgium (GR VIII. D. 17.).[6] Memorials at St Matthew's and St Paul's.

His brother Charles J. served in France, Belgium and Germany as a Lieutenant in the Army Service Corps, transferring to the London Rough Riders, and survived the War.

✠FREEMAN, CHARLES ... L.-Corpl. ... R.F., Jan. 1916, Pte. France. *Killed in Action, June* 11, 1917. M.M., 1917.
   [No address given]

152. FREEMAN, Charles, 23261.[7] Lance-Corporal. 26th (Service) Bn

1 See Appendix 2.
2 CWGC states he was a Private.
3 CWGC.
4 http://mappingouranzacs.naa.gov.au/file-print.html?b=4033662&r=B2455, FRASER F A. Australian papers note the dates of embarkation an disembarkation, revealing the six weeks at sea en route. Printout. Also commemorated on Australian Roll of Honour.
5 Information from SJ. Brother of Harry Fraser of Royston, Darley Street, ??Bodmin, NSW.
6 CWGC.
7 WO 372/7/156224. Discrepancy over day of death. For his MM see WO 372/23/108227. Date of MM 16.08.1917 on MIC but no *London Gazette*

(Bankers), The Royal Fusiliers (City of London Regiment). d. 12 June 1917 aged ?23.

Son of Charles Sharpe Freeman and Clara Freeman of Bank House, Lydney, Gloucestershire.[1] Born at Newbury, Berkshire in 1894. In 1901 he was living at 7, High Street, Gloucester. In 1911 he was a Bank Clerk boarding at 41, Droitwich Road, Worcester. Enlisted at Winchester in Januery 1916. The 'Bankers' Bn was composed largely of Bank Clerks and Accountants.[2] Served in France and Flanders. Awarded the Military Medal. Killed in Action 11 June 1917.[3] Commemorated on Ypres (Menin Gate) Memorial, Ypres (Ieper), West-Vlaanderen, Belgium (PR 6 and 8).[4] No Winchester memorial found.

London Gazette, Supplement 16 August 1917 for his MM.

⌘FREEMANTLE, GEORGE W. ... L-.Corpl. ... Hants, May 1915, Pte. Oxf. And Bucks L.I. Flanders. *Missing, believed Killed, Aug. 22, 1917, Ypres.*
(10, Ranelagh Road)

153. FREEMANTLE, George William, Lance-Corporal,[5] 285155, 2/1st Buckinghamshire Bn Oxford and Buckinghamshire Light Infantry, d. 22 August 1917 aged 18.

Son of the late George Albert and Rosa Constance Freemantle of 10, Ranelagh Road. Born at Twyford in 1899. At school in 1911 aged 12. Enlisted in Southampton, May 1915 and served on the Western Front. Listed as formerly 1505, Hants Cyclists.[6] Entered a theatre of war with Hampshire Regiment at some point after the beginning of 1917. Has a 9th Bn number 356020. Transferred from The Hampshire Regiment. May be assumed Killed in Action 22 August 1917 at Ypres after transfer to Oxford and Bucks.[7] Commemorated on the Tyne Cot Memorial, Zonnebeke, West-Vlaanderen, Belgium (PR Panel

Supplement found for that date. His MM is cited at the end of his *WWSR* entry, see note on Harold Forster, above.
1 CWGC.
2 www.1914-1918 (Long Long Trail). See Lionel Penson.
3 SJ notes 12 June, SDGW, CGWC.
4 CWGC.
5 WO 372/7/159126. SDGW has him as a Private not L.-Corpl.
6 SDGW.
7 *The Oxford and Buckinghamshire Light Infantry Chronicle* records that the 2/1st Bucks Bn marched from Goldfish Chateau camp to the Pommern Castle Sector of the line via Ypres and St Jean on 20 August. 21 August was spent in preparation for the coming attack. Zero hour was 4.45 am 'the casualty rate was high so one can assume he was KIA on 22 August' (courtesy of K. Gray pers. comm.). Additional material from R Hamps Notes. RH.

96 to 98.).[1] Memorials at Peter Symonds School and St Cross Chapel.

His brother Hubert V. served in France as a Private in the Australian Imperial Forces, was taken prisoner by Germans 16 April 1917 and survived the War.

✠**FULFORD, ARCHIBALD C. ... Pte. ... Hants, Sept. 1914, Pte. Oxf. and Bucks L.I., Mesopotamia. Taken Prisoner by Turks, Apl. 29 1916, Kut.** *Died as P.O.W., between Apl. and Dec. 1916.*
(1, Queen's Road)

154. FULFORD, Archibald Cecil, Private, 200909,[2] 1/4th Bn The Hampshire Regiment, d. 31 December 1916 aged 19.

Son of William and Martha Fulford of 1, Queen's Road (2, Ilex Terrace in 1901).[3] . Born 1898. A Clerk in 1911 aged 13. He had three brothers who served in the War A territorial soldier (3009) he enlisted on Salisbury Plain, Wiltshire September 1914. Served in Mesopotamia. He transferred from The Oxford and Buckinghamshire Light Infantry to The Hampshire Regiment. Entered a theatre of war (Mesopotamia) with 1/4th Bn on 18 March 1915. Taken prisoner by Turks 29 April 1916 at Kut and died as a POW between 29 April 1916 and December 1916, his papers stating 31 December.[4] Commemorated on Basra Memorial, Iraq (PR Panel 21 and 63.).[5] Memorials at Christ Church, Peter Symonds and St Thomas's schools.

Clarence V., listed below, was Killed in Action 21August 1917. Horace G. served in France, Salonica, Turkey and the Balkans as a Private, promoted to Corporal in The Hampshire Regiment, and survived the War. Wilfred C. served in Egypt as a Private, was commissioned Lieutenant in The Hampshire Regiment, and survived the War.

✠**FULFORD, CLARENCE, V. ... Sergt.... Can. Inf., Mch. 1916, Pte. France, Belgium. Wounded, May 6, 1917.** *Killed in Action, Aug. 21, 1917, Lens.*
(1, Queen's Road)

155. FULFORD, Clarence Victor, Serjeant, 474212,[6] 46th Bn Canadian

---

1 CWGC.
2 WO 7/173783.
3 SDGW, CGWC.
4 Atkinson, 2, pp. 164ff. Kut surrendered on 24 April: no attack on 29th. R Hamps Notes. RH. states he died at 'Airan', corroborated by Bowker.
5 CWGC.
6 www.canadiangreatwarproject.com/searches/soldier. Contains much personal information.

Infantry (Saskatchewan Regiment), d. 21 August 1917 aged 24.

Son of William and Martha Fulford of 1, Queen's Road. Born 1894. A Gardener Domestic in 1911 aged 17, but a farmer in his Canadian attestation papers. He was a Canadian National who enlisted in March 1916 at Saskatoon, Sask. Served in France and Belgium. Embarked June 1916 for England and arrived on the Western Front in August 1916. He was transferred from the 65th Bn in July 1916, and rose to rank of Serjeant in March 1917. Wounded in the back 6 (or 7) May 1917. Returned to the front and was Killed in Action 21 August 1917 at Lens. Buried in Villers Station Cemetery, Viller-au-Bois, Pas de Calais, France (GR IX. F. 19.).[1] Memorial at Christ Church.

Clarence had three brothers who served in the War. Archibald C., listed above, died as a POW. Horace G. served in France, Salonica, Turkey and the Balkans as a Private, promoted to Corporal in The Hampshire Regiment, and survived the War. Wilfred C. served in Egypt as a Private, was commissioned Lieutenant in The Hampshire Regiment, and survived the War.

✠GALE, ARTHUR W. ... Capt. ... Dragoon Gds., Aug. 1914, Tpr. Life Gds. Flanders. D.S.O. 1916, Despatches 1916. *Killed in Action, April* 10, 1916.
(2, Clifton Road)

156. GALE, Arthur Witherby, Captain, 2nd Life Guards.[2] Household Cavalry and Cavalry of the Line (incl. Yeomanry and Imperial Camel Corps), d. 10 April 1916 aged 41.

Son of the late Alfred Christopher and Sophia Eliza Gale. Born 1875. In 1881 living at Front Street aged 6. In 1891 is mother, a widow, at 7, Ranelagh Road. In 1911 still widowed, at 2, Clifton Road. Educated at Marlborough College, Wiltshire.[3] Arthur enlisted in Winchester, August 1914 and served in Flanders.[4] Attached Royal Field Artillery, (OC, Trench Mortar Batteries, 3rd Div.).[5] Listed in *The London Gazette* 29 August 1914 to be Lieutenant.[6] As 2nd Life Guards, Lieutenant A. W. Gale, Reserve of Officers, to be temporary Captain, dated 9 May, 1915. Awarded the Distinguished Service Order and

---

1 CWGC.
2 WO 372/7/186419. Also recorded in error as Witherly.
3 *The V.C. and D.S.O. A complete record of all those officers, non-commissioned officers and men of His Majesty's naval, military and air forces who have been awarded these decorations from the time of their institution, with descriptions of the deeds and services which won the distinctions and with many biographical and other details.* By O'Moore Creagh and E. M. Humphris. (3 vols, London, n.d.), p. 249. Photograph.
4 SDGW.
5 CWGC.
6 London Gazette

Mentioned in Despatches 1916.¹ Killed in Action 10 April 1916 while flying as an observer: reported alive but wounded when the plane came down, but 'riddled' with bullets and dead by the time comrades reached the aircraft.² Buried in Lijssenthoek Military Cemetery, Poperinge, West-Vlaanderen, Belgium (GR V. A. 26.).³ Memorial at St Thomas's.

His brother Anthony R. served in France as a Major in the Royal Army Ordnance Corps, Inns of Court, Officer Training Corps, and survived the War.

⌘**GARDINER, ARTHUR. ... Pte... Hants, May 10, 1916. Pte. Belgium, France. *Killed in Action, Oct. 14, 1918.*
(85, Wales Street)**

157. GARDINER, Arthur, Private (Signaller), 23378,⁴ 2nd Bn The Hampshire Regiment, d. 14 October 1918 aged 21.

Son of William A. and Rose Gardiner of 85, Wales Street. Born at Alresford in 1898. In 1911 he was a School Butcher's Errand Boy living at East Street, Alresford aged 13. Enlisted in Alresford 10 May 1916. Entered a theatre of war (France) with 11th Bn (Pioneers), The Hampshire Regiment at some point after the beginning of 1916. Served in Belgium and France. Transferred to the 15th (Service) Bn and then to the 2nd Bn.⁵ Killed in Action 14 October 1918. Buried in Dadizeele New British Cemetery, Moorslede, West-Vlaanderen (GR V. C. 4.).⁶ Memorials at St John the Baptist.

His brother William P., listed below, was Killed in Action 2 November 1916.

⌘**GARDINER, WILLIAM P. ... Pte.... Wilts, Jan. 20, 1916, Pte. France. *Killed in Action, Nov. 2, 1916.*
(85, Wales Street)**

158. GARDINER, William Percy, Private, 23046,⁷ 6th (Service) Bn The Duke of Edinburgh's (Wiltshire Regiment), d. 2 November 1916 aged 21.

Son of William A. and Rose Gardiner of 85, Wales Street. Born at Alresford in 1896. Worked as a Fishmonger's Errand Boy in 1911 living at East Street, Alresford

1. *London Gazette* citation not found.
2. http://1914-1918.invisionzone.com/forums/index.php?showtopic=15089 for account of his death etc in The War in the Air Forum.
3. CWGC.
4. WO 372/7/200798.
5. R Hamps Notes. RH. state he was 'Listed as 'sick' in February 1917 Regimental Journal.'
6. CWGC.
7. WO 372/7/202546.

aged 15. Enlisted in Winchester 20 January 1916. Served in Belgium and France. Killed in Action 2 November 1916. Commemorated on Thiepval Memorial, Somme, France (PR Pier and Face 13 A.).[1] Memorial at St John the Baptist.

His brother Arthur, listed above, was Killed in Action 14 October 1918.

✠GARDNER, CHARLES E. ... Stoker ... R.N., July 3, 1918, Stoker. North Sea; H.M.S. *Ascot. Torpedoed and Drowned, Nov.* 10, 1918.
(41, Wales Street)

159. GARDNER, Charles Edward Mafeking, Stoker 2nd Class,[2] K/52284, HMPMS Ascot. Royal Navy, d. 10 November 1918 aged 20.[3]

Son of Frederick and Annie Gardner 41, Wales Street. Born 25 May 1900 at Soberton, Bishops Waltham.[4] Enlisted in Winchester 3 July 1918 and served on the North Sea aboard HM Paddle Minesweeper Ascot. Killed in Action: torpedoed and drowned, 10 November 1918. HMPMS was the last ship to be sunk by direct enemy action in the War.[5] Commemorated on Portsmouth Naval Memorial (PR 30.).[6] Memorial at St John the Baptist.

His brother Frederick W.J., listed below, died of malaria in 1917. His brother Walter G. served on the North Sea as a Stoker in the Royal Navy and survived the War. His father Frederick W. served in India, Mesopotamia and Egypt and became a Serjeant in The Hampshire Regiment (Training Reserve), and survived the War.

✠GARDNER, FREDERICK W. J. ... Pte. ... Hants, Nov. 1915, Pte. India, Egypt, Palestine. *Died of Malaria, Nov.* 2, 1917, *Alexandria.*
(41, Wales Street)

160. GARDNER, Frederick W.J., Private, 201593,[7] 2/4th Bn The Hampshire Regiment, d. 2 November 1917 aged 20.[8]

Son of Frederick and Annie 41, Wales Street. Born at Newtown, Bishops Waltham in 1898. Enlisted in Winchester November 1915 and served in India,

1 CWGC.
2 ADM 188/968/52284.
3 Medals in a Private Collection.
4 1911 census suggests 1901.
5 Hepper, 2006, p. 145.
6 CWGC.
7 WO 372/7/20377.
8 Medals in a Private Collection.

Egypt and Palestine. Entered a theatre of war (Palestine) after the beginning of 1917 with 2/4th Bn. Died of malaria, 2 November 1917 at Alexandria. Buried in Alexandria (Hadra) War Memorial Cemetery, Egypt (GR D. 206.).[1] Memorial at St John the Baptist.

His brother Charles Edward Mafeking, listed above, was Killed in Action 10 November 1918. His brother Walter G. served on the North Sea as a Stoker in the Royal Navy and survived the War. His father Frederick W. served in India, Mesopotamia and Egypt and became a Serjeant in The Hampshire Regiment (Training Reserve), and survived the War.

✠**GARRETT, HARRY D. ... Pte. ... Hants, Aug. 1914, Pte. Egypt, Dardanelles. Wounded, Aug. 8, 1916.** *Died at Sea, Aug. 15, 1916.*
(36, Hyde Street)

161. GARRETT, Henry Daniel,[2] Private, 9974,[3] 10th (Service) Bn The Hampshire Regiment, d. 15 August 1915 aged 19.

Son of Harry and Charlotte Garrett of 2, Hyde Church Lane. Born 1897. A Tailor's apprentice in 1911. Enlisted in Winchester August 1914. Served in Egypt and at Gallipoli (Dardanelles).[4] Entered a theatre of war (Gallipoli) with 10th Bn on 5 August 1915. Wounded 8 August 1916 the first day on which the Hampshires were involved in action at Chunuk Bair.[5] Died at sea, 15 August 1915 of wounds received in action.[6] Commemorated on The Helles Memorial, Turkey (PR Panel 125-134 or 223-226 228-229 and 328.).[7] Memorial at St Bartholomew's.

He had two brothers who served in the War. Arthur served in Germany as a Private in The Royal Warwickshire Regiment transferred to the Army Service Corps. William C. served at Home as a Private in The Hampshire Regiment. Both survived the War.

✠**GERMAIN, HARRY E. ... Lieut. ... Canadians, 1914, Staff Sergt. France. Wounded, June 8, 1917.** *Died of Wounds, July 1917.*
(76, Stockbridge Road)

1   CWGC.
2   'Henry D.'/Harry on memorials.
3   WO 372/7/212930.
4   SDGW
5   Atkinson, 2, pp. 96-9. Chunuk Bair action lasted 8 – 12 August.
6   This and other additional material in this biography from R Hamps Notes. RH. These correct his date of death to 1915 and note he DOW while at sea.
7   CWGC.

162. GERMAIN, Harry Edgar Lieutenant, 3586,[1] 75th Bn Canadian Infantry (Central Ontario Regt), d. 1 July 1917 aged 43.

Son of Thomas and Elizabeth Germain of 10, Parchment Street in 1881. Born 1873. Elizabeth, widow, 1, St John's Street, 1901.[2] Enlisted in The Duke of Edinburgh's (Wiltshire Regiment) in 1893 and served in the Indies.[3] His Canadian attestation papers of 28 September 1915 state that he served thirteen-and-a-half years with the Wiltshire Regiment. Gained certificates in musketry and gym as well as his general education certificates. Previous to enlisting he had been an apprentice for two years. His attestation papers list his trade as grocer and state that he was married, and belonged to the active militia. The *Toronto Star* states that he worked as a messenger for ten years at the head office of the Dominion Bank and that at the time of his death he had a three year old son. Re-enlisted in 1914 according to the *WWSR* but more likely 1915[4] and served in France in the Canadian Infantry.[5] A newspaper at the time reported him as leaving Toronto as a Serjeant-Major in June 1915 and being commissioned in the following January in England. The *Toronto Star* reported that he had been 'severely wounded in the chest and left hand on June 8th.' [1917]. Died of Wounds July 1917 at Calais. Buried in Calais Southern Cemetery (GR Plot B. Row Officers. Grave 5.).[6] Memorial at St Michael's.

His brother Arthur served as a Private in The Hampshire Regiment, the Royal Berkshire Regiment and the Labour Corps in France and survived the War.

✠**GIBSON, ALBERT E. ... Pte. ... H.L.I., 1911, Pte. France. Wounded once. *Killed in Action, Sept. 20, 1914.* (79, Wales Street)**

163. GIBSON, Albert Edward, Private, 11935,[7] 2nd Bn The Highland Light Infantry, d. 20 September 1914 aged 19.

Son of William and Anne Gibson of 79, Wales Street (1901, 86, Wales Street). Born 1894. An Errand Boy in 1911. Enlisted at Winchester in 1911. Served with the British Expeditionary Force in France. with G Coy 2nd Bn HLI.[8] Was wounded once.[9] Killed in Action 20 September 1914. Commemorated on La

1   Reports in *Toronto Star* http://www.veterans.gc.ca/eng/collections/virtualmem/Detail/471018?/Harry%20Edgar%20Germain. Photograph of head and shoulders.
2   1901 Census, SJ.
3   WO 97/4921/108. According to his Army Service Record.
4   or September 28th 1915 (Canadian attestation papers and newspaper reports).
5   Canadians not in France until early 1915. Likely an error in *WWSR* of 1914 for 1915.
6   CWGC.
7   WO 372/8/353.
8   Enlisted with HLI at Winchester. SDGW.
9   DOW according to de Ruvigny (Findmypast website).

Ferté-Sous-Jouarre Memorial, Seine-et-Marne, France.[1] Memorials at St John the Baptist.

✠GIFFORD, NORGA E. ... Capt. ... Leicester, Sept. 1914, 2nd Lieut. France. *Killed in Action, July 14, 1916, Bazentin le Petit.*
(Kinross, Barnes Close)

164. GIFFORD, Norga Ernest, Captain,[2] 7th (Service) Bn The Leicestershire Regiment, d. 14 July 1916 aged 28.

Son of Ernest and Lucy Gifford of Kinross, Barnes Close, St Cross. Born 1889.[3] 1891 family at 43, Wharf Hill. 1901 pupil at Stubbington House School, Stubbington.[4] A Milling Pupil in 1911. Enlisted[5] September 1914 and served in France. Killed in Action 14 July 1916 at Bazentin le Petit i.e. the Battle of the Somme. Commemorated on the Thiepval Memorial, Somme, France (PR Pier and Face 2 C and 3 A.).[6] Memorials at Peter Symonds School and St Cross Chapel.

✠GILLETT, DAVID E. ... Pte. ... Hants, Aug. 1914, Pte. Dardanelles. *Killed in Action, Aug. 10, 1915.*
(3, Cross Street)

165. GILLETT, David Edward, Private, 9971,[7] 10th (Service) Bn The Hampshire Regiment, d. 10 August 1915 aged 34.

Born at Moreton-in-Marsh, Gloucestershire in 1881. Married Ethel Sillence in 1901 and by 1911 they had, Dorothy Ena born 1907 and Harold Edward Victor born 1910. A Gas Burner Maintainer in 1911. Enlisted at Winchester in August 1914. Served at Gallipoli (Dardanelles). Entered a theatre of war (Gallipoli) with 10th Bn on 5 August 1915. Posted as 'missing' in the October 1915.[8] Killed in Action 10 August 1915 at Chunuk Bair.[9] Commemorated on The Helles Memorial, Turkey (PR Panel 125-134 or 223-226 228-229 & 328.).[10] Memorial at St Thomas's.

1 CWGC.
2 WO 372/8/7125. Indexed as Horga.
3 BMD gives 1888.
4 Information from SJ.
5 *WWSR*.
6 CWGC. Norga.
7 WO 372/8/20601.
8 'Missing' reference in October 1915 Regimental Journal. Also other additional material in this biography from R Hamps Notes. RH.
9 See above, Baird, Garrett etc for the same action. Atkinson, 2, p. 97.
10 CWGC.

KIA 10.8.1915.

Entitled to 1914/15 Star, British War Medal & Victory Medal

✠**GILMOUR, WALTER E. ... Pte. ... Hants, Dec. 1914, Pte. Mesopotamia. Wounded, Jan. 21, 1916. *Died of Wounds, Jan.* 24, 1916.**
(36, Hyde Abbey Road)

166. GILMOUR, Walter E., Private, 2924,[1] 1/4th Bn The Hampshire Regiment, d. 24 January 1916 aged 27.

Son of George and Jane Gilmour of 36, Hyde Abbey Road. Born 1889. Educated in Winchester and was a clothier's assistant at Elliot and Sons of Lymington in 1911.[2] Enlisted in Bournemouth in December 1914 and served in India with the Indian Expeditionary Force, and later in Mesopotamia.[3] Entered a theatre of war (Mesopotamia) on 26 August 1915. He was from the 1/7th Bn attached 1/4th Bn. Wounded on 21 January 1916 and Died on 24 January 1916 of Wounds sustained at Umm El Hanna.[4] Buried in Amara War Cemetery (GR I. B. 25.).[5] Memorials at Holy Trinity and St Bartholomew's.

His brother Frank V. served as a Private in The Hampshire Regiment in Mesopotamia. Wounded in March 1917 and survived the War.

✠**GLOVER, THOMAS G. ... Pte. ... Hants, Aug. 1914, Pte. Mesopotamia. Wounded, Jan. 29, 1915. *Killed in Action, Jan.* 21, 1916.**
(64, Chesil Street)

167. GLOVER, Thomas G., Private, 2607 also 200594,[6] 1/4th Bn The Hampshire Regiment, d. 21 January 1916.

Son of James and Louisa Glover of 64, Chesil Street. Born 1892. A Labourer in 1911. Enlisted at Winchester in August 1914.[7] Served in Mesopotamia. Entered a theatre of war with 1/4th Bn (Mesopotamia) on 18 March 1915. so not sure about him being wounded on 29.1.1915 unless it was accidental.[8]

1 WO 372/8/25471.
2 de Ruvigny (Findmypast website).
3 SDGW.
4 R Hamps Notes. RH. for this and other additional material in this biography.
5 CWGC.
6 WO 372/8/38185.
7 SDGW.
8 R Hamps Notes. RH. in doubt about him being wounded on 29 January 1915 unless

Wounded 29 January 1915. Killed in Action 21 January 1916 at the battle of Umm El Hanna. Commemorated on Basra Memorial, Iraq (PR Panel 21 and 63.).[1] Memorial at St Peter Chesil (All Saints).

His brother Albert E. was a Private in The Worcestershire Regiment and the Somerset Light Infantry, served in India and survived the War.

✠**GODDARD, HENRY C. ... Stoker... R.N., Sept. 1914, Stoker. Falkland Islands. *Drowned, Dec. 29, 1916.***
   (7, Lower Wolvesey Terrace)

168. GODDARD, Henry Charles, Stoker 1st Class, 20432,[2] HM Submarine K.13 Royal Navy, d. 29 January 1917 aged 22.[3]

Son of Charles Henry and Emily Faith Goddard of 7, Lower Wolvesey Terrace. Born 29 May 1894. A Farm Labourer in 1911. Enlisted in September 1914. Served in the Falkland Islands. The K.13 sank during trials in Gareloch, Scotland on 29 January 1917 spending 54 hours on the bottom, resulting in some 31 fatalities, Goddard among those drowned.[4] Buried at Faslane Cemetery, Dumbarton (GR Sec. B. Grave 17.).[5] Memorial at St Peter Chesil (All Saints).

His brother William G. was a Private in The Worcestershire Regiment and survived the War.

✠**GODSELL, ALFRED P. ... Gun. ... R.G.A., Sept. 1915, Gun. France. *Killed in Action, Apl. 27, 1918, Brandhoek.***
   (6, Staple Garden)

169. GODSELL, Alfred Percival, Gunner, 352970,[6] 375th Siege Bty Royal Garrison Artillery, d. 27 April 1918 aged 22.

Son of William and Elizabeth Godsell of 6, Staple Gardens. Born at Bishopstoke in 1897.[7] An apprentice to a Printer's Machineman in 1911. Husband of Elizabeth (New Cottages, Sutton Scotney).[8] Enlisted at Southampton in September 1915. Served on the Western Front. Killed in Action 27 April 1918.

   it was accidental.
1 CWGC. KIA at Basra 1916.
2 ADM 188/ 20432/ 20432. K/20432. Gives date of birth.
3 The *WWSR* has 1916 for 1917. Both CWGC and SDGW agree on the 1917 year and month. Apart from *WWSR* all sources agree on 29 January 1917.
4 Hepper, 2006, p. 79.
5 CWGC.
6 WO 372/ 8/45509.
7 In the 1911 census his details match those of 1901, except that his surname is entered as 'Smith'.
8 CWGC.

Commemorated on the Tyne Cot Memorial, Zonnebeke, West-Vlaanderen, Belgium (PR Panel 6 to 7 and 162.).[1] Memorials at St Thomas's Church and School, and at Sutton Scotney.

His brother William J. was a Private in The Hampshire Regiment, served in Egypt, Palestine and France and survived the War.

✠GOODCHILD, GEORGE J. ... L.-Corpl. ... Hants, Aug. 1914, Pte. India, Mesopotamia. Taken Prisoner by Turks, Apl. 28, 1916. *Died, Dec.* 25, 1916, *Angora.*
(40, Eastgate Street)

170. GOODCHILD, George James, Lance-Corporal, 200463,[2] 1/4th Bn The Hampshire Regiment, d. 25 December 1916 aged 32.

Son of James and Esther Goodchild of 40, Eastgate Street. Born 1884.[3] A Baker in 1911. Enlisted in Winchester in August 1914 (2406).[4] Served in India and Mesopotamia. Entered a theatre of war (Mesopotamia) with 1/4th Bn on 18 March 1915. Taken prisoner by Turks 28 April 1916 and died 25 December 1916 at Angora.[5] Buried in Baghdad (North Gate) War Cemetery, Iraq (GR Angora Mem. 73.).[6] Memorials at St John the Baptist.

✠GOODYEAR, ARTHUR W. ... Pte. ... R.M.L.I., 1914, Pte. Dardanelles. *Killed in Action, May* 1915, *Dardanelles.*
(64, Sussex Street)

171. GOODYEAR, Arthur William, Private, 548,[7] Portsmouth Bn RN Div. Royal Marine Light Infantry, d. 3 May 1915 aged 21.

Son of William and Mary Jane Goodyear of 64, Sussex Street. Born 15 October 1891. An Errand Boy for a wine store in 1911. Enlisted in Southampton in September 1914 and embarked with the Royal Marine Brigade in November 1914.[8] Served at Gallipoli (Dardanelles) in the Portsmouth Battalion from February 1915. Killed in Action on 3 May 1915. Commemorated on The Helles Memorial, Turkey (PR Panel 2 to 7.).[9] Memorial at St Thomas's.

1 CWGC.
2 WO 372/8/56726.
3 BMD gives 1883.
4 SDGW.
5 R Hamps Notes. RH. Gives his age as 33. Regimental Journal does not confirm him as a Kut prisoner.
6 CWGC.
7 ADM 188/ 203/ 548. PO/548(S).
8 SDGW.
9 CWGC.

✠**GOULD, HENRY C. H. ... 2nd Lieut. ... R.F.A., Feb. 1916, 2nd Lieut. France. Wounded once.** *Died of Wounds, Apl. 15, 1917, Arras.*
   (Bereweeke House, Bereweeke Road)

172. GOULD, Henry Charles Hamerton, 2nd Lieutenant,[1] 27th Bty, 32nd Bde, Royal Field Artillery, d. 15 April 1917 aged 19.

Son of the Rev. Charles Hamerton Gould and Mary Gould, of Fawley Rectory, Southampton. Born at Holmwood, Surrey in 1898. By 1901 the family were living at Bereweeke House, Bereweeke Road.[2] At Winchester College in 1911. Enlisted in February 1916 and served in France. Wounded once and Died of Wounds (Gas) 15 April 1917. Buried at Aubigny Communal Cemetery Extension, Pas de Calais, France (GR VI. B. 6.).[3] Memorials at St Matthew's, St Paul's, Twyford Preparatory School and Fawley.

✠**GOULDBY, PERCY ... Pte. ... Hants Y., Oct. 1914, Tpr. Hants. Italy, France, Belgium. Wounded, Oct. 27, 1917.** *Killed in Action, Sept. 4, 1918, near Messines.*
   (66, Water Lane)

173. GOULDBY, Percy, 204761,[4] 15th (Service) Bn (2nd Portsmouth) The Hampshire Regiment, d. 4 September 1918, aged 26.

Son of Annie Gouldby of Leigh Road, Eastleigh in 1911. Enlisted in October 1914 in the Hampshire Yeomanry (1377). Entered a theatre of war (France) after the beginning of 1916 with the Hampshire Carabiniers Yeomanry. He was wounded 27 October 1917. Killed in Action 4 September 1918 near Messines. Buried in Voormezeele Enclosure No 3, Ypres (Ieper), West-Vlaanderen, Belgium (GR XVI. L. 23.).[5] Memorials at St John the Baptist and All Saints Church, Eastleigh.

✠**GREEN, JOSEPH C. ... [BLANK] ... Hants, Dec. 1914, Pte. Gallipoli.** *Wounded and Missing (believed Killed).*
   (20, Hyde Church Path)

174. GREEN, Joseph Charles, Private, 14759,[6] 10th (Service) Bn The Hampshire Regiment, d. 10 August 1915.

1 WO 372/8/80381.
2 https://www.winchestercollegeatwar.com/archive/henry-charles-hamerton-gould/ provides more information. We are grateful to Suzanne Foster for this..
3 CWGC.
4 WO 372/8/81381.
5 CWGC.
6 WO 372/8/120551.

Son of Joseph and Mary A. Green of 61, Hyde Street. Born 1879. 1911 husband of Sophia Jane Green of 59, Cheesehill Street. Enlisted in Winchester in December 1914. Served at Gallipoli (Dardanelles). Entered a theatre of war (Gallipoli) with 10th Bn on 5 August 1915. Killed in Action 10 August 1915: this was the Chunuk Bair action.[1] Commemorated on The Helles Memorial, Turkey (Panel 125-134 or 223-226 228-229 & 328.).[2] Memorial at St Bartholomew's.

Listed as wounded in action in October 1915 edition of the Journal. Later confirmed at KIA 10.8.1915.

Entitled 1914/15 Star, British War Medal and Victory Medal.

✠GREENSTOCK, FREDERICK ... Pte. ... Dorset, 1905, Pte. France. Wounded, Oct. 11, 1914. Despatches 1914. *Killed in Action, Oct. 14, 1914.*
(35, Tower Street)

175. GREENSTOCK, Frederick, Private, 7819,[3] 1st Bn The Dorsetshire Regt, d. 14 October 1914 aged 26.

Son of Frank, sometime a Private in The Hampshire Regiment, and Brigid Greenstock of 32, Tower Street. Born 1888. In 1891 and 1901 family living at Winchester Barracks. Greenstock lived from an early age at the Barracks in Winchester and later at Colonel Moberly's,[4] according to the census records from 1891 and 1901.[5] Enlisted in 1905 in Winchester.[6] Served on the Western Front and was Mentioned in Despatches in 1914. Wounded on 11 October 1914. Died of Wounds 14 October 1914.[7] Buried in Bethune Town Cemetery, Pas de Calais, France (GR I. D. 19.).[8] Memorial at St Thomas's.

✠GROVES, ALFRED ... Tpr. ... Lancers, 1901, Tpr. France. *Killed in Action. Nov. 30, 1917.*
(1, St. George's Terrace)

---

1   See Atkinson, 2, pp. 96-9 and Baird, Garratt, Gillett, above. Noteworthy that while those others who died in this action were listed as serving in Dardanelles. Green is listed as serving at Gallipoli. R Hamps Notes. RH. confirms from the Regimental Journal that he was wounded.
2   CWGC.
3   WO 372/8/135020.
4   Atkinson, vol. 1 refers to a Lt-Col. Moberly in The Hampshire Regiment. He apparently provided accommodation for soldiers. RH pers. comm.
5   Military family if the records from the *WWSR* at the same address are his relatives.
6   SDGW.
7   SDGW.
8   CWGC.

176. GROVES, Alfred, Trooper, 4456,¹ 12th (Prince of Wales's Royal) Lancers, d. 30 November 1917 aged 38.

Son of Charles and Emily Groves of 1, St Georges Terrace St Georges Street. Born 1879. Enlisted in 1901 at Winchester according to his Army Service Record.² Formerly a Canvasser. Served in South Africa (Cape Colony), was transferred to the Army Reserve in 1909 and Discharged in 1912. A General Labourer in 1911. Served on the Western Front. Killed in Action 30 November 1917 when Gouzeaucourt was finally retaken from the Germans. Buried at Gouzeaucourt New British Cemetery, Nord, France (GR VIII. C. 1.).³ No Winchester memorial found.

✠GROVES, GEORGE ... L.S. ... R.N., 1905. *Drowned, Nov. 1914, in H.M.S. " Good Hope."*
(4, Lower Brook Street)

177. GROVES, George, Leading Seaman, 211975,⁴ HMS Good Hope⁵ Royal Navy, d. 1 November 1914 aged 29.

Son of Mrs C. Hibberd of 3, Poulson Place, Middle Brook Street. Born 19 November 1884 at Winkfield, Berkshire.⁶ Married Sarah Pearce in 1911 in Winchester (4, Lower Brook Street).⁷ Enlisted in the Royal Navy in 1905 and is recorded serving with the Atlantic Fleet at Gibraltar in 1911. Killed in Action on 1 November 1914 off the coast of Chile.⁸ Commemorated on the Portsmouth Naval Memorial (PR 1.).⁹ No Winchester memorial found.

✠GUDGEON, ATHOL E. ... Lieut. ... R.N.R., Nov. 10, 1914, A.-Lieut. North Sea; H.M.S. *Quail* and *Etterick.* Torpedoed, July 1917. *Died of Wounds, Aug. 27, 1917, Haslar.*
(St. John's Mead, St. John St.)

178. GUDGEON, Athol Edwin, Lieutenant,¹⁰ HMS Ettrick Royal Naval

1 WO 372/ 8/168674. GS/4456.
2 WO 97/5005/86.
3 CWGC. Gouzeaucourt Cemetery was designed by (Sir) Herbert Baker who designed both the Hampshire County and Winchester City memorial west of the cathedral and also the Winchester College War Cloister.
4 ADM 188/370/211975.
5 Unclear why *Good Hope* in inverted commas in the *WWSR*.
6 1911 census suggests 1885.
7 Census and CWGC, SDGW..
8 Hepper, 2006, p. 28.
9 CWGC.
10 ADM 340/60/31. Mechant Service Officers and men serving in armed merchant cruisers. hospital ships, Fleet auxiliaries and transports were often enterd into the

Reserve, d. 27 August 1917 aged 32.

Son of George E.[1] and Hilda R. Gudgeon of St John's Mead, St John's Street. Born 1885.[2] Enlisted 10 November 1914 and served aboard HMS Quail and Ettrick (wrongly spelled in *WWSR*) in the North Sea. Ettrick was torpedoed in July 1917. He Died of Wounds 27 August 1917 at Haslar Naval Hospital. Buried at Winchester (St James Hill) Roman Catholic Cemetery.[3] Memorial at St John the Baptist.

He had three brothers who served in the War. Robert, listed below, Died of Wounds 2 April 1918. Basil was a Chaplain to the forces and served in Palestine. Stanley was an Acting Major in the Royal Garrison Artillery, served in France and was awarded the Military Cross in 1917. Both Basil and Stanley survived the War.

✠**GUDGEON, ROBERT E. ... Capt. ... Hants Y., 1907, Tpr. R.F.A., T.M.B.France. Wounded, Mch. 21, 1918. M.C. 1917. *Died of Wounds, Apl. 2, 1918, Mt. D'Origny.***
   (St. John's Mead, St. John St.)

179. GUDGEON, Robert Eustace, Captain,[4] Trench Mortar Bty Royal Field Artillery, d. 2 April 1918 aged 30.

Son of George E. and Hilda R. Gudgeon of St John's Mead, St John's Street. Born 1888. Enlisted in 1907 and served in France from 1917 according to his medal card. He transferred from the Hampshire Yeomanry with whom he did not serve in a theatre of war. He was awarded the Military Cross in 1917.[5] Wounded 21 March 1918 and Died of Wounds 2 April 1918 while a prisoner of Germans at Mt D'Origny. Buried in St Souplet British Cemetery, Nord, France (GR I. G. 21.).[6] Memorials at St John the Baptist, Winchester and St Swithun's, Hither Green, London.[7]

He had three brothers who served in the War. Athol Edwin, listed bove, died 27 August 1917. Basil was a Chaplain to the forces and served in Palestine. Stanley

    RNR for the duration of the War: often merchant seamen pre-war. (GJEH pers. comm.)
1 At 19, St Thomas Street in 1891..
2 1881 census; BMD.
3 CWGC. Only First World War burial in found in that cemetery in Winchester.
4 WO 372/8/172345.
5 Citation for REG's MC not seen. Additional material in this biography from R Hamps Notes. RH.
6 CWGC.
7 Also memorial at St Swithun's Hither Green, ?Kent?. which refers to 91 and 139 Field Regiment, Royal Artillery. www.lewishamwarmemorials.wiki.com. Also Findagrave.com

was an Acting Major in the Royal Garrison Artillery, served in France and was awarded the Military Cross in 1917. Both Basil an Stanley survived the War.

✠GYE, DENISON A. ... Capt. ... Zion Mule Corps, 1915. R.H.A. Dardanelles, France. *Killed in Action, Feb. 28, 1917, Combles.* (Piper's Field, Chilbolton Avenue)

180. GYE, Denison Allen, Captain,[1] 15th Bde Royal Horse Artillery, d. 28 February 1917 aged 35.

Son of the late Percy Gye and Constance Gye of Piper's Field, Chilbolton Avenue: 'of Kensington and latterly of Winchester.'[2] Born at Paddington, London (Kensington Registration District) in 1882. Enlisted in 1915 and served at Gallipoli (Dardanelles) and France with the Zion Mule Corps,[3] transferring to the Royal Horse Artillery. Killed in Action 28 February 1917 at Combles. Buried at Guards Cemetery, Combles, Somme, France (GR I.D.2.) with Christian symbolism on his grave marker.[4] Memorials at St Matthew's and St Paul's.

✠HAINES, CHARLES ... Rfn. ... K.R.R.C., Nov. 1914, Rfn. France. *Missing, July 1, 1916.* (26, Colson Road)

181. HAINES, Charles, Private, 7556,[5] 2nd Bn The King's Royal Rifle Corps, d. 1 July 1916 aged 22.[6]

Son of Henry and Annie Haines of 10, Canute Road. Born 1895. Husband of Maria Douse (26 Colson Road) in 1914 and they had a son, Charles born 1914 according to birth records.[7] Charles, senior, is listed as an 'Odd' Boy in College House in 1911. Enlisted in November 1914 at Winchester. Served in France. Died of Wounds 1 July 1916 [8] he is commemorated on the Arras Memorial, Pas de Calais, France (PR Bay 7.).[9] Memorial at St John the Baptist.

He had two brothers who served in the War. George, listed below, was Missing, (believed Killed) 3 May 1917. Albert H. served in France as a Private in The

1 No MIC WO 372/. Not with British Army.
2 CWGC. SDGW
3 Jewishvirtuallibrary.com for the Zion Mule Corps.
4 CWGC. One of the latest burals at the Guards Cemetery.
5 WO 372/8/196357. R/7556.
6 SDGW records Died of Wounds.
7 BMD.
8 First day of the Somme; but memorial location, Arras, suggests he was elsewhere.
9 CWGC.

Hampshire Regiment and the Royal Berkshire Regiment, was wounded once and survived the War.

✠HAINES, GEORGE ... Pte. ... E. Surrey, Aug. 1914, Pte. R. Berks. France. Wounded twice. *Missing (believed Killed), May 3, 1917.*
(10, Canute Road)

182. HAINES, George, Private, 25237,[1] 1st Bn Princess Charlotte of Wales's (Royal Berkshire Regiment), d. 3 May 1917[2] aged 25.

Son of Henry and Annie Haines of 10, Canute Road. Born 1893. In 1911 he was a Gardener Nurseryman. Enlisted in London in August 1914. Served on the Western Front. Listed as formerly 2829, army Cyclist Corps.[3] Wounded twice and was Killed in Action 3 May 1917. Commemorated on the Arras Memorial, Pas de Calais, France (PR Bay 7.).[4] Memorials at All Saints and Chilcomb.

He had two brothers who served in the War. Charles, listed above, was Missing, 1 July 1916. Albert H. served in France as a Private in The Hampshire Regiment and the Royal Berkshire Regiment, was wounded once and survived the War.

✠HALL, H. C. ... 2nd Lieut. ... Hants Y., Tpr. Wilts. *Killed in Action,* 1918.
(32, Hyde Street)

183. HALL, Henry Charles, 2nd Lieutenant,[5] The Duke of Edinburgh's (Wiltshire Regiment) attd 15th (Service) Bn (2nd Portsmouth) The Hampshire Regiment, d. 4 September 1918 aged 34.[6]

Son of Henry George and Annie Hall. Born 1885.[7] In 1891 and 1911 family living at 69, High Street. A Yeoman in 1911. Commissioned 29 May 1918. Killed in Action 4 September 1918 attached to the former 15th (Hampshire Carabiniers) Bn The Hampshire Regiment, by then amalgamated.[8] Commemorated on the Tyne Cot Memorial, Zonnebeke, West-Vlaanderen, Belgium (PR Panel 119 to 120).[9] Memorial at St Bartholomew's.

1　WO 372/8/196675.
2　CWGC, SDGW.
3　SDGW.
4　CWGC.
5　WO 372/8/209625.
6　CWGC.
7　BMD gives 1884.
8　See Ernest Alexander.
9　CWGC.

✠**HALLS, HAROLD C. ... Pte. ... Hants Y., Nov. 1915, Tpr. Yorks. France.** *Died,* **Oct. 25, 1918.**
(95, Greenhill Road)

184. HALLS, Harold Charles, Private, 203628,[1] 6th (Service) Bn The Dorsetshire Regiment, d. 25 October 1918 aged 21.

Son of Henry Charles and Minnie Jane Halls of 95, Greenhill Road. Born at Southbourne in 1898. In 1911 at Romney Road, Greenwich, London SE at achool; family at 48, Greenhill Road. Enlisted in November 1915 at Winchester and served on the Western Front. Listed as formerly 2021 Hampshire Carabiniers.[2] Transferred from the Hampshire Yeomanry.[3] No overseas service with Hampshire Yeomanry. Entered a theatre of war with East Yorkshire Regiment. Died 25 October 1918. Buried in Abbeville Communal Cemetery, Somme, France (GR IV. J. 20.).[4] Memorial at St Paul's.

His brother Henry C. served at sea as a Petty Officer in the Royal Navy and survived the War.

✠**HAMILTON, ARTHUR P. ... Lt.-Col. ... R.W.S., 1904, 2nd Lieut. Lond. Irish. France. Wounded, Sept. 25, 1915. M.C. 1915.** *Killed in Action, Sept.* **15, 1916,** *Somme.*
(Brendon, Park Road)

185. HAMILTON, Arthur Percival, Lieutenant-Colonel,[5] The Queen's (Royal West Surrey Regiment) attd 19th Bn London Regiment, d. 15 September 1916 aged 32.

Son of the late Major P. F. P. Hamilton, RA and Mrs Hamilton. Born at Shoeburyness, Essex in 1885.[6] Married Kate G. Kenrick in 1914 (42, Eaton Square, London).[7] Enlisted in 1904 and is recorded in 1911 as being stationed with 2nd Battalion The Queens Regiment of Infantry ATH Companies, Gibraltar. Served in France and was wounded 25 September 1915 and was later awarded the Military Cross for this action. Killed in Action 15 September 1916 on the Somme. Buried in Flatiron Copse Cemetery, Mametz, Somme, France

---

1 WO 372/8/222476.
2 i.e. Hampshire Yeomanry. SDGW.
3 CWGC solely refers to The Dorsetshire Regiment. SDGW adds Hampshire Carabiniers. Check SDGW for Yorksire Regiment not mentioned in CWGC. See Appendix 2.
4 CWGC.
5 WO 372/8/227985.
6 BMD 1884.
7 BMD.

(GR VII. I. 2.).¹ Memorial at St Bartholomew's.

Military Cross Citation.

Supplement to *The London Gazette*, 4 November 1915. 10889.²

Captain Arthur Percival Hamilton, The Queen's (Royal West Surrey Regiment), Adjutant 18th (County of London) Battalion, The London Regiment (London Irish Rifles), Territorial Force.

'For conspicuous gallantry on 25th September, 1915, during the attack at Maroc and Loos. Although severely wounded early in the day, he remained in the German second line trench reorganising and encouraging the men till the consolidation was well advanced. He then had to be ordered to go back for medical attendance.

Captain James Ronald McCurdie, M.B.'

✠**HAMMOND, CHARLES W. ... Pte. Hants, 1913, Pte. India, Mesopotamia. Taken Prisoner by Turks, Apl. 29. 1916. Kut. *Died, Aug.* 1916.**
   (36A, Clifton Road)

186. HAMMOND, Charles Walter, Private, 200333,³ 1/4th Bn The Hampshire Regiment, d. 20 September 1916 aged 19.

Son of John Lovick Hammond and Elizabeth Hammond of 54, St Catherine's Road. Born at Orpington, Kent in 1897. Enlisted at Winchester in 1913 (2157).⁴ Served in India and Mesopotamia. Entered a theatre of war (Mesopotamia) with 1/4th Bn on 18 March 1915.⁵ Taken prisoner by Turks 29 April 1916 at Kut. Died 20 August 1916. Commemorated on the Basra Memorial, Iraq (PR Panel 21 and 63).⁶ Memorials at St Matthew's and St Paul's.

✠**HARRISON, GEORGE J. ... Sergt. ... Hants, 1914, Aug., Pte. Gallipoli, France. Wounded, Mch. 1916. *Died, March* 15, 1919.**
   (13, Clausentum Road)

1   CWGC. Flatiron Copse Cemetery designed by Sir Herbert Baker.
2   *LG* ref. as above..
3   WO 372/8/233862.
4   'at Winchester' from SDGW..
5   R Hamps Notes. RH. for additional material in this biography. Bowker says he died 30 June 1916.
6   CWGC.

187. HARRISON, George J., Serjeant, 4358[1] 3rd (Reserve) Bn The Hampshire Regiment, d. 15 March 1919.[2]

Son of Alfred Harrison of 13, Clausentum Road. Born at Guildford, Surrey. A Bricklayer in 1911. Enlisted 12 August 1914, a Special Reservist. Served at Gallipoli (Dardanelles) and in France. Entered a theatre of war (Gallipoli) on 5 Decmber 1915 just before evacuation with 2nd Bn. Wounded in March 1916. Discharged due to sickness on 25 April 1917.[3] Died at South Stoneham 15 March 1919.[4] No Winchester memorial found.

✠HART, CHARLES N. ... L.-Corpl. ... Hants, Pte. Gallipoli. *Wounded and Missing (believed Killed)*, 1915.
(26, Hyde Street)

188. HART, Charles Newson, Lance-Corporal, 15327,[5] 2nd Bn The Hampshire Regiment, d. 6 August 1916 aged 37.[6]

Born at Notting Hill, London in 1878. A Corn Dealer living with mother Margaret Elizabeth Eliza Hart and his uncle in 1911 at The Prince of Wales, 26, Hyde Street.[7] Enlisted at Winchester. Served at Gallipoli (Dardanelles). Entered a theatre of war (Gallipoli) as a reinforcement for 2nd Bn on 15 June 1915. Initially reported wounded in action 6 August 1915 and then wounded and missing.[8] Killed in Action 6 August 1915. Commemorated on The Helles Memorial, Turkey (PR Panel 125-134 or 223-226 228-229 & 328).[9] Memorial at St Bartholomew's.

✠HARVEY, WILLIAM ... Corpl. ... R.A.S.C., 1915, Pte. R.E. France. *Died of Tuberculosis.*
(12, Hillside Terrace)

189. HARVEY, William, Corporal, Royal Engineers, 246251, formerly ASC SS/13002, formerly WR/266217.[10]

1 WO 372/9/50461.
2 Not a soldier when he died?
3 R Hamps Notes. RH. for this and other additional material in this biography.
4 Not on CWGC or SDGW. His Discharge and date of death makes this an unusual entry in the *WWSR*.
5 WO 372/9/59872.
6 A discrepancy over year of his death: *WWSR* and CWGC give 1915; SDGW and Armed Services BMD give 1916.
7 Census 1911.
8 R Hamps Notes. RH. for additional material in this biography.
9 CWGC.
10 No MIC WO 372/ found. No date of death for him, so could have been post-war. He joined the ASC in 1915 which became the RASC 1919/20. Nothing found in SDGW or CWGC. Information from Census 1911 on parents.

Son of Willam and Emma Jane Harvey (12, Hillside Terrace). William was born 1889, John Henry born 1892, Nellie born 1896, Charles Ernest born 1904 and Frederick Samuel born 1907. Enlisted in 1915. Transferred from the Army Service Corps. Served in France and died of tuberculosis. Memorials at St Peter Chesil (All Saints) and the Primitive Methodist Chapel in Parchment Street.

✠HATT, WILLIAM H. ... [BLANK] ... Hants, 1912. Dardanelles. Wounded, Apl. 1915. *Killed in Action, June* 4, 1915. (5, Alresford Road)

190. HATT, William Henry, Private, 9054,[1] 2nd Bn The Hampshire Regiment, d. 4 June 1915 aged 21.

Son of Charles John and Lavinia Hatt of 5, Alresford Road. Born at Chilcomb in 1895. A Grocer's Porter in 1911. Enlisted in 1912 at Winchester as a regular soldier.[2] Entered a theatre of war (Dardanelles) with 2nd Bn on 25 April 1915. Wounded in action on 28 April 1915 and again on 17 May 1915, left foot. Then for a third time on 4 June 1915. Previously reported wounded in action subsequently reported killed in action 4 June 1915: death from wounds that day.[3] Killed in Action 4 June 1915. Commemorated on The Helles Memorial, Turkey (PR Panel 125-134 or 223-226 228-229 & 328.).[4] Memorials at All Saints and St John the Baptist.

He had two brothers who served in the War. Albert P. served at Gallipoli (Dardanelles), France and Russia as a Private in The Hampshire Regiment and the the Somerset Light Infantry and was wounded April 1915. Frederick J served in France and India as a Private in The Royal Gloucestershire Hussars and the Royal Air Force. They both survived the War.

✠HAWKINS, SIDNEY M. ... 2nd A. M. ... R.F.C., Mch. 1917, 2nd A.M. Home. *Died, Apl.* 9, 1917, *Leeds.* (Piper's Farm, Weeke)

191. HAWKINS, Sidney Michael, Air Mechanic 2nd Class, 63786,[5] Royal Flying Corps, d. 6 April 1917 aged 18.[6]

Son of Caroline and the late Jesse Hawkins of Piper's Farm, Weeke. Born at Sparsholt in 1899. Enlisted in March 1917. Died 6 April 1917 at Leeds. Buried

1   WO 372/9/83279.
2   SDGW.
3   R Hamps Notes. RH. for additional material in this biography from Regimental Journals etc.
4   CWGC.
5   No MIC WO 372/ found.
6   CWGC states 6, not 9 April.

at Sparsholt (St Stephen's) Churchyard (GR Old Ground, north of Avenue.).¹ Memorial St Matthew's, St Paul's and Sparsholt.

✠HAWKINS, WILLLAM A. ... Gun. ... R.F.A., May 1917, Gun. France. Wounded once. *Died of Wounds, Apl. 5, 1918.*
   (15, Osmond's Passage)

192. HAWKINS, William Alfred, Gunner, 238686,² A Bty 174th Bde Royal Field Artillery, d. 5 April 1918 aged 29.

Son of Charles and Eliza Hawkins of 9, Bar End. Born 1889. A Labourer in 1911. Married Annie Berrett in 1914. Husband of Annie Hall of 15, Hyde Street.³ Enlisted in 1917 at Winchester and served on the Western Front.⁴ Wounded once and Died of Wounds 5 April 1918. Buried at Picquigny British Cemetery (GR C. 6.).⁵ Memorial at St Bartholomew's.

✠HAYWARD, WILLIAM A. ... Sergt. ... Hants, 1907, Pte. Dardanelles, France. Wounded, Dec. 1916. *Killed in Action, Dec. 3, 1917, Cambrai.*
   (2, St. Thomas Street)

193. HAYWARD, William Albert, Serjeant, 7746,⁶ 2nd Bn The Hampshire Regiment, d. 3 December 1917 aged 29.

Born at Kings Somborne in 1889.⁷ At his death his parents lived at Littleton. Enlisted in 1907 as a regular soldier and in 1911 was a Private 1st Bn The Hampshire Regiment at Badajos Barracks (Aldershot) Part Area 11c. Served at Gallipoli (Dardanelles) and France. Entered a theatre of war with 2nd Bn on 25 April 1915. Wounded in December 1916. Listed as wounded with GSW to right shoulder in July 1917.⁸ Killed in Action 3 December 1917 at Cambrai. Commemorated on the Cambrai Memorial, Louverval, Nord, France (PR Panel 7.).⁹

1 CWGC.
2 WO 372/9/92875.
3 CWGC.
4 SDGW.
5 CWGC.
6 WO 372/9/109939.
7 BMD. Census suggests 1888.
8 R Hamps Notes. RH. for additional material in this biography from Regimental Journals and a letter following his death referring to his bravery etc.
9 CWGC.

✠**HEAD, FRANK J.... P.O. 1st Class ... R.N., 1901, Boy. North Sea, China.** *Killed in Action, July* **21. 1917, North Sea.**
  (59, Milverton Road)

194. HEAD, Frank Joseph, Petty Officer, 214768,[1] HM Submarine C34 Royal Navy, d. 21 July 1917 aged 29.

Son of William James and Ellen Eliza Head of 14, Romsey Road. Born c. 1887.[2] Joined the Navy in 1901 when he was 16.[3] Served during the War in the North Sea and China. Killed in Action 21 July 1917 in the North Sea.[4] Commemorated on the Portsmouth Naval Memorial (PR 24.).[5] Memorials at St Matthew's, St Paul's, St Thomas's and United Church Jewry Street.

✠**HEAD, GEORGE R. ... R.S.M. ... Hants, 1896, Pte. Mesopotamia.** *Killed in Action, Dec.* **17, 1915.**
  (18, Parchment Street)

195. HEAD, George Robert, Regimental Serjeant Major, 4923,[6] 1/4th Bn The Hampshire Regiment, d. 17 December 1915 aged 35.

Born at East Grinstead, Sussex in 1880.[7] Married Lilian J. M. Head in 1905 (18, Parchment Street). By 1911 they had George born 1907 and Leslie born 1909. Worked as a Butcher prior to enlisting in the Army in 1896 according to his Army Service Record.[8] A Serjeant in 1911 at Territorial Headquarters, Castle Hill, Winchester. A territorial who served as a regular.[9] Served in Mesopotamia during the War and died a Regimental Serjeant Major. Killed in Action 17 December 1915 at the battle of Kut. Buried in Kut War Cemetery, Iraq (GR N. 22.).[10] Memorials at Peter Symonds School and St Thomas's.

✠**HEARD, RICHARD J. ... Corpl. ... Hants, Nov. 24, 1915, Pte. India, Egypt, Palestine, France.** *Killed in Action, July* **24, 1918.**
  (43, Monks Road)

1 ADM 188/ 376/214768.
2 ADM gives birth as 2 February 1886; BMD 1887; Census (1891) 1888.
3 If he was 16 in 1901 he could not have been 29 in 1917. He may therefore have falsified his age in 1901.
4 Hepper, 2006, p. 97 citing TNA PRO ADM 137/3709 states C34 was sunk on 17 July 1917 off Orkney. There was one survivor: not him. [NB Web blog by great nephew. He may have been Coxswain of C34].
5 CWGC has 21 July.
6 WO 372/9/113783.
7 SDGW states Rickinghall, Suffolk.
8 WO 96/646/107 Army Service Record.
9 R Hamps Notes. RH. for this suggestion and other material in this biography.
10 CWGC.

196. HEARD, Richard John, Lance-Corporal, 201708,¹ 2/4th Bn The Hampshire Regiment, d. 25 July 1918 aged 22.

Only son of John (ex-QMS Rifle Brigade) and Fanny Heard of 43, Monks Road. Born at Gosport in 1896. An apprentice Outfitter in 1911 at Townend's High Street, Winchester. Enlisted 24 November 1915 at Winchester. Served in India, Egypt, Palestine and France. Entered a theatre of war with 2/4th Bn after the beginning of 1917.² Killed in Action 25 July 1918.³ Commemorated on the Soissons Memorial, Aisne, France.⁴ Memorial at St Bartholomew's.

✠**HEDGE, BERTIE ... S.M. ... K.R.R.C., Rfn, France Wounded, Sept. 9, 1916. *Died of Wounds, Sept. 9, 1916.*
(8, Poulsome Place)**

197. HEDGE, Bertie John, Company Serjeant Major, 7957,⁵ 2nd Bn The King's Royal Rifle Corps, d. 9 September 1916 age unknown.

Son of George Ernest and Mary Ann Hedge of Knapton Grove, North Walsham, Norfolk. Born at Ridlington, Norfolk c. 1890.⁶ Enlisted in Walsham, Norfolk and in 1911 was a Lance-Corporal 1st Battalion The King's Royal Rifle Corps stationed at New Barracks. Served on the Western Front and became a Company Serjeant Major. Wounded 9 September 1916 and Died of Wounds on the same day. Commemorated on the Thiepval Memorial, Somme, France (PR Pier and Face 13 A and 13 B.).⁷ Memorial Holy Trinity if 'Ted Hedge.'⁸

✠**HEDGES, HARRY ... Pte. ... R.A.S.C., Nov. 1915, Pte. France. *Died of Influenza, Feb. 14, 1919, Charleroi.*
(32, Jewry Street)**

198. HEDGES, Harry, Private, M2/048429,⁹ 135th Mechanical Transport Coy Army Service Corps, d. 14 February 1919 age unknown.

Son of John and Mary Hedges of 29, Parchment Street (1911). Hedges enlisted in November 1915. Address on attestation papers ?Pinhay, Lyme Regis, Bridport, Dorset. Served in France. Died of influenza or pneumonia 14 February 1919

1   WO 372/9/119288.
2   R Hamps Notes. RH. for this and other material in this biography. Also a letter from his commanding officer.
3   CWGC, SDGW contradict *WWSR* here giving 25th.
4   CWGC
5   WO 372/9/127463. Bertie G on MIC.
6   1891 census suggests 1891, 1911 census suggests 1889.
7   CWGC. A memorial to Ted Hedge at Holy Trinity.
8   North Walsham parents etc, Ted Hedge from SJ.
9   WO 372/9/128178. M2/048429 Motor Ambulance? ASCM2. No date of birth found.

at Charleroi.¹ Address of parents on Soldiers Papers in 1919 32, Jewry Street.²
Buried in Charleroi Communal Cemetery, Hainaut, Belgium (GR B. 2.).³ No
Winchester memorial found.

⌘**HERRIDGE, WILLIAM ... [BLANK] ... Dorset, Sept. 1914.
France. Wounded, Mch, 1917.** *Killed in Action, July* **13,
1917.**
  (23, Nuns Road)

199. HERRIDGE, William, Private, 10995,⁴ 1st Bn The Dorsetshire Regiment,
d. 13 July 1917 aged 26.

Son of Charles and Eliza Herridge of 23, Nuns Road (63, Upper Brook Street in
1911).⁵ Born 1892. A Butcher's Delivery Boy in 1911. Enlisted at Southampton
in September 1914. Served on the Western Front. Wounded in March 1917.
Killed in Action 13 July 1917. Buried at Coxyde Military Cemetery, Koksijde,
West-Vlaanderen, Belgium (GR I. H. 13.).⁶ Memorials at St Bartholomew's
and St Thomas's School.

Three other Herridges of 23, Nuns Road are recorded in the *WWSR*. Charles
and Frank served in the Royal Navy, Sidney in The Hampshire Regiment. ⁷

⌘**HERRING, WILLIAM C. ... Pte. ... Hants, Sept. 1914, Pte.
India, Mesopotamia.** *Missing, Jan.* **21, 1916.**
  (38, Tower Street)

200. HERRING, William Charles, Private, 200734,⁸ 1/4th Bn The Hampshire
Regiment, d. 21 January 1916 aged 19.

Son of William and Agnes Herring of 38, Tower Street. Born 1897.⁹ Worked
for Brights (dyers) and Carters of Parchment Street. Enlisted at Hamilton
Camp in September 1914 (2799).¹⁰ Served in Mesopotamia. Entered a theatre
of war with 2/4th Bn on 25 October 1915. Reported missing. Killed in Action

1 See Introduction.
2 SJ provided refs from 'soldiers papers, attestation papers and parents address etc.'
   SDGW. Died after war so no memorial.
3 CWGC.
4 WO 372/9/154697.
5 Census 1911.
6 CWGC.
7 There are three other Herridges from this address in the *WWSR*: who enlisted in
   1900, 1905 (both RN) and 1910 The Hampshire Regiment. All have skeletal entries
   except William.
8 WO 372/9/155196.
9 Census suggests 1898.
10 SDGW

21 January 1916 at Umm El Hanna.¹ Commemorated on Basra Memorial, Iraq (PR Panels 21 and 63).² Memorial at St Thomas's.

⚜HEWINS, THOMAS H. ... L.-Corpl. ... R.E., July 1916, Spr. Wilts. France. *Killed in Action, Dec. 3, 1917.*
   (Jesse Villa, Gordon Avenue)

201. HEWINS, Thomas Harold, Lance-Corporal, 31706,³ 2nd Bn Duke of Edinburgh's (Wiltshire Regiment), d. 3 December 1917 aged 36.

Son of Thomas and Mary Ann Hewins of Stratford-on-Avon, Warwickshire. Born at Stratford-on-Avon, Warwickshire in 1883.⁴ Married Emily (Jesse Villa, Gordon Avenue, Highcliffe Park, Winchester).⁵ Enlisted at Winchester in July 1916.⁶ Transferred from the Royal Engineers. Killed in Action 3 December 1917. Buried in Hooge Crater Cemetery, Ypres (Ieper), West-Vlaanderen, Belgium (GR XVII. J. 14.).⁷ Memorial at All Saints.

⚜HEWLETT, GEORGE H. ... Stoker ... R.N., 1915, Stoker. North Sea, Atlantic, Dardanelles. *Died of Paralysis, Dec. 2, 1918.*
   (26, Wales Street)

202. HEWLETT, George Henry, Stoker 1st Class, 5407,⁸ HMS Europa Royal Navy, d. 2 December 1918 age unknown.

Son of Jesse Frederick and Charlotte Hewlett of 26, Wales Street. Born 2 November 1890.⁹ Enlisted in 1915 and served in the North Sea, Atlantic and at Gallipoli (Dardanelles). Died of paralysis 2 December 1918. Buried in Winchester (St Giles's Hill) Cemetery.¹⁰ Memorial at St John the Baptist.

⚜HIBBERD, ERNEST J. ... L.-Corpl. ... Hants, 1916, Pte. Home. *Died, July, 1919.*
   (28, The Square)

---

1   R Hamps Notes. RH. for this and other material in this biography. Also notes on his civilian life.
2   CWGC.
3   WO 372/9/160587.
4   1911 census gives 'Thomas A.'
5   CWGC.
6   SDGW.
7   CWGC.
8   ADM 188/877/5407. K/5407.
9   SJ.
10 CWGC. No GR.

203. HIBBERD, Ernest J., Lance-Corporal, 223236,[1] The Hampshire Regiment, d. July 1919.

Born 1885. Married Emily in 1907 and in 1911 living at 28a, The Square. Had Lilian Emily born 1908 and Violet May born 1910. In 1911 an Umbrella Maker and Repairer. Enlisted in 1916. Entered a theatre of war with Hampshire Regiment at some point after beginning of 1916 and subsequently transferred to the Labour Corps.[2] Died July 1919.[3] No Winchester memorial found.[4]

⳧HILL, ARTHUR S. ... Rfn. ... K.R.R.C., July 1916, Rfn. Flanders. *Missing (believed Killed), Aug. 3, 1917.*
(69, Fairfield Road)

204. HILL, Arthur Samuel, Private, 31897,[5] 17th (Service) Bn (British Empire League) The King's Royal Rifle Corps, d. 3 August 1917 aged 29.[6]

Son of Edwin and Blanche Hill in 1901 living at 9, Union Street. Born 1888. Enlisted at St Pancras, Middlesex in July 1916.[7] Served on the Western Front and Died of Wounds 3 August 1917.[8] Commemorated on the Ypres (Menin Gate) Memorial, Ypres (Ieper), West-Vlaanderen, Belgium (PR Panel 51 and 53.).[9] Memorials at Holy Trinity, St Matthew's and St Paul's.

⳧HILL, ELIJAH ... [BLANK] ... R.M.L.I., Dec. 1915. France. Wounded once. *Died of Wounds, 1917, Germany.*
(6, St. Leonards Road)

205. HILL, Elijah, Private, 1388,[10] 2nd RM Bn RN Div. Royal Marine Light Infantry, d. 3 May 1917 aged 37.

Born at Garford, Buckinghamshire in 1880. Married Emily Bullock in 1900 and by 1911 they had Hilda born 1904 and Edith Helena Mary born 1907 (4, Nelson Road, Highcliffe Park). A Foreman at the Locomotive Depot of Great Western Railway in 1911. Enlisted in December 1915. Wounded once. Died 3 May 1917 while a POW in Germany. Buried in Cologne Southern Cemetery, Cologne, Nordhein-Westfal, Germany (GR XIII. A. 9.).[11] Memorial at All Saints.

1 The number is from a possible MIC WO 372/.
2 R Hamps Notes. RH.
3 Not on CWGC. BMD for death.
4 ? St Maurice, lost.
5 WO 372/9/183621. R[ifleman]/31897. See also Albert Spencer.
6 See www.1914-18.net/krrc/htm
7 SDGW.
8 SDGW.
9 CWGC.
10 ADM 188/205/1388. PO/1388 (S).
11 CWGC.

✠**HILL, NICHOLAS W. ... Capt. ... Oxf. and Bucks L.I., Oct. 1915, 2nd Lieut. France. Wounded, Nov. 1916.** *Killed in Action, Jan. 16, 1917, near Courcellette.*
(Butts Close, Weeke)

206. HILL, Nicholas Weatherby, Captain,[1] 2nd Bn Oxford and Bucks Light Infantry, d. 16 January 1917 aged 20.[2]

Son of Henry L. G. and Mary Hill[3] of Donhead Cottage, Donhead, Salisbury, Wiltshire. Born 1897. Family in Weeke village 1901.[4] After Horris Hill was a Scholar of Winchester College (1909-15) and won a place at New College, Oxford. Left for Sandhurst 1915. Enlisted in October 1915 and served in France.[5] Won an MC shortly before his death.[6] Killed in Action 16 January 1917 near Courcelette 'while on his way to the front line trenches'. Buried in Courcelette British Cemetery, Somme, France (GR I. D. 13.).[7] Memorials at St Matthew's and St Paul's. There is a window dedicated to him in St Matthew's. London Gazette 13 February 1917.[8]

✠**HOLLAND, ERNEST ... Pte ... Hants, Sept. 1914, Pte. Mesopotamia. Taken Prisoner by Turks, Apl. 29, 1916.** *Died, Oct. 18, 1916, Tarsus.*
(10. St. Leonards Road)

207. HOLLAND, Robert Ernest,[9] Private, 200894,[10] 2/4th Bn The Hampshire Regiment, died 18 October 1916 age 21.

Born at Ponders End, Middlesex son of Mr and Mrs H. Holland of 10, St Leonards Road. Enlisted on Salisbury Plain in September 1914 (2991) and served in Mesopotamia.[11] Must have been attached 1/4th Bn.[12] Taken prisoner by Turks 29 April 1916 and died a POW 18 October 1916. Buried in Baghdad

1 WO 372/9/190720.
2 Service Records at TNA WO 339/52642. Not seen.
3 *Wykehamists who Died in the War 1914-1918*, 4 vols. (Winchester, 1921), vol. ii, p. 22 describe H L G Hill, Esq., as 'of Winchester'. Contains a photograph of NWH. Gives an account of his school life and achievements and notes an MC not listed in the *WWSR*. We are very grateful to Suzanne Foster at the Wincheser College Archive for this information.
4 Census 1901.
5 SDGW.
6 MC.
7 CWGC.
8 For this and other information I am grateful to K.Gray. *The Oxford and Buckinghamshire Light Infantry Chronicle* or *The Rifle Brigade Chronicle*?
9 Ernest only in *WWSR*.
10 WO 372/10/130.
11 SDGW.
12 R Hamps Notes. RH. for this observation and other material in this biography.

(North Gate) War Cemetery, Iraq (GR XXI. O. 48.).[1] Memorial at All Saints.

✠**HOLLAND, JAMES ... Pte ... Hants, Aug. 1914, Pte. Dardanelles. Wounded once. *Died of Wounds, Aug. 21, 1915.***
(3, Mants Lane)

208. HOLLAND, James, Private, 9872,[2] 10th (Service) Bn[3] The Hampshire Regiment, d. 21 August 1915 aged 31.

Son of James and Jane Holland of 3, Mants Lane. Born 1885. A Bricklayer's Labourer in 1911. Enlisted in August 1914 at Winchester. Served at Gallipoli (Dardanelles). Entered a theatre of war with 10th Bn on 5 August 1915. Wounded once[4]. Killed in Action 21 August 1915.[5] Commemorated on The Helles Memorial, Turkey (PR Panel 125-134 or 223-226 228-229 & 328.).[6] No Winchester memorial found.

✠**HOLT, JAMES ... Stoker ... R.N., Stoker. H.M.S. *Princess Royal* and *Begonia*. *Drowned at sea, Oct. 6, 1917.***
(11, Cross Street)

209. HOLT, James, Stoker 1st Class, 18729,[7] HMS Begonia Royal Navy, d. 6 October 1917 aged 23.

Son of Samuel and Maria[8] Holt of 11, Cross Street (20, Water Lane in 1911). Born 23 January 1895. In 1911 he was a Porter. Killed in Action 6 October 1917. The Begonia was a Q-ship decoy which sailed from Devonport in the first week of October 1917 but did not return from the English Channel.[9] Commemorated on the Portsmouth Naval Memorial (PR 26.).[10] No Winchester memorial found.

✠**HOUNSLOW, GEORGE H. ... [BLANK] ... R.G.A. France. Wounded once. M.M. *Died of Wounds, Etaples.***
(30, Brassey Road)

1 CWGC.
2 WO 372/10/1983.
3 SDGW 1/4th Bn.
4 R Hamps Notes. RH.
5 SJ writes KIA not DOW.
6 CWGC.
7 ADM 188/904/18729; K/18729.
8 Mother's name variously recorded. Maria here from 1911 census. Mary on CWGC, May on 'Naval Casualties', Findmypast, Naval Casualties 1914-1919 database. Naval and Military Press.
9 Hepper, 2006, p. 105.
10 CWGC.

210. HOUNSLOW, George Horace, Gunner, 24461,[1] 3rd Siege Bty Royal Garrison Artillery, d. 5 August 1917 aged 30.

Son of William and Florence Ann Hounslow of 30, Brassey Road. Born at Wareham, Dorset in 1888. In 1901 he was a Milk Boy. Enlisted at Winchester and served on the Western Front. Wounded once and received the Military Medal.[2] Died of Wounds at Etaples 5 August 1917. Buried in Etaples Military Cemetery (GR XX. L. 4A.).[3] Memorials at St Matthew's and St Paul's.

✠**HOUSE, HARRY ... Rfn. ... K.R.R.C., Nov. 1915, Rfn. France. Killed in Action, July 15, 1916.**
(2, Hyde Close)

211. HOUSE, Harry Immer,[4] Private, 17177,[5] 16th (Service) Bn (Church Lads Brigade) The King's Royal Rifle Corps, d. 15 July 1916 aged 42.

Son of Isaac Harry and Elizabeth House of 2, Hyde Close. Born 1874. He was a Constructional Fitter in 1911. Enlisted in November 1915.[6] Served on the Western Front. Killed in Action 15 July 1916. Commemorated on the Thiepval Memorial, Somme, France (PR Pier and Face 13 A and 13 B.).[7] Memorial at St Bartholomew's.

✠**HUNT, FRANK E. ... Pte. ... R.M.L.I., Oct. 1916, Pte. France, Belgium. Wounded, October 26, 1417, and October 9, 1918. Died of Wounds, Oct. 10, 1918.**
(34, Kingsgate Road)

212. HUNT, Frank Edward, Private, CH/1696-S-,[8] 1st RM Bn RN Div. Royal Marine Light Infantry, d. 10 October 1918 aged 20.

Son of Frances Edward and Kate Maria Hunt of 34, Kingsgate Road. Born 1898. In 1911 he was a Newsboy at the school where his father worked.[9] Served on the Western Front. The Royal Marine Medal Roll record[10] states that he

1 WO 372/10/55870. WO 372/23/122559 (MM) Gazetted 23.8.16 *Supplement to the Edinburgh Gazette*. August 24 1916. 24461 Gunner G Hounslow.
2 Checked *The London Gazette* for George Horace Hounslow, G.H. Hounslow. 24461 Hounslow. Not found. Two MICs for him exist: one for Service medals, one for MM.
3 CWGC.
4 Harry only on *WWSR*.
5 WO 372/10/56613. R/17177.
6 SDGW.
7 CWGC.
8 ADM 159/146/1696.
9 'Francis' in 1911.
10 Findmypast. Royal Marines Medal Roll 1914-1920.

enlisted 5 October 1916 and embarked with the Royal Marine Brigade 15 December 1916. He had influenza in early 1917 and rejoined 1st Royal Marine Battalion 9 July 1917. He was shot in the right shoulder 26 October 1917 and invalided back to Britain 28 October 1917. Rejoined 1st Royal Marine Battalion 11 September 1918. Wounded again 9 October 1918 and died from a bullet wound to the head in 29th Casualty Clearing Station (accidentally shot by temporary Sub-Lieutenant Faulkner at 8am 9/10/18).[1] Buried at Del Saux Farm Cemetery, Beugny, Pas de Calais, France.[2] Memorial at St Cross Chapel.

⌘INGE, SIDNEY G. ... Pte. ... R.W.S., Oct. 1916, Pte. Lancs. Fus. France. *Killed in Action, Sept. 2, 1918, Eterpigny.*
(90, Fairfield Road)

213. INGE, Sidney George, Private, 38187,[3] 2nd Bn The Lancashire Fusiliers, d. 3 September 1918 aged 33.[4]

Son of May and Amelia Inge of 90, Fairfield Road (Holberry, Hatherly Road, 1911).[5] Native of Canterbury, Kent. He came from Southern Rhodesia to enlist.[6] Enlisted at Herne Bay, Kent in October 1916 and served in France.[7] Transferred from the Royal West Surrey Regiment. Killed in Action 3 September 1918 at Eterpigny. Buried at Eterpigny British Cemetery, Pas de Calais, France (GR A 5.).[8] Memorials at St Matthew's and St Paul's.

⌘JACOB, LESLIE J. ... [BLANK] ... Hants, Sept. 1914. India, Mesopotamia. Taken Prisoner by Turks, Sept. 24, 1916, Kut. *Died, Sept. 1916.*
(57, Western Road)

214. JACOB, Leslie John, Private, 201125,[9] 1/4th Bn The Hampshire Regiment, d. 12 February 1918 or September 1916 aged 23.

Son of John and Winifred Jacob of 39, Stockbridge Road (family at 79, Western Road, 1901 and 1911).[10] Born 1895. A Dentist's Apprentice in 1911. Enlisted in September 1914 at Winchester (3326). Served in India and Mesopotamia. Entered a theatre of war with 1/4th Bn on 25 October 1915.[11] Taken prisoner

1 Findmypast. Royal Marines Medal Roll 1914-1920.
2 CWGC.
3 WO 372/10/150004.
4 CWGC gives 3 September: *WWSR*, 2 September.
5 May Inge in 1911 census Head of Household, with wife Amelia. A mistranscription?
6 According to CWGC.
7 SDGW.
8 CWGC.
9 WO 372/10/184359.
10 William Jacob, who survived, is at 92, Stockbridge Rd on the *WWSR*.
11 R Hamps Notes. RH. Journal confirms taken prisoner at Kut so cannot have been

by Turks on 24 September 1916 and died a POW in September 1916 or 12 February 1918.¹ Buried in the Baghdad (North Gate) War Cemetery, Iraq (GR XXI. P. 7.).² Memorials at St Matthew's, St Paul's and St Thomas's School.

✠JEFFREY, JESSE ... Sergt. ... Hants, 1903, Pte. France. *Killed in Action, Oct. 16, 1916.*
(54, Canon Street)

215. JEFFREYS,³ Jesse, Serjeant, 6966,⁴ 2nd Bn The Hampshire Regiment, d. 16/17 October 1916 aged 26.

Born 1890. An infant resident of the workhouse in Winchester in 1891.⁵ Enlisted at Portsmouth in 1903 as regular soldier. Served in South Africa. A Musician stationed with 2nd Bn The Hampshire Regiment, Wynberg, Cape of Good Hope, South Africa in 1911. A bandsman qualified in stretcher drill and first aid. Served in France. Killed in Action 16/17 October 1916.⁶ Commemorated on the Thiepval Memorial, Somme, France (PR Pier and Face 7 C and 7 B.).⁷ Memorial at St Michael's ('Jeffery').

✠JELLETT, ARTHUR E. ... L.-Corpl. ... Hants, 1914, Pte. India, Mesopotamia. *Killed in Action, Kut.*
(47, Kingsgate Street)

216. JELLETT, Arthur Edward, Lance-Corporal, 201044,⁸ 1/4th Bn The Hampshire Regiment, d. 24 February 1917 aged 21.

Son of Walter and Emma Jellett of 47, Kingsgate Street. Born 1896. An Upholsterer's apprentice in 1911. Worked for E. W. Savage. Enlisted at Winchester in 1914 (3506).⁹ Served in India and Mesopotamia. Entered a

    taken prisoner on 24.9.1916.
1 It seems the 1918 date from CWGC and SDGW is more plausible than 1916. CWGC printed War Grave Register gives 1918. SJ. R Hamps Notes. RH. and Bowker confirm he was a prisoner at Entelli. Date of death not given. Probably died after a while as a POW.
2 CWGC.
3 Jeffrey on *WWSR*.
4 WO 372/10/213608.
5 1891 census.
6 R Hamps Notes. RH. for additional material in this biography. Confirms his death on 17 October.
7 CWGC.
8 WO 372/10/215187. R Hamps Notes. RH. suggests he was 2/4th attached 1/4th. Other additional material in the R Hamps Archive including two laudatory sympathy letters from officers following his death. He died during attacks the day after the crossing of the Tigris on 23 February 1917.
9 SDGW.

theatre of war (Mesopotamia) after the beginning of 1916. Killed in Action at Kut 24 February 1917. Commemorated on the Basra Memorial, Iraq (PR Panel 21 and 63.).[1] Memorial at St Michael's.

Another son served in India.

ⴲJESSON, JOSEPH J. ... Pte. ... Hants, Sept. 1916, Pte. Lab. C. France. *Killed in Action, Dec. 1, 1917.*
(1, Greyfriars Villas)

217. JESSON, Joseph James, Private, 31633,[2] formerly 3rd (Reserve) Bn The Hampshire Regiment, d. 1 December 1917 age 42.

In 1911 his family at 7, Tantony Lane, West Bromwich, Staffordshire. Born West Bromwich. Enlisted on 28 September 1916 and served in France.[3] He was the father of Elsie Jesson of 32, Hyde Close.[4] Transferred to 424388 80th Coy Labour Corps with whom he Died of Wounds [5] 1 December 1917. Buried at Rocquigny-Equancourt Road British Cemetery, Manancourt, Somme, France (GR VI. E. 1.).[6] No Winchester memorial found.

ⴲJOHNSON, ARCHIBALD L. ... P.O. ... R.N., 1914, P.O. Belgium, Russia. *Died, July 17, 1916, Russia.*
(11, Newburgh Street)

218. JOHNSON, Archibald Leonard, Petty Officer Motor Mechanic, 1996,[7] 18th Armoured Car Div. (Russia) Royal Naval Air Service, d. 18 July 1916 aged 27.[8]

Son of Mrs Alice Sarah Johnson of 11, Newburgh Street. Born 15 May 1889 at Petersfield.[9] A Cycle Agent in 1911. Served in Belgium and Russia. Died of disease 18 July 1916 in Russia. Buried at Vladikavkaz Hospital Cemetery, Vladikavkaz, Beslan, Severnaya Osetiya-Alaniya Republic, Russian Federation. Also commemorated on Haidar Pasha Memorial, Turkey.[10] Memorials at St Matthew's and St Paul's.

1 CWGC.
2 WO 372/10/228051. R Hamps Notes. RH. has his second name as Henry and his age.
3 SDGW.
4 CWGC.
5 SJ notes DOW.
6 CWGC.
7 ADM 188/563/1996. F/1996.
8 CWGC.
9 1911 census suggests 1887.
10 CWGC. No Panel Reference. Commemoration moved to Haidar Pasha when maintenance of graves in Russian territory no longer possible.

✠**JOHNSON, FRANK E. D. ... Pte. ... Hants Y., Nov. 1914, Tpr. Hants. France, Belgium.** *Killed in Action, Jan. 31, 1918, St. Julien.*
(1, Birinus Road)

219. JOHNSON, Frank Edwin Davis, Private, 33229,[1] 2nd Bn The Hampshire Regiment, d. 31 January 1918 aged 21.

Only son of Edwin and Emily Johnson of 41, Fairfield Road (1911), later Hope Lennox, Christchurch Road, Bournemouth. Born 1897. Enlisted in November 1914 at Winchester and served on the Western Front.[2] Transferred from the Hampshire Yeomanry 2 December 1916 to The Hampshire Regiment, 15th, then 14th then 2nd Bns. Served with the Machine Gun Corps. Died of Wounds[3] 31 January 1918 at St Julien. Buried at Nine Elms British Cemetery, Poperinge, West-Vlaanderen, Belgium (GR XIII. E. 17.). Memorials at Holy Trinity and Peter Symonds School.

✠**JUDD, ERNEST F. ... Pte. ... Hants, Dec. 1914, Pte. Dorset. France.** *Missing (believed Killed), Apl. 15, 1917.*
(17, Alresford Road)

220. JUDD, Ernest,[4] Private, 22208,[5] 1st Bn The Dorsetshire Regiment, d. 15 April 1917.

Son of George and Ada Judd of 18, Water Lane.[6] Born 1888. In 1911 he was a General Labourer. Enlisted in December 1914 at Winchester. Served in France as 18765 in The Hampshire Regiment then transferred to The Dorsetshire Regiment. Killed in Action 15 April 1917.[7] Commemorated on the Thiepval Memorial, Somme, France (PR Pier and Face 7 B.).[8] Memorials at All Saints and St John the Baptist.

His brother Thomas Alfred, listed below, was Killed in Action at Jutland 31 May 1916.

1 WO 372/11/8271.
2 SDGW.
3 Census 1911 address. Subsequently DOW. R Hamps Notes. RH. for additional material in this biography. States that he was previously wounded and invalided home. Died of wounds to the abdomen.
4 Ernest F in *WWSR*.
5 WO 372/11/85473.
6 The Judd brothers give different addresses for their parents. Maybe because they enlisted at different times, the parents may have moved and so have been recorded as for example Next of Kin at different addresses. They also died in different years.
7 *WWSR* 'Missing (believed Killed)' on this date. R Hamps Notes. RH. note he did not serve in a theatre of war with The Hampshire Regiment.
8 CWGC.

✠JUDD, THOMAS A. ... Stoker ... R.N., 1913, Stoker. North Sea; H.M.S. *Queen Mary*. *Killed in Action, May* 31, 1916, *Jutland*.
(17, Alresford Road)

221. JUDD, Thomas Alfred, Stoker 1st Class, 17111,[1] HMS Queen Mary Royal Navy, d. 31 May 1916 aged 22.

Son of George and Ada Judd 17, Morn Hill (Alresford Road). Born 20 December 1893. In 1911 he was a General Labourer at 22, Colson Road. Enlisted in 1913 and served on HMS Queen Mary in the North Sea. Killed in Action at the Battle of Jutland 31 May 1916.[2] Commemorated on the Portsmouth Naval Memorial (PR 18.).[3] Memorials at All Saints and St John the Baptist.

His brother Ernest served in France as a Private in The Hampshire Regiment then The Dorsetshire Regiment. Killed in Action 15 April 1917 and is listed above.

✠JUPE, BRUCE D. ... Art. ... R.N. H.M.S. *Good Hope*. *Killed in Action, Nov.* 1914, *Chilian Coast*.
(57, Kingsgate Street)

222. JUPE, Bruce Dunning, Engine Room Artificer 4th Class, M/784,[4] HMS Good Hope Royal Navy, d. 1 November 1914 aged 21.[5]

Son of Henry and Eliza Jane Jupe of 57, Kingsgate Street. Born 7 March 1893. Enlisted in the Royal Navy by 1911 when the census record states he was a Boy Artificer 416 with the shore establishment HMS Fisgard. Served aboard HMS Good Hope in the War and was Killed in Action 1 November 1914.[6] De Ruvigny states 'lost in action off Coronel, on the coast of Chile'. Commemorated on the Portsmouth Naval Memorial (PR 3.). Memorials at Peter Symonds School and St Michael's.

De Ruvigny states:

Jupe, Bruce Dunning, Acting ERA 4th Class, M.784, HMS Good Hope, lost in action off Coronel, on the coast of Chile, 1 November 1914.

---

1 ADM 188/901/17111; K/17111.
2 Hepper, 2006, p. 60.
3 CWGC.
4 ADM 188/1019/784.
5 de Ruvigny (Findmypast website) describes him as 'Acting ERA 4th Class M.784'.
6 Hepper, 2006, p. 28.

✠**JUPE, EDWARD ... Tpr. ... Dorset Y., June 9, 1916, Tpr. Hussars. India.** *Died of sunstroke, June 22, 1918, Simla.*
(15, College Street)

223. JUPE, Edward, Private, H/40012,[1] 7th (Queen's Own) Hussars, d. 22 June 1918 aged 39.

Son of Charles J. and Emma Jupe of 54, Kingsgate Street (1891). Born 1879. Married Lily Hannah Hunt 27 November 1904 at Sherborne, Dorset Parish Church.[2] Lily Hannah Jupe at Cold Harbour, Sherborne, Dorset (date?).[3] In 1911 he was living with his wife's family in Sherborne, Dorset, and was working as a Domestic Coachman. By 1911there were Iris May born 1905, Leonard George born 1908 and Tom born 1911. Enlisted 9 June 1916 at Sherborne and served in India.[4] Transferred from the Dorset Yeomanry. Died of sunstroke 22 June 1918 at Simla. Commemorated on the Delhi 1914-1918 War Memorial, India.[5] Memorial at St Michael's.

✠**KEMISH, CHARLES S. B. ... Lieut. and Q.M. ... R.A.S.C.,1888, Dr. Gallipoli. Médaille Militaire.** *Killed in Action, July 14, 1915.*
(16, Gordon Avenue)

224. KEMISH, Charles Sydney Bulpit, Lieutenant Quartermaster,[6] Auxiliary Horse Transport Army Service Corps, d. 14 July 1915 aged 45.

Son of Charles S. and Mary L. Kemish, stepson of Charles Cox (3rd Bn The Rifle Brigade). Born 1867.[7] Married Annie Eliza Mills in 1905 and they had Gladys May in 1906. Therefore also referred to as son-in-law of Mrs E A Mills of 22, Bar End, Winchester. Enlisted in 1888 and served in the Boer (South African) War as a Serjeant in 6 Coy Army Service Corps.[8] Commissioned 23.1.1915. Awarded the Long Service and Good Conduct Medal, and the Médaille Militaire (France).[9] Served at Gallipoli (Dardanelles). Killed in Action 14 July 1915. Buried at Lancashire Landing Cemetery, Turkey (GR A. 45.).[10] Memorials at All Saints and Chilcomb.

1 WO 372/11/88582.
2 BMD.
3 Census 1891 evidence also marriage data and address for wife at Cold Harbour. Census 1911.
4 SDGW. SJ adds 'formerly Corps of Hussars (2315).
5 CWGC. Apparently no burial.
6 WO 372/11/124497.
7 1881 census: he may have down played his age.
8 Boer War Register, 8744, WO 100/231/0.
9 No citations found from Medaille Militaire. Long Service was 18 years (GJEH pers. comm.)
10 CWGC.

✠KETLEY, CHARLES W. ... Corpl. ... R.E., Sept. 1914. Spr. France. Gassed, Sept. 1915. *Killed in Action, Apl.* 11, 1917, *Feuchy.*
(72, Brassey Road)

225. KETLEY, Charles W. Corporal, 42855,[1] Royal Engineers, d. 11 April 1917 age unknown.

Born at Beckenham, Kent.[2] Enlisted in September 1914 in London.[3] Served in France and was awarded the Military Medal.[4] Served in 15th Divisional Signal Coy, Royal Engineers. Killed in Action 11 April 1917 at Feuchy. Buried in Feuchy Chapel British Cemetery, Wancourt, Pas de Calais, France (GR III. C. 6.).[5] Memorial at St Paul's and St Matthew's (Kelley on memorial).

✠KIBBLE, GEORGE F. ... L.-Corpl. ... Wilts, 1906, Pte. France. *Killed in Action,* Oct. 31, 1914.
(7, Silver Hill)

226. KIBBLE, Frank George, Lance-Corporal, 7689,[6] 1st Bn The Duke of Edinburgh's (Wiltshire Regiment), d. 31 October 1914 aged 27.

Son of William Kibble of 7, Silver Hill. Stepson of Emily Sarah Kibble. Born at Norbiton, Surrey in 1888. Mother Sarah died in 1898. Enlisted in 1906 at Southampton and served in South Africa. In 1911 he was at Pietermaritzburg, Natal, South Africa with the 1st Bn The Duke of Edinburgh's (Wiltshire Regiment). Served in France. Killed in Action 31 October 1914. Commemorated on Le Touret Memorial, Pas de Calais, France (PR Panel 33 and 34.).[7] No Winchester memorial found.

His brother William Reddick, listed below, was Killed in Action 9 October 1918.

✠KIBBLE, REDDICK W. ... Gun. ... R.G.A., 1910, Gun. France. *Killed in Action,* Oct. 9, 1918.
(7, Silver Hill)

227. KIBBLE, William Reddick, Gunner, 33246,[8] 99th Siege Bty Royal

1 WO 372/11/149606. Citation for MM WO 372/23/129539 *LG* 21.10.16. Not seen.
2 SJ.
3 SDGW.
4 CWGC. *The London Gazette* checked. No citation.
5 CWGC.
6 WO 372/11/155009.
7 CWGC.
8 WO 372/11/155104.

Garrison Artillery, d. 9 October 1918 aged 27.

Son of William Kibble of 7, Silver Hill. Stepson of Emily Sarah Kibble. Born 1892. His mother, Sarah, died in 1898. William enlisted in 1910 at Winchester and served in Malta.[1] The 1911 census records him at Fort Ricasole, Malta with the 102 Company Royal Garrison Artillery. Served on the Western Front. Died of Wounds 9 October 1918. Buried at Rue-du-Bois Military Cemetery, Fleurbaix, Pas de Calais, France (GR III. C. 19.).[2] No Winchester memorial found.

His brother Frank George, listed above, was Killed in Action 31 October 1914.

✠KILFORD, HENRY W. ... Gun. ... R.G.A., 1911, Gun. India. *Killed in Action, Apl. 18, 1915, Shabkadar.* (35, Middle Brook Street)

228. KILFORD, Henry William, Gunner, 34391,[3] 6th Mountain Bty Royal Garrison Artillery, d. 18 April 1915 aged 24.

Son of Mr and Mrs Kilford of 35, Middle Brook Street. Born at Shirley, Southampton in 1892. Enlisted in 1911 at Winchester and in 1911 was Gunner 30 Coy Royal Garrison Artillery, The Red Barracks, Nothe Fort, Weymouth. Served in India during the War. Killed in Action 18 April 1915. Buried at Shabkadr. Commemorated on the Delhi Memorial (India Gate), India (PR Face 1.).[4] Memorial at Holy Trinity.

✠KNIGHT, CHARLES A. ... [BLANK] ... Canadians, 1914, Pte. France. *Killed in Action, Apl. 10, 1917, Vimy Ridge.* (1, Prinstead Terrace)

229. KNIGHT, Charles Albert, Private, 775985,[5] 38th Bn Canadian Infantry (Eastern Ontario Regiment), d. 10 April 1917 age unknown.

Parents Charles and Emma at 1, Prinstead Terrace, Bar End in 1911. A Canadian National. Enlisted in 1914 and served in France. According to his Canadian attestation papers he was born in Sydney, Australia on 5 February 1884. Married Mary Ann Knight (256, Dufferin Street, Toronto, Ontario)[6]

1 SDGW.
2 CWGC.
3 Some confusion in the records over his name WO 372/11/158838 (HW); 372/11/158855 (WH).
4 CWGC. SJ. Grave can no longer be maintained.
5 http://www.veterans.gc.ca/eng/collections/virtualmem/Detail/586315?Charles%20Albert%20Knight
6 Attestation papers as above. *Toronto Star*, etc. KIA changed to DOW.

and his occupation is listed as Teamster. The *Toronto Star* states that he was employed by the Canadian Bread Company. He enlisted in 1914 (*WWSR*) or more likely 13 March 1916 (Canadian attestation papers) and served in France. The *Toronto Star* states that 'he went overseas with a Peel County battalion'. Died of Wounds 10 April 1917 at Vimy Ridge. Buried in Cabaret-Rouge British Cemetery, Souchez, Pas de Calais, France (GR IV. A. 3.).[1] Memorial at St Peter Chesil.

✠**LANGRIDGE, WALTER S. ... Pte. ... Hants, June 1916, Pte. France.** *Died from exposure, Feb.* **23, 1917.**
(24, Colson Road)

230. LANGRIDGE, Walter Stuart,[2] Private, 25246,[3] 1st Bn The Hampshire Regiment, d. 23 February 1917 aged 36.

Son of Alex and Catherine Langridge of Ashford, Kent. Born at Ashford in 1881. Married Lucy Emlie in 1906 of 24, Colson Road, Winnall.[4] Family at 13, Ashley Terrace (1911).[5] By 1911 they had three children, Alec William born 1907, Louis Walter born 1908 and Gertrude Catherine born 1910.[6] A Tailor Maker in 1911. Enlisted at Winchester in June 1916.[7] Served on the Western Front. Entered a theatre of war with 1st Bn after beginning of 1916. Died from exposure 23 February 1917. Buried in Fins New British Cemetery, Sorel-le-Grand, Somme, France (GR VII. A. 23.).[8] Memorial at St John the Baptist.

✠**LANSLEY, WILLIAM ... Stoker ... R.N., 1902. H.M.S.** *Good Hope.* **Killed in Action, Nov. 1, 1914.**
(54, St. John's Street)

231. LANSLEY, William, Stoker 1st Class, 301754,[9] HMS Good Hope Royal Navy, d. 1 November 1914 aged 30.[10]

Son of Henry and Fanny Lansley of 54, St John's Street. Born at Totford 9 October 1884.[11] In 1901 he was a Carrier's Boy. Enlisted in 1902. Served aboard

1 CWGC.
2 Or Stewart SJ. JB.
3 WO 372/12/902.
4 GWGC.
5 Census 1911.
6 R Hamps Notes. RH. for additional material in this biography. Notes six children at his death. Played football for Winchester.
7 SDGW.
8 CWGC.
9 ADM 188/490/250. [access to this document online barred on 19.03.13].
10 Note different ways the Good Hope losses are noted against individuals.
11 CWGC states b. Winchester 1884, 9 October. Naval Casualty Records give 9 October 1884. 1891 and 1901 censuses give 1885. SJ notes RN and RM War Graves

HMS Good Hope and was Killed in Action off the coast of Chile 1 November 1914.[1] Commemorated Portsmouth Naval Memorial (PR 4.). Memorials at St John the Baptist.[2]

✠**LAVERTY, WILLIAM H. ... S.M. ... K.R.R.C., 1898, Rfn. France.** *Killed in Action, Apl.* **1917.**
  (1, College Street)

232. LAVERTY, William Henry, Serjeant Major,[3] 1218, 3rd Bn The King's Royal Rifle Corps, d. 17 February 1917 aged 34.

Son of James Thomas and Margaret Laverty of 2, College Street, b. 1883.[4] Enlisted in 1898 at Gosport and served in the Boer War where he became a POW (released 10 December 1899 at Stormberg) and wounded 10 December 1901 near Wepener.[5] Served in France during the First World War and was promoted to Serjeant Major. Killed in Action 17 February 1917.[6] Buried at Regina Trench Cemetery, Grandcourt, Somme, France (GR IV. D. 30.).[7] Memorial at St Swithun-upon-Kingsgate.

He had two brothers who served during the War. Arthur A. served in the American Army as a Private, promoted to Serjeant, and John R. served as a Private in The Rifle Brigade. Both survived the War.[8]

✠**LAWRANCE, ALBERT E. ... Pte. ... Glos., Mch. 1916, Pte. Devon. France,Italy.** *Killed in Action, Apl.* **22, 1918.**
  (25, Greenhill Road)

233. LAWRENCE, Albert E., Private, 33643,[9] 1st Bn The Devonshire Regiment, d. 22 April 1918 age unknown.[10]

Enlisted in March 1916. Served in France and Italy and transferred from The Gloucestershire Regiment (5091). Killed in Action 22 April 1918. Buried at

---

   Roll give Winchester birthplace.
1 Hepper, 2006, p. 28.
2 We are grateful to Peter Eagling for visiting St John's Church to research this.
3 WO 372/12/12849. Recorded as Sergeant. Acting Warrant Officer Class 2.
4 Suzanne Foster, pers. comm. Lavertys occupied 1-3 College Street, e.g. parents in 1911. DoB 1883 suggested by 1891 census.
5 WO 100/ Boer War 1889-1902. Soldiers' details.
6 Discrepancy of month of death.
7 CWGC. Photograph of his memorial on St Swithun-upon-Kingsgate Church on Flicka.
8 Augustine, Donald and Reginald probably nephews.
9 WO 372/12/17675. Discrepancy over Lawrance/Lawrence.
10 No place or date of birth found in census.

Morbecque British Cemetery, Nord, France (GR Plot I. Row C. Grave 6.).[1] Memorials at St Paul's and St Matthew's (A.F. on memorial).

✠LAWRENCE, PERCY J. ... Bdr. ... R.F.A., Jan. 1915, Gun. Salonica, France. Wounded, 1916. *Killed in. Action, July* 27 1917.
(13, Greyfriars Terrace)

234. LAWRENCE, Percy J., Bombardier, 66161,[2] 105th Bde Ammunition Col. Royal Field Artillery, d. 27 July 1917 aged 33.

Son of Elijah J. and Jane Lawrence of 13, Grey Friars Terrace, Lower Brook Street. Born at Sonning, Berkshire in 1884.[3] Described as a Gardener (not Domestic) in the 1901 census. Enlisted in London in January 1915 and served in Salonica, France and Flanders. Wounded in 1916. Killed in Action 27 July 1917. Buried in Vlamertinghe New Military Cemetery, West-Vlaanderen, Belgium (GR V. A. 28.).[4] Memorial at Holy Trinity.

Two of his brothers served in the War. William served in India and Mesopotamia as a Private in The Hampshire Regiment and was taken prisoner by Turks in May 1916. Edward served in France with The Northumberland Fusiliers, was commisioned, and was wounded in February 1915 and August 1916. He was awarded the Distinguished Conduct Medal 1915, the Military Cross 1916 and the Médaille Militaire 1914.[5] They both survived the War.

✠LEACH, WILLIAM F. ... R.S.M. ... Hants, 1906, Pte. India, Mesopotamia. Taken Prisoner by Turks, Kut. *Died of Typhus.*
(2, Alswitha Terrace)

235. LEACH, William Frank, Regimental Serjeant Major, 200025,[6] 1/4th Bn The Hampshire Regiment, d. 2 May 1918 aged 30.

Only son of William and Alice Mary Leach of 1, Montgomery Terrace, Bemerton, Salisbury, Wiltshire. Born at St Edmund's, Salisbury in 1889. De Ruvigny[7] states he was educated in Salisbury and then at the Winchester Diocesan Training College which he left in 1909. Enlisted in The Hampshire Regiment 17 September 1907 (187).[8] He was a Schoolmaster at St Thomas's

1 CWGC, recorded as Albert only.
2 WO 372/12/2081. Records Driver not Bombardier.
3 1901. Not found in 1911.
4 CWGC.
5 *WWSR.*
6 WO 372/12/33264. States Acting RSM, likewise CWGC.
7 de Ruvigny (Findmypast website).
8 Left Diocesan Training College in 1909. He joined the Volunteers as a student, an

Boys' School in Winchester Boarding at 2, Alswitha Terrace in 1911. Served with the Indian Expeditionary Force in the Persian Gulf. Entered a theatre of war (Balkans) on 18 March 1915. Served through the siege of Kut. Mentioned in Despatches.[1] Taken prisoner by Turks. Took a leading role in the welfare of the prisoners. Died of typhus 26 April 1918 at Nisibin, Turkey.[2] Commemorated at Baghdad (North Gate) Cemetery, Iraq (PR Nisibin Mem. 239.).[3] Memorials at St Bartholomew's and University of Winchester, King Alfred's College Old Chapel (Winton Memorial Room).

✠LEAL, ALFRED C.... Pte. ... Hants, Nov. 1915, Pte. India. Missing, Jan. 21, 1916.
(10, Greyfriars Terrace)

236. LEAL, Alfred Christian, Private, 201188,[4] 1/4th Bn The Hampshire Regiment, d. 21 January 1916 aged 20.

Son of Edward George and Catherine Slythe Leal of 10, Grey Friars Terrace, Lower Brook Street (1901 58, Eastgate Street). Born 1896. A Grocer's Clerk in 1911. Enlisted in November 1915 at Winchester. Served in India and Mesopotamia. Entered a theatre of war (Mesopotamia) with 1/4th Bn on 18 October 1915. First posted as 'missing' later confirmed Killed in Action 21 January 1916 at Umm El Hanna. Commemorated on the Basra Memorial, Iraq (PR Panel 21 and 63.).[5] No Winchester memorial found.

His brother Charles E. served as a Private in The Hampshire Regiment, transferred to The Devonshire Regiment and survived the War.

✠LEES, HENRY G. ... Pte. ... Hants, June 1916, Pte. France. Killed in Action, Nov. 5, 1917.
(12, Bar End)

---

important part of DCT activity. For his memorial etc see T.B. James *The University of Winchester*. (London: Third Millennium, 2015).
1. CWGC.
2. Atkinson, 2, p. 159 fn 1 All ten officers survived. RSM Leach died in captivity after doing 'outstanding work for his fellow captives.' R Hamps Notes. RH. for additional material in this biography. He appears as 'A. W. Leach'. Leach is one of the best recorded other ranks from the War in the regimental archive which contains a record he made personally of payments from the relief fund to prisoners. Among much else it is recorded that 'his funeral was apparently managed by Germans, and he is one of the few unfortunates who have died in this country who have received a decent burial.'
3. CWGC, SDGW and R Hamps Notes. RH. date his death 2 May 1918. Probably aged 29.
4. WO 372/12/35436 (previous record /4/2405).
5. CWGC.

237. LEES, Henry George ('Spider'), Private, 25172,¹ 14th (Service) Bn (1st Portsmouth) The Hampshire Regiment, d. 5 November 1917 aged 35.

Son of the late Samuel and Anne Lees of 69, Cheesehill (Chesil Street). Born 1883. Married Mary Penton in 1908, 12, Bar End Road. Enlisted in June 1916 at Winchester and served on the Western Front.² Entered a theatre of war (France) with 14th Bn after the beginning of 1916. Killed in Action 5 November 1917.³ Commemorated on the Tyne Cot Memorial, Zonnebeke, West-Vlaanderen, Belgium (PR Panel 88 to 90 and 162.).⁴ Memorial at St Peter Chesil (All Saints) and Chilcomb (George Lees).

His brother William J. served in India, Palestine and France as a Private in The Hampshire Regiment and survived the War.

✠LEVER, GEORGE T. ... Pte. ... Hants. Oct. 1, 1914, Pte. Belgium. *Missing (believed Killed), Oct. 3, 1914.* (11, Milverton Road)

238. LEVER, George Thomas, Private, 7009,⁵ 1st Bn The Hampshire Regiment, d. 19 October 1914 aged 28.⁶

Born 1886. Married Mary Agnes Holt in 1906. They had one son, George born 1908. Mary died 1909. Resident with parents-in-law at 20, Water Lane in 1911. Enlisted as regular c. 1903. Served in Flanders.⁷ Entered a theatre of war (France) with 1st Bn on 23 August 1914. First reported 'missing' and later confirmed as Killed in Action 19 October 1914.⁸ Commemorated on the Ploegsteert Memorial, Comines-Warneton, Hainaut, Belgium (PR Panel 6.).⁹ Memorials at St Matthew's and St Paul's.

✠LEWIS, HUGH F. ... Capt. ... R.W.S., 1900, Lieut. Belgium. Despatches 1915. *Killed in Action, Oct. 19, 1914, Ledeghem.* (Myddelton, Christ Church Rd.)

1 WO 372/12/52282.
2 Note that the *WWSR* records service in 'France', however he is commemorated in Belgium, hence use of the term 'Western Front'.
3 Atkinson, 2, makes no reference to casualties among the 14th Hampshires on this date.
4 CWGC.
5 WO 372/12/68880.
6 Discrepancy in dates 3/19 October.
7 SDGW. R Hamps Notes. RH. for additional material in this biography from Regimental Journals etc.
8 Discrepancy in dates 3/19 October. CWGC and SDGW say 19th.
9 CWGC. Gives no age, relatives etc.

239. LEWIS, Hugh Frederick, Captain,[1] 2nd Bn The Queen's (Royal West Surrey Regiment), d. 19 October 1914 aged 33.

Son of Col. James Frederick Lewis (Royal Engineers) and Amelia Lewis of Winchester (Myddelton, Christchurch Road).[2] Born at Kensington, Middlesex in 1881.[3] Attended Wye College, South-Eastern Agricultural College, Kent.[4] Married Winifred Rachel Griffith in 1910 of Maes Gwyn, Winchester. Enlisted in 1900 and served in the Boer War. In 1911 a Captain, 2nd Battalion The Queen's Regiment of Infantry C and G Companies, Gibraltar. Served in Belgium in the War and was Mentioned in Despatches in 1915.[5] Killed in Action 19 October 1914. The Battalion diary[6] states that Captain Lewis was shot in the head, and most of his party killed, while advancing on buildings held by Germans in the town of Ledeghem. Buried in Ledeghem Military Cemetery, Ledeghem, West-Vlaanderen, Belgium (GR B. 16.).[7] Memorials at Christ Church and St Thomas's.

☩ **LIGHT, ROBERT C. ... Sergt. ... K.R.R.C., rejoined Aug. 1914, Corpl. France.** *Killed in Action, Mch.* **10, 1915,** *Neuve Chapelle.*
(27, St. Catherine's Road)

240. LIGHT, Robert Charles, Serjeant, 1731,[8] 1st Bn The King's Royal Rifle Corps, d. 11 March 1915 aged 34.

Son of the late George and Charlotte Light of 27, St Catherine's Road, Highcliffe. Born at Chilcomb in 1883. Married Bertha Bright in 1907 of Hazeldene Cottage, North Waltham. Served in the Boer War and re-enlisted in August 1914 at Gosport. Served on the Western Front. Died of Wounds [9] 11 March 1915 at Neuve Chapelle. Buried in Chocques Military Cemetery, Pas de Calais, France (GR I. A. 32.). [10] Memorial at North Walsham. No Winchester memorial found.

His brother Thomas Roger served in France as a Private in The Durham Light Infantry and the Labour Corps. He survived the War.

1 WO 372/12/78212.
2 CWGC.
3 Census 1911 suggests birth as 1891.
4 www.kentfallen.com
5 CWGC also Bn War Diary. Queen's Royal Regt..
6 See previous ref, p. 87.
7 CWGC.
8 WO 372/12/88920.
9 SJ.
10 CWGC states 11 March.

⌖**LLOYD, CONWAY W. B. ... C.S.M. ... P.P.C.L.I., Aug. 1914, Pte: France, Belgium.** *Killed in Action, Feb.* **28, 1915,** *St. Eloi.*
(Westbury, City Road)

241. LLOYD, Conway Walter Barnas, Company Serjeant Major, 1501, Princess Patricia's Canadian Light Infantry (Eastern Ontario Regiment),[1] d. 27 February 1915 aged 31.

Son of Walter[2] and Louise M. Lloyd of 92, Forest Road, Torquay, Devon, formerly of Westbury, 13, City Road Winchester (widow in 1911 there). Born 12 January 1884. An Ironmonger's apprentice before enlisting in 1901 in The Hampshire Regiment. Transferred to the Scots Guards in that year and was Discharged at the end of his twelve-year service in 1913.[3] An Ironmonger's Assistant in 1911. Re-enlisted on 24 August 1914 and served in France and Belgium.[4] Killed in Action 27 [or 28] February 1915 at St Eloi. Buried at Voormezeele Enclosure No. 3, Ypres (Ieper), West-Vlaanderen, Belgium (GR III. H. 5.).[5] No Winchester memorial found.

⌖**LLOYD, WILLIAM ... [BLANK] ... R.G.A. France.** *Killed in Action, Aug.* **2, 1917,** *Armentières.*
(63, Chesil Street)

242. LLOYD, William, Gunner, 347417,[6] Royal Garrison Artillery, d. 21 August 1917 age unknown.

William and Isabella Lloyd at 63, Chesil Street in 1911.[7] Served in France and was Killed in Action 21 August 1917 at Armentieres.[8] Buried in Maple Leaf Cemetery, Comines-Warneton, Hainaut, Belgium (GR I. 7.).[9] Memorial at St Peter Chesil.

1 www.collectionscanada.gc.ca/databases/cef/001042-119.02, Canadian online Service Records.
2 CWGC. Next of kin in Service Papers W. W. Lloyd, 14, Bristol Road, Portsmouth; SJ additional material.
3 See Service Records, above. Noted as a Corporal, but if Scots Guards would have been a Lance-Sergeant. Also referred to as a Docker, maybe from 1913. Service Papers note he was 6ft 2ins tall and had a woman tattooed on both arms.
4 Photograph of a medal for C. Lloyd '1501 C.S.Maj. C. Lloyd P.P.C.L.I.'
5 CWGC, just C. Note discrepancy in date of death.
6 WO 372/12/117014. (347417).
7 Right address, but William Lloyd absent in 1911.
8 Discrepancy of date with *WWSR*.
9 CWGC has 34747, so does BMD so possibly a different man.

✠LOADER, ALBERT ... A.B. ... R.N., 1897, Boy. R.F.R. High Seas. *Killed in Action, Feb. 29, 1916, North Sea.*
(16, Hyde Close)

243. LOADER, Albert, Able Seaman, 203514,[1] HMS Alcantara, Royal Navy, d. 29 February 1916 aged 34.

Son of the late Edward and Emily Loader of Winchester (16, Hyde Close).[2] Born 21 April 1883.[3] Enlisted in 1897 and became an Able Seaman. Recorded as being resident aboard HMS Grafton as Able Seaman 416. Served on the High Seas and was Killed in Action 29 February 1916 in the North Sea aboard the Alcantara, an armed merchant cruiser, among the 67 ratings and two officers who lost their lives, when they were caught out by the Rena, in fact the armed surface raider Greif.[4] Commemorated on the Portsmouth Naval Memorial, Hampshire (PR 13.).[5] Memorial at St Bartholomew's.

His brother Thomas B., listed below, Died of Wounds 2 February 1918.

✠LOADER, THOMAS B. ... Pte. ... Hants, Mch. 1916, Pte. Dorset. France, Belgium. Wounded, Aug. 1916, July, and Dec. 1917. *Died of Wounds, Feb. 2, 1918.*
(16, Hyde Close)

244. LOADER, Thomas Bernard, Private, 22302,[6] 1st Bn The Dorsetshire Regiment attached 14th Bn Machine Gun Corps, d. 2 February 1918 aged 31.

Son of the late Edward and Emily Loader of Winchester. Born 1888. A Stable Lad in Upper Chilcomb in 1911. Enlisted in March 1916 at Southampton and served on the Western Front. Listed as formerly 22791, Private, The Hampshire Regiment.[7] Wounded in August 1916 and December 1917. Entered a theatre of war with The Hampshire Regiment. Transferred to Dorsets. Died of Wounds 2 February 1918. Buried in Lijssenthoek Military Cemetery, Poperinge, West-Vlaanderen, Belgium (GR XXVII. F. 20A.).[8] Memorial at St Bartholomew's.

His brother Albert, listed above, was Killed in Action 29 February 1916.

---

1 ADM 188/354/14.
2 Naval Casualties 1914-1919 db. Naval and Military Press, 2010.
3 1911 census suggests 1882.
4 Hepper, 2006, p. 54.
5 CWGC. RN (RFR/PO/B/6022).
6 WO 372/12/116579.
7 SDGW.
8 CWGC.

✠**LOCK, ERNEST ... Pte. ... Canadians, Dec. 1914, Pte. France.**
Killed in Action, Sept. 26, 1916.
(17, St. John's South)

245. LOCK, Ernest, Private, 434580, 10th Bn Canadian Infantry (Alberta Regiment),[1] d. 26 September 1916 age 27.

Son of Ethel Lock. Born at Winchester 12 March 1889.[2] Previously a Farmer. His next of kin is listed as living in Winchester, ?Mrs Ethel Lock. Canadian National. Enlisted December 1914 (*WWSR*) or more likely 27 January 1915 (according to his attestation papers) at Calgary and served in France.[3] Killed in Action 26 September 1916.[4] Commemorated on the Vimy Memorial, Pas de Calais, France. No Winchester memorial found.

✠**LOMER, STANLEY R. ... [BLANK] ... Gordon H. France.** *Killed in Action, Sept. 25, 1915, Hooge.*
(4, Birinus Road)

246. LOMER, Stanley Rupert, Private, 11142,[5] 1st Bn Gordon Highlanders, d. 25 September 1915 aged 23.

Son of the late Wilson and Harriet Lomer of 4, Birinus Road. Born 1892. A Grocer's Porter in 1911. Served on the Western Front. Killed in Action 25 September 1915 at Hooge. Commemorated on the Ypres (Menin Gate) Memorial, Ypres (Ieper), West-Vlaanderen, Belgium (PR Panel 38.).[6] Memorial at St Bartholomew's.

He had two brothers who served in the War. Bertie C. served in India and Mesopotamia as a Sapper in the Royal Engineers. Frank served in The Hampshire Regiment. Both survived the War.

✠**LONG, HERBERT J. S. ... Bdr. ... R.G.A., 1904, Gun. France.**
Wounded once. *Killed in Action, Mch. 26, 1918.*
(4, Victoria Road)

247. LONG, Herbert James Samuel, Acting Bombardier, 20108,[7] 13th Siege

---

1   http://www.veterans.gc.ca/eng/remembrance/memorial/canadian-virtual-war-memorial.
2   Canadian Attestation Papers.
3   Date of enlistment given as 27 January 1915.
4   Attestation Papers Record refers to 'Vitelligo', *recte* vitilego, i.e. left side of abdomen/back.
5   WO 372/12/128140. S/11142.
6   CWGC.
7   WO 372/. Also twgpp.org. War Graves Photographic. Check SDGW.

Bty Royal Garrison Artillery, d. 27 March 1918 aged 31.

Born at Lymington in 1896.[1] Married Annie Mills in 1915: she lived at The Prospect Cottage, Nursling, Southampton.[2] Enlisted in 1904 at Southampton and in 1911 was stationed at No. 8 Company Royal Garrison Artillery, Europa, Gibraltar. Served in France and was wounded once. Died of Wounds 27 March 1918.[3] Buried in Doullens Communal Cemetery Extension No 1, Somme, France (GR V. A. 69.).[4] Memorial at St Bartholomew's.

✠LONGMAN, CECIL R. ... L.-Corpl. ... Hants, Sept. 1914, Pte. France. Despatches 1916. *Killed in Action, Sept.* 9, 1916. (11, Middle Brook Street)

248. LONGMAN, Cecil Reece, Lance-Corporal, 11084,[5] 11th (Service) Bn (Pioneers) The Hampshire Regiment, d. 9 September 1916 aged 32.

Son of Mr and Mrs C. Longman of 11, Northgate Road, Southampton. Born at Southampton in 1884. Married Easter Mary Sheppard in 1907.[6] In 1901 a General Labourer. Enlisted in September 1914 at Southampton and served in France. Entered a theatre of war with 11th Bn on 19 December 1915. Mentioned in Despatches in 1916.[7] Killed in Action 9 September 1916. Commemorated on the Thiepval Memorial, Somme, France (PR Pier and Face 7 C and 7 B.). Memorials at Holy Trinity and Southampton Cenotaph.

✠LOVELAND, ERNEST C. ... Pte. ... Hants, 1913, Pte. Mesopotamia. Taken Prisoner by Turks. *Died as P.O.W.* (4, Egbert Road)

249. LOVELAND, Ernest,[8] Private, 1907,[9] 1/4th Bn The Hampshire Regiment, d. 16 May 1916 aged 21.

Son of William Henry and Lizzie Loveland of 4, Egbert Road. Born at Reading, Berkshire in 1896. An apprentice Mechanical Dentist in 1911. Enlisted in 1913 in Winchester. Entered theatre of war (Mesopotamia) on 18 March 1915. Taken

---

1. Census 1911 suggests 1886.
2. CWGC.
3. SJ DOW?
4. CWGC. Burial place suggests more likely he DOW.
5. WO 372/12/133917.
6. Easter Colenutt, formerly Longman, of 70, Canon Street, by time of CWGC record. Had married again.
7. R Hamps Notes RH. No sign of MiD in Regimntal Journal, *London Gazette* or Regimental History.
8. Ernest C in *WWSR*.
9. WO 372/12/143731.

prisoner by Turks and died as a POW 16 May 1916.¹ Commemorated on the Basra Memorial, Iraq (PR Panel 21 and 63.). Memorial at St Bartholomew's.

He had three brothers who served in the War. Henry W. V., listed below, was Killed in Action 2 April 1917. George H. served in Mesopotamia as a Private, then Serjeant in The Hampshire Regiment and the Army Service Corps. William H. served as a cadet, rose to Serjeant in the Royal Flying Corps and Royal Air Force. Both survived the War.

✠LOVELAND, HENRY W. V. ... Lieut. ... Winnipeg Grenadiers, Sept. 1915, Lieut. R.A.F. France. *Killed in Action, Apl.* 1917. (4, Egbert Road)

250. LOVELAND, Henry W. V., Lieutenant, 78th Bn Canadian Infantry (Manitoba Regiment)² attd 22 Sqdn Royal Flying Corps,³ d. 2 April 1917 aged 29.

Son of William Henry⁴ and Lizzie Loveland of 4, Egbert Road. Born 23 July 1887 at Guildford, Surrey. Had emigrated to Canada in 1910 aboard the Virginian and took Canadian nationality. A Photographic Manager.⁵ Served five years with Wessex Divisional Transport, Army Service Corps.⁶ Enlisted in September 1915 (*WWSR*) or January 1916 (according to his attestation papers) at Winnipeg⁷ and served in France. Killed in Action 2 April 1917.⁸ Buried at Villers Hill British Cemetery, Villers-Guislan, Nord, France (GR V. E. 3.).⁹ Memorial at St Bartholomew's.

He had three brothers who served in the War. Ernest, listed above, died as a POW 16 May 1916. George H. served in Mesopotamia as a Private, then Serjeant in The Hampshire Regiment and the Army Service Corps. William H. served as a Cadet, promoted to Serjeant in the Royal Flying Corps and Royal Air Force. Both survived the War.

---

1 SDGW. R Hamps Notes RH. Not on list of Kut prisoners. However Bowker confirms he was a Kut prisoner.
2 http://www.collectionscanada.gc.ca/databases/cef/index-e.html Library and Archives Canada? No 'w. v.' in Canadian papers.
3 RAF not in Service Record. RAF AIR 76/307/8133 Henry Loveland, Missing 2 April, Killed 3 April.
4 W.H. Loveland next of kin at death.
5 Attestation papers provide snapshot at time of enlistment. Service Papers subsequent career in the forces.
6 Canadian Records.
7 Canadian records say 20 January 1916 at Winnipeg.
8 CR record 'missing killed'
9 CWGC.

☦LOVELOCK, GEORGE A. ... Pte. ... Hants, Aug. 1914, Pte. Dardanelles. *Killed in Action, Aug. 9, 1915.*
(10, Greenhill Road)

251. LOVELOCK, George Allan, Private, 4553,[1] 10th (Service) Bn The Hampshire Regiment, d. 21 August 1915 aged 33.

Son of Thomas and Sarah Lovelock of 15, Elm Road, Weeke. Born 1882. Married Lilian R. Jeffrey in 1910, living at 14, Staple Garden in 1911. A Labourer before enlisting in 1901 in The Rifle Brigade at Winchester. He was Discharged later the same year.[2] In 1911 he was a House Painter Journeyman. A territorial he re-enlisted in August 1914 at Winchester. Served at Gallipoli (Dardanelles). Special Reservist who entered a theatre of war (Gallipoli) on 22 July 1915 with 10th Bn. Initially posted as missing.[3] Killed in Action 21 August 1915. Commemorated on The Helles Memorial, Turkey (PR Panel 125-134 or 223-226, 228-229 & 328.).[4] Memorials at St Matthew's and St Paul's.

☦LOVELOCK, JAMES ... [BLANK] ... Hants, Sept. 1914. India, Egypt. *Killed in Action, Nov. 24, 1917.*
(1, Alswitha Terrace)

252. LOVELOCK, James, Private, 200974,[5] C Coy 2nd/4th Bn The Hampshire Regiment, d. 24 November 1917 aged 21.

Second son of George and Kate Lovelock of King Alfred Place. Born 1897. Enlisted in September 1914 on Salisbury Plain and served in India and Egypt. Entered a theatre of war (Palestine) after beginning of 1917 with 2/4th Bn.[6] Died of Wounds 24 November 1917.[7] Buried in Jerusalem War Cemetery, Israel and Palestine (including Gaza) (GR C. 89.).[8] Memorial at St Bartholomew's.

His brother George served in France as a Private, later Lance-Corporal in the The Lincolnshire Regiment,[9] was wounded 12 April 1917 and survived the War.

☦LUCAS, REGINALD ... Pte. ... Devon, Feb. 12, 1917, Pte. D. of W. Regt. France. *Missing, believed Killed, Nov. 21, 1917.*
(22, Wales Street)

1 WO 327/145/176.
2 WO 97/5364/160.
3 R Hamps Notes. RH.
4 CWGC. Discrepancy in date of death. RH.
5 WO 372/12/145214. C Coy.
6 R Hamps Notes. RH.
7 SDGW.
8 CWGC.
9 The Lincolnshire Regiment from 1881.

253. LUCAS, Reginald Victor, Private, 26465,[1] 2nd/5th Bn The Duke of Wellington's (West Riding Regiment), d. 21 November 1917 aged 28.[2]

Son of Nicholas and Louisa Lucas of Chilcomb. Born 1890. Married Jessie Lilian Westbrook in 1910 of 22, Wales Street. In 1911 he was a Billposter. Enlisted 12 February 1917 at Winchester. Served in France. Transferred from The Devonshire Regiment. Killed in Action 21 November 1917.[3] Commemorated on the Cambrai Memorial, Louverval, Nord, France (PR Panel 6 and 7.).[4] Memorials at St John the Baptist.

✠**LUFFMAN, WALTER ... Pte. ... Hants, Sept. 1914, Pte. Mesopotamia. Wounded, Dec. 14, 1915. *Died of Wounds, Dec. 19, 1915.***
(62, Parchment Street)

254. LUFFMAN, Walter, Private, 2989,[5] 1/4th Bn The Hampshire Regiment, d. 19 December 1915 aged 18.

Son of Walter J. and Minnie A. Luffman of 62, Parchment Street. Born 1898. Enlisted in September 1914 on Salisbury Plain and served in Mesopotamia. Entered a theatre of war (Mesopotamia) with 1/4th Bn on 18 March 1915.[6] Wounded 14 December 1915 and Died of Wounds 19 December 1915. Buried in Kut War Cemetery, Iraq (GR O. 17.).[7] Memorial at Holy Trinity.

✠**LUND, GEOFFREY W. ... C.S.M. ... Hants, 1915, Pte. Dardanelles, France. Wounded twice, gassed. D.C.M. *Killed in Action, Apl. 21, 1917.***
(35, Monks Road)

255. LUND, Geoffrey William, Company Serjeant Major, 7222,[8] 2nd Bn The Hampshire Regiment, d. 21 April 1917 aged 30.

Only son of the Rev. William and Fanny Maud Lund of 36, Welbeck Avenue, Southampton (also late of Harbridge Rectory, near Ringwood). Born at Trotton, Sussex in 1886. Married Mary Jelliff in 1911 (of 35, Monks Road).[9] Enlisted

---

1   WO 372/12/156935. Devonshire regiment not mentioned either in MIC or CWGC. See A. Matthews, same regiment.
2   Inconsistencies with this record. Birth place and marital status.
3   SDGW.
4   CWGC.
5   WO 372/12/160168. SDGW?
6   R Hamps Notes. RH.
7   CWGC.
8   WO 372/23/60401. Also www.highfieldhistory.co.uk
9   BMD. May Lund in CWGC..

at Ringwood. In 1911 recorded as a Lance-Serjeant 413/-/o 1st Bn The Hampshire Regiment, Badajos Barracks Part Area 11c. Re-enlisted in 1915, and served at Gallipoli (Dardanelles) and France. Awarded the Distinguished Conduct Medal on the Somme, 18 April 1916.[1] His service commended in the regimental history.[2] Wounded twice and gassed. Killed in action 21 April 1917 between Manchy and Cambrai Road.[3] Commemorated on the Arras Memorial, Pas de Calais, France (PR Bay 6.). Memorial at St Bartholomew's.

DCM gazetted 11 December 1916. Citation reads:

For conspicuous gallantry in action. He took command of his company when the officers were wounded and showed conspicuous courage and ability in organising the defences.

✠MACKLIN, SYDNEY ... Pte. ... Hants, Aug. 1914, Pte. India, Mesopotamia. *Killed in Action, Feb. 5, 1917, Baghdad.* (11, Colebrook Street)

256. MACKLIN, Sydney, Private, 200767,[4] 1/4th Bn The Hampshire Regiment, d. 5 February 1917 aged 28.

Son of Charles and Isabella Macklin of 63, St John's Street (1901 and 1911). Born 1889. A Bricklayer in 1911. Enlisted in August 1914 (2386) at Hamilton Camp and served in India and Mesopotamia. Entered theatre of war (Mesopotamia) with 1/4th Bn on 18 March 1915.[5] Killed in Action 5 February 1917. Commemorated on the Basra Memorial, Iraq (PR Panel 21 and 63.).[6] No

---

1 Atkinson, 2, p. 194.
2 R Hamps Notes. RH. for additional material and the citation in this biography. Further archive records for Lund incude this press cutting provided by his widow, Mrs M. Lund: 35, Monks Road, Winchester, December 2nd. 1917.
Sir,—The enclosed cutting may be of interest to your readers:- -
Little Eric and his Daddy's Medal.
A woman in black and a toddling boy, Mrs. Lund and her little Eric (3), had come for the D.C.M. of her late husband. Company Sergt.- Major Lund. The King looked at the pair, and asked, "Now, to which one of you shall I give it? It was Eric who settled the question. He looked up at the man in uniform the same colour as daddy's, but of different texture and markings. He was afraid of no King, not he. "My medal," he said. "All right." replied the King, and into Eric 's chubby little hand the medal went. The King stroked him under the chin in a fatherly way, and remarked what a fine little chap Eric was, and asked his age. When I said "Three years old today" (November 8th), the King turned to the Queen, and mentioned the fact to her, and she smiled very graciously at Eric.
3 Atkinson, 2, pp. 194, 217, 451.
4 WO 372/13/34310. SDGW.
5 R Hamps Notes. RH. for this further material in that archive.
6 CWGC.

Winchester memorial found.[1]

✠**MACLACHLAN, RONALD C. ... Brig.-Gen. ... R.B., 1895, 2nd Lieut. France, Belgium. Wounded, July 30, 1916. D.S.O. 1916 Despatches twice. *Killed in Action,* Aug. 11, 1917, near Ypres.**
(Langhouse, Chilbolton Avenue)

257. MACLACHLAN, Robert Campbell, Brigadier-General, Commanding 112th Infantry Bde General Staff[2] late The Rifle Brigade (The Prince Consort's Own), d. 11 August 1917 aged 45.

Son of the late Rev. Archibald Campbell Maclachlan, Patron and Rector of Newton Valence, Alton. Born 24 July 1872 at Newton Valence.[3] Educated Cheam School and Eton, then Sandhurst. Married Elinor Mary Trench (née Cox), widow, of Rookley House, Kings Somborne in 1908 in London. Enlisted in 1895[4] and served in the Boer War. Wounded 6 January 1900 at Wagon Hill. Took part in the 'Thibet' Expedition of 1904 and received the medal. Adjutant of the OTC at Oxford; honorary MA. Served on the Western Front during the War and was promoted in June 1915 to Lieutenant-Colonel. Awarded the Distinguished Service Order in June 1916, both reported in *The London Gazette* (see below).[5] Mentioned in Despatches twice and was wounded 30 July 1916. Killed in Action 11 August 1917 near Ypres by a sniper. Buried in Locre Hospice Cemetery, Heuvelland, West-Vlaanderen, Belgium (GR II. C. 9.).[6] Memorials at St Matthew's, St Paul's and Newton Valence.

The London Gazette, 13 August 1915 p. 6018.

The Rifle Brigade (The Prince Consort's Own), Major (temporary Lieutenant-Colonel) Ronald C. Maclachlan to be Lieutenant- Colonel. Dated 15th June, 1915.

Awarded DSO in June 1916 Lt.-Col. Ronald Campbell Maclachlan, Rif. Brig., comdg. Serv. Bn. *The London Gazette,* 3 June 1916.

1 ? St Maurice, lost.
2 WO 372/24/40754. Additional information, and reference to an Obituary in *The Rifle Brigade Chronicle,* 1916 and photographic image courtesy of K. Gray.
3 1911 census suggests 1872.
4 Given as 8 July 1893 by Creagh and Humphris, below.
5 *The V.C. and D.S.O. A complete record of all those officers, non-commissioned officers and men of His Majesty's naval, military and air forces who have been awarded these decorations from the time of their institution, with descriptions of the deeds and services which won the distinctions and with many biographical and other details.* By O'Moore Creagh and E. M. Humphris. (3 vols, London, n.d.), vol. 3, p. 297. Does not mention wounds of 30 July 1916 but records 'severely wounded 29.12.15'. Photograph.
6 CWGC.

✠**MAIDMENT, HAROLD W. ... L.-Corpl. ... R.B., Sept. 1914, Rfn. France. Wounded, June 21, 1915.** *Killed in Action, Mch. 22, 1918, Ham.*
  (6, Back Street, St. Cross)

258. MAIDMENT, Harold Wilfred, Private, B/1223,[1] 12th (Service) Bn The Rifle Brigade (The Prince Consort's Own), d. 25 March 1918 aged 21.[2]

Son of Harry Latham Maidment and Elizabeth Maidment of 29, Clausentum Road, St Cross. Born 1897. Painting houses with his father in 1911. Enlisted in September 1914 at Winchester. Served in France. Wounded 21 June 1915. Killed in Action 25 March 1918. Commemorated on the Pozieres Memorial, Somme, France (PR Panel 81 to 84.).[3] Memorial at St Cross Chapel.

His brother Frank A. served in France as a Private in The Rifle Brigade, was wounded 31 July and 25 December 1915 and survived the War.

London Gazette, 3 June 1916.

✠**MAIDMENT, HERBERT G. ... Sergt ... R.F., Sept. 21, 1914, Pte. Lond. Malta, Dardanelles, Egypt, France.** *Killed in Action, Sept. 15, 1916, Somme.*
  (1, Gladstone Street)

259. MAIDMENT, Hubert George, Serjeant, 2760,[4] 1st/2nd Bn City of London Regiment (Royal Fusiliers), d. 17 September 1916 aged 24.

Son of William George and Alice Bell Maidment of Gladstone Street. Born 1892. In 1911 he was a Student at College for the Teaching Profession, living at 2, Gladstone Street.[5] Enlisted 21 September 1914. Served in Malta, Gallipoli (Dardanelles), Egypt and France. Killed in Action 17 September 1916 on the Somme. Commemorated on the Thiepval Memorial, Somme, France (PR Pier and Face 9 D and 16 B.).[6] Memorials at Peter Symonds School and the Primitive Methodist Chapel in Parchment Street.

✠**MALE, REGINALD H. ... L.-Corpl. ... Hants Y., Sept. 1914, Tpr. M.G.C. France, Flanders.** *Killed in Action, Sept. 18, 1918.*
  (Trevenna, Stockbridge Road)

---

1. WO 372/13/85261. R/1223, see T. Potter, A. Spencer etc.
2. Discrepancy in date of death: CWGC and SDGW date his death to 25 March 1918. They both have him as a Rifleman (Private), not Lance-Corporal.
3. CWGC.
4. WO 372/13/85254. Discrepancy in names.
5. Not the DTC according to Jake Bain.
6. CWGC. Date of death 17 September SJ.

260. MALE, Reginald Harry, Lance-Corporal, 46366,[1] 6th Bn Machine Gun Corps (Infantry), d. 18 September 1918 aged 21.

Son of George Henry and Caroline Fanny Male of Holland House, Church Street, Malvern, Worcestershire. Born at Wyke Hill, Winchester in 1897.[2] Family living at Trevenna, Stockbridge Road in 1911.[3] Enlisted in September 1914 at Winchester and served on the Western Front. Formerly 1249, the Hampshire Yeomanry but did not serve in a theatre of war with them.[4] Killed in Action 18 September 1918. Buried in Trefcon British Cemetery, Caulaincourt, Aisne, France (GR B. 10.).[5] Memorials at Peter Symonds School, St Paul's and St Matthew's.

✠**MARINER, ALBERT E. ... Pte. ... Glos., Mch. 20, 1916, Pte. France.** *Killed in Action, Apl. 1918, Kemmel.*
(18, St. John's Street)

261. MARINER, Albert Edward, Private, 241880,[6] 8th (Service) Bn The Gloucestershire Regiment, d. 11 April 1918 aged 36.

Son of Henry and Clarissa Mariner of 62, Canon Street. Born 1882. A House Painter in 1911. Enlisted 20 March 1916 at Whitchurch, Hampshire. Served in France and Belgium. Died at Mont Kemmel 11 April 1918.[7] Commemorated on the Tyne Cot Memorial, Zonnebeke, West-Vlaanderen, Belgium (PR Panel 72 to 75.).[8] Memorials at St John the Baptist.

✠**MARINER, JAMES E. ... L.-Corpl. ... Hants, Pte. India, Mesopotamia. Wounded once. Taken Prisoner by Turks, Aug. 29, 1916.** *Died, June 29, 1917, Constantinople.*
(33, Canon Street)

262. MARINER, James Edward, Lance-Corporal, 200067,[9] 1/4th Bn The Hampshire Regiment, d. 29 June 1917 aged 25.

Eldest son of James and Louisa Mariner of 33, Canon Street. Born at Plymouth, Devon in 1892. A House Painter in 1911. A territorial soldier he enlisted at

1 WO 372/13/91485. No mention of Hampshire Yeomanry on WO 372. SDGW formerly 1249 Hampshire Yeomanry. See Ernest Alexander for Hampshire Yeomanry.
2 1911 census gives 'Southampton'.
3 Census 1911.
4 R Hamps Notes. RH.
5 CWGC.
6 WO 372/13/116570.
7 'Died' from SDGW.
8 CWGC.
9 WO 372/13/116594.

Winchester (1392) and served in India and Mesopotamia. Entered a theatre of war (Mesopotamia) with 1/4th Bn on 18 March 1915. Taken prisoner by Turks 29 August 1916 at Kut and died of fever at Constantinople 29 June 1917 as a POW.[1] Buried at Haidar Pasha Cemetery, Constantinople, Turkey (GR II. I. 4.).[2] Memorial at St Michael's.

His brother, Joseph, listed below, died as a POW 27 June 1916.

✠**MARINER, JOSEPH W. ... Pte. ... Hants, .Sept. 1914, Pte. India, Mesopotamia. Taken Prisoner by Turks, Apl. 29, 1916. *Died, June* 27, 1916, *Baghdad.***
   (33, Canon Street)

263. MARINER, Joseph William, Private, 3331,[3] 1/4th Bn The Hampshire Regiment, d. 27 June 1916 aged 20.

Son of James and Louisa Mariner of 33, Canon Street. Born 1896. A General Assistant in School House, ?Winchester College in 1911. Enlisted in September 1914 at Winchester. Served in India and Mesopotamia 2/4th attached 1/4th. Entered a theatre of war with 1/4th Bn on 25 October 1915.[4] Taken prisoner by Turks 29 April 1916 at Kut and died at Baghdad 27 June 1916 as a POW. Buried at Baghdad (North Gate) War Cemetery, Iraq (GR XIV. H. 12.).[5] Memorial at St Michael's.

His brother James, listed above, died as a POW 29 June 1917.

✠**MARSH, BERTIE W... . Pte. ... Hants, Aug. 1914, Pte. Mesopotamia, India, Wounded, 1915 and 1918. *Died of Wounds, June* 2, 1918.**
   (8, Little Minster Street)

264. MARSH, Bertie William, Private, 42508,[6] 2nd Bn The Hampshire Regiment, d. 15 June 1918 aged 26.

Youngest son of Edward and Elizabeth Marsh of 8, Little Minster Street. Born at London in 1892. A Casual Labourer in 1911, family living at 60, Canon Street. Enlisted in August 1914 at Winchester. Served in India and Mesopotamia. Entered a theatre of war (Mesopotamia) with Hampshire Regiment on 18 March 1915. Served in theatre of war with 1/4th, 1st then

1   R Hamps Notes. RH. for additional material in this biography and see archive.
2   CWGC.
3   WO 372/13/116598.
4   R Hamps Notes. RH. for additional material in this biography.
5   CWGC.
6   WO 372/13/126508.

2nd Bns. Transferred in from the Labour Corps on 24 November 1917 and was posted to 4th Reserve Battalion¹ Wounded in 1915 and in 1918. Died of Wounds, Lansdown Hospital, Cardiff, 15 June 1918.² Buried at Cardiff (Cathays) Cemetery, Glamorganshire (GR EB. 72.). Memorial at St Thomas's.

His brother Edward served in India as a Private in The Hampshire Regiment and survived the War.

✠**MARSHALL, ALBERT ... Rfn. ... R.B., rejoined Aug. 1914, Rfn. France. Wounded, May 8, 1915. D.C.M. 1915.** *Died of Wounds, May* **12, 1915,** *Boulogne.*
   (46, St, Faith's Road)

265. MARSHALL/MOORE, Albert, 8110, Private, The Rifle Brigade (The Prince Consort's Own), d. 12 May 1915.

See below Albert Moore.³

✠**MARTIN, SIDNEY J. ... Pte. ... Hants, 1907, Pte. France. Wounded, Nov, 1914, April 1915, June 1918 (gas).** *Died of Wounds (gas), July* **1918.**
   (3, Wales Street)

266. MARTIN, Sidney James, Private, 7742,⁴ 1st Bn The Hampshire Regiment, d. 24 July 1918 aged 30.

Son of John and Emma Martin of 3, Wales Street. Born at Damerham, Wiltshire in 1889.⁵ Enlisted in 1907 and in 1911 was a Private 2nd ?Bn The Hampshire Regiment, stationed at 2nd Battalion Mounted Infantry, Kings Hill, Harrismith, Orange Free State, South Africa. Served in France during the War. Entered theatre of war with 1st Bn on 23 August 1914. Wounded November 1914 and April 1915.⁶ Gassed in June 1918 and died from the effects of gas 24 July 1918. Buried at Winchester (St Giles's Hill) Cemetery.⁷ Memorials at St John the Baptist.

He had two brothers who served in the War. William, listed below, died as

1   R Hamps Notes. RH. for this and other material in this biography.
2   Discrepancy over date of death: CWGC states 15 June.
3   Identification of Marshall/Moore by Gavin Edgerley-Harris and information courtesy of K. Gray.
4   WO 372/13/149886.
5   Entered as Damersham.
6   R Hamps Notes. RH. Discharged due to wounds 10 January 1916. No evidence in the Regimental archive that he was gassed in 1918 or had returned to Army.
7   CWGC.

a POW 21 August 1916. John T. served in France as a Private, promoted to Serjeant, was awarded the Military Medal in 1917 and survived the War.

✠MARTIN, WILLIAM ... Gun. ... R.F.A., 1912, Gun. Mesopotamia. Taken Prisoner by Turks, 1916, Kut. *Died, Aug. 21, 1916, Kut.*
(3, Wales Street)

267. MARTIN, William, Driver, 68304,[1] 63rd Bty Royal Field Artillery, d. 21 August 1916 aged 23.

Son of John and Emma Martin of 3, Wales Street. Born at Fordingbridge in 1893. Enlisted in 1912 at Winchester. Served in Mesopotamia and was taken prisoner by Turks. He died as a POW 21 August 1916 at Kut. Buried in Baghdad (North Gate) War Cemetery, Iraq (GR XXI. E. 21.).[2] Memorials at St John the Baptist.

He had two brothers who served in the War. Sidney, listed above, died 24 July 1918. John T. served in France as a Private, promoted to Serjeant, was awarded the Military Medal in 1917 and survived the War.

✠MASLIN, ALFRED ... Tpr. ... N. Somerset Y., July 1917, Tpr. France. *Killed in Action, May* 26, 1918.
(11, Freelands Buildings)

268. MASLIN, Alfred, Private, 72353,[3] 11th (Service) Bn The Cheshire Regiment, d. 26 May 1918 aged 52.

Born 1866.[4] Married Edith Self in 1895. Nine children 1897-1906. A General Labourer in 1901 living with his parents in law. 1911 a Street Labourer/Scavenger, family at 11, Freelands Buildings in 1911.[5] Enlisted in Winchester. MIC states The Cheshire Regiment, also Prince Albert's (Somerset Light Infantry) not Yeomanry. Killed in Action 26 May 1918. Commemorated on Soissons Memorial, Aisne, France. Memorial at Holy Trinity.[6]

✠MASON, FRANCIS H. ... [BLANK] ... R.E., Aug. 1914. Gallipoli, Salonica, Egypt. Wounded, Aug. 18, 1915. *Died of Pneumonia, Cairo.*
(1, Egbert Road)

1   WO 372/13/150909.
2   CWGC.
3   WO 372/13/155241.
4   Or 1867, 1901 census.
5   Parents unknown.
6   No Panel Ref or Grave Ref on CWGC.

269. MASON, Francis H., Pioneer, 43748,[1] Royal Engineers, d. 2 December 1918 aged 26.

Son of George H. and Emily Celia Mason of 1, Egbert Road. Born 1893. Enlisted in August 1914 and served at Gallipoli (Dardanelles), Salonica, and Egypt with 85th Field Coy, Royal Engineers. He was wounded 18 August 1915. Died of pneumonia at Cairo 2 December 1918. Buried in Cairo War Memorial Cemetery, Egypt (GR Q. 142.).[2] Memorial at St Michael's.

His brother John W. served in India and Persia [Iran] as a Private, promoted to Serjeant in The Hampshire Regiment, and survived the War.

✠**MASON, FRANK ... Corpl. ... R.B., Nov. 1915, Rfn. France. *Killed in Action, Sept. 15, 1916.***
  (51, Canon Street)

270. MASON, Frank, Lance-Corporal, 14400,[3] 8th (Service) Bn The Rifle Brigade (The Prince Consort's Own), d. 15 September 1916 aged 32.

Son of the late Edward and Ellen Elizabeth Mason of 51, Canon Street. Enlisted at Winchester in The Rifle Brigade in 1901 aged 17. Previously a Boot Maker. Discharged in 1913 at the termination of twelve years service, having served in Malta and India. Re-enlisted in November 1915 and served in France. Promoted to Lance-Corporal. Killed in Action 15 September 1916. Commemorated on the Thiepval Memorial, Somme, France (PR Pier and Face 16 B and 16 C.).[4] Memorial at St Bartholomew's.

His brother Charles served in France as a Lance-Corporal in the Canadian Infantry, was wounded 15 September 1916 and survived the War.

✠**MATHEWS, ARTHUR W. ... Gun. ... R.F.A., Oct. 1916, Gun. Yorks. France. *Killed in Action, Aug. 25, 1918.***
  (Upper Chilcomb)

271. MATTHEWS, Arthur William, Private, 34458,[5] 2nd/5th Bn The Duke of Wellington's (West Riding Regiment), d. 25 August 1918 aged 26.

Son of Arthur and Alice Mary Matthews of Upper Chilcomb. Born at Fareham in 1896. A Horseman on a Farm in 1911. Enlisted in October 1916. Served

1 WO 372/13/157357.
2 CWGC.
3 WO 372/13/157117. S/14400. States Private. WO 97/5478/130 provides a calculated date of birth of 1884.
4 CWGC states Lance-Corporal not Corporal.
5 WO 372/13/171554. Spelt Matthews. See R. Lucas, same Regiment.

in the Royal Field Artillery in France. Formerly 42403, Yorkshire Regiment.¹ Killed in Action 25 August 1918. Buried in Mory Abbey Military Cemetery, Mory, Pas de Calais, France (GR V. A. 10.).² Memorial at All Saints.

His brother James A. served in France and Salonica as a Gunner, promoted to Company Quartermaster Serjeant and survived the War.

✠**MATHEWS, WILLIAM S. ... Lieut. ... Hants Y., Sept. 1914, Tpr. K.R.R.C. France. *Killed in Action, Sept.* 15, 1916, *Flers.*
(23, St. Thomas Street)**

272. MATHEWS, William Scott, Lieutenant,³ 18th (Service) Bn (Arts and Crafts) The King's Royal Rifle Corps, d. 15 September 1916 aged 20.

Son of William Robert and Bertha Mathews, of 23, St Thomas Street. Born 1897. A student at Haileybury School in 1911.⁴ Enlisted in September 1914 and served in France. Transferred from the Hampshire Yeomanry.⁵ Killed in Action 15 September 1916 at Flers. Buried in Serre Road Cemetery No. 2, Somme, France (GR XXXIV. J.4.).⁶ Memorials at St Lawrence's and St Thomas's.

✠**MATON, HARRY R. ... [BLANK]... R.A.S.C.,1910. Salonica. *Died, Nov.* 10, 1918.
(10, North View)**

273. MATON, Harry Robert, Driver, 185579,⁷ 209th Coy Army Service Corps, d. 4 October 1918 aged 21.⁸

Son of Alfred and Charlotte Maton of 10, North View. Born 1898. A Grocer's Errand Boy in 1911. Enlisted at Winchester. Served in Salonica. Died 4 October 1918.⁹ Buried in Mikra British Cemetery, Kalamaria, Greece (GR 498.).¹⁰ Memorials at Christ Church and St Thomas's School.

He had two brothers who served in the War. Alfred G. served in France as a Private in The Gloucestershire Regiment and was awarded the Military Medal and Bar. Edward served in France in The Gloucestershire Regiment as a Private,

1 SDGW.
2 CWGC.
3 WO 339/13/4857 for his Service Records.
4 The most likely candidate of this name in 1911.
5 R Hamps Notes. RH. Not found on HCY list for 1913/14.
6 CWGC.
7 WO 372/13/170040. T4/185579. See Introduction for discussion of ASC/RASC.
8 Date of enlistment is 1910 on the *WWSR*, which does not match census occupation records.
9 Discrepancy over date of death: 2 October 1918, SDGW.
10 CWGC.

was promoted to Corporal and was awarded the Military Medal in 1918. Both survived the War.

✠MAY, FREDERICK JAMES ... Pte. ... Hants, 1915, Pte. Dardanelles. *Killed in Action,* 1915.
(Upper Chilcomb)

274. MAY, Frederick, James, Private, 10298,[1] 10th (Service) Bn The Hampshire Regiment, d. 10 August 1915 aged 22.

Son of Edward W. and Sarah Ann May of Upper Chilcomb.[2] Born at Fishers Pond in 1892. A Carter in 1911. Enlisted in 1915 at Winchester. Entered a theatre of war (Gallipoli) with 10th Bn on 5 August 1915.[3] Served at Gallipoli (Dardanelles). Killed in Action 10 August 1915. Commemorated on The Helles Memorial, Turkey (PR Panel 125-134 or 223-226, 228-229 & 328.).[4] Memorial at All Saints.

He had two brothers who served in the War. Cecil served in India and Mesopotamia as a Private in The Hampshire Regiment, then the Military Police. George E. served in France as a Private in the The Royal Warwickshire Regiment and was taken prisoner by Germans. Both survived the War.

✠MAYO, ALEXANDER J. ... Capt. ... R.F.C., Dec. 1915, 2nd Lieut. R.A.F. France. *Killed in Action, Aug.* 9, 1918, *Foucaucourt.*
(6, St. Peter Street)

275. MAYO, Alexander John, Captain,[5] 107 Sqdn Royal Air Force, d. 9 August 1918 aged 22.

Born at Cambridge in 1896. Living at Avebury House, 6, St Peter Street with his Aunt Mary Mayo in 1901 and 1911.[6] Enlisted in the Royal Flying Corps in December 1915 and served in France. Killed in Action 9 August 1918 at Foucaucourt. Buried in Heath Cemetery, Harbonnieres, Somme, France (GR V. H. 9.).[7] Memorial at St Thomas's.

1 WO 372/13/184214.
2 Address also given as Old Down, Longwood, Winchester. CWGC.
3 R Hamps Notes. RH.
4 CWGC.
5 No MIC found. IWM Index Private papers shows two Flying Log Books.
6 See Wm Mayo.
7 CWGC.

✠MAYO, WILLIAM C. ... Lieut. ... C.U.R.V., Oct. 1905. Sherwood For. *Killed in Action, Aug. 9, 1915, Suvla Bay.*
(6, St. Peter Street)

276. MAYO, William Charles, Lieutenant,[1] 9th (Service) Bn The Sherwood Foresters (Nottinghamshire and Derbyshire Regiment), d. 7 August 1915 aged 27.

Born at Cambridge in 1888.[2] Living at Avebury House, 6, St Peter Street with his Aunt Mary Mayo in 1901 and 1911. Enlisted in October 1905. Served with the Cambridge University Rifle Volunteers, then transferred to the Sherwood Foresters. Killed in Action 7 August 1915 at Suvla Bay.[3] Commemorated on The Helles Memorial, Turkey (PR Panel 150 to 152.).[4] No Winchester memorial found.

✠MEACHER, EDWIN J. ... Corpl. ... Hants, 1909, Pte. Dardanelles. *Killed in Action, Apl. 28, 1915.*
(11, Eastgate Street)

277. MEACHER, Edwin James, Lance-Corporal, 8459,[5] 2nd Bn The Hampshire Regiment, d. 28 April 1915 aged 23.

Son of George Henry and Sabina Meacher of 11, Eastgate Street. Born 1892. Enlisted in 1909 at Winchester and in 1911 was a Cook at Wellington Lines Aldershot. Served at Gallipoli (Dardanelles). Entered theatre of war with 2nd Bn on 25 April 1915. Initially posted as wounded and missing on 28 April 1915.[6] Killed in Action 28 April 1915. Commemorated on The Helles Memorial, Turkey (PR Panel 125-134 or 223-226 228-229 & 328.).[7] Memorials at Holy Trinity and St John the Baptist.

His brother Albert E. V. served in France with the Royal Berkshire Regiment, transferred to the Royal Engineers, The King's Own Yorkshire Light Infantry according to the *WWSR*.[8] He survived the War.

✠MEACHER, JOHN H. ... L.-Corpl. ... R. Marines, 1012, Pte. R.N.D. France. *Killed in Action, Apl. 28, 1917, Arras.*
(29, Tower Street)

1 No WO reference found.
2 Cousin of Alexander Mayo above.
3 SDGW gives 7-11 August.
4 CWGC.
5 WO 372/13/192052.
6 R Hamps Notes. RH.
7 CWGC.
8 Discrepancy: date conflicts with his WO 372/ MIC.

278. MEACHER, John Henry, Lance-Corporal, PO16215,[1] 2nd RM Bn RN Div. Royal Marine Light Infantry, d. 28 April 1917 aged 23.

Son of John and Fanny Meacher of 29, Tower Street. Born 14 January 1894 at St Paul's.[2] In 1911 he was a Gardener. Enlisted 15 January 1912. Served in France during the War. Embarked with the Royal Marine Brigade in December 1916 and was part of the Royal Battalion draft February 1917. Missing, assumed dead, 28 April 1917 at Arras. Commemorated on the Arras Memorial, Pas de Calais, France (PR Bay 1.).[3] Memorial at St Thomas's.

His brother Frederick served in the North Sea as a Stoker in the Royal Navy and survived the War.

✠**MERRITT, ALFRED E. ... Sergt. ... Hants, 1901, Pte. Dardanelles, France. Despatches 1917.** *Killed in Action, Apl. 23, 1917.*
   (9, Lawn Street)

279. MERRITT, Alfred Ernest, Serjeant, 6392,[4] 2nd Bn The Hampshire Regiment, d. 23 April 1917 aged 31.

Son of Mary Merritt.[5] Born at Chichester, Sussex in 1886.[6] A Carter before enlisting in The Hampshire Regiment in 1901 at Portsmouth when he was 17, was a Drummer.[7] In the Army Reserve in 1911. Re-enlisted at Winchester and served at Gallipoli (Dardanelles) and France. Entered a theatre of war with 1st Bn on 23 August 1914, in hospital at Leeds 10 December 1914.[8] Mentioned in Despatches in 1917.[9] Killed in Action 23 April 1917. Commemorated on the Arras Memorial, Pas de Calais, France (PR Bay 6.).[10] Memorial at Holy Trinity.

✠**MERRITT, GEORGE. H. ... L.-Corpl. ... Hants, Jan. 1915, Pte. France. Wounded, Dec. 4, 1915, and June 1916.** *Killed in Action, Mch. 17, 1918.*
   (Upper Chilcomb)

1   ADM 159/189/16215. Image ref. 1501. Gives number as PO16215.
2   1911 census and Naval Casualties 1914-1919. Naval and Military Press 2010 agree date of birth.
3   CWGC.
4   WO 372/24/43270.
5   WO 96/648/235.
6   SDGW Born and resided at Compton. Army Service Record calculates 1884.
7   According to his Army Service Record.
8   R Hamps Notes. RH.
9   MiD *LG* 22 May 1917 p. 5032. R Hamps Notes. RH. shows him in Sir Douglas Haig's Despatch of April 9th. That Mentioned in Despatches list published in the *London Gazette*, May 15th, 1917.
10 CWGC.

280. MERRITT, George Henry, Private, 14912,[1] 2nd Bn The Hampshire Regiment, d. 17 March 1918 aged 29.[2]

Son of Frank Samuel and Ellen Merritt of Bury Court, Bentley. Born at Compton in 1889. A Farm Labourer in 1911. Enlisted in January 1915. Served in France. Entered a theatre of war with 1st Bn on 26 May 1915. Wounded 4 December 1915 and June 1916. Died of wounds[3] 17 March 1918. Buried in Nine Elms British Cemetery, Poperinge, West-Vlaanderen, Belgium (GR X. C. 19.).[4] Memorials at All Saints, Chilcomb and East Worldham.

✠**MIDDLETON, BERTRAM C. ... L.-Corpl. ... A.P.C., Nov. 1914, Pte. Arg. and Suth. H. France. Wounded, Apl. 12, 1918. *Died of Wounds, May* 21, 1918.**
(7, Cheriton Road)

281. MIDDLETON, Bertram Charles, Private, 16457,[5] 2nd Bn[6] Argyll and Sutherland Highlanders, d. 21 May 1918 aged 25.

Son of John and Charlotte Middleton of 7, Cheriton Road. Born 1893. In 1911 working as a Law Clerk. Enlisted in November 1914 at Winchester. Served in France. Transferred from the Army Pay Corps. Wounded 12 April 1918 and Died of Wounds 21 May 1918. Buried in Winchester (West Hill) Old Cemetery.[7] Memorials at St Matthew's, St Paul's and St Thomas's School.

His brother Harold W. served on the Home Front as a Serjeant in the Royal Engineers and survived the War.

✠**MILES, WILLIAM ... Pte. ... Hants, Oct. 1916, Pte. France. Wounded, Nov. 1, 1917. *Killed in Action, Oct.* 2, 1918.**
(31, St. John's Terrace)

282. MILES, William, Private, 31805,[8] 2nd Bn The Hampshire Regiment, d. 2 October 1918 aged 42.

1 WO 372/13/215577 records Private rather than Lance-Corporal.
2 CWGC and SDGW have him as a Private
3 SDGW and R Hamps Notes. RH. citing Regimental Journals state he died of wounds. The archive also contains details of his wounds and hospitals where he was treated in England. Journal for May 1917 states he was awarded the French Croix de Guerre, but not recorded elsewhere.
4 CWGC.
5 WO 372/13/225217. S/16457. CWGC and SDGW have him as a Private. NB SJ writes 'Lance-Corporal an appointment not a rank, so reverts to Private if dies.'
6 1/8th Bn in SDGW.
7 CWGC.
8 WO 372/13/232265.

Son of Ann Miles of Weyhill, Andover. Born at Weyhill in 1872. Married Emma Temple in 1899 (31, St John's Terrace).[1] By 1911 they had six children and lived at 56, St John's Terrace. Frank born 1900, Frederick born 1902, Edith born 1904, Harry born 1906, Horace born 1907 and Sidney born 1910. A Groom in 1911. Eight children at his death. Enlisted in October 1916 at Winchester. Served in France. Entered theatre of war after beginning of 1916 with 15th Bn. Subsequently transferred to 2nd Bn.[2] Wounded 1 November 1917. Killed in Action 2 October 1918. Buried in Duhallow A.D.S. Cemetery, Ypres (Ieper), West-Vlaanderen, Belgium (GR VII. E. 23.).[3] Memorial at St John the Baptist.

☩**MILES, WILLIAM G. ... Pte. ... Hants, Sept. 1914, Pte. Mesopotamia. Taken Prisoner by Turks, Apl. 29, 1916, Kut. Died.**
   (93, Lower Brook Street)

283. MILES, William George, Private, 200893,[4] 1/4th Bn The Hampshire Regiment, d. 30 January 1917 aged 26.

Eldest son of William and Florence Miles of 93, Lower Brook Street (family at 58, Colebrook Street in 1901 and 1911). Born 1891. An Architect's Assistant in 1911. Worked with G Smith and Son, surveyors, also an Assistant to Mr Clarke of Walthamstow.[5] Enlisted in September 1914 at Winchester (2990).[6] Served in Mesopotamia. Entered a theatre of war with 1/4th Bn on 18 March 1915. Taken prisoner by Turks 29 April 1916 at Kut and died as a POW 30 January 1917. Commemorated on the Basra Memorial, Iraq (PR Panel 21 and 63.).[7] No Winchester memorial found.

☩**MILLARD, ALFRED J. ... Pte. ... . Hants, Aug, 1914. Dardanelles. Wounded and taken Prisoner by Bulgarians, Dec. 7, 1915. *Died, Jan.* 18, 1916, *Dupnitza.***
   (13, Colebrook Street)

1   BMD.
2   R Hamps Notes. RH. other information in the archive including that he 'Attested under Derby Scheme on 18.11.1915 called up 20.10.1916 and posted to 3rd Bn age 39 and 7 months.'
3   CWGC.
4   WO 372/13/232411.
5   R Hamps Notes. RH. for this and other information in this biography. Further details in the Regimental Archive. Bowker says he died 7.5.1916 on the 'Shumran bend' near Kut which date disagrees with other sources.
6   SDGW gives Salisbury Plain.
7   CWGC. William Miles memorials at St John the Baptist, could be William above or possibly this man.

284. MILLARD, Alfred James, Private, 9919,[1] 10th (Service) Bn The Hampshire Regiment, d. 18 January 1916 aged 19.

Son of Alfred and Ann Millard of 10, Water Lane (13, North Walls in 1911). Born 1897. Enlisted in August 1914 at Winchester and served at Gallipoli (Dardanelles) and Serbia. Wounded and taken prisoner by Bulgarians 7 December 1915 and died a POW 18 January 1916 at Dupnitza. Buried in Sofia War Cemetery, Bulgaria (GR I. F. 6.).[2] No Winchester memorial found.[3]

✠MILLER, ARTHUR E. ... L.-Corpl. ... Hants. Apl. 1916, Pte. France. *Killed in Action. Apl. 12, 1917, Arras.*
(37, Colson Road)

285. MILLER, Arthur Edward, Lance-Corporal, 23319,[4] 1st Bn The Hampshire Regiment, d. 12 April 1917 aged 25.

Second son of Henry Joshua and Elizabeth Miller of 37, Colson Road, Winnall. Born 1892. Married Daisy Beatrice Dewey in 1912 (39, North Street, Portsmouth).[5] Enlisted in April 1916 at Winchester. Served in France. Entered a theatre of war with 1st Bn at some point after the beginning of 1916.[6] Killed in Action 12 April 1917 at Arras. Commemorated in the Arras Memorial, Pas de Calais, France (PR Bay 6.).[7] Memorials at St John the Baptist.

His brother Ernest served in France as a Private in The Hampshire Regiment and survived the War.

✠MILLER, CHARLES K. ... Corpl. ... R.F.A., 1913, Gun. France. Wounded once. Taken Prisoner by Germans and escaped. *Died of Wounds, Apl. 2, 1917.*
(15, Hyde Abbey Road)

286. MILLER, Charles Knight, Corporal, 71750,[8] D Bty 159th Bde Royal Field Artillery, d. 2 April 1918 aged 22.

Son of Charles and Alice Miller of 15, Hyde Abbey Road. Born 1896. Husband of M. E. Miller of Long Eaton, Derby. Enlisted in 1913 at Winchester and served in France. Wounded once, taken prisoner and escaped. Died of Wounds

1 WO 372/14/1898.
2 CWGC.
3 ? St Maurice, lost.
4 WO 372/14/3841. D. DB.
5 R Hamps Notes. State husband of Mrs A. E. Miller, 20, St. John's Street, Winchester.
6 R Hamps Notes. RH.
7 CWGC.
8 WO 372/14/4638.

2 April 1917. Buried in Etaples Military Cemetery, Pas de Calais, France (GR XXXIII. C. 15.).[1] Memorials at St Bartholomew's and St Thomas's.

He had two brothers who served in the War. Herbert R. served in the Hampshire Yeomanry, then the Royal Army Ordnance Corps. Sydney W. served in West Africa, Salonica and Serbia in the Army Service Corps (Mechanical Transport) as a Private. He was promoted to Lance-Corporal. Both survived the War.

✠**MITCHELL, HARRY F. ... Pte. ... Hants, 1914, Pte. France. Killed in Action, Mch. 23, 1918.**
(60, Sussex Street)

287. MITCHELL, Harry F., Pioneer, 11212,[2] 11th (Service) Bn (Pioneer) The Hampshire Regiment, d. 23 March 1918 aged 26.

Only son of John and Emma Mitchell of Armsworth, Old Alresford. John and Emma Mitchell, 60, Sussex Street, Winchester (late of Armsworth, Alresford).[3] Born at Houghton, Stockbridge in 1892. Husband of Emma Mitchell. In 1911 he was a General Estate Labourer. Enlisted in 1914. Served in France. Entered a theatre of war with 11th Bn on 19 December 1915. Killed in Action 23 March 1918. Buried at Ste Emilie Valley Cemetery, Villers-Faucon, Somme, France (GR II. A. 20.).[4] Memorials at St Thomas's and Old Alresford.

✠**MITCHELL, JAMES J. ... Sergt. ... Hants, rejoined, Sergt. Home. Died, May 8, 1917.**
(38, Hyde Abbey Road)

288. MITCHELL, James J., Serjeant, 5226,[5] Depot The Hampshire Regiment,[6] d. 8 May 1917 aged 49.

Born at Portsmouth in 1880. Enlisted at Sheffield in 1886 and served in the army for twenty years according to his Discharge papers. While in the army he was awarded a Long Service and Good Conduct Medal and he qualified as a Gymnast. Husband of Jean Mitchell of 38, Hyde Abbey Road.[7] In 1911 was a Serjeant in The Hampshire Regiment, living at Colonel Moberly's.[8] An

1   CWGC.
2   WO 372/14/35546.
3   R Hamps Notes. RH. for this and other information in this biography. Further details in the Regimental Archive including a letter referring to his bravery and the circumstances of his death.
4   CWGC.
5   WO 372/ MIC not found 4.6.13.
6   RH.
7   Widow at same address.
8   See Greenstock.

Instructor at the Depot.¹ He died 8 May 1917 at the Red Cross Hospital, St Thomas's Street. Buried at Winchester (West Hill) Old Cemetery (SQ.38.G.2787).² Memorial at St Bartholomew's.

✠**MOORE, ALBERT ... Rfn. ... R.B., rejoined Aug. 1914, Rfn. France. Wounded, May 7, 1915. D.C.M., Russian Order of St. George 1914.** *Died of Wounds, May* **12, 1915,** *Boulogne.* **(17, St. Clement Street)**

289. MOORE, Albert, Private, 8110,³ 1st Bn The Rifle Brigade (The Prince Consort's Own), d. 12 May 1915 aged 35.

Son of the late Albert and Ellen Marshall Moore. Born at Aldershot in 1880. Married Emily M. Winkworth in 1914. CWGC gives an address for her of 17, St Clement Street.⁴ A Bricklayer's Labourer in 1911. Re-enlisted at Winchester under his mother's name Marshall, entered again, see above, as Marshall. First went to France 23 August 1914. Served in France and was awarded the Distinguished Conduct Medal in 1915 and the Russian Order of St George (4th Class) posthumously. His DCM citation is below. Wounded 7 May 1915 at Boulogne and Died of Wounds 12 May 1915. Buried in Boulogne Eastern Cemetery, Pas de Calais, France (GR VIII. C. 28.).⁵ Memorials at St Cross Chapel and St Thomas's.

DCM Citation 18.2.15. Citation *LG* 1 Apr. 1915.⁶

8110 Private A. Moore, 1st Bn Rifle Brigade. For gallant conduct on 19 December 1914, in carrying up ammunition on six occasions to the firing line whilst under fire.

Medal of St George 4th Class (Russia). 28 August 1915 (Posthumous).

✠**MORRAH, JOHN ... Major ... K.O.R. Lancs., 1896, 2nd Lieut. France. Despatches 1915.** *Killed in Action,* **Oct. 18, 1914. (25, Cranworth Road)**

290. MORRAH, John Henry, Major,⁷ 1st Bn The King's Own (Royal Lancaster

1 R Hamps Notes. RH. Further details in the Regimental Archive including a detailed account of his family services background and his funeral.
2 CWGC. 3/5226.
3 WO 372/ 14/65828; /23/62490.
4 CWGC.
5 CWGC.
6 *LG.*
7 WO 372/14/94412; /24/44725 MiD.
   www.kingsownmuseum.pws.com/galleryship005.htm. Sandhurst winning team

Regiment), d. 18 October 1914 aged 39.

Son of Col J. A. Morrah (60th Rifles) and Mary Morrah of The Willows, St Cross. Born at Derby, Derbyshire in 1876. Enlisted in 1896 and served in the Boer War in the Mounted Infantry. Severely wounded 17 December 1901 at Vredefort. Married Maud Florence Macgregor in London 1903: they had Margery born 1905 by 1911. His father died before 1911. Address for wife 129, Hamlet Gardens, Ravenscourt Park, London.[1] Went to France 23 August 1914. Served in France. Posthumously Mentioned in Despatches in 1915. Killed in Action 18 October 1914. Buried in Le Touquet Railway Crossing Cemetery, Comines-Warneton, Hainaut, Belgium (GR A. 6.).[2] Memorials at St Matthew's, St Paul's and St Thomas's.

LG 9 Mar. 1896 p. 1882. Honorary Queen's Cadet Royal Military College to be 2nd Lieut.

LG 9 Feb. 1915 p. 1659. 1st Bn.

✠MORRIS, CHARLES ... Pte. ... Hants, Aug. 1914, Pte. France. *Killed in Action, July* 1, 1916.
(11, Hedges Buildings)

291. MORRIS, Charles, Private, 9932,[3] 1st Bn The Hampshire Regiment, d. 1 July 1916 aged 21.

Son of William and Alice Morris of 11, Hedges Buildings, Alresford Road. Born 1895. An Errand Boy in 1911. Enlisted in August 1914 at Winchester. Served in France. Entered a theatre of war (Gallipoli) with 10th Bn on 5 August 1915, later transferred to the 1st Bn on the Western Front.[4] Killed in Action 1 July 1916. Commemorated on the Thiepval Memorial, Somme, France (PR Pier and Face 7 C and 7 B.).[5] Memorials at All Saints, St John the Baptist and Chilcomb (Morriss).

✠MOULD, JOHN A. S. ... Pte. ... Hants, Aug. 1914, Pte. France. *Died, Sept.* 20, 1916.
(15, St. John's Road)

292. MOULD, John Alfred Samuel, Private, 2266[6] 4th Bn The Hampshire

---

    etc. Photo 1897 in uniform. More on service in Boer War.
1 CWGC.
2 CWGC.
3 WO 372/14/96731. ?10th Bn Gallipoli. Atkinson, 2, pp. 170-1 'plunged in'.
4 Ditto
5 CWGC. First day of the Somme.
6 WO 372/ MIC not found.

Regiment, d. 20 September 1916 aged 19.

Son of John and Ellen Mould of 15, St John's Road.¹ Born 1897. A Printer's Errand Boy in 1911 living with his parents at 10, Percy Terrace, Water Lane. Joined on 19 March 1914 and served on the Home Front. Discharged 26 August 1914 as medically unfit.² Died 20 September 1916.³ Memorial at St John the Baptist.

✠MUDDIMAN, OLIVER ... Corpl. ... Coldstream Gds., 1898, Pte. France. *Missing (believed Killed)*, Sept. 22, 1914.
(61, Canon Street)

293. MUDDIMAN, Oliver, Lance-Corporal, 4868,⁴ 1st Bn Coldstream Guards, d. 14 September 1914 aged 30.

Son of Alfred and Kate Muddiman of 61, Canon Street.⁵ Born 1884. Married May Louisa Everett in 1907. A Milkman in 1901. Enlisted in 1898 at Aldershot.⁶ Died, 14 September 1914.⁷ Commemorated on La Ferté-Sous-Jouarre Memorial, Seine-et-Marne, France.⁸ Memorial at St Michael's.

He had four brothers who served in the War. William served in France as a Trooper, commissioned as Lieutenant and Quartermaster with the Hussars. Bertie served in France as a Trooper, then Lance-Corporal in the Hussars and then in the Coldstream Guards, and was wounded 5 December 1915. Stephen served as an Able Seaman in the Mercantile Marine in 1907. Later aboard HMAS Panama. Ernest served in France as a Gunner in the Royal Horse Artillery. They all survived the War.

✠MULDOWNEY, JOHN ... Pte. ... American Legion, June 1916, Pte. France. Wounded, July 15, 1917. *Killed in Action, Aug. 8, 1918.*
(15A, Greenhill Road)

294. MULDOWNEY, John, Private, 818241,⁹ 26th Bn (formerly 140th Bn)

1 Census 1911.
2 SJ. R Hamps Notes. RH. No mention in Regimental Journal.
3 CWGC reference not found; no GR.
4 WO 372/14/130904. www.wwlphotos.com/ColdstreeamGuards Photo.
5 See Canon Street pamphlet for Muddiman.
6 SDGW.
7 SDGW for 'Died' SJ. See also de Ruvigny entry.
8 CWGC. Also 4568 SDGW.
9 www.collectionscanada.gc.cahttp://www.veterans.gc.ca/eng/collections/virtualmem/Detail/278243 Ref. RG, 150.6467-08-pdf. His two Canada Memorial Cross sold by Spink 2011. Spink Catalogue 24 November 2011 (London: Spink and Co.2011), p. 123.

Canadian Infantry (New Brunswick Regiment), d. 8 August 1918 age 20.

Lived at 35, Moreland Street, Roxbury, Mass., USA. Son of Mrs Rose Muldowney of Tree Cottage, Greenhill Road, Winchester. Born April 1898. A Labourer. Enlisted in June 1916 at Saint John, New Brunswick. According to the *WWSR* he served in France in the American Legion, however this seems unlikely. He was a Canadian National. Served in the Canadian Infantry.[1] He had bronchitis in December 1916 but was pronounced fit for duty later that month according to his army medical records. Wounded 15 July 1917.[2] Killed in Action 8 August 1918. Buried in Wood Cemetery, Marcelcave, Somme, France (GR A.2.).[3] Memorials at St Matthew's, St Paul's and St Thomas's School.

✠MUNDY, ALFRED ... Pte. ... Hants, Nov. 11, 1915, Pte. France. *Killed in Action, Sept.* 9, 1916.
(14, Granville Place)

295. MUNDY, Alfred, Private, 21373,[4] 11th (Service) Bn (Pioneer) The Hampshire Regiment, d. 9 September 1916 aged 27.

Second son of the late Joseph Mundy and of Mary Ann Mundy of Avington, Itchen Abbas (formerly of 14, Granville Place).[5] Born 1891. A Painter in 1911. Enlisted in November 1915 at Winchester. Served in France. Entered a theatre of war with 11th Bn after the beginning of 1916.[6] Reported missing, later as Killed in Action 9 August 1916. Commemorated on the Thiepval Memorial, Somme, France (PR Pier and Face 7 C and 7 B.).[7] Memorial at St Peter Chesil.

His brother George, listed below, was Killed in Action 12 April 1915.

✠MUNDY, GEORGE ... Pte. ... Dorset, Aug. 1914, Pte, France. *Killed in Action, Apl.* 12, 1915.
(14, Granville Place)

296. MUNDY, George, Private, 6776, 1st Bn The Dorsetshire Regiment, d. 17 April 1915 aged 21.[8]

Son of Mary Ann Mundy of Avington, Itchen Abbas (Formerly 14, Granville

---

1 CWGC.
2 *WWSR.*
3 CWGC.
4 WO 372/14/142854.
5 CWGC. See George Mundy below.
6 R Hamps Notes. RH. for this and other information in this biography.
7 CWGC.
8 WO 372/14/143049; also CWGC give date of death as 17 April.

Place).¹ Born 1896. An Errand Boy in 1911. Enlisted in August 1914 at Southampton. Served in France. Killed in Action 17 April 1915.² Buried in Woods Cemetery, Zillebeke, Ypres (Ieper), West-Vlaanderen, Belgium (GR I. B. 23.).³ Memorial at St Peter Chesil.

His brother Alfred, listed above, was Killed in Action 9 September 1916.

✠**MUNT, THOMAS W. ... Pte. ... Hants, 1911, Pte. R.E. India, Mesopotamia,Kut. Taken Prisoner by Turks, Apl. 26, 1916. Died, Sept. 30, 1916, Afion-Kara-Ilissan.**
(13, King Alfred Place)

297. MUNT, Thomas,⁴ Private, 200165,⁵ 1/4th Bn The Hampshire Regiment, d. 30 September 1916 aged 23.

Son of Thomas and Louisa Munt of 13, King Alfred Place (sometime of Salcot Lodge, Worthy Road, Winchester). Born 1894. In 1911 he was a Printer's Compositor, before enlisting at Winchester (1795). Served in India and Mesopotamia. Transferred from the Royal Engineers and was promoted to Signaller. Entered a theatre of war (Mesopotamia) with 1/4th Bn on 18 March 1915.⁶ Taken prisoner by Turks 26 April 1916 at Kut and died a POW 30 September 1916 at Afion-Kara-Hissan in Turkey. Buried at Baghdad (North Gate) War Cemetery, Iraq (GR XXI. M. 18.).⁷ Memorial at St Bartholomew's.

His brother Cyril F. served in Egypt, Palestine and Syria in the Hampshire Yeomanry, the Hussars and the Staffordshire Yeomanry. He survived the War.

✠**NEWBY, WILLIAM E. ... Stoker ... R.N., 1912, Stoker. North Sea; H.M.S.** *Queen Mary.* **Killed in Action, May 31, 1916, Jutland.**
(1, Ashley Terrace)

298. NEWBY, William Ernest Herbert, Stoker 1st Class, K/16532,⁸ HMS Queen Mary Royal Navy, d. 31 May 1916 aged 23.

1   Also recorded as of Avington, Itchen Abbas.
2   Discrepancy over date of death.
3   CWGC.
4   Thomas W. in *WWSR.*
5   WO 372/14/147334.
6   R Hamps Notes. RH. for this and other information in this biography. Gives date of death as 20 September. Bowker says he died at 'Airan'. Mr and Mrs Munt received a letter, in the archive, through the Comite Internationale de la Croix-Rouge, commiserating over their son's death and giving some reassurance about Turkish care of POWs.
7   CWGC.
8   ADM 188/900/165832. Check 5832 or 532.

Son of the late John Newby and Annie Eliza Goodenough (formerly Newby) of 1, Ashley Terrace, Gladstone Street. Born at Kilmeston, 12 July 1892.[1] An apprentice Hot and Cold Water Fitter in 1911. A Whitesmith when he enlisted in 1912. Served aboard the Queen Mary in the North Sea. Killed in Action 31 May 1916 at the battle of Jutland. Commemorated on the Portsmouth Naval Memorial, Portsmouth (PR 19.).[2] Memorials at St Matthew's and St Paul's.

✠**NEWMAN, ARTHUR W. ... L.-Corpl. ... Hants, 1906, Band Boy. Egypt, France. Wounded, Apl. 1918. *Died of Wounds, Apl.* 1918.**
(29, Colson Road)

299. NEWMAN, Arthur,[3] Private, 27934, 6th (Wiltshire Yeomanry) Bn The Duke of Edinburgh's (Wiltshire Regiment), d. 13 April 1918 aged 29.

Second son of the late Frank (a Sergeant in The Hamspshire Regiment) and Mary Jane Newman of 29, Colson Road. Enlisted in 1906 at Winchester. Born 1889. A Drummer in 1911 with The Hampshire Regiment stationed at Wynberg Cape of Good Hope, South Africa. Served in Egypt, Flanders and France during the War. Formerly 6787, The Hampshire Regiment. Entered a theatre of war after beginning of 1916 with The Hampshire Regiment then transferred to The Wiltshire Regiment.[4] Initially reported missing on 10 April. Later noted as wounded, Died of Wounds 13 April 1918. Buried at Harlebeke New British Cemetery, Harelbeke, West-Vlaanderen, Belgium (GR II. D. 11.).[5] Memorial at St John the Baptist.

✠**NEWMAN, REGINALD W. ... Pte. ... Hants, Nov. 1911, Boy. France. Wounded, Apl. 9 and July 22, 1917. *Died of Wounds, Sept.* 3, 1918**
(29, Colson Road)

300. NEWMAN, Reginald Wilfred, Private, 8968,[6] 1st Bn The Hampshire Regiment, d. 2 September 1918 aged 20.

Youngest son of late Serjeant F. Newman (2nd Bn The Hampshire Regiment) and Mrs M. J. Newman of 29, Colson Road, Winnall. Born 1898.[7] Living

1. Census 1911. Ratings Service Papers say b 12 July 1892 at Winchester. 1901 census 1893; 1911 census suggests 1892.
2. CWGC. Hepper, 2006, p. 60. Nine survivors.
3. WO 372/14/205929. Arthur W in *WWSR*.
4. SDGW. R Hamps Notes. RH. for this and other information in this biography. See photo 1910 Journal p. 202.
5. CWGC.
6. WO 372/14/208519. Discrepancy over date of death MIC gives 2 September.
7. Identification most likely in 1901 and 1911.

at Colonel Moberly's in 1901.¹ Enlisted in November 1911 at Winchester, Drummer. Served in France during the War. Entered a theatre of war with 1st Bn at some point after the beginning of 1916. Wounded 9 April and 22 July 1917. Killed in Action 2 September 1918. Buried in Dury Crucifix Cemetery, Pas de Calais, France (GR III. C. 50.).² Memorial at St John the Baptist.

✠**NEWTON, ALAN H. ... 2nd Lieut. ... Middlesex, May 1915, 2nd Lieut. France. Wounded, Apl. 7, 1916.** *Died of Wounds, Apl. 7, 1916, Albert.*
   (Morn Dale, Bereweeke Road)

301. NEWTON, Alan Herbert, 2nd Lieutenant,³ 2nd Bn The Duke of Cambridge's Own (Middlesex Regiment), d. 7 April 1916 aged 24.

Son of the late Thomas Edwin and Gertrude Newton of 1, Clifton Hill, Winchester.⁴ Born 1892. In 1911 was a student Land Agent. Enlisted in May 1915. Served in France. Died of Wounds 7 April 1916 at Albert. Buried in Millencourt Communal Cemetery Extension, Somme, France (GR C. 38.).⁵ Memorials at St Matthew's, St Paul's and St Cross Chapel.

✠**NORGATE, PERCY D. ... Sig. ... R.G.A., Apl. 1917, Sig. France. Taken Prisoner by Germans, Mch. 21, 1918.** *Died, Aug. 10, 1918, Valenciennes.*
   (4, Brassey Road)

302. NORGATE, Percy Douglas, Gunner,⁶ 153118, 233rd Siege Bty Royal Garrison Artillery, d. 10 August 1918 aged 38.

Son of the late Mr and Mrs Michael Norgate of Bighton. Born at Bighton in 1880. Married Annie Elizabeth Barnett in 1915 of 46, Andover Road. A Manager of a Grocery in 1911, living as a boarder. Enlisted in April 1917 at Winchester. Served in France. Taken prisoner 21 March 1918 – the first day of the German Spring Offensive - and died 10 August 1918 at Valenciennes. Buried at Valenciennes (St Roch) Communal Cemetery, Nord, France (GR V. E. 20.).⁷ Memorials at Holy Trinity, St Matthew's, St Paul's and Bighton (D. Norgate).

---

1 Check 1901, 1911. See Greenstock for Moberly.
2 CWGC. SDGW KIA.
3 WO 372/14/211506; 339/497/18, Service Papers. No photo found.
4 CWGC.
5 CWGC.
6 WO 372/15/361. MIC, SDGW and CWGC have him as a Gunner.
7 CWGC.

✠**OFFER, ALBERT... Pte. ... Hants, June 1916, Pte. France, Salonica. Wounded, Sept. 1, 1918.** *Died of Wounds, Sept. 17, 1918.*
(2, Abbey Passage)

303. OFFER, Albert, Private, 380211,[1] 10th (Service) Bn The Hampshire Regiment, d. 17 September 1918 aged 33.

Eldest son of Albert and Sophia Offer 27, Canon Street in 1901 and 1911, later Sophia at 2, St Cross Road. Born at Cheriton in 1886. Married Gertrude Cobb in 1910, they lived at 2, Abbey Passage. A Nurseryman in 1911. Enlisted in June 1916 at Winchester. Served in France and Salonica. Formerly 31385, The Worcestershire Regiment.[2] Entered a theatre of war (France and Flanders) with 15th Battalion, The Hampshire Regiment.[3] Transferred to the 10th Battalion, Hampshire Regiment in Salonika. Wounded 1 September 1918 and Died of Wounds 17 September 1918. Buried in Mikra British Cemetery, Kalamaria, Greece (GR 295.).[4] Memorials St John the Baptist and St Michael's.

✠**OFFER, Cecil H... Sergt. ... Hants, 1911, Pte. India, Persian Gulf.** *Killed in Action Jan. 21, 1916.*
(2, Abbey Passage)

304. Offer, Cecil Henry. Lance-Sergeant,[5] 200116, later corporal, 1686 1/4th Hampshire Regiment, d. 21 January 1916.

Son of Albert and Sophia Offer 27, Canon Street in 1901 and 1911. Born 1893.[6] In 1911 a Chemical Laboratory Assistant. A territorial soldier, he enlisted in Winchester in 1911.[7] Served in India and Persian Gulf. Entered a theatre of war (Mesopotamia) with 1/4th Battalion, Hampshire Regiment on 18 March 1915.[8] Initially posted as missing, later confirmed as Killed in Action 21 January 1916 at Umm El Hanna. Commemorated on Basra Memorial, Iraq. (PR 21 and 63). Memorials at St Bartholomew's, St John the Baptist and St Michael's.

✠**OFFER, JOHN A. ... A.B. ... R.N., 1911, Boy. English Channel. North Sea; H.M.S.** *Impregnable, Colossus, Bulwark,* **and**

---

1 WO 372/15/44335. Does not mention The Worcestershire Regiment. SDGW. .
2 SDGW.
3 R Hamps Notes. RH. for this and other information in this biography. Regimental Archive refers to him as 'the dearly-loved husband of Mrs. A. Offer, of 18, St. John's Road'. Regimental Journal says wounded 3 September.
4 CWGC.
5 WO 372/15/44351 Corporal. Lance-Sergeant (CWGC).
6 Census 1911 Place of birth.
7 SDGW.
8 R Hamps Notes. RH. for this and other information in this biography.

Black Prince. Killed in Action, May 31, 1916, Jutland.
(105, Colebrook Street)

305. OFFER, John Alfred, Able Seaman, J/13594,[1] HMS Black Prince Royal Navy, d. 31 May 1916 aged 20.

Son of the late Alfred Richard Offer and Jessie Louisa Offer of 105, Lower Colebrook Street. Born 11 June 1895 St Maurice. An Errand Boy in 1911. Enlisted 11 June 1913, his 14th birthday, as a Boy having previously been a Baker's Boy.[2] Served on HMS Impregnable, Colossus and Bulwark. Killed in Action 31 May 1916 at the Battle of Jutland while serving on HMS Black Prince which blew up and sank with no survivors.[3] Memorial on the Portsmouth Naval Memorial, (PR 13.).[4] No Winchester memorial found.[5]

✠**OFFER, WILLIAM J. ... Pte. ... Hants, Sept. 1914, Pte. Gallipoli, France. Wounded, Apl. 1, 1916. *Killed in Action, Apl. 23, 1917, Mouchez.***
(77, Lower Brook Street)

306. OFFER, William, Private, 10891,[6] 2nd Bn The Hampshire Regiment, d. 23 April 1917 aged 26.

Son of William and Amy Offer of 77, Lower Brook Street. Born 1891. A Fellmonger's Labourer in 1911. Worked for Mr N H Forder Woolstapler. Married with one child, lived at 73, Lower Brook Street. Enlisted in September 1914 at Winchester. Served at Gallipoli (Dardanelles) and in France. William Offer entered a theatre of war (Gallipoli) with 2nd Bn on 24 August 1915. Wounded 1 April, August and September 1916.[7] Killed in Action 23 April 1917 at Mouchez. Commemorated on the Arras Memorial, Pas de Calais, France (PR Bay 6.).[8] No Winchester memorial found.

✠**OPENSHAW, HAROLD M. ... Lieut. ... Norfolk, 1900, 2nd Lieut. France. Wounded, Aug. 24, 1914. Taken Prisoner by Germans. *Died in Hospital, Thulin.***
(Fairlawn, Sleepers Hill)

1 ADM 188/674/13594.
2 Not his 14th birthday if born in 1896. Census 1911.
3 Hepper, 2006, p. 63.
4 CWGC.
5 ? St Maurice, lost.
6 WO 372/15/44419.
7 R Hamps Notes. RH. for this and other information in this biography. Gives his address as 73, Lower Brook Street, his parents at 77. More detail of his wounds and note that although missing on 23 April, his body was not found until 11 June.
8 CWGC.

307. OPENSHAW, Harold Michael, Lieutenant,[1] 1st Bn The Norfolk Regiment, d. 28 August 1914 aged 24.

Son of Lt.-Col. and Mrs B. D. Openshaw of Fairlawn, 11, Christchurch Road.[2] Born at Edinburgh, Midlothian in 1890.[3] In 1901 he was at boarding school in Kent. In 1911 he was a 2nd Lieutenant 1st Bn The Norfolk Regiment, stationed at Malplaquet Barracks, Churchill House Staff House, Aldershot. Served in France. Wounded 24 April and taken prisoner by Germans. Died in Thulin Hospital, Belgium 28 April 1914 and was buried in Thulin New Communal Cemetery. His grave is lost and he is now commemorated on the Kipling Memorial at Cement House Cemetery, Langemark-Poelkapelle, West-Vlaanderen, Belgium.[4] Memorial at Christ Church.

✠OSBORNE, PERCY ... Tpr. ... R. Dragoons, Tpr. France. *Killed in Action, Nov. 13, 1914.*
(5, The Weirs)

308. OSBORNE, Percy Henry, Private, 5509,[5] C Sqdn 1st (Royal) Dragoons, d. 13 November 1914 aged 27.

Son of Alfred Osborne of 5, The Weirs. Born 1884.[6] A General Labourer in 1911. Enlisted at Winchester. Served in France. Killed in Action 13 November 1914. Commemorated on the Ypres (Menin Gate) Memorial, Ypres (Ieper), West-Vlaanderen, Belgium (PR Panel 5.).[7] Memorial at St Peter Chesil.

His brother Alfred served in France as a Trooper in the Dragoon Guards, was wounded in 1916 and survived the War.

✠PACK, JOHN T. ... [BLANK] ... R.N., 1895. *Killed in Action, Jan. 12, 1918, H.M.S. Opal.*
(44, Upper Brook Street)

309. PACK, John Thomas, Able Seaman, 191353 (PO), HMS Opal Royal Navy, d. 12 January 1918 aged 37.[8]

1 WO 372/15/57893. Photo of him at ww1photos.com/NorfolkRegiment-Directory.
2 Sleepers Hill and Christ Church Rd are not contiguous. Chris Grover pers. comm. states that Fairlawn was a Sleepers Hill address at this date. Christchurch Road was the nearest highway.
3 *WWSR* has him enlisting in 1900, when he was apparently only 10.
4 CWGC.
5 WO 372/15/67455.
6 Discrepancy over age. Birth date from 1911 census.
7 CWGC.
8 Only census records for John Pack do not match with the birth date in Naval Casualties 1914-1919 Database. Naval and Military Press 2010.

Born 27 November 1880.[1] An Errand Boy. Enlisted 27 November 1898.[2] HMS Opal, a destroyer, steamed on to rocks and broke her back. One survivor.[3] Killed in Action[4] 12 January 1918. Buried in Lyness Royal Naval Cemetery, Orkney (GR B. 192.).[5] Memorials at Holy Trinity and St John the Baptist.

His brother Edward served in India, Egypt, Palestine and France as a Private in The Hampshire Regiment, was wounded 26 August 1918 and survived the War.

⌘**PAGE, HENRY C. ... Spr. ... Hants, Dec. 1915, Pte. R.E. France.** *Killed in Action, Aug.* **21, 1916.**
  (3, St. George's Terrace)

310. PAGE, Henry Charles, Pioneer, 128843,[6] Royal Engineers, d. 21 August 1916.

Born at Wonston in 1879.[7] Enlisted in December 1915 at Winchester and served in France. Formerly 21892, The Hampshire Regiment.[8] Entered theatre of war after beginning of 1916 with Hampshire Regiment.[9] Served with 5th RN Special Bde Corps of Royal Engineers. Killed in Action 21 August 1916. Commemorated on the Thiepval Memorial, Somme, France (PR Pier and Face 8 A and 8 D.).[10] No Winchester memorial found.

⌘**PAGE, THOMAS ... C.S.M. ... K.R.R.C., Pte. Home.** *Died.*
  (11, Monks Road)

311. PAGE, Thomas Alfred,[11] Company Serjeant Major, 9028,[12] The King's Royal Rifle Corps Depot, d. 2 October 1916 aged 45.

Son of the late Thomas and Elizabeth Page of Shermanbury, Sussex. Born at

---

1 Brother Edward at 44, Upper Brook Street. Next of Kin.
2 ADM 188/327/191353. Discrepancy in his enlistment records: *WWSR* states 1895; ratings papers say boy second class 1896 and also refer to enlistment in 1898. Maybe an issue of his age?
3 Hepper, 2006, pp. 115,116.
4 His naval record states that he died of something other than disease, accident or enemy action – i.e. he drowned. *WWSR* states Killed in Action.
5 CWGC.
6 WO 372/15/89455.
7 1881 census suggests 1879. 1911 suggests Harry Page born 1880 with a wife and four children, same birth date and place but 7, St Georges not 3, St Georges Terrace. Married Emily in 1899. They had four children by 1911. Ernest born 1901, Reginald born 1903, Lucy born 1906 and Frederick born 1909. Likely to be this man.
8 SDGW.
9 R Hamps Notes. RH.
10 CWGC.
11 Thomas only in *WWSR*.
12 No MIC identified.

Steyning, Sussex in 1870.¹ Married Alice Botting in 1907 (11, Monks Road).² Enlisted at Chichester and served in the Boer War, where he was wounded 7 August 1900 at Amersfoort. In 1911 was a Corporal 1st Bn The King's Royal Rifle Corps, New Barracks, Gosport. Served on the Home Front during the War. Died 2 October 1916. Buried in Portsdown (Christ Church) Military Cemetery, Hampshire (GR B. 67.).³ Memorial at St Bartholomew's.

✠PARR, BENJAMIN .... L.S. ... R.N., 1897, Boy. Grand Fleet, Mediterranean. *Died of Pneumonia*, Oct. 5, 1915.
   (7, Alresford Road)

312. PARR, Benjamin, Leading Seaman, 231854,⁴ HMS Lychais Royal Navy, d. 5 October 1918 aged 31.

Son of Frank and Annie Parr of Batley, Yorkshire. Born at Batley 4 January 1887. Became a Miner. Married Emily Arnold in 1913 (Emily Kate Parr 7, Morn Hill Road).⁵ In 1901 he was living with his uncle and aunt and working as a Pony Driver in a pit in Yorkshire. Enlisted in a Lancashire Regiment in May 1904 and transferred to the Royal Navy in August 1904 according to his Army Service Record.⁶ Naval Record says he signed up for twelve years on 4 January 1905. Served with the Grand Fleet in the Mediterranean during the War. Died of influenza,⁷ 5 October 1918. Buried in Gibraltar (North Front) Cemetery, Gibraltar (GR E. 4048.).⁸ Memorials at All Saints and St John the Baptist.

✠PARRACK, RICHARD R. ... Pte. ... Hants, rejoined Aug. 4, 1914. Pte. Dardanelles, Egypt, France. Wounded once. *Wounded and Missing*, Oct. 16, 1916.
   (13, Chester Road)

313. PARRACK, Richard Ralph, Private, 5698,⁹ 2nd Bn The Hampshire Regiment, d. 17 October 1916 aged 36.

1   1871 census suggests 1870, 1911 suggests 1869.
2   BMD.
3   CWGC.
4   ADM 188/410/231854. PO/231854. If this man in *WWSR* he would have joined the Navy at some ten years old. Gives date of death as 5 October 1918, not 1915, and the cause as influenza. Need to compare with record of army service with regard to a Lancashire Regiment – East Lancashire or Lancashire Fusiliers, and also date of transfer, 1905? Tattoos of mother and child in memory of his mother. 1891 census suggests birth as 1888.
5   BMD.
6   WO 96/695/249.
7   Naval Casualties says disease.
8   CWGC.
9   WO 372/15/128114.

Son of James and Helen Parrack of 1, Tower Street, Alton.[1] Born at Bentworth in 1881. Married Emily Harding in 1907. By 1911 they had Emily Maisey, born 1909 and Alice Helen born 1911. (Emily Offer (formerly Parrack) 1, Tower Street, Alton. Served in the Jidballi and Somaliland Expeditions (1902-04).[2] In 1911 he was a House Painter. Re-enlisted 4 August 1914. Served at Gallipoli (Dardanelles), Egypt and France. Entered a theatre of war (Gallipoli) with 2nd Bn on 25 April 1915.[3] Wounded and Missing 17 October 1916. Commemorated on the Thiepval Memorial, Somme, France (PR Pier and Face 7 C and 7 B.).[4] Memorials at St John the Baptist, Winchester and at Alton: main memorial, All Saints Church and St Lawrence Church.

✠PATTERSON, CECIL J. ... O.S. ... RN., 1902, O.S. H.M.S. Good Hope. Killed in Action, Nov. 1, 1914. Chilian Coast. (47, St. Catherine's Road)

314. PATTERSON, Cecil James,[5] Able Seaman, 208036,[6] HMS Good Hope Royal Navy, d. 1 November 1914 aged 30.

Son of Charles and Emma Patterson of 47, St Catherine's Road. Born 8 October 1884.[7] Enlisted on 8 October 1902 for twelve years. Formerly a Telegraph Messenger. In 1911 was an Able Seaman, stationed at Royal Naval College, Osborne, Whippingham, Isle of Wight. Killed in Action 1 November 1914 off the Chilean coast when HMS Good Hope was lost with all hands. Commemorated on the Portsmouth Naval Memorial (PR 2.).[8] Memorial at All Saints.

He had three brothers who served in the War. Ernest served as a Private in the National Reserve and The Gloucestershire Regiment on the Home Front. Harry served in the North Sea as an Able Seaman in the Royal Navy. Sydney A. served in France as a Driver in the Royal Field Artillery. All three survived the War.

1   CWGC gives Helen Offer of Alton.
2   CWGC.
3   R Hamps Notes. RH. for this and other material in this biography. Noted as wounded in action Dec 1916 Journal. Note of posthumous baby: PARRACK .—On May 11th, Eva Kate Parrack (Babady), infant daughter of Mrs. R. Parrack, 14, Tower Street, Alton, and Pte. R. R. Parrack, Hampshire Regiment (wounded and missing since October 18th, 1916).
4   CWGC.
5   CWGC gives Cyril. SJ writes 'Cyril on official records'.
6   ADM 188/363/208036. Tattoos: pierced heart right arm; flag left arm; LOVE left forefinger.
7   1891 and 1911 censuses suggest 1885 for birth.
8   CWGC. Hepper, 2006, p. 28. Note Lansley etc for varying references to this action.

☦**PAYNE, HENRY J. ... Pte. ... T.R., Dec. 1916, Pte. M.G.C. . France.** *Killed in Action, Aug. 5, 1917.*
(68, Brassey Road)

315. PAYNE, Henry John, Private, 85422,[1] 123rd Coy Machine Gun Corps (Infantry), d. 5 August 1917 aged 30.

Son of David and Annie Payne of Compton, Newbury, Berkshire. Born at Compton, Berkshire in 1888. Married Edith Mary (68, Brassey Road).[2] In 1911 he was a Grocer's Assistant lodging at Beale, Berkshire. Enlisted in December 1916 at Winchester. Served in France and transferred from the Training Reserve. Killed in Action 5 August 1917. Commemorated on the Ypres (Menin Gate), Ypres (Ieper), West-Vlaanderen, Belgium (PR Panel 56.).[3] Memorials at St Matthew's, St Paul's, the Primitive Methodist Chapel in Parchment Street and University of Winchester King Alfred's College Old Chapel (Winton Memorial Room).

☦**PEARMAN, THOMAS B. ... Rfn. ... R.B., 1900, Rfn. France.** *Killed in Action, May 4, 1915.*
(20, Victoria Road)

316. PEARMAN, Thomas Brown, Private, 8082,[4] 4th Bn The Rifle Brigade (The Prince Consort's Own), d. 14 May 1915 aged 32.[5]

Son of William J. and Jane Pearman. Born at Glemsford, Suffolk in 1883.[6] Enlisted in 1900 at London and served in France during the War. In 1901 in The Rifle Brigade at New Barracks, Alverstoke, Gosport. 1911 at Winchester Barracks. Killed in Action 14 May 1915. Commemorated on the Ypres (Menin Gate) Memorial, Ypres (Ieper), West-Vlaanderen, Belgium (PR Panel 46 - 48 and 50.).[7] Memorial at St Bartholomew's.

☦**PEARMAN, WILLIAM H. ... Pte. ... Northants, Aug. 1914, Pte. France. Wounded, 1915.** *Killed in Action, Oct. 1916.*
(13, Staple Garden)

317. PEARMAN, William Henry, Private, 10100,[8] 5th (Service) Bn

---

1 WO 372/15/160852.
2 CWGC.
3 CWGC.
4 WO 372/15/173728.
5 CWGC and SDGW state date of death as 14 May 1915. *WWSR* misprint?
6 Birth year suggested by 1891 census. Not found in other censuses except 1901 of which SJ writes : 'Born at Glemsford, Sussex (*sic*). Crossed out and Sudbury put in!'.
7 CWGC.
8 WO 372/15/173751 states he died of wounds.

(Pioneers) The Northamptonshire Regiment, d. 20 October 1916 aged 23.

Son of George and Bessie Pearman of 13, Staple Garden. Born 1894.[1] Enlisted in August 1914 at Hants, Northampton[2] and served in France. Wounded in 1915. Died of Wounds[3] 20 October 1916. Buried in Heilly Station Cemetery, Mericourt-l'Abbe, Somme, France (GR V. C. 43.).[4] Memorial at St Thomas's.

He had two brothers who served in the War. Alfred served in France, Salonica and Palestine as a Private, promoted to Company Quartermaster Serjeant in the Middlesex Regiment and the Machine Gun Corps. George served on the Home Front as a Private, promoted to corporal in the Army Service Corps. They both survived the War.

✠PEARSON, GEORGE A. ... Pte. ... Canadians, Aug. 1914, Pte. France. *Killed in Action,* July 25, 1916.
(85, Lower Brook Street)

318.   PEARSON, George Arthur, Private, 11275, 4th Bn Canadian Infantry (Central Ontario Regiment), d. 25 July 1916 aged 22.[5]

Son of John and Ellen Pearson of 85, Lower Brooks (*sic*) Street. Born at Kentish Town, London 1 January 1892.[6] An Errand Boy in 1911. Emigrated to Canada in May 1913 aboard the Ausonia, and took Canadian nationality. On the passenger transcript he appears as a General Labourer.[7] Belonged to the 36th Regiment militia at the time of his enlistment in August 1914 or September 1914 and served in France.[8] Killed in Action 25 July 1916 'while attached 1st Brigade wiring party, and at work in a sap at the ?Bleft, Ypres, at about 10pm on July 25th 1916 he was killed by an enemy mine which exploded directly beneath the party'.[9] Commemorated on the Ypres (Menin Gate) Memorial, Ypres (Ieper), West-Vlaanderen, Belgium (PR Panel 18 - 24 - 26 - 30.).[10] No Winchester memorial found.

1   1901 census.
2   SDGW.
3   SDGW alters KIA to DOW.
4   CWGC.
5   Slip in *WWSR* here, July should be in italics.
6   Most likely match in 1911 census suggests born 1894.
7   Reference for passenger transcript and Canadian attestation papers where he is down as a General Labourer.
8   *WWSR*; www.collectionscanada.gc.ca/RG150 . Canadian Attestation Papers. Gives enlistment date as 22 September 1914. Place of enlistment is illegible on his records. Gives Next of Kin as Ellen Pearson of Lower Brook Street.
9   SJ adds this quote.
10 CWGC. Brooks Street.

✠**PENSON, LIONEL R. ... C.Q.M.S. ... R.F., Aug. 1915, Pte. France. Wounded. *Died of Wounds, Aug. 6, 1917, Etaples.* [No address given]**

319. PENSON, Lionel Robert, Company Quarter Master Serjeant, 19380,[1] 26th (Service) Bn (Bankers) The Royal Fusiliers (City of London Regiment), d. 6 August 1917 aged 32.[2]

Eldest son of Robert and Esther Penson of Idbury, Oxfordshire where he was born in 1886.[3] Enlisted in August 1915 at Oxford. Served in The Royal Fusiliers, wounded. Died of Wounds 6 August 1917. Buried at Etaples Military Cemetery, Pas de Calais, France (GR XXII.O.18A.).[4] No Winchester memorial found. Commemorated on South Leigh War Memorial, Oxfordshire.

✠**PERRIN, ALFRED J. ... Sergt. ... R.B., 1905, Rfn. Belgium, France. *Killed in Action, May 8, 1915, Ypres.* (34, Water Lane)**

320. PERRIN, Alfred John, Serjeant, 6925,[5] 4th Bn The Rifle Brigade (The Prince Consort's Own), d. 8 May 1915 age unknown.

Born at Clerkenwell, Middlesex.[6] Enlisted in 1905 at Dalston, Middlesex, resided at Islington Middlesex.[7] Served in France. Killed in action 8 May 1915 at Ypres. Commemorated on the Ypres (Menin Gate) Memorial, Ypres (Ieper), West-Vlaanderen, Belgium (PR Panel 46 - 48 and 50.).[8] Memorials at St John the Baptist.

✠**PERRY, PERCY ... Pte. ... Lancers, rejoined Aug. 1914, Tpr. A.V.C., R.F. France. *Killed in Action, May 9, 1918.* (21, Victoria Road)**

321. PERRY, Percy George,[9] Private, GS/69524,[10] 7th (Extra Reserve) Bn The Royal Fusiliers (The City of London Regiment), d. 9 May 1918 aged 30.

Son of Albin George and Emily Perry. Born 1887. Married Harriet Marsh of 14

1   WO 372/15/196012.
2   See also Charles Freeman.
3   1891 census. Not found in other censuses.
4   CWGC. www.scribd.com records him as commemorated on South Leigh War Memorial.
5   WO 372/15/204090.
6   SDGW: not found in censuses.
7   SDGW.
8   CWGC.
9   Percy only in *WWSR*.
10 WO 372/15/208066. GS/69524.

Canada Road, Woolston in 1917. In 1911 he was a Private in the 12th (Prince of Wales's) Royal Lancers, stationed at Cantonments Potchefstroom, Transvaal, South Africa. Re-enlisted in August in 1914. Served in France, arriving among the early troops, on 15 August 1914. Transferred from 12th Lancers (139) to the Army Veterinary Corps (897), then The Royal Fusiliers. Killed in Action 9 May 1918. Buried in Mesnil Communal Cemetery Extension, Somme, France (GR I. A, 1.).[1] Memorial at St Bartholomew's.

His father and brother served in the War. Albin, his father served in Mesopotamia and India as a Private in The Hampshire Regiment, then a Sapper, Royal Engineers. Frank, his brother served in France as a Private in The Leicestershire Regiment, then transferred to the Royal Air Force. They both survived the War.

✠**PHILLIPS, ARTHUR ... L.-Corpl. ... Hants, Aug. 1914, Pte. Dardanelles. *Killed in Action, Aug. 10, 1915, Gallipoli.***
   (1, Hyde Close)

322.   PHILLIPS, Arthur, Lance-Corporal, 10007,[2] 10th (Service) Bn The Hampshire Regiment, d. 10 August 1915 aged 21.

Fourth son of the late George and Emily Phillips of 1, Hyde Close. Born 1893. Enlisted in 1906 aged 13 at Winchester. His previous occupation is listed as 'Boy'. He was Discharged free under special army order in 1907. In 1911 he was a Grocer's Porter. Re-enlisted in August 1914. Served at Gallipoli (Dardanelles). Entered a theatre of war (Gallipoli) with 10th Bn on 5 August 1915.[3] Killed in Action 10 August 1915 at Gallipoli (Dardanelles). Commemorated on The Helles Memorial, Turkey (PR Panel 125-134 or 223-226 228-229 & 328.).[4] Memorial at St Bartholomew's.

He had three brothers who served in the War. Walter, listed below, was Killed in Action 3 December 1917. Alfred served India and Egypt as a Private in The Hampshire Regiment and survived the War.

✠**PHILLIPS, WALTER ... Pte. ... Hants, May 1916, Pte. France. *Killed in Action, Dec. 3, 1917.***
   (1, Hyde Close)

323.   PHILLIPS, Walter, Private, 202537,[5] 2nd Bn The Hampshire Regiment, d. 3 December 1917 aged 19.

1   CWGC.
2   WO 372/15/220901.
3   R Hamps Notes. RH. for this and other material in this biography. Previous service does not appear in the Journal.
4   CWGC records son of Emily Phillips.
5   WO 372/15/228544. SJ notes 202537 is a 4th Bn number.

Youngest of five sons of the late George and Emily Phillips of 1, Hyde Close. Born 1898. In 1911 he was a Butcher's Errand Boy. Also worked for H. Collis, Dairyman of Hyde Street. Enlisted in May 1916 at Winchester.¹ Served in France. Entered a theatre of war with 2nd Bn at some point after beginning of 1917.² Killed in Action 3 December 1917. Commemorated on the Cambrai Memorial, Louverval, Nord, France (PR Panel 7.).³ Memorial at St Bartholomew's.

He had two brothers who served in the War. Arthur, listed above, was Killed in Action 10 August 1915. Alfred served India and Egypt as a Private in The Hampshire Regiment and survived the War.

✠PHILLIS, CHARLES ... Pte. ... Hants, Sept. 1914, Pte. India. Wounded, Feb. 7, 1917. *Died of Wounds, Feb.* 13, 1917. (15. Monks Road)

324. PHILLIS, Charles, Private, 200907,⁴ 1/4th Bn The Hampshire Regiment, . 13 February 1917 aged 25.

Son of Alfred and Harriet Phillis of 15, Monks Road. Born 1892. A Carpenter in 1911. Enlisted September 1914 on Salisbury Plain (3006). Served in India. Entered a theatre of war with 1/4th Bn on 18 March 1915.⁵ Died of Wounds 13 February 1917. Buried Amara War Cemetery, Iraq (GR XIV. F. 25.).⁶ Memorial at St Bartholomew's.

His brother Leonard served in The Gloucestershire Regiment in in France, was wounded and survived the War.

✠PHILPOT, CHARLES J. ... Pte. ... Can. Gds., 1916, Pte. France. *Killed in Action,* Sept. 23, 1916. (Bar End)

325. PHILPOT, Charles John ⁷, Private, 178011,⁸ 1st Bn (formerly 87th) Bn⁹ Canadian Infantry (Canadian Grenadier Guards), d. 23 September 1916.

1 SDGW.
2 R Hamps Notes. RH. for this and other material in this biography.
3 CWGC.
4 WO 372/15/230012.
5 R Hamps Notes. RH.
6 CWGC.
7 CWGC.
8 www.collections Canada.gc.ca./RG150. CWGC states he died serving with 1st Bn Canadian Infantry (Western Ontario).
9 SJ adds 1st Bn.

Born 20 September 1872 at Winchester. Emigrated to Canada on The Parisian 3 May 1894 from Liverpool. A Labourer on the ship's transcript. Attestation papers give him as a Milkman. Enlisted 26 October 1915 in Montreal. Husband of Elizabeth Philpot (née Bellinger) 1901 of Bar End Road then Clark Street, Montreal.[1] Killed in Action 23 September 1916. Commemorated on Vimy Memorial, Pas de Calais, France (No PR given).[2] Memorial at St Peter Chesil.

✠PIPER, ALFRED G. ... Corpl. ... Hants, 1912, Pte. M.G.C.. France Wounded four times, 1914, 1915, and 1916. *Killed in Action, Aug.* 21, 1918.
(16, St. Clement Street)

326. PIPER, Alfred George, Corporal, 21135,[3] 63rd Coy Machine Gun Corps (Infantry), d. 21 August 1918 aged 23.

Son of Alfred J. and Mary A. Piper. Born at Whitchurch in 1895. Married Florence Bytha Middleton (formerly Piper) in 1917 (16, St Clement Street).[4] In 1911 he was a Labourer in a Jam Factory. Enlisted in 1912 at Winchester. Formerly 9124. The Hampshire Regiment.[5] Regular soldier entered a theatre of war with 1st Bn on 23 August 1914. Served in France.[6] Wounded four times: in 1914, 1915 and 1916. Transferred to Machine Gun Corps. Killed in Action 21 August 1918. Commemorated on the Vis-en-Artois Memorial, Pas de Calais, France (PR Panel 10.).[7] Memorials at St Thomas's and Whitchurch.

✠PIPER, CHARLES S. ... L.-Corpl. ... Hants, Aug. 1916, Pte. R.A.S.C. France. *Died, Jan.* 4, 1919.
(72, Hyde Street)

327. PIPER, Charles Sidney, Lance-Corporal, 323631[8], attd A Siege Park Army Service Corps, d. 4 January 1919 aged 36.

Son of Charles and Elizabeth Piper of Winchester. Born at Hampton Hill, Middlesex in 1882. Married Lydia Lilian in 1904: the Pipers lived at 15, Cathedral View, Highcliffe, Winchester (1911, at 72, Hyde Street).[9] They had

1 CWGC states husband of Elizabeth Annie Bellinger Nettleship (formerly Philpot) of 6019, St Audre Street, Montreal.
2 CWGC. No Panel Reference.
3 WO 372/16/14742.
4 BMD.
5 SDGW.
6 R Hamps Notes. RH. for this and other material in this biography.
7 CWGC.
8 WO 372/16/14828, has number as M/323631.
9 CWGC. Census 1911.

three children by 1911. Cyril William Charles born 1904, Dorothy Lilian born 1905 and Sydney Walter born 1907. A Grocer's Porter in 1911. Enlisted in August 1916. Served in France, first with The Hampshire Regiment but no service in a theatre of war with Hampshire Regiment.[1] Died 4 January 1919. Buried in Etaples Military Cemetery, Pas de Calais, France (GR LXXII. A. 15.).[2] Memorial at the Primitive Methodist Chapel in Parchment Street.

☩**POPE, SAMUEL H. ... L.-Corpl. ... Hants, Aug. 1914. Pte. Mesopotamia, India.** *Died, Apl.* **10, 1918.**
(12, Lawn Street)

328. POPE, Samuel H.[3] Lance-Corporal, 37341, Royal Defence Corps 166th Protection Company formerly Private, 2411, 4th Bn, The Hampshire Regiment, d. 10 April 1918 aged 54.[4]

Husband of Emily Pope. Enlisted 6 August 1914, possibly a pre-war territorial. Served in India and Mesopotamia. Entered theatre of war on 18 March 1915 so must have served in Mesopotamia.[5] Discharged 8 November 1917 due to ill health 'general disability following malaria'.[6] Died 10 April 1918 at Winchester. No Winchester memorial found.

☩**POTTER, THOMAS ... [BLANK] ... K.R.R.C. Salonica, France.** *Killed in Action, Jan.* **17, 1917.**
(82, Lower Brook Street)

329. POTTER, Thomas, Lance-Corporal,[7] 9503,[8] 4th Bn The King's Royal Rifle Corps, d. 17 January 1917 aged 38.

Born in Worcestershire in 1877. Married Elizabeth Ann (82, Lower Brook Street).[9] Served in the Boer War.[10] In 1911 he was a Private, The King's Royal Rifle Corps stationed at Winchester Barracks. Enlisted in Birmingham. Served in Salonica and France during the War. Died in a railway accident 17 January 1917.[11] Buried in Les Gonards Cemetery, Versailles, Yvelines, France (GR 5.

1   R Hamps Notes. RH. for this and other material in this biography.
2   CWGC.
3   MIC and CWGC references not found 19.06.13. No date of birth found.
4   SJ adds much detail here. https://www.forces-war-records.co.uk/collections/86 *Silver War Badge Roll List.* Naval and Military Press.
5   R Hamps Notes. RH. for this and other material in this biography.
6   SDGW for Enlistment and death etc SJ adds malaria etc.
7   SJ notes Rifleman. See note on Lance-Corporal at death above. See also Albert Spencer.
8   WO 372/16/53257.
9   CWGC.
10 CWGC; SDGW. Served for twenty years.
11 SDGW 'Died'. Discrepancy over age at death.

15.).¹ No Winchester memorial found.

✠POVEY, GEORGE O. ... Corpl. ... R.M.L.I., Pte. R.N.D. At Sea, France. *Killed in Action, Apl.* 23, 1917.
(1, Lower Wolvesey Terrace)

330. POVEY, George Otty, Lance-Corporal, PO/16867,² 1st RM Bn RN Div. Royal Marine Light Infantry, d. 23 April 1917 aged 23.

Son of John and Dora Povey of 1, Lower Wolvesy (sic) Terrace. Born 12 January 1894 at St Martin's, Winnall. A College Porter in 1911.³ Enlisted 12 March 1912 in The Hampshire Regiment at Winchester, according to his Royal Naval Division record. Transferred to the Royal Marine Light Infantry 16 May 1913 and embarked with the Royal Marine Brigade 3 December 1916 to serve in France. Killed in Action 23 April 1917. The Battalion diary for the 23 April states 'Large carrying party to Gavrelle - 2 Other Ranks wounded, 5 killed.'⁴ Commemorated on the Arras Memorial, Pas de Calais, France (PR Bay 1.).⁵ Memorials at St Peter Chesil (All Saints) and the Primitive Methodist Chapel in Parchment Street.⁶

He had to brothers who served in the War. Percy, listed below, was Killed in Action 10 August 1915 at Suvla Bay. Bertram served in Salonica, Egypt and at Gallipoli (Dardanelles) as a Driver in the Army Service Corps. He survived the War.

✠POVEY, PERCY ... Pte. ... Hants, Sept. 1914, Pte. Dardanelles. *Killed in Action, Aug.* 10, 1915, *Suvla Bay.*
(1, Lower Wolvesey Terrace)

331. POVEY, Percy Gerald, Private, 10160,⁷ 10th (Service) Bn The Hampshire Regiment, d. 10 August 1915 aged 23.

Son of John and Dora Povey of 1, Lower Wolvesey Terrace. Born 1892. A Butcher's Boy in 1911. Enlisted September 1914 at Southampton. Served at Gallipoli (Dardanelles). Entered theatre of war (Gallipoli) with 10th Bn when he landed at Gallipoli 5 August 1915. Initially posted as missing but later

---

1   CWGC.
2   ADM 159/191/16867.'Burn mark R nipple.'
3   Possibly Winchester College? Not found in Winchester College records although a 'Povey' came second in the College Servants' Race in 1897, perhaps a relation. Suzanne Foster, pers. comm.
4   RND Battalion Diary entry.
5   CWGC.
6   All Saints, a different memorial at St Peter, Chesil.
7   WO 372/16/58173.

confirmed as Killed in Action 10 August 1915 at Suvla Bay.[1] Commemorated on The Helles Memorial, Turkey (PR Panel 125-134 or 223-226 228-229 & 328.).[2] Memorials at St Peter Chesil (All Saints) and the Primitive Methodist Chapel in Parchment Street.[3]

He had two brothers who served in the War. George, listed above, was Killed in Action 23 April 1917. Bertram served in Salonica, Egypt and at Gallipoli (Dardanelles) as a Driver in the Army Service Corps. He survived the War.

✠POWNEY, WILLIAM B. ... L.-Corpl. ... R. Berks, 1899, Pte. France. *Killed in Action, May 16, 1915, Richebourg.*
(76, Stockbridge Road)

332.   POWNEY, William Benjamin, Lance-Corporal, 5779,[4] 1st Bn Princess Charlotte of Wales's (Royal Berkshire Regiment) d. 16 May 1915 aged 41.

Son of Joseph and Mary Ann Martha Powney of Salisbury. Born at Salisbury, Wiltshire in 1875. A Cutter's Assistant in 1891. Enlisted in Reading in 1899.[5] Served in France. Died of Wounds, Sunday 16 May 1915. Buried Bethune Town Cemetery, Pas de Calais, France (GR III.C.82.).[6] Memorials at St Matthew's and St Paul's, also commemorated in the Salisbury Book of Remembrance at St Thomas's, Salisbury.[7]

✠PRANGLE, ALBERT ... Pte. ... Hants Y., 1914. Tpr. Hants. France. *Killed in Action, Mch 23, 1918, Bapaume.*
(13, Water Lane)

333.   PRANGLE, Albert (Bert), Private, 204827,[8] 15th (Hampshire Carabiniers) Bn The Hampshire Regiment, formerly Hampshire Yeomanry[9] d. 23 March 1918 aged 26.

Son of the late Walter and Charlotte Prangle of Winchester. Married Rose E. Rose (7, Bridge Street)[10] in 1916. Enlisted in 1914 and served in France (1230). Entered theatre of war after beginning of 1916 with Hampshire Carabiniers

---

1   R Hamps Notes. RH. for this and other material in this biography.
2   CWGC.
3   SDGW.
4   WO 372/16/66976. States Died of Wounds.
5   A Private W. Powney (935) served in The Lancashire Fusiliers in the Boer War 1899-1902. See Anglo-Boer War Records 1899-1902 for his decorations etc.
6   CWGC.
7   www.wiltshire-opc.org.uk
8   WO 372/16/68313. SJ notes 'a 4th Bn number.' Not found in the census.
9   See note to Alexander, re 15th Hampshires.
10 BMD.

Yeomanry.[1] Killed in Action 23 March 1918 at Bapaume. Commemorated on the Arras Memorial, Pas de Calais, France (PR Bay 6.).[2] Memorials at St John the Baptist.

✠PRESSLEE, ALBERT ... Pte. ... Hants, 1914, Pte. Dardanelles. *Killed in Action, Aug. 10, 1915.*
(2, St. Clement Street)

334. PRESSLEE, Albert or Bertram, Private, 9977,[3] 10th (Service) Bn The Hampshire Regiment, d. 10 August 1915 aged 17.

Son of Joseph Presslee of 203, High Street, Streatham, London (also recorded as son of Joseph and Emily Presslee, 38, Colson Road, Winnall).[4] Born at Liss, Petersfield in 1898. Bertram in 1901 and 1911. Family at Petersfield in 1901, at Winnall in 1911. Errand Boy in 1911. Served at Gallipoli (Dardanelles). Entered theatre of war with 10th Bn on 5 August 1915.[5] Killed in Action 10 August 1915. Commemorated om Helles Memorial, Turkey (PR 125-134, 223-226, 228-229, 328).[6] Memorial at Wesleyan Methodist Chapel, St Peter's Street.

His brother Laban served as a Private in The Hampshire Regiment in India, Mesoptamia and France. He survived the War.

✠PRICHARD, WILLIAM C. ... [BLANK] ... Devon, Nov. 1914. France. *Killed in Action, Sept. 25, 1915.*
(7, Boundary Street)

335. PRICHARD, William,[7] Private, 14326,[8] 8th (Service) Bn The Devonshire Regiment, d. 25 September 1915 aged 25.

Son of Mrs E. Bradford of 7, Boundary Street. Born 1889.[9] In 1911 he was a Footman at Ashford, Kent. Enlisted in November 1914 at Southampton. Served in France. Killed in Action 25 September 1915. Commemorated on the Loos Memorial, Pas de Calais, France (PR Panel 35 to 37.).[10] Memorial at Holy Trinity.

1 R Hamps Notes. RH. for this and other material in this biography.
2 CWGC.
3 WO 372/16/75243.
4 SJ adds bracketed material.
5 R Hamps Notes. RH. for this and other material in this biography.
6 CWGC.
7 William C in *WWSR*.
8 WO 372/16/86902.
9 Most likely identification in 1911.
10 CWGC.

✠**PRIDEAUX, JOHN T. ... Pte. ... Hants, Sept. 1914, Pte. Dardanelles,Balkans. Wounded, Sept. 19, 1915. *Missing, believed Killed, Dec. 7, 1915.***
(3, Domum Road)

336. PRIDEAUX, John Thomas, Private, 13021,[1] 10th (Service) Bn The Hampshire Regiment, d. 7 December 1915 aged 20.

Son of Charles William and Laura Prideaux of 3, Domum Road.[2] Born 1895. In 1911 was a Domestic Indoors Boy. Enlisted in September 1914 at Winchester. Served at Gallipoli (Dardanelles) and the Balkans. Entered a theatre of war with 10th Bn on 5 August 1915.[3] Wounded 19 September 1915. Killed in Action 7 December 1915.[4] Commemorated on the Doiran Memorial, Greece.[5] Memorial at St Peter Chesil.

His father and brother served in the War. His father Charles W. served in France as a Pioneer in the Royal Engineers. Herbert, his brother served on the Home Front as a Private in The Worcestershire Regiment. They both survived the War

✠**PRINCE, GEORGE H. A. ... Pte. ... Hants, Aug. 1914, Pte. Dardanelles,France. *Killed in Action, July 1, 1916, Somme.***
(45, Colebrook Street)

337. PRINCE, George Henry Alexander, Private, 9918,[6] A Coy 1st Bn The Hampshire Regiment, d. 1 July 1916 aged 22.

Son of George and Alice Prince of 45, Upper Colebrook Street. Born 1895 in St Maurice. An Errand Boy in 1911. Enlisted August 1914 at Winchester. Served at Gallipoli (Dardanelles) and France. Entered theatre of war with 10th Bn (Gallipoli) on 5 August 1915, later transferred to 1st Bn.[7] Killed in Action 1 July 1916 on the Somme. Buried in Redan Ridge Cemetery No.2, Beaumont-Hamel, Somme, France (GR B. 24.).[8] No Winchester memorial found.[9]

His brother John M. served on the Home Front as a Private in the Army Service Corps and survived the War.

1 WO 372/16/87522. B Coy.
2 Entered as 'Dornum Road'.
3 R Hamps Notes. RH.
4 SDGW substitutes KIA for 'Missing etc...'
5 CWGC.
6 WO 372/16/90270.
7 R Hamps Notes. RH.
8 CWGC.
9 ? St Maurice, lost.

✠**PRIOR, GEORGE ... Pte. ... Canadians, Pte. France. *Killed in Action, Apl.* 9, 1917, *Vimy Ridge.***
   (21, Cranworth Road)

338. PRIOR, George, Private, 907538,[1] 5th Bn Canadian Infantry (Saskatchewan Regiment), d. 9 April 1917 aged 33.

Son of George Thomas and the late Sarah Prior. Born at Dean, Bedford, England 7 February 1887. A Canadian National.[2] Formerly a Farmer. Next of Kin Mary Prior, Sister, of Shawingan, Newton Road, Northampton, England. Resident at Candahar, Saskatchewan when he enlisted at Regina, Saskatchewan 28 March 1916. Served in France and was Killed in Action 9 April 1917 at Vimy Ridge. Commemorated on the Vimy Memorial, Pas de Calais, France.[3] Memorials at St Matthew's and St Paul's.

✠**PRITCHARD, REGINALD ... [BLANK] ... Hants, Nov. 1914. Home. *Died, Nov.* 28, 1916.**
   (44, Lansdowne Terrace)

339. PRITCHARD, Reginald Frank,[4] The Hampshire Regiment, d. 28 November 1916.

Second son of Walter and Alice Pritchard of 44, Lansdowne Terrace, Middle Brook Street. A Baker in 1911. Born 1893. Enlisted in November 1914. Served on the Home Front. Died 28 November 1916 at County Hospital Winchester.[5] No Winchester memorial found.

He had two brothers who served in the War. Cecil served in the North Sea as an Able Seaman in the Royal Navy. Walter John served in the North Sea and Russia as a carpenter, promoted to Petty Officer in the Royal Navy. Both survived the War.

✠**PULLINGER, WILLIAM ... Corpl. ... R. Berks., 1914, Pte. France. *Killed in Action, July* 1, 1916, *Somme.***
   (3, Staple Garden)

340. PULLINGER, William Henry Jno, Lance-Corporal, 12828,[6] 6th

---

1   www.collectionscanada.gc.ca/RG150.
2   CWGC.
3   CWGC.
4   MIC not found.
5   R Hamps Notes. RH. for this and other material in this biography.
6   WO 372/16/107841. Notes he was demoted from Lance-Corporal to Private. Promoted again up to Corporal?

(Service) Bn Princess Charlotte of Wales's (Royal Berkshire Regiment),[1] d. 1 July 1916 aged 30.

Son of Jane Travers, stepson of Walter Travers of 3, Staple Gardens. In 1901 he was a Photographer's Errand Boy. In 1911 a Domestic Chauffeur at Little Somborne Park.[2] Enlisted in 1914 at Reading, Berkshire. Served in France. Killed in Action 1 July 1916 on the Somme. Commemorated on the Thiepval Memorial, Somme, France (PR Pier and Face 11 D.).[3] Memorial at St Thomas's.

✠**READ, LEONARD S. ... Pte. ... Hants, Sept. 1914, Pte. India, Persian Gulf, Mesopotamia. *Killed in Action, July* 24, 1915, *Nasariyeh.***
(13, Tower Street)

341. READ, Leonard Stanley, Private, 2841,[4] 1/4th Bn The Hampshire Regiment, d. 24 July 1915 aged 21.

Son of late Augustus O. and Sarah Jane Read of 13, Tower Street. Born 1894. A Book Binder apprentice in 1911. Enlisted in September 1914 at Hamilton Camp. Served in India, the Persian Gulf and Mesopotamia. Entered theatre of war with 1/4th Bn on 18 March 1915.[5] Killed in Action 24 July 1915 at Nasariyeh. Buried in Basra War Cemetery, Iraq (GR II. R. 10.).[6] Memorial at St Thomas's.

His brother Kempton C. served in France as a Pioneer, promoted to Sapper in the Royal Engineers and survived the War.

✠**READINGS, WILLIAM ... Corpl. ... E. Lancs., 1894, Pte. France. Wounded, 1917. *Killed in Action.***
(10, Staple Garden)

342. READINGS, William C., Corporal, 9957,[7] 2nd Bn The East Lancashire Regiment, d. 22 November 1917 age unknown.

Born Woolton Lancashire in 1879.[8] Enlisted in 1894. In 1911 serving in India aged 16. Served in France during the War. Wounded in 1917 and was Killed in Action 22 November 1917. Buried in Passchendaele New British Cemetery,

1   www.6throyalberks.co.uk. Photograph and biography.
2   1911 census suggests birth as 1896 should be 1886.
3   CWGC.
4   WO 372/16/166300.
5   R Hamps Notes. RH.
6   CWGC.
7   WO 372/16/168266.
8   1881 census. This seems the most likely candidate.

Zonnebeke, West-Vlaanderen, Belgium (GR XV. C. 27.).[1] Memorial at St Thomas's.

✠**REEVES, JOHN H. ... Sergt. ... R.B., 1915, Rfn. Home.** *Died, July* **15, 1918.**
   (40, Sussex Street)

343.   REEVES, John Harold, Serjeant, 9147,[2] Depôt The Rifle Brigade (The Prince Consort's Own), d. 15 July 1918 aged 49.

Born at Burghfield, Berkshire in 1869. Married Alice Camilla Hine in 1894. They had three children by 1911 when recorded at 54, Sussex Street. Harold George Winton born 1897, Reginald Raymond born 1902 and Edna Mary born 1904. A Printer's Compositor in 1911. Enlisted in 1915. Served on the Home Front. Died 15 July 1918. Buried in Winchester (West Hill) Old Cemetery (GR 16530.).[3] No Winchester memorial found.

✠**REYNOLDS, EDWARD C. ... Pte. ... Lond., Mch. 1917, Pte. France. Wounded and taken Prisoner by Germans, Nov. 24, 1917.** *Died of Wounds, Dec.* **21, 1917,** *Seigsburg.*
   (19, Clausentum Road)

344.   REYNOLDS, Edward Charles, Private, 515361,[4] 1st /14th (County of London) Bn The London Regiment (London Scottish), d. 21 December 1917 aged 36.

Son of Alfred S. Reynolds, of Peterborough. Married Edith Annie (19, Clausentum Road, St Cross).[5] In 1911 a boarder at 6, St Catherine's Road. Enlisted in March 1917 at Winchester and served in D Coy in France. Wounded and taken prisoner by Germans, 24 November 1917. Died of Wounds 21 December 1917 at Siegburg. Buried in Cologne Southern Cemetery, Cologne, Nordhein-Westfal, Germany (GR VIII. E. 11.).[6] No Winchester memorial found.

✠**RICHARDS, FREDERICK C. ... Pte. ... Hants, 1912, Pte. India, Mesopotamia. Wounded, Dec. 11, 1915. Taken Prisoner by Turks, Apl. 29, 1916, Kut.** *Died, June* **17, 1916,** *Nesibin.*
   (29, Western Road)

1   CWGC.
2   MIC not found. See Clark, Reginald J S/.
3   CWGC has S/9147. Possible influenza casualty?
4   WO 372/16/201671.
5   CWGC.
6   CWGC.

345. RICHARDS, Frederick C. Private, 200163[1] (1793), A Coy 1/4th Bn The Hampshire Regiment, d. 30 January 1917 aged 21.

Youngest son of the late Edward and Sarah Richards of 29, Western Road. Born 1895. In 1911 he was an Assistant in the Railway Refreshment Bar. Enlisted in 1912 at Winchester. Served during the War in A Coy in India and Mesopotamia. Entered a theatre of war with 1/4th Bn on 25 October 1915.[2] Wounded 11 December 1915 and taken prisoner by Turks 29 April 1916 at Kut. Died a POW 30 January 1917. Commemorated on the Nisibin Memorial Baghdad (North Gate) War Cemetery, Iraq (PR Nisibin Mem. 250.).[3] Memorials at St Matthew's, St Paul's and St Thomas's.

✠**RICHARDSON, EDWARD M. ... Pte. ... Hants, Oct. 1915, Pte. France.** *Killed in Action, Sept. 3, 1916, Glanchy.*
   (31, Middle Brook Street)

346. RICHARDSON, Edward Maurice, Private, 20382,[4] 14th Bn The Hampshire Regiment, d. 3 September 1916 aged 18.

Son of William and the late Edith Richardson, of Middle Brook Street. Born 1898. In 1901 at 84, Lower Brook Street. 1911 living at Gordon Avenue, Highcliffe Park, at school aged 13. Enlisted in October 1915 and served in France. Killed in Action 3 September 1916 at Glanchy. Buried at Hamel Cemetery, Beaumont-Hamel, Somme, France.[5] Memorial at Holy Trinity (Maurice Edward Richardson).

He had two brothers who served during the War. Frank A. served in East Africa and Russia in The Royal Marine Light Infantry. William P. served in France as a Private in The Hampshire Regiment then the Machine Gun Corps. They both survived the War.

✠**RICKMAN, FREDERICK ... Drummer ... Hants, 1906, Drummer. Dardanelles. Wounded, 1915.** *Killed in Action, 1915.*
   (65, Colebrook Street)

---

1   WO 372/16/212618.
2   R Hamps Notes. RH. for this and other material in this biography. The Archive reveals he died as a prisoner of war between 29th April, 1916, and January 30th, 1917. However, Bowker says date of death was 30.6.1916 'on the march'.
3   CWGC records only Frederick.
4   R Hamps Notes. RH. for this and other material in this biography. His number suggested as 203062.
5   R Hamps Notes. RH. indicated confusion about the order of his names/initials (E. M. or M. E.) also notes he is on CWGC as W. M. Richardson.

347. RICKMAN, Frederick Arthur, Private, 7834,[1] 2nd Bn The Hampshire Regiment, d. 6 August 1915 aged 22.

Son of Charles and Ellen Rickman of 65, Colebrook Street. Born at Pennington in 1893. A Golf Caddie for a Mr Munday prior to enlisting in 1906 in The Hampshire Regiment at Winchester as a boy soldier. He was 14 years old according to his Army Service Record. In 1911[2] was a Drummer 2nd Bn The Hampshire Regiment, resident at Wynberg, Cape of Good Hope, South Africa. Served at Gallipoli (Dardanelles). Entered a theatre of war with 2nd Bn on 25 April 1915.[3] Wounded in 1915. Killed in Action 6 August 1915 noted as 'the worst day in the peninsula' when eighteen officers and 284 other ranks were killed or reported missing.[4] Commemorated on The Helles Memorial, Turkey (PR Panel 125-134 or 223-226 228-229 & 328.).[5] No Winchester memorial found.[6]

He had three brothers who served during the War. Tom, listed below, was Killed in Action 27 September 1916. Charles served as a Private in The Hampshire Regiment, transferred to The Duke of Cornwall's Light Infantry. George served in Salonica as a Gunner in The Royal Garrison Artillery. They both survived the War.

✠**RICKMAN, TOM ... Sergt. ... Scots Gds., Aug. 1914, Tpr. France. Wounded, Oct. 1915. D.C.M. 1915.** *Killed in Action, Sept.* **1916.**
  (65, Colebrook Street)

348. RICKMAN, Thomas William,[7] Lance-Serjeant, 6484,[8] 1st Bn Scots Guards, d. 27 September 1915 aged 28.[9]

Son of Charles and Ellen Rickman of 65, Colebrook Street. Born at Sway 1888.[10] Married Mary Bridget in 1909 resident at "M" Block, Peabody Buildings, Orchard Street Estate, Westminster, London. They had Margaret Ellen born 1911. In 1911 Rickman was a Soldier Foot Guards, living at Caterham, Surrey.

1 WO 372/16/228975.
2 1901 census suggests 1893, 1911 1894, Army Service Record 1892. Three potential dates of birth.
3 R Hamps Notes. RH. for this and other material in this biography.
4 Atkinson, 2, p. 96.
5 CWGC.
6 ? St Maurice, lost.
7 Tom only in *WWSR*.
8 WO 372/16/229035; /23/65451 for his citation. www.lawrences.co.uk undated sale of his medals, pictured.
9 *WWSR* has his death in 1916 and his date of wounding after the date of his death in the military records. SDGW says d. 1915.
10 1911 census suggests birth as 1888; 1901 as 1890.

Re-enlisted in August 1914 at Winchester. Served in France. Awarded the Distinguished Conduct Medal in 1915 and was wounded in October 1915. Killed in Action 27 September 1915. Commemorated on the Loos Memorial, Pas de Calais, France (PR Panel 8 and 9.).[1] No Winchester memorial found.[2]

DCM citation Announced *The London Gazette* 3 March 1915.

6484 Private T. Rickman, 1st Bn, The Scots Guards (*The London Gazette* 1 April 1915).

'For gallant conduct and ability between 27 October and 11 November 1914, north of the Menin road, when he carried out reconnaissance duties at great risk, and obtained much valuable information relative to the enemy's positions.'

He had three brothers who served during the War. Frederick, listed above, was Killed in Action 6 August 1915. Charles served as a Private in The Hampshire Regiment, transferred to The Duke of Cornwall's Light Infantry. George served in Salonica as a Gunner in The Royal Garrison Artillery. They both survived the War.

✠ROBERTS, FRANK A. ... Pte. ... Hants, Nov. 1914, Pte. India, Mesopotamia. *Killed in Action, Jan. 21, 1916, Arah.*
   (1, Queen's Terrace)

349.   ROBERTS, Frank Alfred, Private, 3434,[3] 2/4th Bn The Hampshire Regiment, d. 21 January 1916 aged 22.

Son of David John and Mary Roberts of 1, Queen's Terrace, Queen's Road. Born at Fareham in 1894. An Errand Boy in 1911. Enlisted in November 1914 at Winchester. Served in India and Mesopotamia with H Coy. Entered theatre of war with 1/4th Bn on 25 October 1915.[4] Killed in Action 21 January 1916 at Arah. Commemorated on the Basra Memorial, Iraq (PR Panel 21 and 63.).[5] Memorials at Christ Church and St Peter Chesil.

His brother Leslie, listed below, was Killed in Action 20 September 1917.

✠ROBERTS, HERBERT R. ... Pte. ... Worc., 1916, Pte. M.G.C. France. *Killed in Action, May 27, 1918.*
   (5, St. John's North)

1   CWGC.
2   ? St Maurice, lost.
3   WO 372/17/22405.
4   R Hamps Notes. RH. for this and other material in this biography. Regimental Journal says he was 1/4th Bn.
5   CWGC.

350. ROBERTS, Herbert Richard, Private, 89471,¹ 8th Bn Machine Gun Corps (Infantry), d. 27 May 1918 aged 30.

Son of the late Albert Richard Roberts and Jane Roberts, widow, in 1911 living at 13, Owens Road. Born 1888. In 1911 he was a Linotype Operator. Enlisted in 1916 at Dudley. Served in France. Formerly 38270, The Worcestershire Regiment.² Killed in Action 27 May 1918. Commemorated on the Soissons Memorial, Aisne, France.³ Memorial at St Thomas's School.

✠ROBERTS, LESLIE W. ... Pte. ... Dorset, Jan. 1917, Pte. R.A.S.C. (M.T.), Yorks. France, Belgium,. Wounded July 17, 1917. *Killed in Action, Sept.* 20, 1917.
(1, Queen's Terrace)

351. ROBERTS, Leslie William, Private, 33672,⁴ 9th (Service) Bn Alexandra Proncess of Wales's (Yorkshire Regiment), d. 20 September 1917 aged 19.

Son of David John and Mary Roberts of 1, Queen's Terrace, Queen's Road. Born at Fareham in 1899. Enlisted in January 1917 in The Dorsetshire Regiment (5259) at Winchester and served in France and Belgium. Transferred to the Army Service Corps (Mechanical Transport) and then the Yorkshire Regiment. Wounded 17 July 1917 and was Killed in Action 20 September 1917. Commemorated on the Tyne Cot Memorial, Zonnebeke, West-Vlaanderen, Belgium (PR Panel 52 to 54 and 162A.).⁵ Memorials at Christ Church and St Peter Chesil.

His brother Frank, listed above, was Killed in Action 21 January 1916.

✠ROGERS, ARTHUR W. ... Corpl. ... Hants, Dec.1914, Pte. R.E. (Sigs.). India, Mesopotamia. *Died, Sept.* 27, 1918, *Poona.*
(7, Crowder Terrace)

352. ROGERS, Arthur Whitlock, Corporal, 201304,⁶ 2nd /4th Bn The Hampshire Regiment, d. 27 September 1918 aged 24.

Son of George Alfred and Agnes Rogers of Arthurdene, Hookpit, Kings Worthy. Born 1895. An Errand Boy in 1911. Family living at 21, Avenue Road, 1911. Enlisted in December 1914 at Winchester. Served in India.⁷ Transferred

1   WO 372/17/25002.
2   SDGW.
3   CWGC. There is no PR.
4   WO 372/17/4698.
5   CWGC, SDGW.
6   WO 372/17/67727.
7   R Hamps Notes. RH. Only overseas service in India. MIC does not mention Royal

from the Royal Engineers (Signallers). Died 27 September 1918 at Poona. Commemorated on the Kirkee 1914-1918 Memorial, India (PR Face 6.).[1] Memorials at St Thomas's and Kings Worthy.

Only overseas service in India. MIC does not mention Royal Engineers. Entitled to British War Medal only.

✠**ROSE, JAMES ... [BLANK] ... Hants, Sept. 1914. France. Wounded twice.** *Killed in Action, Sept.* **13, 1918. (5, Greyfriars Terrace)**

353. ROSE, James, Private, 14330,[2] 2/4th Bn The Hampshire Regiment, d. 13 September 1918 aged 34.

Third of four sons of Alfred and Eliza Rose of 5, Greyfriars Terrace, Lower Brook Street. Employed by Mr Browning of North Walls before enlisting. Enlisted in September 1914 at Winchester. Entered a theatre of war (France) with 1st Bn on 2 June 1915.[3] Subsequently transferred to 2nd Bn then 2/4th Bn. Wounded twice and was Killed in Action 13 September 1918. Buried in Lowrie Cemetery, Havrincourt, Pas de Calais, France (GR C. 6.).[4] Memorial at Holy Trinity.

He had three brothers who served in the War. Alfred served in France as a Private in The Royal Fusiliers, and was gassed. Frederick and William both served in France as Privates in the Army Service Corps. All three survived the War.

✠**ROWELL, WILLIAM G. ... Stoker ... R.N., 1912, Stoker. North Sea; H.M.S.** *Hampshire. Drowned, June* **5, 1916. (8, Cross Street)**

354. ROWELL, William George, Stoker 1st Class, K/18751,[5] HMS Hampshire Royal Navy, d. 5 June 1916 aged 20.

Son of the late William Rowell and Lucia Rowell of 8, Cross Street, Town

Engineers. Entitled to British War Medal only.
1 CWGC.
2 WO 372/17/86758.
3 R Hamps Notes. RH. for this and other material in this biography. Regimental archive has his age as 29.
4 CWGC, SDGW. Not found in 1911 census.
5 ADM 188/904/18751. 'Scar on f'head'. Service always 'VG'.

Road.[1] Born 15 December 1894.[2] Enlisted 28 April 1913.[3] During the War he served in the North Sea aboard HMS Hampshire.[4] Drowned 5 June 1916. Commemorated on the Portsmouth Naval Memorial (PR 19.).[5] Memorial at St Thomas's.

⚔ROWLANDS, JOHN H. ... L.-Corpl. ... R. Berks, Pte. Devon. Egypt. Wounded once. *Died, June* 25, 1918.
(5, Hyde Close)

355. ROWLANDS, John Henry, Acting Corporal, 47962,[6] 1st /5th Bn The Devonshire Regiment, d. 25 June 1918 aged 38.

Son of Sam and Mary Ann Rowlands. Stepson of Edward Savage. Born at Aldershot in 1881. Married Annie Louisa Jessie Rowlands (née Hoskins) in 1911 (of 5, Hyde Close).[7] His father had died prior to 1901. His mother died in 1909. In 1901 he was a Journeyman Baker. A House Painter in 1911 boarding at 2, Greyfriars Terrace. Enlisted at Winchester. Served with the Egyptian Expeditionary Force. Transferred from the Royal Berkshire Regiment and was wounded. Died 25 June 1918. Buried in Cairo War Memorial Cemetery, Egypt (GR O. 200.).[8] Memorial at St Bartholomew's.

⚔RUMBOLD, ARTHUR ... [BLANK] ... Dorset. Gallipoli, France, Belgium. *Killed in Action, Dec.* 1918, *near Ypres.*
(4, St. George's Terrace)

356. RUMBOLD, Arthur, Private, 3/8263,[9] D Coy 1st Bn The Dorsetshire Regiment, d. 10 December 1917 aged 26.

Son of Henry and Emily Rumbold of 4, St George's Terrace. Born 1890. A Plumber's Labourer in 1911 boarding at 1, Windsor Terrace, Durrington, Salisbury, Wiltshire. Enlisted at Swansea, Glamorganshire. Served at Gallipoli (Dardanelles) and in France and Belgium. Formerly 13824, Prince Albert's (Somerset Light Infantry).[10] Killed in Action 10 December 1917 near Ypres. Commemorated on the Tyne Cot Memorial, Zonnebeke, West-Vlaanderen,

1 SJ. 'Son of Mrs L Varney (??Verney) (formerly Rowell) of 8, Cross Street. Another source Mother Louica Staples of 8, Cross Street.' Naval Casualties 1914-1919.
2 Not found in the census.
3 *WWSR* records enlistment 1912.
4 This was the ship carrying Kitchener who also drowned when HMS Hampshire struck a minefield. Hepper, 2006, p. 64.
5 CWGC.
6 WO 372/17/108205 records him as Acting-Corporal.
7 BMD.
8 CWGC records him as Lance-Corporal.
9 WO 372/17/118596: 3/8263.
10 SDGW..

Belgium (PR Panel 92.).¹ No Winchester memorial found.

✠RUMBOLD, PERCY B. ... Corpl. ... Hants, June 1915, Pte. France. *Killed in Action, July 1, 1916, Beaumont Hamel.* (2, St. James' Villas)

357. RUMBOLD, Percy B., Lance-Corporal, 18260,² 1st Bn The Hampshire Regiment, d. 1 July 1916 aged 32.

Son of William and Lucy Rumbold. Born 1884. In 1891 living with family at 4, Eastgate Street. In 1901 he was working as an Outfitter's Apprentice. In 1911 he was an Assistant in Southsea, Portsmouth living at 25-35, Palmerston Road, Southsea. Enlisted in June 1915 at Edinburgh. Served in France. Entered a theatre of war with 1st Bn after beginning of 1916.³ Killed in Action 1 July 1916 on the first day of the Battle of the Somme at Beaumont Hamel. Buried in Sucrerie Military Cemetery, Colincamps, Somme, France (GR I. D. 78.).⁴ Memorial at Peter Symonds School.

✠RUSSELL, LEONARD C. B. ... Capt. ... R.B., Aug. 1914, 2nd Lieut. France. *Killed in Action, Oct 7, 1916, Gaudecourt.* (St. Cross Mede, St. Cross Rd.)

358. RUSSELL, Leonard Cosmo Bolles, Captain,⁵ 12th (Service) Bn The Rifle Brigade (The Prince Consort's Own), d. 7 October 1916 aged 21.

Only son of Major Leonard and Mrs Agnes Russell of St Cross Mede. Born 19 March 1895 at Folkestone, Kent. In 1911 he was a boarder at Winchester College (Southgate House) then Sandhurst, captain of athletics team record for throwing a cricket ball. Third generation in the regiment after his grandfather (1839-68) and father (1878-1903). Enlisted in August 1914 gazetted to 3rd Bn, but never joined it, going to a Service Bn instead. Served in France. Killed in Action 7 October 1916 'leading [his Company] in an attack on some German trenches' at Gaudecourt. 'His keenness, his utter devotion to duty, and his great personal courage are things we will all remember. He was absolutely worshipped by his men' wrote a brother officer.⁶ Buried in Bancourt British Cemetery, Pas de

---

1 CWGC records him as 318263 an error for oblique. An OCR error.
2 WO 372/17/118661 records him as Acting-Corporal. SJ enters this as Lance-Corporal. Check SDGW.
3 R Hamps Notes. RH.
4 CWGC.
5 WO 372/17/127969. Misread as 'Cornes Bollis' in on-screen MIC Index.
6 For further information and a photograph see https://www.winchestercollegeatwar.com/archive/leonard-cosmo-bolles-russell Additional information from *The Rifle Brigade Chronicle* (1916) and photographic image courtesy of K. Gray. Further information from Suzanne Foster, to whom we are most grateful.

Calais, France (GR V. E. 19.).¹ Memorials at St Cross Chapel, one of which is his original grave wooden cross.

His father, Leonard G. served on the Home Front in The Rifle Brigade and survived the War.

✠SAWLE, WALTER ... Boy ... R.N., Nov. 1918, Boy. H.M.S. *Impregnable. Died of pneumonia, Feb.* 25, 1919.
(35, Nuns Road)

359.   SAWLE, Walter, Boy 2nd Class, J/93962,² HMS Impregnable Royal Navy, d. 25 February 1919 aged 15.

Son of William Henry Sawle and Caroline Paris Sawle of 35, Nuns Road. Born 17 September 1903 at Southampton.³ Enlisted in November 1918. Died of pneumonia 25 February 1919 at Royal Naval Hospital Plymouth. Buried in Winchester (West Hill) Old Cemetery (GR 25. 2098.).⁴ No Winchester memorial found.

✠SCADDAN, ALFRED ... Pte. ... Kent Cyc., Oct. 1915, Pte. Buffs. France. *Missing, believed Killed, Oct.* 5, 1916.
(10, Andover Road)

360.   SCADDEN, Alfred, Private, G/15680,⁵ 7th (Service) Bn The Buffs (East Kent Regiment), d. 5 October 1916 aged 27.

Son of William and Annie Scadden of 10, Andover Road. Born 1889.⁶ Enlisted at Tonbridge, Kent in October 1915 and served in France. Transferred from the Kent Cyclists. Killed in Action 5 October 1916. Commemorated on the Thiepval Memorial, Somme, France (PR Pier and Face 5D.).⁷ Memorials at St Matthew's and St Paul's.

✠SCOTT, CYRIL ... Pte. ... Wilts, Jan. 1916, Pte. France. *Killed in Action, June* 14, 1917.
(32, Nuns Road)

---

1   CWGC. See also www.1914-1918.invisionzone.com (Guedecourt).
2   ADM 188/834/93962. Probably the youngest Winchester boy to die.
3   1911 census suggests 1904 birth.
4   CWGC. Naval Casualties 1914-1919.
5   WO 372/17/184103. Indexed as 'Scaddon'. SDGW. SJ states 'Indexed as Scuddan on CWGC and SDGW.
6   1891 census. Not readily found in other censuses.
7   CWGC. Scuddan, Alfred d. 5 October 1916. SJ record KKIA not Missing.

361. SCOTT, Cyril, Private, 23014,[1] 6th (Service) Bn The Duke of Edinburgh's (Wiltshire Regiment), died 14 June 1917 aged 23.

Son of Burton George and Emma Scott of St Ives, Arthur Road. Born at Dunstable, Bedfordshire, 1894.[2] A Hay and Straw Builder in 1911. His brother Ernest was a Straw Dealer so maybe they worked together. Enlisted in January 1916. Served in France. Died of Wounds 14 June 1917. Buried in Locre Hospice Cemetery, Heuvelland, West-Vlaanderen, Belgium (GR I. A. 8.).[3] Memorial at St Bartholomew's.

His brother Ernest William served as a Wheeler, promoted to Bombardier, in The Royal Field Artillery, was wounded once and gassed three times, and survived the War.

✠**SCOTT, EDWARD C. ... Lieut. ... R.A., 1912, Lieut. France. Killed in Action, Nov. 21, 1914, *Armentières*.**
  (The Garth, Lankhills Road)

362. SCOTT, Edward Claud, 2nd Lieutenant,[4] The Royal Garrison Artillery, d. 21 November 1914 aged 22.

Son of General Hugh Aboakir Scott, RA and Laura Milicent Scott, of The Garth, Lankhills Road. Born at St Helier, Jersey in 1892. Educated at Repton, Derbyshire, in 1911 he was a Military Student. Commissioned 2nd Lieutenant in The Royal Garrison Artillery 23 December 1911 and joined the 5th Siege Battery 19 February 1912. Embarked for France 27 September 1914. Killed in Action near Armentieres 21 November 1914.[5] Buried at Ration Farm Military Cemetery, La Chapelle-d'Armentieres, Nord, France (GR VIII. A. 3.).[6] Memorial at St Bartholomew's.

✠**SEWARD, JOHN W. ... Sergt. ... R.B., 1904, Rfn. India, France. Wounded four times. Killed in Action, Aug. 26, 1917.**
  (16, Stockbridge Road)

363. SEWARD, John W., Serjeant, 26123,[7] 101st Coy Machine Gun Corps (Infantry), d. 26 August 1917 aged 30.

1 WO 372/17/196142.
2 Most likely identification 1911.
3 CWGC, SDGW. SJ changes KIA to DOW.
4 No MIC found. WO 339/8140, Service Papers not seen.
5 de Ruvigny. Poor quality photo on de Ruvigny's roll. Not found via Repton School.
6 CWGC. Image of face at www.findagrave.com.
7 WO 372/17/228300.

Son of John and Esther Seward of 46, Canon Street, 1911. Born 1887.[1] An Errand Boy in 1901. Enlisted in 1904 and in 1911 was a Private 2nd Bn The Rifle Brigade (The Prince Consort's Own), resident at Fort William, Calcutta, India. Served during the War in India and France. Went to France 7 November 1914. Formerly 355, Lance-Corporal in The Rifle Brigade.[2] Wounded four times and was Killed in Action 26 August 1917. Commemorated on the Thiepval Memorial, Somme, France (PR Pier and Face 5 C and 12 C.).[3] Memorials at St Matthew's and St Paul's.

He had two brothers who served in the War. Charles served in Mesopotamia as a Private in The Hampshire Regiment, transferred to The Northumberland Fusiliers and was wounded once. George served as a Private in The Hampshire Regiment and transferred to the Royal Air Force. They both survived the War.

ⴕSHARPE, ALFRED ... Pte. ... Hants, Mch. 1916, Pte. India, Egypt, France. Wounded once. *Killed in Action, July 28, 1918.*
   (2, Granville Place)

364.   SHARP,[4] Alfred, Private, 202406,[5] 2/4th Bn The Hampshire Regiment, d. 28 July 1918 aged 33.

Second son of the late Robert and Emma Sharp of 2, Granville Place. Born 1886.[6] A General Labourer in 1901. In 1911 was a Gardener. Enlisted in March 1916 at Winchester. Served in India, Egypt and France. Entered a theatre of war with 2/4th Bn some point after the beginning of 1917.[7] Wounded once and Killed in Action 28 July 1918. Commemorated on the Soissons Memorial, Aisne, France.[8] Memorial at St Peter Chesil (All Saints) (Sharpe).

He had two brothers who served during the War. Frederick served in France as a Gunner in The Royal Garrison Artillery and was wounded March 22 1918. William served on the Home Front as a Private in The Labour Corps for the last month of the War. Both survived.

ⴕSHEARS, SAMUEL ... [BLANK] ... Hants, Aug. 1914. Home. *Died, Feb.* 5 1919.
   (12, Ashley Terrace)

1   1901 suggests 1887, 1911 1886.
2   SDGW.
3   CWGC.
4   Sharpe in *WWSR*.
5   WO 372/18/7533.
6   1891 and 1901 censuses suggest 1886, 1911 1885.
7   R Hamps Notes. RH.
8   CWGC. No PR. SDGW.

365. SHEARS, Samuel,[1] 144693 (formerly 1449) The Hampshire Regiment, The Hampshire Regiment Labour Corps 380th Home Service Labour Company), d. 5 February 1919 aged 51.

Born about 1868 at Wallop.[2] Lived at 12, Ashley Terrace. Husband of Mabel A. Shears. They had two children, Mabel Rose born 1898 and Samuel George born 1900. He had three stepchildren, Frances A., Leonard L. and Jessie E. His wife died in 1911. A Railway Carrier's Carman in 1901 and 1911. Enlisted 26 May 1884 (1449). Discharged 30 January 1894 physically unfit (epilepsy), intending to live at 11, ?Terrace Row. ? Joined Territorials 1908, re-enlisted in August 1914. Discharged 1 August 1918 permanently unfit (chronic bronchitis).[3] Served on the Home Front. Died 5 February 1919.[4] Memorials in St Matthew's and St Paul's.

His son Samuel George served on the Western Front as a Corporal in The Hampshire Regiment and The Worcestershire Regiment. He survived the War.

✠**SHEFFERD, CECIL ... L.-Corpl. ... Hants, 1914, Pte. India, Mesopotamia. Wounded, Mch. and July, 1915. Taken Prisoner by Turks.** *Died as P.O.W.*
(94, Fairfield Road)

366. SHEFFERD, Cecil, Private,[5] 200107,[6] 1/4th Bn The Hampshire Regiment, d. 4 September 1916 aged 23.

Eldest son of Thomas and Jane Shefferd (widow in 1911) of Grangemont, Fairfield Road.[7] Born at Northington in 1893. Worked for the Council as a Clerk in 1911. Enlisted in 1914 (1660). Served in India and Mesopotamia. Entered theatre of war with 1/4th Bn on 18 March 1915.[8] Wounded in March and July 1915. Taken prisoner by Turks at Kut and died a POW 4 September 1916. Buried in Baghdad (North Gate) War Cemetery, Iraq (GR XXI. T. 23.).[9] Memorials at St Matthew's, St Paul's, Hampshire County Council and Peter Symonds and St Thomas's schools..[10]

1 MIC not found.
2 1901 census suggests 1870 at Wallop, 1911 suggests 1868 at Andover.
3 Military career from SJ.
4 CWGC. No S. Shears.
5 Recorded in the *WWSR* as Lance-Corporal. .
6 WO 372/18/27760.
7 Census 1911.
8 R Hamps Notes. RH. for this and other material in this biography. His age in the archive is given as 24. Bowker says he died at 'Yasbaschi'.
9 CWGC.
10 www.dnfa.co.uk. 'A Great War Memorial Plaque'to Private Cecil Shefferd, with supporting paper confirming his date of death was sold by Dreweatt's of Bloomsbury on 28 September 2012 for £80.

He had three brothers who served during the War. Charles D. served in Mesopotamia as a Sapper, promoted to Serjeant in the Royal Engineers. George served in France as a Private in The Hampshire Regiment. Ronald served in France in The Royal Army Medical Corps. They all survived the War.

✠SHEPPARD, WILLIAM J. ... [BLANK] ... Hants, Oct. 1916, Pte. France. *Killed in Action, Feb. 1, 1917.*
(13, Lawn Street)

367. SHEPPARD, William Jesse, Private, 29837,[1] 14th (Service) Bn (1st Portsmouth) The Hampshire Regiment, d. 1 February 1917 aged 38.

Son of Jesse and Elizabeth Sheppard of 11, Middle Brook Street. Born 1891.[2] Married Nellie Maria (née Pope) in 1905 (13, Lawn Street).[3] By 1911 they had three children: Nellie Marion Rose, born 1906, Gladys Lilian May born 1908 and Jen Alexander born 1910. A Builder's Labourer in 1911. Enlisted in October 1916 at Winchester. Served in France. Entered a theatre of war with 2/4th Bn at some point after beginning of 1916.[4] Killed in Action 1 February 1917. Commemorated at Vlamertinghe Military Cemetery, Ypres (Ieper), West-Vlaanderen, Belgium (GR V. G. 1.).[5] Memorial at Holy Trinity (Jess Sheppard).

✠SHERWOOD, FRANK E. ... [BLANK] ... Hants, Aug. 1914. Dardanelles. *Killed in Action, Aug. 10, 1915.*
(Highcliffe Park Farm)

368. SHERWOOD, Frank Edwin, Private, 9780,[6] 10th (Service) Bn The Hampshire Regiment, d. 10 August 1915 aged 23.

Son of George and Lydia Sherwood of Highcliffe Park Farm, Winchester. Born at Alresford in 1892.[7] George Sherwood died in 1911. A Farm Labourer in 1911. Enlisted in August 1914 at Winchester. Served at Gallipoli (Dardanelles). Entered a theatre of war with 10th Bn on 5.8.1915. Initially posted as missing.[8] Killed in Action 10 August 1915. Commemorated on The Helles Memorial, Turkey (PR Panel 125-134 or 223-226 228-229 & 328.).[9] Memorial at All Saints.

1 WO 372/18/38279.
2 1911 census. Not found earlier.
3 BMD.
4 R Hamps Notes. RH.
5 CWGC. Winch memorial? SDGW?
6 WO 372/18/43266.
7 1911 census, not found earlier.
8 R Hamps Notes. RH.
9 CWGC.

His brother George was Killed in Action 30 November 1914.

⛭SHERWOOD, GEORGE ... Pte. ... Hants, rejoined Aug. 1914, Pte. France. *Killed in Action, Nov. 30, 1914.*
  (Highcliffe Park Farm)

369.   SHERWOOD, George Henry,[1] Private, 5899,[2] 1st Bn The Hampshire Regiment, d. 30 November 1914 aged 33.

Son of the late George and Lydia Sherwood of Highcliffe Park Farm, Winchester. Born at Andover in 1889. George Sherwood, senior, d. in 1911. George, junior, is registered at Fort Rawalpindi, India as a soldier in 1911. Served in the South African campaign.[3] Transferred to Army Reserve 1908. Re-enlisted in August 1914 at Winchester. Served with the British Expeditionary Force in France. Entered a theatre of war with 1st Bn on 12 September 1914.[4] Killed in Action 30 November 1914. Buried at Lancashire Cottage Cemetery, Ploegsteert, Comines-Warneton, Hainaut, Belgium (GR I. C. 14.).[5] Memorial at All Saints.

His brother Frank, listed above, was Killed in Action 10 August 1915.

⛭SHORE, ALFRED G. ... A.-C.Q.M.S. ... Hants (T.F.), Pte. Hants. India, Mesopotamia. Wounded once. Taken Prisoner by Turks, Kut. *Died, as P.O.W.*
  (Little Minster Street)

370.   SHORE, Alfred George, Company Quartermaster Serjeant, 200022,[6] 1/4th Bn The Hampshire Regiment, d. 31 July 1916 aged 28.

Son of Alfred Edwin and Jessie Jane Shore of 8, Little Minster Street. Born 1888. A Carter in 1911. As with his father and brother (see below) Shaw was transferred from The Hampshire Regiment (Territorial Force). Enlisted at Winchester (97). Served in India and Mesopotamia. Wounded once. Taken prisoner at Kut and died a POW 31 July 1916. Commemorated on the Basra Memorial, Iraq (PR Panel 21 and 63.).[7] Memorial at St Thomas's Church.

His father Alfred Edwin served in India and Mesopotamia as a Private, promoted to company Serjeant Major in The Hampshire Regiment. His brother William V. served in India and Mesopotamia as a Private, promoted to Serjeant

1   George only in *WWSR*.
2   WO 372/18/43326.
3   CWGC.
4   R Hamps Notes. RH. for this and other material in this biography.
5   CWGC.
6   WO 372/18/52091. Not 'Acting' in WO records.
7   CWGC.

in The Hampshire Regiment. Both survived the War.

✠SIMMONDS, ALBERT W. ... Pte. ... Hants, 1913, Pte. France. Wounded, Oct. 15, 1914. *Killed in Action, May* 13, 1915. (Railway Cottages, St. Cross)

371. SIMMONDS, Albert Walter,[1] Private, 9343,[2] 1st Bn The Hampshire Regiment, d. 13 May 1915 aged 18.

Son of Walter and Rose A. Simmonds, of Railway Cottage, Mead Road. Born at Kings Worthy in 1897. In 1911 he was a Baker's Assistant. Enlisted in 1913 at Winchester. Served during the War in France. Entered theatre of war with 1st Bn 23 August 1914. [3]Wounded 15 October 1914, in hospital in France. Killed in Action 13 May 1915. Commemorated on the Ypres (Menin Gate) Memorial, Ypres (Ieper), West-Vlaanderen, Belgium (PR Panel 35.).[4] Memorial at St Cross Chapel.

✠SIMMONS, JOHN ... 2nd Lieut. ... R.W.S., 1888, Band Boy. R.B. France. *Killed (accidentally), Aug.* 21, 1916, *Aldershot.* (4, Greenhill Road)

372. SIMMONS, John, 2nd Lieutenant,[5] 3rd Bn attd Bombing School The Rifle Brigade (The Prince Consort's Own), d. 21 August 1916 aged 42.

Born at Marylebone, London in 1874. Married Helen Mary Barrow in 1900: lived at 4, Greenhill Road. Enlisted in 1888 as a Band Boy and served in the Royal West Surrey Regiment. A Colour Serjeant (Serjeant-Major 7178) 5th Bn Rifle stationed at Cambridge Barracks and Recruiting Office, Francis Street Woolwich in 1911. First served in France 12 January 1915. Killed accidentally at Aldershot 21 August 1916. Buried in Aldershot Military Cemetery (PR AH. 347.).[6] Memorials at St Bartholomew's, St Matthew's, St Paul's, and Wesleyan Methodist Chapel, St Peter's Street.

His son John G. served in Germany as a Boy in The Royal Flying Corps, then The Royal Air Force and survived the War.

✠SINGLE, ALBERT E. ... Rfn. ... R.B., 1905, Rfn. Home. *Died,* 1916, *Winchester.* (11, St. John's Street)

1 SDGW Albert William.
2 WO 372/18/67816.
3 R Hamps Notes. RH. for this and other material in this biography.
4 CWGC. SDGW.
5 WO 372/18/70588.
6 CWGC.

373. SINGLE, Albert Edward, Private,[1] The Rifle Brigade (The Prince Consort's Own), d. 1916 aged 39.[2]

Born 1887.[3] Enlisted prior to the 1891 census when he was registered as a Private in The Rifle Brigade resident with 4th Battalion Rifle Brigade & Troops, Parkhurst Isle of Wight. In 1911 he was stationed at Cambridge Barracks and Recruiting Office, as a Bugler 6th Bn The Rifle Brigade. Served on the Home Front during the War and died in 1916 at Winchester.[4] Memorials at St John the Baptist.

✠**SIPPETTS, JACK ... Pte. ... Hants, Sept. 1914, Pte. Mesopotamia. *Killed in Action.***
(12, High Street)

374. SIPPETTS, Jack Frederick,[5] Serjeant, 200777 (formerly 2851),[6] 1/4th Bn The Hampshire Regiment, d. 5 October 1918 aged 26.

Son of Richard and Jemima Sippetts of 3, Castle Cottage, Forest Row, Sussex. Born at Forest Row, Sussex in 1893. In 1911 he was a Draper's Assistant in a Department Store in Basingstoke.[7] Enlisted in September 1914 at Hamilton Camp. Served in Mesopotamia. Entered a theatre of war after beginning of 1916.[8] Killed in Action 5 October 1918.[9] Buried in Tehran War Cemetery, Iraq (III. D. 4.).[10] No Winchester memorial found.[11]

✠**SLATER, HARRY F. ... [BLANK] ... R.F.A., Sept. 7, 1914. Gallipoli. *Killed in Action, Aug. 9, 1915.***
(55, Upper Brook Street)

375. SLATER, Harry Francis, Gunner, 11442,[12] 66th Bde Royal Field Artillery, d. 8 August 1915 aged 26.

1 MIC not found; CWGC.
2 SJ suggests 'Probably died after Discharge.'
3 1891 and 1901 censuses.
4 No burial found.
5 Jack only in *WWSR*.
6 WO 372/18/88046. SDGW.
7 See Introduction. Both Jack Sippetts and Leonard Balls worked as Draper's Assistants, at 12, High Street, (Sherriff and Ward's shop, Mark Allen pers. comm.) when they gave the High Street address. Both joined the 1/4th Hampshires and both were entered in the *WWSR* with a 12, High Street address.
8 R Hamps Notes. RH. for this and other material in this biography.
9 R Hamps Notes. RH. confirm KIA. SJ says 'Died'.
10 CWGC.
11 ? St Maurice, lost.
12 WO 372/18/101233. SDGW.

Son of William and Sarah Slater. Born at Wimbledon, Surrey in 1889. Married Lily R. Hampton in 1912. She apparently married again as she is recorded as Tyers (formerly Slater) of 7, Magdalen Hill.¹ An Assistant in a shop in 1911. Enlisted 7 September 1914 at Southampton and served at Gallipoli (Dardanelles) with C Bty 66th Bde. Died 8 August 1915.² Buried at Lancashire Landing Cemetery, Turkey (GR G. 4.).³ No Winchester memorial found.

✠**SMART, EDWARD T. ... Dr. ... R.H.A., Aug. 1914, Dr. France. Wounded once.** *Died of Tuberculosis, Mch. 2, 1916.*
(8, Freelands Buildings)

376. SMART, Edward Thomas, Driver, 34883,⁴ 7th Bde Royal Horse Artillery, d. 2 March 1916 aged 34.

Son of William and Jesse Smart of Kings Somborne (1891). Born at London in 1881. In 1911 widowed mother at 85, Canon Street.⁵ Married Rose Ellen Johnson in 1905 (of 9, Freelands Buildings, Middle Brook Street). They had two children, Muriel Jessie born 1908 and George Henry Lewis born 1910. He was stepfather to Edward Charles Johnson. Joined in 1904, to Reserves 1907. In 1911 he was a Groom. Enlisted in August 1914 and his army work as a Driver of horses was a good fit with his pre-war occupation. Served in France. Discharged 28 December 1914 as no longer fit for War Service. Wounded once. Died after Discharge of tuberculosis 2 March 1916. Buried in Kings Somborne New Cemetery (GR I.5.).⁶ No Winchester memorial found.⁷

✠**SMITH, ALBERT E. ... Stoker ... R.N., 1904, Stoker. Pacific Ocean.** *Killed in Action,* **1914, H.M.S.** *Good Hope.*
(5, Staple Garden)

377. SMITH, Albert Ernest, Stoker 1st Class, SS/100458,⁸ HMS Good

1 SJ adds address. NOK? Census 1911 AKA 7, Alresford Road.
2 SDGW substitutes 'Died' for KIA.
3 CWGC.
4 WO 372/18/111470.
5 Brigade info, and census, parents, enlistment and reenlistment etc from SJ.
6 CWGC. It is not clear why the CWGC recognised Edward Smart as he died so long after Discharge. (SJ) In common with many large houses in the country during the war local landowners made their premises available to sick and wounded servicemen. Marsh Court, between Kings Somborne and Stockbridge was the property of Herbert Johnson and was used for these purposes during the war. Johnson funded the war memorials at both Kings Somborne and Stockbridge (both by Lutyens who designed the National Cenotaph and these memorials well as Marsh Court itself) and a village hall at Kings Somborne in memory of his nephew who was killed in the war. There is, however, no known connection between Smart and Marsh Court.
7 Might not be expected because of circumstance in previous note.
8 ADM 188/1106/100458. (RFR/PO/IC/148).

Hope Royal Navy, d. 1 November 1914 aged 30.

Son of Peter Smith and Emily Smith of 5, Staple Garden. Born 23 November 1884. Married Sarah R. Smith (Macklin). In 1911 Moreton Macklin, Smith's father-in-law was Head of Household at 5, Staple Gardens. Enlisted in 1904 initially for five years. Bricklayer in 1911. Reenlisted from the Fleet Reserve in July 1914 and served aboard HMS Good Hope. Killed in Action 1 November 1914 off the coast of Chile.[1] His *WWSR* record uniquely refers to service in 'Pacific Ocean' where the Good Hope was lost. Commemorated on the Portsmouth Naval Memorial (PR 4.).[2] Memorials at St John the Baptist and St Thomas's.[3]

De Ruvigny states:[4]

'Smith, Albert Ernest, Stoker 1st Class (RFR II 8044) SS/100458, HMS Good Hope; lost in action off Coronel, on the coast of Chili, 1 November 1914.'[5]

✠SMITH, ALFRED C. ... Pte. ... Somerset L.I., May 1916, Pte. Surrey Rif. France. *Killed in Action, Oct. 8, 1916, Somme.* (30, Monks Road)

378.   SMITH, Alfred Charles, Private, 653183, (formerly 6699)[6] 1st /21st (County of London) Bn The London Regiment (First Surrey Rifles), d. 8 October 1916 age unknown.

Enlisted May 1916 at Winchester and served in France. Listed as formerly 4071 5th Surrey Rifles[7] and transferred from Prince Albert's (Somerset Light Infantry).[8] Killed in Action on the Somme 8 October 1916. Commemorated on the Thiepval Memorial, Somme, France (PR Pier and Face 13 C.).[9] Memorial at St Bartholomew's.

✠SMITH, ALFRED J. ... Pte. ... Hants, Aug. 1914, Pte. Dardanelles. Wounded, Aug. 1915. *Died of Wounds, July 1917.* (44, Water Lane)

1   Hepper, 2006, p. 28.
2   CWGC.
3   SJ queries St John memorial, adds St Thomas.
4   de Ruvigny.
5   SJ cites (RFR/PO/1C/138). Naval Casualties 1914-1919.
6   WO 372/18/119983. SDGW.
7   SDGW. SJ adds 'East Surrey Regiment'.
8   *WWSR.*
9   CWGC.

379. SMITH, Alfred J., Private, 4550,[1] 3rd (Reserve) Bn The Hampshire Regiment, d. 7 July 1917 aged 37.

Son of Charles and Ellen Martha Smith of 44, Water Lane. Enlisted in The Hampshire Royal Artillery in 1901.[2] Previously a Building Labourer for a Mr Jenkins. Discharged with good character in July 1911, Special Reservist.[3] A Builder's Labourer in 1911. Re-enlisted in August 1914. Served at Gallipoli (Dardanelles). Special Reservist. Entered a theatre of war with 10th Bn on 22 July 1915.[4] Wounded August 1915 and Died of Wounds 7 July 1917. Buried in Winchester (St Giles's Hill) Cemetery.[5] Memorial at St John the Baptist.

His brother Edward served in France as a Driver in the Royal Field Artillery. He was taken prisoner by Germans 21 March 1918 and survived the War.

✠**SMITH, ARCHIBALD C. ... Pte. ... Hants, Dec. 1916, Pte. Mesopotamia. *Died, July* 13, 1917, *Baghdad*. (13, Cheriton Road)**

380. SMITH, Archibald C., Private, 203512,[6] 1/4th Bn The Hampshire Regiment, d. 13 July 1917 aged 35.

Son of Harry Giles and Ann Smith 'formerly of 53, Western Road in 1911'.[7] Born at Alresford in 1882. Married Annie Sophia Wiseman in 1908. Lived at 13, Cheriton Road. By 1911 they had Frederick Harry George, born 1909 and Robert Archibald Charles, born 1911. A Journeyman Tailor in 1911. Enlisted in December 1916 at Winchester. Served in Mesopotamia. Entered a theatre of war with 1/4th Bn after beginning of 1917.[8] Died 13 July 1917[9] at Baghdad. Buried in Baghdad (North Gate) War Cemetery, Iraq (GR XV. E. 11.).[10] Memorials at St Matthew's, St Paul's and St Thomas's.

1 WO 372/18/117503. Alfred Smith.
2 Possibly Garrison Artillery?
3 According to his Army Service Records. WO 96/1368/39.
4 R Hamps Notes. RH. for this and other material in this biography. More in Regimental Archive.
5 CWGC. An account of his funeral and burial in R Hamps Notes.
6 WO 372/18/120007.
7 Census 1911.
8 R Hamps Notes. RH. for this and other material in this biography. Notes include this reference: 'In civilian life he was an expert hand in the employ of Messrs. F. Flight & Sons, military tailors, of Winchester, who appealed for him before the local Tribunal on two or three occasions.'
9 SDGW states 31 July 1917.
10 CWGC. Winchester memorials to A.C. Smith are found in these churches which could be to this man, especially as Alfred C. Smith above is apparently commemorated at St Bartholomew's

✠**SMITH, CHARLES F. ... Pte. ... Hants, rejoined Aug. 1914, Pte. India, Persian Gulf.** *Killed in Action, June* **12, 1915,** *Basra.*
(Southall Cottage, Alresford Rd.)

381. SMITH, Charles Frederick, Private, 2413,[1] 1/4th Bn The Hampshire Regiment, d. 12 June 1915 age unknown.

Re-enlisted in August 1914 at Winchester. Served in India and the Persian Gulf. Killed in Action 12 June 1915 at Basra.[2] Buried in the Basra War Cemetery, Iraq (GR VI. B. 8.).[3] Memorials at All Saints and St John the Baptist.

✠**SMITH, EDWIN A. ... Pte. ... Hants, Sept. 1914, Pte. India, Persia, Mesopotamia.** *Killed in Action, Feb.* **23, 1917.**
(11, Fairfield Road)

382. SMITH, Edwin Alfred (Teddy), Private, 200771,[4] 1/4th Bn The Hampshire Regiment, d. 24 February 1917 aged 25.

Eldest son of Edwin H. and Charlotte E. Smith of 11, Fairfield Road. Born 1888. A Wood Carver in 1911. Enlisted in September 1914 at Hamilton Camp (2844). Served in India, Persia and Mesopotamia. Entered a theatre of war with 1/4th Bn on 18 March 1915.[5] Killed in Action 24 February 1917. Commemorated on the Basra Memorial, Iraq (PR Panel 21 and 63.).[6] Memorials at St Paul's and St Matthew's (B. A. on memorial).[7]

His brother Clement O. served in France as a Private, promoted to Corporal in the Training Reserve, then The Royal Warwickshire Regiment.

✠**SMITH, FREDERICK C. ... Corpl. ... Hants, June 1916, Pte. France.** *Killed in Action, Aug.* **24, 1917,** *Ypres.*
(4, Hedges Buildings)

383. SMITH, Frederick Charles, Corporal, 25170,[8] 2nd Bn The Hampshire Regiment, d. 24 August 1917 aged 35.

1   WO 372/18/126867 and SDGW. Not identified in the census.
2   R Hamps Notes. RH. do not state that he 'Entered a theatre of war' but that he died of disease at Basra. SDGW also says 'Died'.
3   CWGC.
4   WO 372/18/131602. Discrepancy in date of death and age related to census birth. SDGW.
5   R Hamps Notes. RH. for this and other material in this biography. A medallist for Winchester Football Club.
6   CWGC.
7   SJ suggest 'B. A. on memorial'.
8   WO 372/18/136375. SDGW.

Son of Peter and Emily Smith of Chilcomb (sometime of Staple Garden). Born 1883.[1] Married Emma Kate Stockwell in 1902. Lived at 4, Hedges Buildings, Magdalen Hill (aka Morn Hill). By 1911 they had one son, Frederick Charles born 1908. In 1911 F. C. senior was a Bricklayer. Worked for Mr O. H. Paul of Parchment Street). Enlisted in June 1916 at Winchester. Served in France. Entered a theatre of war with 2nd Bn at some point after the beginning of 1916.[2] Killed in Action 24 August 1917 at Ypres. Commemorated on the Tyne Cot Memorial, Zonnebeke, West-Vlaanderen, Belgium (PR Panel 88 to 90 and 162.).[3] Memorials at All Saints and St John the Baptist.

ⴕSMITH, HORACE ... Tpr. ... D.C.L.I., 1907, Pte. Dragoon Gds. France, Belgium. Wounded three times, 1914 and 1918. Died, Mch. 1918.
(14, Gladstone Street)

384. SMITH, Horace, Private, D/3211,[4] 5th (Princess Charlotte of Wales's) Dragoon Guards, d. 31 March 1918 aged 33.

Son of Horace and Julia Smith. Born 1885. A cadet at Thames Nautical Training HMS Worcester in 1901.[5] Enlisted in 1907 at Winchester and served in France and Belgium during the War. Transferred from The Duke of Cornwall's Light Infantry. Wounded three times from 1914 to 1918 and Died of Wounds 31 March 1918. Buried in St Sever Cemetery Extension, Rouen, Seine-Maritime, France (GR P. IX. E. 3B.).[6] Memorials at St Matthew's, St Paul's and St Thomas's School.

ⴕSMITH, ROBERT W. ... Sergt. ... R.B., 1898, Rfn. France. Died, Aug. 6, 1916, Abbeville.
(2, Westgate Lane)

385. SMITH, Robert William, Serjeant, 6336,[7] 1st Bn The Rifle Brigade (The Prince Consort's Own), d. 6 August 1916 aged 35.

Son of Robert and Emma Smith. Born in 1882 and resided at Norwich, Norfolk.[8] Enlisted in 1898 in Norwich. A Bugler in The King's Royal Rifle

1   1883 in 1901; 1882 in 1911. R Hamps Notes. RH. for this and other material in this biography where this Smith family's loss of three sons and a grandson was noted.
2   R Hamps Notes.
3   CWGC.
4   WO 372/18/146829. SDGW.
5   1901 and 1891 censuses.
6   CWGC.
7   WO 372/18/169314. SDGW.
8   SJ adds 'and resided. Winchester connection unclear.' Census, JB notes New Road Woolwich in 1911 – different man?

Corps resident at Cambridge Cottages, Woolwich in 1911. During the War he served on the Western Front. Died of Wounds 6 August 1916 at Abbeville. Buried in Abbeville Communal Cemetery, Somme, France (GR VI. K. 8.).[1] Memorial at St Thomas's.

**✠SMITH, SYDNEY E. ... Pte. ... R.M.L.I., 1913, Pte. North Sea, Dardanelles, Salonica, France. *Killed in Action, Apl. 1, 1918.*
(13, Union Street)**

386. SMITH, Sydney Ernest, Private, PO/16708,[2] 2nd RM Bn RN Div. Royal Marine Light Infantry, d. 7 April 1918 aged 22.

Son of the late Ernest George and Sarah Jane Smith of 13, Union Street. Born 13 December 1895 at St Giles, Reading, Berkshire.[3] A Tailor's apprentice in 1911. Enlisted 21 January 1913 at Southampton and served during the War in North Sea, at Gallipoli (Dardanelles), Salonica and France. Killed in Action 7 April 1918. Commemorated on the Pozieres Memorial, Somme, France (PR Panel 1).[4] Memorial at Holy Trinity.

His father served on the Home Front as a Private in The Rifle Brigade (The Prince Consort's Own) and survived the War.

**✠SMITH, WILFRID S. ... [BLANK] ... R.G.A., Nov. 1, 1916. Home. *Accidentally Drowned, Nov. 4, 1916, Plymouth.*
(66, Kingsgate Street)**

387. SMITH, Wilfred Sidney, Gunner, 126307,[5] No. 3 Depot Royal Garrison Artillery, d. 4 November 1916 aged 26.

Son of Sidney and Elizabeth Anna Smith of 66, Kingsgate Street. Born 1890. An Assistant in his father's Tailoring business in 1911. Enlisted 1 November 1916 at Winchester. Drowned accidentally 4 November 1916 at Plymouth. Buried at Winchester (West Hill) Old Cemetery (GR 1753.).[6] Memorial at St Michael's.

**✠SNOOK, CYRIL A. ... Sergt. ... R.G.A., 1913, Gun. France. Wounded and Gassed, Sept. 25, 1917. M.M. 1917. *Died of Wounds,* 1918.
(53, St. Catherine's Road)**

1 CWGC.
2 ADM 159/190/16708. Discrepancy in dates of death.
3 1911 census gives 1896.
4 CWGC.
5 MIC not identified.
6 CWGC.

388. SNOOK, Cyril A., Serjeant, 352341,[1] Hampshire. [RGA - (TF)][2] Royal Garrison Artillery, d. 7 May 1918 aged 24.

Son of Leah Snook of 53, St Catherine's Road. Born 1894. A Clerk with the National Service League in 1911. Enlisted in 1913 at Winchester. Served in France during the War. Awarded the Military Medal in 1917.[3] Gassed and wounded 25 September 1917 and Died of Wounds 7 May 1918. Buried in Winchester (St Giles's Hill) Cemetery.[4] Memorials at All Saints and Peter Symonds School.

✠**SOFFE, GEORGE ... Pte. ... Hants, Aug. 1914, Pte. India, Mesopotamia. Taken Prisoner by Turks, Apl. 29, 1916, Kut. Died, June 20, 1916, *Mosul*.**
   (17, St. Paul's Hill)

389. SOFFE, George, Private, 2471,[5] 1/4th Bn The Hampshire Regiment, d. 26 June 1916 aged 34.

Fifth son of John T. and Charlotte Soffe of 8, Upper Stockbridge Road. Born at Church Oakley in 1881. A Domestic Under Gardener in 1901. In 1911 he was boarding with a family in Romsey and working as a Domestic Gardener. Enlisted in August 1914 at Winchester (2471). Served in India and Mesopotamia. Entered a theatre of war with 1/4th Bn on 18 March 1915.[6] Taken prisoner by Turks 29 April 1916 at Kut and died a POW 26 June 1916 at Mosul. Commemorated on the Basra Memorial, Iraq (PR Panel 21 and 63.).[7] Memorials at St Matthew's and St Paul's.

He had three brothers who served in the War. Henry J., listed below, was Killed in Action 20 October 1916. Arthur J. served on the Home Front as a Gunner in the Royal Marine Artillery. Ernest T. served at Salonica as a Private, promoted to Corporal in The Hampshire Regiment and the Machine Gun Corps. They both survived the War.

✠**SOFFE, HENRY J. ... Pte. ... Hants, 1915, Pte. France. *Killed in Action Oct.* 20, 1916, *Goudecourt*.**
   (17, St. Paul's Hill)

1   WO 372/18/192563. SDGW.
2   SDGW.
3   No citation for MM found. Award states Royal Garrison Artillery.
4   CWGC. No GR. Photo of grave inscription.
5   WO 372/18/195748.
6   R Hamps Notes. RH. for this and other material in this biography.
7   CWGC.

390. SOFFE, Henry (Harry), Private, 17710,[1] 2nd Bn The Hampshire Regiment, d. 20 October 1916 aged 45.

Third son of John T. (Tom) and Charlotte Soffe of 18, Upper Stockbridge Road. Born at Church Oakley in 1872. Married Maria Louise Campbell in 1901.[2] Lived at 4, Victoria Road, Freemantle, Southampton.[3] They had Dorothy Louise born 1902 and Henry Thomas born 1904. Henry worked as a Domestic Groom according to the 1891 census. In 1911 he was a Domestic Gardener living with his wife and children at St Bartholomew, Hyde. Enlisted in 1915 at Southampton. Served in France. Entered a theatre of war (Egypt) as a reinforcement for the 2nd Bn on 1 December 1915.[4] Killed in Action 20 October 1916 at Goudecourt. Buried in Bancourt British Cemetery, Pas de Calais, France (GR X. B. 9.). Memorials at St Matthew's and St Paul's.

He had three brothers who served in the War. George, listed above, was Killed in Action 26 June 1916. Arthur J. served on the Home Front as a Gunner in the Royal Marine Artillery. Ernest T. served at Salonica as a Private, promoted to Corporal in The Hampshire Regiment and the Machine Gun Corps. They both survived the War.

✠**SOUTHCOTT, CHARLES F. ... Sergt. ... Hants (T.F.), Pte. Persian Gulf. Wounded once. *Died*, Dec. 16, 1917.**
(5, Ilex Terrace)

391. SOUTHCOTT, Charles Forbes, Serjeant, 380126,[5] 17th Bn The Hampshire Regiment,[6] d. 17 December 1917 aged 39.

Born at New Cross, Kent in 1877. Husband of Edith Charlotte Southcott from 1900. Lived at 7, Princes Place, Stanmore, Winchester. In 1881 he was living with a cousin in Cottenham, Cambridgeshire. A Cabinet Maker living with his wife at 15, Eastgate Street in 1911. Enlisted at Winchester (13). Served in the Persian Gulf. Wounded once. Died 16 December 1917.[7] Buried in Winchester (West Hill) Old Cemetery (GR 1875).[8] Memorials at Christ Church and Holy Trinity.

1 WO 372/18/195752. SDGW.
2 Also noted as Marie.
3 Census 1911. CWGC.
4 R Hamps Notes. RH. for this and other material in this biography. Archive has him as 44.
5 WO 372/18/202575. 4/13 – Regimental Number? SDGW.
6 See Appendix 2 footnote for the 17th Hampshires.
7 R Hamps Notes. RH. for this and other material in this biography. Gives his age as 40. Served with 4th attached 2/4th died with 7th Bn. A popular figure in the city in military and Conservative circles, he was accorded an impressive funeral which is recorded in the archive.
8 CWGC.

⚔SOUTHCOTT, HERBERT ... Pte. ... R.A.F., June 1918, Pte. Home. *Died, July 1, 1918, Blandford.*
(77, Canon Street)

392. SOUTHCOTT, Herbert, Private 2nd Class, 197507,[1] Repair Depot Royal Air Force, d. 1 July 1918 age unknown.

Son of a cathedral Lay Clerk, William Veysey, and Sophia Southcott residing in 1911 at 77, Canon Street. Born 1873. Herbert Southcott was living with his wife at 22, ?Marvels Lane, Grove Park, Lee, SE London in 1911. Enlisted June 1918 and served on the Home Front. Died 1 July 1918 at Blandford, Dorset. Buried in Winchester (West Hill) Old Cemetery (GR 1958).[2] Memorial at St Michael's.

⚔SPENCER, ALBERT ... Pte. ... Hants, Feb. 1916, Pte. Egypt. *Missing, believed Killed.*
(6, Percy Terrace)

393. SPENCER, Albert, Private, 331221,[3] 1/8th (Isle of Wight Rifles, Princess Beatrice's) Bn The Hampshire Regiment, d. 19 April 1917 aged 26.

Son of Sarah Mullins. Born at Andover in 1891. A Farm Labourer in 1911. Enlisted in February 1916 at Winchester (2980). Served in Egypt. Entered a theatre of war with 1/8th Bn after beginning of 1916.[4] Killed in Action 19 April 1917. Buried in Gaza War Cemetery, Israel and Palestine (including Gaza) (GR XXI. G. 5.).[5] Memorials at St John the Baptist.

⚔SPENCER, JOSEPH ... L.-Corpl. ... Hants, 1911, Pte. India, Mesopotamia. *Killed in Action, Feb. 17, 1916, Kut.*
(2, St. John's Park Terrace)

394. SPENCER, Joseph, Lance-Corporal, 1822,[6] 1/4th Bn The Hampshire Regiment, d. 17 February 1916 aged 20.

Son of Henry J. and Rose Spencer of 2, St John's Park Terrace. Enlisted in 1911 at Winchester. Served in India and Mesopotamia during the War. Entered a theatre of war with 1/4th Bn on 18 March 1918.[7] Killed in Action 17 February

1 MIC not found. Census and family data from SJ.
2 CWGC.
3 WO 372/18/214386. SDGW? SJ adds (Rifleman). See Fielder, Maidment, T Potter etc.
4 R Hamps Notes. RH.
5 CWGC.
6 WO 372/18/216909. Not found in census. SDGW.
7 R Hamps Notes. RH.

1916 at Kut. Buried in Kut War Cemetery, Iraq (GR H. 3.).¹ Memorials at St John the Baptist.

✠STACEY, FRANK ... Corpl. ... Lond. (Civil Service Rif.), 1916, Rfn. Mesopotamia, Egypt. *Killed in Action, Dec.* **14, 1917.**
(12, Westgate Lane)

395. STACEY, Frank Lance-Corporal, 574712,² 2nd/17th (County of London) Bn The London Regiment (Poplar and Stepney Rifles) d. 8 December 1917 aged 30.

Son of Noah and Alice Stacey of 12, Westgate Lane.³ Born 1887. Employed as a Doctor's Boy in 1901; a Gardener in 1911. Enlisted in 1916 at Bow, London while resident at Saffron Waldon, Essex. Served in Mesopotamia and Egypt. Killed in Action 8 December 1917. Commemorated on Jerusalem Memorial, Israel and Palestine (including Gaza) (PR 47-53.).⁴ Memorial at St Thomas's School.

✠STACEY, FREDERICK ... Corpl. ... Glos., Mch. 1916, Pte. Hants. France. Wounded, Apl. 23, 1918. *Died of Wounds,* ***Apl.* 24, 1918.**
(12, Westgate Lane)

396. STACEY, Frederick, Corporal, 28566,⁵ 1st Bn The Hampshire Regiment, d. 24 April 1918 aged 27.

Son of Noah and Alice Stacey of 12, Westgate Lane. Born 1891. A Plumber's Labourer in 1911. Enlisted in March 1916 at Winchester. Served in France. He was formerly 27416 The Gloucestershire Regiment.⁶ Previously husband of Mrs William Shaw of 45, Queen Street, Hulme, Manchester.⁷ Entered a theatre of war with 1st Bn Hampshire Regiment at some point after the beginning of 1916.⁸ Wounded 23 April 1918 and Died of Wounds 24 April 1918. Buried in La Pougnay⁹ Military Cemetery, Pas de Calais, France (GR VII. E. 13.). Memorial at St Thomas's.

1   CWGC gives his number as 1823.
2   WO 372/19/6271. Nothing about Civil Service Rifles on his MIC. Frank Stacey 17th London Regiment. No reference to MIC on SDGW. SJ writes 'I have no details.'
3   Census 1891, 1901, 1911. CWGC.
4   CWGC.
5   WO 372/19/6278.
6   SDGW.
7   CWGC.
8   R Hamps Notes. RH.
9   'Lapugnay'. CWGC.

✠**STAGG, CHARLES T. ... Rfn. ... K.R.R.C., rejoined Aug. 1914, Rfn.** *Killed in Action, July 10, 1917.*
(85, Chesil Street.)

397. STAGG, Charles Thomas, Private,[1] 6586, 2nd Bn The King's Royal Rifle Corps, d. 10 July 1917 aged 29.

Born 1888. Enlisted in the 3rd Bn The King's Royal Rifle Corps as a Private in 1911, registered as living in Dagshai, India. Re-enlisted August 1914 at Winchester. Served in France. Mentioned in Despatches 20 October 1914.[2] Died of Wounds[3] 10 July 1917. Commemorated on the Nieuport Memorial, West-Vlaanderen, Belgium.[4] Memorial at St Peter Chesil.

✠**STAGG, HENRY ... Pte. ... Hants, Mch. 1916, Pte. India, Mesopotamia.** *Died of Fever, Sept. 3, 1918, Basra.*
(7, Upper Brook Street)

398. STAGG, Henry, Private, 307159,[5] 2nd /7th Bn The Hampshire Regiment, d. 3 September 1918 aged 31.

Son of Florence Stagg. Born 1887. A Carman Coal Merchant in 1911. Enlisted in March 1916 at Winchester. Served in India and Mesopotamia. Entered a theatre of war (Mesopotamia) with 2/7th Bn after beginning of 1917. [6]Died of fever 3 September 1918 at Basra. Buried in Amara War Cemetery, Iraq (GR XIV. C. 10.).[7] Memorial at Holy Trinity.

✠**STAINER, TOM ... [BLANK] ... R.A.S.C., 1917. France.** *Died, Dec, 4, 1918.*
(38, Eastgate Street)

399. STAINER, Tom, Private, A/382130,[8] Army Service Corps (Canteens), d. 4 December 1918 age unknown.

In 1911 family living at 5, St Swithun Villas, Canon Street headed by Tom Stainer and his wife Annie Emily Stainer. Their son was also Tom and this could be him.[9] Served in France in the ASC Expeditionary Force Canteen

1   See Maidment, Spencer, T. Potter, Fielder etc.
2   *London Gazette* p. 58661.
3   SJ substitutes DOW for KIA SDGW.
4   CWGC. No PR.
5   WO 372/19/9043. SDGW.
6   R Hamps Notes. RH.
7   CWGC.
8   WO 372/19/9454.
9   Census 1911.

at Lillers. Died 4 December 1918. Buried in Lille Southern Cemetery, Nord, France (GR I.C.8.).¹ Memorials at St John the Baptist.

✠**STANLEY, JOHN H. ... A.B. ... R.N., 1913. North Sea ; H.M.S.** ***Negro.*** **Drowned, Dec. 20, 1915.**
    (57, Water Lane)

400.   STANLEY, John Henry, J/20376,² Able Seaman 1, Royal Navy, HMS Negro, d. 20 December 1916 aged 19.

Son of Jane Stanley of 30, Eastgate Street.³ Born 15 May 1897 at Fareham. Enlisted 6 December 1912. Served in the North Sea. HMS Negro was run down by HMS Hoste in a collision off Scapa Flow 26 December 1916 with the loss of 47 men.⁴ Commemorated on Portsmouth Naval Memorial (PR 13).⁵ Memorials at St John the Baptist.

✠**STEEL, FRANK ... Pte. ... Glos., Mch. 1916, Pte. R.W.K. France. Wounded, Apl. 3, 1917, and Aug. 27, 1918.** ***Died of Wounds, Aug. 27, 1918.***
    (21, Eastgate Street)

401.   STEEL, Frank, Private, G/21528,⁶ 7th (Service) Bn The Queen's Own (Royal West Kent Regiment) d. 27 August 1918.

Born 1883. In 1901 he was a Draper's Porter living with his brother William. In 1911 a Slaughterman. Enlisted March 1916 at Winchester. Served in France with the Royal West Kent Regiment. Formerly 5165 The Gloucestershire Regiment.⁷ Wounded 3 April 1917. Killed in Action⁸ 27 August 1918. Commemorated on Vis-en-Artois Memorial (PR 7). Memorial at Holy Trinity.⁹

✠**STEELE, WALTER C. ... Pte. ... Hants, 1910, Pte-.India, Mesopotamia, Egypt. Wounded, Apl. 1915 and Nov. 1917.** ***Killed in Action, Oct. 10, 1918.***
    (47, Wales Street)

---

1   CWGC.
2   ADM 188/687/20376.
3   Naval Casualties 1914-1919.
4   Check Hepper 2006, p. 76.
5   CWGC.
6   WO 372/19/29249. SJ has number as G/21528 not 2158.
7   SDGW.
8   SDGW KIA.
9   CWGC.

402. STEELE, Walter Charles (Jock),[1] Private, 200146,[2] 1/4th Bn The Hampshire Regiment, d. 10 October 1918 aged 33.

Son of Edward and Elizabeth A. Steele of Compton (at 47, Wales Street in 1911). Born at Compton in 1886. His father died in 1902.[3] Enlisted in 1910 (1753) at Winchester and served in India, Mesopotamia and Egypt during the War. Entered a theatre of war with 1/4th Bn on 18 March 1915.[4] Wounded April 1915 and November 1917. Died 10 October 1918 at Basra. Buried in Tehran War Cemetery, Iran (GR III. D. 14.).[5] Memorial at St John the Baptist.

✠STEVENS, ERNEST ... 2nd Lieut. ... 2nd Lieut. Sea. H., 1900, R.Q.M.S. France. Wounded, Feb. 2, 1915. *Died of Wounds, Feb. 2, 1915*
 (11, Western Road)

403. STEVENS, Ernest, 2nd Lieutenant,[6] 1st Bn Seaforth Highlanders (Ross-shire Buffs, The Duke of Albany's), d. 2 February 1915 aged 34.

Son of Samuel and Emily Stevens of 21, Sussex Street. Born 1880. Husband of Ethel Stevens (two addresses on MIC The Bungalow, Holly Road, Green Street, Green, Orpington. Kent and ?Caineville School, Mussoorie, India).[7] A Colour Serjeant (RQMS 8248) with the Seaforth Highlanders, resident in 'Chanbattia' in 1911. Served in France with the Seaforth Highlanders. Commissioned 20 January 1915. Died of Wounds 2 February 1915. Buried at Le Touret Military Cemetery, Richebourg-L'Avoue, France (GR II.D.4.).[8] Memorials at St Matthew's, St Paul's and St Thomas's.

Samuel, of the same address, served as a Lieutenant in The Hampshire Regiment and survived the War.

✠STICKLAN, CHARLES H. ... Bug. ... Hants, 1893, Bug. France. *Killed in Action, May 3, 1915.*
 (14, Little Minster Street)

404. STICKLAN, Herbert Charles,[9] Private, 3/8831,[10] 1st Bn The Hampshire

1 William Charles in 1911 census.
2 WO 372/19/32107. And SDGW state 'Died' not 'Killed in Action'.
3 BMD.
4 SDGW for this and other material in this biography. Notes place of death as Basra, but burial in Tehran.
5 CWGC.
6 WO 372/19/43142. Commission from National Army Museum Records.
7 SJ adds RQMS.
8 CWGC.
9 Charles H in *WWSR*.
10 WO 372/19/59604. SDGW.

Regiment, d. 3 May 1915 aged 33.

Born at Shawford 1880.[1] Husband of Charlotte S. Sticklan of 14, Little Minster Street. Enlisted in 1893 at Grange Camp, Special Reservist. Served in France. Received the Long Service and Good Conduct Medal. Entered theatre of war with 1st Bn on 12 November 1914.[2] Killed in Action 3 May 1915. Commemorated on the Ypres (Menin Gate) Memorial, Ypres (Ieper), West-Vlaanderen, Belgium (PR Panel 35.).[3] Memorial at St Thomas's.

✠**STONE, ARCHIBALD ... [BLANK] ... Somerset L.I., Jan. 1916. R. Berks. France.** *Killed in Action. May* **8, 1917,** *Henninel.* **(22, Bar End)**

405. STONE, Archibald, Private,[4] 6th (Service) Bn Princess Charlotte of Wales's (Royal Berkshire Regiment), d. 8 May 1917 age unknown.

Born at Southampton.[5] Living at Earls Court, Middlesex when he enlisted at Winchester in January 1916. Served in France with The Berkshire Regiment. Formerly 21125 The Somerset Light Infantry. Killed in Action 8 May 1917. Buried London Cemetery, Neuville-Vitasse, Pas de Calais, France (GR I.13.47.).[6] Memorial at St Peter Chesil.

✠**STRIPP, ALFRED ... Pte. ... Hants, Nov. 1915, Pte. India, Egypt, Palestine.** *Killed in Action, Apl.* **9, 1918.** **(46, Water Lane)**

406. STRIPP, Alfred, Private, 241746,[7] 2/5th Bn The Hampshire Regiment, d. 9 April 1918 aged 26.

Son of Henry and Hannah Stripp of 46, Magdelene Cottages, Water Lane. Born 1893. A General Labourer in 1911. Enlisted in November 1915 at Southampton and served in India, Egypt and Palestine. Entered a theatre of war with 2/5th Bn after beginning of 1917.[8] Killed in Action 9 April 1918. Buried in Ramleh War Cemetery, Israel and Palestine (including Gaza) (GR T. 39.).[9] Memorials at St John the Baptist.

1 BMD.
2 R Hamps Notes. RH. for this and other material in this biography. Spells his name Sticklen. Previous service as regular or territorial. But no trace of previous service found in Regimental Archive.
3 CWGC. Age 33, discrepancy over age and birth.
4 WO 372/19/70917.
5 SDGW.
6 CWGC.
7 WO 372/19/90940.
8 R Hamps Notes. RH.
9 CWGC.

His brother Arthur served in France as a Lance-Corporal (enlisted in 1905) in The Rifle Brigade (The Prince Consort's Own), then The Labour Corps. He was wounded once and survived the War.

✠SUMMERBELL, CHARLES ... Pte. ... Hants, Pte. Dardanelles, Salonica. Wounded once. *Died.*
(25, Hyde Close)

407. SUMMERBELL, Charles, Private, 17794,[1] 1st Bn The Hampshire Regiment died 7 June 1917, aged 35.

Son of John and Margaret Summerbell of 107, Colebrook Street (1901, 1911). Born 1879.[2] Husband of Rose Louisa Summerbell of 25, Hyde Close. Enlisted 26 May 1915. Entered a theatre of war (Gallipoli) with 10th Bn on 3 October 1915.[3] Discharged 2 August 1916 as no longer fit for War Service due to tuberculosis of right lung. Served with The Hampshire Regiment in Salonica and Gallipoli (Dardanelles).[4] No Winchester memorial found.[5]

His brother William served in Royal Engineers and is listed below.

✠SUMMERBELL, WILLIAM ... Dr. ... R.E., 1905, Dr. Salonica, Serbia, Dardanelles. *Died.*
(25, Hyde Close)

408. SUMMERBELL, William, 14559,[6] Royal Engineers, age and date of death unknown.

---

1 WO 372/19/107598. MIC states 'Discharged' no date of death. Additional material from SJ and BMD.
2 BMD.
3 R Hamps Notes. RH. for this and other material in this biography. Also a note 'late' Hampshire Regiment. Also 'SWB enlisted 26.5.1915. Discharged due to wounds on 2.8.1916' ?South Wales Borderers, dates and evidence of discharge appear to conflict with evidence of service with and discharge from The Hampshire Regiment.
4 His medals sold at Eastbourne Auction Rooms, 15 September 2012, Lot 571. Included 1914/15 Star, War Medal and Victory Medal (VM indicates he has served in an active theatre of War). Value £20-£30.
5 Not found on CWGC as died after Discharge. Parents' connection with Colebrook Street might have led to memorialisation on lost St Maurice memorial.
6 WO 372/19/107627 may refer to this man. No reference found to Discharge/death. 1914 Star medal issued to those who served in France between 5 August and 22 November 1914. His unit suggests he was a regular soldier. www.wartimememoriesproject. States that the 17th Field Company Royal Engineers went to France mid-August 1914. Not on CWGC, presumably died after Discharge. Parents' connection with Colebrook Street might have led to memorialisation on lost St Maurice memorial.

Son of John and Margaret Summerbell of 107, Colebrook Street (1901, 1911). Served with 17th Field Company, Corps of Royal Engineers. No Winchester memorial found.

His brother Charles served in The Hampshire Regiment and is listed above.

✠SWAYNE, DENNIS ... Pte. ... R. Sussex, Aug. 1914, Pte. France. Wounded, July 10, 1916. *Died of Wounds, July 11, 1916.*
(19, St. John's Road)

409.   SWAYNE, Albert Dennis,[1] Private, L/8133,[2] 7th (Service) Bn The Royal Sussex Regiment, d. 11 July 1916 aged 28.

Only son of Francis and Anna Swayne of 19, St Johns Road, Magdalen Hill. Born at Sherrington, Wiltshire in 1887. In 1911 serving as a Private 1st Bn The Royal Sussex Regiment, resident at Rawalpindi Punjab India. Re-enlisted in August 1914 at Chichester and served in France. Wounded 10 July 1916 and Died of Wounds next day 11 July 1916. Buried in Boulogne Eastern Cemetery, Pas de Calais, France (GR VIII. D. 13.).[3] Memorials at St John the Baptist.

✠TAYLOR, CHARLES W. ... Sergt. ... Hants, Pte. Indian Supply Corps. India. Taken Prisoner by Turks, Apl. 29, 1916, Kut. *Died, Dec. 29, 1916.*
(5, Westgate Lane)

410.   TAYLOR, Charles (Charlie) W., Serjeant, 8065,[4] 2nd Bn the Hampshire Regiment, d. 29 December 1916, aged 29.

A son of Charles Taylor at 5, Westgate Lane in 1901. Enlisted in Winchester. Born 1890 St Thomas's. Enlists c 1908. In 1911 a regular soldier, Private in The Hampshire Regiment serving in South Africa at Wynberg, Cape of Good Hope. Served in India and Mesopotamia. Entered theatre of war with 2nd Bn on 9 November 1914.[5] Taken Prisoner by Turks 29 April 1916. Died 29 December 1916. Buried Baghdad (North Gate) War Cemetery, Iraq (GR Angora Memorial 164).[6] Memorial at St Thomas's Church and School.

1   Dennis only in *WWSR*.
2   WO 372/19/126914.
3   CWGC.
4   WO 372/19/159431.
5   R Hamps Notes. RH. for this and other material in this biography. Illustrated in the 1913 Journal, p. 139.
6   CWGC.

His brother Albert served in France as a Private in The Royal Berkshire Regiment and Labour Corps. He survived the War.

✠TEE, THOMAS V. ... Stoker ... R.N., Nov. 1915, Stoker. Grand Fleet. *Died, Feb.* 22, 1915, *R.N. Hospital, Gosport.* (5, Lower Brook Street)

411. TEE, Thomas Victor, Stoker 2nd Class, 29237, HMS Victory Royal Navy, d. 22 February 1916 aged 18.[1]

Son of the late Henry and Ellen Tee of 5, Lower Brook Street. Born 13 March 1897. In 1911 Thomas was working in the woods with his father. His father died in 1913. Enlisted in November 1915. Served with the Grand Fleet. Died from broncho-pneumonia 22 February 1916 at the Royal Navy Hospital, Gosport. Buried in Winchester (West Hill) Old Cemetery (GR 42-3. 16208.).[2] No Winchester memorial found.[3]

He had two brothers who served in the War. Walter Frank, listed below, was Killed in Action 7 June 1917. William served in France as a Driver in the Army Service Corps and survived the War.

✠TEE, WALTER F. ... Pte. ... Hants Y., Nov. 1915, Tpr. Hants. France. *Killed in Action, June* 7, 1917. (5, Lower Brook Street)

412. TEE, Walter Frank, Private, 26890,[4] 15th (Service) Bn (2nd Portsmouth) The Hampshire Regiment,[5] d. 7 June 1917 aged 37.

Eldest son of the late Henry and Ellen Tee of 5, Lower Brook Street. A Jobbing Gardener in 1911. His father died in 1913. Enlisted in November 1915. Served in France with the Hampshire Yeomanry.[6] Killed in Action 7 June 1917 when the 15th Hampshires suffered 41 killed and missing while lying out to avoid the barrage before zero hour at 03.10am.[7] Commemorated on the Ypres (Menin Gate) Memorial, Ypres (Ieper), West-Vlaanderen, Belgium (PR Panel 35.).[8] No Winchester memorial found.

1 ADM 188/925/29237. K/29237. Discrepancy of year of death 22 February 1916 on MIC which must be correct as he did not enlist until November 1915. Error on *WWSR*.
2 CWGC.
3 SJ suggests Lower Brook Street could have been on St Maurice lost memorial.
4 WO 372/19/187578
5 See Appendix 2 for Hampshire Yeomanry.
6 Died before amalgamation on 27 September 1917, so did not serve with 15th Bn? See Appendix 2 for Hampshire Yeomanry.
7 Atkinson, 2, pp. 226-7.
8 CWGC. SJ suggests LBS cd have been on St Maurice lost memorial.

He had two brothers who served in the War. Thomas Victor, listed above, died of disease 22 February 1916. William served in France as a Driver in the Army Service Corps and survived the War.

☦TEMPLE, HENRY J. ... Pte. ... Hants, Sept. 1914, Pte. France. *Killed in Action, Apl. 9, 1916, Loos.*
(26, Wharf Hill)

413.   TEMPLE, Henry John, Private, 4807,[1] 11th (Service) Bn (Pioneers) The Hampshire Regiment, d. 9 Apr 1916 aged 39.

Son of Henry and Emma Temple. Married Lydia Neville in 1898 of 26, Wharf Hill. Son Henry born 1901. In 1901 he was a Bricklayer's Labourer, in 1911 a General Labourer. Enlisted at Winchester in September 1914, a Special Reservist. Served with The Hampshire Regiment in France. Entered a theatre of war (France) with 11th Bn on 18 December 1914. Killed in Action 9 April 1916 at Loos when the Pioneers were in the front line and communication trenches.[2] Buried St Patrick's Cemetery, Loos, Pas de Calais, France (GR III.J.9).[3] Memorial at St Peter Chesil (All Saints).

☦THOMPSON, RICHARD J. ... Sergt ... R.F.A., 1906. Gun. France. M.M. 1916. *Killed in Action, July 21, 1916, Festubert.*
(41, Sussex Street)

414.   THOMPSON, Richard J., 54572,[4] Serjeant, 117th Bty, Royal Field Artillery d. 21 July 1916 age unknown.

Born Cork, Ireland.[5] Enlisted at Cork in 1906. Served with the Royal Field Artillery in France. Awarded Military Medal in 1916.[6] Died 21 July 1916.[7] Buried Dantzig Alley British Cemetery, Mametz, Pas de Calais, France (GR III.F.6).[8] Memorials at St Matthew's and St Paul's.

☦TILL, HARRY ... 2nd Lieut. ... Hants, Pte. Glos. France, Belgium. *Killed in Action, Oct. 4, 1917, Ypres.*
(119, High Street)

1   WO 372/19/190427. 3/4807.
2   Atkinson, 2, p. 135.
3   CWGC.
4   WO 372/20/3404. NB Festubert different battle to The Somme.
5   SDGW.
6   Citation for MM not found at www.london-gazette.co.uk.
7   SDGW states 'Died'.
8   CWGC. Wife, parents etc unknown.

415. TILL, Henry (Harry),[1] 2nd Lieutenant,[2] 1st Bn The Gloucestershire Regiment, d. 4 October 1917 aged 33.

Fourth son of George William (Baker and Confectioner) and Evelyn S. Till of 119, High Street later of Devona, Hookpit, Winchester. Family at 51, St Catherine's Road 1891, 1901.[3] G. W. Till remarried Kate Ellen in 1907. In 1911 Henry Till serving overseas, resident at Wynberg, Cape of Good Hope, South Africa. A 'private secretary to a gentleman in North Wales' before re-enlisting a the outbreak of war. During the War he served in France and Belgium. Entered a theatre of war on 18 December 1914 with 11th Bn.[4] Transferred from The Hampshire Regiment as CQMS A/WO/cl. II 3/4757 (i.e. Acting Warrant Officer II); commissioned in The Gloucestershire Regiment as 2nd Lieutenant 26 June 1917. Killed in Action 4 October 1917 at Ypres. Commemorated on the Tyne Cot Memorial, Zonnebeke, West-Vlaanderen, Belgium (PR Panel 72 to 75.).[5] No Winchester memorial found.

✠TOLLMAN, CHARLES V. ... A.B. ... R.N., 1913, O.S. North Sea H.M.S. *Queen Mary*. **Killed in Action, May 31, 1916, Jutland.** (32, Water Lane)

416. TOLLMAN, Charles Victor, Ordinary Signalman, 22699,[6] HMS Queen Mary Royal Navy, d. 31 May 1916 aged 18.

Son of Thomas and Frances Emma Tollman of 32, Water Lane. Born 28 November 1898 at Balingdon, Sudbury, Suffolk.[7] Apprenticed to a Tailor in 1911. Enlisted 28 January 1913 and served in the North Sea during the War. Killed in Action at the Battle of Jutland 31 May 1916.[8] Commemorated on the Portsmouth Naval Memorial (PR 15.).[9] Memorials at St John the Baptist.

His brother Thomas James, listed below, was Killed in Action 1 July 1916.

1   Harry in *WWSR*.
2   WO 372/20/31641.
3   1911 census.
4   R Hamps Notes. RH. for this and other material in this biography. Regimental records give various numbers for him: 3/4787 Harry TILL (not 3/4757 as above); also 'Previously 6395 H Till') because he enlisted in the Hampshire Regiment in 1901 and was promoted Sergeant in 1909, was discharged in 1913 and later re-enlisted.
5   CWGC.
6   ADM 188/692/22699. J/22699.
7   Naval Casualty Records for birth. Balingdon 'Essex'a suburb of Sudbury, Suffolk.
8   Hepper, 2006, p. 60.
9   CWGC.

✠**TOLLMAN, THOMAS J. ... Pte. ... Middlesex, July 1915, Pte. France.** *Killed in Action, July 1, 1916, Somme.*
(32, Water Lane)

417. TOLLMAN, Thomas James, Private, 2453,¹ 16th (Service) Bn (Public Schools) The Duke of Cambridge's Own (Middlesex Regiment), d. 1 July 1916 aged 21.

Son of Thomas and Frances Emma Tollman of 32, Water Lane. Born at Fareham. Assistant to William Scott, Grocer, Provision, Wine and Beer Merchant in Southall in 1911. Enlisted in July 1915 at Hounslow, Middlesex. Served in France. Killed in Action 1 July 1916. Buried in Auchonvillers Military Cemetery, Somme, France, (GR II. E. 15.).² Memorials at St John the Baptist.

His brother Charles Victor, listed above, was Killed in Action 31 May 1916.

✠**TONG, HERBERT L. ... L.-Corpl. ... Wilts, 1916, Pte. France.** *Killed in Action. Apl. 12, 1917, Somme.*
(11, Stockbridge Road)

418. TONG, Herbert Lewis, Lance-Corporal, 23003,³ 2nd Bn The Duke of Edinburgh's (Wiltshire Regiment), d. 12 April 1917 aged 21.

Son of Edward and Louisa Jane Tong of 11, Stockbridge Road. Apprenticed to a Chemist in 1911. Enlisted in 1916 at Winchester. Served in France. Died of Wounds⁴ 12 April 1917 on the Somme. Buried in Warlingcourt Halte British Cemetery, Saulty, Pas de Calais, France (GR VII. F. 7.).⁵ Memorials at Peter Symonds School, St Matthew's, St Paul's and St Lawrence's.

He had two brothers who served during the War. Augustine Henry served on the Home Front as a Petty Officer in The Royal Naval Air Service. Sydney James served in Italy in The Royal Naval Air Service, then The Royal Air Force. Both survived the War.

✠**TRIMBLE, WILLIAM C. ... Pte. ... R.W. Fus., Aug. 1914, Pte. France. Wounded once.** *Died of Wounds, Givenchy.*
(18, Chesil Street)

1 WO 372/20/48069. SDGW gives PS/2453.
2 CWGC. Number only.
3 WO 372/20/54675.
4 SDGW: Died of Wounds.
5 CWGC.

419. TREMBLE, William Charles.¹ Private, 17015, 1st Bn Royal Welsh Fusiliers²

Son of Frederick and Joanna Trimble (Tremble). Born Abingdon, Berkshire 1894.³ Family at Chesil Street, 1901 (School House, 18, Chesil Street). A Fruiterer in 1911 (Resident London). Enlisted August 1914 Llanelly, Carmarthen. Served in France. Killed in Action 3 September 1916 at Givenchy. Thiepval Memorial, Somme, France (PR Pier and Face 4A).⁴ Memorial at St Peter Chesil.

☨**TUCKER, ALFRED E. ... Stoker ... R.M.L.I., 1899. R.N. North Sea, Jutland. *Died*.**
   (73, Middle Brook Street)

420. TUCKER, Alfred Ethelbert, Stoker 1st Class, 309995,⁵ HMS Victory Royal Navy, d. 7 January 1917 aged 36.

Son of Alfred and Rosamond Tucker of 73, Middle Brook Street. Born 13 October 1880 at Godalming, Surrey. Enlisted 14 December 1898 in RMLI (PO/10126). Transferred to Royal Navy in 1906.⁶ Recorded in 1911 as Stoker 1st Class 416 aboard HMS Grafton. During the War he served in the North Sea and at Jutland.⁷ Died of bronchitis 7 January 1917. Buried in Winchester (West Hill) Old Cemetery (GR 41.5.16397).⁸ No Winchester memorial found.

He had two brothers who served in the War. Ernest served in the North Sea as a steward in the Royal Navy. Stanley R. served on the Home Front as a Steward, then an Air Mechanic in The Royal Naval Air Service and The Royal Air Force. Both survived the War.

☨**TUFFIN, J. ARNOLD ... Gun. ... R.G.A., May 1917, Gun. France. Wounded once. *Died of Wounds*. May 29, 1918.**
   (32, Christ Church Road)

---

1   No MIC found. Only found on *WWSR* and in the census. SJ identified him in CWGC and SDGW as Tremble who fits this entry and supplied the information.
2   The Royal Welsh Fusiliers.
3   Birthplace also given as Oxford.
4   CWGC.
5   ADM 188/506/309995.
6   Information of enlistment, RMLI, RN transfer from SJ.
7   Survived Jutland.
8   CWGC.

421.   TUFFIN, Josiah Arnold,[1] Gunner, 163729,[2] 1st /1st[3] North Midland Heavy Bty Royal Garrison Artillery, d. 30 May 1918 aged 37.

Son of Josiah and Maria Tuffin of Southampton. Born at Southampton in 1880. Husband of Eva Y. Tuffin of 32, Christchurch Road. A Joiner in 1901 living with his uncle at Thornton, Marnhull. An Inter-Denominational Evangelist in 1911. Enlisted at Brighton in May 1917. Served in France. Wounded once and Died of Wounds 30 May 1918. Buried in Dormans French National Cemetery, Marne, France (GR B. 3.).[4] Memorial at Christ Church.

✠TUNKS, EDWARD J. A. ... 2nd Lieut. ... Arg. and Suth. H., 1915, Pte. France. *Killed in Action*, 1918.
(Rippledene, Sussex Street)

422.   TUNKS, Edward Joseph Austin (Jack), 2nd Lieutenant,[5] 4th Bn The Hampshire Regiment, d. 14 April 1918 aged 20.[6]

Son of Joseph John and Alice Mary Budd Tunks of 62, High Street. Born 1898. At 21 and 45, Southgate Street in 1901 and 1911. Winchester College Choir School, then Guildhall Schhol, London. Enlisted in 1915 and served in France. He started as a Private in the Argyll and Sutherland Highlanders; transferred to the 4th Bn The Hampshire Regiment, then commissioned. Entered a theatre of war with Argyll and Sutherland Highlanders (3806) on 8 May 1917.[7] Actually attached to 2/4th Bn when killed but serving with 1st Bn The Hampshire Regiment which was engaged in the attack on the Lys when he was Killed in Action 14 April 1918.[8] Buried in Cabaret-Rouge British Cemetery, Souchez, Pas de Calais, France (XX. D. 24.).[9] Memorials at St Lawrence's, St Matthew's, St Paul's and St Thomas's.

His father and brother served during the War. His father Joseph John served in India as a Private, promoted to Serjeant in The Hampshire Regiment. Wounded once. His brother Cyril served in The Royal Naval Air Service, then The Royal Air Force. Both survived the War.

1   J. Arnold in *WWSR*. Josiah Arnold in SDGW.
2   WO 372/20/90985. Discrepancy over date of death CWGC and SDGW give 30 May 1918..
3   CWGC.
4   CWGC.
5   WO 372/20/93801.
6   SDGW dates his death to 3 April. *WWSR* gives his regiment as Argyll and Sutherland Highlanders. CWGC and SDGW give his regiment at The Hampshire Regiment. See above for a reason.
7   and an explanation, see above for the confusion over his regiment. Various tributes from fellow officers in the archive.
8   Atkinson, 2, pp. 338-9.
9   CWGC. Gives death as 14 April 1918.

✠**TURNER, FREDERICK J. ... [BLANK] ... Hants, Sept. 1914, Pte. Dardanelles. Wounded, Aug. 1915. *Killed in Action*, 1915.**
(10, Little Minster Street)

423. TURNER, Frederick John, Private, 11281,[1] 10th (Service) Bn The Hampshire Regiment, 'presumed dead' 21 August 1915, aged 24.

Son of John and Emily Turner of 10, Little Minster Street. Enlisted at Winchester 1914. Served at Gallipoli (Dardanelles). Entered theatre of war with 10th Bn on 5 August 1915.[2] Killed in Action 21 August 1915. Commemorated on The Helles Memorial, Turkey (PR 125-34 or 223-226 228-9 328). Memorial at St Thomas's.

✠**TURNER, WILLIAM G. ... [BLANK] ... Hants, Sept. 1914. Persian Gulf. Taken Prisoner by Turks, May 1916. *Died*, 1916, *Nesblin*.**
(10, Little Minster Street)

424. TURNER, William George, Private, 201056,[3] 1/4th Bn The Hampshire Regiment, d. 30 June 1916 aged 24.

Son of John and Emily Turner of 10, Little Minster Street. Born 1892. A Van Man in 1911. Enlisted in September 1914 at Winchester (3236). Served in the Persian Gulf. Entered a theatre of war 25 October 1915 with 1/4th Bn.[4] Taken prisoner by Turks May 1916 and died a POW 30 June 1916 at Nisibin. Commemorated on the Nisibin Memorial, Baghdad (North Gate) War Cemetery, Iraq (PR 262).[5] Memorial at St Thomas's.

✠**TYLER, FREDERICK C. ... Corpl. ... Hants Y., Nov. 1915, Pte. Hants. France. Wounded, May 26, 1917. *Died of Wounds, June* 13, 1917.**
(16, King Alfred Place)

1 Two possibilities here both Frederick J Turner in The Hampshire Regiment. WO 372/20/102328 the more likely candidate. 422(b) WO372/20/102328.Same number? This man, born in Winchester and Killed in Action is the preferred candidate. 422. There is also TURNER, Frederick J., Private, 8247, 2nd Bn The Hampshire Regiment, date of death unknown. Served at Gallipoli (Dardanelles). Buried Pieta Military Cemetery, Malta. (GR D.III.3).
2 R Hamps Notes. RH. for this and other material in this biography.
3 WO 372/20/110724.
4 R Hamps Notes. RH. for this and other material in this biography. Bowker says he was 1st/6th Bn and died at Baghdad. List of Administrative Centre 4th Hampshire Regiment says he was 2/4th Bn att 1/4th.
5 CWGC.

425. TYLER, Frederick Chapman, Lance-Corporal, 27011,[1] 15th (Service) Bn (2nd Portsmouth) The Hampshire Regiment,[2] d. 13 June 1917 aged 26.

Son of the late Frederick Tyler and Mary Smeeth (formerly Tyler) of 16, King Alfred Place. Born Hyde Close 1889. His father died in 1892. A Boot Repairer in 1911.[3] Enlisted in November 1915 at Winchester. Served in France in the Hampshire Yeomanry, before amalgamation with The Hampshire Regiment. Did not enlist in the Hampshire Carabiniers Yeomanry.[4] Wounded 26 May 1917. Died of Wounds 13 June 1917. Died at Canadian Military Hospital, Beachborough Park. Buried in Winchester (West Hill) Old Cemetery (GR 1823.).[5] Memorial at St Bartholomew's.

His brother William Chapman, listed below, was Killed in Action 24 February 1917.

✠**TYLER, WILLIAM C. ... Corpl. ... Hants., Aug. 1914, Pte. India, Mesopotamia. *Killed in Action, Feb,* 1917. (16, King Alfred Place)**

426. TYLER, William Chapman, Private,[6] 200595,[7] 1/4th Bn The Hampshire Regiment, d. 24 February 1917 aged 28.

Eldest son of the late Frederick Tyler and Mary Smeeth (formerly Tyler) of 16, King Alfred Place. Born St Peter, Colebrook in 1889. His father died in 1892. A Boot Repairer in 1911. A territorial soldier, he enlisted in August 1914 at Winchester (2608). Served in India and Mesopotamia in The Hampshire Regiment. Entered theatre of war with 1/4th Bn on 18 March 1915.[8] Killed in Action 24 February 1917. Commemorated on the Basra Memorial, Iraq (PR Panel 21 and 63.).[9] Memorial at Holy Trinity.

His brother Frederick Chapman, listed above, Died of Wounds 13 June 1917.

1. WO 372/20/119033. Gives no information on cause/mode of death.
2. For Hampshire Yeomanry see Appendix 2.
3. Both brothers Boot Repairers.
4. R Hamps Notes. RH. for this and other material in this biography. Regimental records suggest no service with Hampshire Carabiniers Yeomanry in a theatre of war. A full account of his funeral at St Bartholomew Hyde.
5. CWGC.
6. *WWSR* has him as Corporal. CWGC as a Private.
7. WO 372/20/120021. Both MIC and CWGC record him as a Private. Formerly 4/2608, i.e. 4th Bn 2608.
8. R Hamps Notes. RH. for this and other material in this biography. Spells his mother's name Smeath. Gives his age as 27 not 28. A goalkeeper for Winchester Football Club.
9. CWGC.

✠**VACHER, GEORGE H. ... 2nd Lieut. ... R. Warwick, Aug. 1914, 2nd Lieut. France.** *Killed in Action, Oct.* **1914,** *Zandvoorde.*
(36, Edgar Road)

427. VACHER, George Herbert, 2nd Lieutenant,[1] 4th Bn Bn The Royal Warwickshire Regiment, died 11 November 1914 aged 20.

Son of Herbert Perkins Vacher and Elizabeth Gautherot Vacher of Wayford, Edgar Road. Born 1894. At school in 1911. Enlisted in August 1914 and served in France. Killed in Action 11 November 1914 attached 2nd Bn. Commemorated on the Ploegsteert Memorial, Comines-Warneton, Hainaut, Belgium (PR Panel 2 and 3.).[2] Memorial at St Cross Chapel.

De Ruvigny states:[3]

'2nd Lieut., The Royal Warwickshire Regt., oldest s. of Herbert P (and Elizabeth G.) Vacher, of Weyford, Winchester; served with the Expeditionary Force in France and Flanders, and was Killed in Action between the end of Oct. and 7 Nov. 1914'

His brother William E. served in France as a 2nd Lieutenant, promoted to Captain in The Worcestershire Regiment, Trench Mortar Battery. He was taken prisoner by Germans in 1918 and survived the War.

✠**VANDELEUR, JOHN B. ... [BLANK] ... Leicester. Belgium.** *Killed in Action Nov.* **7, 1914,** *Ploegstraat.*
(1, Romsey Road)

428. VANDELEUR, John Beauclerk, Lieutenant,[4] 3rd Bn The Leicestershire Regiment attd 3rd Bn The Worcestershire Regiment, died 7 November 1914.[5]

Son of Col. John S. Vandeleur, CB, and Frederic Jane Vandeleur (widow 1911) of 1, Romsey Road.[6] Born 1887. Served in Belgium during the War. Killed in

1 WO 372/20/132844. Also his Service Papers at WO 339/14432 (unexamined).
2 CWGC.
3 de Ruvigny.
4 WO 372/20/135252.
5 The following is from http://www.limerickcity.ie/Library/LocalStudies/Obituariesd eathnoticesinquestreportsfuneralreportsetcfromTheLimerickChronicle/ Vandeleur, John Beauclerk 28/11/1914 Ballinacourty, Castleconnell, 3rd Battalion, The Leinster regiment [The Prince of Wales's Leinster Regiment (Royal Canadians]). Leinster regiment; First World War casualty. Is this a different man? Different date, similar sounding regiment?
6 According to the CWGC he was Native of Ballynagurty, Castle Connell, Co. Limerick but the all census records have him born at Winchester. In 1891 parents listed at 23, High Street as John O. and Jane F Vandeleur. 1901 living at Rosslyn,

Action 7 November 1914 at Ploegstraat. Commemorated on the Ypres (Menin Gate) Memorial, Ypres (Ieper), West-Vlaanderen, Belgium (PR Panel 33.).[1] Memorials at Holy Trinity, St Matthew's, St Paul's and St Thomas's.

✠**WADE, WILLIAM ... Pte. ... Hants Y., May 1916, Tpr. Hants. France. Wounded, Feb. 1, 1917.** *Killed in Action, June 3, 1917, Ypres.*
(1A, Newburgh Street)

429. WADE, William, Private, 33258,[2] 14th (Service) Bn (1st Portsmouth) The Hampshire Regiment, died 3 June 1917 aged 31.

Only son of William and Elizabeth Wade of 1A, Newburgh Street. Born 1886. A Butcher in 1911 and had served as a butcher for Mr Hunt of Andover Road for eighteen years before he enlisted. Enlisted in the Hampshire Yeomanry in May 1916 at Winchester. Served in France. Entered a theatre of war with 15th Bn at some point after beginning of 1916.[3] Wounded 1 February 1917. Killed in Action 3 June 1917 at Ypres. Buried in Vlamertinghe Military Cemetery, Ypres (Ieper), West-Vlaanderen, Belgium (GR VII. F. 9.).[4] Memorial at St Thomas's Church and School.

✠**WAKE, FREDERICK W. ... A.-Sergt. ... Hants, Mch. 1916, Pte. Mesopotamia.** *Died. Aug. 29, 1919, Basra.*
(64, Fairfield Road)

430. WAKE, Frederick William, Serjeant, 307105,[5] 2nd/7th Bn The Hampshire Regiment, d. 29 August 1919.[6]

Son of The late Henry and Anne Wake of 'Midstead'.[7] Enlisted March 1916. Hampshire. Served in Mesopotamia. Entered a theatre of war (Mesopotamia) with 2/7th Bn at some point after beginning of 1917.[8]

Died 29 August 1919. Nothing about his demise on his MIC. Perhaps he died

---

    Hyde Park, Winchester.
1 CWGC.
2 WO 372/20/160840. SDGW.
3 R Hamps Notes. RH. for this and other material in this biography. No overseas service with Hampshire Carabiniers Yeomanry. 15th Bn then 14th Bn. No information on cause of death.
4 CWGC.
5 WO 372/20/167312. Not identified in the census.
6 CWGC agrees 29 August 1919. A very late date of death for the *WWSR*.
7 Medstead?
8 R Hamps Notes. RH.

of influenza? Buried Basra War Cemetery, Iraq (GR II.E.11).¹ Memorials at St Matthew's, St Paul's, HCC and Medstead.

✠WARD, DONALD H. C. ... L.-Corpl. ... Devon Cyc., Sept. 1916, Pte. France. *Killed in Action, Oct. 7, 1917, Hooge.* (51, Chesil Street)

431.   WARD, Donald Henry Charles, Private, 291033,² 9th (Service) Bn The Devonshire Regiment, died 10 October 1917 aged 19.³

Son of Charles and Caroline Ward of 51, Cheesehill (Chesil) Street. Born 1898. At school in 1911. Enlisted in September 1916 at Winchester and served in France. Killed in Action 7 October 1917 at Hooge. Commemorated on the Tyne Cot Memorial, Zonnebeke, West-Vlaanderen, Belgium (PR Panel 38 to 40.).⁴ Memorials at St Matthew's, St Paul's and St Peter Chesil.

✠WARD, GEORGE W. ... [BLANK] ... Hants, Sept. 1914, Pte. France, Gallipoli. *Killed in Action, Apl. 29, 1916.* (2, Water Lane)

432.   WARD, George W., Private, 10719, ⁵ Private, 2nd Bn The Hampshire Regiment, d. 29 April 1916 age unknown.

Son of Thomas Henry and Annie Maria Ward of 2, Water Lane. Born St John's 1894. In 1911 family at 17, Water Lane. Enlisted at Winchester.⁶ The 1st Bn went to France in 1914; the 2nd was ?in India which makes this account odd. Returned to England.⁷ Entered a theatre of war (Gallipoli) with 2nd Bn on 29 August 1915. Subsequently transferred with them to Western Front. ⁸Killed in Action 29 April 1916. Comemmorated on the Thiepval Memorial, Somme, France (PR Pier and Face 7C. and 7B.).⁹ Memorials at St John the Baptist.

His brother Thomas, listed below, served in The Dorsetshire Regiment.

---

1   CWGC.
2   WO 372/20/217425. The 9th Bn were not Cyclists. SDGW and CWGC agree on 9th Bn The Devonshire Regiment.
3   *WWSR* has him as a Lance-Corporal and Devon Cyclists.
4   CWGC.
5   WO 372/20/219146. George only on MIC.
6   SDGW.
7   GJEH pers. comm.
8   R Hamps Notes. RH. for this and other material in this biography.
9   CWGC.

✠**WARD, THOMAS ... Pte. ... Dorset, 1905, Pte. France.** *Killed in Action,* **Oct. 13, 1914.**
   (2, Water Lane)

433.   WARD, Thomas, Private, 7588,[1] 1st Bn The Dorsetshire Regiment, died 13 October 1914 aged 26.

Son of Thomas Henry and Annie Maria Ward of 2, Water Lane. Born 1887. Enlisted in 1905 at Winchester and in 1911 was a Private 2nd Battalion The Dorsetshire Regiment, resident at Wanowrie Lines Poona, India. During the War he served in France. Killed in Action 13 October 1914. Commemorated on the Le Touret Memorial, Pas de Calais, France (PR Panel 22 and 23.).[2] Memorials at St John the Baptist.

His brother George W. served in The Hampshire Regiment and is listed above.

✠**WARD, WILLIAM GEORGE ... Pte. ... Devon, Apl. 1916, Pte. France.** *Killed in Action,* **Sept. 22, 1916.**
   (30, St. John's Terrace)

434.   WARD, William George, Private, 21972,[3] 12th (Labour) Bn The Devonshire Regiment, died 22 September 1916 aged 35.

Son of Richard A. and Jane Ward of Winchester. Born 1883. A General Dealer in 1901. In 1911 living with his brother and working as a Railway Carman. Enlisted in April 1916 at Winchester. Served in France with C Coy. Killed in Action 22 September 1916. Buried in Fricourt New Military Cemetery, Somme, France (GR A. 4.).[4] Memorials at St John the Baptist.

✠**WATSON, ARTHUR F. ... Sig. ... Hants, Mch. 1916, Sig. India, Palestine.** *Killed in Action,* **Apl. 9, 1918.**
   (3, St. Peter Street)

435.   WATSON, Arthur Francis, Private, 201801,[5] 2nd/5th Bn The Hampshire Regiment, died 10 April 1918 aged 30.

Second son of John Edward (of the London Bazaar, High Street) and Amy Susanna Watson of 3, St Peter Street. He worked in Logs and Fancy, Stationer, with his father and brother John in 1911. Enlisted in March 1916 at Winchester.

1   WO 372/21/4713.
2   CWGC.
3   WO 372/21/6134. SDGW.
4   CWGC. C. Company.
5   WO 372/21/31947. SDGW.

Served in India and Palestine with A Coy. Entered a theatre of war with 2/5th Bn (Palestine) after beginning of 1917.¹ Killed in Action 10 April 1918. Buried in Ramleh War Cemetery, Israel and Palestine (including Gaza) (GR T. 11.).² Memorials at Peter Symonds School and St Thomas's.

His three brothers served during the War. Donald Edward served on the Home Front as a cadet in The Royal Navy. John Gordon served in India as a Private, promoted to Serjeant in The Hampshire Regiment, then the Indian Ordnance Department. Victor Garfield served in France as a Private, promoted to Serjeant in The Hampshire Regiment, then The Machine Gun Corps. All three survived the War.

✠**WAUD TETLEY, CLARENCE E. ... Lieut. ... Lancs. Fus., Aug. 1914, 2nd Lieut. Gallipoli. Despatches 1915.** *Missing, believed Killed, Aug. 21, 1915, Suvla Bay.*
(The Lodge, Bereweeke Road)

436. WAND TETLEY, Clarence C.,³ Lieutenant,⁴ 9th (Service) Bn The Lancashire Fusliers, d. 22 August 1915 aged 26.

Son of Ernest Wand and Mrs Emily Tetley of The Lodge, Winchester. Educated at Eastbourne College and Oriel College, Oxford University; half-blue hockey; played rugby for Harlequins 1st XV 1909-12. Served in Gallipoli (Dardanelles). Mentioned in Despatches.⁵ Killed in Action 22 August 1915. Commemorated on The Helles Memorial, Turkey (PR Panel 58-72 or 218-219).⁶ Memorials at St Matthew's and St Paul's.

✠**WEBB, ALFRED ... Pte. ... Dorset, Apl. 1917, Pte. India, Mesopotamia.** *Killed in Action,* **1918.**
(33, St. John's Terrace)

437. WEBB, Alfred, Private, 203426,⁷ 1/4th Bn the Dorsetshire Regiment, d. 10 October 1918 age unknown.

---

1   R Hamps Notes. RH. for this and other material in this biography. Possible conflict of dates 'He joined up in March, 1910, and proceeded to India three months later' but ws working with his father in Winchester in 1911.
2   CWGC.
3   Appears as Clarence Ernest; Charles Ernest; Charles C. in different records. Also both as Wand-Tetley and Waud-Tetley. Eastbourne College has a photographn from 1907 in rugby clothes. Nothing found on census.
4   WO 372/24/64751. Lists his decorations. Discrepancy over the day of his death.
5   *LG* 28 January 1916 p. 199 for MiD.
6   CWGC.
7   WO 372/21/54159.

Enlisted in April 1917 in Winchester. Served with the Hampshires in India and Mesopotamia. Died[1] 10 October 1918. Buried Baghdad (North Gate) War Cemetery, Iraq (GR VI.L.10).[2] Memorials at St John the Baptist.

✠**WEBB, ROBERT A. ... Corpl. ... Hants, Sept. 1914, Pte. Egypt, India, France.** *Killed in Action,* **1918.**
(43, St. Catherine's Road)

438.   WEBB, Robert Austin,[3] Serjeant, 200902, [4]2nd/4th Bn The Hampshire Regiment, died 16 September 1918 aged 24.

Eldest son of Robert and stepson of Louisa Webb of 43, St Catherine's Road. Born at Highcliffe, Winchester in 1894. In 1911 he was an Assistant Gardener in a private house, working alongside his father. Enlisted in September 1914 on Salisbury Plain. Served in Egypt, India and France. Entered theatre of war with 2/4th Bn after the beginning of 1917.[5] Mentioned in Despatches, 14 June 1918.[6] Died of Wounds[7] sustained in France 12 June on 16 September 1918. Buried at Sunken Road Cemetery, Boisleux-St. Marc, Pas de Calais, France (GR II. B. 27.).[8] Memorials at All Saints and Chilcomb (Corporal on Memorial).

✠**WEBB, WILLIAM F. ... Rfn. ... Lond. P.O. Rif. Feb. 1917, Rfn. France.** *Killed in Action,* **Sept. 20, 1917, St. Julien.**
(53, Southgate Street)

439.   WEBB, William F., Private, 374745,[9] 2/8th (City of London) Bn The London Regiment (Post Office Rifles), d. 20 September 1917 age unknown.

Born at Millbrook. Resident in Winchester at time of enlistment at Winchester in February 1917.[10] Served in France. Killed in Action 20 September 1917. Commemorated on Ypres (Menin Gate) Memorial, Ypres (Ieper), West-Vlaanderen, Belgium (PR Panel 54).[11] Memorial at St Thomas's.

1   SDGW records 'Died'.
2   CWGC.
3   Listed on the 1911 census as Austin, and on SDGW as Austin Robert.
4   WO 372/24/65587.
5   R Hamps Notes. RH. for this and other material in this biography. Mentioned by General Allenby with other Hampshires in a despatch of those worthy of 'special mention' from GHQ, Egyptian Expeditionary Force, April 3rd, 1918.
6   *LG.* 14 June 1918 p. 7053. See also WO 372/21/54789.
7   SDGW records Died of Wounds.
8   CWGC.
9   WO 372/21/60563. SDGW.
10 SDGW.
11 CWGC.

✠WEDGE, CHARLES ... Pte. ... Wilts.,1911. Pte. France. Wounded 1914. *Killed in Action, Mch.* **11, 1915.**
(6, Andover Road)

440. WEDGE, Charles Edward, Private, 7802, [1] 2nd Bn The Duke of Edinburgh's (Wiltshire Regiment), d. 11 March 1915 age unknown..

Son of James and Mary Ann Wedge living at 1, Jubilee Villas, Kingsgate Street, in 1891. Mother died 1895 and father remarried to Agnes. Living at 8 Andover Road.[2] Enlisted in 1911 at Portsmouth. Served in France with The Wiltshire Regiment. Wounded in 1914. Killed in Action 11 March 1915. Commemorated on Le Touret Memorial, Pas de Calais, France (PR Panel 33, 34).[3] Memorials at St Matthew's and St Paul's.

His brother James Wedge served with the Royal Navy as a Chief Gunnery Instructor. He was killed in 1918 and is listed below.

✠WEDGE, JAMES C. T. ... C. Gun. Instr. ... R.N., 1894. Belgian Coast, Dardanelles, Dover Patrol. *Killed,* **Oct. 21, 1918,** *mine explosion.*
(6, Andover Road)

441. WEDGE, James Charles Thomas, Chief Petty Officer, 171150.[4] Royal Navy, M21 d. 20 October 1918 age unknown.

Son of James and Mary Ann Wedge living at 1, Jubilee Villas, Kingsgate Street, in 1891. Mother died 1895 and father remarried to Agnes. Living at 8, Andover Road.[5] Born 30 December 1877 at Bloomsbury, London. In 1881 family at Ladywood Summer House, Broseley, Shropshire. Enlisted 10 January 1894. In 1901 family at 11, Victoria Road. Married Emily Maud Forsdick in 1905 at Portsmouth. (Her address as wife and Next of Kin. given as Emily M. Wedge, 8, Highfield Street, Fratton, Portsmouth as Next of Kin).[6] A Seaman Petty Officer in 1911, living at 16 Netley Street, Fratton Park, Portsmouth. One daughter in 1911, Constance Maud, born 1908. Served on the Belgian Coast, at the Dardanelles and the Dover Patrol.[7] M21 hit two mines off Dover before sinking. Five people lost their lives.[8] Commemorated on Portsmouth Naval

1 WO 372/21/67255. Charles Edward.
2 For further family details see James Wedge, below.
3 CWGC.
4 ADM 188/280/171150. Discrepancy over day of death. CWGC and Naval Casualties agree 20th.
5 BMD for Mary Ann Wedge in 1895.
6 Naval Casualties.
7 CWGC states Mentioned in Despatches, but not found.
8 Hepper 2006, p. 143.

Memorial (PR Panel 28).¹ Memorials at St Matthew's and St Paul's.

His brother Charles served in The Wiltshire Regiment and is listed above.

✠WHICHER, EDWIN W. ... Tpr. ... Derby Y., Sept. 1, 1918, Tpr. Home. *Died, Sept. 24, 1918, Canterbury.*
(2, Avenue Road)

442. WHITCHER,² Edwin Walter, Private, 30267,³ 2nd /1st Derbyshire Yeomanry, d. 24 September 1918 aged 37.

Son of Frederick and Elizabeth Whitcher of 10, Hillside Terrace, Bar End. Married Annie Wild in 1908. Lived at 2, Avenue Terrace (sic).⁴ In 1901 and in 1911 he was working as a Bricklayer's Labourer, like his father and brother. In 1911 at 12, Staple Gardens. Enlisted 1 September 1918. Served on the Home Front. Died 24 September 1918 at Canterbury. Buried in Winchester (St Giles's Hill) Cemetery.⁵ Memorials at St Matthew's, St Paul's and St Peter Chesil.

✠WHITE, FREDERICK A. ... L.-Corpl. ... Grenadier Gds. France. *Killed in Action, Apl. 13, 1918.*
(36, Stockbridge Road)

443. WHITE, Frederick Alexander, Lance-Corporal, 20024,⁶ 4th Bn Grenadier Guards, d. 13 April 1918 aged 30.

Son of William and Emily White of 18, Stockbridge Road in 1911. Born at Evercreech, Somerset in 1889. Living at Horrington, Wells, Someset in 1911. Married Rosie Beaver in 1917. Rose White lived at 6, Gatling Road, Plumstead, London. An Asylum Attendant in the Somerset and Bath Lunatic Asylum in 1911. Enlisted in Newport and served in France with No 1 Coy Grenadier Guards . Killed in Action 13 April 1918. Buried in Aval Wood Military Cemetery, Vieux-Berquin, Nord, France (GR III. C. 2.).⁷ Memorials at St Matthew's, St Paul's and United Church, Jewry Street.

---

1 CWGC. Here the vessel is referred to in an OCR error as HMS May: printed Register has M21. Refers to Wedge as an Acting C.P.O.
2 Whicher in *WWSR*. Whitcher elsewhere.
3 No MIC found.
4 CWGC.
5 CWGC. D/30267. No GR.
6 WO 372/21/127182. SDGW.
7 CWGC.

✠WHITE, HAROLD W. ... Pte. ... Inns of Court O.T.C., June 1915, Pte. Home. *Died, Dec.* 1916, *Winchester.*
(3, Connaught Terrace)

444. WHITE, Harold Wickham, Private, 5533, Inns of Court O.T.C., d. December 1916 age unknown.

Son of Walter and Rosa White of 64, Eastgate Street (1891). Born 1888. His father died in 1899. Mother a widow at 14, Ranelagh Road (1901). A Tailor's Clerk in 1911 living at 74, Easatgate Street. Served on the Home Front. Enlisted 9 August 1915. Discharged sick 24 June 1916.[1] Memorial at Peter Symonds School.

✠WHITE, HAVILAND ... Stoker ... R.N., Aug. 1914, Stoker. China ; H.M.S. *Venus. Died, Sept.* 19, 1918.
(3A, King Alfred Place)

445. WHITE, Harry Haviland, Leading Stoker, 283351,[2] RN Leading Stoker with HMS Victory,[3] d. 19 September 1918.

Son of William and Eliza White of 3, King Alfred Place. Born 23 May 1877 at Bournemouth. Served from 7 September 1896. Married Ellen M. Dumper in 1912 (his widow of 21, Castle Street, Plymouth, next of kin).[4] Two children by 1916, Doris M. born 1913, Harry W born 1916.[5] Served in China. Died of empyema (chronic puss in lungs) 19 September 1918. Buried Winchester (West Hill) Old Cemetery (GR 32.2960).[6] Memorial at St Bartholomew's.

✠WHITE, LEONARD F. ... Pte. ... R.F.C., Feb. 1917, 2nd A.M. R.I. Fus. France. Wounded, Apl. 11, 1918. *Died of Wounds, Apl.* 12, 1918, *Ypres.*
(West Highlands, Romsey Road)

446. WHITE, Leonard Furnell, Private, 45789,[7] 9th (North Irish Horse Yeomanry) (Service) Bn Princess Victoria's Royal Irish Fusiliers, d. 12 April 1918 aged 19.

---

1   An unusual case of a death in the *WWSR* of man who had apparently been Discharged before he died. Not found on the CWGC because Discharged before he died.
2   ADM 188/453/283351.
3   Victory not Venus. CWGC, First World War Naval Casualties record.
4   Naval Casualties 1914-1919.
5   England and Wales Birth Transcriptions 1837-2007.
6   CWGC.
7   WO 372/21/122923. RFC records not found.

Son of Charles and Fanny White of The Cottage, West Highlands, Romsey Road. Enlisted in February 1917 in the Royal Flying Corps (59391) and served in France as 2nd Air Mechanic before transferring to the Fusiliers. Wounded 11 April 1918 and Died of Wounds 12 April 1918 at Ypres. He is buried in Lijssenthoek Military Cemetery, Poperinge, West-Vlaanderen, Belgium (GR XXVI. H. 19.).[1] Memorials at Christ Church and St Thomas's School.

⚔WHITE, WILLIAM E. ... Pte. ... Hants, Aug. 1914, Pte. Mesopotamia. Taken Prisoner by Turks, Apl. 29, 1916, Kut. *Died, July* 22, 1916.
(32, Fairfield Road)

447. WHITE, William Edward, Private, 200904,[2] 1/4th Bn The Hampshire Regiment, d. 22 July 1916 aged 20.

Son of William and Kate White of 32, Fairfield Road. Apprenticed as a Whitesmith in 1911. Worked with his father at Kingdon and Co., Ironmongers, High Street. Enlisted in August 1914 on Salisbury Plain (3002). Served in Mesopotamia. Entered a theatre of war with 1/4th Bn on 18 March 1915.[3] Taken prisoner by Turks 29 April 1916 at Kut and died a POW 22 July 1916. Buried in Baghdad (North Gate) War Cemetery, Iraq (GR XXI. X. 40.).[4] Memorials at St Matthew's, St Paul's and St Thomas's School.

⚔WILLIS, EDWIN G. ... A.B. ... R.N., 1883. North Sea. *Killed in Action, May* 31, 1916, *Jutland.*
(5, Percy Terrace)

448. WILLIS, Edward, Able Seaman, 204410,[5] HMS Invincible. Died 31 May 1916.

Born 24 December 1883 at Alresford. No parents given. Previous occupation House Boy. Husband of Florence Willis (5, Percy Terrace, Water Lane).[6] However, if these records are for this man the *WWSR* enters his entry to service as 1883: it would be highly unusual if not unique in the *WWSR* to find a date of

1 CWGC.
2 WO 372/21/127039. Confirms 'Died'.
3 R Hamps Notes. RH. for this and other material in this biography. Notes that news of his death did not arrive with his parents until during 1917. Gives his age as 21.
4 CWGC.
5 Uncertain identity. ADM 188/355/204410 refers to Edward (Not Edwin or Edwin G.). Information here refers to Edward Willis. Refers to various days served in the cells in his record. Died 31 May 1916 at Jutland. See Printout. Nothing found on Findmypast of Edwin Willis or Edward Willis, or plain Willis.
6 SJ supplied NOK data.

birth in the 1921 account of his service. References to HMS Invincible in MIC and CWGC. Killed in Action 31 May 1916 at Jutland. Commemorated on Portsmouth Naval Memorial (PR Panel 14).[1] Memorials at St John the Baptist.[2]

✠WINCHCOMB, FREDERICK J. ... Stoker ... R.N., 1912. Stoker. North Sea; Submarine G. 8. *Killed in Action, Dec. 1917.*
(34, Wharf Hill)

449. WINCHCOMB, Frederick John, Stoker 1st Class, K/14708,[3] HM S/M G8 Royal Navy, d. 3-14 January 1918 aged 24.[4]

Son of Daniel and Olive Sarah Winchcomb of 34, Wharf Hill. Born 19 October 1893.[5] Former occupation Miller. Married to Ellen Winchcomb of 42, Codd Street, South Bank, Yorkshire. Enlisted in 1912 and served in the North Sea during the War. Killed in Action 3-14 January 1918[6]. Commemorated on the Portsmouth Naval Memorial (PR 30.).[7] Memorial at St Peter Chesil.

✠WINKWORTH, HARRY ... Chief Cook ... R.N., 1893, Cook's Mate. North Sea. *Drowned, Oct. 15, 1914.*
(17, St. Clement Street)

450. WINKWORTH, Harry, Chief Ship's Cook, 176650,[8] HMS Hawke, Royal Navy, d. 15 October 1914 aged 40.

Son of Stephen and Mary Winkworth of 17, St Clement's Street. Born 16 November 1873 at Shepton Mallet, Somerset. Formerly a Fishmonger. Enlisted in 1893. Served in the North Sea during the War. Drowned 15 October 1914 when the cruiser HMS Hawke was lost with the 500 deaths, maybe half her complement.[9] Commemorated on the Chatham Naval Memorial, Kent (PR 6.).[10] Memorial at St Thomas's.

1 CWGC.
2 Edwin, Edwin G. HMS Invincible at St John the Baptist.
3 ADM 188/896/14708. K/14708.
4 *WWSR* gives his death as Dec 1917. Doubt about his date of death: his Naval Rating Record (ADM 188/) has a final entry for 14 January 1918 which authorities accord as the date of the loss of Submarine G8. Winchcomb is referred to as 'Lost on Duty'.
5 Naval Casualties 1914-1919.
6 See Hepper 2006, p.116 which refers to 14 January. Also A.S. Evans, *Beneath the Waves: a History of HM Submarine Losses 1904-71.* (London: William Kimber, 1986), p. 108. CWGC and Naval Casualties give 3 January 1918.
7 CWGC.
8 ADM 188/291/176650.
9 Hepper 2006, p. 27. Torpedoed by U-9 off Aberdeen.
10 CWGC.

His half brother Arthur served in France as a Private in The Hampshire Regiment, then the Royal Berkshire Regiment and The Labour Corps or Labour Company. He survived the War.

✠WINKWORTH, WILLIAM ... Rfn. ... R.B, 1903, Rfn. France. Wounded, 1914. *Killed in Action, May* 10, 1915, *Ypres.*
(20, Parchment Street)

451. WINKWORTH, William, Private, 9432,[1] 4th Bn The Rifle Brigade (The Prince Consort's Own), d. 10 May 1915, aged 31.

Son of Thomas Winkworth of 6, Bank Street, Ashford, Kent. Born Winchester 1884. Living in Water Lane aged 7, 1891. Enlisted in 1903 at Winchester. Husband of Bessie Winkworth of 5, Nutley Lane, Reigate, Surrey.[2] In 1911 a Journeyman Baker living with Bessie and Ernest Winter Arnold at 2, Holly Cottages, Smelthy Lane, Lower Kingswood, Reigate. Served in France. Wounded in 1914. Killed in Action 10 May 1915. Commemorated on Ypres (Menin Gate) Memorial, Ypres (Ieper), West-Vlaanderen, Belgium (PR Panels 46-48, 50).[3] No Winchester memorial found.

✠WINTER, CHARLES J. ... Stoker ... R.N., Stoker. North Sea, Jutland; H.M.S. *Queen Mary. Killed in Action, May* 31, 1915, *Jutland.*
(Pond Cottage, Weeke)

452. WINTER, Charles John, Stoker 1st Class, 1129943,[4] RN served on Queen Mary. Killed in Action at Jutland 31 May 1916 age not given.

Son of Sarah Winter of Pond Cottages,[5] Weeke. Born 30 June 1890 at Winchester. A Gardener prior to service. Enlisted 16 October 1912. Served on board HMS Queen Mary. Killed in Action at Jutland 31 May 1916.[6] Commemorated on Portsmouth Naval Memorial (PR Panel 20).[7] Memorials at St Matthew's and St Paul's.

1 WO 372/22/22864. Rifleman.
2 CWGC for NOK. BMD. Census 1911.
3 CWGC.
4 ADM 188/1118/112943. SS/112943 CWGC and Naval Casualties. *WWSR* prints 1915 in error for Jutland.
5 Naval Casualties 1914-1919.
6 Hepper, 2006, p. 60.
7 CWGC.

✠WOOD, ROBERT C. ... Rfn. ... K.R.R.C., 1906, Rfn. France, Belgium. *Killed in Action, Nov. 14, 1914, Ypres.*
(10, Gordon Avenue)

453. WOOD, Robert Charles, Private, 7397,[1] 2nd Bn The King's Royal Rifle Corps, d. November 14 1914.

Son of Louisa Wood. Married Mary J. McKenzie in 1914. Born 1888. Enlisted in Winchester in 1906. Served in Flanders. Killed in Action 14 November 1914 at Ypres. Commemorated on Ypres (Menin Gate) Memorial, Ypres (Ieper), West-Vlaanderen, Belgium (PR Panels 51 and 53).[2] Memorial at All Saints.

✠WOODS, FREDERIC G. ... Pte. ... Hants, Dec.1914, Pte. India. *Died of Malaria.*
(26, Nuns Road)

454. WOODS, Frederick George, Private, 205567,[3] 2nd Bn The Bedfordshire Regiment, d. 6 December 1918 aged 18.

Son of Mr (Bandmaster in the The Hampshire Regiment) and Mrs W.H. Woods of 26, Nuns Road. Born Shorncliffe, Kent in 1900. At school in 1911. Enlisted in The Hampshire Regiment, but serving with 2nd Garrison Bn, The Bedfordshire Regiment at the time he died of malaria on 6 December 1918.[4] Served only in India. Died at Karachi. Commemorated on The Delhi Memorial (India Gate), Face I, India.[5] Memorial at St Bartholomew's.[6]

✠WORSAM, JOHN E. ... Pte. ... T.R., Mch. 1917, Pte. Hants, R. Berks. France. *Killed in Action, Mch. 29, 1918, Arras.*
(33, St. Catherine's Road)

455. WORSAM, John Elliot, Private, 39198,[7] 1st Bn Princess Charlotte of Wales's (Royal Berkshire Regiment), d. 23 March 1918 aged 19.

Son of John and Edith Worsam of 33, St Catherine's Road. Born 1899. At school in 1911. Enlisted in March 1917 at Winchester. Served France and was posted

1 WO 372/22/48479.
2 CWGC.
3 WO 372/22/61578. 3390 in The Bedfordshire Regiment.
4 R Hamps Notes. RH. for this and other material in this biography. Gives his age as 19.
5 CWGC.
6 At University of Winchester King Alfred's College Old Chapel (Winton Memorial Room). Frederick W. Woods is commemorated.
7 WO 372/22/77050. Makes no mention of service in The Hampshire Regiment. Refers alternatively to service in Prince Albert's (Somerset Light Infantry).

from the Training Reserve to The Hampshire Regiment before transferring to the Royal Berkshire Regiment. Entered a theatre of war with Somerset Light Infantry (41865). Did not serve in theatre of war with Hampshire Regt.[1] Died of Wounds 29 March 1918 at Arras. Buried in Doullens Communal Cemetery Extension No.1, Somme, France (GR V. C. 9.).[2] Memorial at All Saints.

His brother George James served in Mesopotamia and Aden as a Driver in The Royal Field Artillery and survived the War.

✠WRIGHT, WILLIAM C. ... Pte. ... Hants, Aug. 1914, Pte. Egypt, Dardanelles. *Killed (accidentally), Aug. 10, 1915.*

456. WRIGHT, William Charles, Private, 9944,[3] 10th (Service) Bn The Hampshire Regiment, d. 10 August 1915 aged 21.

Son of the late Henry and Emily Wright. Born St Maurice. In 1901 and 1911 at 23, Wharf Hill, in 1901 as a boarder with William Ward, his mother a servant designated a 'Cripple.' She was also there in 1911 when William is not found. Enlisted in August 1914 at Winchester and served in Egypt and at Gallipoli (Dardanelles). Entered a theatre of war with 10th Bn on 5 August 1915.[4] Killed in Action 10 August 1915.[5] Commemorated on The Helles Memorial, Turkey (PR Panel 125-134 or 223-226 228-229 & 328.).[6] Memorials at St John the Baptist. Appears on Easton War Memorial: Lychgate Memorial and also memorialised inside the church.[7]

✠WROE, HAROLD B. ... Pte. ... Hants, 1913, Pte. India, Mesopotamia. *Killed in Action, July* 1915, *Nasireyah.* (11, Alswitha Terrace)

457. WROE (WRAE), Harold Bertram, Private, 1908,[8] 1/4th Bn The Hampshire Regiment, d. 15 July 1915 aged 21.

Son of William George and Ellen Wroe of 33, Western Road (1911). Born at Peshawar, India in 1895. In 1911 he was a Junior Clerk. Enlisted in 1913. Served in India and Mesopotamia during the War. Entered theatre of war on 18

1 R Hamps Notes. RH.
2 CWGC. SDGW records Died of Wounds.
3 WO 372/22/98424.
4 R Hamps Notes. RH. Cannot confirm accidental death. Medal Index Card and Regimental Journal state Killed in Action.
5 SDGW records Killed in Action.
6 CWGC.
7 GJEH pers. comm. SJ states 'not on Lychgate'.
8 WO 372/22/100280; WO 372/22/80550. Uncertainty about this name. Bertram Wrae recorded as signing up: MIC Subsequently corrected to Bertram Wroe.

March 1915 with 1/4th Bn.¹ Killed in Action 15 July 1915 at Nasireyah. Buried in Basra War Cemetery, Iraq (GR V. L. 1.).² Memorials at St Bartholomew's and St Thomas's School.³

✠WYATT, ALFRED H. ... A.B. ... R.N., 1894, O.S. North Sea. *Killed in Action,* May 31, 1916, *Jutland.*
(67, Hyde Street)

458. WYATT, Alfred Henry, Able Seaman, 181053,⁴ HMS Invincible, Royal Navy, d. 31 May 1916 aged 39.

Son of Alfred Henry and Emily Wyatt of 67, Hyde Street. Born 22 August 1876 at Aldershot. At 10, Staple Gardens in 1881.⁵ Enlisted in 1894. In 1911 he was resident at The Royal Sailor's Rest, Portsmouth. Served in the North Sea during the War. Killed in Action at the Battle of Jutland 31 May 1916. Commemorated on the Portsmouth Naval Memorial (PR Panel 14.).⁶ Memorial at St Bartholomew's.

His brother Ernest, listed below, Died of Wounds 11 September 1915.

✠WYATT, ERNEST W. ... C.S.M. ... R.B., 1894, Rfn. France. Wounded, Sept. 1915. *Died of Wounds,* Sept. 11, 1915, *Ypres.*
(67, Hyde Street)

459. WYATT, Ernest Walter, Private,⁷ 3197,⁸ 3rd Bn The Rifle Brigade (The Prince Consort's Own), d. 11 September 1915 aged 37.

Son of Alfred Henry and Emily Wyatt of 67, Hyde Street. Born at Aldershot in 1878.⁹ Enlisted in 1894 at Winchester. Served in France during the War. Awarded the Long Service and Good Conduct medals. Wounded September 1915 and Died of Wounds 11 September 1915 at Ypres. Buried Lijssenthoek Military Cemetery, Poperinge, West-Vlaanderen, Belgium (GR III. A. 20.).¹⁰ Memorial at St Bartholomew's.

1 R Hamps Notes. RH.
2 CWGC. Appears as Bertram (not H. or Harold). Bertram Wrae does not appear on CWGC.
3 SJ notes 'just Bertram or B on memorials'.
4 ADM 188/301/181053.
5 Mother notified 10, Staple Gardens, Naval Casualties 1914-1919.
6 CWGC.
7 Promoted to Company Serjeant Major according to the *WWSR*: a discrepancy of rank. Rifleman on CWGC.
8 WO 372/22/101042.
9 1891 census suggest a birth date of 1878. Not found in 1911 census.
10 CWGC.

APPENDICES

APPENDIX 1

A. Cecil Piper (ed), *Winchester War Service Register. A Record of the Service of Winchester Men in the Great War 1914-1918* (Winchester: Warren and Co. 1921) (*WWSR*).

We are grateful to Alan Bungey for supplying a digitised version of the *Winchester War Service Register*, from which this facsimile has been made.

Winchester
War Service Register

A RECORD OF THE SERVICE OF
WINCHESTER MEN IN THE GREAT WAR
1914—1918

Edited for the Committee by
A. CECIL PIPER
City Librarian of Winchester

"SEMPER HONOR, NOMENQUE TUUM, LAUDESQUE MANEBUNT"
Virgil

𝕎inchester
PRINTED BY WARREN AND SON, LIMITED, HIGH STREET
1921

COMMITTEE

ALDERMAN A. R. DYER
(MAYOR, 1920 and 1921).

ALDERMAN A. EDMEADES, C.B.E., D.L., J.P.
(MAYOR, 1914–1919).

COUNCILLOR J. S. FURLEY, M.A.

MAJOR F. R. BOYLE.

MISS F. D. GALE.

MR. W. R. MATHEWS.

MR. A. C. PIPER.

MR. H. W. WARREN.

CAPTAIN A. J. WHISTLER.

MR. C. S. WOOLDRIDGE
(*Hon. Secretary and Treasurer*).

FOREWORD

WHATEVER form of Memorial is adopted by the City of Winchester to commemorate the sacrifice made by its citizens and their sons for their Country in the Great War, one part of it should necessarily be a record of the names of all who served in it. This book is intended to furnish such a record. It contains, so far as it has been possible to ascertain them, the names of all men domiciled in Winchester at the outbreak of the War who have served in any branch of His Majesty's Forces, from the Declaration of War to the Signing of the Armistice. More details of individual service could in most cases undoubtedly have been obtained, but in many others this was impossible; their memorial has perished with them, and it has been thought better to confine the details to what could be given on a uniform system than to risk the disparagement of those who have rendered equal service, but whose record it has not been possible to obtain.

It is regretted that this book was not published immediately after the signature of Peace; the material for it was all collected shortly after that date, but the cost of publication was so great that it would have been impossible to issue it at a price that would bring the book within the reach of all. It was only when the publication was recognised by the Winchester War Memorial Committee as an integral part of that Memorial that this difficulty has been overcome.

The thanks of the compilers are due to those who have helped them by collecting and furnishing information, and there have been many who have given time and trouble that their fellow-citizens who have served should be amongst those " who have left a name behind them."

The particulars of service given in the Register are as follows: The names are arranged in strict alphabetical order of surnames, the address being given under each name. Where no address is found, it has either been impossible to obtain it, or the person has since left Winchester. The rank in next column is that of the highest rank attained. Then follow the name of the unit first joined and the date and rank on joining; units to which transferred; theatres of war in which served; honours gained; nature of any casualties, with dates. Names with a cross prefixed signify those who were killed or died during the War. A list of all abbreviations used, with the meanings, will be found on pages vi—viii.

SUMMARY

Number of Names included on the Roll	3454

CASUALTIES

Killed in Action	287
Missing, believed Killed	23
Killed Accidentally	2
Died of Wounds	45
Died of Disease	91
Drowned	11
TOTAL KILLED AND DIED	**459**
Wounded once	559
" twice	133
" three times	27
" four times	10
" six times	1
" accidentally	3
TOTAL NUMBER WOUNDED	**733**
Gassed once	95
" twice	9
" three times	4
" four times	1
TOTAL NUMBER GASSED	**109**
Torpedoed once	5
" twice	1
" three times	2
TOTAL NUMBER TORPEDOED	**8**
Taken Prisoner	98
Taken Prisoner and Escaped	5
TOTAL NUMBER TAKEN PRISONER	103

SUMMARY

HONOURS

C. M. G.	4
O. B. E.	4
M. B. E.	2
C. I. E.	1
D. S. O. and Bar	3
D. S. O.	14
M. C. and Bar	4
M. C.	31
D. C. M. and Bar	1
D. C. M.	22
D. S. C.	2
D. S. M.	7
D. F. M.	1
M. M. and Bar	2
M. M.	44
M. S. M.	22
Despatches once	67
,, twice	13
,, three times	10
,, four times	3
TOTAL NUMBER OF MENTIONS	93
Cavalier de Savoie	1
Chevalier Légion d'Honneur	2
Chevalier of St. Maurice and St. Lazare	1
Croix de Guerre	15
Italian Bronze Medal	1
Médaille Militaire	4
Officer of the Order of the Redeemer	1
Order of Leopold I	1
Russian Order of St. Anne	1
Russian Order of St. George	1
Serbian Gold Cross	1
Serbian Silver Medal	1
Serbian White Eagle	1
TOTAL NUMBER OF HONOURS	288

ABBREVIATIONS

A.B. Able Seaman.
A.G.S. Army Gymnastic Staff.
A.I.F. Australian Imperial Forces.
A.M. Air Mechanic.
A.-Major. Acting Major.
A.P.C. Army Pay Corps.
A.-Paymaster. Acting Paymaster.
A.-Q.M.S. Acting Quartermaster Sergeant.
A.-Sergt. Acting Sergeant.
A.-Ship's Corpl. Acting Ship's Corporal.
A.-Staff S.M. Acting Staff Sergeant Major.
A.V.C. Army Veterinary Corps.
Agric. Coy. Agricultural Company.
Amer. Army. American Army.
Arg. and Suth. H. Argyll and Sutherland Highlanders.
Arm. Cars. Armoured Cars.
Armd. Motor Car. Armoured Motor Car.
Art. Artificer.
Artists' Rif. Artists' Rifles.
Attd. Attached.
Aus. Cyc. C. Australian Cyclist Corps.
Aus. L.H. Australian Light Horse.
Aus. L.I. Australian Light Infantry.
B.Q.M.S. Battery Quartermaster Sergeant.
Bdr. Bombardier.
Bedford Vol. Bedford Volunteers.
Bedford Y. Bedford Yeomanry.
Berks Y. Berkshire Yeomanry.
Bn. Battalion.
Bombay Vol. Rif. Bombay Volunteer Rifles.
Border R. Border Regiment.
Boy T. Boy Telegraphist.
Brig.-Gen. Brigadier-General.
Brit. R.C. British Red Cross.
Bug. Bugler.
C. Engr. Chief Engineer.
C.F. Chaplain to the Forces.
C. Gun. Instr. Chief Gunnery Instructor.
C.M.G. Companion of Order of St. Michael and St. George.
C.P.O. Chief Petty Officer.
C.Q.M.S. Company Quartermaster Sergeant.
C.S.M. Company Sergeant Major.
C.-Sergt. Colour Sergeant.
C. Steward. Chief Steward.
C.U.R.V. Cambridge University Rifle Volunteers.
Camel T.C. Camel Transport Corps.
Can. Arty. Canadian Artillery.
Can. Cav. Canadian Cavalry.
Can. Eng. Canadian Engineers.
Can. F.A. Canadian Field Artillery.
Can. Field Amb. Canadian Field Ambulance.
Can. Fus. Canadian Fusiliers.
Can. Gds. Canadian Guards.

Can. Inf. Canadian Infantry.
Can. Light Horse. Canadian Light Horse.
Can. M.G.C. Canadian Machine Gun Corps.
Can. M.P. Canadian Military Police.
Can. M. Rif. Canadian Mounted Rifles.
Can. R.G.A. Canadian Royal Garrison Artillery.
Can. Rif. Canadian Rifles.
Can. Ry. C.C. Canadian Railway Construction Corps.
Can. Scot. Canadian Scottish.
Capt. Captain.
Cav. (Ind. Army). Cavalry (Indian Army).
Cav. M.G.C. Cavalry Machine Gun Corps.
Cav. Res. Cavalry Reserve.
Ceylon Planters' Rif. C. Ceylon Planters' Rifle Corps.
Ceylon Rif. Ceylon Rifles.
Chev. Chevalier.
Chev. St. M. and St. L. Chevalier of St. Maurice and St. Lazare.
Chinese Lab. C. Chinese Labour Corps.
Civil Service Rif. Civil Service Rifles.
Col. Colonel.
Coldstream Gds. Coldstream Guards.
Comdr. Commander.
Com. Gun. Commissioned Gunner, R.N.
Con. Ran. Connaught Rangers.
Corpl. Corporal.
D.C.L.I. Duke of Cornwall's Light Infantry.
D.C.M. Distinguished Conduct Medal.
D.F.M. Distinguished Flying Medal.
D.L.I. Durham Light Infantry.
D. of W. Cav. Bde. Duke of Westminster's Cavalry Brigade.
D. of W. Regt. Duke of Wellington's Regiment.
D.S.C. Distinguished Service Cross.
D.S.M. Distinguished Service Medal.
D.S.O. Distinguished Service Order.
Derby Y. (Cyc.). Derbyshire Yeomanry (Cyclists).
Devon Cyc. Devon Cyclists.
Devon Y. Devon Yeomanry.
Dorset Y. Dorset Yeomanry.
Dr. Driver.
Dragoon G. Dragoon Guards.
Dub. Fus. Dublin Fusiliers.
E.A. Mounted Rif. East African Mounted Rifles.
E. Africa. East Africa.
E. Kent. East Kent Regiment.
E. Lancs. East Lancashire Regiment.
E. Surrey. East Surrey Regiment.
E. Yorks. East Yorkshire Regiment.
Egypt. Lab. C. Egyptian Labour Corps.
Elec. Electrician.
Eng.-Comdr. Engineer-Commander.
Erinpura R. Erinpura Regiment.
Essex Y. Essex Yeomanry.

ABBREVIATIONS

French R.C.   French Red Cross.
G.H.Q.   General Head Quarters.
Glamorgan Vol.   Glamorgan Volunteers.
Glos.   Gloucester Regiment.
Gordon H.   Gordon Highlanders.
Gren. Gds.   Grenadier Guards.
Gun.   Gunner.

H.A.C.   Honourable Artillery Company.
H.L.I.   Highland Light Infantry.
H.M.A.S.   His Majesty's Australian Ship.
H.M. Hosp. Boats.   His Majesty's Hospital Boats.
H.M. Hosp. S.   His Majesty's Hospital Ship.
H.M.S.   His Majesty's Ship.
H.M.T.   His Majesty's Transport.
Hants.   Hampshire Regiment.
Hants Cyc.   Hampshire Cyclists.
Hants Y.   Hampshire Yeomanry.

I. of W. Militia.   Isle of Wight Militia.
I. of W. Regt.   Isle of Wight Regiment.
Ind. A.C.   Indian Army Corps.
Ind. Cav.   Indian Cavalry.
Ind. M.C.   Indian Medical Corps.
Ind. Mountain Art.   Indian Mountain Artillery.
Ind. Ord. Dept.   Indian Ordnance Department.
Innis. D.   Inniskilling Dragoons.
Innis. Fus.   Inniskilling Fusiliers.
Irish Gds.   Irish Guards.

K.A. Rif.   King's African Rifles.
K. Liverp.   King's Liverpool Regiment.
K.O.R. Lancs.   King's Own Royal Lancaster Regt.
K.O.S.B.   King's Own Scottish Borderers.
K.O.Y.L.I.   King's Own Yorkshire Light Infantry.
K.R.R.C.   The King's Royal Rifle Corps.
Kashmir Rif.   Kashmir Rifles.
Kent Cyc.   Kent Cyclists.
King Edw. Horse.   King Edward's Horse.

L.A.M.B.   Light Armoured Motor Battery.
L.-Corpl.   Lance-Corporal.
L.M.   Leading Mechanic.
L.S.   Leading Seaman.
L.-Sergt.   Lance-Sergeant.
L.T.   Leading Telegraphist.
Lab. C.   Labour Corps *or* Labour Company.
Lancs.   Lancashire Regiment.
Lancs. Fus.   Lancashire Fusiliers.
Lieut.   Lieutenant.
Lieut.-Comdr.   Lieutenant-Commander.
Life Gds.   Life Guards.
Lond.   London Regiment.
Lond. Elec. Eng.   London Electrical Engineers.
Lond. Fus.   London Fusiliers.
Lond. Irish.   London Irish.
Lond. P.O. Rifles.   London Post Office Rifles.
Lond. R.B.   London Rifle Brigade.
Lond. Rangers.   London Rangers.

Lond. Rough Riders.   London Rough Riders.
Lond. Scot.   London Scottish.
Lond. Y.   London Yeomanry.
Loyal N. Lancs.   Loyal North Lancashire Regiment.
Lt.-Col.   Lieutenant-Colonel.

M.A.C.   Motor Ambulance Corps.
M.B.E.   Member of Order of British Empire.
M.B.R.   Motor Boat Revenue.
M.C.   Military Cross.
M.F.P.   Military Foot Police.
M.G.C.   Machine Gun Corps.
M.M.   Military Medal.
M.M.G.C.   Motor Machine Gun Corps.
M.M.P.   Military Mounted Police.
M.P.   Military Police.
M.S.M.   Meritorious Service Medal.
Manch.   Manchester Regiment.
Mech.   Mechanician.
Merc. Fleet Aux.   Mercantile Fleet Auxiliary
Merc. Marine.   Mercantile Marine.
Mid.   Midshipman.
Motor Boat Res.   Motor Boat Reserve.

N. Devon Y.   North Devon Yeomanry.
N. Fus.   Northumberland Fusiliers.
N. Irish Horse.   North Irish Horse.
N. Somerset Y.   North Somerset Yeomanry.
N. Staffs.   North Staffordshire Regiment.
Nat. Res.   National Reserve.
Native Lab. C.   Native Labour Corps.
Northants.   Northampton Regiment.
Northants Y.   Northamptonshire Yeomanry.

O.B.E.   Officer of Order of British Empire.
O.C.B.   Officers' Cadet Battalion.
O.S.   Ordinary Seaman.
O.T.C.   Officers' Training Corps.
Off. Cook.   Officers' Cook.
Off. of Redeemer.   Officer of the Order of the Redeemer.
Ord. Survey.   Ordnance Survey.
Oxf. and Bucks L.I.   Oxford and Buckinghamshire Light Infantry.

P.O.   Petty Officer.
P.O.W.   Prisoner of War.
P.P.C.L.I.   Princess Patricia's Canadian Lt. Infantry.
Pte.   Private.
Punjabi R.   Punjabi Regiment.

Q.M.   Quartermaster.
Q.M.S.   Quartermaster Sergeant.
Q.O. Oxf. Hus.   Queen's Own Oxford Hussars.
Queen's Westm.   Queen's Westminster Rifles.

Pnr.   Pioneer.

R.A.   Royal Artillery.
R.A.F.   Royal Air Force.
R.A.M.C.   Royal Army Medical Corps.

ABBREVIATIONS

R.A.O.C. Royal Army Ordnance Corps.
R.A.S.C. Royal Army Service Corps.
R.A.S.C. (M.T.). Royal Army Service Corps (Mechanical Transport).
R.B. The Rifle Brigade.
R. Berks. Royal Berkshire Regiment.
R. Bucks. Hus. Royal Buckinghamshire Hussars.
R. Can. R. Royal Canadian Regiment.
R.D.C. Royal Defence Corps.
R. Dragoons. Royal Dragoons.
R. Dub. Fus. Royal Dublin Fusiliers.
R.E. Royal Engineers.
R.E. Kent M. Rif. Royal East Kent Mounted Rifles.
R.F. Royal Fusiliers.
R.F.A. Royal Field Artillery.
R.F.C. Royal Flying Corps.
R.F.R. Royal Fleet Reserve.
R.G.A. Royal Garrison Artillery.
R. Glos. Hus. Royal Gloucestershire Hussars.
R. Guernsey L.I. Royal Guernsey Light Infantry.
R.H.A. Royal Horse Artillery.
R.H.G. Royal Horse Guards.
R.I. Fus. Royal Irish Fusiliers.
R.I.R. Royal Irish Regiment or Royal Irish Rifles.
R. Innis. Fus. Royal Inniskilling Fusiliers.
R. Liverp. Royal Liverpool Regiment.
R.M.A. Royal Marine Artillery.
R.M. Eng. Royal Marine Engineers.
R.M.L.C. Royal Marine Labour Corps.
R.M.L.I. Royal Marine Light Infantry.
R. Marines. Royal Marines.
R. Munster Fus. Royal Munster Fusiliers.
R.N. Royal Navy.
R.N.A.S. Royal Naval Air Service.
R.N. Coll. Royal Naval College.
R.N.D. Royal Naval Division.
R.N.D.R. Royal Naval Division Reserve.
R.N. Devon Hus. Royal North Devon Hussars.
R.N.R. Royal Naval Reserve.
R.N.V.R. Royal Naval Volunteer Reserve.
R.Q.M.S. Regimental Quartermaster Sergeant.
R.S.M. Regimental Sergeant Major.
R. Scots Fus. Royal Scots Fusiliers.
R. Scots Greys. Royal Scots Greys.
R. Sussex. Royal Sussex Regiment.
R.T.O. Railway Transport Officer.
R.W.F. Royal Welsh Fusiliers.
R.W.K. Royal West Kent Regiment.
R.W.S. Royal West Surrey Regiment.
R. Warwick. Royal Warwickshire Regiment.
Rajputana Inf. Rajputana Infantry.
Regt. Regiment.
Remount Dept. Remount Department.
Rfn. Rifleman.

S.A. Force. South African Force.
S.A. Imp. Light Horse. South African Imperial Light Horse.
S.A. Inf. South African Infantry.
S.A. Lab. C. South African Labour Corps.
S.A. Rifles. South African Rifles.
S.A. Transport. South African Transport.
S. Africa. South Africa.
S.B.A. Sick Berth Attendant.
S. Lancs. South Lancashire Regiment.
S.M. Sergeant Major.
S.Q.M.S. Squadron Quartermaster Sergeant.
S.S.A. Ship's Steward's Assistant.
S. Smith. Shoeing Smith.
S. Staffs. South Staffordshire Regiment.
S.W.B. South Wales Borderers.
Sea. H. Seaforth Highlanders.
2nd Lieut. Second Lieutenant.
Sergt. Sergeant.
Sherwood For. Sherwood Foresters.
Shropshire L.I. Shropshire Light Infantry.
Sig. Signaller or Signalman.
Somerset L.I. Somerset Light Infantry.
Spr. Sapper.
Staff S.M. Staff Sergeant Major.
Staff Sergt. Staff Sergeant.
Staffs. Staffordshire Regiment.
Sub-Lieut. Sub-Lieutenant.
Surg.-Comdr. Surgeon-Commander.
Surg.-Lieut. Surgeon-Lieutenant.
Surrey Y. Surrey Yeomanry.
Sussex Y. Sussex Yeomanry.
T. Telegraphist.
T.B. Torpedo Boat.
T.B.D. Torpedo Boat Destroyer.
T.F. Territorial Force.
T.M.B. Trench Mortar Battery.
T.R. Training Reserve.
Tank C. Tank Corps.
Tpr. Trooper.
Tptr. Trumpeter.
W. Africa. West Africa.
W.O. War Office.
W.O. Warrant Officer.
W. Somerset Y. West Somerset Yeomanry.
W.T. Wireless Telegraphist.
W. Yorks. West Yorkshire Regiment.
Warwick Y. Warwickshire Yeomanry.
Welsh R. Welsh Regiment.
Westm. Dragoons. Westminster Dragoons.
Wilts. Wiltshire Regiment.
Wilts Y. Wiltshire Yeomanry.
Winnipeg Rif. Winnipeg Rifles.
Worc. Worcester Regiment.
Worc. Y. Worcester Yeomanry.

Y. Sig. Yeoman of Signals.
York and Lancs. Yorkshire and Lancashire Regiment.
Yorks. Yorkshire Regiment.
Yorks Hus. Yorkshire Hussars.
Yorks L.I. Yorkshire Light Infantry.

Winchester War Service Register

✠ ABRAHAM, ARTHUR J. ... ... Pte. ... Lond. P.O. Rifles, Dec. 1917, Rfn. R.W.S. France.
(89, Upper Brook Street) Gassed, Sept. 20, 1918. *Died, Sept.* 21, 1918.

ADAMS, ALBERT E. V. ... Pte. ... Hants, Mch. 1917, Pte. France.
(10, Cathedral View)

ADAMS, ALFRED ... ... Rfn. ... R.B., May 1917, Rfn. Home.

ADAMS, ARCHIBALD B. A. ... Pte. ... Hants Y., Aug. 1914, Tpr. Hants. France.
(18, Gordon Avenue) Wounded, Oct. 14, 1918. M.M. 1918.

ADAMS, ARTHUR R. ... ... Pte. ... R.A.O.C., Sept. 1917; Pte. Home.
(10, Cathedral View)

ADAMS, EDGAR D. J. ... ... Pte. ... Hants, Aug. 1914, Pte. France, Salonica.
(18, Gordon Avenue)

ADAMS, EDWARD ... ... W.O. A.G.S., rejoined Sept. 1914, C.-S.-M. Home.
(4B, City Road) (Class 1)

ADAMS, ETHELBERT ... ... Pte. ... Devon, 1916, Pte. Hants, Lab. C. Home.
(Durngate House, North Walls)

ADAMS, FRANCIS G. ... ... Staff-Sergt. R.A.O.C., 1912, Pte. France, Egypt.
(10, Cathedral View)

✠ ADAMS, FREDERICK ... ... R.S.M. ... Can. Cav., Sept. 1914, Pte. France. Wounded,
(5, Maidstone Terrace) 1915. *Killed in Action, Mch.* 12, 1918.

ADAMS, FREDERICK C. ... Spr. ... R.E., June, 1916. France.
(28, Middle Brook Street)

ADAMS, GEORGE ... ... Sergt. ... R.B., 1891, Rfn. Home.
(10, Cathedral View)

ADAMS, HENRY R. N. ... Dr. ... R.F.A., Aug. 1914, Dr. France.
(18, Gordon Avenue)

ADAMS, JOHN ... ... Corpl. ... R.A.S.C., 1911, Dr. Salonica, Egypt.
(9, Wales Street)

✠ ADAMS, JOHN R. ... ... L.S. ... R.N., 1910, O.S. North Sea. Despatches, 1917.
(Hill View, Bar End) *Killed in Action, Dec.* 1, 1916.

ADAMS, MAURICE ... ... Gun. ... R.G.A., July 1917, Gun. France.
(26, Eastgate Street)

ADAMS, PHILIP W. G. H. ... A.-Q.M.S. Hants Y., Mch. 1916, Tpr. Worcester, Chinese
(18, Gordon Avenue) Lab. C. France.

ADDISON, WILLIAM E. ... Sergt. ... K.R.R.C., 1903, Rfn. Home.
(14, Monks Road)

AGAR, ROBERT ... ... Corpl. ... Lond., May 1916, Pte. France. Wounded, Oct.
(Cemetery Lodge) 1917.

AINLEY, ALBERT J. ... ... Pte. ... Hants, Nov. 1915, Pte. R.E., Cheshire, Lab. C.
(19, St. Giles' Hill Hutments) France. Wounded, Sept. 25, 1916.

ALBOROUGH, ALBERT ... ... Pte. ... Hants, Dec. 1914, Pte. M.G.C. Mesopotamia.
(3, Greyfriars Terrace)

B

WINCHESTER WAR SERVICE REGISTER

ALBOROUGH, ALFRED E. ... Pte. ... Hants, Sept. 1914, Pte. Mesopotamia.
(3, Greyfriars Terrace)

ALBOROUGH, CHARLES H. ... Pte. ... R.A.S.C., Jan. 1915, Pte. R.I.Fus. France,
(5, Poulsome Place) Salonica. Wounded twice.

ALBOROUGH, ROBERT ... Corpl. ... Hants, Apl. 29, 1918, Pte. France, Germany.
(3, Greyfriars Terrace)

ALDER, EDWARD ... ... Pte. ... Glos., Mch. 1915, Pte. Lab. C. France.
(45, St. Faith's Road)

ALDERMAN, ALBERT ... ... Tpr. ... Hants Y., Tpr.
(2, Worthy Lane)

ALDERTON, ALBERT L. ... L.-Corpl. R.E., Jan. 1915, Tptr. Home.
(32, Kingsgate Street)

ALDERTON, ARTHUR G. ... Sergt. ... R.N.A.S., Apl. 1915, 1st A.M. R.A.F. Home.
(32, Kingsgate Street)

ALDERTON, CHARLES D. ... Pte. . ... Wilts, Feb. 1916, Pte. Home.
(32, Kingsgate Street)

ALDERTON, FRANK H. ... C.Q.M.S. R. Berks, Feb. 1917, Pte. France, Russia.
(32, Kingsgate Street) Wounded. Dec. 25, 1917.

ALDERTON, WILLIAM H. ... Spr. ... R.E., Apl. 1915, Spr. France, Mesopotamia.
(32, Kingsgate Street) Gassed, July 1916.

ALDOUS, JOHN ... ... Spr. ... R.E., Oct. 1916. France, Belgium.
(28, Cheriton Road)

ALEXANDER, ALFRED G. ... 1st T.H. R.N., Aug. 1911. North Sea; H.M.S. *Cleopatra*.
(7, Percy Terrace) Wounded three times, 1915 and 1916.

✠ ALEXANDER, ARTHUR E. ... L.-Corpl. R. Berks, May 1916, Pte. Dorset. India, Mesopo-
(44, Nuns Road) tamia. *Died in Hospital*, 1918.

✠ ALEXANDER, DOUGLAS G. ... Cadet ... Hants Y., 1913, Tpr. R.F.C. France, Belgium,
(Lawn House, Eastgate Street) Egypt. *Killed in Egypt*, Oct. 8, 1918.

✠ ALEXANDER, ERNEST H. ... Pte. ... Hants Y., June 1915, Tpr. Hants. France, Belgium.
(1, Wales Street) Wounded, Nov. 1917. *Killed in Action*, Oct. 14, 1918.

ALEXANDER, FREDERICK E. Pte. ... Middlesex, May 1916, Pte. France. Gassed, Jan.
(2, Lower Wolvesey Terrace) 30, 1917.

ALEXANDER, FREDERICK J. ... Stoker ... R.N., Mch. 1915. North Sea; H.M.S. *Resolution*,
(7, Percy Terrace) *Ramillies*.

ALEXANDER, FREDERICK W. ... L.-Corpl. Hants Y., Aug. 1915, Tpr. Hants. Italy, France.
(95, Upper Brook Street) Wounded, May 1917, Sept. 1918.

ALEXANDER, HARRY J. ... Pte. ... R.A.S.C., 1913, Dr. K.O.R.Lancs. Gallipoli,
(104, Colebrook Street) France.

ALEXANDER, STUART V. ... L.-Corpl. R.G.A., Aug. 1914, Gun. Hants Y. Home.
(Lawn House, Eastgate Street)

ALEXANDER, SYDNEY O. ... Lieut. ... R.G.A., Aug. 1914, Tpr. Hants Y., O.C.B., R.W.K.
(Lawn House Eastgate Street) France, Belgium.

ALEXANDER, THOMAS ... ... Pte. ... Hants Y., Nov. 1916, Tpr. Hants. France, Italy,
(2, St. George's Terrace) Germany.

✠ ALEXANDER, THOMAS A. ... Blacksmith's R.N., 1904, Stoker. H.M.S. *Good Hope*. *Killed in*
(1, Wales Street) Mate ... *Action*, Nov. 1, 1914, *Falkland Islands*.

WINCHESTER WAR SERVICE REGISTER

ALEXANDER, WALTER H. (1, Wales Street)	...	Dr.	... R.A.S.C. (M.T.), May 1917, Dr. Home.
ALEXANDER, WALTER J. (78, Lower Brook Street)	...	Pte.	... Hants, rejoined, Aug. 1914, Pte. France. Wounded, Apl. 26, 1915.
ALEXANDER, WILLIAM E. (14, Water Lane)	...	Pte.	... Hants, July 1916, Pte. Devon. Home.
ALLEN, ALBERT ... (68, Water Lane)	...	Rfn.	... A.V.C., Jan. 1917, Pte. R.B. France.
ALLEN, ALFRED B. (17, Union Street)	...	Pte.	... Canadians, 1917, Pte. Home.
✠ ALLEN, ARTHUR H. (17, Union Street)	...	Sergt.	... Hants, Sept. 1914, Pte. India, Mesopotamia. Wounded, July 29, 1915. *Died, Mch.* 2, 1919, *as result of wounds.*
ALLEN, EDWARD (68, Water Lane)	...	Pte.	... Hants, Mch. 1916, Pte. India, Mesopotamia.
ALLEN, ERNEST A. (4, Hillside Terrace, Bar End)	...	Sergt.	... Hants Lab. Coy., Feb. 1917, Pte. Chinese Lab. C. France.
ALLEN, FRANK (25, Wharf Hill)	...	Gun.	... R.F.A., Nov. 1917, Gun. France.
ALLEN, FREDERICK (68, Water Lane)	...	Dr.	... R.A.S.C., May 1916, Dr. France.
ALLEN, FREDERICK J. (8, Wales Street) ...	...	Corpl.	... Hants, Nov. 1915, Pte. India, Egypt, France. M.M. 1918.
ALLEN, FREDERICK P. ... (17, Union Street)	...	Pte.	... Hants, Oct. 1915, Pte. India, Egypt, Palestine.
ALLEN, GEORGE H. (87, Greenhill Road)	...	Rfn.	... R.B., Aug. 1914, Rfn. France. Wounded and taken prisoner by Germans, 1914.
ALLEN, HENRY G. (17, Union Street)	...	Pte.	... Canadians, 1916, Pte. Home.
ALLEN, JAMES W. (60, Lower Brook Street)	...	Pte.	... R.A.S.C., Jan. 1915, Pte. France.
ALLEN, JOHN ... (68, Water Lane)	...	Pte.	... Hants, Aug. 1916, Pte. India.
ALLEN, RICHARD (68, Water Lane)	...	Gun.	... R.G.A., Aug. 1914, Gun. France.
ALLEN, ROBERT N. (24, St. John's North)	...	Pte.	... R.A.O.C., Nov. 1916, Pte. Mesopotamia, Palestine, Egypt.
ALLEN, SAMUEL W. G. (17, Union Street)	...	Pte.	... R.A.M.C., Pte. Home.
ALLEN, THOMAS E. (7, Nelson Road)	...	A.B.	... R.N., 1900, Boy. R.F.R. H.M.S. *Fishguard.*
ALLEN, WILLIAM G. (8, Wales Street)	...	Sergt.	... Hants (T.F.), Sept. 1902, Pte. Mesopotamia, India. Wounded, Feb. 4, 1917.
ALLSOPP, FREDERICK S. (8, Egbert Road)	...	Pte.	... Worc., June 1916, Pte. Hants. Home.
ALNER, FRANK ... (7, Chester Road)	...	Bandsman	K.R.R.C., Aug. 1915, Bandsman. Home.

WINCHESTER WAR SERVICE REGISTER

ALNER, PERCY W. ... ... Pte. ... Hants, May 1915, Pte. Mesopotamia, Persia.
(7, Chester Road)

ANDERSON, ALEXANDER H. ... S.B.A. ... R.N., 1908, S.B.A. North Sea, West Indies; H.M.S.
(14, Greenhill Road)   Princess Royal. Wounded, May 31, 1916.

ANDREWES, GERRARD L. ... Lieut. ... Suffolk, Nov. 1915, 2nd Lieut. Lab. C. Belgium.
(Chilcomb Rectory)

ANDREWES, WILLIAM G. ... Sub.-Lieut. R.N.Coll., 1912, Cadet. Grand Fleet. Baltic;
(Chilcomb Rectory)   H.M.S. *Canada* and *Walrus*.

ANDREWS, ALBERT ... ... Corpl. ... Lancers, Aug. 1914, Corpl. M.M.P. France.
(8, St. John's South)

ANDREWS, ALBION ... ... Corpl. ... R.A.S.C., 1911, Pte. France.
(8, St. John's South)

ANDREWS, ARTHUR ... ... O.S. ... R.N., Aug. 1917, O.S. Home.
(1, Cross Keys Passage)

ANDREWS, ARTHUR J. ... ... Pte. ... R.A.S.C. (M.T.), June 1916, Pte. Salonica.
(8, Water Lane)

ANDREWS, BRIAN ... ... Spr. ... R.G.A., Aug. 1915, Gun. R.E. France. Gassed
(73, Hyde Street)   once.

ANDREWS, CHARLES J. ... ... Gun. ... R.G.A., Mch. 3, 1916, Gun. France, Belgium.
(73, Hyde Street)

ANDREWS, DANIEL G. ... ... Major ... Hants. Home.
(The Hermitage, St. Giles Hill)

ANDREWS, EDWARD C. ... ... Pte. ... Hants, 1916, Pte. Home.
(32, Canon Street)

✠ ANDREWS, FRANK ... ... A.B. ... R.N., 1914. North Sea. *Died*, 1916.
(63, Parchment Street)

ANDREWS, FRANK ... ... L.-Corpl. Hants Y., Mch. 1917. Dorset. France, Belgium.
(5, Water Lane)   Wounded, Aug. 11, 1918.

ANDREWS, FREDERICK ... ... O.S. ... R.N., July 1917, O.S. North Sea.
(1, Cross Keys Passage)

ANDREWS, FREDERICK ... ... L.-Corpl. ... Hants, July 1914, Pte. Mesopotamia.
(5, Water Lane)

ANDREWS, FREDERICK C. ... Pte. ... R.A.S.C. (M.T.), Sept. 1915, Pte. M.A.C. France,
(12A, Water Lane)   Flanders.

ANDREWS, GEORGE ... ... Pte. ... Nat. Res., Sept. 3, 1914, Pte. R.D.C., Hants,
(41, Eastgate Street)   T.M.B. Home.

ANDREWS, GEORGE ... ... Pte. ... T.R., Pte. Hants. France. Gassed.
(73, Hyde Street)

ANDREWS, GEORGE D. ... Major ... Hants, Oct. 1914, 2nd Lieut. Mesopotamia
(The Hermitage, St. Giles' Hill)   Wounded three times. M.C., Despatches
                            three times.

ANDREWS, HARRY F. ... ... S.M. ... Hussars, 1914, Tpr. M.M.P. France, Germany,
(8, St. John's South)   Gassed. M.M., Belgian Croix de Guerre.

✠ ANDREWS, JAMES C. W. ... Corpl. ... R.G.A., 1907, Gun. France. Wounded, Aug. 15,
(1, Cross Keys Passage)   1915. *Killed in action, Sept. 23, 1917, Vimy
                            Ridge.*

WINCHESTER WAR SERVICE REGISTER

ANDREWS, PERCY (8, St. John's South)	Corpl.	R.E. (Postal Sec.), Sept. 1914, Pte. France.	
ANDREWS, PERCY (6, St. Thomas Street)	Pte.	Hants, Nov. 1915, Pte. India.	
ANDREWS, REGINALD (41, Eastgate Street)	Pte.	T.R., Apl. 1, 1917, Pte. Devon. France. Wounded, Apl. 22 and Nov. 5, 1918.	
ANDREWS, REGINALD (Pilgrims' Rest, Arthur Road)	Pte.	Devon, 1907, Pte. France. Gassed once.	
✠ ANDREWS, WILLIAM (8, St. John's South)	Bdr.	R.H.A., Aug. 1914, Gun. France. *Killed in Action, Nov. 5, 1914.*	
ANDREWS, WILLIAM (8, St. John's South)		R.N.A.S., 1917. Home.	
ANDREWS, WILLIAM G. (41, North Walls)	A.M.	R.N.A.S., Nov. 1917, A.M. R.A.F. Home.	
ANDREWS, WILLIAM H. (5, Water Lane)		Devon, Oct. 1916, Pte. R.A.F. Egypt, Palestine.	
✠ ANDREWS, WILLIAM J. (41, North Walls)	Gun.	R.F.A., Sept. 1914, Gun. Flanders, France. Wounded, Dec. 3, 1914. *Died of Wounds, Dec. 4, 1914.*	
ANNETTS, ARTHUR G. (65A, Water Lane)	Pte.	R.A.S.C., Feb. 1915, Dr. M.G.C. France.	
ANSELL, HENRY J. (25, Nuns Road)	Spr.	R.E., June 1916, Spr. France.	
ANSELL, J. C. (12, High Street)	Pte.	R.A.O.C., Oct. 1915, Pte. Home.	
ARCHARD, VICTOR S. (35, Southgate Street)	Sergt.-Instr.	M.M.G.C., Nov. 17, 1915, Gun. Tank C. France. Wounded, Apl. 9, 1917. Torpedoed, Apl. 17, 1917.	
ARLOTT, JOHN (Chilcomb)		R.F.A., Aug. 1914. R.A.S.C. (M.T.). France.	
ARNOLD, ALBERT B. (5, Thurloe Place)	L.-Corpl.	Hants, 1916, Pte. R. Innis. Fus. France, Belgium. Wounded twice, 1917. Gassed, 1917.	
ARNOLD, ALFRED (1, Upper Wolvesey Terrace)	Sergt.	Hants, Aug. 1914, Pte. Essex. France, Belgium. Wounded, Mch. 16, 1915.	
ARNOLD, FRANK (36, Tower Street)	Corpl.	Hants, Nov. 1914, Pte. India, Egypt, Palestine, France, Germany. Wounded, Sept. 13, 1918.	
ARNOLD, JAMES A. (1, Greenhill Avenue)	Pte.	Hants, 1896, Bandsman. Lab. C. Home.	
ARNOLD, LEVI F. (Upper Chilcomb)	L.-Corpl.	Hants, Nov. 1914, Pte. India, Palestine.	
ARNOLD, THOMAS B. (5, Thurloe Place)	Corpl.	S.W.B., 1915, Pte. R.A.S.C., R. Innis. Fus., Hants, R.I.R. France, Belgium. Wounded, Nov. 1917.	
ARNOLD, WILLIAM G. (7, Alresford Road)	L.S.	R.N., 1901, Boy. Persian Gulf.	
ASHFORD, CHARLES (23, St. Giles' Hill Hutments)	Pte.	Hants, Aug. 4, 1914, Pte. France. Wounded, Aug. 1914. Taken Prisoner by Germans, Aug. 25, 1914.	

WINCHESTER WAR SERVICE REGISTER

ASHFORTH, CHARLES (10, West End Terrace)	Rfn.	R.B., 1901, Rfn. France, Belgium.
ASLET, WILLIAM B. (44, Colebrook Street)	L.-Corpl.	K.R.R.C., Aug. 1917, Rfn. France, Russia. Gassed, 1918.
ASLET, WILLIAM R. (44, Colebrook Street)	Sergt.	K.R.R.C., rejoined, Sept. 1915, Sergt. Home.
✠ ASLETT, ALBERT G. (38, St. Catherine's Road)	Corpl.	R.G.A., Aug. 1914. France. Wounded, May 1915. *Killed in Action*, 1918.
ATTREE, ERDLEY E. (90, Wales Street)	Pte.	Hants, Aug. 1914, Pte. Gallipoli, Serbia. Wounded. Aug. 1915. Taken Prisoner by Bulgarians, Aug. 7, 1915.
ATTREE, WILLIAM T. (90, Wales Street)	Pte.	Hants, Jan. 1914. R. Marines. North Sea; H.M.S. *Calgarion*. Torpedoed twice.
ATTWOOD, ALBERT (10, Staple Garden)	Corpl.	Hants, Aug. 1914, Pte. India, Mesopotamia.
ATTWOOD, EDGAR S. (10, Highcliffe Road)	Pte.	R.A.M.C., Feb. 1915, Pte. France.
ATTWOOD, FREDERICK H. H. (10, Highcliffe Road)	Sergt.	K.R.R.C., 1905, Rfn. Egypt, India, France. Wounded, Oct. 1914.
ATTWOOD, PERCY (10, Staple Garden)	Spr.	R.N., 1914. Hants, R.E. Italy.
✠ ATTWOOD, WILLIAM (10 Staple Garden)	Pte.	R. Sussex, Aug. 1914, Pte. France. *Killed in Action*, Sept. 1915.
ATTWOOD, WILLIAM G. (10, Highcliffe Road)	Gun.	R.G.A., Oct. 1915, Gun. Home.
AUDSLEY, ERNEST A. (33, Milverton Road)	Spr.	R.E., 1910, Boy. France, Mesopotamia.
AUDSLEY, SAMUEL H. (33, Milverton Road)	C.Q.M.S.	Hants, Dec. 1914, Pte. R.E. Dardanelles.
AUDSLEY, WILLIE N. (33, Milverton Road)	Pte.	Hants, Aug. 1915, Pte. Mesopotamia. Wounded, Jan. 31, 1917.
✠ AVERY, CHARLES W. (21, Canon Street)	Pte.	Hants, Sept. 1914, Pte. Mesopotamia. *Killed in Action, Jan. 21, 1916.*
AVERY, PERCY A. (21, Canon Street)	A.-Sergt.	Hants, Sept. 1914, Pte. Mesopotamia. M.S.M., Médaille Militaire.
AVIS, JOHN C. (1, East Cliff)	Stoker	R.N., May 1916, Stoker. Gibraltar, Malta, Australia, New Zealand; H.M.S. *Royal Sovereign* and *Marguerite*.
AXE, CHARLES (11, Alresford Road)	L.-Corpl.	Devon, Oct. 1916, Pte. R.E. Home.
✠ AXE, THOMAS A. (23, Union Street)	P.O.	R.N., 1902. Grand Fleet. *Killed in Action, June 1, 1916, Jutland.*
AYLING, HERBERT J. (31, Romsey Road)	Pte.	Hants, Aug. 1915, Pte. France.
AYLING, WILLIAM C. (23, Hyde Abbey Road)	L.-Corpl.	Hants, Aug. 1914, Pte. India, Egypt, France. Wounded, Nov. 18, 1917.

WINCHESTER WAR SERVICE REGISTER

AYLING, WILLIAM F. (2, Avenue Terrace)	...	**Sergt.**	... R.E., Nov. 1914, Corpl. France, Mesopotamia, Palestine.
AYLWARD, EDWARD B.	...	**Major**	... Glos., (T.F.) Pte. R.G.A., Ind. Mountain Art. India.
BACON, REGINALD J. (28, Union Street)	...	**Tpr.**	... Devon, Feb. 1917, Pte. Surrey Y. Home.
BAILEY, ARTHUR J. (11, Chester Road)	...	**Sergt.**	... Hants, Pte. India, Egypt, Palestine, France, Belgium, Germany.
BAILEY, ERNEST (1, Poulsome Place)	...	**Tpr.**	... Dragoons, May 1916, Tpr. France.
BAILEY, FRANK K. (1, Poulsome Place)	...	**O.S.**	... R.N., 1911, O.S. Grand Fleet.
BAILEY, HARRY L. (The Dell, Wharf Hill)	...	**Pte.**	... R.M.A., 1903, Pte. Home.
BAILEY, WILLIAM C. (3, Southgate Street)	...	**Bdr.**	... R.G.A., Nov. 1915, Gun. Egypt.
BAILEY, WILLIAM H. (45, North Walls)	...	**A.B.**	... R.N., Aug. 1914, Boy. North Sea; H.M.S. *King George V.*
BAILY, FREDERICK G. (11, Water Lane)	...	**1st A.M.**	... R.F.C., Feb. 1917, 2nd A.M. Home.
✠ BAIRD, WILLIAM A. (4, Cossack Lane)	...	**Pte.**	... Hants, Aug. 1914, Pte. Dardanelles. *Killed in Action, Aug. 10, 1915.*
BAKER, ALBERT W. (65, St. John's Street)	...	**A.B.**	... R.N., 1907. Grand Fleet.
BAKER, ARTHUR C. (37, St. Faith's Road)	...	**2nd Lieut.**	... R.F.C., Sept. 1917, Boy. Home.
BAKER, C.	...	**Pte.**	... Hants, 1915, Pte. Gallipoli.
BAKER, EDWARD S. (65, St. John's Street)	...	**Gun.**	... Hants Y., Oct. 1914, Tpr. R.H.A. Home.
BAKER, EDWARD ST. L. (65, St. John's Street)	...	**L.-Corpl.**	... Hants, Aug. 1914, Pte. India, Mesopotamia, Persia.
BAKER, ERNEST A. (St. Clare, Owen's Road)	...	**Sergt.**	... R.A.F. France.
BAKER, ERNEST W. (80, Colebrook Street)	...	**Pte.**	... R.A.M.C., Apl. 1917, Pte. Home.
✠ BAKER, GEORGE C. (56, Sussex Street)	...	**Pte.**	... T.R., Sept. 1917, Pte. Lond., att. R.B. France. *Killed in Action, June 2, 1918, Albert.*
BAKER, REGINALD H. (71, Eastgate Street)	...	**Pte.**	... R.W.S., July 1916, Pte. France. Wounded twice.
BAKER, SIDNEY T. (St. Clare, Owen's Road)	...	**Pte.**	... Warwick, Sept. 1915. R.I.R. France, Germany.
BAKER, WILLIAM (16, Little Minster Street)	...	**Dr.**	... R.A.S.C., 1915, Dr. Home.

WINCHESTER WAR SERVICE REGISTER

BALDING, FREDERICK P. ... Pte. ... Hants, Aug. 20, 1914, Pte. France. Wounded
(56, North Walls) Apl. 1915, May 1915, July 1, 1916.

BALDING, HENRY M. ... Pte. ... Glos., Nov. 1914, Pte. Lond. Elec. Eng., Lab. C.
(55, North Walls) France. Wounded and gassed 1917.

BALDWIN, JAMES ... Pte. ... Hants. France. Wounded three times.
(11, Wharf Hill)

BALDWIN, RICHARD ... Pte. ... Worc., Mch. 1917, Pte. Home.
(77, Upper Brook Street)

BALL, JOHN E. ... Sergt. ... R.B., 1900, Rfn. M.F.P. France.
(20, North Walls)

✠ BALL, JOHN W. ... Rfn. ... R.B., Aug. 1914, Rfn. France. *Killed in Action,*
(6, Chester Road) *Aug. 26, 1914, in Retreat from Mons.*

✠ BALL, LEONARD A. ... Pte. ... Hants, Sept. 1914, Pte. Mesopotamia. *Died, July*
(12, High Street) *11, 1916, Amara.*

BALL, REGINALD H. C. ... L.-Corpl. ... T.R., Feb. 1917, Pte. R. Warwick. France.
(16, St. Swithun Street) Wounded, 1917.

BALL, STANLEY J. ... Sig. ... Sea Scout, Jan. 1915. R.N. (Minesweepers). North
(16, St. Swithun Street) Sea.

BALLARD, CALEB ... Spr. ... R.E., Sept. 1916, Spr. Mesopotamia, India.
(35, Colson Road)

BALLARD, CECIL H. ... Sergt. ... R.G.A., June 1914, Gun. France. Gassed, Nov. 28,
(56, St. Catherine's Road) 1917.

BANKS, WALTER E. ... 2nd Lieut. ... Lond., Apl. 27, 1917. O.C.B. Northants. France.
(76, Hatherley Road) Wounded, Sept. 18, 1918.

BANTING, WALTER ... Pte. ... Nat. Res., Jan. 1915. R.D.C. Home.
(52, Brassey Road)

BARFOOT, BERTRAM J. ... Spr. ... R.E., 1914, Spr. Belgium, France, Germany.
(40, Parchment Street)

BARGE, HENRY J. ... Pte. ... A.V.C., Aug. 1916, Pte. France.
(13, Chester Road)

✠ BARING, GUY V. ... Lt.-Col. ... Coldstream Gds., Aug. 6, 1914, Major. France.
(60, Kingsgate Street) Despatches twice. *Killed in Action, Sept. 15,*
1916, Somme.

BARKER, CHRISTOPHER ... L.-Corpl. ... Hants, Aug. 1915, Pte. France. Wounded, July 1,
(2, Alexandra Terrace) 1916; Aug. 2, 1918.

BARKER, EDWARD W. ... Gun. ... R.N., 1910, Boy. North Sea.
(2, Alexandra Terrace)

BARKER, GEORGE H. ... Lieut. ... Hants, 1900, Pte. France, Belgium. Wounded,
(35, North Walls) Sept. 21, 1917. M.C., 1917.

BARKER, HERBERT ... Tpr. ... N. Devon Y., Mch. 1917, Tpr. France. Taken
(2, Alexandra Terrace) Prisoner by Germans, Sept. 23, 1918.

BARNARD, EDWARD C. ... Sergt. ... Hants, Aug. 1914, Pte. India.
(7, St. John's South)

BARNES, ALEXANDER ... Pte. ... Hants, rejoined 1914, Pte. France.
(28, Canon Street)

BARNES, CHARLES E. ... Stoker ... R.N., Oct. 1915, Stoker. Indian Ocean, Mediter-
(63, Wales Street) ranean.

WINCHESTER WAR SERVICE REGISTER

BARNES, MARK (9, Nelson Road)	Pte.	Hants Y., Nov. 1915, Tpr. Hants. France.
BARNETT, CECIL E. (6, St. James' Villas)	Lieut.	Lond., Mch. 1917, Pte. O.C.B. France. M.C., 1918.
BARNETT, GEORGE P. (6, St. James' Villas)	Lieut.	Lond., Mch. 1917, Pte. O.C.B. France.
✠ BARNEY, HAROLD G. (14, Hyde Abbey Road)	Pte.	Hants, Oct. 1916, Pte. France. *Killed in Action, Oct. 10, 1917, Langemarck.* 2ND BN 203393
BARRATT, ERNEST F. (One Ash, Petersfield Road)	Spr.	Nat. Res., Sept. 1914, Pte. R.D.C., Hants, R.E. Home.
BARRETT, CHARLES J. (42, Colebrook Street)	Dr.	R.A.S.C., Aug. 1914, Dr. Salonica.
✠ BARRETT, EDGAR F. (1, Ivy Terrace, Bar End)	Pte.	Hants, Feb. 3, 1918, Pte. Germany. *Died, May 7, 1919, Cologne.*
BARRETT, FREDERICK T. (42, Colebrook Street)	A.B.	R.N., 1912, Boy. North Sea; H.M.S. *Iron Duke* and *Impregnable.* Wounded (accidentally), 1918.
BARRETT, LEONARD V. (1, Ivy Terrace, Bar End)	Corpl.	R.A.S.C. (M.T.), Mch. 1917, Pte. France.
BARRETT, REGINALD F. (1, Ivy Terrace, Bar End)	Off. Cook	R.N., Oct. 1915, Off. Cook. Egypt, India, North Sea; H.M.S. *Beagle.* Wounded, Aug. 10, 1918.
BARRETT, WALTER J. (55, Middle Brook Street)	Pte.	Hants, Sept. 1914, Pte. France, Dardanelles. Wounded, Sept. 1915; 1917.
BARRETT, WILLIAM H. (49, Upper Brook Street)	Pte.	Hants, Dec. 1914, Pte. Home.
✠ BARRINGTON, WILFRED (Hillside Cottage, Sleeper's Hill)	Pte.	Devon, Dec. 1917, Pte. France. *Killed in Action, Aug. 30, 1918, Beugny.*
BARROW-SIMONDS, JOHN (Abbotts Barton, Worthy Rd.)	Lieut.	Hants, July 1915, 2nd Lieut. France. Taken Prisoner by Germans, Apl. 23, 1917.
BARTLETT, ALEC L. (72A, High Street)	Corpl.	Hants, Sept. 1914, Pte. India, Mesopotamia.
✠ BARTLETT, ALLAN O. (72A, High Street)	Lieut. and Q.M.	Hants, Sept. 1914, Pte. Camel Corps. India, Palestine. *Killed in Action, October,* 1918.
BARTLETT, EDWARD J. (69, Sussex Street)	Pte.	Herts, Oct. 1916, Pte. Home.
✠ BARTLETT, GUY G. (26, Edgar Road)	2nd Lieut.	R.E. (Motor Despatch Rider), Apl. 1916, Corpl. R.F.C. Flanders. *Killed in Action, Mch.* 1918.
BARTLETT, PHILIP (55, Middle Brook Street)	O.S.	R.N., 1917, O.S. North Sea.
BARTLETT, ROBERT (55, Middle Brook Street)	Stoker	R.N., 1901, Stoker. North Sea.
BARTLETT, THOMAS W. (4, Upper Wolvesey Terrace)	Corpl.	Wilts, rejoined Aug. 1914, Pte. R. Berks. France. Wounded, July 11, 1915.
BARTLETT, WILLIAM F. (55, Middle Brook Street)	Stoker	R.N., 1900, Stoker. North Sea, Gibraltar.
BARTLETT, WILLIAM J. (55, Middle Brook Street)	Pte.	R.A.S.C., Oct. 1914, Pte. Salonica.

WINCHESTER WAR SERVICE REGISTER

BARTON, ERNEST W. E. (South Hall, Kingsgate Street)	Dr.		Brit.R.C., Oct. 1915, Ambulance Motor Driver. France, Italy.
BASCOMB, FREDERICK A. (1, Stanmore Villas)	Spr.		R.E., Sept., 1916, Spr. France, Belgium, Germany.
BASTABLE, CHARLES E. (6, Prison Quarters)	L.-Corpl.		S.W.B., Aug. 1914, Pte. France, India, Germany. Wounded, Mch. and July 1916.
BASTABLE, GORDON (6, Prison Quarters)	C.Q.M.S.		Hants, May 1915, Pte. Egypt, France, Italy, Germany. Wounded, Nov. 17, 1916. D.C.M., 1917.
BASTER, CHARLES (82, Chesil Street)	Sergt.		R.B. France. Wounded four times.
BATCHELLOR, ERNEST W. (3, Jewry Street)	A.-Paymaster		K.R.R.C., Aug. 1916, Rfn. A.P.C. Home.
BATCHELOR, FREDERICK E. (47, North Walls)	Pte.		Hants, Aug. 1916, Pte. Wilts. India, Egypt.
BATCHELOR, REGINALD G. (1, St. John's Park Terrace)	Gun.		R.N., 1912, O.S. North Sea.
BATCHELOR, WILLIAM (8, King Alfred Terrace)	Pte.		R.F.C., June 1916, Pte. Home.
✠ BATES, ALAN (Mill House, St. Cross)	L.-Corpl.		Hants, Aug. 1914, Pte. Mesopotamia. Wounded twice. Taken Prisoner by Turks, Mch. 1917. *Died, Nov. 12, 1917, Amara.*
BATES, CYRIL H. (Mill House, St. Cross)	L.-Corpl.		Hants, Aug. 1914, Pte. Mesopotamia. Wounded, Mch. 1917.
BATH, ALBERT (57, Upper Brook Street)			Hants. Home.
BATH, FREDERICK G. (57, Upper Brook Street)	Sergt.		R.M.A., Pte. North Sea, St. Helena. Wounded, Sept. 22, 1914.
BATH, FREDERICK G. ST. J. (St. John's Hospital)	Pte.		Hants, Nov. 1915, Pte. Mesopotamia, India. Wounded, Feb. 7, 1917.
BATH, JOHN (57, Upper Brook Street)	Pte.		T.R., Pte. Devon. France.
BATH, ST. JOHN A. C. (St. John's Hospital)	A.-Sergt.		R.A.O.C., 1913, Pte. France, E. Africa.
BAVERSTOCK, GEORGE J. (10, Wales Street)	Sergt.		R.G.A., Nov. 1915, Gun. R.E. France. Wounded, Mch. 1918.
BAWDEN, ALBERT A. (3, Queen's Road)	A.-Ship's Corpl.		R.N., rejoined Aug. 1914, A.B. North Sea, Canada, Archangel; H.M.S. *Devonshire*.
BEALE, JOHN (18, Wales Street)	Dr.		R.A.S.C., 1914, Dr. Egypt, Salonica, Mesopotamia.
BEALE, THOMAS (18, Wales Street)	A.B.		R.N., 1915, Boy. North Sea.
BEARD, EDWIN T. (23, Clifton Road)	A.B.		R.N., 1904, A.B. Dardanelles, North Sea; H.M.S. *Swiftsure* and *Hydra*.
BEARD, PERCY R. (23, Clifton Road)	Stoker		R.N., 1909, Stoker. Dardanelles, Gallipoli, Salonica, Italy.
BEAUCHAMP, PERCY W. (7, Gladstone Street)	Pte.		R. Berks, June 1916, Pte. Home.

WINCHESTER WAR SERVICE REGISTER

BEAUMONT, WILLIAM F. (45, Upper Brook Street)	Dr.	R.N.A.S., Aug. 1917, Dr. Home.
BEAUMONT, WILLIAM H. (45, Upper Brook Street)	Pte.	Nat. Res., Sept. 1914. Hants. Home.
BEAVIS, LIONEL (20, Clausentum Road)	Pte.	R.A.S.C. (M.T.), Oct. 1916, Pte. France.
BECKETT, JOSEPH (102, Brassey Road)	A.-Staff S.M.	Sherwood For., 1895, Pte. A.P.C. Egypt, Salonica. Despatches 1916, M.S.M. 1917.
BECKETT, WILLIAM (46, Lansdown Terrace)	P.O.	R.N.R., 1913, O.S. Malta.
✠ BECKINGHAM, ALBERT (7, Hedges Buildings)	C.Q.M.S.	R.B., rejoined Aug. 1914, Rfn. France. Wounded once. M.M. 1916, Despatches 1916. *Killed in Action, Apl. 16, 1917, Arras.*
BECKINGHAM, RICHARD (38, Western Road)	Spr.	R.E., Mch. 1915. Bug. France, Russia. Wounded, Oct. 30, 1918.
BECKLES, WILLIAM H. (37, Upper Brook Street)	Boy	R.N., Mch. 1917, Boy. North Sea. Wounded, Dec. 17, 1917.
✠ BELL, ALFRED G. (13, Water Lane)	Rfn.	R.B., 1908, Rfn. France. *Killed in Action, Aug. 26, 1914.*
BELL, ARTHUR (89, Wales Street)	...	R.N., 1909. North Sea, Atlantic, Mediterranean; H.M.S. *Hampshire*.
BELL, ERNEST (89, Wales Street)	...	R.A.S.C., 1915. Dardanelles, Egypt.
BELL, FREDERICK (9, Cross Street)	Rfn.	R.B., 1899, Rfn. France. Taken Prisoner by Germans, Aug. 1914.
BELL, FREDERICK (89, Wales Street)	Corpl.	R. Berks, 1914, Pte. France, Salonica.
✠ BELL, GAWAIN M. (Culver's Close)	Major	Hants, Oct. 1914, Capt. France. D.S.O. 1917. *Killed in Action, July 31, 1917, Ypres.*
BELL, HARRY W. (10, Hedges Buildings)	L.-Corpl.	Wilts, Aug. 1916, Pte. Somerset L.I., R.D.C. France.
✠ BELL, PERCY (89, Wales Street)	...	R.G.A., 1909. France. *Killed in Action, Mch. 10, 1915, Neuve Eglise.*
BELL, WALTER S. (1, Magdalen Hill)	Sergt.	Hants, Oct. 1914, Pte. Mesopotamia, Persia.
BELL, WILLIAM (89, Wales Street)	...	R. Marines, 1909. North Sea; H.M.S. *Galatea* and *Furious*.
BELL, WILLIAM R. (3, Tower Street)	Drummer	Hants, May 1914, Bug. India, Persian Gulf. Taken Prisoner by Turks, Dec. 1916.
✠ BELLINGER, ANDREW E. (42, Tower Street)	Conductor	R.A.O.C., 1896, Pte. Gallipoli, Palestine. Despatches twice. *Died of exposure.*
✠ BELLINGER, HENRY G. (42, Tower Street)	Corpl.	R.B., rejoined 1914, Rfn. P.P.C.L.I. France. *Killed in Action, Jan. 8, 1915, St. Eloi.*
BELLINGER, JESSE (42, Tower Street)	Pte.	R.N.A.S., 1915, Pte. Home.
BELLINGER, LEONARD C. (42, Tower Street)	Rfn.	R.B., rejoined 1916, Rfn. Home.

WINCHESTER WAR SERVICE REGISTER

BELLINGER, REGINALD ... Staff-Sergt. R.A.O.C., 1904, Pte. Egypt.
(42, Tower Street)

✠ BENDLE, WILLIAM J. ... ... Pte. ... Hants, Sept. 1914, Pte. Mesopotamia. Taken
(12, King Alfred Terrace) Prisoner by Turks, Apl. 1916. Died, May 5, 1916, *Shanram.*

BENHAM, ALFRED C. ... ... Pte. ... Hants, Bandsman. M.G.C. Egypt, France,
(Eastgate House, Eastgate St.) Dardanelles. Wounded twice.

BENHAM, ERNEST H. ... ... Sergt. ... R.A.S.C., Nov. 1915, Pte. Salonica.
(8, Fairfield Road)

BENHAM, THOMAS G. ... ... Pte. ... Nat. Res., Sept. 1914, Pte. Hants. France.
(8, Fairfield Road) Wounded, Sept. 4, 1918.

BENNETT, ALFRED E. ... ... Pte. ... H.M.T. *Aragon*, Aug. 1914, Steward. R.B., M.G.C.
(8, Culver Road) Dardanelles, France. Wounded twice, 1918.

BENNETT, GEORGE ... ... Corpl. ... Hants, May 1915, Pte. France. Wounded, 1916;
(36B, Clifton Road) Oct. 26, 1917.

BENNETT, HAROLD J. ... ... Corpl. ... Arg. and Suth. H., Oct. 1915, Pte. Sea. H. France.
(19, Western Road)

BENNETT, JAMES H. ... ... C.Q.M.S. ... R.B., 1889, Rfn. France. Wounded, 1915. D.C.M.
(8, Culver Road) 1915.

BENNETT, THOMAS F. ... ... Sergt. ... Hants, Aug. 1914. Home.
(19, Western Road)

✠ BENNETT, VICTOR ... ... Pte. ... Hants, Oct. 1915, Pte. India, Palestine, France.
(8, Culver Road) *Killed in Action, Nov. 4, 1918.* M.M. 1918.

BENNETT. WILLIAM ... ... Corpl. ... R.A.S.C., Aug. 1914, Pte. Gallipoli, Egypt, Palestine.
(8, Culver Road)

BENNING, GRANGER W. ... ... R.N.A.S., May 16, 1917. R.A.F. Home.
(53, Milverton Road)

BERRY, FRANK N. ... ... P.O. ... R.N., 1911, Cook's Mate. Malta, North Sea.
(38, St. Faith's Road) (2nd Class)

BERRY, FRED ... ... L.M. ... R.N.A.S., Aug. 1916, 1st A.M. R.A.F. Home.
(35, St. Faith's Road)

✠ BERRY, FREDERICK J. ... ... Sergt. ... K.R.R.C., Jan. 1906, Rfn. France. *Killed in Action, Feb. 11, 1916, Givenchy.*
(17, Clausentum Road)

BERRY, GEORGE ... ... Sergt. ... R.G.A., 1912, Gun. France, S. Africa. Wounded,
(2, Lower Wolvesey Terrace) 1917.

BERRY, WILLIAM G. ... ... P.O. ... R.N., 1912, Carpenter. China, North Sea.
(38, St. Faith's Road) (2nd Class)

BEST, FREDERICK W. ... ... Lord Strathcona's Horse. Can. Light Horse.
(30B, Hyde Street) France. Gassed once.

BEST. REGINALD J. ... ... R.E., Jan. 1917. Palestine.
(31, Andover Road)

BETTERIDGE, ARTHUR A. ... Pte. ... R.B., 1906, Rfn. Lab. C. France. Wounded,
(51, Nuns Road) Sept. 14, 1914.

BETTERIDGE, JAMES ... ... 3rd A.M. R.F.C., Apl. 1917, 3rd A.M. Home.
(62, St. Catherine's Road)

WINCHESTER WAR SERVICE REGISTER

BEVIS, CHARLES H. (27, Hyde Street)	Sergt.	A.P.C., Nov. 1914, Pte. Glos., R. Warw. France.
BEVIS, THOMAS (6, Sussex Street)	Pte.	R.B., 1897, Bug. R.A.S.C. Home.
BIDDLE, FRANK W. (3, Queen's Terrace)	Pte.	R.A.S.C., Nov. 1916, Pte. Home.
BIDDLE, HENRY A. (17, Upper Wolvesey Terrace)	Pte.	Hants, Oct. 1915, Pte. India, Palestine, France.
BIDE, ARTHUR R. (4, Romsey Road)	A.M.	R.N.A.S., Jan. 1918, A.M. R.A.F. Grand Fleet.
BIDE, WILFRED J. (4, Romsey Road)	L.T.	R.N., June 1914, W.T. North Sea, Baltic.
BIDEN, HUGH A. (Woodlands, Worthy Road)	Pte.	Somerset L.I., June 22, 1917, Pte. France, Belgium.
BIDWELL, ERNEST W. (106, Colebrook Street)	Pte.	Hants, Dec. 1914, Pte. France. Taken Prisoner by Germans, Dec. 3, 1917.
✠ BIGNELL, JESSE (34, Stockbridge Road)	Corpl.	Essex, Dec. 1914, Pte. France. Wounded, Oct. 10, 1915, and Aug. 2, 1917. *Killed in Action, Oct. 8, 1917.*
BIGNELL, WALTER F. (2, Dell Road)	2nd Corpl.	R.E., 1917, Spr. France.
BIGNELL, WILLIAM (34, Stockbridge Road)	Sergt.	Hants Cyc., Aug. 1914, Pte. India, Egypt, France.
BILLINGS, FRANK A. J. (1, Culver Road)	L.-Sergt.	K.R.R.C., June 1916. Lab. C. France, Belgium.
BILLINGSLEY, JOHN H. (91, Colebrook Street)	Pte.	Hants, rejoined Sept. 1914, Pte. Home.
BILSON, RICHARD K. (40, Lower Brook Street)	Sergt.	K.R.R.C., Aug. 1916, Sergt. France.
BINSTEAD, CHARLES F. (23, Middle Brook Street)	Corpl.	Hants, May 1915, Pte. France. Wounded, July 1916 and Oct. 1917. M.M. 1918.
✠ BINSTEAD, GEORGE A. (23, Middle Brook Street)	Pte.	Hants (T.F.), 1913, Pte. India, Mesopotamia. Wounded once. *Died of Wounds, Dec. 22, 1915, Kut.* 1894 1/4TH T⊂ BN
BINSTEAD, GEORGE W. (23, Middle Brook Street)	Sergt.	K.R.R.C., Feb. 1915, Rfn. Home.
BINSTEAD, WILLIAM C. (23, Middle Brook Street)	Gun.	Hants (T.F.), Sept. 1914, Pte. Armd. Motor Car. India, Mesopotamia.
BIRD, STANLEY A. (8, St. James' Villas)	Rfn.	R.B., Dec. 8, 1915, Rfn. Dorset, Manch., D.C.L.I., Lab. C., attd. K.R.R.C. Home.
BIRMINGHAM, FREDERICK (18, St. Swithun Street)	Gun.	R.G.A., 1915, Gun. R.F.A. France, Germany.
BIRMINGHAM, JAMES (24, Lower Brook Street)	Rfn.	K.R.R.C., 1916, Rfn. France.
BIRT, STANLEY R. (White House, St. Cross Road)	Sergt.	Hants Y., 1914, Tpr. R.A.S.C. (M.T.). France, Egypt, Palestine, Syria.

Bishop, Alfred H. (33, North Walls)	W.O.	R.N., 1901, Writer. Gibraltar. M.S.M.	
Bishop, Charles (33, North Walls)	W.T.	R.E. Sigs., Sept. 1915, Spr. Palestine.	
Bishop, Charles F. (6, Hedges Buildings)	Boy	R.N., Feb. 1918, Boy. Belgium, French coast.	
Bishop, Edward C. (50, Fairfield Road)	Pte.	Hants, Feb. 1917, Pte. R. Berks., Glos. France, Belgium.	
Bishop, Ernest (33, North Walls)	Spr.	R.E. Sigs., May 1915, Spr. Dardanelles.	
✠ Bishop, Frederick (33, North Walls)	Staff Capt.	Cheshire, Sept. 1914, Pte. France. M.C., Despatches. *Died of influenza*.	
Bishop, George (12, Chesil Street)	Pte.	Hants, Feb. 1914, Pte. Mesopotamia. Wounded, July 25, 1915.	
Bishop, George J. (12, Chesil Street)	C.S.M.	Hants, Aug. 1914, Sergt. Somerset L.I. Home.	
Bishop, Herbert (33, North Walls)	Pte.	Devon, Jan. 1917, Pte. R.F.C. Home.	
Bishop, Herbert W. (3, Greenhill Road)	Pte.	Devon, May 1917, Pte. R.A.F. Home.	
Bishop, Leonard (33, North Walls)	Spr.	R.E. Sigs., Jan. 1916, Spr. France.	
Bishop, Reginald (33, North Walls)	2nd Lieut.	Hants Y., Sept. 1914, Tpr. Cheshire. France. Wounded, Nov. 1918.	
Bishop, Walter J. (6, Hedges Buildings)	Pte.	Hants, June 1917, Pte. France, Germany. Wounded, 1918.	
Bishop, William J. (6, Hedges Buildings)	Pte.	R.A.M.C., Nov. 1915, Pte. France.	
Blackman, Arthur M. (5 Leckford Cottages)	Gun.	R.F.A., Nov. 5, 1914, Gun. France. Wounded, Oct. 12, 1917, and July 9, 1918.	
Blackman, Ernest E. (5, Leckford Cottages)	Pte.	R. Bucks Hus., Apl. 19, 1915, Tpr. M.G.C. Egypt. Wounded once.	
Blackman, John W. (4, Greyfriars Terrace)	Pte.	T.R., Feb. 1917, Pte. Somerset L.I. France. Wounded, Dec. 30, 1917.	
Blackman, Walter W. (5, Leckford Cottages)	Pte.	R.A.S.C. (M.T.), May 31, 1915, Pte. France.	
Blackmore, Arthur G. (22, Stockbridge Road)	Pte.	Hants, Nov. 1917, Pte. India, Egypt, Mesopotamia. Wounded once.	
Blackwell, Harry (25, Milverton Road)	Bandsman	Hants, 1910, Bandsman. India.	
Blake, Albert G. (9, St. James' Lane)	1st A.M.	R.F.C., Mch. 1916, 2nd A.M. France.	
Blake, Arthur G. (17, Brassey Road)		R.A.S.C., June 1915. Mesopotamia.	
Blake, Charles F. (21, St. John's Road)	Pte.	R.A.M.C., Nov. 1914, Pte. R.A.S.C. Home.	

WINCHESTER WAR SERVICE REGISTER

Name (Address)	Rank	Service
BLAKE, CHRISTOPHER (2, Greenhill Avenue)	Sergt.	Hants, Sept. 1914, Sergt. Salonica.
BLAKE, CHRISTOPHER C. (89, Lower Brook Street)	Gun.	R.F.A., Nov. 1915, Gun. Mesopotamia, India.
BLAKE, FREDERICK A. (89, Lower Brook Street)	Fireman	Merc. Mar., 1913, Trimmer. Mediterranean.
BLAKE, FREDERICK G. (8, St. George's Street)	Pte.	Hants, Aug. 1915, Pte. R. Liverp. Egypt. Wounded twice.
BLAKE, SYDNEY S. (8, Western Road)	Art.	R.N., Nov. 1915. North Sea, Russia.
BLAKE, WILLIAM H. (18, Alresford Road)	Pte.	Hants, Aug. 1914, Pte. Dorset. Home.
✠ BLANDFORD, ARCHIE (14, St. John's North)	Sergt.	Can. Rif., Feb. 1915, Rfn. France. *Killed in Action, Apl. 9, 1917, Vimy Ridge.*
BLANDFORD, REGINALD F. (14, St. John's North)	Corpl.	Hants, Sept. 1914, Pte. France. Wounded, Aug. 5, 1917.
BLATCH, JOHN (11, Hedges Buildings)	Pte.	Lond., Aug. 1914, Pte. France. Wounded, Nov. 1915, and July 1917. Gassed, Dec. 1917.
✠ BLIGH, EDWARD H. S. (Prior's Barton, Kingsgate Street)	Lieut.	R.N.D., Drake Bn., Oct. 1914. Sub-Lieut. Gallipoli. Despatches, Sept. 1915. *Killed in Action, Sept. 10, 1915.*
BLOMFIELD, EDWARD V. (Rosehill, St. James' Lane)	Lieut.	R.E., Oct. 1915, 2nd Lieut. Salonica, France.
BLOOMFIELD, ARTHUR E. (4, Ivy Terrace, Bar End)	Pte.	Hants, 1898, Pte. Bedford. India.
BLOTT, F. H.	Tpr.	R. Sussex Y., 1914, Tpr. R.G.A.
BLOUNT, ALFRED H. (17, City Road)	Pte.	A.P.C., 1914, Pte. Home.
BLOUNT, WILFRED H. (17, City Road)	Pte.	Devon, 1917, Pte. D.C.L.I. France, Belgium. Wounded, 1918.
BLUNDEN, CHARLES (57, Water Lane)	Rfn.	R.B., 1914, Rfn. France, Mesopotamia.
BLUNDEN, FRANK H. (43, Middle Brook Street)	Corpl.	K.R.R.C., Rfn. France.
BLUNDEN, JAMES W. (43, Middle Brook Street)	L.-Corpl.	Dorset, Aug. 14, 1914, Pte. France. Wounded once. Taken Prisoner by Germans, 1914.
BLYTH, HERBERT (32A, Water Lane)	Pte.	Hants, Oct. 1915, Pte. France, Belgium, Mesopotamia.
BLYTH, JACK (32A, Water Lane)	Pte.	R.B., Sept. 1916, Rfn. Lond. P.O. Rif., Hants. Home.
BLYTH, JAMES (32A, Water Lane)	Pte.	Wilts, Jan. 22, 1915, Pte. France, Belgium. Taken Prisoner by Germans, Apl. 10, 1918. M.M. 1917.
BLYTH, WILLIAM (32A, Water Lane)	Pte.	Hants, June 8, 1916, Pte. France, Belgium. Gassed once.
BOARD, REGINALD H. (51, Parchment Street)	Pte.	Hants Y., 1916, Tpr. Hants. France, Italy.

WINCHESTER WAR SERVICE REGISTER

BODGER, BERTIE W. (11, Owen's Road)	...	Staff-Sergt.	R.A.O.C., May 1916. France.
BOGHURST, WILLIAM E. (46, Colebrook Street)	...	2nd Lieut.	R.B., Aug. 1914, Rfn. Hants. France, Palestine. Wounded, Dec. 30, 1914.
✠ BOGIE, ANDREW W. (22, St. Paul's Hill)	...	C.Q.M.S.	Hants, 1914, Sergt. Mesopotamia. Despatches, M.S.M. Taken Prisoner by Turks at Kut. *Died, Sept. 22, 1916, Yarbaschi.*
BOLT, CHARLES A. (96, Brassey Road)	...	Pte.	R.A.S.C. (M.T.), Sept. 1914, Pte. M.G.C., M.A. France. Wounded, Aug. 1915. Croix de Guerre, 1918.
BOLT, HERBERT L. (96, Brassey Road)	...	Pte.	T.R., Dec. 1916, Pte. R.F.C. Russia.
BOND, ARTHUR (3, Gladstone Street)	...		R.G.A., June 1916. Lab. C. Home.
BOND, ARTHUR W. (61, Wharf Hill)	...	Pte.	Hants, Jan. 1915, Pte. France, Salonica.
BOND, HENRY V. (3, Gladstone Street)	...	Pte.	Hants, Sept. 1914, Pte. M.G.C., D.C.L.I. India, Palestine, Egypt.
BONE, ALFRED (Lower Chilcomb)	...	Sergt.	E. Surrey, Sept. 1914, Pte. E. Kent. France. Wounded, Oct. 11, 1915.
BONE, CHARLES E. (73, Colebrook Street)	...	Pte.	Hants, Sept. 1914, Pte. Devon. France.
BONE, FRANK (Nelsonvale, Highcliffe Park)	...	Spr.	R.E., Aug. 1914, Spr. Wounded once. Taken Prisoner by Germans.
BONE, HARRY G. (33, Bar End Road)	...	Pte.	Hants, Nov. 1915, Pte. Wilts. India, Palestine. Wounded, Sept. 19, 1918.
BONE, WILLIAM H. (73, Colebrook Street)	...	Rfn.	R.B., rejoined Aug. 1914. France. Gassed once.
BONIFACE, WALTER G. (2, Cossack Lane)	...		Devon, June 1916. Home.
BOORER, HARRY J. F. (16, King Alfred Terrace)	...		R.F.C., Jan. 1917. Home.
BOSANQUET, ARTHUR F. G. (10, St. Cross Road)	...	Lieut.	S.A. Rifles, Sept. 1914, S.M. Africa.
✠ BOSANQUET, EDWARD C. B. (10, St. Cross Road)	...	Capt.	S.A. Imp. Light Horse, Sept. 1914, Corpl. Home. *Drowned by enemy action, Sept. 12, 1918.*
BOSWORTH, ERNEST (32, Hyde Close)	...	Sergt.	Hants, 1887, Pte. Canadians. France. Gassed once.
BOSWORTH, FREDERICK (32, Hyde Close)	...	Corpl.-Major	D.L.I., Sept. 1914, Pte. R.H.G. France. Wounded once.
BOSWORTH, THOMAS P. (32, Hyde Close)	...	Corpl.	R.A.S.C. (M.T.), Nov. 1914, Pte. France.
✠ BOSWORTH, WILFRED J. (32, Hyde Close)	...	C.Q.M.S.	Hants, 1889, Pte. R. Innis. Fus. Aden. *Missing.*
BOUNDS, ARCHIBALD F. (25, Colebrook Street)	...		R.N.A.S., Jan. 13, 1918. R.A.F. Italy.

WINCHESTER WAR SERVICE REGISTER

BOUNDS, GEORGE F. (25, Colebrook Street)	Sergt.	Hants, Nov. 28, 1914, Pte. Attd. R.E. India, Persia, Mesopotamia.
BOURNE, GEORGE W. (23, Lower Brook Street)		Oxf. and Bucks L.I. R.A.S.C. Home.
BOUVERIE, C. W. PLEYDELL-		*See* PLEYDELL-BOUVERIE.
BOWMAN, SIDNEY C. (Colebrook Street)	C.Q.M.S.	Hants, 1907, Pte. France. Wounded, July 1, 1915. M.M.
BOWSHER, CHARLES J. (45, Kingsgate Road)	A.B.	R.N., Sept. 1915, Boy. North Sea; H.M.S. *Warspite*.
BOWSHER, EDWARD T. (45, Kingsgate Road)	Bdr.	R.H.A., Aug. 1915, Gun. R.G.A., Warwick. France, Italy.
BOWYER, HENRY (13, Ashley Terrace)	Corpl.	R.A.S.C., 1913, Dr. Dardanelles, Egypt, Salonica.
BOYES, A. E. (10, Brandon Terrace)	Pte.	Hants, 1914, Pte. Home.
BOYES, ARTHUR J. (10, Brandon Terrace)	A.B.	R.N., 1917, O.S. North Sea.
BOYES, ARTHUR J. P. (20, Middle Brook Street)	Pte.	Hants Y., Tpr. Hants. France, Italy. Wounded, June 30, 1918.
BOYES, EDWARD (59, Wales Street)	L.-Corpl.	Hants, Sept. 1914, Pte. India, Mesopotamia.
BOYES, JOSEPH W. (1, Domum Road)	L.-Corpl.	R.A.S.C., Dr. R.G.A. France, Belgium, Italy, Egypt. Gassed, Apl. 1915.
BOYES, SIDNEY F. (10, Brandon Terrace)	Stoker	R.N., 1914, Stoker. North Sea, Russia, Black Sea.
✠ BOYES, SYDNEY W. C. (20, Middle Brook Street)	L.-Corpl.	Hants, Aug. 1914, Pte. S.W.B. Mesopotamia, Salonica, France. *Killed in Action, Nov. 24, 1917*.
BOYLE, FRANCIS A. (7, Highland Terrace)	Dr.	R.A.S.C. (M.T.), June 1916, Dr. France.
BOYLE, FRANCIS R. (Fairfield, Clifton Road)	Major	R.M.L.I., 1890, 2nd Lieut. Mediterranean, Italy, West Indies.
BRACKNELL, SIDNEY W. (42D, Eastgate Street)	1st A.M.	R.N.A.S., Apl. 1917, 1st A.M. R.A.F. Home.
BRADBURY, HENRY (1, Tower Road)	L.-Corpl.	Worc., June 1916, Pte. Hants, Manch. France, Belgium.
BRADFORD, FRANK R. (7, Boundary Street)	Pte.	Hants, Dec. 1915, Pte. Oxf. and Bucks L.I. France.
✠ BRAITHWAITE, PHILIP P. (9, The Close)	Capt.	Cav. (Ind. Army), Dec. 1914, 2nd Lieut. Jacob's Horse. India, France, Palestine. Wounded, Sept. 12, 1917. Despatches. *Killed in Action, Sept. 23, 1918*.
BRAMBLE, HERBERT C. (37, Nuns Road)	Sergt.	R.G.A., 1904, Gun. R.F.A. France. Wounded, Dec. 18, 1917.
BRAMBLE, REYNOLD J. (37, Nuns Road)	Pte.	M.G.C., May 1916, Pte. Egypt.

WINCHESTER WAR SERVICE REGISTER

✠ BRAMBLE, WILFRED E. ... Pte. ... Hants, Dec. 1916, Pte. Mesopotamia. *Died*, 1919,
(37, Nuns Road) India.

BRAMBLEY, ARTHUR ... Pte. ... Hants, Oct. 1914, Pte. Lab. C. Home.
(6, Alresford Road)

BRAMLEY, A. W. JENNINGS *See* JENNINGS BRAMLEY.

BRAMLEY, CECIL ... Pte. ... Dorset, Feb. 1918, Pte. France.
(10, Colebrook Place)

BRAY, JOHN ... ... Gun. ... R.F.A., Oct. 1914, Gun. Home.
(26, Water Lane)

BRAY, THOMAS F. ... ... Pte. ... R.A.M.C. (Indian), Pte. Egypt, Palestine, Syria.
(43, Clifton Road)

BREADMORE, CHARLES W. ... Staff Major R.A.S.C., Nov. 1915, Lieut. France, Italy, Belgium.
(188, Stockbridge Road) Despatches 1916, 1918, 1919.

BREADMORE, CYRIL W. ... Capt. ... R.A.S.C. (M.T.), Oct. 1914, 2nd Lieut. France,
(188, Stockbridge Road) Belgium. Despatches 1915, 1919.

BREADMORE, DOUGLAS S. ... Sergt. ... A.I.F., Mch. 1916, Pte. France, Belgium. Wounded,
(188, Stockbridge Road) June 1917, May 1918, July 1918, Aug. 1918.

✠ BREADMORE, PERCY G. ... Pte. ... R. Berks, Nov. 1914, Pte. France. Wounded,
(188, Stockbridge Road) Aug. 1916. *Killed in Action, Apl. 28, 1917, Gouzeaucourt.*

BREADMORE, REGINALD G. ... Major ... R.A.S.C., Oct. 1914, 2nd Lieut. Egypt, Salonica.
(188, Stockbridge Road) Despatches 1917 and 1918, O.B.E. 1919.

BREALEY, ALBERT E. ... ... Lieut. ... R.B., May 1917, Rfn. R.F.C. France.
(1, Cheriton Road)

BREALEY, ARTHUR ... ... Corpl. ... R.B., Mch. 1914, Rfn. France. Wounded, June 21,
(1, Cheriton Road) 1915.

BREALEY, THOMAS ... ... R.S.M. ... R.B., rejoined Sept. 1914, C.-Sergt. Home.
(1, Cheriton Road)

BREALEY, THOMAS E. ... ... L.-Sergt. Devon, Oct. 1916, Pte. A.P.C. Home.
(36, Egbert Road)

BREALEY, WILLIAM H. ... Sergt. ... R.B., 1909, Rfn. France. Wounded, Nov. 27,
(1, Cheriton Road) 1914, and Oct. 1, 1915.

✠ BREWER, CHARLES W. ... Rfn. ... K.R.R.C., rejoined Aug. 1914, Rfn. France. *Killed*
(4, Cross Street) *in Action, Sept. 14, 1914, Aisne.*

BREWER, EDWIN ... ... A.B. ... R.N., 1913, A.B. Dardanelles, Grand Fleet; H.M.S.
(24, Hyde Abbey Road) *Queen Elizabeth.*

BREWER, GEORGE ... ... Sergt. ... Hants, Aug. 1914, Pte. M.G.C. France, Egypt.
(71, Greenhill Road) Wounded, July 1, 1916, and May 1, 1918.

✠ BREWER, HARRY J. S. ... Gun. ... R.G.A., Oct. 1915, Gun. France, Belgium. *Killed*
(24, Hyde Abbey Road) *in Action, July 15, 1917, Nieuport.*

BRICKELL, ALBERT F. ... ... Pte. ... Devon, Dec. 1916, Pte. Home.
(28, Egbert Road)

BRICKNELL, ALFRED J. ... Pte. ... R.F.A., Oct. 1916, Gun. York and Lancs., R.A.F.
(5, Gladstone Street) France. Wounded, Apl. 9, 1917.

BRICKWOOD, ALBERT E. ... L.-Corpl. R.A.S.C., Pte. W. Yorks. France. Wounded,
(61, Upper Brook Street) Sept. 1918.

WINCHESTER WAR SERVICE REGISTER

BRICKWOOD, EDWARD W. (61, Upper Brook Street)	Gun.	R.G.A., July 5, 1916. France, Malta.
BRIGDEN, WILLIAM E. (8, Thurloe Place)	Sergt.	Kent Cyc., 1915, Pte. R.A.S.C., R.E. Home.
✠ BRIGGS, GEORGE L. C. (Qu'Appelle, Sleeper's Hill)	Sub-Lieut.	R.N., Sept. 1913, Mid. H.M.S. *Princess Royal* and *Genista. Killed in Action, Oct.* 23, 1916.
BRIGHT, ALBERT (18, Upper Brook Street)	P.O. (1st Class)	R.N. North Sea. Wounded, June 1, 1916. D.S.M., Croix de Guerre.
BRIGHT, ALFRED A. (4, Percy Terrace)	Corpl.	R.A.S.C., Aug. 1915, Pte. E. Lancs. France.
BRIGHT, ARTHUR R. (2, Southgate Street)		R.F.C., Jan. 1918. R.A.F. Home.
✠ BRIGHT, ERNEST (15, Canon Street)	Corpl.	Dorset, Pte. France. *Killed in Action,* 1915, *Hill* 60.
✠ BRIGHT, ERNEST G. (2, Southgate Street)	Pte.	R.M.L.I., Sept. 1914, Pte. Hants. Belgium, Egypt, Dardanelles, North Sea, France. Wounded, June 23, 1915. *Killed in Action, Apl.* 11, 1917, *Arras.* 25944 1ST BN
BRIGHT, GEORGE (20, Upper Brook Street)	Pte.	Hants, Aug. 11, 1914, Pte. N. Fus. Home.
BRIGHT, HAROLD (18, Upper Brook Street)	L.-Corpl.	Hants, 1914, Pte. France.
✠ BRIGHT, HARRY C. (2, Southgate Street)	L.-Corpl.	Hants, June 1914, Pte. Devon. Dardanelles, France. *Killed in Action, Sept.* 4, 1916, *Somme.*
BRIGHT, JAMES H. (16, Andover Road)	Pte.	R.F.A., Oct. 16, 1916, Gun. D.L.I. France. Wounded, Sept. 4, 1917.
BRIGHT, LEONARD (St. Donald's, Highcliffe Park)	A.B.	R.N., 1904, O.S. Mediterranean.
BRIGHT, PERCY (18, Upper Brook Street)		R.N., 1911. North Sea.
BRIGHT, THOMAS P. (1, Middle Road)	Stoker	R.N., 1913, Stoker. North Sea; H.M.S. *Iron Duke.*
BRIGHT, WALTER (18, Upper Brook Street)	P.O. (Class I)	R.N. North Sea. D.S.M.
✠ BRIGHT, WILLIAM A. (15, Colson Road)	A.-Sergt.	R.G.A. (T.F.), 1912, Gun. France. *Killed in Action, July* 20, 1917, *Dickebusch.*
BRIMFIELD, HENRY (55, Lower Brook Street)	Chief Stoker	R.N., 1898, Stoker. North Sea.
BRIND, HAROLD J. (56, Greenhill Road)	Pte.	Glos., Mch. 1916. France, Belgium, Italy, Austria, Albania, Egypt.
BRINDLE, WILLIAM J. (42, Water Lane)		R.F.A. France. Wounded, Aug. 1916.
BRINE, FRANK H. (26, St. Thomas Street)	C.S.M.	Middlesex, Apl. 1916, Pte. R.A.O.C. France.
✠ BROAD, CHARLES G. (12, Back Street, St. Cross)	Pte.	R. Warwick, Sept. 1918, Pte. Home. *Died, Oct.* 14, 1918.

WINCHESTER WAR SERVICE REGISTER

BROAD, WILLIAM G. (29, Bar End)	Pte.	Hants, Dec. 1914, Pte. India, Mesopotamia.
BROADFIELD, ALBERT (46, Colebrook Street)	Pte.	Devon, Nov. 10, 1915, Pte. Wilts. France.
BROADWAY, CHARLES	Corpl.	R.F.C., Feb. 1916, 2nd A.M. Italy.
BROADWAY, TOM (27, Nuns Road)	Pte.	Hants, Mch. 1916, Pte. Worc. Home.
BROCK, HERBERT T. (164, High Street)	Pte.	Hants Y., June 1915, Tpr. Hants. France, Italy.
BROCK, PERCIVAL (164, High Street)	Corpl.	Lancers, Sept. 1914, Tpr. Dragoon G. France.
BROCK, WILLIAM (164, High Street)	S.M.	R.A.S.C., Aug. 1914, Dr. France.
BROCKHURST, EDWARD (16, Little Minster Street)	Gun.	R.G.A., 1914, Gun. France. Wounded, Mch. 1916.
BROOKER, JOHN (11, Hyde Street)	Pte.	Worc., Aug. 1916, Pte. Lab. C., K.R.R.C. France.
BROOKER, WILLIAM (4, Foundry Lane)	Pte.	Somerset L.I., Mch. 1915, Pte. Wilts. France. Wounded, Sept. 25, 1917.
✠ BROOKS, ALBERT E. (27, Trinity Terrace)	Pte.	Hants Cyc., Oct. 1915, Pte. Hants. France. Killed in Action, Sept. 3, 1916, Somme.
BROOKS, HAROLD H. (27, Trinity Terrace)		R.A.S.C. (M.T.), May 1917, Pte. Mesopotamia.
BROOKS, HENRY (50, Nuns Road)	Corpl.	R.A.F. Home.
BROOKS, ROBERT V. (10, St. John's Road)	Rfn.	Lond., Jan. 1916, Rfn. France, Belgium.
BROOMFIELD, JAMES (40, Brassey Road)	Sergt.	R.E., May 1916, Spr. Home.
BROWN, ALFRED H. (6, Castle Terrace)	Dr.	R.A.S.C., 1914, Dr. Salonica.
BROWN, ARTHUR G. (27, Clausentum Road)	Sig.	R.G.A., June 1916, Sig. France, Italy.
BROWN, BENJAMIN C. (48, Greenhill Road)	Corpl.	Hants, Apl. 1916, Pte. R.A.S.C. Flanders, Germany.
BROWN, CHARLES (61, Water Lane)	Corpl.	Hants, Sept. 1914, Pte. R. Berks, N. Fus., R.A.F. France. Wounded Nov. 15, 1915, and May 8, 1916.
BROWN, DONALD M. (102, High Street)	Pte.	Artists' Rif., 1916, Pte. France.
BROWN, EDWIN C. (50, Chesil Street)	Tpr.	Lancers, 1910, Tpr. Res. Cav. France. Wounded, Jan. 11, 1916.
BROWN, ERNEST E. (9, Hyde Abbey Road)	Corpl.	R.A.S.C. (M.T.), Oct. 1916, Pte. France.
BROWN, ERNEST E. (23, Wales Street)	A.M.	Hants, June 1916, Pte. R.A.F. Home.

WINCHESTER WAR SERVICE REGISTER

Brown, Ezra (11, City Road)	Lieut.	Hants, Mch. 1915, 2nd Lieut. T.M.B. France. Wounded, 1917. M.C. 1917.
Brown, George R. (102, High Street)	Lieut.	R.E., Oct. 1914, Spr. R.G.A. France.
Brown, Henry J. (57, St. Catherine's Road)	Sergt.	Hants, Apl. 1916, Pte. France.
Brown, Hugh A. (Becton Lodge, Berewecke Road)	A.-Major	R.F.A., Aug. 1914, Cadet. India, France.
Brown, James S. (18, Granville Place)	Pte.	Hants, Pte. France, Belgium, Germany. Belgian Croix de Guerre.
✠ Brown, John (5, Freelands Buildings)	C.S.M.	K.R.R.C., Sept. 1914, Sergt. Yorks. France. Wounded, May 24, 1916. *Killed in Action, Oct. 6, 1916.*
Brown, John T. (Pond Cottage, Weeke)	Pte.	Hants, Sept. 2, 1914, Pte. Warwick, Somerset L.I., Devon. France.
Brown, Leonard (6, Middle Brook Street)	Pte.	Middlesex, May 1915, Pte. France. Wounded, Sept. 27, 1915, and in 1916.
✠ Brown, Osbert H. (102, High Street)	Major	R.B., Sept. 1914, Rfn. France. Wounded, July 1916. D.S.O. 1916, M.C. 1916, Despatches 1917. *Killed in Action, Nov. 1, 1916, Armentières.*
Brown, Percy H. (19, Andover Road)	Pte.	Hants, July 20, 1917, Pte. D.C.L.I. France.
Brown, Robert N. (168, High Street)	Pte.	Hants, June 1916, Pte. Mesopotamia.
Brown, William (5, Freelands Buildings)	Sergt.	Hants, Sept. 1914, Pte. France.
Brown, William A. (57, St. Catherine's Road)	Bdr.	R.F.A., 1911, Gun. R.G.A. France. Wounded, Aug. 15, 1918.
Brown, William A. J. (73, Upper Brook Street)	Corpl.	Hants, Sept. 1914, Pte. Mesopotamia.
Brown, William V. (34, Fairfield Road)	Staff-Sergt.	Hants, Oct. 1914, Pte. India, Persia.
Browne, Meyrick G. (Rockingham, Andover Road)	Capt.	E. Lancs., Sept. 1914, 2nd Lieut. France. Wounded, May 1915, June 1915, July 1, 1916. Taken Prisoner by Germans, July 1, 1916.
Browning, Edward C. (42, North Walls)	L.-Corpl.	Hants Y., Nov. 1914, Tpr. Hants. France, Italy.
Browning, Walter F. (42, North Walls)	Tpr.	Hants Y., Oct. 1914, Tpr. Berks Y. France, Egypt.
✠ Browning, William J. (42, North Walls)	Sergt.	Warwick, June 1915, Pte. France. *Killed in Action, Dec. 5, 1917, Cambrai.*
Brunning, Frederick (29, Eastgate Street)	Pte.	A.V.C., Apl. 17, 1917, Pte. France, Belgium, Germany.
Bryant, Henry W. (47, Nuns Road)	R.S.M.	R.B., rejoined Apl. 1915, R.S.M. Home.

WINCHESTER WAR SERVICE REGISTER

BRYANT, JOHN (33, Colson Road)	...	Pte.	R.A.S.C. (M.T.), July 1916, Pte. Mesopotamia, India.
BRYANT, PERCY W. (12, North Walls)	...	Pte.	R. Berks, Oct. 1916, Pte. Tank C., R.A.F. France. Wounded, Oct. 1917.
✠ BRYANT, RICHARD G. (12, North Walls)	...	Pte.	Hants, Jan. 1916, Pte. France. *Killed in Action. Oct. 1, 1917, Ypres.*
✠ BRYON, G. H. (43, Parchment Street)	...	Pte.	D.L.I., 1916, Pte. France, Belgium. *Killed in Action, Sept. 21, 1917.*
✠ BUCK, JAMES H. (17, Andover Road)	...	Pte.	Hants, 1915, Pte. India. *Died of Enteric, 1916, Quetta.*
BUCKLAND, ARTHUR E. (23, St. Swithun Street)	...	Bdr.	R.G.A. (T.F.), Feb. 1914, Gun. Anti-Aircraft. France.
✠ BUCKLAND, CHARLES H. (23, St. Swithun Street)	...	Pte.	Glos., May 1916, Pte. M.G.C. France. Wounded once. *Killed in Action, Aug. 27, 1917.*
BUCKLAND, SIDNEY G. (15, Canute Road)	...	Pte.	Hants, Dec. 1915, Pte. Home.
BUCKLE, WILLIAM D. (58, Greenhill Road)	...		Herts, Oct. 1916, Pte. Home.
BUDD, ALAN G. (1, Cross Street)	...	Pte.	Hants, 1907, Pte. France. Wounded, Sept. 15, 1914.
BUDD, GEORGE J. (9, Greenhill Road)	...		R.N.V.R., Mch. 1917. North Sea, Baltic.
BUDGEN, EDWARD T. (28, Colson Road)	...	Sergt.	Hants, rejoined Aug. 1914, Pte. Home.
BUGG, ERNEST A. (7, Chesil Terrace)	...	Corpl.	R.F.C., June 1917. R.A.F. Home.
✠ BUGG, NOBLE G. (7, Chesil Terrace)	...	Gun.	R.G.A., July 1915, Gun. France. *Died of Pneumonia, Feb. 4, 1919.*
BULL, CHARLES (75, Lower Brook Street)	...	L.-Corpl.	Hants, 1893, Pte. France.
✠ BULL, JOHN (54, Canon Street)	...	Pte.	Hants Y., June 1916, Tpr. Hants. France. *Killed in Action, Feb. 15, 1917*
BULPETT, JAMES H. (2, Upper Brook Street)	...	Spr.	R.E., 1916, Spr. France.
BULPETT, WILLIAM (1, Greyfriars Terrace)	...	A.B.	R.N., Dec. 1916, A.B. North Sea.
BULPITT, WILLIAM (13, Wharf Hill)	...	Pte.	Hants, June 1916, Pte. Home.
BUMSTEAD, HENRY C. (21, Wales Street)	...	Pte.	Nat. Res., Sept. 1914, Pte. R.D.C. Home.
BUNBURY, BERTRAM J.	...	Lieut.	R.B., Aug. 1914, 2nd Lieut. France.
BUNBURY, CHARLES H. ST. P.		Lieut.-Col.	Yorks, Apl. 1898. Bedford, Lancs. Fus. France.
BUNBURY, EVELYN J.	...	2nd Lieut.	Bombay Vol. Rif., Aug. 1914, Rfn. Gren. Gds. France.
✠ BUNBURY, WILFRED J.	...	Capt.	N. Fus., Aug. 1914, 2nd Lieut. France. Wounded, May 1915. *Killed in Action, April 15, 1917, Arras.*

WINCHESTER WAR SERVICE REGISTER

BUNCE, ALBERT E. (Deacon Hill, Chilcomb)	...	Pte.	Hants, Sept. 1915, Pte. France. Wounded, Mch. 1916.
BUNCE, ALFRED J. (Deacon Hill, Chilcomb)	...	Pte.	Hants, May 1915, Pte. France. Wounded, Mch. 1916.
BUNCH, HORACE W. (Auburndale, Stockbridge Road)	...	Capt.	Hants (T.F.), 1904, Pte. Essex. Gallipoli. Wounded, Aug. 13, 1915.
BUNKER, CHARLES B. (8, City Road)	...	Lieut.	Hants (T.F.), 1914. R.A.S.C. Home.
BUNKER, SPENCER G. (8, City Road)	...	Corpl.	Hants Y., Oct. 1914, Tpr. Hants. France, Italy. M.M. 1918.
BURBAGE, EDWARD (30, Upper Brook Street)	...	Pte.	R. Berks., June 20, 1916, Pte. Lab. C. France.
BURCHETT, CHARLES A. (19, St. John's South)	...	L.-Corpl.	Hants Y., Nov. 1914. R.W.S., Hants. France.
BURFITT, GEORGE (34, Hyde Street)	...	Corpl.	Gren. Gds., Jan. 1917, Tpr. Home.
BURFITT, JAMES H. (1, St. Swithun's Villas)	...	L.-Corpl.	R.E. Sigs. Mesopotamia.
BURFITT, STANLEY G. (34, Hyde Street)	...	Tpr.	R.H.G., Jan. 1918, Tpr. Home.
BURGENS, ARTHUR S. (49, Egbert Road)	...	C.S.M.	K.R.R.C., 1899, Rfn. France.
✠ BURGESS, FRANK (10, Ashley Terrace)	...	Sergt.	K.R.R.C., Sept. 1914, Rfn. France. *Believed Killed in Action, Mons.*
BURGESS, FREDERICK J. (77, Colebrook Street)	...	Gun.	R.M.A., Jan. 1916, Gun. Home.
BURGESS, FREDERICK L. (107, Colebrook Street)	...	Corpl.	K.R.R.C., Aug. 1915, Band Boy. Home.
BURGESS, JAMES W. (107, Colebrook Street)	...	Spr.	Hants, Sept. 1914, Pte. R.E. India, Egypt.
BURGESS, REGINALD (54, Sussex Street)	...	L.-Corpl.	K.R.R.C., 1910, Rfn. France.
BURGESS, RICHARD G. (7, Hillside Terrace)	...	Pte.	R.A.S.C. (M.T.), Mch. 1915. France, Italy.
BURGESS, WALTER E. (75, Middle Brook Street)	...	Pte.	Devon, Aug. 25, 1916. Home.
BURGESS, WILLIAM J. (77, Colebrook Street)	...	Dr.	R.F.A., Aug. 1914, Dr. France. Gassed, Jan. 1917.
BURKE, EDMUND F. C. (26, St. Thomas Street)	...	Corpl.	Hants Y., Nov. 1914, Tpr. Hants. Mesopotamia.
BURKE, FRANCIS (62, Colebrook Street)	...	Band Boy	Hants, Apl. 1915, Band Boy. Home.
BURKE, JAMES (62, Colebrook Street)	...	Pte.	Hants, Mch. 1915, Pte. Oxf. and Bucks L.I., Hants. France, Russia. Gassed, 1918.
BURKE, JOHN H. (62, Colebrook Street)	...	Drummer	Hants, June 1916, Pte. Dorset. France.

WINCHESTER WAR SERVICE REGISTER

BURKE, REGINALD (62, Colebrook Street)	...	Pte.	Hants, 1903, Band Boy. France, Dardanelles. Wounded, 1918. Gassed, 1916 and 1918.
BURKE, THOMAS (62, Colebrook Street)	...	Corpl.	Hants, 1898, Band Boy. Worc. France.
BURNER, DAVID W. (11, Romsey Road)	...	Pte.	Works Bn., Mch. 1917, Pte. Home.
BURNETT, CHARLES B. (4, Ashley Terrace)	...	Sergt.	Hants (T.F.), 1903, Pte. Hants. India, Mesopotamia. Wounded, Jan. 7, 1916.
BURNETT, CHARLES H. (4, Highland Terrace)	...	Pte.	R.A.S.C. (M.T.), Feb. 1916, Pte. France.
✠ BURNETT, HENRY (13, Boundary Street)	...	Pte.	Hants, Sept. 1914, Pte. Persian Gulf. *Killed in Action, July 5, 1915.*
BURNETT, JOHN (13, Boundary Street)	...	Pte.	Hants, Aug. 1914, Pte. Dardanelles. Wounded, Aug. 12, 1915.
BURNISTON, CHARLES E. (34, Hatherley Road)	...	R.Q.M.S.	Hants, rejoined Aug. 1914, R.Q.M.S. Home.
BURROWS, BENTLEY (31, Water Lane)	...	Gun.	R. G. A. (Anti-Aircraft), Sept. 1915, Gun. Mesopotamia.
✠ BURROWS, JOHN J. (19, Colebrook Street)	...	Gun.	R.G.A., Nov. 1915, Gun. France. Wounded, Dec. 19, 1917. *Died of Wounds, Dec. 21, 1917, Rouen.*
BURROWS, WILLIAM (31, Water Lane)	...	Corpl.	Life Gds., 1910, Tpr. France.
BURT, LEONARD (117, Upper Brook Street)	...	Pte.	Devon, Pte. Home.
BURT, WALTER (117, Upper Brook Street)	...	Corpl.	R.G.A., Dec. 1914, Gun. France, Italy. Wounded twice.
✠ BURTON, ALBERT T. (4, Westgate Lane)	...	Stoker	R.N., Nov. 1910, Stoker. North Sea; H.M.S. Queen Mary. *Killed in Action, May 31, 1916, Jutland.*
BURTON, ARTHUR G. (50, Canon Street)	...	Pte.	Hants, Sept. 1914, Pte. India, Mesopotamia. Wounded, Jan. 25, 1917.
BURTON, EDWARD J. (4, Westgate Lane)	...	L.-Corpl.	R.F.A., 1910, Gun. D.C.L.I. France.
BURTON, ERNEST (4, Westgate Lane)	...	Stoker	R.N., Oct. 1917, Stoker. North Sea.
BURTON, ERNEST J. (8, Greenhill Avenue)	...	2nd Lieut.	R.F.C., Sept. 1917, Cadet. Home.
BURTON, FRANK J. (19, Middle Brook Street)	...	Pte.	Devon, Oct. 1916, Pte. A.V.C. Home.
BURTON, GEORGE (8, Greenhill Avenue)	...	Spr.	R.E., rejoined Oct. 1914, Spr. France. Wounded, Oct. 1916.
BURTON, HENRY (4, Westgate Lane)	...	L.-Corpl.	Hants Y., 1914, Tpr. Hants. Mesopotamia, India.
BURTON, HENRY W. (8, Greenhill Avenue)	...	Pte.	Hants, Nov. 1915, Pte. India, Egypt, France. Wounded, Nov. 4, 1918.

WINCHESTER WAR SERVICE REGISTER

BURTON, WALTER J. (9, Queen's Road)	...	Sea Scoutmaster	Coastguard Service, Jan. 1, 1916, Sea Scoutmaster. Home.
BURTON, WILLIAM C. (4, Westgate Lane)	...	Stoker	R.N., 1913, Stoker. North Sea, Baltic, Falkland Islands; H.M.S. *Princess Royal*, *Royalist*, and *Cordelia*.
✠ BURTON, WILLIAM F. (22, Colebrook Street)	...	Rfn.	R.B., Mch. 1915, Rfn. France, Belgium. Wounded, Aug. 8, 1917. Gassed, 1918. *Killed in Action, Oct. 2, 1918, Ypres*.
BUTCHER, ARTHUR (6, Percy Terrace)	...	Rfn.	R.B., Sept. 4, 1914, Rfn. Belgium, France. Wounded twice. Gassed three times.
BUTCHER, HERBERT T. (3, Crowder Terrace)	...	Spr.	R.E., Dec. 28, 1914, Spr. Dardanelles, Salonica, Palestine.
BUTCHER, WALTER Z. (143, High Street)	...	Corpl.	Hants Y., May 1915, Tpr. Dragoon Gds., Northants Y., M.M.P. France, Italy.
BUTCHER, WILLIAM (2, St. Swithun's Villas)	...	Pte.	R.A.S.C. (M.T.), Feb. 1917, Pte. Home.
BUTCHER, ZEBEDEE Z. (143, High Street)	...		R.A.S.C., Oct. 1917. France.
BUTLER, CYRIL A. G. (8, St. Thomas Street)	...	Steward	R.N., Mch. 1917. North Sea, Baltic; H.M.S. *Royalist*.
BUTLER, EDGAR O. (8, St. Thomas Street)	...	Pte.	R.A.S.C., Oct. 1915, Pte. France.
BUTLER, FRANCIS H. C. (South End, St. Cross Road)	...	Capt.	Hants, Oct. 1914, 2nd Lieut. India, Mesopotamia, Egypt, Palestine. Despatches, 1917.
BUTT, ARTHUR H. (Maybury, Stockbridge Road)	...	Sergt.	Hants, Sept. 1914, Pte. India.
BUTT, GEORGE F. (Redbourne, East Hill)	...	Lieut.	Hants, Dec. 1914, 2nd Lieut. France. Wounded, Jan. 1915.
BUTT, GEORGE F. (25, Egbert Road)	...	1st A.M.	R.N.A.S., Aug. 1916, 1st A.M. R.A.F. Home.
BUTT, STANLEY G. (Maybury, Stockbridge Road)	...	L.-Corpl.	K.R.R.C., July 1916, Rfn. France. Taken Prisoner by Germans, Nov. 30, 1917.
BYE, FRANK R. W. (4, Morn Hill)	...	Corpl.	R.A.S.C. (M.T.), Sept. 1916, Pte. Home.
BYRNE, ARTHUR H. (2, Ivy Terrace, Bar End)	...	Dr.	R.F.A., rejoined Nov. 1915, Dr. R.G.A. France.
CABLE, EDGAR (19, Queen's Road)	...	Sig.	R.N., 1911, Boy. North Sea; H.M.S. *Iron Duke*.
CABLE, GEORGE (10, Queen's Road)	...	1st A.M.	R.F.C., Feb. 1917, 2nd A.M. France.
CABLE, VICTOR J. (19, Queen's Road)	...	Corpl.	R.F.A., 1913, Gun. France. Gassed, Nov. 3, 1917. M.M., 1916.
CABLE, WILLIAM H. (19, Queen's Road)	...	Pte.	Devon, May 1916, Pte. Lab. C. Home.

WINCHESTER WAR SERVICE REGISTER

CAINEY, ARTHUR C. S. ... Sergt. ... A.G.S., Sergt.-Instr. Home.
(14, Brassey Road)

✠ CALLEN, SIDNEY J. ... Pte. ... Hants, Sept. 1914, Pte. Egypt, Palestine. *Killed in Action, Nov. 22, 1917.*
(13, Egbert Road)

CAMM, CUTHBERT B. ... Staff Capt. Hants, Dec. 12, 1914, Lieut. W.O. Staff. India, Egypt.
(The Hermitage, Weeke)

CAMP, ARTHUR ... Pte. ... R.A.M.C., Sept. 1914, Pte. France.
(12, High Street)

CAMPBELL, JOSEPH L. ... Sergt. ... Hants, May 1, 1915, Pte. R.A.S.C. France.
(6, Southgate Street)

✠ CANCELLOR, DESMOND B. ... Lieut. ... Hants, Apl. 1917, 2nd Lieut. France. Wounded, July 23 and Aug. 22, 1917. M.C. 1918. *Killed in Action, Nov. 1918, near Préseau.*
(23, Edgar Road)

CANNINGS, ARTHUR G. ... Pte. ... R.A.S.C. (M.T.), Oct. 1915, Pte. France.
(20, Queen's Road)

CAPES, GARETH W. ... Capt. ... Hants, Sept. 1914, 2nd Lieut. India, Mesopotamia, Palestine, France.
(13, St. Cross Road)

CAPLIN, THOMAS P. ... Pte. ... Hants, Aug. 1914, Pte. France.
(84, Wales Street)

CARDY, WILLIAM J. ... Sergt. ... Hants, Sept. 1914, Pte. R.A.S.C. Persian Gulf, India.
(Wolvesey Palace)

CARPENTER, CHARLES W. ... L.-Corpl. Dorset, 1907, Pte. India, Persian Gulf, France. Wounded, Nov. 10, 1914, Jan. 30, 1915, Sept. 16, 1917.
(16, The Weirs)

CARPENTER, GEORGE W. ... Pte. ... R.M.L.I., Apl. 1917. Grand Fleet.
(2, Greenhill Terrace)

CARPENTER, JOHN T. ... Pte. ... R.W.S., Feb. 1915, Pte. France. Wounded, Sept. 27, 1915, July 1, 1916.
(16, The Weirs)

CARPENTER, WILLIAM H. ... Pte. ... Hants, Oct. 1916, Pte. Egypt. Wounded, Apl. 19, 1917.
(45, St. John's Street)

CARPENTER, WILLIAM J. E. ... Spr. ... R.E., Aug. 1914, Spr. Gallipoli, Mesopotamia.
(11, Upper Wolvesey Terrace)

CARSE, ADAM ... L.-Corpl. Wilts, Aug. 1916, Pte. France.
(The Hawthorns, Kingsgate St.)

CARTER, ALBERT ... Pte. ... R.A.F., May 1918, Pte. Home.
(2, Tangier Terrace)

CARTER, ALFRED B. ... Pte. ... Hants, July 1916. India, Egypt.
(48, Eastgate Street)

CARTER, ALFRED J. ... Gun. ... R.N., 1902, Boy. North Sea.
(20, Parchment Street)

CARTER, ALFRED R. ... A.B. ... R.N., 1913, O.S. H.M.S. *Cochrane.*
(25, Water Lane)

✠ CARTER, ARTHUR F. ... L.-Corpl. Hants (T.F.), 1894, Pte. Hants. India. *Died, Feb. 15, 1916.*
(4, Penarth Place)

CARTER, BERTRAM I. ... Lieut. ... R.N., 1910, P.O. (2nd Class). R.N.A.S., R.A.F. North Sea.
(20, Parchment Street)

WINCHESTER WAR SERVICE REGISTER

CARTER, CHARLES H. (6, Parchment Street)	Pte.	Hants, Pte. France.	
CARTER, CHARLES M. (75, Hyde Street)	Pte.	Worc., 1918, Pte. Home.	
CARTER, EDWARD W. (69, Water Lane)	Gun.	R.G.A., rejoined Aug. 1914, Gun. France.	
CARTER, FREDERICK S. (8, Culverwell Gardens)	Sergt.	Hants Cyc., 1912, Pte. France.	
✠ CARTER, GEORGE (46, North Walls)	Pte.	Hants, June 1916, Pte. France. Wounded, July 31, 1917. *Killed in Action, July 31, 1917, St. Julien.*	
CARTER, JOHN (57, Middle Brook Street)	Rfn.	Suffolk, Oct. 1915, Pte. K.R.R.C. France.	
✠ CARTER, JOHN (1, Queensland Terrace)	Sig.	R.E., Sept. 1917, Sig. France. *Killed.*	
CARTER, JOSEPH (19, St. Clement's Street)	Corpl.	Wilts, May 1915, Pte. M.G.C. France. Wounded, Mch. 11, 1916, Aug. 12, 1917.	
CARTER, LEWIS M. (108, Colebrook Street)	Lieut.	Hants, Sept. 1914, L.-Corpl. R.G.A. Singapore.	
CARTER, STANLEY T. (108, Colebrook Street)	Major	R.G.A., 1908, Lieut. Aden, India.	
CARTER, THOMAS (19, St. Clement Street)	Pte.	R.A.S.C. (M.T.), May 1915, Pte. Salonica.	
CARTER, WILFRED J. (79, Middle Brook Street)	Dr.	R.A.S.C., Dr. France, Salonica.	
CARTER, WILLIAM (27, Canon Street)	Pte.	Welsh, Pte. Dardanelles, Salonica. Wounded, Aug. 8, 1915.	
CARTER, WILLIAM C. (9, Cheriton Road)	Corpl.	R.A.M.C., Sept. 1914, Pte. France.	
CARTER, WILLIAM D. (24, Wales Street)	Gun.	R.M.A., May 1916, Gun. Mudros, Salonica, Mesopotamia.	
CARTER, WILLIAM R. (75, Hyde Street)	Bdr.	R.G.A., 1915, Gun. Egypt, Palestine.	
CARTER, WILLIAM S. (5, St. John's Road)	Bandsman	Hants, Nov. 1910, Bandsman. Mesopotamia, Persia.	
CASE, REGINALD F. (15, St. Clement Street)	Cook	R.N., Sept. 1916, O.S. Gibraltar.	
CASE, WALTER C. (15, St. Clement Street)	Pte.	R.F., Jan. 1916, Pte. R.W.F. Mesopotamia.	
✠ CASSIDY, GERALD (13, Eastgate Street)	Boy	R.N., 1913, Boy. H.M.S. *Powerful* and *Crescent.* Died, Mch. 1919.	
CASSIDY, JOHN A. (13, Eastgate Street)	Cadet	R.I.R., July 1917, Cadet. France.	
CASTLE, ARCHIBALD C. (37, Brassey Road)	C.Q.M.S.	Hants (T.F.), 1907, Pte. Hants. India, Mesopotamia.	
CASTLE, FREDERICK L. (10, Hatherley Road)	2nd Lieut.	Inns of Court O.T.C., Pte. O.C.B. France, Germany. Wounded, Sept. 1918.	

WINCHESTER WAR SERVICE REGISTER

✠ CAUSTON, JERVOISE P. (Master's Lodge, St. Cross)	Capt.	...	Hants, 1914, 2nd Lieut. India, France. *Killed in Action, Apl. 22, 1918, near Bethune.*
CAVE, ARTHUR S.	Major	...	R.T.O., Aug. 5, 1914, Major. Home.
CAVE, PERCY R. (20, Nuns Road)	Pte.	...	Devon, Apl. 1916, Pte. Home.
CAWDREY, CHARLES W. (31, Sussex Street)	Rfn.	...	R.B., July 1916, Rfn. Home.
CAWTE, EDWARD V. (31, Wales Street)	2nd Lieut.	...	Artists' Rif., Jan. 1918, Pte. O.C.B. Home.
✠ CHALK, ARCHIBALD (4, St. Clement Street)	Rfn.	...	R.B., Aug. 4, 1914, Rfn. France. *Killed in Action, Aug. 26, 1914.*
✠ CHALK, ARTHUR (75, Chesil Street)	Pte.	...	R.M.L.I., Dec. 1916, Pte. France. *Killed in Action, Oct. 1917, Passchendaele.*
CHALK, EDWIN (4, St. Clement Street)	R.S.M.	...	R.B., Rfn. M.P., R.A.F. Home. Despatches.
CHALK, FRANK A. (4, St. Clement Street)	Corpl.	...	R.F.C., July 1915, 3rd A.M. Home.
CHALK, WALTER J. (4, St. Clement Street)	Corpl.	...	H.A.C., Aug. 1914, Gun. Palestine.
CHALK, WILLIE A. (4, St. Clement Street)	1st A.M.	...	R.A.F., Feb. 1916, 3rd A.M. Home.
CHALKE, HORACE R. (1, Step Terrace)	Lieut.	...	R.F., Nov. 1915, Pte. R. Berks. France.
CHALKLEY, EDWARD (78, Hatherley Road)	C.Q.M.S.	...	Hants, Aug. 4, 1914, Bandsman. Home.
CHALLEN, WALTER (22, Brassey Road)	C.Q.M.S.	...	K.R.R.C., 1900, Rfn. Lab. C. Home.
CHANDLER, ALBERT (4, Magdalen Hill)	Pte.	...	Hants, Aug. 1916, Pte. Lab. C., R.D.C. France.
CHANDLER, ALEXANDER G. (3, South View)	Pte.	...	Hants, Pte. Germany.
✠ CHANDLER, ERNEST (7, Maidstone Terrace)	Rfn.	...	R.B., 1888, Rfn. France. *Killed in Action, Mch. 11, 1915, Neuve Chapelle.*
✠ CHANDLER, FRANK (7, Maidstone Terrace)	Rfn.	...	Hants, 1902, Pte. R.B. France. *Killed in Action, Dec. 19, 1914, Armentières.*
CHANDLER, GEORGE (15, Owen's Road)	Spr.	...	R.E., Oct. 1915, Spr. Russia.
CHANDLER, HENRY T. (3, South View)	Pte.	...	Essex, Pte. Palestine, Egypt.
CHANDLER, HERBERT (7, Maidstone Terrace)	Pte.	...	R.A.S.C. (M.T.), Oct. 1916, Pte. France.
CHANT, FREDERICK C. (76, Sussex Street)	Pte.	...	Hants, Apl. 1915, Pte. France, Salonica.
CHANT, FREDERICK G. (76, Sussex Street)	Pte.	...	Hants Y., May 1915, Tpr. Hants. France.
CHAPMAN, FRANCIS C. (3, Romsey Road)	Rfn.	...	K.R.R.C., Sept. 25, 1905, Band Boy. France. Wounded, Nov. 10, 1914.

WINCHESTER WAR SERVICE REGISTER

✠ Chapman, Frank J. (4, Andover Road)	...	Pte.	Hants, Sept. 1914, Pte. India, Persian Gulf. Taken Prisoner by Turks, Apl. 29, 1916, Kut. *Died of Enteric*, Oct. 1916.
Chapman, James W. (8, Percy Terrace)	...		A.V.C., Dec. 1915. R.F.A. France. Wounded, 1917.
Chapman, Reginald A. (12, Victoria Road)	...	Dr.	R.A.S.C. (M.T.), Oct. 1916, Dr. German E. Africa.
Chappell, James A. (78A, Canon Street)	...	Bandsman	K.R.R.C., Nov. 1916, Band Boy. Home.
Chappell, William (78A, Canon Street)	...	Rfn.	Bedford Militia, 1891, Pte. R.A.S.C., K.R.R.C. Belgium, France. Wounded, July 6, 1915.
Chappell, William F. (78A, Canon Street)	...	A.B.	R.N., 1913. Dardanelles, North Sea; H.M.S. *Audacious* and *Queen Elizabeth*.
Charlton, Alfred (4, Tower Street)	...	Sergt.	Hants, Aug. 1915, Corpl. Home.
✠ Chaston, Edward A. (13, Edgar Road)	...	L.-Corpl.	Hants Y., Aug. 1914, Tpr. Hants. Italy, France. *Killed in Action*, Oct. 14, 1918, *Menin*.
Chaston, Richard D. (13, Edgar Road)	...	Pte.	R. Warwick, Sept. 26, 1918, Pte. Home.
✠ Chatfield, William L. (4, Ranelagh Road)	...	Pte.	Hants Y., Jan. 1915. Hants. France. Wounded, July 31, 1917. *Killed in Action*, Nov. 4, 1918, *Beaudignies*.
Cheater, Albert G. (7, Queen's Road)	...	Gun.	R.G.A., Dec. 1915, Gun. France. Wounded, Feb. 27, 1917.
Chevis, Albert (15, Union Street)	...	Pte.	R. Berks, June 1916, Pte. France.
Chevis, Charles A. T. (8, Greyfriars Terrace)	...		R.N.A.S., Oct. 1917. R.A.F. Home.
Chevis, William G. (8, Chester Road)	...	A.B.	R.N., 1916, Boy. North Sea; H.M.S. *King George V*.
Chilcott, Albert E. (26, Hyde Close)	...	L.-Corpl.	R.F.A., Jan. 1917, Gun. Tank C. France.
Child, Francis J. (Mayfield, Christ Church Road)	...	Capt.	R.A.M.C., May 1917, Lieut. France.
Child, Frederick J. C. (Water Works Cottage, St. Giles' Hill)	...	Gun.	R.G.A., Nov. 1915, Gun. India.
Child, William G. (Water Works Cottage, St. Giles' Hill)	...	Corpl.	R.A.S.C. (T.F.), 1910. Dardanelles, Salonica.
Childs, Herbert W. (62, Eastgate Street)	...	A.B.	R.N., Mch. 1916, O.S. North Sea.
Chisnell, George (1, St. John's Street)	...		R.A.F., Aug. 1, 1918. Home.
Chivers, Edward G. (3, Gordon Terrace)	...	Steward	R.N., 1912, Steward. North Sea, Mediterranean; H.M.S. *Iron Duke*. Wounded, June 1, 1916.
Chivers, Henry (11, Boundary Street)	...	Gun.	R.G.A., Apl. 1916, Gun. Belgium.

WINCHESTER WAR SERVICE REGISTER

Churcher, Ernest C. (3, Avenue Road)	L.-Corpl.	R.A.S.C., 1915, Pte. Lancs. France. *Wounded, Oct. 5, 1918.*
Churcher, Harold J. (3, Avenue Road)	Corpl.	Hants, 1914, Pte. Egypt, Palestine, France, Germany. *Wounded, Dec. 1, 1917.*
✠ Churcher, Henry T. (3, Avenue Road)	C.S.M.	Hants, 1914, Pte. Egypt, France. *Killed in Action, Sept. 19, 1918.* M.M., 1918.
Clampitt, William J. (6, Alresford Road)	Pte.	Hants, Jan. 1915, Pte. France. *Wounded, May 28, 1915, and June 8, 1916.*
Clark, A. H. (12, High Street)	Tpr.	Hants Y., Sept. 1914, Tpr. Cav., M.G.C. France.
Clark, Arthur T. (5, Canute Road)	Sergt.	R.A.S.C., 1914, Pte. France.
Clark, Edward G. (24, Clifton Road)	Staff Q.M.S.	R.B., Mch. 28, 1915, C.Sergt. Home.
Clark, Frederick (83, Chesil Street)	Pte.	Hants, Aug. 1914, Pte. D.C.L.I. India, Mesopotamia, France. *Wounded, Sept. 1917.*
✠ Clark, Gerald M. (24, Ranelagh Road)	Major	O.T.C., 1906, Capt. Northants. France. Despatches 1916. *Killed in Action, July 14, 1916.*
✠ Clark, Henry P. (8, Mants Lane)	Pte.	A.V.C., Jan. 1916, Pte. Oxf. and Bucks L.I. France. *Killed in Action, Dec. 22, 1917, Cambrai.*
Clark, John C. (83, Chesil Street)	Sergt.	R. Guernsey L.I., Feb. 1915, Pte. France.
Clark, Reginald (142, Stockbridge Road)		A.V.C., Dec. 1915. R.G.A. France.
✠ Clark, Reginald J. (40, Fairfield Road)	Rfn.	R.A.O.C., June 1916, Pte. R.B. France. *Missing, Nov. 30, 1917.*
Clark, William (46, Lower Brook Street)	Pte.	Devon, Mch. 1917, Pte. Italy.
Clark, William J. (Sunnycote, St. Faith's Road)	Capt.	Hants (T.F.), 1889, Pte. Hants. India, Palestine.
Clarke, Arthur C. (7, Upper Wolvesey Terrace)	C.P.O.	R.N., 1897, Boy. Grand Fleet.
Clarke, William (25, Andover Road)	Pte.	Hants, Mch. 1915, Pte. Germany, Russia.
Clarke, William, Junr. (25, Andover Road)	L.-Corpl.	Hants, Sept. 1914, Pte. Somerset L.I. India.
Clarke, William J. (30, Bar End)	Spr.	R. Berks, June 1916, Pte. R.E. France.
✠ Clarke, William J. (85, Colebrook Street)	Pte.	Hants, Aug. 1914, Pte. Egypt, Mesopotamia. *Drowned, Jan. 23, 1915.*
Clements, Archibald (13, King Alfred Place)	Gun.	R.G.A., Sept. 1914, Gun. Anti-Aircraft. France.
Clements, Charles F. (7, Clausentum Road)	Pte.	R. Marines, Feb. 1915. North Sea.
Clements, Stewart O. (4, Avenue Road)	Sergt.	R.E., 1900, Spr. Belgium, France, Italy. D.C.M. 1915, M.M. 1915, Despatches 1919.

WINCHESTER WAR SERVICE REGISTER

Name (Address)	Rank	Service
CLEVERLY, CECIL A. (2, King Alfred Terrace)	Corpl.	R.E., Sept. 1914, Spr. France. Wounded, Apl. 6, 1918.
CLEWER, EDWARD (3, St. Catherine's Road)	Sergt.	Nat. Res., Sept. 1914. R.F.C. Mesopotamia, France.
CLIFF, EDWARD G. (17, St. John's Park Terrace)	Pte.	Hants, 1916, Pte. Wilts. Mesopotamia. Wounded, 1917.
CLINTON, EDWARD C. (24, Monks Road)	Sergt.	K.R.R.C., 1895, Band Boy. France.
✠ CLOWES, CHARLES G. E. (Milnthorpe, Airlie Road)	Lieut.	K.R.R.C., 1912, 2nd Lieut. France, Belgium. Wounded, Oct. 8, 1914. *Killed in Action, Feb. 15, 1915, Ypres.*
CLOWES, JOHN L. (Milnthorpe, Airlie Road)	A.-Major	K.R.R.C., Aug., 1914 2nd Lieut. M.G.C. France, Salonica, Belgium, Germany. Despatches, Belgian Croix de Guerre.
COATES, ERNEST (4, St. Thomas Street)	Pte.	R.E., May 1916, Spr. R.A.O.C. France.
COBB, GEORGE (3, Abbey Passage)	Tpr.	Hants Y., Nov. 1915, Tpr. Home.
✠ COBB, JAMES A. (3, Abbey Passage)	Tpr.	Hussars, Aug. 1914, Tpr. France, Belgium. *Killed in Action, May 13, 1915, Ypres.*
COBB, WILLIAM P. (3, Abbey Passage)	Sig.	Hants Y., Nov. 1915, Tpr. Border R., E. Lancs. France.
COBERN, STANLEY F. (72, Parchment Street)	L.-Corpl.	R. Berks, Oct. 1915, Pte. Home.
COBERN, THOMAS M. (72, Parchment Street)	Pte.	R.A.M.C., Sept. 1914, Pte. France.
✠ COBERN, WESLEY V. (72, Parchment Street)	Rfn.	R.B., 1903, Rfn. France. *Killed in Action, Oct. 18, 1914, Armentières.*
✠ COBERN, WILFRED G. (72, Parchment Street)	Corpl.	Hants (T.F.), Pte. Hants. India, Persian Gulf. *Killed in Action, June 15, 1915, Basra.* 2570
COBERN, WILLIAM A. H. (72, Parchment Street)	Corpl.	Hants (T.F.), 1916, Pte. Glamorgan Vol. Home.
COCKSHEAD, ARTHUR H. (4, Queen's Terrace)	Band Boy	R. Marines, 1912, Band Boy. Mediterranean, Dardanelles; H.M.S. *London*.
COCKSHEAD, FRANK W. (4, Queen's Terrace)	Bandmaster	R. Marines, 1909, Band Boy. North Sea; H.M.S. *New Zealand*, H.M.A.S. *Sydney*.
COCKSHEAD, THOMAS R. (4, Queen's Terrace)	Sergt.	Hants, Aug. 1914, Pte. Erinpura R., R.A.S.C. India, Mesopotamia, Persia.
CODDINGTON, HENRY B. (51, Southgate Street)	Major	Hants, rejoined Sept. 1914, Capt. Home.
COKER, JAMES (4, Hyde Street)	Pte.	R.A.S.C. (M.T.), May 1915, Pte. Salonica, Egypt.
COLE, CHARLES H. (Wellisford House, Weeke)	Pte.	Artists' Rif. O.T.C., June 1917, Pte.
COLE, FREDERICK G. (8, Water Lane)	Gun.	R.F.A., Nov. 1914, Gun. Home.

WINCHESTER WAR SERVICE REGISTER

COLE, GEORGE L. (Wellisford House, Weeke)	...	C.F.	C.F., Sept. 1916, Capt. Flanders, Germany.
COLE, JAMES E. (59, St. John's Street)	...	L.-Corpl.	R.E., 1915, Spr. France. Wounded, Aug. 21, 1917. M.M., 1917.
COLERICK, WILLIAM H. (11, Saxon Road)	...		R.N.A.S., 1917. R.A.F. France, Egypt.
✠ COLES, FRANK (2, Andover Road)	...	C.S.M.	Hants (T.F.), Aug. 1914, Pte. India, Mesopotamia. Taken Prisoner by Turks, Apl. 29, 1916. Kut. *Died of Dysentery, Sept. 18, 1916.*
✠ COLES, SYDNEY J. (44, Western Road)	...	Pte.	Hants, Sept. 1914, Pte. India, Mesopotamia. *Missing, believed killed, Jan. 21, 1916.*
COLES, WILLIAM H. (38, Andover Road)	...	Pte.	Hants, June 1916, Pte. France. Gassed, Sept. 3, 1918.
COLLESTER, ROBERT (137, High Street)	...	C.S.M.	K.R.R.C., Rfn. Amer. Army. France. Wounded twice.
COLLINS, ALFRED (38, Colson Road)	...	Pte.	R. Marines, 1902, Pte. China, Mediterranean.
COLLINS, ALFRED G. (1, St. Faith's Road)	...	Pte.	Hants, July 1916, Pte. India, Mesopotamia.
COLLINS, ARTHUR (29, St. Thomas Street)	...	C.S.M.	R.A.S.C., 1914, Corpl. Tptr. Camel Corps. Gallipoli, Egypt. M.S.M. 1916.
COLLINS, BERNARD W. (Park Road Nursery)	...	Pte.	Hants, 1912, Pte. India, Mesopotamia, Persia.
COLLINS, CHARLES (19, Colson Road)	...	P.O. (1st Class)	R. Marines, 1902, Pte. R.N. North Sea.
COLLINS, EDWIN J. (1, Greyfriars Villas)	...	Pte.	Hants, May 1916, Pte. France. Wounded and Gassed, Aug. 1917.
COLLINS, HAROLD J. (31, Monks Road)	...	Pte.	Hants, Sept. 1914, Pte. Mesopotamia, India. Wounded twice.
✠ COLLINS, HERBERT F. (Park Road Nursery)	...	Pte.	Hants Y., Nov. 1914, Tpr. Hants. France. *Killed in Action, Mch. 1918, Cambrai.*
COLLINS, JOHN (10, Greenhill Avenue)	...	C.Q.M.S.	Lancers, 1899, Bandsman. M.G.C. France. Despatches.
COLLINS, JOHN A. (7, North Walls)	...	Pte.	Hants, Feb. 1916, Pte. Welsh R. Salonica, Constantinople.
COLLINS, REGINALD F. (37, Water Lane)	...		R.N.A.S., July 1917. Home.
COLLINS, REGINALD G. (31, Monks Road)	...	Corpl.	Hants, Pte., 1915. France. Wounded once.
COLLINS, WALTER (9A, Magdalen Hill)	...	Spr.	R.E., Nov. 1915, Spr. Home.
COLLINS, WILLIAM (69, Canon Street)	...	2nd Corpl.	R.E., Nov. 1915, Spr. France. Gassed, Oct. 1916 and Sept. 1917. Wounded, Oct. 28, 1918.
COLLIS, CHARLES (26, Clausentum Road)	...	C.P.O.	R.N., rejoined June 1915, C.P.O. Home. H.M.S. *Gartshore.*
COLLIS, EDWARD G. (Canon Street)	...	Sergt.	Hants, 1912, Pte. India, Egypt.

WINCHESTER WAR SERVICE REGISTER

COLLIS, FREDERICK T. (43, Nuns Road)	Sergt.	Hants, 1897, Bandsman. R.E. India, Persian Gulf. Wounded, Jan. 21, 1916.
COLLIS, GEORGE (41, Upper Brook Street)	Pte.	Hants, July 1915, Pte. France. Wounded, July 1, 1916.
COLLIS, SYDNEY (26, Clausentum Road)	Pte.	Hants, Dec. 1916, Pte. R.E. France. Wounded, Oct. 1918.
COLLISS, HERBERT R. H. (12, Gladstone Street)	Corpl.	R.A.S.C., Mch. 6, 1917, Pte. Salonica.
CONDUIT, BERNARD N. W. (3, West End Terrace)	Lieut.	Hants Y., 1910, Tpr. H.A.C., R.F.A. France, Flanders.
CONDUIT, LIONEL B. (3, West End Terrace)	Major	Warwick Y., 1913, Tpr. R.A.S.C. (M.T.). Egypt, Gallipoli, Salonica. Despatches four times.
CONEY, JOHN (The Lodge, Milnthorpe, Airlie Road)	Rfn.	K.R.R.C., 1899, Rfn. France. Wounded, Oct. 23, 1914.
COO, CHARLES E. (7, Culverwell Gardens)		R.A.F., rejoined Aug. 1, 1918. Home.
✠ COOK, ARTHUR B. K. (6, The Close)	2nd Lieut.	R.F., Feb. 1915, 2nd Lieut. France. *Killed in Action, July 7, 1916, Ovillers.*
COOK, ARTHUR J. (71, Sussex Street)	Rfn.	K.R.R.C., 1902, Rfn. France.
COOK, FRANK (11A, Owen's Road)	Pte.	Hants Cyc., Mch. 1917, Pte. France.
COOK, FRANK W. E. (20, Tower Street)	A.-Major	R.H.A., 1905, Gun. France, Russia. Wounded, Apl. 1918. M.C. 1917.
COOK, HENRY T. (Wyke Mark Cottage)	Pte.	R.A.S.C. (M.T.), Oct. 1916, Pte. France.
COOKE, ERNEST A. (5, Upper Brook Street)	Pte.	Hants, June 1915, Pte. France. Wounded twice, 1918.
COOKE, HARRY (5, Upper Brook Street)	Sergt.	K.R.R.C., 1897, Rfn. E. Kent, Gordon H. France, Flanders.
COOKE, LEONARD A. (5, Upper Brook Street)	Dr.	R.F.A., Oct. 1914, Dr. France.
COOMBES, FREDERICK R. (70, Water Cottages)	Pte.	A.V.C., Oct. 1914, Pte. R. Berks, Hants. France, Belgium.
COOMBES, GEORGE H. (49, North Walls)	Corpl.	Hants Y., Oct. 25, 1915, Tpr. Hants. France, Italy, Germany. Wounded, Sept. 1917 and Mch. 1918.
COOMBES, JAMES (106, Colebrook Street)	Sergt.	R.A.S.C., 1912, Dr. T.R., Warwick, Worc. France.
COOMBES, LESLIE R. (70, Water Cottages)	Pte.	A.I.F., 1914, Pte. Gallipoli, France, Salonica. Gassed once.
COOPER, ALBERT (52, Winnall)	Pte.	Dorset, 1905, Pte. India, Persian Gulf. Taken Prisoner by Turks, Apl. 29, 1916, Kut.
COOPER, ARTHUR C. (52, Winnall)	Gun.	R.G.A., 1906, Gun. India, Egypt, France, Salonica.

WINCHESTER WAR SERVICE REGISTER

Name (Address)	Rank	Service
COOPER, FRANCIS G. (52, Winnall)	Gun.	A.V.C., Apl. 1915, Pte. R.F.A. France.
COOPER, GEORGE (2, Highfield Terrace)	L.-Corpl.	Hants, May 1915, Pte. R.D.C. France.
COOPER, HARRY W. (Connemara, Bereweeke Road)	Gun.	R.F.A., Aug. 1916, Gun. Home.
COOPER, HENRY G. (2, Highfield Terrace)	L.-Corpl.	Hants, Sept. 1914, Pte. Mesopotamia.
COOPER, JOSEPH (11, Queen's Road)	S.M.	R.H.A., rejoined Sept. 1914, S.M. K.R.R.C., R.F.A. Home.
COPLEY, HENRY W. (89, Chesil Street)	Sergt.	Nat. Res. Lond., R.F. Home.
COPPARD, EDWIN J. S. (1, Cathedral View)	P.O.	R.N., 1910, Stoker. North Sea; H.M.S. *Malaya*.
CORBEY, JAMES T. (6, Gordon Avenue)	Pte.	Hants Y., May 1916, Tpr. Hants. France. Wounded, Oct. 22, 1918.
CORPS, FREDERICK C. (The Castle)	Pte.	Hants, Aug. 1914, Pte. Mesopotamia, Persia. Wounded, 1915.
COSHAM, FRANK (96, Fairfield Road)	Sergt.	R.B., Aug. 1915, Rfn. Home.
COSIER, THOMAS H. (6, Egbert Road)	Pte.	R.A.M.C., Apl. 1917, Pte. R.E. Home.
COSTER, JOHN A. (89c, Chesil Street)	Corpl.	R.G.A., 1907, Gun. France, China.
COURTNESS, WILLIAM G. (7, Westgate Lane)	L.-Corpl.	R.B., 1900, Rfn. Home.
COURTNEY, HENRY G. (Marlfield, St. James' Lane)	Lieut.	R.G.A., Dec. 1915, 2nd Lieut. Macedonia. Despatches.
COUSINS, ROBERT (66, Canon Street)	Pte.	R.A.S.C., Dec. 1914, Pte. M.A.C. Salonica. Wounded, 1918.
COUZENS, FREDERICK (7, Water Lane)	Pte.	Hants, June 24, 1916, Pte. R.A.S.C. France.
COUZENS, JOHN (52, Lansdowne Terrace)	Pte.	R.A.S.C., Oct. 26, 1918, Pte. Somerset L.I.
COUZENS, WILLIAM (15, Water Lane)	Sergt.	R.G.A., Jan. 1915, Corpl. France.
COVEY, ALBERT E. (2, Westgate Lane)	Pte.	Hants, Oct. 1915, Pte. India, Mesopotamia.
✠ COVEY, EDWIN H. (2, Westgate Lane)	Pte.	A.I.F., Oct. 1914, Pte. Gallipoli, France. *Killed in Action, July 2, 1916, Armentières.*
✠ COVEY, PERCY (2, Westgate Lane)	Pte.	A.I.F., Oct. 1914, Pte. Gallipoli. *Killed in Action, Aug. 6, 1915.*
COWAN, DAVID L. (Little Meade, Cheriton Road)	Lieut.	R.N.R., Oct. 1914, Sub-Lieut. China, Dardanelles, Mediterranean, Atlantic, North Sea. D.S.C. 1915, Despatches twice.
✠ COWAN, DOUGLAS H. (Little Meade, Cheriton Road)	2nd Lieut.	Hants, 1912, 2nd Lieut. France. *Killed in Action, Aug. 26, 1914, Cambrai.*

WINCHESTER WAR SERVICE REGISTER

Cowan, Graeme S. (Little Meade, Cheriton Road)	Lieut.	Ceylon Rif., 1914. R.A.F. Home.
Cowan, William B. (Little Meade, Cheriton Road)	Staff Capt.	Canadians, Jan. 1915, Pte. Hants, Warwick. France.
Cowland, Walter S. (10, College Street)	Major	Hants, Sept. 1914, 2nd Lieut. Gallipoli, Macedonia. Wounded once. D.S.O., Croix de Guerre avec Palme, Despatches twice.
Cox, Albert E. (4, Alswitha Terrace)	Gun.	R.F.A., Gun. R.H.A. France. Gassed, Aug. 1917. Wounded, Sept. 1918.
Cox, Edward E. (The Lodge, Recreation Ground)	Bug.	Hants, May 1914, Bug. Mesopotamia. Wounded, Feb. 24, 1917, and in 1918.
Cox, Francis W. M. (6, St. Cross Road)	Lieut.	K.R.R.C., June 1916, Rfn. R.E. France, America (propaganda), Germany.
✠ Cox, Frank (1, Culver Road)	Pte.	N. Fus., Sept. 25, 1914, Pte. France. *Killed in Action, Aug. 8, 1917, Nieuport.*
✠ Cox, Frederick G. (1, Culver Road)	Stoker	R.N., 1904. H.M.S. *Queen Mary*. *Killed in Action, May 31, 1916, Jutland.*
Cox, Herbert (1, Culver Road)	Spr.	R.E., Feb. 1918, Spr. Home.
Cox, Horace J. (Nanzela, Andover Road)	Sig.	Hants, Sept. 1914, Pte. India, Palestine, France.
Cox, Reginald H. (Nanzela, Andover Road)	Pte.	Devon, Sept. 1917, Pte. Tank C. France.
Cox, Sidney C. (The Lodge, Recreation Ground)	Stoker	R.N., 1905, Stoker. Mediterranean, Dardanelles.
✠ Cox, Thomas (1, Culver Road)	Pte.	R.A.M.C., Sept. 15, 1914, Pte. France. *Killed in Action, July 1, 1916, Albert.*
Cox, Walter (1, Culver Road)	Pte.	Hants, 1915, Pte. India.
Coxon, George (6, The Close)	Corpl.	Hants, 1916, Pte. India, Baluchistan, Egypt, Palestine, France, Belgium, Germany.
Coxon, Harry C. (15, Sussex Street)	Sergt.	Hants Cyc., June 1915, Pte. M.G.C. France, Belgium, Germany. Wounded, 1917 and Mch. 30, 1918. Taken Prisoner by Germans and escaped.
Coyne, James (4, Riflemen's Cottages)	C.S.M.	R.B., C.S.M. France. Wounded, Aug. 9, 1915.
Coyne, James A. (4, Riflemen's Cottages)	A.M.	R.A.F., July 27, 1917. A.M. Home.
Cress, Albert E. W. (33, Middle Brook Street)	Pte.	Hants, Sept. 1914, Pte. Mesopotamia. Taken Prisoner by Turks, Mch. 27, 1915, Kut.
Cress, Charles J. J. (33, Middle Brook Street)		R.A.S.C., Aug. 1915, Pte. France.
Cress, Frederick W. H. (33, Middle Brook Street)	Corpl.	R.B., Sept. 1914, Rfn. France. Wounded, July 27, 1916.
Crockett, Frank H. (51, Brassey Road)	1st A.M.	R.F.C., June 1916, A.M. Home.

WINCHESTER WAR SERVICE REGISTER

CROFT, CHARLES (1, South View)	...	Pte.	R.B., Mch. 1914, Rfn. Oxf. and Bucks L.I. France. Wounded, Dec. 1914.
CROFT, DESMOND W. (Egmont, St. James' Lane)	...	Major	S.W.B., 1914, 2nd Lieut. France. Wounded, 1917 and 1918. M.C. 1916, D.S.O. 1918, Despatches 1917 and 1918.
CROFT, HAROLD G. (4, Kingsgate Street)	...	Lieut.	Hants, Aug. 1914, Pte. Loyal N. Lancs. India, Mesopotamia.
CROFT, HARRY (1, South View)	...	L.-Corpl.	Hants, Dec. 1914, Pte. India, Mesopotamia. Wounded, 1915.
CROFT, REGINALD J. (50, St. Faith's Road)	...	L.-Sergt.	Devon, Feb. 1917, Pte. A.P.C. Home.
CROSS, CHARLES (47, St. Faith's Road)	...	Pte.	Hants, Aug. 1914, Pte. Home.
CROSS, CLAUD E. (20, Egbert Road)	...		R.E., May 1917. R.F.C. France, Germany.
CROSS, EDMUND F. (20, Egbert Road)	...	Sergt.	Hants, 1908, Boy. Wounded, May 9, 1915.
✠ CROSS, ERNEST (12, St. John's Street)	...	Pte.	Hants, Sept. 1914, Pte. India, Persian Gulf. *Died, July 28, 1916, Quetta.*
CROSS, HENRY (20, Egbert Road)	...	R.S.M.	Hants, rejoined Sept. 1914, R.S.M. Home. M.S.M.
CROSS, S. ARCHIBALD (4, St. Swithun Street)	...		Sussex Y., Nov. 1914, Tpr. R. Sussex. Dardanelles, Egypt, Palestine, France.
CROSSWELL, WILLIAM E. (49, Brassey Road)	...		R.A.M.C., May 1917. R. Warwick, M.G.C. India.
CROWDY, ARTHUR A. G. (2, Beaufort Road)	...	Lieut.	R.A.S.C., 1914, 2nd Lieut. Home.
CRUTE, ARTHUR L. (11, Sussex Street)	...	Pte.	Hants Cyc., Sept. 1915, Pte. Hants. France, Mesopotamia, Persia.
CRUTE, WILLIAM H. (13, Gordon Avenue)	...	1st A.M.	R.F.C., Apl. 1916, A.M. Mesopotamia, Egypt, France. Wounded, Sept. 24, 1918.
✠ CRUTE, WILLIAM H. (12, Lower Brook Street)	...	Pte.	Hants, Nov. 1914, Pte. Mesopotamia, France. Wounded, Jan. 21, 1916. *Killed in Action, 1917.*
CUNYNGHAM, DAVID H. (48, Christ Church Road)	...	Lieut.	R. Scots Fus., 2nd Lieut. Belgium, Salonica. Wounded, Mch. 29, 1915.
CURRELL, ALFRED L. (3, Ivy Terrace, Bar End)	...	L.-Corpl.	Wilts, Jan. 21, 1916, Pte. Norfolk. France, Belgium. Wounded, Aug. 19, 1916.
CURSON, ALBERT (7, Wharf Hill)	...	Dr.	R.H.A., Aug. 1914, Dr. France, Egypt. Wounded once.
CURTIS, GEORGE (48, Lower Brook Street)	...	Stoker	R.N., 1899, Stoker. North Sea.
CURTIS, JAMES E. (St. Margaret's, Culver Close)	...	Sergt.	K.R.R.C., Feb. 1915, Rfn. Home.
CURTIS, JOHN C. (St. Margaret's, Culver Close)	...	L.-Corpl.	Hants, Mch. 1914, Pte. India, Palestine, Egypt.
CURTIS, WALTER, sen. (St. Margaret's, Culver Close)	...	L.-Corpl.	Hants, 1908, Pte. Home.

WINCHESTER WAR SERVICE REGISTER

CURTIS, WALTER, jun. (St. Margaret's, Culver Close)	Corpl.	A.P.C., Oct. 1914, Pte. Cheshire, R. Warwick. Italy, France. Wounded, June 1918.
CURTIS, WILFRED (4, Sussex Street)	Bdr.	R.G.A., 1907, Gun. France. Wounded, July 31, 1917, and Sept. 18, 1917.
CURTIS, WILLIAM (St. Margaret's, Culver Close)	L.-Corpl.	Hants, Mch. 1914, Pte. France. Gassed, 1917.
DACRE, HARRY E. (21, Parchment Street)	Stoker	R.N., 1911, Stoker. North Sea.
DAISH, FREDERICK A. (Hill View, Fordington Road)	R.S.M.	R.G.A., 1898, Gun. France.
DAISH, GEORGE A. (3, Penarth Place)	L.-Corpl.	T.R., Sept. 1917, Pte. R.I.R. France, Germany.
DAISH, GEORGE J. (Hill View, Fordington Road)	Sergt.	A.V.C., July 1916, Pte. France. Wounded, 1917.
DAISH, GERALD E. (Hill View, Fordington Road)	Army Schoolmaster	Army Schoolmaster, 1909. Army H.Q. India.
DAISH, LEONARD G. (Hill View, Fordington Road)	Capt.	R.E., 1913, Spr. R. Innis. Fus. Palestine, Salonica, Egypt, France.
DAISH, PERCY W. (3, Penarth Place)	Sergt.	Hants, Dec. 1915, Pte. Mesopotamia, Persia.
DAISH, WILLIAM (64, Greenhill Road)	P.O.	R.N., Apl. 1917, Armourer. Grand Fleet, Gibraltar, North Sea, Malta; H.M.S. *Barham* and *Donovan*.
DALE, ALBERT S. (5, Culverwell Gardens)	Gun.	R.N., 1915. North Sea; H.M.S. *Impregnable*, *Repulse*, and *Inconstant*.
DARTER, GEORGE A. (3, Penarth Place)	Staff Q.M.S.	R.A.O.C., 1908, Pte. Palestine.
DASHWOOD, VERE E. C. (St. Cross Lodge, St. Cross Road)	Major	R. Sussex, 1906, 2nd Lieut. M.G.C. France, Salonica, United States, Mesopotamia. M.C. 1915, Despatches 1914, 1915, and 1919.
DAVIDGE, ARTHUR E. (75, Upper Brook Street)	Corpl.	R.B., rejoined Aug. 1914, Rfn. France. Wounded and taken Prisoner by Germans, Aug. 26, 1914.
DAVIDGE, ARTHUR J. (54, Fairfield Road)	Corpl.	R.E., Aug. 1914, Spr. France, Gallipoli, Egypt, Palestine.
↦ DAVIDGE, ERNEST (81, Upper Brook Street)	L.-Corpl.	Hants, July 1916, Pte. R. Berks. France. Wounded, Apl. 28, 1916. Taken Prisoner by Germans, Apl. 28, 1917. *Died, May 6, 1917.*
DAVIDGE, HERBERT F. (54, Fairfield Road)	Sergt.	A.P.C., Aug. 1914, Pte. Hants. France, Germany. Wounded, June 30, and Sept. 15, 1916.
DAVIDGE, LOUIS H. (54, Fairfield Road)	Spr.	R.E., Aug. 1914, Spr. France.
DAVIDGE, ROBERT G. (54, Fairfield Road)	Sergt.	R.F.C., Feb. 1918, Cadet. R.A.F. Home.
DAVIDGE, WILLIAM (42, Lansdown Terrace)	Pte.	Hants, Feb. 1917, Pte. D.C.L.I. Italy. Wounded, Oct. 1917.

WINCHESTER WAR SERVICE REGISTER

DAVIDSON, THOMAS ST. C. ... Lieut.-Col. ... R. Lancs., Sept. 1914. Lieut.-Col. France, Salonica.
(Landor House, St. Cross Road)

DAVIS, ARTHUR G. ... ... Staff-Sergt. ... Hants, Sept. 1916, Pte. I. of W. Regt. India,
(2, Ranelagh Road) Mesopotamia. Despatches.

✠ DAVIS, FRANCIS ... ... Pte. ... Wilts, 1906, Pte. France, Belgium. *Killed in*
(46, Wales Street) *Action, Nov. 1914, in Retreat from Mons.*

DAVIS, FREDERICK ... ... A.-Sergt. ... Hants, Nov. 9, 1914, Pte. India, Baluchistan.
(2, Boscobel Road) Despatches.

DAVIS, GEORGE ... ... Rfn. ... K.R.R.C., 1905, Rfn. India, France. Wounded,
(29, Middle Brook Street) Sept. 17, 1914.

DAVIS, GEORGE ... ... Pte. ... Hants Y., Mch. 1, 1917, Tpr. R.A.S.C. Home.
(16, St. Giles' Hill Hutments)

DAVIS, HARRY ... ... Pte. ... Dorset, June 1916, Pte. R. Berks., Worc. Home.
(6, Ivy Terrace, Bar End)

DAVIS, HARRY ... ... L.-Corpl. ... R.E., 1907, Pte. Salonica.
(46, Wales Street)

DAVIS, HUMPHREY K. ... Staff-Sergt. ... Can. F.A., Sept. 1915, Gun. France. Wounded,
(2, Ranelagh Road) Apl. 27, 1917. Despatches.

DAVIS, MAX ... ... Pte. ... Hants Y., Nov. 1914, Tpr. Hants. France,
(2, Ranelagh Road) Italy. Wounded once.

DAWES, HENRY J. ... ... Corpl. ... R.A.S.C., Nov. 1914, Pte. Gallipoli, Egypt,
(13, St. John's Street) Palestine.

✠ DAWKINS, FRANK ... ... Pte. ... Devon Y., Mch. 1917, Tpr. Cheshire. *Killed in*
(8, Greenhill Terrace) *Action, Apl. 29, 1918.*

DAWKINS, GEORGE ... ... Stoker ... R.N., Sept. 1916, Stoker. H.M.S. *Constance*.
(8, Greenhill Terrace)

DAWKINS, HUGH A. ... ... Pte. ... Lond., July 1915, Pte. M.G.C. France.
(The Glen, Stanmore Lane)

DEAN, ALFRED M. ... ... Corpl. ... R.N.A.S., Jan. 5, 1915, 1st A.M. R.A.F. Belgium,
(55, Western Road) France, Dardanelles, Italy.

DEAN, AUGUSTUS D. ... ... Hants, Sept. 5, 1914. R.E. France.
(16, College Street)

DEAR, CHARLES ... ... Pte. ... Hants, Apl. 1915, Pte. France.
(33, Bar End Road)

✠ DEAR, DOUGLAS G. ... ... Pte. ... Hants, Jan. 1914, Pte. India, Mesopotamia.
(12, St. Leonard's Road) *Killed in Action, Jan. 21, 1916, Kut.*

DEAR, HENRY R. ... ... R.M.A., July 1906. Belgium, France.
(12, Back Street, St. Cross)

DEARDEN, JAMES H. ... ... R.A.F., 1917. France.
(14, Alswitha Terrace)

DEARSLEY, ARTHUR ... ... Sergt. ... R.F.A., 1915, Gun. R.A.S.C. France.
(36, Parchment Street)

DEDMAN, GEORGE F. ... ... Spr. ... Devon, Oct. 3, 1917, Pte. R.E. Germany.
(25, Middle Brook Street)

DEMATOSE, WALTER J. ... ... Pte. ... Hants, Apl. 1915, Pte. France.
(19, Canon Street)

WINCHESTER WAR SERVICE REGISTER

DENN, CHARLES T. (29, Tower Street)	Rfn.	R.B., 1908, Bug. France. Wounded, Sept. 22, 1914.
DENNETT, ARTHUR S. (16, Upper High Street)	C.S.M.	Hants, 1904, Pte. Tank C. France, Belgium. Wounded, 1915 and Mch. 1918.
DENNETT, HORACE L. (16, Upper High Street)	C.S.M.	Hants, Sept. 1914, Pte. India, Egypt, Palestine, France. D.C.M., 1918.
DENNISTOUN, GEORGE H. (The Lodge, Bereweeke Road)	Comdr.	R.N. Lake Nyassa, Samoa. D.S.O. 1916.
✠ DENNISTOUN, JAMES R. (The Lodge, Bereweeke Road)	Lieut.	N. Irish Horse, 2nd Lieut. R.A.F. France. Wounded and taken Prisoner by Germans, June 26, 1916. *Died of Wounds, Aug. 9, 1916, at Ohrdruf.*
DERHAM, CECIL G. (5, Castle Terrace)	Pte.	Hants Cyc., Jan. 1915, Pte. India, Russia.
DERHAM, EDMUND P. (5, Castle Terrace)	L.-Corpl.	Hants, 1912, Pte. R. Warwick. France. Wounded, Mch. 30, 1918.
DEVINE, ALBERT J. (58, St. Catherine's Road)	Pte.	Dorset, July, 1918 Pte. Home.
DEVINE, WILLIAM F. (58, St. Catherine's Road)	Sig.	R.G.A., Mch. 1916, Gun. R.E. France. Wounded and Gassed, May 1918. M.M. 1918.
DEWDNEY, GEORGE (3, St. Cross Road)	1st A.M.	R.N.A.S., Mch. 1917, 2nd A.M. R.A.F. Home.
DIAMOND, GEORGE W. (64, Hyde Street)	C.Q.M.S.	R.B., 1899, Rfn. France.
DICKEN, EDWARD B. C. (Norton, Park Road)	Lt.-Comdr.	R.N., 1902. Mediterranean. Chev. St. M. and St. L. 1916, D.S.C. 1917, Off. of Redeemer 1918.
DICKEN, JOHN A. (Norton, Park Road)	Lieut.	R.N., 1909. Grand Fleet.
DICKER, JOHN (9, Nelson Road)	Pte.	Somerset, 1918, Pte. Home.
✠ DICKER, PERCY J. (9, Nelson Road)	Pte.	Middlesex, Aug. 1915, Pte. R.A.M.C. France. Wounded, Nov. 1916. *Killed in Action, Aug. 2, 1917.*
✠ DICKINSON, E.	1st A.M.	Hants Y., 1914, Tpr. R.A.F. France, Belgium. *Died, Feb. 22, 1919, St. Omer.*
DILLOW, ARTHUR V. (3, St. John's Road)	Pte.	Hants, May 1918, Pte. Home.
DILLOW, HERBERT E. (3, St. John's Road)	Pte.	Lond., Feb. 1916, Pte. France, Salonica, Egypt.
DILLOW, MARK T. (1, Highcliffe Road)		R.N. North Sea.
DIMENT, BERNARD A. (24, Brassey Road)	Gun.	R.G.A., Jan. 1917, Gun. India.
DINEEN, FREDERICK J. (107A, Colebrook Street)	C.P.O.	R.N., 1898, Boy. Dardanelles, North Sea; H.M.S. *Queen.*
DINEEN, LAWRENCE (107A, Colebrook Street)	L.-Corpl.	Hants, Sept. 1914, Pte. India, Mesopotamia.

WINCHESTER WAR SERVICE REGISTER

DINEEN, MICHAEL H. ... ... L.-Corpl. ... R.E., June 1916, Spr. Home.
(107A, Colebrook Street)

DINEEN, THOMAS R. ... ... R.S.M. ... Dorset, 1894, Pte. R. Guernsey L.I. Home.
(107A, Colebrook Street)

DIPPER, THOMAS J. ... ... L.-Corpl. ... Hants, June 1916, Pte. France.
(18, Elm Road)

DIVER, CECIL ... ... Conductor ... R.A.S.C., Aug. 1914, Pte. France. M.S.M.
(Durngate House, North Walls)

DIXON, WILLIAM ... ... Pte. ... Wilts, Jan. 1916, Pte. Mesopotamia, India, Persia.
(38, Clifton Road)

✠ DOBSON, FRANCIS W. ... ... Tpr. ... Coldstream Guards, Aug. 1914, Tpr. France. Wounded and Missing, believed Killed, Dec. 22, 1914, *Givenchy*.
(County School for Girls, Cheriton Road)

DOBSON, LAWRENCE F. ... ... Pte. ... R.A.S.C. (M.T.), 1915, Pte. France, Italy, Egypt, Mesopotamia.
(23, City Road)

DOBSON, TOM N. ... ... Corpl. ... K.R.R.C., Oct. 1914, Rfn. Lond. Rangers. France. Wounded, July 20, 1918.
(County School for Girls, Cheriton Road)

DOLLERY, FREDERICK G. ... Pte. ... Hants, Sept. 1914, Pte. Mesopotamia.
(44, Lower Brook Street)

DOLLERY, WILLIAM H. G. ... Pte. ... R.A.M.C., Oct. 1915, Pte. France.
(24, Brassey Road)

DOLTON, ALFRED A. ... ... Spr. ... R.E., Sept. 1917, Spr. Home.
(59, Lower Brook Street)

DOLTON, GEORGE ... ... Pte. ... Glos., 1916, Pte. France. Wounded, Oct. 1916.
(28, Canon Street)

DOMINY, CYRIL V. ... ... A.-C.Q.M.S. R.A.S.C., 1911, Dr. Gallipoli. Despatches.
(4, West End Terrace)

DOMNEY, GEORGE A. ... ... Pte. ... Hants, Oct. 1916, Pte. Home.
(8, Freelands Buildings)

DOMONEY, ERNEST G. ... ... Pte. ... Hants, 1893, Pte. France.
(44, Wales Street)

DONGER, WILLIAM J. ... ... P.O. ... R.N.A.S., Mch. 7, 1917, A.M. R.A.F. Italy.
(Ardenza, Courtenay Road)

DONISTHORPE, ARTHUR F. ... L.-Corpl. ... Hants, Nov. 1917, Pte. Lab. C. Home.
(45, Tower Street)

DONOGHUE, BENJAMIN ... ... Rfn. ... K.R.R.C., Aug. 1914, Rfn. France, Italy.
(22, Nuns Road)

DOODY, CYRIL W. ... ... Lieut. ... R.E., Aug. 1915, 2nd Lieut. Home.
(6, Hatherley Road)

DOODY, FREDERIC W. ... ... Pte. ... Hants, Dec. 1915, Pte. France. Wounded and taken Prisoner by Germans, Feb. 1, 1917.
(6, Hatherley Road)

DOREY, WILLIAM ... ... C.-Sergt. ... R. Marines. Recruiting Sergt. Home.
(6, North Walls)

DORRELL, ERNEST R. ... ... R.N.A.S., Sept. 1917. R.A.F. Home.
(89, Greenhill Road)

WINCHESTER WAR SERVICE REGISTER

✠ Douglas, Charles E. G. ... Pte. ... Hants, 1913, Pte. India, Persian Gulf. *Died, June* 15, 1915, *Basra.*
(22, Cheriton Road)

Douglas, Frederick S. ... Sig. ... R.E., 1910, Boy. Flanders, Germany. Wounded, Sept. 16, 1914.
(8, West End Terrace)

Douglas, George H. ... Spr. ... R.E., 1911, Spr. France, Salonica. Wounded, Jan. 5, 1915.
(8, West End Terrace)

Douse, Ernest ... Tpr. ... Hants Y., Mch. 1917, Tpr. R.N. Devon Hus. France, Germany. Wounded once.
(26, Colson Road)

Dowling, Bertram F. ... Pte. ... Hants, Sept. 1914, Pte. Mesopotamia, India. Wounded, July 24, 1915.
(81, Chesil Street)

Dowling, Frank ... Spr. ... Dorset, Sept. 25, 1915, Pte. N. Fus., R.E. India, Mesopotamia.
(81, Chesil Street)

Downer, Edward C. ... Pte. ... A.V.C., Nov. 1915, Pte. Home.
(3, Bar End)

Downham, Alfred E. ... Pte. ... Devon, Dec. 1917. France, Belgium. Wounded, Sept. 23, 1918.
(3, Upper Wolvesey Terrace)

Downham, Charles E. ... Pte. ... Dorset, Feb. 1913, Pte. Wounded, Sept. 10, 1914.
(3, Upper Wolvesey Terrace)

Downham, George W. ... Pte. ... Hants, 1910, Pte. Dardanelles, France.
(3, Upper Wolvesey Terrace)

Downie, George W. ... Bug. ... Hants, May 1915, Bug. Home.
(31, Romsey Road)

Dowse, Alfred J. ... Pte. ... Hants, May 1916, Pte. Dorset. France. Wounded, Sept. 27, 1916.
(45, Colson Road)

✠ Dowse, Clifford T. ... Pte. ... Hants Y., Apl. 1916, Tpr. Hants. France. *Killed in Action, Sept.* 14, 1918.
(5, Andover Road)

✠ Dowse, Henry A. ... Y. Sig. ... R.N., 1898, Boy. North Sea; H.M.S. *Faulkner. Died, May* 18, 1916, *Glasgow.*
(56–58, Colebrook Street)

Dowse, Ralph E. ... Pte. ... Hants, Pte. R.F.C. Home.
(2, Princes Buildings)

Dowse, Walter G. ... Pnr. ... R.E., Pnr. France.
(2, Princes Buildings)

Dowse, William J. ... Pte. ... R.A.S.C. (M.T.), Oct. 1916, Pte. Con. Ran. Mesopotamia.
(56–58, Colebrook Street)

Drake, Arthur H. ... Pte. ... H.M. Hosp. Boats, Jan. 1915, Nurse. Cav. Res., Devon. France.
(21, Tower Street)

✠ Drake, Thomas H. ... Tpr. ... E.A. Mounted Rif., Aug. 1914, Tpr. E. Africa. *Killed in Action, Nov.* 3, 1914, *Longido.*
(Wyke Hill House, Weeke)

Drewe, Charles J. ... Bdr. ... R.G.A., Oct. 1915, Gun. Anti-Aircraft. France.
(85, St. Cross Road)

Drewe, Wilfred J. ... Pte. ... Hants, Sept. 1914, Pte. Warwick. France. Wounded, Mch. 24, 1918.
(85, St. Cross Road)

Drewe, William ... Spr. ... Hants, Sept. 1914, Pte. R.E. Salonica.
(18, Water Lane)

Drewitt, Albert H. ... Corpl. ... R.F.C., Aug. 1916, 2nd A.M. Home.
(14, Gordon Avenue)

WINCHESTER WAR SERVICE REGISTER

DRISCOLL, WILLIAM U. ... Sergt. ... R.M.A., rejoined Aug. 1914, Sergt. North Sea, Dardanelles; H.M.S. *Bacchante*.
(30, Nuns Road)

DU BOULAY, N. W. HOUSSEMAYNE Brig.-Gen. R.A., 1880, Lieut. France. C.M.G., 1916.
(24, St. Thomas Street)

DU BOULAY, P. HOUSSEMAYNE Major ... Egypt Lab. C., July 1915, Lieut. Gallipoli, Egypt, Palestine.
(24, St. Thomas Street)

DU BOULAY, R. F. HOUSSEMAYNE Lieut. ... Native Lab. C., S. Africa, 1917, 2nd Lieut. France.
(24, St. Thomas Street)

✠ DUFFIN, WILLIAM J. ... Pte. ... Hants, Aug. 1914, Pte. France. *Killed in Action*, *Apl.* 1, 1915, *France*.
(8, Hedges Buildings)

DUKE, BERNARD G. ... Pte. ... Hants, Nov. 1915, Pte. R.N.A.S., R.A.F. Home.
(48, St. Catherine's Road)

DUMBLETON, HORATIO N. ... Col. ... W.O. Committee on Billets, 1914, Col. Home.
(Barton Segrave, Bereweeke Rd.)

DUMMER, ALFRED ... Spr. ... Devon, 1915, Pte. R.E. France.
(11, Tower Street)

DUMMER, BERTRAM D. ... Staff Sergt. R.A.O.C., Nov. 1917, Pte. Home.
(5, Tower Road)

DUMMER, CHARLES ... Pte. ... Hants, June 1916, Pte. France.
(11, Tower Street)

DUMMER, CHARLES F. ... Pte. ... Hants, June 1916, Pte. India.
(30, Wales Street)

DUMMER, CHARLES V. H. ... Pte. ... Hants, June 1916, Pte. France, Belgium. Gassed, Apl. 1917.
(9, Colebrook Place)

DUMMER, CYRIL ... Pte. ... Hants, Sept. 1916, Pte. France. Wounded twice, 1917 and 1918.
(30, Wales Street)

DUMMER, DOUGLAS B. ... Staff Sergt. R.A.O.C., 1916, Pte. Home.
(5, Tower Road)

DUMMER, EWART H. ... Pte. ... Hants, Mch. 1916, Pte. Devon. France, Belgium.
(30, Wales Street)

✠ DUMMER, FREDERICK ... Pte. ... R. Berks, 1915, Pte. France. *Killed in Action*, *Oct.* 23, 1916, *France*.
(11, Tower Street)

DUMMER, GEORGE G. ... Pte. ... Somerset L.I., 1917, Pte. R. Innis. Fus. France.
(30, Wales Street)

DUMMER, JOHN W. ... Gun. ... R.N., 1903, Boy. Dardanelles, North Sea; H.M.S. *Irresistible* and *Comet*. Torpedoed three times.
(30, Wales Street)

DUMMER, RICHARD ... Pte. ... Hants, 1915, Pte. Lab. C. Egypt, India. Wounded, Apl. 9, 1918.
(11, Tower Street)

DUMMER, THOMAS E. ... Corpl. ... Dorset, 1905, Pte. India, Mesopotamia, Egypt.
(30, Wales Street)

DUMPER, ARTHUR F. ... L.-Corpl. Hants (T.F.), 1900, Pte. Hants. France.
(63, Lower Brook Street)

DUMPER, EDWARD M. ... Gun. ... R.G.A., Nov. 1914, Gun. France.
(12, Kingsgate Street)

DUMPER, JOSEPH ... Spr. ... R.E., Jan. 1917, Spr. France.
(2, Culver Road)

WINCHESTER WAR SERVICE REGISTER

Dumper, Joseph H. (2, Culver Road)	...	Pte.	T.R., Aug. 1914, Pte. R.N. Devon Hus. France.
Dunford, Albert (3, St. Paul's Hill)	...	Pte.	Hants, Oct. 1915, Pte. Somerset L.I. France. Wounded, Aug. and Nov. 1916, Apl. 1917.
Dunford, Albert E. (60, North Walls)	...	Pte.	Hants, Sept. 1914, Pte. India, Mesopotamia. Wounded, Jan. 1916.
Dunford, Edward (3, St. Paul's Hill)	...	Corpl.	R.E., Apl. 1916, Spr. France, Italy. Wounded, 1918.
Dunford, Edwin W. (14, Upper High Street)	...	Corpl.	R.E., Apl. 1916, Spr. S. Staffs. France, Italy. Wounded, Aug. 22, 1918.
Dunford, George (3, St. Paul's Hill)	...	L.-Corpl.	R. Sussex, Apl. 1916, Pte. France. Wounded and Gassed, 1918.
Dunlavey, Emmanuel (11, St. James' Terrace)	...	Lieut.	K.R.R.C., 1909, Rfn. France, Flanders. Wounded, Sept. 25, 1915, and Apl. 13, 1916. D.C.M.
✠ Dunmill, John B. (St. Clement's, Hyde Street)	...	Bdr.	R.G.A., 1917, Gun. France. *Killed in Action, Feb. 2, 1918.*
✠ Dunn, Frank (6, Arthur Road)	...	Pte.	Lond., Feb. 1917, Pte. France. *Killed in Action.*
Dureli, Clement V. (The College, Winchester)	...	Lieut.	R.G.A., Apl. 25, 1916, 2nd Lieut. France. Despatches, 1918.
Durnford, Arthur C. (28, Brassey Road)	...		R.A.S.C., Apl. 1915. France, Greece, Salonica.
Durnford, Philip B. (28, Brassey Road)	...	Pte.	Hants Cyc., May 1915, Pte. India, Siberia.
Durnford, William F. H. (2, Greenhill Road)	...	Pte.	R.A.M.C., Apl. 1916, Pte. Home.
Durrant, William (22, Parchment Street)	...	Corpl.	R.A.S.C., 1914, Pte. France.
✠ Dyer, Arthur F. R. (6, Grafton Road)	...	Capt.	Hants Y., 1902, Tpr. Hants, K.A. Rif. E. Africa. *Killed in Action, Sept. 30, 1917, Nitua.*
Dyer, Godfrey M. (Palm Hall, St. Giles' Hill)	...	Lieut.	Lancers, 1917, 2nd Lieut. Indian Army. India, Syria.
Dyett, Oliver W. (3, Brassey Road)	...	Steward	R.N., Off. Steward. Home.
Dyke, Albert (13, St. Leonard's Road)	...	Pte.	Dorset, Jan. 1916, Pte. Devon. France. Gassed once.
Dyke, Edgar (13, St. Leonard's Road)	...	Pte.	Hants, 1917, Pte. France.
Dymond, Frank (9, Poulsome Place)	...	Sergt.	R.B., 1898, Rfn. France.
✠ Eade, Charles A. (11A, Union Street)	...	Drummer	Hants, 1913, Drummer. India, Mesopotamia. *Killed in Action, Jan. 21, 1916.*
Eade, Edward A. (11A, Union Street)	...	Sig.	R.N., Oct. 1914. North Sea, Russia.

WINCHESTER WAR SERVICE REGISTER

✠ EADE, HARRY A. F. ... Pte. ... Hants, May 1914, Band Boy. France. *Killed in Action, May* 1918, *France.*
(18, North View)

EADE, WILLIAM C. ... Pte. ... Hants, Sept. 1914, Pte. France. Wounded, 1916 and 1917. Taken Prisoner by Germans, Mch. 1918.
(11A, Union Street)

EADE, WILLIAM J. ... Sergt. ... Hants, rejoined Sept. 1914, Sergt. Home.
(18, North View)

EADE, WILLIAM R. G. ... Pte. ... Hants, May 1914, Pte. India, Palestine, France.
(18, North View)

EADES, CHARLES ... Pte. ... Hants, Aug. 1915, Pte. Egypt.
(95, Upper Brook Street)

EAGLES, FRANK ... Pte. ... Middlesex, Apl. 1916, Pte. France. Wounded once.
(4, Union Street)

EAMES, EDGAR E. ... ... R.A.F., Sept. 16, 1918. Home.
(33, Tower Street)

EAMES, FREDERICK ... Corpl. ... R.M.L.I., 1909, Pte. North Sea.
(32, St. Faith's Road)

EAMES, GEORGE W. ... Pte. ... Hants, Sept. 1914, Pte. Gallipoli. Wounded, Aug. 10, 1915.
(33, Tower Street)

EAMES, WALTER ... Pte. ... Hants, Aug. 1916, Pte. R.A.F. Home.
(33, Tower Street)

EARLY, ALFRED ... ... Hants. R.E. France.
(33, Clifton Road)

EARLY, ALFRED E. ... ... R.A.S.C. (M.T.), July 1917. Home.
(1, New Road, Bar End)

EARLY, CHARLES R. ... Dr. ... R.A.S.C. (M.T.), Aug. 1914, Dr. France.
(33, Clifton Road)

EARLY, EDWARD ... Pte. ... Dorset, Aug. 1914, Pte. France. Wounded and taken Prisoner by Germans, Oct. 13, 1914.
(33, Clifton Road)

EARLY, FREDERICK ... Pte. ... R.M.L.C., Mch. 1918, Pte. France.
(33, Clifton Road)

EARLY, GEORGE ... Pte. ... Can. M.G.C., Jan. 1917, Pte. France.
(33, Clifton Road)

EARLY, WILFRED ... Gun. ... R.G.A., Dec. 24, 1915, Gun. France. Wounded, Nov. 17, 1917.
(90A, Chesil Street)

EASTHER, EDWARD A. ... ... R.N.A.S., Mch. 1917. Mudros.
(70, Eastgate Street)

EASTHER, HARRY E. ... Pte. ... Hants, Aug. 1916, Pte. Bedford. India.
(7, Newburgh Street)

EASTHER, WALTER C. ... Pte. ... Notts and Derby, Mch. 1916, Pte. K.O.S.B. Home.
(Milland House, Bar End)

EASTMAN, JESSE ... Corpl. ... R.A.S.C., Dec. 27, 1914, Pte. Dardanelles, France, Belgium. Wounded, Nov. 10, 1918.
(30, St. John's Terrace)

EDGERTON, ARTHUR G. ... C.F. ... C.F., 1917. France, Belgium.
(10, Thurloe Place)

EDMONDS, ARTHUR T. ... Corpl. ... Hants, Feb. 1916, Pte. France. Wounded, Oct. 14, 1918.
(26, Edgar Road)

WINCHESTER WAR SERVICE REGISTER

EDMONDS, PERCY J. (32, Christ Church Road)	A.-Capt.	Hants Y., Sept. 1914, Pte. R.F.A. France, Palestine.
EDMUNDS, ALBERT N. (31, Kingsgate Street)	Pte.	R.A.S.C., 1916, Pte. France.
EDMUNDS, ERNEST (6, Canon Street)	Pte.	Hants, May 1916, Pte. France. Wounded, Nov. 5, 1916.
EDWARDS, CHARLES (5, Highfield Terrace)	C.S.M.	Hants, Sept. 10, 1914, Sergt. A.G.S. France.
EDWARDS, EDWARD H. (11, St. James' Lane)	Corpl.	Aus. L.I., Oct. 1914, Pte. Egypt, Gallipoli, France. M.M., 1918.
✠ EDWARDS, FREDERICK (1, Greenhill Road)	Pte.	Hants, Mch. 1916, Pte. India, Egypt, Palestine. Wounded, Apl. 10, 1918. Taken Prisoner by Turks. *Died of Wounds, May 25, 1918, Jabez.*
EDWARDS, FREDERICK C. (3, Cathedral View)	Pte.	R.D.C., Sept. 1914, Pte. Leicester. France.
EDWARDS, HARRY (3, Westgate Lane)	R.Q.M.S.	R.B., 1903, Rfn. France. Wounded, Oct. 3, 1914, and Mch. 10, 1917.
EDWARDS, HERBERT (42, Upper Brook Street)	O.S.	R.N., Jan. 1917, O.S. North Sea.
EDWARDS, SIDNEY (42, Upper Brook Street)	Stoker	R.N., 1912, Stoker. Egypt, Dardanelles.
EDWARDS, SIDNEY A. (51, Wharf Hill)	Pte.	Devon, Feb. 1917, Pte. Wilts. France. Wounded six times. Taken Prisoner by Germans, Mch. 23, 1918.
EDWARDS, THOMAS J. (1A, Chester Road)	L.A.C.	R.N.A.S., Dec. 28, 1916, 1st A.M. R.A.F. France, Belgium.
EDWARDS, WILLIAM H. (1, Greenhill Road)	Gun.	R.G.A., Apl. 1916, Gun. France.
ELCOCK, ARTHUR (7, Ashley Terrace)	A.-Sergt.	Hants, Sept. 28, 1914, Pte. India, Siberia.
ELDERFIELD, CECIL R. (32, North Walls)	Pte.	R.E., Aug. 1914, Pte. Dardanelles, Serbia, Palestine, Salonica.
ELDERFIELD, PERCY L. (32, North Walls)	Staff Sergt.	Hants, Sept. 1914, Pte. Mesopotamia, India. Despatches 1916, 1917, and 1918, M.S.M. 1917, Serbian Silver Medal 1917.
ELDRIDGE, GEORGE S. (37, Milverton Road)	2nd A.M.	R.N.A.S., Oct. 1917, 2nd A.M. R.A.F. Home.
ELFORD, ALFRED (5, Boundary Street)	L.-Corpl.	Hants Y., Oct. 1915, Tpr. Hants. France, Belgium. Wounded, June 6, 1917.
ELFORD, WILLIAM E. (2, St. John's Street)	Pte.	Hants, 1897, Pte. France.
ELGEE, ERNEST A. (Chilcomb Manor)	Capt.	Remount Dept., 1915, Lieut. Home.
✠ ELGEE, HUGH (Chilcomb Manor)	Capt.	S.W.B., 2nd Lieut. Egyptian Army. Dardanelles. *Killed in Action, July 6, 1915, Gallipoli.*
ELKINS, ALFRED E. (16, Granville Place)	L.-Corpl.	Hants, Dec. 1914, Pte. R. Sussex. Mesopotamia, Persia, Afghanistan.

ELKINS, CHARLES H. (4A, Jewry Street)	Sergt.	Hants Y., rejoined Aug. 1914, L.-Corpl. R.G.A. France, Belgium.	
ELKINS, ERNEST H. (16, Granville Place)	Pte.	Hants, Nov. 1916, Pte. Leicester. Mesopotamia, Palestine, Syria.	
✠ ELKINS, FREDERICK (16, Granville Place)	Pte.	Dorset, Sept. 1914, Pte. Dardanelles. *Killed in Action, Aug. 19, 1915.*	
✠ ELKINS, FREDERICK A. (31, Eastgate Street)	Pte.	Hants, Sept. 11, 1914, Pte. India, Mesopotamia. Taken Prisoner by Turks. *Died, Aug. 7, 1916, Baghdad.* 3246 14TH (T.F.) BN	
✠ ELKINS, HERBERT J. (16, Granville Place)	Pte.	Hants, Aug. 1914, Pte. Dardanelles, France. Wounded, Aug. 10, 1915. *Died, Mch. 4, 1916, Rouen.* 9928 1ST BN	
ELKINS, JAMES (14, Hedges Buildings)	Pte.	Herts, Oct. 1916, Pte. Bedford, Lab. C. Home.	
ELKINS, ROBERT (Hamilton House, Canon St.)	P.O. (1st Class)	R.N., 1904, Stoker. North Sea.	
ELLERBY, WILLIAM J. (Fyfield, St. Faith's Road)	T.	R.N.V.R., Jan. 2, 1917, T. North Sea, White Sea, Aden. Despatches, 1917.	
ELLIOTT, FRANK L.	Com. Gun.	R.N., 1891, Boy. Gibraltar, Persian Gulf, Mesopotamia, North Sea; H.M.S. *Britomart, Southampton,* and *Birmingham.* Wounded, Apl. 4, 1918.	
ELLIS, ERNEST C. (63, Canon Street)	L.-Corpl.	Oxf. and Bucks L.I., 1899, Pte. India, Mesopotamia. Taken Prisoner by Turks at Kut.	
ELLIS, FREDERICK A. (63, Canon Street)	L.-Corpl.	Hants, 1911, Pte. India, Mesopotamia.	
ELLIS, PERCIVAL (63, Canon Street)	Dr.	R.A.S.C., Mch. 1915, Dr. Dardanelles, Egypt, Salonica.	
EMERY, CHARLES T. (1, Back Street, St. Cross)	Stoker	R.N., rejoined Dec. 1915, Stoker. Escort Duty at Sea.	
EMERY, WILLIAM E. (1, Back Street, St. Cross)	Pte.	R. Warwick, Oct. 18, 1918, Pte. Home.	
EMMETT, ALBERT E. (22, Eastgate Street)	L.-Corpl.	R.B., May 1916, Rfn. N. Fus. France.	
ENGLEFIELD, GEORGE H. (2, Saxon Road)	3rd A.M.	R.F.C., Oct. 1916, 3rd A.M. Home.	
ENGLEFIELD, THOMAS C. (14, Canute Road)	Bdr.	R.M.A., 1916, Gun. France, Belgium. Gassed twice, 1917. Despatches.	
EPPS, AUSTIN A. T. R. (34, Greenhill Road)	A.-R.Q.M.S.	R.B., 1897, Rfn. Home.	
ETHERIDGE, CHARLES R. (30, The Wharf)	Corpl.	R.N.A.S., Mch. 1917, A.M. R.A.F. Home.	
EUSTACE, JOSEPH (30, Tower Street)	Pte.	Hants, Aug. 1914, Pte. R.A.O.C. Dardanelles, France. Wounded, July 1915 and Aug. 1917.	
EVE, REGINALD W. (5, Stockbridge Road)	Lieut.	D.C.L.I., Dec. 1914, Pte. W. Somerset Y. France. Wounded, May 1915.	
EVE, VICTOR H. (5, Stockbridge Road)	Sergt.	Hants, Mch. 1916, Pte. Bedford. India.	

WINCHESTER WAR SERVICE REGISTER

✠ EVEREST, HAROLD R. (34, Hyde Close)	...	Rfn.	K.R.R.C., Sept. 1915, Rfn. France. Wounded, Sept. 18, 1916. *Died of Wounds, Sept.* 24, 1916, *Etaples.*
✠ EVEREST, REGINALD B. (34, Hyde Close)		Pte.	P.P.C.L.I., Dec. 1915, Pte. France. *Killed in Action, Oct.* 4, 1916, *France.*
EVERETT, ALBERT E. (5, Cathedral View)	...	A.B.	R.N., 1910. Boy. Home.
EVERETT, WILLIAM H. (Valentia, Park Road)		Lieut.	Central India Horse, Feb. 7, 1918, 2nd Lieut. India.
✠ EYLES, ARTHUR E. (13, Bridge Street)	...	Pte.	Hants, Jan. 1915, Pte. Dardanelles. *Killed in Action, Aug.* 6, 1915.
EYLES, CHARLES (4, Boundary Street)	...		R.A.S.C. (M.T.), Jan. 1917. France.
✠ EYLES, WILLIAM J. (10, Upper Brook Street)	...	Pte.	Hants, rejoined Mch. 1915, Pte. Dardanelles. Wounded, Aug. 6, 1915. *Died of Wounds, Oct.* 20, 1918.
FABER, CONRAD F. (15, Elm Road)	...	Corpl.	R.A.S.C., Aug. 1914, Pte. Egypt, Salonica.
FABIAN, ARTHUR W. (9, St. John's Road)	...	L.-Corpl.	Hants Y., Nov. 1914, Tpr. Hants. France, Italy.
FABIAN, HEDLEY G. (9, St. John's Road)	...	Tpr.	Hants Y., Nov. 1914, Tpr. Dragoon Gds., Grenadier Gds. France.
FACEY, JOHN F. (61, St. John's Street)		L.-Corpl.	K.R.R.C., Aug. 1914, Rfn. France. Wounded, July 28, 1915.
✠ FACEY, WILLIAM H. (25, Eastgate Street)	...	Staff Sergt.	R.E., 1900, Spr. Home. *Died, Aug.* 4, 1916, *Gravesend.*
FAITHFULL, ALFRED E. (8, Cathedral View)		1st A.M.	R.N.A.S., Mch. 1917, 2nd A.M. R.A.F. Home.
FAITHFULL, ARTHUR W. V. (62, Hyde Street)	...	Pte.	Hants, Sept. 1914, Pte. Mesopotamia.
FAITHFULL, FRANCIS E. N. (40, Christ Church Road)	...	Lieut.	Oxf. and Bucks L.I., 1915, 2nd Lieut. Rajputana Inf. Mesopotamia, India, Persia. Wounded, October 1915.
FAITHFULL, JOHN (7, Granville Place)	...	Gun.	R.G.A., 1904, Gun. Mesopotamia.
FAITHFULL, MALCOLM E. (40, Christ Church Road)	...	Lieut.	Inns of Court O.T.C., Oct. 1916, Pte. R.A.F. Home. Despatches.
FAITHFULL, REGINALD E. (66, Greenhill Road)		Staff Sergt.	R.F.A., Mch. 1917, Dr. Tank C. France.
FAITHFULL, WILLIAM J. (4, Nelson Road)	...	A.M.	R.A.F., A.M. Home.
FANCY, ARTHUR N. (22, Elm Road)	...	Pte.	Wilts, Aug. 1915, Pte. R.E. France. Gassed once.
FARMER, EDGAR (42, Upper Brook Street)	...	Sergt.	Hants, Sept. 1914, Pte. France. Wounded, Feb., 1916.

✠ FARMER, JOSEPH V. L. (42, Upper Brook Street)	Stoker	R.N., 1913, Stoker. North Sea, Salonica, France; H.M.S. *Paragon*. *Killed in Action*, Mch. 18, 1917, *off Dover*.	
FARMER, WILLIAM (42, Upper Brook Street)	Gun.	R.G.A., rejoined, 1914, Gun. France.	
FARNHAM, ALBERT E. (1, Riflemen's Cottages)		R.A.S.C. (M.T.), Oct. 1914. France, Belgium.	
FARNHAM, CECIL C. (1, Riflemen's Cottages)		R.M.L.I., May 1917. Russia, Turkey.	
FARNHAM, FREDERICK (1, Riflemen's Cottages)		Hussars, 1910. France, Belgium. Wounded twice.	
FARNHAM, PERCIVAL (1, Riflemen's Cottages)		Hussars, 1909. France. Wounded twice.	
FARRANT, WILLIAM G. (71, Upper Brook Street)	Corpl.	E. Surrey, 1906, Pte. Lond. France. Wounded, May 8, 1915, and Nov. 6, 1916.	
FARRELL, JAMES (10, Colebrook Place)	Pnr.	R.E., Aug. 1915, Pnr. France.	
FARRELL, THOMAS W. (7, St. John's Street)	Pte.	Hants, Sept. 1914, Pte. France. Wounded, Apl. 1915.	
FARROW, ERNEST H. (4, Gordon Avenue)	Sergt.	R.G.A., 1904, Gun. France. Wounded twice.	
FAYERS, WALTER C. (19, Parchment Street)	L.-Corpl.	Hants, Nov. 1915, Pte. R.D.C. Home.	
FEAR, EDWIN J. E. (Barfield, Bar End)	Lt.-Col.	Essex, 1901, 2nd Lieut. R.G.A. Home.	
FELTHAM, ERNEST N. (106, Stockbridge Road)	Sergt.	R.B., Mch. 1915, Rfn. Home.	
FELTHAM, ROBERT W. (106, Stockbridge Road)	B.Q.M.S.	M.G.C., Nov. 1915, Gun. L.A.M.B. Mesopotamia.	
FELTHAM, WALTER G. (106, Stockbridge Road)	Dr.	R.A.S.C., Sept. 1914, Dr. Salonica, Dardanelles.	
FELTON, FRANKLYN (41, St. Faith's Road)	Sergt.	Hants, June 1916, Pte. Home.	
FENNELL, FRANK W. R. (79, Hyde Street)	Lieut.	Hants Y., 1912, Tpr. M.G.C. France. Wounded, 1918.	
FENNELL, JAMES W. (79, Hyde Street)	Pte.	R.F.C., 1916, Pte. R.A.F. Home.	
FIELD, FREDERICK (29, Andover Road)	A.B.	R.N., 1893, A.B.	
FIELDER, ARTHUR C. (15, Chester Road)	Rfn.	R.B., rejoined, 1914, Rfn. France. Wounded and taken Prisoner by Germans, Aug. 29, 1914. Escaped, Nov. 1917. M.M.	
FIELDER, ARTHUR W. (62, Brassey Road)	Pte.	Lovat's Scouts, Oct. 1915, Pte. Con. Ran. Salonica, Egypt.	
✠ FIELDER, EDGAR J. (39, Upper High Street)	Lieut.	Hants, Sept. 1914, Pte. R. Lancs. France. *Killed in Action*, Apl. 8, 1917, *Arras*.	
✠ FIELDER, FRANK (39, Upper High Street)	C.S.M.	Hants, Aug. 1914, Pte. Gallipoli. *Missing*, Aug. 1915, *Suvla Bay*.	

WINCHESTER WAR SERVICE REGISTER

FIELDER, FREDERICK P. R. B. (62, Brassey Road)	Corpl.	...	Hants, June 1918, Pte. Germany.
✠ FIFIELD, JACK ... (1, Elm Road)	Pte.	...	Hants, May 1916, Pte. France. *Killed in Action*, Aug. 17, 1918, *Kemmel*.
FIGGINS, FRANK (63, St. John's Street)	A.B.	...	R.N., Oct. 1914, A.B. High Seas.
FIGGINS, THOMAS (63, St. John's Street)	A.B.	...	R.F.R., Aug. 1914, A.B. High Seas.
FINCH, ARTHUR F. (75, Sussex Street)	Sergt.	...	R.A.S.C. (M.T.), Oct. 1914, Pte. France. Wounded, June 1, 1918. M.M.
FINCH, JAMES H.- (2, New Road, Bar End)	Sergt.	...	R.A.S.C., 1913, Dr. France.
FINCH, JOHN (9, Canon Street)	Pte.	...	Hants, May 21, 1914, Pte. M.G.C. Mesopotamia, India, Egypt, France. Wounded, Jan. 27, 1917.
FINCH, RICHARD (9, Canon Street)		...	R.N. North Sea.
FINCH, THOMAS (9, Canon Street)	Sergt.	...	A.V.C., Feb. 1915, Pte. France. Wounded, 1918.
FINCH, WILLIAM... (22, Greenhill Road)	Sergt.	...	A.V.C., Apl. 1915, Pte. France.
FINCH, WILLIAM G. (5, Magdalen Hill)	Sergt.	...	K.R.R.C., rejoined Aug. 1914. France.
FINDEN, HARRY (5, Cossack Lane)		...	Hants, rejoined Aug. 1917. R.E. Home.
FISHER, EDWIN G. (1, Hyde Street)	Spr.	...	R.E., Jan. 1915, Spr. France.
FISHER, RICHARD H. (12, Ashley Terrace)	Corpl.	...	Hants, Dec. 1915, Pte. France, Belgium. Wounded, Apl. 12, 1917.
FISHER, RICHARD H. (10, Romsey Road)	Pte.	...	R.A.M.C., June 1917, Pte. Lab. C. France. Wounded, Mch. 1918.
FISHER, WILLIAM B. (1, Hyde Street)	Pte.	...	Hants, Apl. 1916, Pte. France. Wounded once.
✠ FITT, FREDERICK H. (21, St. Thomas Street)		...	A.I.F., 1917. France. *Killed in Action, Aug.* 1918.
FITT, RICHARD W. (21, St. Thomas Street)	W.T.	...	R.N.V.R., 1915, W.T. White Sea.
FLEET, ALFRED (38, St. John's Street)	Pte.	...	Devon, Nov. 1916, Pte. R.A.F. France.
FLEMING, CHARLES R. ... (7, Clifton Terrace)	Sergt.	...	Hants, Mch. 1915, Pte. Bedford. India.
FLEMING, GEORGE H. ... (7, Elm Road)	L.-Corpl.	...	Arg. and Suth. H., Oct. 1915, Pte. France. Wounded, Apl. 23, 1916, and Mch. 21, 1918.
FLETCHER, REGINALD A. P. (36, Hyde Close)	Tptr.	...	Hants Y., Oct. 1914, Boy. Hants. Home.
FLETCHER, STANLEY W. (36, Hyde Close)	R.S.M.	...	Hussars, 1890, Tpr. Hants Y. India.

E

WINCHESTER WAR SERVICE REGISTER

FLIGHT, FREDERICK H.   Hants Y., rejoined Aug. 4, 1914. King Edw.
(Edendarroch, Barnes Close)   Horse. France. Gassed once.

✠ FLUX, CHARLES   Pte.   Hants, 1911, Pte. India, France, Mesopotamia,
(49, Wharf Hill)   Dardanelles. Wounded three times. *Died from Pneumonia, Oct. 13, 1918, Mesopotamia.*

✠ FLUX, GEORGE H.   Sergt.   Hants, Aug. 1914, Pte. Mediterranean. *Drowned*
(13, Upper Wolvesey Terrace)   *in H.M.S. "Royal Edward," Aug. 13, 1915.*

FLUX, NICHOLAS   Pte.   R. Berks, June 1916, Pte. Devon, Lab. C. France.
(12, Wales Street)

FLUX, WALTER   Pte.   Hants, July 1916, Pte. France.
(6, Freelands Buildings)

✠ FLYNN, WILLIAM   Sergt.   S.W.B., Aug. 1914, Corpl. Dardanelles, Mesopo-
(10, Freelands Buildings)   tamia. Wounded, Aug. 12, 1915. *Killed in Action, Apl. 9, 1916.*

FOOT, JOHN   Corpl.   Hants, Aug. 1914, Pte. France. Wounded twice.
(28, Hyde Street)

✠ FORBES, JOHN   Pte.   Sea.H., June 1915, Pte. France. *Killed in*
(25, Sussex Street)   *Action, Aug. 19, 1916, France.*

FORD, ARTHUR C.   Bdr.   R.G.A., 1913, Boy. France. Gassed once.
(92, Brassey Road)

✠ FORD, C. H.   Pte.   Hants (T.F.), 1914, Pte. India, Mesopotamia.
    Killed in Action, Jan. 21, 1916, Kut.

FORD, CHARLES H.   Drummer   Lond., Oct., 1917, Drummer. Home.
(3, Greyfriars Villas)

FORD, CHARLES O.   Bdr.   R.G.A., May 1915, Boy. Home.
(92, Brassey Road)

FORD, GEORGE   Pte.   R.A.O.C., Oct. 1915, Pte. France.
(12, High Street)

FORD, HUBERT W.   R. Marines, 1912, Pte. North Sea, Mediterranean,
(10, Colebrook Place)   Black Sea; H.M.S. *Commonwealth, Lord Nelson,* and *Emperor of India.*

✠ FORD, VICTOR W.   Sergt.   Hants, 1912, Pte. India, Mesopotamia. Taken
(10, Colebrook Place)   Prisoner by Turks, Apl. 1916, Kut. *Died, Sept. 21, 1916.*

FORD, WILLIAM G.   Tpr.   Lond. Y., May 1916, Tpr. Egypt.
(3, Greyfriars Villas)

✠ FORDER, FRANCIS J.   Pte.   Hants, May, 1910, Pte. India, Mesopotamia.
(75, Parchment Street)   Taken Prisoner by Turks, Apl. 1916, Kut. *Died, July 7, 1916, Baghdad.*

FORSDICK, CHARLES G.   Sergt.   A.P.C., 1914, Pte. R.G.A. France, Germany.
(8, Ranelagh Road)

FORSTER, CHARLES   Rfn.   Hants, Mch. 1916, Pte. R.B. India, Egypt.
(2, The Weirs)

✠ FORSTER, HAROLD T.   Major   R. Berks, Pte. Northants. France, Belgium.
(14, Avenue Road)   Wounded, Oct. 1914. *Wounded and Missing (believed Killed), May 29, 1918.* D.S.O. and Bar, M.C. and Bar.

WINCHESTER WAR SERVICE REGISTER

FORSTER, WILLIAM J. ... (2, The Weirs)	Pte.	Hants, July 1917, Pte. Bedford. India.
FORSYTH, HARRY (9, Westgate Lane)	Sergt.	R.B., 1885, Rfn. France, Germany. Wounded, May 7, 1915.
FOSTER, ARTHUR F. ... (146, Stockbridge Road)	Corpl.	R.A.S.C. (M.T.), Jan. 1917, Pte. R.F., R. Sussex. France, Germany.
FOSTER, STANLEY (35, Upper Brook Street)	Stoker	R.N., July 1913, Stoker. Grand Fleet.
FOSTER, SYDNEY J. ... (6, Upper High Street)	Pte.	Somerset L.I., Mch. 1916, Pte. Wilts. Salonica.
FOULDS, HARRY (34, Nuns Road)	...	R.F.A., 1914. France, Egypt, Belgium, Salonica.
FOWLER, WILLIAM C. (24, Hyde Street)	Bdr.	R.G.A., Nov. 1915, Gun. France.
FOYLE, LESLIE J. C. ... (83, Middle Brook Street)	Spr.	R.A.M.C., Apl. 1917, Pte. R.E. France, Germany, Egypt. Wounded and taken Prisoner, May 27, 1918.
FRAMPTON, HENRY N. (7, Parchment Street)	Lieut.	R.E. Kent M. Rif., rejoined Aug. 1914. Hants. Dardanelles, Egypt, Salonica. Wounded once.
FRAMPTON, SYDNEY J. (36, Clifton Road)	Gun.	R.G.A., May 1916, Gun. France. Gassed once.
✠ FRANCIS, ALBERT E. ... (11, Andover Road)	Corpl.	Hants Y., May 1916, Tpr. Hants. France. *Killed in Action, Mch. 25, 1918, Arras.*
FRANCIS, ALBERT E. ... (23, Upper Brook Street)	Corpl.	Hants Y., 1915, Tpr. M.P. Home.
FRANCIS, FRANK (23, Upper Brook Street)	Pte.	Hants Y., 1915, Tpr. Hants. France.
FRANCIS, H. (23, Lower Brook Street)	...	R.A.S.C. Home.
FRANCIS, REGINALD T. (23, Upper Brook Street)	Pte.	Hants, 1914, Pte. Devon. France, Dardanelles. Wounded twice.
FRANKLIN, ARTHUR G. (55, St. John's Street)	Gun.	R.M.A., Sept. 1917, Gun. Home.
FRANKLIN, JOHN H. ... (62, St. Cross Road)	S.Q.M.S.	Hants Y., Aug. 4, 1914, Corpl. Home.
FRANKS, THOMAS G. ... (11, St. Paul's Hill)	Sergt.	R.B., 1895, Rfn. France.
FRASER, ALEXANDER J. (Culduthel, Links Road)	Major	R. Berks. France. Wounded, Mch. 11, 1915, and Aug. 7, 1916. M.C., Despatches twice.
FRASER, CHARLES J. ... (Links Road)	Lieut.	Lond. Rough Riders, Mch. 1915, Pte. R.A.S.C. France, Belgium, Germany.
FRASER, FRANCIS H. ... (Culduthel, Links Road)	...	D. of W. Regt. Staff. France. Wounded, Nov. 10, 1915. D.S.O., M.C., Despatches.
✠ FRASER, FRANK A. ... (Links Road) ...	Sig.	A.I.F., May 1916, Sig. France. *Killed in Action, Oct. 9, 1917, France.*
FRASER, HARRY (4, King Alfred Terrace)	Pte.	Lond. Scot., Apl. 1915, Pte. France, Salonica, Egypt, Palestine.

WINCHESTER WAR SERVICE REGISTER

✠ FREEMAN, CHARLES	...	L.-Corpl.	R.F., Jan. 1916, Pte. France. *Killed in Action, June* 11, 1917. M.M., 1917.
FREEMAN, GEORGE F. (84, Brassey Road)	...		R.M. Eng., June 1917. Home.
FREEMANTLE, ALBERT A. (81, Canon Street)	...	Stoker	R.N., July 1914, Stoker. North Sea.
FREEMANTLE, ERNEST (3, Clifton Terrace)	...	Sergt.	Hants, Sept. 7, 1914, Pte. Dardanelles, Egypt. Wounded, Aug. 6, 1916.
✠ FREEMANTLE, GEORGE W. (10, Ranelagh Road)	...	L.-Corpl.	Hants, May 1915, Pte. Oxf. and Bucks L.I. Flanders. *Missing, believed Killed, Aug.* 22, 1917, *Ypres.*
FREEMANTLE, HUBERT V. (10, Ranelagh Road)	...	Pte.	A.I.F., Mch. 1916, Pte. France. Taken Prisoner by Germans, Apl. 16, 1917.
FREEMANTLE, REGINALD M. (83, St. Cross Road)	...		R. Sussex, Sept. 1914. R.G.A. France. Wounded once.
FRENCH, CECIL G. (45, St. Catherine's Road)	...	Dr.	R.A.S.C., Aug. 1914, Dr. R.H.A. Egypt, Dardanelles.
FRENCH, CHARLES L. (45, St. Catherine's Road)	...	Corpl.	A.P.C., Dec. 1914, Pte. Home.
FRENCH, PERCY E. (6, Highcliffe Road)	...	Gun.	R.G.A., Mch. 1915, Gun. France.
FRIEND, ARCHIBALD F. (59, Colebrook Street)	...	Sergt.	Hants, Aug. 1914, Pte. India, Mesopotamia. M.S.M.
FRIEND, FREDERICK (8, St. John's Road)	...	L.-Corpl.	R.E., Jan. 1917, Spr. France.
FRIEND, LIONEL H. (28, The Square)	...	L.-Corpl.	Wilts, Jan. 1916, L.-Corpl. France. Wounded, Apl. 9, 1917. Taken Prisoner by Germans, Mch. 21, 1918.
FRIPP, THOMAS B. (71, Milverton Road)	...	Pte.	Hants, 1904, Pte. Dorset, Manch., Lab. C. Home.
FROOME, MONTAGUE (15, St. James' Villas)	...	Pte.	Hants, Feb. 1916, Pte. Wilts. Palestine, India, Egypt.
FROOME, STANLEY (16, St. James' Villas)	...	Sergt.	A.I.F., Pte. France. Wounded once.
FROST, FRANK (16, Cranworth Road)	...	L.-Corpl.	Lab. C., May 1917, Pte. Home.
FRY, WALTER F. (Hatherley Road)	...	Capt.	Devon, 1915, 2nd Lieut. Egypt. Despatches.
FUDGE, THOMAS E. S. (47, Andover Road)	...		T.R., Feb. 1917. R. Warwick. France. Wounded, Sept. and Oct. 1917.
FULBROOK, JOHN T. (53A, St. John's Street)	...		R.B., Aug. 1914. Home.
✠ FULFORD, ARCHIBALD C. (1, Queen's Road)	...	Pte.	Hants, Sept. 1914, Pte. Oxf. and Bucks L.I. Mesopotamia. Taken Prisoner by Turks, Apl. 29, 1916, Kut. *Died as P.O.W. between Apl. and Dec.* 1916.
✠ FULFORD, CLARENCE V. (1, Queen's Road)	...	Sergt.	Can. Inf., Mch. 1916, Pte. France, Belgium. Wounded, May 6, 1917. *Killed in Action, Aug.* 21, 1917, *Lens.*

WINCHESTER WAR SERVICE REGISTER

FULFORD, HORACE G. ... (1, Queen's Road)	...	Corpl. ...	Hants, Sept. 1914, Pte. France, Salonica, Turkey, Bulgaria, Serbia, Rumania.
FULFORD, WILFRED C. (1, Queen's Road)		Lieut. ...	Hants, Aug. 1914, Pte. Egypt.
FUREY, JAMES ... (11, Little Minster Street)	...	R.S.M. ...	R.B., 1898, Rfn. France. Wounded, Aug. 31, 1917. Taken Prisoner by Germans, May 27, 1918. M.C. 1916, D.C.M. 1917.
FUTCHER, WILLIAM (81, Canon Street)	...	Gun. ...	R.H.A., 1909, Gun. India, Mesopotamia. Taken Prisoner by Turks.
GALE, ALFRED C. (2, Clifton Road)	...	Major ...	Hants, Dec. 1914, Lieut. Anti-Aircraft. Home.
GALE, ANTHONY R. (2, Clifton Road)	...	Major ...	Inns of Court O.T.C., Nov. 1914. R.A.O.C. France.
✠ GALE, ARTHUR W. (2, Clifton Road)	...	Capt. ...	Dragoon Gds., Aug. 1914, Tpr. Life Gds. Flanders. D.S.O. 1916, Despatches 1916. *Killed in Action, April* 10, 1916.
GALE, WILLIAM (5, Fairfield Road)	...	Pte. ...	Hants, rejoined Aug. 1914, Pte. Dardanelles. Wounded, Aug. 10, 1915.
GALE, WILLIAM J. (18, St. Faith's Road)	...	Steward	R.N.A.S., Oct. 3, 1917, Steward. R.A.F. Home.
GALLAGHER, EDWARD M. (54, Sussex Street)	...	C.S.M. ...	R.B., 1900, Rfn. France. Wounded and Gassed, 1916.
GALLOP, ARTHUR E. ... (5, Freelands Buildings)	...	Sergt. ...	R.B., Rfn. France. Wounded, May 28, 1915, and Sept. 1, 1916.
GAMBLE, ALBERT E. ... (Hospital Lodge, Romsey Road)		Sergt. ...	R.A.S.C., Nov. 1914, Pte. K.R.R.C. France.
GAMBLE, JAMES ... (Hospital Lodge, Romsey Road)	...	C.P.O. ...	R.N., 1876. H.M.S. *Excellent.* Home.
GAMBLE, REGINALD J. (Hospital Lodge, Romsey Road)	...	P.O. ... (1st Class)	R.N., 1900. North Sea, Dardanelles; H.M.S. *Queen Elizabeth.*
GAMBLE, WALTER E. ... (9, Prison Quarters)	...	2nd A.M.	R.N.A.S., Jan. 1918, Boy. R.A.F. India.
GAMBLING, ERNEST ... (9, St. Catherine's Road)	...	A.M. ...	R.N.A.S., Feb. 1916, A.M. R.A.F. Home.
GANDY, JOHN S. ... (1, Lansdowne Avenue)	...		R.G.A. France.
✠ GARDINER, ARTHUR (85, Wales Street)	...	Pte. ...	Hants, May 10, 1916, Pte. Belgium, France. *Killed in Action, Oct.* 14, 1918.
GARDINER, CHRISTOPHER A. (5, Alswitha Terrace)	...	2nd Lieut.	R.A.M.C., Jan. 1915, Pte. R.G.A. Gallipoli.
✠ GARDINER, WILLIAM P. (85, Wales Street)	...	Pte. ...	Wilts, Jan. 20, 1916, Pte. France. *Killed in Action, Nov.* 2, 1916.
✠ GARDNER, CHARLES E. (41, Wales Street)	...	Stoker ...	R.N., July 3, 1918, Stoker. North Sea; H.M.S. *Ascot. Torpedoed and Drowned, Nov.* 10, 1918.

WINCHESTER WAR SERVICE REGISTER

GARDNER, FREDERICK E. C. ... (152, Stockbridge Road)	S.M.	...	R.A.S.C. (M.T.), Sept. 1915, Pte. R.E. France, Belgium.
GARDNER, FREDERICK W. (41, Wales Street)	Sergt.	...	Hants (T.F.), 1889, Pte. India, Mesopotamia, Egypt.
✠ GARDNER, FREDERICK W. J. (41, Wales Street)	Pte.	...	Hants, Nov. 1915, Pte. India, Egypt, Palestine. *Died of Malaria, Nov. 2, 1917, Alexandria.*
GARDNER, WALTER (Chilcomb)	...	...	Hants Y., May 1916. M.G.C. France.
GARDNER, WALTER G. (41, Wales Street)	Stoker	...	R.N., June 20, 1918, Stoker. North Sea.
GARFITT, JOHN S. (85, Greenhill Road)	Corpl.	...	K.R.R.C., 1901, Rfn. Northants, Lab. C., R.A.S.C. France.
GARMAN, WILLIAM G. ... (36, Greenhill Road)	C.S.M.	...	R.B., rejoined 1914, Sergt. Salonica.
GARRETT, ARTHUR (36, Hyde Street)	Pte.	...	Hants, 1918, Pte. R. Warwick, R.A.S.C. Germany.
✠ GARRETT, HARRY D. ... (36, Hyde Street)	Pte.	...	Hants, Aug. 1914, Pte. Egypt, Dardanelles. Wounded, Aug. 8, 1916. *Died at Sea, Aug. 15, 1916.*
GARRETT, WILLIAM C. (36, Hyde Street)	Pte.	...	Hants, Oct. 1917, Pte. Home.
GASCOIGNE, HERBERT ... (114, Stockbridge Road)	Pte.	...	Canadians, Nov. 1914, Pte. France.
GASSER, GEORGE (12, High Street)	Gun.	...	R.F.A., Sept. 1914, Gun. France.
GASSER, THOMAS J. ... (1, Chesil Cottages)	Pte.	...	Hants, 1912, Pte. India, Mesopotamia. Wounded, Jan. 6 and 21, 1916.
GATES, ROBERT S. (18, Brassey Road)	Pte.	...	R.A.S.C. (M.T.), May 1916, Pte. S.W.B. France. Taken Prisoner by Germans, Sept. 19, 1918.
GATRELL, ARTHUR E. ... (35, Hyde Close)	L.-Corpl.	...	Hants, Nov. 1914, Pte. India, Mesopotamia. Despatches.
GAY, ALBERT A. (12B, Romsey Road)	Boy T.	...	R.N., Dec. 1916, Boy. North Sea; H.M.S. *Queen Elizabeth* and *Peregrine.*
GAY, ALBERT D. (12B, Romsey Road)	Storeman		R.A.F., Sept. 1918, Storeman. Home.
GAYLER, HENRY (Abbey Hill Cott., Worthy Rd.)	Corpl.	...	R.B., rejoined May 1916, Rfn. Home.
GEARING, CHARLES (3, Freelands Buildings)	...		T.R. D.C.L.I. France. Wounded once.
GEARING, GEORGE A. (12, Princes' Buildings)	Pte.	...	Hants, Aug. 1914, Pte. Home.
GEE, WILLIAM E. (5, Romsey Road)	Boy	...	R.F.C., Nov. 1917, Boy. R.A.F. Home.
GEORGE, ARTHUR (3, Clausentum Road)	L.S.	...	R.N., 1911. North Sea, Baltic, Russia.
GEORGE, CHARLES T. ... (17, Jewry Street)			Hants, 1893. France.

WINCHESTER WAR SERVICE REGISTER

GEORGE, HARRY (3, Clausentum Road)	Pte.	Glos., June 1918, Pte. Lab. C. France.
GEORGE, WALTER (3, Clausentum Road)	L.S.	R.N., 1911, Boy. North Sea, Baltic.
GERAULT, ALBERT E. (148, Stockbridge Road)	Sergt.	R.A.S.C., Sept. 1914. Wilts. France.
GERAULT, GILBERT L. (148, Stockbridge Road)	Sig.	R.E., May 1917, Sig. Italy.
GERAULT, REGINALD (148, Stockbridge Road)		R.A.S.C., Aug. 1914. France, Salonica.
GERMAIN, ARTHUR H. (76, Stockbridge Road)		Hants, Mch. 1916, Pte. R. Berks, Lab. C. France.
✠ GERMAIN, HARRY E. (76, Stockbridge Road)	Lieut.	Canadians, 1914, Staff Sergt. France. Wounded, June 8, 1917. *Died of Wounds, July* 1917, *Calais.*
GIBB, FREDERICK G. (31A, High Street)	2nd Lieut.	Hants, Sept. 1914, Pte. Punjabi R. Mesopotamia.
✠ GIBSON, ALBERT E. (79, Wales Street)	Pte.	H.L.I., 1911, Pte. France. Wounded once. *Killed in Action, Sept.* 20, 1914.
GIBSON, BENJAMIN J. (52, North Walls)	2nd Lieut.	R.G.A., 1907, Gun. France.
GIBSON, GEORGE T. (7, Ilex Terrace)	Drummer	Hants, 1914, Drummer. India, Mesopotamia.
GIBSON, JAMES P. (52, North Walls)		Lancs. Fus., 1915. Home.
GIBSON, JOHN H. (The Cottage, Westgate Lane)	Pte.	Hants, Pte. India, Egypt.
GIBSON, JOHN H. H. (16, The Weirs)	Pte.	Hants, Oct. 1915, Pte. India, Egypt.
GIBSON, ROBERT (68, Water Lane)	C.S.M.	R.B., 1902, Rfn. France. M.S.M.
GIBSON, ROBERT C. (52, North Walls)	Pte.	Hants, Nov. 1914, Pte. France. M.M. 1917.
GIBSON, WILLIAM C. (48, North Walls)	Pte.	Hants, Sept. 4, 1914, Pte. Lab. C. France.
GIBSON, WILLIAM E. R. (52, North Walls)	Pte.	R.A.S.C., 1915, Pte. France, Salonica. Wounded, 1917.
GIFFORD, JACK R. (Lynch Cottage, Bereweeke Avenue)	A.-Major	R.F.A., Nov. 1915, 2nd Lieut. France. Gassed, Apl. 8, 1918. M.C. 1917.
✠ GIFFORD, NORGA E. (Kinross, Barnes Close)	Capt.	Leicester, Sept. 1914, 2nd Lieut. France. *Killed in Action, July* 14, 1916, *Bazentin le Petit.*
GIFFORD, STANLEY (19, Saxon Road)		Hants Y., Sept. 1914. Home.
GILBERT, ALFRED (82, Canon Street)	Rfn.	K.R.R.C., 1912, Rfn. France. Taken Prisoner by Germans, Oct. 1914.

WINCHESTER WAR SERVICE REGISTER

GILBERT, FRANK (82, Canon Street)			R.A., 1912. India.
GILES, EDWARD C. (7, Greenhill Avenue)			R.N., 1893.
✠ GILLETT, DAVID E. (3, Cross Street)		Pte.	Hants, Aug. 1914, Pte. Dardanelles. *Killed in Action, Aug.* 10, 1915.
GILLETT, WILLIAM T. (4, Cross Street)		Spr.	R.E., Aug. 1914, Spr. France.
GILLETT, WILLIAM T., jun. (4, Cross Street)		Bug.	R.E., Mch. 1917, Bug. Home.
GILLIAN, FREDERICK G. (34, Jewry Street)			R.B., Sept. 1916, Rfn. R.A.F. Home.
GILLINGHAM, EDWARD E. (31, St. John's Road)		Dr.	R.A.S.C., Sept. 1914, Dr. Salonica.
GILLINGHAM, HERBERT (1, Chester Road)		Dr.	R.A.S.C., 1914, Dr. Salonica, Egypt.
GILLINGHAM, HORACE L. (1, Chester Road)		Pte.	A.V.C., 1915, Pte. France. Gassed once.
GILLINGHAM, PERCY (30, North Walls)		Pte.	R.A.M.C., 1914, Pte. Home.
GILLINGHAM, PERCY F. (22, Saxon Road)			R.A.M.C., 1916. Home.
GILLINGHAM, SIDNEY C. (1, Chester Road)		Pte.	Hants, Oct. 1916, Pte. Worc. France, Salonica, Egypt. Wounded, Nov. 20, 1917.
GILLMAN, WILLIAM F. (27, Highcliffe Road)			R.E., Sept. 1916. France.
GILLSON, ROBERT M. T. (The Beeches, Andover Road)		A.-Lt.-Col.	Wilts, 1899, 2nd Lieut. France. Wounded, Mch. 10 and Sept. 25, 1915; July 8, 1916. D.S.O. 1916, Russian Order of St. Anne 1916, Despatches four times.
GILMOUR, FRANK V. (36, Hyde Abbey Road)		Pte.	Hants, Oct. 1914, Pte. Mesopotamia. Wounded, Mch. 1917.
GILMOUR, GEORGE (37, Monks Road)		A.-Q.M.S.	R.B., C.-Sergt. Bedford Vol. Home. '
✠ GILMOUR, WALTER E. (36, Hyde Abbey Road)		Pte.	Hants, Dec. 1914, Pte. Mesopotamia. Wounded, Jan. 21, 1916. *Died of Wounds, Jan.* 24, 1916.
GILMOUR, WILLIAM G. (20, St. Clement Street)		Gun.	R.A., Gun. France. Gassed, May 1918.
GILMOUR, WILLIAM J. (Uplands Lodge, Romsey Rd.)		Gun.	R.G.A., Nov. 1915, Gun. France.
GINN, STANLEY (64, Hyde Street)		Capt.	Hants, 1912, Pte. E. Yorks. France, Egypt. Wounded twice.
GLADDEN, CLAUDE W. (80, Wales Street)		L.-Corpl.	A.V.C., 1910, Pte. France.
GLASS, THOMAS S. (37, Kingsgate Street)		Pte.	Hants Y., Nov. 1916, Tpr. R.W.K. Home.
GLASS, WILLIAM D. (Teg Down Farm)		Lieut.	Hants, 1911, Pte. E. Lancs. India, Mesopotamia.

WINCHESTER WAR SERVICE REGISTER

GLASSPOOL, HARRY (62, Lower Brook Street)			Somerset L.I., Mch. 1916. Dorset. France.
GLENISTER, FREDERICK G. (7, Leckford Cottages)		C.-Sergt.	R.B., rejoined Aug 5, 1914, Corpl. France.
GLEW, REGINALD A. (10, Culverwell Gardens)			Devon. R.W.S., Monmouth. Home.
GLOVER, ALBERT E. (64, Chesil Street)		Pte.	Worc., Sept. 1916, Pte. Somerset L.I. India.
GLOVER, CHRISTOPHER (7, Cranworth Road)		L.-Corpl.	Devon, 1900, Pte. France, Italy. Wounded, Oct. 1914.
GLOVER, CHRISTOPHER T. (29, Arbour Terrace)		Pte.	Hants, Oct. 1915, Pte. Somerset L.I. India, Egypt.
GLOVER, EDGAR (7, Cranworth Road)		Pte.	Hants, Jan. 1914, Pte. India, Mesopotamia, Persia.
✠ GLOVER, THOMAS G. (64, Chesil Street)		Pte.	Hants, Aug. 1914, Pte. Mesopotamia. Wounded, Jan. 29, 1915. *Killed in Action, Jan.* 21, 1916.
GLOVER, WILLIAM (7, Cranworth Road)			Hants, rejoined July 1917, Pte. R.A.M.C. Home.
GOATER, FRANK L. (31, Cheriton Road)		Pte.	K.R.R.C., Sept. 1916, Rfn. Lab. C. France.
GODDARD, BERNARD R. (25, Edgar Road)		Capt.	4th Hants (T.F.), 2nd Lieut., 1897. India, Palestine. Wounded, Nov. 23, 1917. Despatches 1917.
GODDARD, FRANK (12, Highcliffe Road)		Gun.	R.G.A., Nov. 1914, Gun. Dardanelles, France. Wounded, Jan. 16, 1916.
✠ GODDARD, HENRY C. (7, Lower Wolvesey Terrace)		Stoker	R.N., Sept. 1914, Stoker. Falkland Islands. *Drowned, Dec.* 29, 1916.
GODDARD, WILLIAM G. (7, Lower Wolvesey Terrace)		Pte.	Worc., Aug. 5, 1915, Pte. Home.
GODFREY, EDWARD F. (Piper's Farm, Weeke)		Sergt.	R.F.C., Feb. 1916, 2nd A.M. R.A.F. Egypt.
GODLEY, EDWIN T. (47, Tower Street)		C.S.M.	Hants, rejoined Aug. 1914, Sergt. Bedford. India.
✠ GODSELL, ALFRED P. (6, Staple Garden)		Gun.	R.G.A., Sept. 1915, Gun. France. *Killed in Action, Apl.* 27, 1918, *Brandhoek.*
GODSELL, WILLIAM J. (6, Staple Garden)		Pte.	Hants, Mch. 1916, Pte. Egypt, Palestine, France.
GODWIN, ARTHUR H. V. (64, Eastgate Street)		Major	Hants, July 1916, Pte. Border R. India, Persia.
GODWIN, FREDERICK W. (34, Romsey Road)		Stoker	R.N., May 1915, Boy. North Sea.
GODWIN, ROBERT S. (64, Eastgate Street)		Corpl.	R.A.O.C., Sept. 1915. France.
GODWIN, WILLIAM J. (19, Highcliffe Road)		Sergt.	Hants, Nov. 1915, Pte. France.
GOLDING, EDWARD C. (8, Granville Place)		Pte.	A.V.C., Sept. 1917, Pte. Home.

WINCHESTER WAR SERVICE REGISTER

GOLDING, ERNEST J. (6, Colebrook Place)	Pte.		Hants Y., Sept. 1914, Tpr. Hants. France, Italy. Wounded, May 1918.
GOODALL, ALBERT J. (57, St. John's Street)	Pte.		Hants, 1915, Pte. France.
GOODALL, SAMUEL (5, Mants Lane)	A.B.		R.N., 1910. North Sea, Mediterranean; H.M.S. *Hercules* and *Caesar*.
GOODCHILD, FREDERICK D. (71, Upper Brook Street)	A.B.		R.N., July 1914, Boy. North Sea.
GOODCHILD, GEORGE F. (71, Upper Brook Street)			R.A.S.C., 1915. Italy, France.
✠ GOODCHILD, GEORGE J. (40, Eastgate Street)	L.-Corpl.		Hants, Aug. 1914, Pte. India, Mesopotamia. Taken Prisoner by Turks, Apl. 28, 1916. *Died, Dec. 25, 1916, Angora.*
GOODCHILD, WALTER D. (71, Upper Brook Street)	Stoker		R.N., 1913, Stoker. North Sea.
GOODCHILD, WILLIAM J. (93, Upper Brook Street)	Sergt.		R.B., Aug. 4, 1914, Rfn. France. Wounded, July 6, 1916, and Apl. 1918. D.C.M.
GOODCHILD, WILLIAM R. (100, Colebrook Street)	S.M.		Can. M. Rif., Nov. 1914, Rfn. France. D.C.M. and Bar, M.M.
GOODE, FRANCIS W. (4, South View)	R.S.M.		R.B., 1898, Rfn. France. Wounded three times, Mch. 14, 1915, Nov. 11, 1918.
GOODENOUGH, MATTHEW G. (13, Wales Street)			Coldstream Gds., Apl. 1918. Home.
GOODMAN, ROBERT C. (2, Riflemen's Cottages)	Rfn.		K.R.R.C., May 1915, Rfn. Home.
✠ GOODYEAR, ARTHUR W. (64, Sussex Street)	Pte.		R.M.L.I., 1914, Pte. Dardanelles. *Killed in Action, May 1915, Dardanelles.*
GORTON, CHRISTOPHER H. (Badingham, Bereweeke Rd.)	Pte.		A.I.F., Oct. 1916, Pte. France. Wounded, Nov. 1917.
GORTON, HORACE G. (Badingham, Bereweeke Rd.)	Lieut.		R.N., Lieut. H.M.S. *Platypus*, *Zealandia*, *Vernon*, and *Maidstone*.
GORTON, ROBERT P. (Badingham, Bereweeke Rd.)	Lieut.		R.A.S.C., June 1917, 2nd Lieut. France.
GOSLING, ALFRED (7, Cossack Lane)	Pte.		Hants, Sept. 1914, Pte. France, Dardanelles. Wounded, Sept. 1916. M.M. 1917.
GOSLING, CHARLES (7, Cossack Lane)	Pte.		Hants Y., Nov. 1917, Tpr. Hants. France. Taken Prisoner by Germans, Mch. 28, 1918.
GOSLING, LEONARD (7, Cossack Lane)	Stoker		R.N., 1913, Stoker. Grand Fleet, H.M.S. *Furious*.
✠ GOULD, HENRY C. H. (Bereweeke House, Bereweeke Road)	2nd Lieut.		R.F.A., Feb. 1916, 2nd Lieut. France. Wounded once. *Died of Wounds, Apl. 15, 1917, Arras.*
✠ GOULDBY, PERCY (66, Water Lane)	Pte.		Hants Y., Oct. 1914, Tpr. Hants. Italy, France, Belgium. Wounded, Oct. 27, 1917. *Killed in Action, Sept. 4, 1918, near Messines.*
GOULDING, ARCHIBALD F. C. (150, Stockbridge Road)	Pte.		R.A.S.C. (M.T.), Sept. 20, 1916, Pte. France, Macedonia, Serbia.

WINCHESTER WAR SERVICE REGISTER

GOULDING, CECIL F. ... (1, Alexandra Terrace)		R.A.S.C. (M.T.), Apl. 20, 1916. France, Belgium, Germany.
GRACE, REGINALD T. ... (St. Margaret's, Culver Close)	Corpl.	Bedford Y., Nov. 1914, Tpr. R.A.S.C. (M.T.). Mesopotamia, India, France.
GRANT, ALBERT L. ... (22, St. Thomas Street)	Dr.	R.H.A., Dec. 1916, Dr. Home.
GRANT, ARTHUR E. ... (22, St. Thomas Street)	L.-Corpl.	Hants, Sept. 1914, Pte. India, Mesopotamia.
GRANT, FREDERICK A. (Guildhall, High Street)	Corpl.	K.R.R.C., Aug. 1916, Rfn. A.P.C. Home.
GRANT, FREDERICK C. ... (22, St. Thomas Street)	Sergt.	Hants, Feb. 1916, Pte. India, Egypt, France, Germany.
GRANT, FREDERICK W. (11, Hyde Close)	Pte.	Hants, July 1914, Pte. India.
GRANT, GEORGE H. ... (Cemetery Lodge, Alresford Rd.)	L.-Corpl.	Hants, Apl. 1915, Pte. India, Egypt.
GRANT, GERALD A. ... (36B, Clifton Road)	Dr.	R.A.S.C., 1911, Dr. France, Egypt.
GRANT, LEONARD H. ... (5, Canon Street)	Pte.	Hants, July 1914, Pte. Bedford. India.
GRANT, LIONEL E. ... (22, St. Thomas Street)	Sergt.	Welsh, Sept. 1914, Pte. France, Salonica. Gassed. 1918.
GRANT, NORMAN H. ... (22, St. Thomas Street)	Pte.	Hants, July 1916, Pte. India, Egypt, France, Germany. Wounded, July 22, 1918.
GRANT, WILLIAM ... (36B, Clifton Road)	...	Hants, 1915. Home.
GRAVES, ARCHIBALD W. (45, Monks Road)	Pte.	T.R., Pte. Hants. Home.
GRAVES, FREDERIC S. ... (45, Monks Road) ...	Pte.	Essex, Pte. Norfolk. France. Wounded once. Taken Prisoner by Germans, Apl. 15, 1918.
GRAY, A. E. ...	Pte.	Devon Cyc., 1916, Pte. Lab. C. France.
GRAY, ALFRED C. ... (21, Union Street)	Pte.	R. Warwick, Jan. 1918, Pte. France.
GRAY, ERIC ... (20A, St. Peter's Street)	Spr.	E. Surrey, 1914, Pte. R.E. France.
GRAY, JOHN ... (20A, St. Peter's Street)	Pte.	Hants, 1916, Pte. Home.
GRAY, THOMAS W. ... (21, Union Street)	Pte.	R. Berks, Oct. 1916. R.M.L.I. France. Wounded, Sept. 4 and Sept. 27, 1918.
GREASELEY, ALFRED ... (1, Poulsome Place)	Rfn.	K.R.R.C., 1910, Rfn. Salonica. Wounded, Nov. 10, 1914.
GREEN, ALBERT G. ... (33, Greenhill Road)	Pte.	Hants, May, 1916, Pte. Palestine, Egypt, India. Wounded, Dec. 1917.
GREEN, ALFRED J. ... (31, St. Catherine's Road)	Corpl.	R.A.S.C. (M.T.), Sept. 1916, Pte. Home.
GREEN, BERTIE ... (31, St. Catherine's Road)	Pte.	Hants, Jan. 1918, Pte. Somerset L.I. France.

WINCHESTER WAR SERVICE REGISTER

GREEN, ERNEST (33, Greenhill Road)	... Pte.	...	Hants, Oct. 1915, Pte. India, Mesopotamia.
GREEN, FREDERICK (33, Greenhill Road)	... Pte.	...	Hants, 1911, Pte. Mesopotamia, Persia.
GREEN, FREDERICK A. (65, Wales Street)	... Sergt.	...	R. Berks, 1911, Pte. Belgium, France. Gassed, Mch. 1915, and Jan. 1917.
GREEN, FREDERICK C. J. (34, Parchment Street)	... Corpl.	...	M.M.P., Feb. 1915, L.-Corpl. France.
GREEN, GEORGE A. (10, Tower Street)	... Pte.	...	Hants, Dec. 1915, Pte. M.G.C. France.
GREEN, GEORGE C. (10, Tower Street)	... Pnr.	...	R.A.S.C., rejoined 1915, Pte. R.E. France.
GREEN, HAROLD (33, Greenhill Road)	... Corpl.	...	R.E., 1911, Spr. France. Wounded, Nov. 1914.
GREEN, HAROLD A. (54, Parchment Street)	... Corpl.	...	Hants Y., Nov. 1914. Tpr. Hants. France. Wounded, Mch. 4 and Sept. 22, 1917. M.M. 1917.
GREEN, JAMES (32, Greenhill Road)	... C.S.M.	...	R.B., 1897, Bandsman. France. Wounded, May 21, 1916.
GREEN, JOHN C. (10, Tower Street)	... Pte.	...	Hants, Nov. 1915, Pte. India, Mesopotamia.
✠ GREEN, JOSEPH C. (20, Hyde Church Path)	...		Hants, Dec. 1914, Pte. Gallipoli. *Wounded and Missing (believed Killed).*
GREEN, PERCY W. (71, Sussex Street)	... Sergt.	...	R.F.C., Oct. 1915, 2nd A.M. R.A.F. France, Belgium.
GREEN, RAYMOND (8, Sussex Street)	... Spr.	...	R.E., Nov. 1915, Spr. Salonica.
GREEN, S. F.	... L.-Corpl.		Hants Y., 1914, Tpr. Hants. France, Belgium. Wounded, Aug. 20, 1918.
GREEN, WILLIAM (63, Milverton Road)	... 2nd A.M.		R.F.C., Aug. 1917, 2nd A.M. R.A.F. France.
GREEN, WILLIAM G. (31, St. Catherine's Road)	... L.-Corpl.		D.L.I., Sept. 1916, Pte. France. Wounded, June 26, 1917.
GREEN, WILLIAM J. R. (10, Tower Street)	... Pte.		Hants, Nov. 1915, Pte. India, Mesopotamia. Wounded, Feb. 9, 1917.
GREENER, CHARLES E. (44, Upper Brook Street)	... Dr.	...	R.A.S.C., Dec. 1914, Dr. Mesopotamia.
GREENER, RONALD (60, Canon Street)	... Pte.	...	Hants, Nov. 1916, Pte. France.
GREENFIELD, GEORGE C. (10, Alswitha Terrace)	... Bandsman		Hants, 1913, Bandsman. Mesopotamia, India.
GREENSTOCK, CHARLES (35, Tower Street)	... Sergt.	...	Hants, 1907, Boy. Dardanelles. Wounded, Aug. 6, 1915. Despatches, 1915.
GREENSTOCK, DAVID (35, Tower Street)	... C.S.M.	...	R.E., rejoined 1914, Corpl. France. D.C.M. 1917, Despatches 1918, Belgian Croix de Guerre, 1918.

WINCHESTER WAR SERVICE REGISTER

✠ Greenstock, Frederick (35, Tower Street)	...	Pte.	Dorset, 1905, Pte. France. Wounded, Oct. 11, 1914. Despatches 1914. *Killed in Action, Oct.* 14, 1914.
Greenstock, Thomas ... (35, Tower Street)	...	Staff Sergt.	Somerset L.I., rejoined 1914, Pte. France. Wounded, 1917.
Gregory, Cyril (5, Abbey Passage)	...	Pte.	Hants, 1911, Pte. India, Mesopotamia.
Gregory, Wilfred G. (5, Abbey Passage)	...	Bdr.	R.G.A., 1910, Gun. France. Wounded, July 1916 and May 1917.
Greig, John P. S. ... (3, St. James' Crescent)	...	A.-Major	R.E., 1908, 2nd Lieut. Flanders. Croix de Guerre 1917.
Griffin, Arthur (6, Clausentum Road)	...	Corpl.	Hants, Pte. France, Germany.
Griffin, Arthur E. ... (15, Eastgate Street)	...	Pte.	Hants, Nov. 1915, Pte. France.
Griffin, Bertram (3, Cranworth Road)	...	Pte.	Hants, Sept. 1914, Pte. Dardanelles. Wounded, Aug. 9, 1915.
Griffin, Douglas H. (Prison, Romsey Road)	...	Pte.	T.R., Dec. 1917, Pte. R. Warwick. France.
Griffin, Edmund W. (10, Union Street)	...	Pte.	Hants, June 1916, Pte. Salonica.
Griffin, Frank (3, Cranworth Road)	...	Pte.	Devon Y., Nov. 1915, Tpr. R.A.S.C. Egypt, Palestine, France.
Griffin, Herbert W. (15, Eastgate Street)	...	Pte.	T.R., May 1917, Pte. Somerset L.I. France.
Griffith, Charles E. (Maes Gwyn, Sleeper's Hill)	...	Major	R.G.A., 1900, 2nd Lieut. Flanders, France.
Griffith, Hugh F. R. (Maes Gwyn, Sleeper's Hill)	...	Capt.	Hants, 1905, 2nd Lieut. R. Can. R. Flanders, France.
Griffith, Llewelyn ... (Maes Gwyn, Sleeper's Hill)	...	Major	Welsh, 1902, 2nd Lieut. Indian Army. France, India. Despatches 1915.
Grist, Reginald W. ... (27, Wales Street)	...	Dr.	R.A.S.C., Dec. 1915, Dr. Salonica, Malta.
Grist, William A. (6, Mant's Lane)	...	Sergt.	Hants (T.F.), 1912, Pte. India, Egypt, Palestine, France. Wounded, 1917 and June 1918.
Grout, Arthur G. (168, High Street)	...	Sergt.	Hants Y., Nov. 1914, Tpr. Hants. France.
Grout, Harry ... (3, Nuns Walk)	...	A.-C.Q.M.S.	K.R.R.C., 1894, Rfn. France.
Grove-Jones, Leonard (12, Arthur Road)	...		R.A.F., June 17, 1918. Home.
✠ Groves, Alfred (1, St. George's Terrace)	...	Tpr.	Lancers, 1901, Tpr. France. *Killed in Action, Nov.* 30, 1917.
Groves, Arthur (1, St. George's Terrace)	...	Bdr.	R.G.A., 1911, Gun. France. Wounded, June 2, 1917.
Groves, Austin J. (89a, Chesil Street)	...	1st A.M.	R.N.A.S., A.M. R.A.F. Home.

WINCHESTER WAR SERVICE REGISTER

GROVES, ERNEST (1, St. George's Terrace)		Pte.	R. Warwick, Jan. 9, 1918, Pte. France. Wounded, Sept. 2, 1918.
✠ GROVES, GEORGE (4, Lower Brook Street)		L.S.	R.N., 1905. *Drowned, Nov. 1914, in H.M.S. "Good Hope."*
✠ GUDGEON, ATHOL E. (St. John's Mead, St. John St.)		Lieut.	R.N.R., Nov. 10, 1914, A.-Lieut. North Sea; H.M.S. *Quail* and *Etterick*. Torpedoed, July 1917. *Died of Wounds, Aug. 27, 1917, Haslar.*
GUDGEON, BASIL F. H. (St. John's Mead, St. John St.)		C.F.	C.F., Nov. 1917, Capt. Palestine.
✠ GUDGEON, ROBERT E. (St. John's Mead, St. John St.)		Capt.	Hants Y., 1907, Tpr. R.F.A., T.M.B. France. Wounded, Mch. 21, 1918. M.C. 1917. *Died of Wounds, Apl. 2, 1918, Mt. D'Origny.*
GUDGEON, STANLEY E. (St. John's Mead, St. John St.)		A.-Major	R.G.A. (T.F.), Mch. 1914, 2nd Lieut. France. M.C. 1917.
GUMMERSON, ERNEST (1, Greenhill Terrace)		S.Q.M.S.	Lancers, 1901, Tpr. France. Gassed, May 14, 1915.
GURD, WILLIAM H. (19, Owen's Road)		Sergt.	Hants, Aug. 1914, Sergt. Gallipoli. Wounded, Aug. 9, 1915.
✠ GYE, DENISON A. (Piper's Field, Chilbolton Avenue)		Capt.	Zion Mule Corps, 1915. R.H.A. Dardanelles, France. *Killed in Action, Feb. 28, 1917, Combles.*

HACKETT, HAROLD J. (26, Fairfield Road)		Sergt.	R. Warwick, Aug. 22, 1918, Pte. Germany.
HACKETT, WILLIAM H. (26, Fairfield Road)		Writer	R.N., Nov. 22, 1914, Writer. Home.
HADLEY, HAROLD G. H. (32, St. Catherine's Road)		Cook's Mate	R.N., June 1915, 2nd Cook's Mate. Dover Patrol.
HAINES, ALBERT H. (10, Canute Road)		Pte.	T.R., May 1917, Pte. Hants, R. Berks. France. Wounded once.
HAINES, ALFRED GEORGE (9, Brandon Terrace)		Pte.	T.R., Sept. 1917, Pte. Somerset L.I., Lab. C. France. Wounded, Apl. 14, 1918.
HAINES, ARTHUR G. (17, Cross Street)		Spr.	R.E., Oct. 1916, Spr. France, Belgium. Gassed, July 1917.
✠ HAINES, CHARLES (26, Colson Road)		Rfn.	K.R.R.C., Nov. 1914, Rfn. France. *Missing, July* 1, 1916.
✠ HAINES, GEORGE (10, Canute Road)		Pte.	E. Surrey, Aug. 1914, Pte. R. Berks. France. Wounded twice. *Missing (believed Killed), May* 3, 1917.
HAINES, HARRY (9, Brandon Terrace)		Sergt.	Hants, Sept. 1914, Pte. India, Persian Gulf, Mesopotamia, Egypt, Palestine, France. Wounded, Nov. 22, 1916, and Aug. 26, 1918.
HAINES, HERBERT C. (148, Stockbridge Road)		L.-Corpl.	R.A.S.C. (M.T.), Oct. 1916, Pte. France. Gassed, 1917.
HALL, ALBERT B. (88, Wales Street)		Pte.	Hants (T.F.), 1906, Pte. Hants, Yorks. India, Mesopotamia.

WINCHESTER WAR SERVICE REGISTER

HALL, ARCHIBALD F. (54, Lansdowne Terrace)	Bdr.	R.G.A., Dec. 1916, Gun. France, Germany.
HALL, ARTHUR J. (23, Andover Road)	Pte.	Hants, 1907, Pte. Mesopotamia.
HALL, CHARLES (44, Sussex Street)	Pte.	R.A.O.C., 1917, Pte. Home.
HALL, EDWARD (82, Wales Street)	Gun.	R.G.A., Nov. 1915, Gun. France, Germany.
HALL, ERNEST C. (42, Hatherley Road)	1st A.M.	R.N.A.S., Aug. 25, 1916, A.M. R.A.F. France.
HALL, FREDERICK J. (64, Colebrook Street)	Pte.	R.A.S.C. (M.T.), Apl. 1917, Pte. France. Gassed, Nov. 1918.
HALL, GEORGE E. (9, Canute Road)	Gun.	R.G.A., Feb. 1916, Gun. France.
HALL, GERALD A. (5, Nuns Road)	Pte.	R.A.S.C., June 1916, Baker. R.F. France, Belgium, Italy.
✠ HALL, H. C. (32, Hyde Street)	2nd Lieut.	Hants Y., Tpr. Wilts. *Killed in Action*, 1918.
HALL, HARRY (25, Hyde Abbey Road)	Tpr.	Lond. Y., May 1915, Tpr. Egypt. Wounded once.
HALL, HECTOR A. (88, Wales Street)	Spr.	R.E., Nov. 1915, Spr. Egypt.
HALL, HERBERT G. (9, Canute Road)	2nd A.M.	R.A.F., Mch. 23, 1916, 2nd A.M. Home.
HALL, JAMES FREDERICK (64, Colebrook Street)	Sergt.	Devon, Mch. 1916, Pte. Wilts, K. Liverp. France.
HALL, JOSHUA (30, Colson Road)	C.S.M.	R.B., rejoined Sept. 1914, Rfn. Lond. France.
HALL, LEONARD R. (23, Andover Road)	Pte.	Hants, Apl. 1916, Pte. Wilts. Salonica.
HALL, PERCIVAL H. (44, Brassey Road)	Gun.	R.G.A., May 1916, Gun. Home.
HALL, RICHARD (3, Hyde Church Lane)		Coldstream Gds., Dec. 2, 1916, Tpr. France. Wounded, Sept. 8, 1917, and Aug. 21, 1918.
HALL, ROLAND F. (23, Andover Road)	Pte.	Hants, Apl. 1916, Pte. Wilts. France, Salonica.
HALL, T. P. (32, Hyde Street)	2nd Lieut.	Hussars, 2nd Lieut. Home.
HALL, THOMAS W. (3, Chester Road)	Pte.	Hants, May 1915, Pte. Mesopotamia, India, Afghanistan.
HALL, WILLIAM E. (10, St. Catherine's Road)	Pte.	Devon, Apl. 1916, Pte. France. Wounded, Jan. 5, 1917.
✠ HALLS, HAROLD C. (95, Greenhill Road)	Pte.	Hants Y., Nov. 1915, Tpr. Yorks. France. *Died*, Oct. 25, 1918.
HALLS, HENRY C. (95, Greenhill Road)	P.O.	R.N., Aug. 1914, P.O. North Sea, White Sea, Mediterranean.

WINCHESTER WAR SERVICE REGISTER

HALLS, WALTER R. (Dell Cottage, Andover Road)	Pte.	A.V.C., July 1916, Pte. France.
HAMILTON, ALAN F. (Brendon, Park Road)	Capt.	Hants, Oct. 1914. India, Mesopotamia, Persia, Turkestan.
✠ HAMILTON, ARTHUR P. (Brendon, Park Road)	Lt.-Col.	R.W.S., 1904, 2nd Lieut. Lond. Irish. France. Wounded, Sept. 25, 1915. M.C. 1915. *Killed in Action, Sept.* 15, 1916, *Somme*.
HAMILTON, HANS P. (Brendon, Park Road)	Capt.	Hereford, Oct. 1914, 2nd Lieut. French R.C. France.
HAMLYN, ALBERT F. (4, Staple Garden)	Sergt.	Hussars, 1913, Tpr. D. of W. Cav. Bde., Arm. Cars. France, Egypt. D.C.M. 1917.
HAMLYN, ARTHUR (4, Staple Garden)	Pte.	Hants, 1916, Pte. Wilts. India.
HAMLYN, ARTHUR F. G. (22, Alresford Road)	Pte.	Hants, Feb. 1916, Pte. Wilts. Mesopotamia, India, Balkans.
HAMLYN, HENRY C. (112, Colebrook Street)	Pte.	Hants, Dec. 1914, Pte. Devon. India, Mesopotamia, France.
HAMMOND, CHARLES E. (3, Nuns Road)	L.-Corpl.	R. Sussex, Apl. 1915, Pte. India.
✠ HAMMOND, CHARLES W. (36A, Clifton Road)	Pte.	Hants, 1913, Pte. India. Mesopotamia. Taken Prisoner by Turks, Apl. 29, 1916. Kut. *Died, Aug.* 1916.
HAMMOND, ERIC F. (36A, Clifton Road)	Pte.	R.A.O.C., June 10, 1918, Pte. Home.
HAMMOND, HERBERT J. (8, Stanmore Lane)	A.M.	R.N.A.S., May 1, 1917, A.M. Home.
HAMMOND, JOHN L. (36A, Clifton Road)	Staff Q.M.S.	R.B., rejoined Feb. 1915, R.Q.M.S. Home.
HAMMOND, THOMAS N. (36A, Clifton Road)	W.O. (Class I)	Army Schoolmaster, 1907, W.O. (Class II). India.
HAMPTON, CHARLES (24, Middle Brook Street)	Pte.	Hants, Aug. 1914, Pte. France, Dardanelles. Wounded, June 4, 1915.
HAMPTON, PHILIP H. (55, Hyde Street)		M.M.G., Mch. 1916. France, India.
HAMPTON, WALTER M. (4, Chester Road)	Pte.	Hants, Pte. Gallipoli, Salonica.
HANCOCK, SYDNEY J. (35, Jewry Street)	L.-Corpl.	R.A.S.C., Apl. 1917, Pte. R.F. France.
HANKIN, CHARLES E. (88, Colebrook Street)	Pte.	Hants, 1916, Pte. Egypt. Wounded, Oct. 13, 1917.
HANKIN, NICHOLAS F. (2, Ladysmith Cottages)	Stoker	R.N., 1913, Stoker. Dardanelles, North Sea.
HANKIN, WALTER J. (2, Ladysmith Cottages)	Corpl.	Hants, 1914, Pte. Egypt, France. Wounded once.
HANKIN, WILLIAM H. (2, Ladysmith Cottages)		Grenadier Gds. Home.
HANSFORD, GEORGE W. K. (8, Cheriton Road)	Dr.	R.A.S.C., Sept. 1914, Dr. M.A.C. France. Gassed three times.

WINCHESTER WAR SERVICE REGISTER

HANSON, CHARLES J. (7, Crowder Terrace)	...	Sergt.	R.B., 1909, Rfn. France. Wounded, May 3, 1917, and Mch. 1918.
HARDER, ALBERT (22, Water Lane)	...	L.S.	R.N., 1909. North Sea, Suez Canal, Russia.
HARDER, WILFRED (54, Canon Street)	...	...	T.R., Feb. 1917, Pte. Lancs. Home.
HARDING, CHARLES W. (32, St. John's Terrace)	...	Spr.	R.E., Sept. 1915, Spr. France.
HARDING, GEORGE (17, Bar End)	...	A.B.	R.N., 1901. North Sea.
HARDING, WILLIAM J. (10, Cross Street)	...	Spr.	Hants, 1901, Pte. R.E. Home.
HARDY, FRANCIS K. (Ashton, Chilbolton Avenue)	...	Major	York and Lancs., 1903, 2nd Lieut. France. D.S.O. 1918, Despatches 1915.
HARDY, JAMES (22, Water Lane)	...	Rfn.	R.B., 1904, Rfn. France. Wounded once.
HARFIELD, JAMES A. (6, Nelson Road)	...	Gun.	R.M.A., Gun. France.
HARFIELD, WILLIAM G. (9, Percy Terrace)	...	Corpl.	Hants, July 1914, Pte. France, Italy. Wounded, 1917.
HARMAN, ARCHIBALD (Park View, North Walls)	...	Pte.	Hants, Dec. 1914, Pte. India, Mesopotamia. Wounded, Jan. 21, 1916.
HARMAN, CHARLES (Park View, North Walls)	...	Corpl.	R.H.A., Apl. 1914, Gun. Anti-Aircraft. France. M.M. 1917.
HARPER, GEORGE T. (12, Granville Place)	...	Rfn.	R.B., Aug. 1914. France. Wounded, Nov. 11, 1914.
HARRIS, EDGAR T. (11, Nuns Road)	...	...	R.A.S.C., Aug. 6, 1914. France. Wounded, Oct. 1914.
HARRIS, FREDERICK (45, Hyde Street)	...	Spr.	Can. Eng., Apl. 1915, Spr. Home.
HARRIS, GUY C. (Wyke Croft, Wecke)	...	Sub-Lieut.	R.N., Mch. 1917, Mid. Baltic, Finland; H.M.S. *Temeraire* and *Watchman*.
HARRIS, JAMES A. (46, Greenhill Road)	...	Pte.	Hants, Pte. R. Sussex. France.
HARRIS, JAMES H. (Wyke Croft, Wecke)	...	Capt.	Hants, Feb. 1914, 2nd Lieut. India, Mesopotamia. Taken Prisoner by Turks, Apl. 29, 1916, Kut, and escaped Aug. 1918. M.C. 1918.
HARRIS, PATRICK G. (46, Greenhill Road)	...	Stoker	R.N., 1905, Stoker. North Sea, Atlantic.
HARRIS, THOMAS J. (13, Greenhill Avenue)	...	Pte.	Hants, Oct. 1914, Pte. Home.
HARRIS, WILLIAM W. (35, Upper Brook Street)	...	Corpl.	R.F.A., Oct. 1915, Gun. France. Gassed, Nov. 8, 1917.
HARRISON, ALAN S. (Merton, St. Faith's Road)	...	Capt.	R.A.S.C., May 1915, Dr. R. Dub. Fus. France, Palestine, Egypt.
HARRISON, GEORGE (Merton, St. Faith's Road)	...	2nd Lieut.	R.A.S.C. (M.T.), Feb. 1917, Pte. T.R., R.A.F.

F

WINCHESTER WAR SERVICE REGISTER

✠ HARRISON, GEORGE J. ... (13, Clausentum Road)	Sergt.	Hants, 1914, Aug., Pte. Gallipoli, France. Wounded, Mch. 1916. *Died, March 15, 1919.*	
HARRISON, JOHN T. ... (13, Clausentum Road)	1st A.M. ...	R.N.A.S., Aug. 1915, 2nd A.M. R.A.F. France, Mediterranean, Mudros.	
HARRISON, OLIVER F. ... (13, Clausentum Road)	2nd Lieut.	R.N.A.S., Aug. 1915, 2nd A.M. R.A.F. Home.	
HARRISON, ROBERT ... (Merton, St. Faith's Road)	2nd Lieut.	R.A.S.C. (M.T.), Feb. 1917, Pte. T.R., R.A.F.	
HARRISON, SAMUEL G. ... (13, Clausentum Road)	Pte.	R.A.S.C., Oct. 1914, Pte. Sher. For. France. Taken Prisoner by Germans, Mch. 24, 1918. Despatches 1917.	
HARROD, FRANK H. ... (Ivy Dene, East Hill)	Staff Capt.	Hants, Apl. 1915, 2nd Lieut. France. M.C. 1916, Croix de Guerre.	
✠ HART, CHARLES N. ... (26, Hyde Street)	L.-Corpl.	Hants, Pte. Gallipoli. *Wounded and Missing (believed Killed),* 1915.	
HARVEY, RICHARD E. ... (10, Chester Road)	Pte.	Hants, June 1916, Pte. Lab. C. France, Belgium.	
✠ HARVEY, WILLIAM ... (12, Hillside Terrace)	Corpl.	R.A.S.C., 1915, Pte. R.E. France. *Died of Tuberculosis.*	
HASKELL, CHARLES F. ... (26, St. John's Road)	Pte.	Hants Y., Feb. 1917, Tpr. Hants. France, Germany. Wounded, May 22, 1918.	
HASKELL, HERBERT F. ... (5, Cranworth Road)	L.-Corpl.	R.E., Sept. 1916, Spr. R.N.D.R. France, Belgium.	
HASKELL, REGINALD ... (42, Eastgate Street)	Tpr.	Nat. Res., Sept. 1914, Pte. Hants Y.	
HATCHER, ERNEST ... (7, Clausentum Road)	Pte.	R. Berks., Apl. 1915, Pte. France.	
HATCHER, GEORGE ... (24, Colebrook Street)	Steward ...	R.N., 1905, Off. Steward. North Sea, Baltic; H.M.S. *Alarm, Lurcher, Malaya* and *Wolsey.*	
HATCHER, WILFRED W. ... (7, Clausentum Road)	Pte.	Hants, Oct. 1916, Pte. France.	
HATCHETT, ALFRED ... (27, Canon Street)	1st A.M.	Lond., Feb. 1917, Pte. R.A.F. Italy.	
HATCHETT, HENRY ... (49, Canon Street)	Dr.	R.E., Oct. 1914, Dr. France, Italy.	
HATCHETT, WILLIAM A. ... (14, St. Faith's Road)	2nd Lieut.	R.E., 1900, Spr. R.A.F. France, Belgium.	
HATT, ALBERT P. ... (5, Alresford Road)	Staff Sergt.	Hants, 1905, Pte. Somerset. Dardanelles, France, Russia. Wounded, Apl. 1915.	
HATT, FREDERICK J. ... (5, Alresford Road)		Hants, Mch. 1917, Pte. R. Glos. Hus., R.A.F. France, India.	
✠ HATT, WILLIAM H. ... (5, Alresford Road)		Hants, 1912. Dardanelles. Wounded, Apl. 1915. *Killed in Action, June 4, 1915.*	
HAWKER, ARTHUR E. ... (4, Saxon Road)	Sergt.	Hants Y., Nov. 1914, Tpr. Home.	
HAWKINS, ALBERT ... (21, St. Swithun's Street)	Gun.	R.G.A., Mch. 1916, Gun. E. Africa.	

WINCHESTER WAR SERVICE REGISTER

HAWKINS, GEORGE A. ... Bdr. ... R.G.A., Dec. 1916, Gun. Home.
(25, Clausentum Road)

HAWKINS, GEORGE V. ... ... R.A.M.C., Feb. 1915. Hants. Egypt.
(130, Stockbridge Road)

HAWKINS, REDVERS M. ... ... R.N., Nov. 1915. North Sea; H.M.S. *Inflexible*
(130, Stockbridge Road) and *Iron Duke*.

✠ HAWKINS, SIDNEY M. ... ... 2nd A.M. ... R.F.C., Mch. 1917, 2nd A.M. Home. *Died,*
(Piper's Farm, Weeke) *Apl. 9, 1917, Leeds.*

HAWKINS, THOMAS J. ... ... Lieut. ... A.P.C., Jan. 1915, Pte. R.B., Somerset L.I.
(130, Stockbridge Road) Home.

✠ HAWKINS, WILLIAM A. ... Gun. ... R.F.A., May 1917, Gun. France. Wounded once.
(15, Osmond's Passage) *Died of Wounds, Apl. 5, 1918.*

HAWKINS, WILLIAM E. ... Tpr. ... Hants Y., Nov. 1915, Tpr. Essex Y. France.
(4, St. George's Street)

HAYDEN, ALEXANDER ... ... Pte. ... Hants, Aug. 1914, Pte. India, Mesopotamia.
(11, Westgate Lane) Taken Prisoner by Turks, Apl. 29, 1916, Kut.

HAYDEN, ALFRED J. ... ... Corpl. ... Hants, Aug. 1914, Pte. R.E. India, Mesopotamia.
(19, Tower Street)

HAYDEN, JOHN C. ... ... Corpl. ... Hants, Aug. 1915, Pte. M.G.C. Home.
(91, Wales Street)

HAYDEN, SYDNEY W. ... ... Corpl. ... R.E., Mch. 1915, Pnr. Flanders, France.
(19, Tower Street)

HAYDEN, WILLIAM J. ... ... C.S.M. ... Hants, 1900, Pte. France, Mesopotamia, Russia.
(4, Alresford Road) Wounded, Dec. 14, 1914, and Apl. 26, 1915.
D.C.M. 1915, M.M. 1918, Despatches 1914
and 1915.

HAYES, PERCY R. ... ... Pnr. ... R.E., Feb. 1917, Pnr. France, Germany.
(11, Prison Quarters)

HAYLES, ERNEST J. ... ... R.F.C., July 8, 1918. R.B. Home.
(34, Brassey Road)

HAYNES, REGINALD ... ... Sergt. ... Glos., May 1916, Pte. Italy, France.
(38, Bar End Road)

HAYTER, EDWARD T. ... L.S. ... R.N. (R.F.R.), 1914, A.B. North Sea, Atlantic.
(6, Wales Street)

HAYTER, FRANK ... ... Pte. ... Canadians, Sept. 1914, Pte. Hants. Mesopotamia,
(6, Wales Street) India. Wounded, Apl. 1917.

HAYTER, HENRY C. ... ... A.B. ... R.N., 1895, A.B. Dardanelles.
(45, Andover Road)

HAYTER, JOSEPH ... ... Sergt. ... Hants, Dec. 1914, Pte. T.M.B. India, Egypt.
(2, Union Street)

HAYTER, WILLIAM ... ... D.L.I., Sept. 1916. Yorks. Hus. Home.
(39, Hyde Street)

HAYWARD, ARTHUR ... ... Pte. ... Hants, Sept. 13, 1915, Pte. Wilts. Salonica,
(2, St. Thomas Street) France. Wounded, Oct. 1918.

HAYWARD, CYRIL W. ... 2nd Lieut. Hants, Sept. 1914, Pte. Mesopotamia, India,
(The Old House, St. Cross Road) Burma.

WINCHESTER WAR SERVICE REGISTER

HAYWARD, EDWARD (2, St. Thomas Street)	Pte.	Hants, 1907, Pte. Dardanelles, France, Mesopotamia, Persia. Wounded, May 6, 1915, Aug. 8 and Dec. 1, 1916. Taken Prisoner by Turks, Sept. 12, 1918.
HAYWARD, HUBERT B.... (The Old House, St. Cross Road)	2nd Lieut.	Hants Y., 1914, Tpr. Indian Army. France, Afghanistan. Wounded once.
HAYWARD, WALTER (2, St. Thomas Street)		Hants, Feb. 1915, Pte. France.
✠ HAYWARD, WILLIAM A. (2, St. Thomas Street)	Sergt.	Hants, 1907, Pte. Dardanelles, France. Wounded, Dec. 1916. *Killed in Action, Dec. 3, 1917, Cambrai.*
HAYWOOD, ROGER (62, Chesil Street)	L.-Corpl.	Hants, Feb. 1915, Pte. France. Wounded, Aug. 25, 1915.
HEAD, ALFRED W. (60, Wharf Hill)	Pte.	R.M.L.I., 1913, Pte. North Sea, France. Gassed, Sept. 1918.
HEAD, ARTHUR W. (59, Milverton Road)	Pte.	Hants, 1912, Pte. India, Mesopotamia.
HEAD, BERT (60, Wharf Hill)	Pte.	Hants, Sept. 1916, Pte. Lab. C. Home.
✠ HEAD, FRANK J. (59, Milverton Road)	P.O. 1st Class	R.N., 1901, Boy. North Sea, China. *Killed in Action, July 21, 1917, North Sea.*
✠ HEAD, GEORGE R. (18, Parchment Street)	R.S.M.	Hants, 1896, Pte. Mesopotamia. *Killed in Action, Dec. 17, 1915.*
HEAD, HARRY (60, Wharf Hill)	Pte.	R.M.L.I., July 1917, Pte. Mudros.
HEAD, HARRY M. (59, Milverton Road)	Pte.	Glos., Feb. 1916, Pte. R. Berks, R.D.C. France. Wounded, Aug. 1916.
HEAD, LEONARD G. (27, Brassey Road)	Corpl.	R.A.S.C., Aug. 8, 1914. France, Italy.
✠ HEARD, RICHARD J. (43, Monks Road)	Corpl.	Hants, Nov. 24, 1915, Pte. India, Egypt, Palestine, France. *Killed in Action, July 24, 1918.*
HEATHER, HAROLD T. (34, Sussex Street)	Gun.	R.G.A., Jan. 1917, Gun. India, Mesopotamia.
HEATHER, HERBERT (34, Sussex Street)	Lieut.	R.A.O.C., Jan. 1917, Pte. R.E. France.
HEATHER, NORMAN (34, Sussex Street)	W.O. (Class II)	R.A.M.C., Jan. 1915, Pte. France. Wounded, Sept. 28, 1915. M.M. 1916, M.S.M.
✠ HEDGE, BERTIE J. (8, Poulsome Place)	S.M.	K.R.R.C., Rfn. France. Wounded, Sept. 9, 1916. *Died of Wounds, Sept. 9, 1916.*
HEDGECOTT, ARTHUR V. (77, Wales Street)	Pte.	Wilts, Mch. 1915, Pte. Salonica, Egypt, France. Wounded three times, 1916–17.
HEDGECOTT, ELDRED E. (77, Wales Street)	Tpr.	Dragoon Gds., 1910, Tpr. France, Egypt. Wounded, June 13, 1915, and Apl. 11, 1917.
HEDGECOTT, ERNEST W. (77, Wales Street)		R.F.C., Jan. 1917. R.A.F. France.
HEDGER, FRANCIS E. (9, Nuns Road)	Pte.	Hants Y., Nov. 1915, Tpr. Hants. France. Wounded, Sept. 20, 1917.

WINCHESTER WAR SERVICE REGISTER

HEDGES, CHARLES (32, Jewry Street)	...	L.-Corpl.	Hants Y., Aug. 1914, Tpr. France. Wounded, 1918.
HEDGES, ERNEST E. (36, Jewry Street)	...	Pte.	R.A.S.C., 1916, Pte. France.
✠ HEDGES, HARRY (32, Jewry Street)	...	Pte.	R.A.S.C., Nov. 1915, Pte. France. *Died of Influenza, Feb. 14, 1919, Charleroi.*
HEDGES, JESSE (32, Jewry Street)	...	Pte.	R.A.S.C., Oct. 1915, Pte. Welsh. France.
HEDGES, PERCY J. (32, Jewry Street)	...	Pte.	Devon Cyc., Jan. 1917, Pte. R.N. Devon Hus., R.A.S.C. France.
HEDLEY, LEONARD (12, High Street)	...	Cadet	Hants Y., May 1915, Tpr. Norfolk, R.A.F. Home.
HEMMING, JOHN (2, Queen's Terrace)	...	Spr.	R. Berks., June 1916, Pte. R.E. Home.
HENNING, ARCHIBALD (79, Chesil Street)	...	Corpl.	Dorset, Sept. 1914, Pte. France, Belgium. Gassed once.
HENNING, DAVID S. (2, Newburgh Street)	...	Pte.	Essex, Oct. 1916, Pte. Home.
HENNING, FREDERICK H. (79, Chesil Street)	...	P.O.	R.N., 1900, Boy. China, Australia, North Sea; H.M.S. *Minotaur*, H.M.A.S. *Sydney*.
HENNING, GEORGE D. (2, Newburgh Street)	...	Cadet	R.A.F., June 1918, Cadet. Home.
HENNING, HORACE (79, Chesil Street)	...	Pte.	R.A.S.C. (T.F.), Pte. France, Belgium.
HENNING, PERCY (79, Chesil Street)	...	P.O.	R.N., 1903, Boy. North Sea, White Sea.
HENNING, WILLIAM J. (79, Chesil Street)	...	W.O.	R.N., 1900, Boy. Atlantic, North Sea; H.M.S. *Martin* and *Owl*.
HERRIDGE, ALFRED H. (1, Dean Lane, Weeke)	...	Gun.	R.G.A., Jan. 1915, Gun. France.
HERRIDGE, ARTHUR F. (1, Dean Lane, Weeke)	...	Pte.	R.A.M.C., Oct. 1915, Pte. Mesopotamia.
HERRIDGE, CHARLES (23, Nuns Road)	...	W.O.	R.N., 1900. North Sea.
HERRIDGE, CHARLES E. (1, Dean Lane, Weeke)	...	Corpl.	R.G.A., Jan. 1915, Gun. France.
HERRIDGE, FRANK (23, Nuns Road)	...	...	R.N., 1905. North Sea.
HERRIDGE, FREDERICK (18, Bar End)	...	Sergt.	Hants, 1914, Pte. France.
HERRIDGE, HARRY (41, Lower Brook Street)	...	Pte.	Hants, Sept. 1914, Pte. Home.
HERRIDGE, SIDNEY (23, Nuns Road)	...	...	Hants, 1910. India.
HERRIDGE, WALTER J. (25, Greenhill Road)	...	Pte.	Lab. C., July 1917, Pte. Home.

WINCHESTER WAR SERVICE REGISTER

✠ HERRIDGE, WILLIAM ... ...   Dorset, Sept. 1914. France. Wounded, Mch. 1917. *Killed in Action, July* 13, 1917.
(23, Nuns Road)

✠ HERRING, WILLIAM C. ... Pte. ... Hants, Sept. 1914, Pte. India, Mesopotamia. *Missing, Jan.* 21, 1916.
(38, Tower Street)

✠ HEWINS, THOMAS H. ... ... L.-Corpl. ... R.E., July 1916, Spr. Wilts. France. *Killed in Action, Dec.* 3, 1917.
(Jesse Villa, Gordon Avenue)

HEWITT, ERNEST E. G. ... Boy T. ... R.N., Mch. 1917, Boy T. H.M.S. *King George V.*
(12, Cheriton Road)

✠ HEWLETT, GEORGE H. ... Stoker ... R.N., 1915, Stoker. North Sea, Atlantic, Dardanelles. *Died of Paralysis, Dec.* 2, 1918.
(26, Wales Street)

HEWLETT, WILLIAM J. ... Pte. ... R.M.L.I., Sept. 1916, Pte. Home.
(26, Wales Street)

HIBBERD, ALBAN S. ... ... L.-Corpl. ... Hants, Nov. 1914, Pte. M.F.P. India, Mesopotamia.
(2, Back Street, St. Cross)

HIBBERD, CHARLES ... ... L.S. ... R.N., 1913, Boy. Grand Fleet, Dardanelles.
(7, Alresford Road)

HIBBERD, EDWARD V. ... ... 2nd A.M. ... R.F.C., Oct. 1917, 2nd A.M. R.A.F. Home.
(8, The Weirs)

✠ HIBBERD, ERNEST J. ... ... L.-Corpl. ... Hants, 1916, Pte. Home. *Died, July,* 1919.
(28, The Square)

HIBBERD, HENRY ... ... Boy ... R.N., Feb. 1917, Boy. Mudros.
(7, Alresford Road)

HIBBERD, JESSE V. ... ... Pte. ... R.A.S.C., Jan. 1914, Dr. N. Staffs. Egypt, Dardanelles, India.
(2, Back Street, St. Cross)

HIBBERD, JOHN C. ... ... Pte. ... R.A.S.C., Oct. 1915, Pte. France.
(1, Union Street)

HICKETTS, ALBERT E. ... Staff Q.M.S. R.G.A., Oct. 3, 1896. Home.
(43, Owen's Road)

HICKS, FRANK B. ... ... Pte. ... Hants, June 1916, Pte. Salonica. Wounded once.
(16, Monks Road)

HICKS, FREDERICK M. ... ... Capt. ... Hants, Sept. 1914, 2nd Lieut. R.F.C. Gallipoli, Salonica, Palestine. Wounded, Aug. 10, 1915. Despatches 1915, Croix de Guerre.
(7, Kingsgate Street)

HICKS, HARRY ... ... Corpl. ... R.G.A., rejoined Oct. 1914. Home.
(2, Nuns Walk)

HICKS, SIDNEY A. ... ... Dr. ... R.A.S.C., Aug. 1914, Dr. France.
(5, New Road, Bar End)

HIDER, RANDOLPH B. ... ... Sergt. ... A.P.C., Nov. 1914, Pte. Oxf. and Bucks, Shropshire, Wilts. France. Wounded, Nov. 1918.
(14, Clausentum Road)

HIGGINS, CHARLES A. G. ... Rfn. ... R.B., 1910, Rfn. Salonica.
(12, Cathedral View)

HIGGINS, CHARLES H. P. ... Sergt. ... R.B., rejoined, Sergt., Lond. Irish. Home.
(12, Cathedral View)

HIGGINS, CLARENCE H. ... ... Irish Gds., 1912. R.B. Home.
(12, Cathedral View)

HIGGINS, EDWIN P. ... ... Corpl. ... R.B., 1912, Rfn. Salonica.
(12, Cathedral View)

WINCHESTER WAR SERVICE REGISTER

Higgins, Henry (8, Avenue Road)	...	L.-Sergt.	A.P.C., Pte. Dorset. Home.
Higgins, Thomas L. (51, High Street)	...	Pte.	Lond. Scot., Sept. 1917, Pte. Coldstream Guards. France.
Higgs, Harry (38, Nuns Road)	...	Pte.	Hants, 1916, Pte. Home.
Higson, William G. (1, Hillside Terrace)	...	Mate	R.N., 1903, Boy. North Sea, Dardanelles, Mediterranean. D.S.M. 1915.
Hilborne, William S. (26, Greenhill Road)	...	Pte.	Hants Y., Mch. 1917, Tpr. R.N. Devon Hus., Glos. France, Russia.
✠ Hill, Arthur S. (69, Fairfield Road)	...	Rfn.	K.R.R.C., July 1916, Rfn. Flanders. *Missing (believed Killed), Aug. 3, 1917.*
Hill, Charles H. (54, Greenhill Road)	...	Spr.	Devon, June 1916, Pte. R.E. Home.
✠ Hill, Elijah (6, St. Leonards Road)	...		R.M.L.I., Dec. 1915. France. Wounded once. *Died of Wounds, 1917, Germany.*
Hill, Henry C. (31, Front Street, St. Cross)	...	Pte.	R.A.S.C. (M.T.), Sept. 1916. Home.
Hill, Henry L. G. (Butts Close, Weeke)	...	Major	War Office, Directorates of Recruiting and Mobilization. O.B.E.
✠ Hill, Nicholas W. (Butts Close, Weeke)	...	Capt.	Oxf. and Bucks L.I., Oct. 1915, 2nd Lieut. France. Wounded, Nov. 1916. *Killed in Action, Jan. 16, 1917, near Courcellette.*
Hill, Percy A. (22, Colson Road)	...	Pte.	Hants Y., Aug. 1914, Tpr. M.G.C. France, Wounded once.
Hill, Stephen R. (67, Fairfield Road)	...	Corpl.	R.A.S.C., rejoined Sept. 1914, Pte. R.E. France, Italy.
Hillary, Frederick W. (9, Owens Road)	...	Sergt.	A.P.C., Feb. 22, 1915, Pte. Home.
Hillier, Arthur R. (4, Christ Church Road)	...	Corpl.	Devon, Nov. 1916, Pte. A.P.C., R.B., R.I.R. France.
Hillier, Frederic W. (49, St. Catherine's Road)	...	Pte.	Glos., Mch. 1915, Pte. France. Wounded, Aug. 22, 1917.
Hillier, Howard (1, Cromwell Terrace)	...	Pte.	R.A.M.C., May 1917, Pte. France.
Hillyer, Frank (11, North Walls)	...	Pte.	Hants Y., Oct. 1915, Pte. Lancers, K. Liverp., R.A.O.C. Home.
Hillyer, Walter G. (29, Elm Road)	...		E. Surrey, 1917, Pte. France, Russia.
Hine, Cecil C. B. (12a Romsey Road)	...	Bandsman	R.B., Oct. 1917, Bandsman. Home.
Hine, Charles (12a Romsey Road)	...	Pte.	A.V.C., Apl. 1915, Pte. France.
Hine, Frederick (3, Greenhill Terrace)	...	Pte.	R.A.O.C., Aug. 1916, Pte. France.
Hine, Herbert (3, Greenhill Terrace)	...	Pte.	Hants, Sept. 1915, Pte. India, Mesopotamia. Wounded, Feb. 5, 1917.

WINCHESTER WAR SERVICE REGISTER

HINE, PERCY C. ... ... R.N.A.S., Jan. 1918. R.A.F. Home.
(3, Greenhill Terrace)

HINE, REGINALD ... ... L.-Corpl. R.A.M.C., Sept. 1915, Pte. France, Belgium.
(3, Greenhill Terrace)

HINTON, ALEXANDER ... ... Pte. ... Hants, June 6, 1918, Pte. Home.
(151, High Street)

HINTON, ARTHUR ... ... Pte. ... Hants Y., Nov. 1914, Tpr. Hants. France.
(151, High Street)

HINTON, STANLEY ... ... Bdr. ... R.G.A., Oct. 1915, Gun. France.
(151, High Street)

HINTON, WILFRED G. ... ... Steward ... R.N.A.S., May 1917, Steward. R.A.F. Egypt.
(151, High Street)

HINVES, REGINALD N. ... Corpl. ... R.A.S.C., 1911, Pte. France, Salonica.
(22, Hatherley Road)

HINXMAN, ALAN ... ... Capt. ... Westm. Dragoons, Aug. 1914, Tpr. Tank C.
(Kitnocks, St. Thomas Street) France.

HINXMAN, EDWIN M. ... Bdr. ... R.G.A., June 14, 1917, Gun. France, Belgium.
(20, Sussex Street)

HINXMAN, HARRY E. ... ... Corpl. ... Dorset, June 12, 1916, Pte. Devon, Lab. C., R.E.
(134, Stockbridge Road) Home.

HINXMAN, ROLAND ... ... Capt. ... Lond. R.B., Aug. 1914, Rfn. R.F.A. France.
(Kitnocks, St. Thomas Street)

HISCOCK, WALTER H. C. ... Pte. ... R.A.S.C., June 1915, Pte. France.
(34, Canon Street)

HOARE, ALBERT G. ... ... Spr. ... R.E., Sept. 1916, Spr. Mesopotamia.
(22, St. John's Road)

HOBBS, ALFRED G. ... ... Corpl. ... Life Gds., 1911. France.
(7, Swan Lane)

HOBBS, CHARLES V. ... ... Pte. ... Hants, July 1914, Pte. Mesopotamia, Persia,
(47, Brassey Road) India, Russia.

HOBBS, FRANCIS... ... ... Pte. ... Hants, Sept. 1914, Pte. Egypt, India.
(47, Brassey Road)

HOBBS, FRANK H. ... ... Sergt. ... Hants, Aug. 5, 1914, Pte. R.D.C. Home.
(44, North Walls)

HOBBS, FRANK W. ... ... S. Smith ... Hants Y., Nov. 26, 1914, Tpr. R.H.A. Egypt,
(44, North Walls) Palestine.

HOBBS, FREDERICK F. B. ... A.-Capt. ... R.G.A., Nov. 25, 1914, 2nd Lieut. France.
(Glenroy, Stockbridge Road)

HOBBS, GEORGE ... ... R.A.S.C. (M.T.), July 1917. Italy.
(29, Brassey Road)

HOBBS, HERBERT ... ... R.A.O.C., Mch. 1917. Home.
(47, Brassey Road)

HOBBS, WALTER J. ... ... A.-Pay- A.P.C., Nov. 7, 1914, Pte. Hants. France,
(2, Clausentum Road) master Belgium. Despatches 1919.

HOBDAY, THOMAS E. L. ... Spr. ... Hants, June 18, 1918, Pte. R.E. Home.
(3, Castle Terrace)

WINCHESTER WAR SERVICE REGISTER

HODDER, GEORGE W. ... (1, Chester Road)	A.B.	R.N., 1901. Russia, North Sea. D.S.M.
HODDER, JOHN F. ... (12, Christ Church Road)	L.-Corpl.	Oxf. and Bucks L.I., 1913. France, Italy.
HODGES, ALBERT P. ... (16, Brassey Road)	Gun.	R.G.A., May 27, 1916, Gun. France, Italy.
HODGKINS, JAMES H. ... (12, Water Lane)		R.M.L.I., Sept. 1914, Pte. France.
HODGSON, ROBERT ... (5, Canute Road)	Sergt.	K.R.R.C., rejoined Aug. 1915, Sergt. Home.
HOGAN, WILLIAM P. ... (12, St. George's Street)	Pte.	A.V.C., Jan. 12, 1917, Pte. Home.
HOLGATE, HENRY ... (13, Nuns Road)	C.S.M.	K.R.R.C., 1899, Rfn. France. Despatches 1917.
HOLLAND, ALBERT V. ... (12, Tower Street)	Pte.	Worc., Feb. 1916, Pte. Home.
HOLLAND, ARTHUR ... (12, Tower Street)	Corpl.	Hants, Aug. 1914, Corpl. India, Mesopotamia. Wounded, Feb. 24, 1917.
✠ HOLLAND, ERNEST ... (10, St. Leonards Road)	Pte.	Hants, Sept. 1914, Pte. Mesopotamia. Taken Prisoner by Turks, Apl. 29, 1916. *Died, Oct. 18, 1916, Tarsus.*
HOLLAND, FREDERICK ... (12, Tower Street)	A.B.	R.N., 1909, A.B. Patrol Duty, English Channel.
✠ HOLLAND, JAMES ... (3, Mants Lane)	Pte.	Hants, Aug. 1914, Pte. Dardanelles. Wounded once. *Died of Wounds, Aug. 21, 1915.*
HOLLAND, PERCY ... (12, Tower Street)	Dr.	R.A.S.C. (M.T.), Mch. 1916, Pte. France.
HOLLAND, WILLIAM G. ... (3, Mants Lane)	Pte.	Hants, Aug. 1914, Pte. Salonica.
HOLLIDAY, CHARLES W. ... (36, Jewry Street)	Corpl.	R.F.C., Aug. 1915, A.M. R.A.F. India.
HOLLIDAY, HAROLD R. ... (36, Jewry Street)	A.M.	R.N.A.S., Feb. 1918, A.M. R.A.F. Russia.
HOLLOWAY, DOUGLAS ... (13, Lower Brook Street)	Sergt.	K.R.R.C., 1893, Rfn. Home.
HOLLOWAY, EDWARD ... (16, Hyde Abbey Road)	Spr.	R.E., June 1916, Spr. France.
HOLLOWAY, FRANK J. ... (31, Arbour Terrace)	Pte.	N. Staffs., Sept. 1916, Pte. France. Wounded, 1917.
HOLLOWAY, FREDERICK G. ... (31, Arbour Terrace)	Pte.	Hants, Jan. 1917, Pte. Lab. C. France.
HOLLOWAY, OVERNILE ... (36, Colson Road)	A.B.	R.N.R., Jan. 1895. R.N. North Sea. Wounded once.
HOLLOWAY, WILLIAM ... (9, Mants Lane)	Pte.	Hants, Dec. 1914, Pte. Gallipoli. Wounded, Sept. 26, 1915.
HOLMES, HERBERT J. ... (2, Chesil Cottages)	Sergt.	Hants, Jan. 1913, Pte. India, Mesopotamia, Egypt, France. Wounded, Nov. 1917, and July 20, 1918.

WINCHESTER WAR SERVICE REGISTER

HOLMES, WALTER H. ... (2, Chesil Cottages) — A.-Sergt. — Hants, Sept. 1914, Pte. India, Mesopotamia.

✠ HOLT, JAMES ... (11, Cross Street) — Stoker — R.N., Stoker. H.M.S. *Princess Royal* and *Begonia*. Drowned at sea, Oct. 6, 1917.

HOLT, ROBERT L. ... (Westfield, Chilbolton Avenue) — Cadet — R.F.A., Sept. 11, 1918, Cadet. Home.

HOLT, SAMUEL ... (11, Cross Street) — Pte. — Hants, Aug. 1914, Pte. Home.

HOLWAY, ALBION L. ... (38, Egbert Road) — Corpl. — R.A.M.C., 1910, Pte. France, Italy.

HOLWAY, ERNEST J. ... (38, Egbert Road) — Corpl. — Hants, Dec. 1914, Pte. India, Mesopotamia.

HOLYOAK, FRANK ... (4, St. James' Street) — Corpl. — R.E., Sept. 27, 1915, Corpl. France.

HONEY, CHARLES W. ... (41, Hyde Street) — W.O. (Class I) — R.A.S.C., 1907, Dr. Dardanelles, Egypt.

HONEY, HAROLD J. ... (12, St. John's Road) — Gun. — R.G.A., Nov. 1915, Gun. Anti-Aircraft. Home.

HOOD, GEORGE W. B. ... (7, Step Terrace) — Pte. — Essex, Oct. 26, 1916, Pte. Hants. Home.

HOOKER, FREDERICK R. ... (Western Road) — Pte. — Hants, Sept. 30, 1914, Pte. India, Palestine, Egypt, France.

HOOKER, WILLIAM J. ... (Western Road) — Sergt. — Hants, Sept. 5, 1914, Pte. India, Egypt, Palestine, France. Wounded, Nov. 20, 1917, and July 22, 1918.

HOOPER, ALEXANDER ... (36, Water Lane) — L.-Corpl. — Hants, Feb. 16, 1915, Pte. Wilts. Gallipoli, Egypt, France. Wounded, Oct. 18, 1916, Oct. 9, 1917, and Apl. 10, 1918. M.M. 1917.

HOPGOOD, JOHN S. ... (36, St. Catherine's Road) — Sergt. — Hants, May 1915, Pte. Mediterranean, France. Wounded, Aug. 5, and Oct. 20, 1916. M.M.

HOPKINS, PERCY ... (21, Highcliffe Road) — Pte. — Wilts, Aug. 1916, Pte. M.G.C. France.

HORSMAN, WILLIAM H. ... (31, Nuns Road) — Sergt. — R.G.A., Jan. 1916, Gun. France.

HOTSTON, ROBERT J. ... (15, St. Swithun Street) — Pte. — Devon, Dec. 1916, Pte. Home.

HOUNSLOW, FRANK R. ... (30, Brassey Road) — Pte. — Wilts, Feb. 1916, Pte. India, Mesopotamia. Wounded, 1916.

✠ HOUNSLOW, GEORGE H. ... (30, Brassey Road) — R.G.A. France. Wounded once. M.M. *Died of Wounds, Etaples*.

HOUSE, CECIL J. ... (42, Hyde Street) — Sergt. — R.A.S.C. (M.T.), May 1916, Pte. Mesopotamia.

HOUSE, CYRIL J. ... (42, Hyde Street) — Pte. — Hants Y., Nov. 1915, Tpr. Lab. C. Home.

HOUSE, EDGAR W. ... (6, St. Swithun Street) — Pte. — Hants, June 1916, Pte. Lab. C. Home.

HOUSE, GEORGE F. ... (2, Hyde Close) — Pte. — Hants, Mch. 1916, Pte. Salonica.

WINCHESTER WAR SERVICE REGISTER

✠ House, Harry ... (2, Hyde Close)	...	Rfn.	K.R.R.C., Nov. 1915, Rfn. France. *Killed in Action, July* 15, 1916.
House, Victor N. (42, Hyde Street)	...	L.-Corpl.	Hants, Feb. 1916, Pte. Lab. C. France. Wounded, Oct. 23, 1916.
Houssemayne Du Boulay	...		*See* Du Boulay.
Howard, Thomas (87, Chesil Street)	...	Pte.	A.V.C., Jan. 1916, Pte. France.
Hughes, Herbert V. (Caer Gwent, Worthy Road)	...	Lieut.	Norfolk, Oct. 1914, 2nd Lieut. R.E. France, Italy.
Hunt, Albert J. (2, Nuns Road)	...	Pte.	R.A.S.C. (M.T.), Sept. 1916, Pte. France.
Hunt, Bertram H. (52, Andover Road)	...	Pte.	Hants Y., Nov. 1915, Tpr. Hants. France. Wounded, June 7, 1917.
Hunt, Charles E. (52, Andover Road)	...	Pte.	Hants Y., May 1916, Tpr. M.G.C. France.
✠ Hunt, Frank E. (34, Kingsgate Road)	...	Pte.	R.M.L.I., Oct. 1916, Pte. France, Belgium. Wounded, October 26, 1917, and October 9, 1918. *Died of Wounds, Oct.* 10, 1918.
Hunt, John (4, North Walls)	...	Pte.	R.A.M.C., 1911, Pte. France. Wounded, 1917, Gassed, 1917. M.M.
Hunt, Thomas E. (34, Kingsgate Road)	...	Pte.	Hants, Oct. 1914, Pte. India.
Hunter, Walter (5, Crowder Terrace)	...	L.-Corpl.	Hants (T.F.), Pte. Home.
Hunter, Walter C. (91, Colebrook Street)	...	Corpl.	R.F.A., 1898, Dr. France. Wounded, Oct. 1918.
Huntley, John C. (7, Nuns Road)	...	Corpl.	R.N.A.S., July 1917. R.A.F. Home.
Hutchings, Charles (37, Lower Brook Street)	...	Pte.	Hants, Sept. 1914, Pte. India, Mesopotamia.
Hutchings, Ernest (37, Lower Brook Street)	...		R.N.A.S., Oct. 1917. R.A.F. Home.
Hutchings, John (15, Romsey Road)	...	A.B.	R.N., Aug. 1914, A.B. Home.
Hutchings, Vernon H. (31, Western Road)	...	Sergt.	R.B., Aug. 24, 1916, Rfn. T.R., K.R.R.C., R.B. France, Belgium.
Hutchings, William (37, Lower Brook Street)	...	Gun.	R.N., 1911, O.S. Grand Fleet.
Hutchins, Charlie W. (154, High Street)	...	Gun.	R.G.A., Nov. 1916, Gun. Italy, Egypt, Palestine.
Hyde, Leonard (11, St. Clement Street)	...	Corpl.	R.A., 1915, Gun. Home.
Hyde, Thomas C. (4, St. John's Road)	...	Sergt.	Hants Y., Dec. 1914, Tpr. Hants. France, Italy.

WINCHESTER WAR SERVICE REGISTER

INGE, HARRY (80, Hatherley Road)	... Pte.	...	R.W.S., Oct. 31, 1916, Pte. Belgium, Italy, France. Wounded, Mch. 9, 1917, and Mch. 23, 1918.
✠ INGE, SIDNEY G. (90, Fairfield Road)	... Pte.	...	R.W.S., Oct. 1916, Pte. Lancs. Fus. France. *Killed in Action, Sept. 2, 1918, Eterpigny.*
INGRAM, WILLIAM (73, Milverton Road)	... Pte.	...	R.A.S.C. (M.T.), July 13, 1918, Pte. Glos. Home.
JACKSON, ALBERT E. (2, Foundry Lane)	... B.Q.M.S.		R.F.A., 1902, Gun. France.
JACKSON, EDWIN C. (8, Cranworth Road)	... Pte.	...	Hants, Apl. 1914, Pte. R. Warwick. France.
JACKSON, ERNEST (9, Sussex Street)	... Sergt.	...	R.F.C., Oct. 1915, 2nd A.M. R.A.F. Home.
JACKSON, HORACE A. (74, Kingsgate Street)	... Lieut.	...	Inns of Court O.T.C., Jan. 10, 1916, Pte. K.R.R.C. France. Wounded, Feb. 17, 1917, and Mch. 21, 1918.
JACKSON, REGINALD T. (3, Lower Brook Street)	... Pte.	...	R.A.O.C., Apl. 1917, Pte. Home.
JACKSON, REGINALD W. (8, Cranworth Road)	... Spr.	...	Hants, 1908, Pte. R.E. France.
JACKSON, WILFRED E. (8, Cranworth Road)	... Lieut.	...	Hants, 1912, Pte. * Punjabi R. India, Mesopotamia, Salonica, Turkey.
JACKSON, WILLIAM J. (30, Union Street)	... Pte.	...	Hants, Sept. 1914, Pte. Home.
JACKSON, WILLIAM T. (21, Upper High Street)	... Sergt.	...	R. Marines, 1909, Bandsman. Falkland Islands, North Sea, Gallipoli, Red Sea, E. Africa, Cameroons, East Indies.
JACOB, ERNEST E. (34, Bar End Road)	... Sergt.	...	M.M.P., June 1915, Corpl. Belgium, France, Germany.
✠ JACOB, LESLIE J. (57, Western Road)	...		Hants, Sept. 1914. India, Mesopotamia. Taken Prisoner by Turks, Sept. 24, 1916, Kut. *Died, Sept.* 1916.
JACOB, WILLIAM (92, Stockbridge Road)	Sergt.	...	Hants (T.F.), 1894, Bandsman. N. Fus. India, Mesopotamia.
JAGO, HENRY (63, Sussex Street)	... Sergt.	...	T.R., July 1917. R. Warwick. France.
JAMES, FREDERICK J. (47, Egbert Road)	... Corpl.	...	R.B., 1907, Rfn. France. Wounded, Sept. 25, 1914 and Mch. 21, 1918. Taken Prisoner by Germans, Mch. 21, 1918.
JAMES, HARRY (13, Magdalen Hill)	... L.-Corpl.		Hants, Sept. 1914, Pte. Home.
JAMES, HENRY (21, St. Peter's Street)	... Major	...	R.F.A., 1910, 2nd Lieut. India, Mesopotamia. Despatches 1918 and 1919.
JAMES, WILLIAM (3, Avenue Road)	... Pte.	...	Hants, Sept. 1914, Pte. R. Berks. France. Wounded twice. Taken Prisoner by Germans, Mch. 1918.

WINCHESTER WAR SERVICE REGISTER

JAMES, WILLIAM H. ... (58, St. John's Street)	L.-Corpl.	Devon Y., Feb. 15, 1917, Tpr. M.F.P., Hants. Home.
JARVIS, WILLIAM J. ... (30, Middle Brook Street)	Sergt.	N. Fus., 1905, Pte. France. Wounded, Sept. 14, and Nov. 8, 1914, Feb. 24, 1915, Aug. 31, 1917.
JEFFREY, ALBERT E. ... (25, Tower Street)	Bandsman	Hants, 1913, Bandsman. India, Persian Gulf, Egypt, Palestine, France.
JEFFREY, ARTHUR E. (154, Stockbridge Road)	1st A.M.	R.N.A.S., June 1916, 1st A.M. R.A.F. Home.
JEFFREY, CHARLES A. (26, Upper High Street)	Sig.	R.G.A., Oct. 1916, Sig. France, Salonica. Wounded, Nov. 3, 1917.
JEFFREY, EDWIN ... (53, Upper Brook Street)		R.A.S.C. France.
JEFFREY, FREDERICK ... (Christ's Hospital)	Pte.	Glos., May, 1915, Pte. France.
JEFFREY, FREDERICK ... (25, Upper Brook Street)	Corpl.	Dorset, 1904, Pte. France. Gassed, May 2, 1915, and Nov. 15. 1917.
JEFFREY, GEORGE H. (73, Parchment Street)	Pte.	Can. Scot., 1915, Pte. France. Wounded, Apl. 9, 1917.
JEFFREY, GRANVILLE L. W. ... (111, High Street)	L.-Corpl.	Hants, Jan. 1916, Pte. Home.
JEFFREY, HAROLD P. (154, Stockbridge Road)	L.-Corpl.	Buffs, Sept. 1914. India, Aden, Mesopotamia. Wounded, Jan. 26, 1917.
✠ JEFFREY, JESSE ... (54, Canon Street)	Sergt.	Hants, 1903, Pte. France. *Killed in Action, Oct. 16, 1916.*
JEFFREY, PERCY C. ... (1-2, Hedges Buildings)	Sergt.	Hants, Oct. 1916, Pte. Home.
JEFFREY, SYDNEY H. ... (154, Stockbridge Road)	Gun.	R.F.A., Nov. 1916, Gun. France, Germany.
JEFFREY, WILLIAM C. ... (39, Nuns Road)	Spr.	Hants (T.F.), 1898, Bandsman. R.E. Home.
✠ JELLETT, ARTHUR E. ... (47, Kingsgate Street)	L.-Corpl.	Hants, 1914, Pte. India, Mesopotamia. *Killed in Action, Kut.*
JELLETT, CHARLES L. ... (12, Upper Wolvesey Terrace)	Pte.	Hants, June 1916, Pte. India, Egypt, France, Germany, Palestine. Wounded, July 23, 1918.
JELLIFF, FREDERICK J. ... (65, Upper Brook Street)	L.-Corpl	R.E., June 1916, Spr. France. Wounded, May 27, 1918.
JELLY, EDWIN M. ... (9, Cranworth Road)	Pte.	A.P.C., Feb. 1915, Pte. Hants. India.
JENNINGS, HERBERT L. (59, Hatherley Road)	Pte.	Hants Cyc., June 24, 1915, Pte. R.A.F. Home.
JENNINGS BRAMLEY, ALWYN W. (Meadow House, Kingsgate St.)	Lt.-Col.	Hussars, 1895, 2nd Lieut. Egyptian Army. Suez Canal, Egypt, Palestine. D.S.O. 1916, Serbian White Eagle 1916.
JENVEY, DANIEL J. ... (14, Wales Street)	Stoker	R. Marines, 1903, Pte. R.N. North Sea.
JENVEY, EDGAR ... (36, Monks Road)	L.-Corpl.	Hants, Sept. 1914, Pte. India, Palestine.

WINCHESTER WAR SERVICE REGISTER

JENVEY, HUGH (12, Canon Street)	Corpl.	Hants, Sept. 1914, Pte. France. Wounded, Oct. 1918.	
JENVEY, JOHN C. R. (16, Wales Street)	Stoker	R.N., Dec. 1917, Stoker. North Sea.	
JENVEY, WILLIAM (36, Monks Road)	Pte.	Dorset Y., May 1916, Tpr. R.A.S.C. Home.	
JERMANY, JOHN J. (Gas Works)	Elec.	R.N., Nov. 1915, Elec. North Sea, Atlantic.	
JERRAM, GEORGE A. (2, Victoria Road)	C.S.M.	Hants (T.F.), 1895, Pte. India, Mesopotamia. Wounded, July 27, 1915.	
JERRAM, VICTOR A. (65, St. John's Street)	Pte.	R.A.S.C., Oct. 1917, Pte. Home.	
JESSON, HAROLD P. (3, Ranelagh Road)	Capt.	R.E., Jan. 1904. France. Despatches 1916.	
✠ JESSON, JOSEPH J. (1, Greyfriars Villas)	Pte.	Hants, Sept. 1916, Pte. Lab. C. France. *Killed in Action, Dec. 1, 1917.*	
JESSON, ROGER (3, Ranelagh Road)	Lieut.	K. Liverp., Aug. 1914, Pte. N. Staffs. Gallipoli. Wounded, Aug. 8, 1915. Despatches 1916.	
JEWELL, ALFRED E. (16, Colson Road)	Corpl.	K.R.R.C., Mch. 1916, Rfn. France. Wounded, May 27, 1917.	
JEWELL, WILLIAM E. (15, Chesil Street)	Pte.	R.M.L.I., 1913, Pte. North Sea, Belgium.	
✠ JOHNSON, ARCHIBALD L. (11, Newburgh Street)	P.O.	R.N., 1914, P.O. Belgium, Russia. *Died, July 17, 1916, Russia.*	
JOHNSON, ARTHUR H. (64, St. Cross Road)	Lieut.	Artists Rif., Mch. 1916, Cadct. R.G.A. France, Flanders. Wounded, Apl. 1918.	
✠ JOHNSON, FRANK E. D. (1, Birinus Road)	Pte.	Hants Y., Nov. 1914, Tpr. Hants. France, Belgium. *Killed in Action, Jan. 31, 1918, St. Julien.*	
JOHNSON, GEORGE (7, The Close)	Corpl.	K.R.R.C., 1907, Rfn. France. Wounded three times.	
JOHNSTON, ANDREW H. (6, Queen's Terrace)	C.P.O.	R.N., P.O (Class 2). North Sea; H.M.S. *Cyclops*.	
JOHNSTON, GEORGE S. (1, Jubilee Villas)	Corpl.	R.E., May 1916, Spr. Mesopotamia, India.	
JONES, CHARLES R. (49, Sussex Street)	2nd A.M.	R.N.A.S., 1916, A.M. R.A.F. Home.	
JONES, CHARLES W. (41, Colson Road)	Sergt.	Hants (T.F.), 1894, Pte. Hants. India, Mesopotamia.	
JONES, JAMES (4, Lower Wolvesey Terrace)	Dr.	R.A.S.C., Sept. 1914, Dr. France. Wounded twice.	
JONES, L. GROVE-		*See* GROVE-JONES.	
JONES, LEWIS A. (6, Queensland Terrace)	Spr.	R.E., Aug. 1916, Spr. Home.	
JONES, PERCY (102, Colebrook Street)	Rfn.	R.B., Aug. 6, 1914, Rfn. France. Wounded, Feb. 1916.	

WINCHESTER WAR SERVICE REGISTER

Jones, William (1, Percy Terrace)	Pte.	Hants, Mch. 1917, Pte. Home.
Jordan, Charles P. (62, Sussex Street)	C.S.M.	K.R.R.C., 1905, Rfn. France. Torpedoed, 1915.
Jordan, Robert (17, Canon Street)	Pte.	Hants, Nov. 1914, Pte. Mesopotamia.
Journeaux, Percy F. (15, Cranworth Road)	Lieut.	R.A.S.C., May 21, 1918, Pte. France.
Joyce, Donovan W. (Pinaster, West Hill)		R.N.R., 1917, Cadet. Atlantic.
Joyce, Ernest (3, St. John's Street)	1st A.M.	R.N.A.S., Oct. 1917, 1st A.M. R.A.F. Home.
Joyce, Ernest W. (3, St. John's Street)	2nd A.M.	R.N.A.S., Dec. 12, 1917, A.M. R.A.F. Home.
Joyce, Joseph J. (46, St. John's Street)	Spr.	Devon, July 1916, Pte. R.E. Home.
✠ Judd, Ernest F. (17, Alresford Road)	Pte.	Hants, Dec. 1914, Pte. Dorset. France. *Missing (believed Killed), Apl. 15, 1917.*
Judd, George D. (114, Stockbridge Road)	O.S.	R.N., Aug. 1914, O.S. E. Africa, S. Africa.
Judd, Reginald A. (9, St. James' Street)		Hants Y., Sept. 1914, Tpr. Hants. France, Italy. Wounded, July 21, 1918.
✠ Judd, Thomas A. (17, Alresford Road)	Stoker	R.N., 1913, Stoker. North Sea; H.M.S. *Queen Mary. Killed in Action, May 31, 1916, Jutland.*
Judd, William H. (17, Alresford Road)	A.B.	R.N., 1902, Boy. North Sea; H.M.S. *Neptune.*
Judkins, Bernard E. H. (20, St. Peter's Street)	Capt.	Hussars. France, Mesopotamia.
Judkins, Leonard E. H. (20, St. Peter's Street)	Capt.	York and Lancs. France, Belgium. Wounded once.
✠ Jupe, Bruce D. (57, Kingsgate Street)	Art.	R.N. H.M.S. *Good Hope. Killed in Action, Nov. 1914, Chilian Coast.*
✠ Jupe, Edward (15, College Street)	Tpr.	Dorset Y., June 9, 1916, Tpr. Hussars. India. *Died of sunstroke, June 22, 1918, Simla.*
Jupe, Francis H. (57, Kingsgate Street)	A.-Sergt.	Hants, Aug. 1916, Pte. Mesopotamia, India.
Jupe, Leonard G. (15, College Street)	P.O. (1st Class)	R.N., 1906, Boy. North Sea. Wounded, 1914.
Kavanagh, William (63, Water Lane)	Sig.	R.I.R., Nov. 20, 1916, Pte. R.E. France, Belgium. Wounded, Sept. 4, 1917. Gassed, Dec. 21, 1917, and Mch. 4, 1918.
Kearley, (16, St. James' Terrace)	Sergt.	France.

WINCHESTER WAR SERVICE REGISTER

KEEL, CHARLES H. ... ... Sergt. ... Hants, Aug. 1914, Pte. France.
(6, Upper Wolvesey Terrace)

KEENE, FREDERICK F. ... L.-Corpl. R.A.S.C., May 1915, Pte. France.
(62, Greenhill Road)

KEEVILL, PERCY A. R. ... Capt. ... K.R.R.C., 1911, Rfn. France. Wounded three
(3, Queensland Terrace) times. M.C. and Bar 1916–17.

KEEVILL, WALLACE R. ... Staff Sergt. K.R.R.C., 1905, Boy. R.A.O.C. Egypt, Gallipoli,
(3, Queensland Terrace) Singapore, China. Wounded, 1915.

KELLIE, JOHN ... ... Pte. ... R.A.S.C., Nov. 1915, Pte. France. Wounded,
(6, St. George's Street) Nov. 29, 1916.

KELLIE, THOMAS ... ... Stoker ... R.N., 1912, Stoker. North Sea.
(6, St. George's Street)

✠ KEMISH, CHARLES S. B. ... Lieut. and R.A.S.C., 1888, Dr. Gallipoli. Médaille Militaire.
(16, Gordon Avenue) Q.M. *Killed in Action, July* 14, 1915.

KEMP, ROBERT ... ... A.-Sergt. Nat. Res., Sept. 1914, Pte. R. Berks, Lab. C.
(27, Sussex Street) Home.

KENNY, ALBERT H. ... ... Tpr. ... Hants Y., May 1916, Tpr. France.
(14, Culver Road)

✠ KETLEY, CHARLES W. ... Corpl. ... R.E., Sept. 1914, Spr. France. Gassed, Sept.
(72, Brassey Road) 1915. *Killed in Action, Apl.* 11, 1917, *Feuchy.*

KEW, WILLIAM ... ... Pte. ... Hants, Aug. 1914, Pte. Egypt. Wounded twice.
(18, Bar End Road)

KEYWOOD, GEORGE ... ... Pte. ... Hants, 1910, Pte. Dardanelles, France. Wounded,
(9, Middle Brook Street) May 9, 1916.

✠ KIBBLE, GEORGE F. ... ... L.-Corpl. Wilts, 1906, Pte. France. *Killed in Action,*
(7, Silver Hill) *Oct.* 31, 1914.

✠ KIBBLE, REDDICK W. ... Gun. ... R.G.A., 1910, Gun. France. *Killed in Action,*
(7, Silver Hill) *Oct.* 9, 1918.

KIGHT, ERNEST E. ... ... Pte. ... Hants, Nov. 1916, Pte. Lincoln, Lab. C. France.
(2A, Newburgh Street)

KIGHT, WILLIAM H. ... ... Pte. ... Hants Y., June 1916, Tpr. Hants. Belgium,
(5, Prinstead Terrace) France, Italy. Wounded, Mch. 25, 1918.

KILFORD, FRANK A. ... ... R.N., 1912. Grand Fleet.
(35, Middle Brook Street)

✠ KILFORD, HENRY W. ... Gun. ... R.G.A., 1911, Gun. India. *Killed in Action,*
(35, Middle Brook Street) *Apl.* 18, 1915, *Shabkadar.*

KILFORD, ROBERT ... ... P.O. ... R.N., 1903. China.
(35, Middle Brook Street)

KILROY, WILLIAM J. ... ... Pte. ... R.B., 1899, Rfn. M.G.C. France.
(25, Canon Street)

KIMBER, ALBERT ... ... Pte. ... Hants, June 1914, Pte. France. Wounded, 1916.
(26, Clifton Road)

KIMBER, ALFRED ... ... Hants. France. Wounded, Apl. 26, 1915.
(26, Clifton Road)

KIMBER, FREDERICK W. ... Pte. ... R.A.M.C., Nov. 1915, Pte. Salonica, France.
(5, Chesil Terrace)

WINCHESTER WAR SERVICE REGISTER

KIMBER, WILLIAM (6, Wales Street)	...	Pte.	Hants, 1896, Pte. France.
KINAHAN, JAMES M. (2, Lower Brook Street)	...	Drummer	Hants, 1890, Drummer. Home.
KING, CHARLES S. (Edington, Barnes Close)	...	Major	R.G.A., Lieut. France, Germany. M.C. 1918.
KING, ERNEST S. (60, Parchment Street)	...	L.-Corpl.	Hants Y., 1912, Tpr. France.
KING, FREDERICK (26, Middle Brook Street)	...	Pte.	Hants, Sept. 1914, Pte. France. Wounded, Apl. 26, 1915, and Mch. 19, 1916. M.S.M. 1917.
KING, FREDERICK W. (31, Greenhill Road)	...	Tpr.	Hants Y., Oct. 1916, Tpr. Q.O. Oxf. Hus. France.
KING, REGINALD A. (60, Parchment Street)	...	C.S.M.	Welsh R., Pte. Salonica.
KING, WILLIAM E. (4, Penarth Place)	...	L.-Sergt.	Devon, Oct. 1916, Pte. A.P.C. Home.
KINGSTON, MILBERT (10, Gordon Avenue)	...	Pte.	Hants, Sept. 1914, Pte. Home.
KINSHOTT, WILLIAM H. (44, Chesil Street)	...	Corpl.	Hants, 1907, Bandsman. France.
KIRBY, FREDERICK (71, Middle Brook Street)	...	L.-Corpl.	Dorset, 1908, Pte. France. Wounded, Sept. 15, 1914, and July 5, 1915.
KIRBY, ROBERT M. (35, Lower Brook Street)	...	Pte.	R.A.S.C., July 1914, Pte. Shropshire. Dardanelles, Egypt, Salonica.
KIRBY, WALTER R. (7, College Street)	...	Capt.	Hants, Oct. 1914, 2nd Lieut. India, Palestine, Egypt. Despatches 1918.
KITCHENER, ALFRED W. (52, Canon Street)	...	Pte.	Hants Y., June 1916, Tpr. Hants, Worc. France. Gassed once.
KITLEY, GEORGE T. (8, Leonard's Road)	...	Stoker	R.N., 1894, Stoker. Pacific; H.M.S. *Kent*.
KITLEY, HARRY (58, Wharf Hill)	...	L.-Corpl.	Hants Y., Oct. 1916, Tpr. M.F.P. Home.
KNELLER, ERNEST (45, Lower Brook Street)	...	Pte.	Hants, June 1916, Pte. France, Mesopotamia. Wounded, Oct. 1916.
KNELLER, GEORGE (8, Magdalen Hill)	...	Pte.	R.M.L.I., 1899, Pte. North Sea, Russia.
KNIGHT, ALBERT E. (74, Lower Brook Street)	...	Dr.	R.F.A., Aug. 1916, Dr. Salonica.
KNIGHT, ARTHUR F. (13, St. Clement Street)	...	L.-Corpl.	R.A.S.C. (M.T.), May 1916, Pte. Salonica, Roumania.
✠ KNIGHT, CHARLES A. (1, Prinstead Terrace)	...		Canadians, 1914, Pte. France. *Killed in Action*, Apl. 10, 1917, *Vimy Ridge*.
KNIGHT, EDGAR (13, St. Clement Street)	...	C.Q.M.S.	Hants, 1915, Pte. India, Egypt, France, Germany.
KNIGHT, EDWARD C. (12, Prison Quarters)	...	L.-Corpl.	Hants, 1918, Pte. Home.

WINCHESTER WAR SERVICE REGISTER

KNIGHT, EDWARD P. (22, St. Swithun Street)	L.-Corpl.	T.R., July 1917, Pte. Oxf. and Bucks L.I. Hants. Home.
KNIGHT, GEORGE (66, Sussex Street)		Devon, Sept. 1916. Lab. C. France.
KNIGHT, RALPH B. (9, Little Minster Street)		Dorset, June 10, 1916. Somerset L.I. France. Wounded twice, 1918.
KNIGHT, WILLIAM (13, St. Clement Street)	Tpr.	Aus. L.H., Jan. 1916, Tpr. Egypt.
KNIGHTS, ROBERT (81, Colebrook Street)	Bdr.	R.F.A., 1902, Dr. France. Gassed four times.
KNOWLES, FRANK (97, Upper Brook Street)		Hants, Oct. 1915, Pte. Shropshire. France.
KOTCH, ARTHUR H. (61, Parchment Street)	C.Q.M.S.	R.A.S.C., 1910, Dr. Dardanelles.
KOTCH, HAROLD J. (61, Parchment Street)	Corpl.	R.G.A., Nov. 1915, Gun. Home.
KUHN, GEORGE J. (72, High Street)	Cook's Mate	R.N., Mch. 1915, Cook's mate. Mesopotamia, Hong Kong.

LAKE, FRANK (12, North View)	Pte.	T.R., Apl. 1917, Pte. Somerset L.I. Cheshire. France.
LAKE, GEOFFREY J. M. (11, St. John's North)	W.O. (Class 1)	Lond. (T.F.), Aug. 1914, Sergt. France.
LAKE, SIDNEY M. (12, North View)	Corpl.	Hants, 1913, Pte. Dardanelles, France. Wounded, Nov. 2, 1914, Aug. 6, 1915, Oct. 16, 1917, Oct. 9, 1918.
LAKE, WILLIAM H. (12, North View)	P.O.	Merc. Fleet Aux., Nov. 1914. North Sea, Mediterranean.
LALLY, JOHN (5, Greenhill Terrace)	S.M.	R.B., Sergt. Home. Despatches 1918.
LAMBERT, JAMES F. (3, Milverton Road)	L.-Corpl.	Hants Y., Mch. 1916, Tpr. Hants. France. Wounded, June 7, 1917.
LAMBERT, THOMAS W. (Railway Mews, Station Hill)	Pte.	Hants Y., 1915, Tpr. Hants. France, Italy. Wounded twice, 1918.
LAMBERT, WILLIAM J. (Railway Mews, Station Hill)	Sergt.	Hants Y., 1915, Tpr. Home.
LAMING, JESSE E. (36B, Clifton Road)	Sergt.	R.A.S.C., 1911, Dr. Salonica.
LAMING, LEONARD L. (35A, Canon Street)	Pte.	A.V.C., Dec. 1915, Pte. Home.
LAMMIE, THOMAS (65, Lower Brook Street)	Stoker	R.N., Apl. 1913, Stoker. North Sea.
LAMOND, ALEXANDER W. (52, Hatherley Road)	Capt.	Scots Gds., 1907, Pte. York and Lancs. France, Germany. Despatches three times, 1915 and 1917. Croix de Guerre 1915.

WINCHESTER WAR SERVICE REGISTER

LAMOND, HARRY D. (52, Hatherley Road)	C.S.M.		K.R.R.C., May 1916, Rfn. R.B., A.P.C., R.F. Egypt.
LAMOND, HENRY (52, Hatherley Road)	Lieut.		K.R.R.C., rejoined Mch. 1915, W.O. (Class 1). General List. Home. Despatches 1917 and 1918.
LAMOND, KENNETH L. (52, Hatherley Road)	Sergt.		K.R.R.C., June 1915, Rfn. France. Wounded, Nov. 5, 1917, and Oct. 12, 1918.
LAMPARD, ARCHIBALD J. (48, St. Faith's Road)	Corpl.		Hants, Dec. 1914, Pte. India, Egypt, Palestine, France, Germany. Wounded, July 22, 1918.
LAMPARD, ERNEST G. (15, St. Catherine's Road)	Sergt.		A.P.C., Feb. 1915, Pte. Home.
LAMPARD, FREDERICK (68, Sussex Street)	Gun.		R.G.A., 1906, Gun. France.
LAMPARD, HORACE E. (16, Culver Road)	2nd A.M.		R.N.A.S., Aug. 1916, 2nd A.M. R.A.F. France
LAMPARD, LEONARD (68, Sussex Street)	Pte.		Hants, 1914, Pte. Mesopotamia.
LAMPARD, LEONARD S. (20, Highcliffe Road)	2nd A.M.		R.F.C., Nov. 1917, 2nd A.M. R.A.F. France.
LAMPARD, PERCY M. (16, Culver Road)	L.-Corpl.		Hants, 1907, Pte. India, Mesopotamia.
LANDRAY, WILLIAM E. (36, Sussex Street)	Sergt.		A.P.C., 1914, Pte. Home.
LANDRAY, WILLIAM J. (36, Sussex Street)	Pte.		R.A.S.C., Pte., 1915. Salonica, Constantinople.
LANE, ALBERT (42, Parchment Street)	Pte.		Hants, Sept. 1914, Pte. Mesopotamia.
LANE, ROBERT M. (6, St. Giles' Hill Hutments)	Pte.		Hants, Sept. 1914, Pte. R.E., Lab. C. France.
LANE, WALTER (21, Middle Brook Street)	Spr.		Dorset, Jan. 1917, Pte. Hants, R.E. France, Germany. Wounded, Oct. 1, 1918.
LANGFORD, RICHARD (8, Princes Buildings)	Saddler		R.F.A., Aug. 1914, Saddler. France.
LANGMAN, FREDERICK J. (25, Lower Brook Street)			Devon. Apl. 1917, Pte. Lab. C. France. Wounded, Apl. 1918.
✠ LANGRIDGE, WALTER S. (24, Colson Road)	Pte.		Hants, June 1916, Pte. France. *Died from exposure, Feb. 23, 1917.*
LANSDELL, EDWARD C. (8, Upper High Street)	Bdr.		R.G.A. (T.F.), Jan. 1915, Gun. Anti-Aircraft. Home.
LANSLEY, GEORGE (54, St. John's Street)	Pte.		Hants, Sept. 15, 1914. France, India. Wounded, 1915.
LANSLEY, HENRY (54, St. John's Street)	Pte.		Hants, Aug. 1917, Pte. Home.
✠ LANSLEY, WILLIAM (54, St. John's Street)	Stoker		R.N., 1902. H.M.S. *Good Hope*. *Killed in Action, Nov. 1, 1914.*
LAVERTY, ARTHUR A. (1, College Street)	Sergt.		Amer. Army, 1917, Pte. Home.

WINCHESTER WAR SERVICE REGISTER

LAVERTY, AUGUSTINE H. (1, College Street)	...	Cadet Pilot	Hants, 1915, Pte. R.A.F. India, Egypt, Palestine.
LAVERTY, DONALD G. ... (1, College Street)	...	C.P.O.	R.N.A.S., May 1915, L.M. R.A.F. Home.
LAVERTY, EDWIN I. ... (1, Nelson Road)	...	P.O.	R.N., Nov. 1915, Carpenter. North Sea; H.M.S. *Monarch*.
LAVERTY, JOHN R. ... (1, College Street)	...	Rfn.	R.B., 1915, Rfn. Home.
LAVERTY, REGINALD N. (1, College Street)	...	Pte.	M.M.G., 1915, Pte. Tank C. France. Wounded, Sept. 16, 1916.
✠ LAVERTY, WILLIAM H. (1, College Street)	...	S.M.	K.R.R.C., 1898, Rfn. France. *Killed in Action, Apl.* 1917.
LAVINGTON, GEORGE ... (105, High Street)	...		Hants, Aug. 1914. N. Fus. Home.
LAWES, GEORGE E. ... (83, Upper Brook Street)	...	Corpl.	R.B., Sept. 1916, Rfn. A.P.C. Home.
LAWLER, RUPERT ... (21, Monks Road)	...	Bdr.	R.G.A., Oct. 1915, Gun. France.
LAWLER, THOMAS ... (21, Monks Road)	...		Hants Y., Aug. 1914. Hants. France, Italy. Wounded once.
✠ LAWRANCE, ALBERT E. (25, Greenhill Road)	...	Pte.	Glos., Mch. 1916, Pte. Devon. France, Italy. *Killed in Action, Apl.* 22, 1918.
LAWRENCE, EDWARD ... (13, Greyfriars Terrace)	...	Capt.	Lancers, 1907, Tpr. N. Fus. France. Wounded, Feb. 1915, and Aug. 1916. D.C.M. 1915, M.C. 1916, Médaille Militaire 1914.
LAWRENCE, GILBERT L. (15, Clifton Road)	...	L.-Corpl.	R.A.S.C. (M.T.), 1914, Pte. France.
LAWRENCE, HENRY A. (13, Greyfriars Terrace)	...	2nd Corpl.	R.E., 1901, Dr. France.
✠ LAWRENCE, PERCY J. ... (13, Greyfriars Terrace)	...	Bdr.	R.F.A., Jan. 1915, Gun. Salonica, France. Wounded, 1916. *Killed in Action, July* 27, 1917.
LAWRENCE, ROBERT T. (13, Greyfriars Terrace)	...	P.O. (Class 1)	R.N., North Sea. Torpedoed, Aug. 1915.
LAWRENCE, THEODORE H. (Harpsdene, Nelson Road)	...	Spr.	Hants Y., Apl. 1916, Pte. Hants, R.E. France. Wounded, June 15 and July 31, 1917.
LAWRENCE, WILLIAM A. (15, Clifton Road)	...	Sergt.	R.F.C., Aug. 1914, 2nd A.M. R.A.F. Belgium, France.
LAWRENCE, WILLIAM G. (13, Greyfriars Terrace)	...	Pte.	Hants, Aug. 1914, Pte. India, Mesopotamia. Taken Prisoner by Turks, May 1916.
LAWTON, WILLIAM H. (69, Middle Brook Street)	...	Rfn.	Hants, Pte. R. Berks, R.E., R.B. France. Wounded, June 1917.
LAY, ETHELBERT ... (1, Owens Road)	...	A.M.	R.N.A.S., Feb. 1918, A.M. R.A.F. Home, H.M.S. *Furious*.
LAYTON, ROBERT A. ... (Wharf Hill)	...	Pte.	R.A.S.C. (M.T.), June 1916, Pte. Home.

WINCHESTER WAR SERVICE REGISTER

✠ LEACH, WILLIAM F. ... R.S.M. ... Hants, 1906, Pte. India, Mesopotamia. Taken Prisoner by Turks, Kut. *Died of typhus.*
(2, Alswitha Terrace)

✠ LEAL, ALFRED C. ... Pte. ... Hants, Nov. 1915, Pte. India. *Missing, Jan. 21, 1916.*
(10, Greyfriars Terrace)

LEAL, CHARLES E. ... Pte. ... Hants, Jan. 1917, Pte. Devon. Home.
(10, Greyfriars Terrace)

LEAR, ALBERT W. ... Corpl. ... R.A.S.C. (M.T.), Nov. 1915. France.
(46, Nuns Road)

LEE, ALFRED ... Pte. ... R.A.S.C., Aug. 1916, Pte. Home.
(18, St. John's North)

LEE, FREDERICK J. ... L.-Corpl. ... Hants, Apl. 1917, Pte. France.
(18, St. John's North)

LEE, MARTIN T.... ... ... Hants, 1913. Palestine.
(49, Owens Road)

LEE, REGINALD E. ... L.-Corpl. ... Bedford, Pte. Northants. France, Egypt. Wounded, Oct. 1914.
(4, Alswitha Terrace)

✠ LEES, HENRY G. ... Pte. ... Hants, June 1916, Pte. France. *Killed in Action, Nov. 5, 1917.*
(12, Bar End)

LEES, WILLIAM J. ... Pte. ... Hants, Mch. 1916, Pte. India, Palestine, France.
(69, Chesil Street)

LEGG, HARRY A. ... 2nd Corpl. ... Hants, Dec. 1914, Pte. R.E. India, Mesopotamia.
(40, Andover Road)

LEGGE, CECIL ... Corpl. ... Hants, 1912, Pte. M.G.C. Mesopotamia, Palestine, India. Wounded twice. Taken Prisoner by Turks, Apl. 29, 1916, Kut.
(19, City Road)

LEMON, WILLIAM ... Corpl. ... R.A.S.C., Aug. 1914, Pte. Egypt, Salonica.
(Durngate House, North Walls)

LESSITER, CHARLES W. ... L.-Corpl. ... R.A.S.C. (M.T.), Nov. 1915, Pte. France. Gassed, July 22, 1917.
(80, Lower Brook Street)

LESSTER, ARTHUR A. ... C.P.O. ... R.N.A.S., Aug. 1915, A.M. R.A.F. Home.
(3, Clifton Terrace)

LETFORD, RICHARD H. ... Pte. ... R.A.S.C., Feb. 1915, Pte. France, Belgium, Germany.
(127, Upper Brook Street)

✠ LEVER, GEORGE T. ... Pte. ... Hants, Oct. 1, 1914, Pte. Belgium. *Missing (believed Killed), Oct. 3, 1914.*
(11, Milverton Road)

LEWINGTON, ALFRED O. ... A.M. ... R.F.C., July 1916, A.M. R.A.F. France, Germany.
(Christ's Hospital)

LEWINGTON, ARCHIBALD A. ... Pte. ... Hants, June 1917, Pte. D.C.L.I. France, Italy. Wounded, June 28, 1918.
(Christ's Hospital)

LEWINGTON, ERNEST ... ... Hants Y., Nov. 17, 1914. Hants. France. Wounded, Mch. 27, 1918. M.M. 1918.
(3, Romsey Road)

LEWIS, ALBERT G. ... Corpl. ... R.G.A., 1914, Gun. France, Gibraltar, Italy, Salonica, Mesopotamia. Wounded, 1915. M.M. 1918.
(2, Colson Road)

LEWIS, CHARLES M. ... ... R.N.A.S., Sept. 1917. R.A.F. Home.
(11, South View)

WINCHESTER WAR SERVICE REGISTER

Lewis, Edward R. (11, South View)	...	Pte.	R. Munster Fus., 1910, Pte. France.
Lewis, Ernest H. (46, Lower Brook Street)	...	Pte.	Hants, Oct. 1916, Pte. India.
Lewis, Frank (12, High Street)	...	A.-Sergt.	Hants, Aug. 1914, Pte. Bedford. Mesopotamia, India.
Lewis, Frederick (10, Poulsome Place)	...	Pte.	Welsh, May 1916, Pte. Lab. C. France.
Lewis, Frederick H. (14, Hyde Street)	...		R.A.S.C., Apl. 1916. R.G.A. France, Germany.
Lewis, Henry J. (38, Greenhill Road)	...	Q.M.S.	K.R.R.C., 1902, Rfn. Home. M.S.M. 1919, Despatches.
Lewis, Herbert (14, Canute Road)	...	Corpl.	R.E., May 1915, Corpl. France, Salonica.
✠ Lewis, Hugh F. (Myddelton, Christ Church Rd.)	...	Capt.	R.W.S., 1900, Lieut. Belgium. Despatches 1915. *Killed in Action, Oct. 19, 1914, Ledeghem.*
Lewis, Leslie (83, High Street)	...	Corpl.	R.B., Sept. 1915, Rfn. Home.
Lewis, Stanley H. (2, Colson Road)	...	Pte.	Warwick, Oct. 1917, Pte. R.I.F. France. Wounded once.
Lewis, William (14, Canute Road)	...		Lond. Scot., Sept. 1916. Home.
Light, Frederick (55, Lower Brook Street)	...		R.N., 1897. North Sea. P.O.W. in Holland.
Light, John (30, Water Lane)	...	Pte.	Hants, 1894, Pte. Suffolk. Home.
Light, Prinches A. (43, Fairfield Road)	...	Corpl.	R.A.O.C., Mch. 1915, Pte. Dardanelles, Egypt, Cyprus.
✠ Light, Robert C. (27, St. Catherine's Road)	...	Sergt.	K.R.R.C., rejoined Aug. 1914, Corpl. France. *Killed in Action, Mch. 10, 1915, Neuve Chapelle.*
Light, Thomas R. (27, St. Catherine's Road)	...	Pte.	D.L.I., June 1916, Pte. Lab. C. France.
Light, William J. (27, St. Catherine's Road)	...	Pte.	T.R., Mch. 1917, Pte. R.W.S. France, Germany.
Lillington, Percy W. (5, Saxon Road)	...		Hants Y., 1915. M.P. Home.
Lincoln, Harry W. (10, Fairfield Road)	...	P.O. (1st Class)	R.N., rejoined Aug. 1914. R.N.R. Gallipoli, Russia, North Sea.
Lingham, Melville G. (6, Union Street)	...	Pte.	Wilts, Aug. 1914, Pte. Dardanelles. Wounded three times.
✠ Lloyd, Conway W. B. (Westbury, City Road)	...	C.S.M.	P.P.C.L.I., Aug. 1914, Pte. France, Belgium. *Killed in Action, Feb. 28, 1915, St. Eloi.*
Lloyd, John (33, Romsey Road)	...	Pte.	Devon, Apl. 1915, Pte. Lab. C. Home.
✠ Lloyd, William (63, Chesil Street)	...		R.G.A. France. *Killed in Action, Aug. 2, 1917, Armentières.*

WINCHESTER WAR SERVICE REGISTER

✠ Loader, Albert (16, Hyde Close)	A.B.	R.N., 1897, Boy. R.F.R. High Seas. *Killed in Action, Feb.* 29, 1916, *North Sea.*
Loader, George (58, Parchment Street)	Spr.	R.E., July 1916, Spr. Salonica, Russia.
✠ Loader, Thomas B. (16, Hyde Close)	Pte.	Hants, Mch. 1916, Pte. Dorset. France, Belgium. Wounded, Aug. 1916, July, and Dec. 1917. *Died of Wounds, Feb.* 2, 1918.
Loasey, Arthur L. (137, High Street)		R.F.A., Aug. 1917. Home.
Lock, Alfred J. (90, Colebrook Street)	Corpl.	R.F.A., May 1914, Gun. France, Salonica. Gassed, 1915. D.C.M. 1915, Serbian Gold Cross 1916.
✠ Lock, Ernest (17, St. John's South)	Pte.	Canadians, Dec. 1914, Pte. France. *Killed in Action, Sept.* 26, 1916.
Lock, George (90, Colebrook Street)	Bandsman	Hants, June 1914, Band Boy. India, Mesopotamia.
Lock, Harry (90, Colebrook Street)		Tank C., July 1917, Gun. France.
Lock, James (90, Colebrook Street)	Pte.	Hants, Aug. 1914, Pte. Gallipoli. Wounded, Aug. 6, 1915.
Lofting, George T. (Station House, L. & S.W.R.)	Dr.	R.A.S.C. (M.T.), Dr. France.
Lomer, Bertie C. (4, Birinus Road)	Spr.	R.E., Spr. India, Mesopotamia.
Lomer, Frank (4, Birinus Road)		Hants, Nov. 10, 1915. Home.
Lomer, Frederick G. (4, Birinus Road)	Corpl.	Hants. India.
✠ Lomer, Stanley R. (4, Birinus Road)		Gordon H. France. *Killed in Action, Sept.* 25, 1915, *Hooge.*
Long, Harold (4, Victoria Road)	A.B.	R.N., 1908, Boy. Falkland Islands, Dardanelles, Grand Fleet; H.M.S. *Duke of Edinburgh, Inflexible,* and *Blenheim.*
✠ Long, Herbert J. S. (4, Victoria Road)	Bdr.	R.G.A., 1904, Gun. France. Wounded once. *Killed in Action, Mch.* 26, 1918.
Long, Lawrence M. (8, Monks' Road)	Gun.	R.G.A., Aug. 1916, Gun. France.
✠ Longman, Cecil R. (11, Middle Brook Street)	L.-Corpl.	Hants, Sept. 1914, Pte. France. Despatches 1916. *Killed in Action, Sept.* 9, 1916.
Longman, William (5, St. Paul's Hill)	Pte.	Dorset, Aug. 1914, Pte. France. Wounded, and taken Prisoner by Germans, Aug. 24, 1914.
✠ Loveland, Ernest C. (4, Egbert Road)	Pte.	Hants, 1913, Pte. Mesopotamia. Taken Prisoner by Turks. *Died as P.O.W.*
Loveland, George H. (4, Egbert Road)	Sergt.	Hants, Aug. 1914, Pte. R.A.S.C. Mesopotamia.
✠ Loveland, Henry W. V. (4, Egbert Road)	Lieut.	Winnipeg Grenadiers, Sept. 1915, Lieut. R.A.F. France. *Killed in Action, Apl.* 1917.

WINCHESTER WAR SERVICE REGISTER

LOVELAND, WILLIAM H. (4, Egbert Road)	Sergt.	R.F.C., Nov. 1917, Cadet. R.A.F. Home.
LOVELL, A. N. (Butt's Close, Weeke)	Major	Hants Y., Oct. 1914, Major. France.
LOVELOCK, CHARLES J. (13, Hyde Close)	Dr.	R.A.S.C., June 1916, Dr. Salonica, Egypt.
LOVELOCK, ERNEST E. W. (29, Owens Road)	Pte.	Hants, Nov. 1915, Pte. Home.
LOVELOCK, GEORGE (1, Alswitha Terrace)	L.-Corpl.	Lincoln, Feb. 1916, Pte. France. Wounded, Apl. 12, 1917.
✠ LOVELOCK, GEORGE A. (10, Greenhill Road)	Pte.	Hants, Aug. 1914, Pte. Dardanelles. *Killed in Action, Aug. 9, 1915.*
✠ LOVELOCK, JAMES (1, Alswitha Terrace)		Hants, Sept. 1914. India, Egypt. *Killed in Action, Nov. 24, 1917.*
LOVICK, ALFRED F. A. (26, Monks Road)	C.S.M.	R.G.A., rejoined, C.S.M. Home.
LOWE, WILLIAM E. (36, Union Street)		Nat. Res., Sept. 1914, Pte. R.D.C. Home.
LOWE, WILLIAM G. (13, Queen's Road)	Spr.	Lond. (Civil Service Rif.), Aug. 1914, Pte. R.E. France, Belgium.
✠ LUCAS, REGINALD (22, Wales Street)	Pte.	Devon, Feb. 12, 1917, Pte. D. of W. Regt. France. *Missing, believed Killed, Nov. 21, 1917.*
LUCAS, WILLIAM T. (Deacon Hill, Chilcomb)	Pte.	Hants, Nov. 1915, Pte. India.
✠ LUFFMAN, WALTER (62, Parchment Street)	Pte.	Hants, Sept. 1914, Pte. Mesopotamia. Wounded, Dec. 14, 1915. *Died of Wounds, Dec. 19, 1915.*
✠ LUND, GEOFFREY W. (35, Monks Road)	C.S.M.	Hants, 1915, Pte. Dardanelles, France. Wounded twice, gassed. D.C.M. *Killed in Action, Apl. 21, 1917.*
LUNN, WILLIAM H. (3, Clifton Road)	Corpl.	R.A.S.C. (M.T.), Feb. 1916, Pte. France.
LYNCH, JAMES (1, Penarth Place)	L.-Corpl.	R.W.S., 1913, Pte. France. Wounded, Mch. 18 and Sept. 20, 1918.
LYNCH, ROBERT (1, Penarth Place)	L.-Corpl.	R.W.S., 1914, Pte. Home.
LYON, WALTER G. (8, St. John's Park Terrace)	Sergt.	Hants, 1893, Pte. France.
LYONS, WILLIAM J. (1, Highfield Terrace)	L.-Corpl.	Devon, Nov. 1916, Pte. Lab. C. France.
McCALL, REGINALD D. (1, Royal Oak Passage)	Pte.	Hants, Jan. 1914, Pte. India, Mesopotamia.
McCALL, WILLIAM T. (1, Royal Oak Passage)	Lieut.	Hants (T.F.), 1887, Pte. Hants, R.D.C. India, Mesopotamia.

WINCHESTER WAR SERVICE REGISTER

McCarthy, George H. (32, Arbour Terrace)	...	Essex Y., Aug. 1914. M.G.C. France. Wounded, 1916 and 1917. Taken Prisoner by Germans, 1917.
McDonald, D. ...	L.-Corpl.	Worc., Mar. 1915, Pte. Wounded.
MacDuff, John H. (28, Water Lane)	1st A.M.	Oxf. and Bucks L.I., 1917, Pte. R.A.F. France, Belgium, Germany.
Mackersy, William A. (12, Durngate Place)	Lieut.	Lond., May 1915, Pte. Lab. C., Chinese. Flanders, France.
McKey, Francis W. (47, Greenhill Road)	C.-Sergt.	K.R.R.C., rejoined Nov. 1914, C.-Sergt. Home.
McKey, Francis W., jun. (47, Greenhill Road)	Corpl.	K.R.R.C., 1912, Boy. France, Russia.
McKey, Herbert F. (47, Greenhill Road)	Sergt.	K.R.R.C., 1910, Boy. R. Sussex. France. Taken Prisoner by Germans, Mch. 21, 1918.
McKie, Harry F. (90, Stockbridge Road)	Gun.	R.G.A., June 1916, Gun. France. Gassed, Dec. 20, 1917.
Macklin, Albert A. (39, Union Street)	Spr.	Hants, Pte. R.E. France. Wounded, July 13, 1917.
Macklin, Alfred (39, Andover Road)	Sergt.	M.M.G.C., 1914, Pte. France.
Macklin, Edgar W. (69, Chesil Street)	Pte.	Hants, Nov. 1914, Pte. India, Palestine, France.
Macklin, Frederick M. (113, Upper Brook Street)	Pte.	Essex, Oct. 1916, Pte. R.W.S., Lab. C. France.
Macklin, George H. (91, Colebrook Street)	Corpl.	Hants, Sept. 1914, Pte. M.F.P. Mesopotamia, India.
Macklin, Stanley G. (12, Brassey Road)	Spr.	R.E., Feb. 1917, Spr. France.
✠ Macklin, Sydney (11, Colebrook Street)	Pte.	Hants, Aug. 1914, Pte. India, Mesopotamia. *Killed in Action, Feb. 5, 1917, Baghdad.*
Mackrell, Sydney G. (15, Culver Road)	L.-Corpl.	R.M.L.I., Feb. 1917, Pte. Mudros.
✠ Maclachlan, Ronald C. (Langhouse, Chilbolton Avenue)	Brig.-Gen.	R.B., 1895, 2nd Lieut. France, Belgium. Wounded, July 30, 1916. D.S.O. 1916, Despatches twice. *Killed in Action, Aug. 11, 1917, near Ypres.*
Maidment, Frank A. (6, Back Street, St. Cross)	Rfn.	R.B., Aug. 1914, Rfn. France. Wounded, July 31 and Sept. 25, 1915.
✠ Maidment, Harold W. (6, Back Street, St. Cross)	L.-Corpl.	R.B., Sept. 1914, Rfn. France. Wounded, June 21, 1915. *Killed in Action, Mch. 22, 1918, Ham.*
✠ Maidment, Herbert G. (1, Gladstone Street)	Sergt.	R.F., Sept. 21, 1914, Pte. Lond. Malta, Dardanelles, Egypt, France. *Killed in Action, Sept. 15, 1916, Somme.*
Mainwaring, Walter (1, Magdalen Hill)	Bandsman	Hants, 1914, Bandsman. Mesopotamia.
Major, Charles (34, St. John's Street)	Pte.	A.V.C., Nov. 10, 1915, Pte. Egypt.

WINCHESTER WAR SERVICE REGISTER

✠ MALE, REGINALD H. ... L.-Corpl. Hants Y., Sept. 1914, Tpr. M.G.C. France, (Trevenna, Stockbridge Road) Flanders. *Killed in Action, Sept.* 18, 1918.

MANLEY, ERIC R. ... Lieut. ... R.F., Sept. 1914, Pte. D.L.I., R.A.F. France, (Brookside, St. Cross) Belgium.

MANSBRIDGE, HERBERT J. ... Corpl. ... R.E., 1916, Spr. France.
(2, Hadleigh Villas)

MANSON, ALICK ... R.H.A., 1905. R.F.A. France. Wounded, Aug. 2, (St. Philip's, Sleeper's Hill) 1915.

MARCHANT, ALFRED J. ... L.-Corpl. Hants, June 1916, Pte. Egypt, India, France.
(21, Elm Road)

MARCHANT, ERNEST A.... ... Pte. ... Hants (T.F.), rejoined Aug. 1914, Pte. Home.
(14, North Walls)

MARCHANT, HARRY ... Pte. ... Hants, July 1917, Pte. Glos. France, Russia.
(14, North Walls) Wounded, June and Aug. 1918.

✠ MARINER, ALBERT E. ... Pte. ... Glos., Mch. 20, 1916, Pte. France. *Killed in*
(18, St. John's Street) *Action, Apl.* 1918, *Kemmel.*

MARINER, ALBERT H. ... Pte. ... Hants, Nov. 1915, Pte. Home.
(2, St. Swithun's Terrace)

✠ MARINER, JAMES E. ... L.-Corpl. Hants, Pte. India, Mesopotamia. Wounded once.
(33, Canon Street) Taken Prisoner by Turks, Aug. 29, 1916. *Died, June* 29, 1917, *Constantinople.*

✠ MARINER, JOSEPH W. ... Pte. ... Hants, Sept. 1914, Pte. India, Mesopotamia.
(33, Canon Street) Taken Prisoner by Turks, Apl. 29, 1916. *Died, June* 27, 1916, *Baghdad.*

MARINER, WILLIAM ... Spr. ... Devon, Pte. R.E. France, Belgium.
(8, Pageant Villas)

MARINER, WILLIAM ... Bandsman Hants, 1898, Bandsman. Home.
(17, Victoria Road)

MARKS, LEONARD G. ... Pte. ... Hants, Aug. 1914, Pte. Mesopotamia.
(12, High Street)

MARLOW, JESSE C. ... Sergt. ... Hants, Sept. 1914, Pte. France.
(35, Eastgate Street)

MARLOW, THOMAS H. ... Pte. ... Nat. Res., Aug. 1914, Pte. Dorset. Wounded
(Canon Street) once.

MARRINER, HERBERT G. ... R.A.S.C., June 1915. France, Belgium.
(24, Andover Road)

MARRINER, JOHN R. ... Corpl. ... Hants Y., May 1916, Tpr. M.G.C. Egypt.
(43, Brassey Road)

✠ MARSH, BERTIE W. ... Pte. ... Hants, Aug. 1914, Pte. Mesopotamia, India.
(8, Little Minster Street) Wounded, 1915 and 1918. *Died of Wounds, June* 2, 1918.

MARSH, EDWARD ... Pte. ... Hants, rejoined Aug., 1914, Pte. India.
(8, Little Minster Street)

MARSH, EDWARD C. T. ... Pte. ... K.R.R.C., 1907, Rfn. R.A.M.C. France, Salonica,
(16, Upper Brook Street) Malta. Wounded twice.

MARSH, EDWIN J. ... Pte. ... Somerset L.I., May 15, 1917, Pte. France, Egypt.
(6, Wharf Hill)

WINCHESTER WAR SERVICE REGISTER

Marsh, George (2, Union Street)	...	Pte.	Hants, May 1916, Pte. India, Egypt.
Marsh, Henry (21, Victoria Road)	...		R.N.A.S., May 1917. R.A.F. Home.
Marsh, Jim (35, Union Street)	...	Pte.	Hants, June 1916, Pte. Salonica. Wounded, Apl. 25, 1917.
Marsh, William H. (4, East Cliffe)	...		Hants, Apl. 10, 1915. Lab. C. France, Salonica, Turkey. Wounded, Apl. 24, 1917.
✠ Marshall, Albert (46, St. Faith's Road)	...	Rfn.	R.B., rejoined Aug. 1914, Rfn. France. Wounded, May 8, 1915. D.C.M. 1915. *Died of Wounds, May* 12, 1915, *Boulogne*.
Marshall, Alfred (46, St. Faith's Road)	...	Sergt.	Innis. D., rejoined Oct. 1914, Corpl. Home.
Marshall, Arthur W. (46, St. Faith's Road)	...	C.P.O.	R.N., 1901, Boy. R.N.A.S., R.A.F. North Sea. D.F.M.
Marshall, Edgar S. (46, St. Faith's Road)	...	Pte.	Hants, Aug. 1914, Pte. India, Mesopotamia.
Marshall, Joseph (8, Romsey Road)	...	Pte.	Hants, rejoined Nov. 1916, Pte. Home.
Marshall, Victor C. (46, St. Faith's Road)	...	P.O. (2nd Class)	R.N., 1909, Boy. Zeebrugge, Ostend.
Marshall, William (46, St. Faith's Road)	...	P.O. (2nd Class)	R.N., 1899, Boy. North Sea.
Martin, Harry (45, St. Faith's Road)	...	Dr.	R.E., Aug. 1918, Dr. Home.
Martin, James H. (20, Andover Road)	...	Stoker	R.N., Jan. 1917, Stoker. English Channel.
Martin, John T. (3, Wales Street)	...	Sergt.	Hants, 1906, Pte. France. M.M. 1917.
Martin, Lawrence (1, Stanmore Lane)	...	Cook's Mate	R.N., 1915, Cook's Mate. North Sea.
Martin, Lawrence (34, Tower Street)	...	Pte.	R.A.S.C. (M.T.), Aug. 1914, Pte. France.
Martin, Robert J. (11, Kingsgate Street)	...	Cadet	R.F.C., Nov. 1917, Cadet. R. Berks. France. Wounded, Sept. 18, 1919.
✠ Martin, Sidney J. (3, Wales Street)	...	Pte.	Hants, 1907, Pte. France. Wounded, Nov. 1914, April 1915, June 1918 (gas). *Died of Wounds* (gas), *July* 1918.
Martin, William (4, City Road)	...	C.S.M.	R.A.S.C., 1914, Pte. France, Belgium, Italy.
✠ Martin, William (3, Wales Street)	...	Gun.	R.F.A., 1912, Gun. Mesopotamia. Taken Prisoner by Turks, 1916, Kut. *Died, Aug.* 21, 1916, *Kut*.
✠ Maslin, Alfred (11, Freelands Buildings)	...	Tpr.	N. Somerset Y., July 1917, Tpr. France. *Killed in Action, May* 26, 1918.
Maslin, Alfred (11, Freelands Buildings)	...	Pte.	R. Marines, June 1917, Pte. France.
Mason, Albert E. (1, Egbert Road)	...	Pte.	Hants, Oct. 1916, Pte. France. Wounded, Dec. 2, 1917, Sept. 5 and Oct. 17, 1918.

WINCHESTER WAR SERVICE REGISTER

MASON, CHARLES ... ... L.-Corpl. ... Can. Inf., Oct. 1914, Pte. France. Wounded, (51, Canon Street) Sept. 15, 1916.

MASON, CHARLES J. ... ... A.M. ... R.A.F., Dec. 1917, A.M. Home. (10, Water Lane)

✠ MASON, FRANCIS H. ... ... R.E., Aug. 1914. Gallipoli, Salonica, Egypt. (1, Egbert Road) Wounded, Aug. 18, 1915. *Died of Pneumonia, Cairo.*

✠ MASON, FRANK ... ... Corpl. ... R.B., Nov. 1915, Rfn. France. *Killed in Action,* (51, Canon Street) *Sept. 15, 1916.*

MASON, JOHN H. ... ... Lieut. ... A.P.C., Apl. 1, 1917, Corpl. Home. (35, Arbour Cottages)

MASON, JOHN W. ... ... Sergt. ... Hants, 1913, Pte. India, Persia. (1, Egbert Road)

MASON, MOSES ... ... L.-Corpl. ... R.B., 1908, Rfn. France. Wounded, July 12, (11, Colebrook Place) 1916, and Aug. 1918. Gassed, 1917.

MASON, WILLIAM W. ... ... Hants, Apl. 1916. India, Egypt, Arabia, Palestine. (42B, Eastgate Street)

✠ MATHEWS, ARTHUR W.... ... Gun. ... R.F.A., Oct. 1916, Gun. Yorks. France. *Killed* (Upper Chilcomb) *in Action, Aug. 25, 1918.*

MATHEWS, JAMES A. ... ... C.Q.M.S. ... R.F.A., 1904, Gun. France, Salonica. (Upper Chilcomb)

✠ MATHEWS, WILLIAM S. ... ... Lieut. ... Hants Y., Sept. 1914, Tpr. K.R.R.C. France. (23, St. Thomas Street) *Killed in Action, Sept. 15, 1916, Flers.*

MATON, ALFRED G. ... ... Pte. ... Glos., 1903, Pte. France. M.M. and Bar. (10, North View)

MATON, EDWARD ... ... Corpl. ... Glos., Aug. 1915, Pte. Northants. France. M.M. (10, North View) 1918.

✠ MATON, HARRY R. ... ... R.A.S.C., 1910. Salonica. *Died, Nov. 10, 1918.* (10, North View)

MATTHEWS, FRANCIS L. ... Devon. Glos. France. Gassed once. (1, Freeland Buildings)

MATTHEWS, GEORGE W. ... ... Sig. ... Hants, Aug. 1914, Sig. Ind.A.C. India, Persian (108, St. Cross Road) Gulf.

MATTHEWS, THEODORE H. ... Wheeler ... R.A.S.C., Aug. 1914, Wheeler. France. (14, Romsey Road)

MATTINGLEY, WILLIAM J. ... Gun. ... R.G.A., May 1916, Gun. Home. (9, Water Lane)

MATTOCK, ARCHIBALD W. ... Spr. ... Hants, Sept. 1914, Pte. R.E. France. Wounded, (26, Front Street, St. Cross) Sept. 26, 1917.

MATTOCK, CECIL B. ... ... Pte. ... Devon, May 1917, Pte. R.A.F. Home. (58, Water Lane)

MAUDE, THOMAS R. ... ... Pte. ... Artists' Rif., Feb. 14, 1918, Pte. Lond. Asia (Rosehill, St. James' Lane) Minor, Egypt.

MAUGHAN, ROBERT W. ... Sergt. ... R.A.M.C., Aug. 6, 1914, Pte. France, Salonica. (10, Princes Buildings)

MAULE, HARRY J. H. ... ... R.W.S., Nov. 18, 1915. Mesopotamia. Wounded, (35, Southgate Street) 1916.

WINCHESTER WAR SERVICE REGISTER

May, Cecil (Upper Chilcomb)	... Pte.	...	Hants, Nov. 1915, Pte. M.P. India, Mesopotamia.
May, Charles G. (33, Owens Road)	... Pte.	...	Hants Y., Sept. 1914, Tpr. R.A.S.C. (M.T.). France.
May, Frank A. (33, Owens Road)	... Corpl	...	Hants Y., Feb. 1914, Tpr. R.E. France. Wounded, June 7, 1917.
✠ May, Frederick James (Upper Chilcomb)	... Pte.	...	Hants, 1915, Pte. Dardanelles. *Killed in Action*, 1915.
May, Frederick John (49, Eastgate Street)	... Pte.	...	R.A.S.C. (M.T.), Apl. 1916, Pte. France.
May, George E. (Upper Chilcomb)	... Pte.	...	Warwick, Sept. 1916, Pte. France. Taken Prisoner by Germans.
May, Herbert A. (33, Owens Road)	... Corpl.	...	R.A.F., May 14, 1918, Pte. Home.
Mayne, Albert E. (9, West End Terrace)	... Sig.	...	R.E., Nov. 20, 1915, Sig. France.
✠ Mayo, Alexander J. (6, St. Peter Street)	... Capt.	...	R.F.C., Dec. 1915, 2nd Lieut. R.A.F. France. *Killed in Action, Aug. 9, 1918, Foucaucourt*.
✠ Mayo, William C. (6, St. Peter Street)	... Lieut.	...	C.U.R.V., Oct. 1905. Sherwood For. *Killed in Action, Aug. 9, 1915, Suvla Bay*.
Meacher, Albert E. V. (11, Eastgate Street)	...		R. Berks, July 1916. R.E., K.O.Y.L.I. France.
✠ Meacher, Edwin J. (11, Eastgate Street)	... Corpl.	...	Hants, 1909, Pte. Dardanelles. *Killed in Action, Apl. 28, 1915.*
Meacher, Frederick (29, Tower Street)	... Stoker	...	R.N., 1915, Stoker. North Sea.
Meacher, Harold (29, Nuns Road)	...		R.A.F., 1916. Home.
✠ Meacher, John H. (29, Tower Street)	... L.-Corpl.	...	R. Marines, 1912, Pte. R.N.D. France. *Killed in Action, Apl. 28, 1917, Arras*.
Meacher, Percival C. (11, Greenhill Road)	... Bandsman		Hants, 1912, Bandsman. India, Persian Gulf, Egypt, Palestine, France, Germany.
Meadham, Arthur J. (45, Chesil Street)	...		R.E., Feb. 1917. Home.
Mears, Raphael H. O. (31, Milverton Road)	... Corpl.	...	Hants, Aug. 1916, Pte. Devon, A.P.C., R.B., A.P.C. Home.
Meigh, George (15, Saxon Road)	... Sergt.	...	R.A.S.C. (M.T.), Pte. Home.
Merchant, James R. (2, West End Terrace)	... Spr.	...	R.E., Sept. 3, 1917, Spr. France, Belgium.
✠ Merritt, Alfred E. (9, Lawn Street)	... Sergt.	...	Hants, 1901, Pte. Dardanelles, France. Despatches 1917. *Killed in Action, Apl. 23, 1917.*
Merritt, Alfred H. D. (1, Canon Street)	... A.B.	...	R.N., Jan. 19, 1917, A.B. H.M.S. *Comus*.
Merritt, David (27, Lower Brook Street)	... Pte.	...	Hants, 1908, Pte. Lab. C. Home.

WINCHESTER WAR SERVICE REGISTER

MERRITT, GEORGE H. ... ... Pte. ... Hants, Sept. 6, 1914, Pte. Lab. C. Home.
(1, Canon Street)

✠ MERRITT, GEORGE H. ... ... L.-Corpl. Hants, Jan. 1915, Pte. France. Wounded, Dec.
(Upper Chilcomb) 4, 1915, and June 1916. *Killed in Action, Mch. 17, 1918.*

MERRITT, LEONARD W. ... Pte. ... Hants, Aug. 1917, Pte. M.G.C. France. Wounded,
(Upper Chilcomb) Mch. 1918.

MERRITT, WALTER J. ... ... Pte. ... Hants, July 1916, Pte. France.
(56, Wales Street)

MESSENGER, THOMAS G. ... Pte. ... Hants, June 1916, Pte. Lab. C. France.
(19, Water Lane)

MESSINGHAM WILLIAM J. ... Drummer Hants, 1894, Drummer. Home.
(26, St. Catherine's Road)

METTYEAR, FREDERICK G. ... Sig. ... R.E., Nov. 23, 1915, Sig. France. Wounded,
(39, North Walls) May 6, 1917.

METTYEAR, VICTOR ... ... Spr. ... Hants (T.F.), Aug. 1914, Pte. R.E. Egypt,
(39, North Walls) Salonica.

MICKLAM, CYRIL B. S. ... Lieut. ... Hants, Sept. 1914, Pte. R.E. Home.
(Ivanhoe, Hyde Abbey Road)

✠ MIDDLETON, BERTRAM C. ... L.-Corpl. A.P.C., Nov. 1914, Pte. Arg. and Suth. H. France.
(7, Cheriton Road) Wounded, Apl. 12, 1918. *Died of Wounds, May 21, 1918.*

MIDDLETON, HAROLD W. ... Sergt. ... R.E., July 1916, Spr. Home.
(7, Cheriton Road)

MIDGLEY, ERNEST ... ... Sergt. ... R.B., 1914, Sergt. France. Taken Prisoner by
(50, Parchment Street) Germans, 1914.

MILBURN, LESLIE ... ... Capt. ... R.A.M.C., Lieut., 1918. Italy.
(1, Sparkford Road)

MILDENHALL, EDWIN J. ... Pte. ... Welsh, May 1916, Pte. R.W.F. France. Wounded,
(9, King Alfred Place) June 12, 1917.

MILDENHALL, WILLIAM A. ... Gun. ... R.G.A., June 1916, Gun. France, Belgium.
(7, King Alfred Place) Wounded, Jan. 10, 1917.

MILES, ALFRED F. ... ... Pte. ... T.R., Pte. Glos. Home.
(31, St. John's Terrace)

MILES, ALFRED G. ... ... Pte. ... Hants, Oct. 1915, Pte. France.
(93, Lower Brook Street)

MILES, EDWARD E. ... ... Rfn. ... R.B., 1900, Rfn. France. Taken Prisoner by
(10, Alresford Road) Germans, Aug. 26, 1914.

MILES, HARRY ... ... Mech. ... R.N., 1900, Stoker. North Sea, Russia.
(106, Brassey Road)

✠ MILES, WILLIAM ... ... Pte. ... Hants, Oct. 1916, Pte. France. Wounded, Nov.
(31, St. John's Terrace) 1, 1917. *Killed in Action, Oct. 2, 1918.*

✠ MILES, WILLIAM G. ... ... Pte. ... Hants, Sept. 1914, Pte. Mesopotamia. Taken
(93, Lower Brook Street) Prisoner by Turks, Apl. 29, 1916, Kut. *Died.*

✠ MILLARD, ALFRED J. ... ... Pte. ... Hants, Aug. 1914, Pte. Dardanelles, Serbia.
(13, Colebrook Street) Wounded and taken Prisoner by Bulgarians, Dec. 7, 1915. *Died, Jan. 18, 1916, Dupnitza.*

WINCHESTER WAR SERVICE REGISTER

MILLARD, WILLIAM T. (8, Water Lane)	...	Corpl.	... Hants, 1912, Pte. India, Mesopotamia. Wounded, July 1915.
✠ MILLER, ARTHUR E. ... (37, Colson Road)		L.-Corpl.	Hants, Apl. 1916, Pte. France. *Killed in Action, Apl.* 12, 1917, *Arras.*
✠ MILLER, CHARLES K. ... (15, Hyde Abbey Road)		Corpl.	... R.F.A., 1913, Gun. France. Wounded once. Taken Prisoner by Germans and escaped. *Died of Wounds, Apl.* 2, 1917.
MILLER, EDWARD G. B. (3, Gordon Avenue)		Corpl.	... S.A. Inf., Dec. 1915, Pte. E. Africa.
MILLER, ERNEST ... (37, Colson Road)		Pte.	... Hants, Jan. 1918, Pte. France.
MILLER, FREDERICK W. (27, Andover Road)	...		Hants, Nov. 1915. Mesopotamia.
MILLER, GORDON R. W. (3, Gordon Avenue)		L.-Corpl.	Glos., Mch. 1917, Pte. Wilts, M.G.C. France. Wounded and Gassed, Oct. 1918.
MILLER, HERBERT R. ... (15, Hyde Abbey Road)		Pte.	... Hants Y., Feb. 1917, Tpr. R.A.O.C. Home.
MILLER, REGINALD ... (1, Hyde Abbey Road)		2nd A.M.	R.F.C., Dec. 1916, 2nd A.M. R.A.F. France, Belgium, Germany.
MILLER, SYDNEY W. ... (15, Hyde Abbey Road)		L.-Corpl.	R.A.S.C. (M.T.), Aug. 1915, Pte. W. Africa, Salonica, Serbia.
MILLER, WILLIAM G. ... (37, Wales Street)		Rfn.	... R.B., Aug. 1914, Rfn. France.
MILLER, WILLIAM J. ... (68, Wales Street)		Corpl.	... Hants, 1912, Pte. R.D.C. Home.
MILLS, ALFRED ... (20, Colson Road)		Sergt.	... Hants, Feb. 1915, Pte. France, Salonica.
MILLS, CECIL G. ... (24, Jewry Street)		2nd A.M.	R.N.A.S., Aug. 24, 1916, 2nd A.M. R.A.F. France.
MILLS, EDWARD F. ... (28, Greenhill Road)		Bug.	... Hants, Sept. 1914, Bug. India, Persian Gulf, Mesopotamia. Wounded, 1916.
MILLS, ERNEST G. ... (114, High Street)		Pte.	... Cheshire, 1917, Pte. India.
MILLS, ERNEST W. ... (22, Bar End)		Corpl.	... R.B., 1902, Rfn. France, Salonica.
MILLS, FREDERICK ... (14, Cross Street)		L.-Corpl.	Worc., Oct. 1916, Pte. Oxf. and Bucks L.I. France.
MILLS, HENRY C. ... (22, Bar End)		Stoker	... R.N., Jan. 1916, Stoker. Russia, North Sea.
MILLS, HERBERT ... (14, Cross Street)		Pte.	... Hants, June 1915, Pte. India, Egypt, France.
MILLS, JOHN T. ... (114, High Street)		L.-Corpl.	Hants, Aug. 1914, Pte. Mesopotamia. Taken Prisoner by Turks.
MILLS, REUBEN ... (49, St. John's Street)		Spr.	... R.E., Sept. 1916, Spr. Mesopotamia.
MILLS, WILLIAM ... (11, Gordon Avenue)		2nd A.M.	R.E., Oct. 1915, Spr. R.A.F. Home.

WINCHESTER WAR SERVICE REGISTER

MILLS, WILLIAM J. (78, Canon Street)	2nd Lieut.	R.G.A., Jan. 1915, Gun. Queen's Westm. Flanders, Palestine, Egypt.
MILMAN, JOHN (77, Hyde Street)	Corpl.	R.N.A.S., 1916, A.M. Home.
MITCHELL, ALBERT B. (66, Colebrook Street)	Pte.	D.C.L.I., Mch. 1916, Pte. Lab. C. France, Belgium.
MITCHELL, CHARLES G. (51, Sussex Street)	T.-R.S.M.	Dub. Fus., 1894, Pte. K.R.R.C. France. M.S.M.
MITCHELL, EDGAR J. (21, Fairfield Road)	Steward	R.N., 1911, S.B.A. Ægean Sea.
MITCHELL, FREDERICK W. (13, St. James' Lane)	Lieut.	R.F.A., 1898, Gun. France. Wounded, Sept. 14, 1914. M.S.M., Despatches 1918.
✠ MITCHELL, HARRY F. (60, Sussex Street)	Pte.	Hants, 1914, Pte. France. *Killed in Action, Mch. 23, 1918.*
MITCHELL, HUBERT A. W. (38, Hyde Abbey Road)	Drummer	Hants, Sept. 1915, Drummer. Home.
✠ MITCHELL, JAMES J. (38, Hyde Abbey Road)	Sergt.	Hants, rejoined, Sergt. Home. *Died, May 8,* 1917.
MITCHELL, JOSEPH H. (58, Sussex Street)	C.S.M.	R.B., 1896, Boy. R.F., Lab. C., R.B. France. Wounded, Mch. 12, 1915, May 9, and Oct. 17, 1915, Oct. 19, 1916. D.C.M. 1916, M.S.M. 1919.
MITCHELL, PHILIP (21, Fairfield Road)	Bdr.	R.F.A., 1911, Bug. France. Wounded, Sept. 29, 1916.
MITCHELL, RALPH (21, Fairfield Road)	S.S.A.	R.N., Sept. 1914, S.S.A. S. Africa.
MITCHELL, RICHARD W. (51, Sussex Street)	C.S.M.	K.R.R.C., 1893, Boy. Salonica, France, Belgium. M.S.M. 1917.
MITCHELL, WILLIAM (8, Upper Wolvesey Terrace)		R.A.S.C. Home.
MITCHELMORE, FREDERICK P. (72, Stockbridge Road)	Pte.	R. Marines, 1898, Pte. Mudros.
MITCHELMORE, WILFRED J. (72, Stockbridge Road)	A.B.	R.N., 1897, A.B. North Sea.
MITCHENER, PERCY (33, Water Lane)	Sergt.	Hants, Aug. 26, 1914, Pte. Dorset, Lab. C. Gallipoli. Wounded, Aug. 10, 1915.
MITCHENER, WILFRED (55, Canon Street)	Band Boy	Hants, June 1917, Band Boy.
MOBLEY, ALBERT P. (3, St. Swithun's Villas)		Somerset L.I., Apl. 1916. R. Warwick. Home.
MONAGHAN, JOSEPH C. (1, King Alfred Terrace)	Dr.	H.A.C., Sept. 1915, Dr. R.F.A. Flanders, France.
MONAGHAN, LEO F. (1, King Alfred Terrace)	Gun.	R.G.A., Sept. 1914, Gun. Flanders, France. M.M. 1918.
MONAGHAN, THOMAS A. (1, King Alfred Terrace)	Pte.	Irish Gds., July 1916, Pte. France.
MONGER, HENRY G. (17, Stockbridge Road)		R.N.A.S., Oct. 1917. Home.

WINCHESTER WAR SERVICE REGISTER

Monk, Arthur H. (30, Elm Road)	Corpl.	R.A.S.C. (M.T.), Pte. France, E. Africa. Gassed, Nov. 13, 1916. Wounded, Aug. 28, 1917.
Monk, George S. (11, Brassey Road)	Corpl.	R.A.F., Sept. 3, 1917, Carpenter. Home.
Montgomery, Patrick (25, Christ Church Road)	Pte.	Hants, Mch. 1916, Pte. M.G.C. France, India. Wounded, Oct. 7, 1916.
Moody, Edwin J. (33, Cheriton Road)	Sergt.	Hants, Aug. 1914, Pte. Bedford. India.
Moody, Eldred B. (Christ's Hospital)	Corpl.	R.B., 1899, Rfn. France, Germany.
Moody, Wilfred H. (23, Colson Road)	R.S.M.	R.E., 1898, Spr. Ord. Survey. Lemnos, Egypt, Palestine.
Moon, Ernest (10, Ashley Terrace)	A.-S.M.	Dragoon Gds., 1906, Tpr. India, France. Wounded, Sept. 20, 1916.
Moon, Robert W. (10, Ashley Terrace)		R. Marines, Oct. 1915. North Sea; H.M.S. *Hercules*.
Moon, Thomas (10, Ashley Terrace)		R.N., 1912. North Sea.
✠ Moore, Albert (17, St. Clement Street)	Rfn.	R.B., rejoined Aug. 1914, Rfn. France. Wounded, May 7, 1915. D.C.M., Russian Order of St. George 1914. *Died of Wounds, May 12, 1915, Boulogne.*
Moore, Frank (26, Arbour Terrace)		D.C.L.I., Mch. 1916. France.
Moore, Frederick J. (19, St. Swithun Street)	A.-S.M.	Hants, 1904, Pte. Home.
Moore, George H. (18, Hyde Street)	Corpl.	Hussars, Sept. 1914, Pte. France, Salonica. Despatches 1916.
Moore, Thomas (20, St. Swithun Street)		R.A.S.C. (M.T.), Oct. 1917, Pte. France, Belgium, Germany.
Moore, William C. (18, Hyde Street)	Pte.	Hants, 1907, Boy. India, Egypt, Dardanelles. Wounded, Apl. 29, 1915.
Moran, John (1, St. Giles' Hill Hutments)	Gun.	R.G.A., 1914, Gun. France. Wounded and Gassed, Mch. 5, 1915.
Moreton, Clifton W. (3, St. Swithun Street)	L.-Corpl.	R.E., Feb. 1917, Pnr. France, Mesopotamia. Gassed once.
Moreton, William S. (3, St. Swithun Street)	Lieut.	Nat. Res., 1913, Corpl. R.E. Home.
Morey, William (86, Colebrook Street)	Bandsman	Hants, Mch. 1915, Bandsman. Home.
Morgan, Charles E. (101, Upper Brook Street)	Stoker	R.N., Apl. 1914, Stoker. North Sea; T.B.D. 80.
Morley, Bernard F. (17, St. John's Park Terrace)	Rfn.	Lond., Oct. 1917, Rfn. Wounded once.
Morley, Terence C. (17, St. John's Park Terrace)	Drummer	Lond., Oct. 1917, Drummer. Home.

MORRAH, HERBERT A. (25, Cranworth Road)	Lieut.	R.N.V.R., Oct. 1917, Lieut. Home.	
✠ MORRAH, JOHN H. (25, Cranworth Road)	Major	K.O.R.Lancs., 1896, 2nd Lieut. France. Despatches 1915. *Killed in Action, Oct. 18, 1914.*	
MORRELL, INWOOD (19, Culver Road)	Stoker	R.N., Aug. 1914, Stoker. H.M.S. *Minerva*.	
MORRIS, ALFRED (11, Hedges Buildings)	Pte.	Hants, 1895, Pte. France.	
✠ MORRIS, CHARLES (11, Hedges Buildings)	Pte.	Hants, Aug. 1914, Pte. France. *Killed in Action, July 1, 1916.*	
MORRIS, ERNEST (7, Water Lane)	L.-Corpl.	R.E., June 1916, Spr. Devon. Home.	
MORRIS, FRANK (13, Water Lane)	L.-Corpl.	Hants, 1912, Pte. India, Gallipoli, Egypt, France. Gassed, Jan. 9, 1917.	
MORRIS, GEORGE (2, Gordon Road)	Pte.	Hants Y., 1915, Tpr. Lab. C. Home.	
MORRIS, WILLIAM (Grove Cottage, Quarry Road)	Sergt.	Hants, Sept. 7, 1914, Pte. D.C.L.I. France. Wounded, Aug. 22, 1917.	
MORRIS, WILLIAM (11, Hedges Buildings)	Pte.	Hants, Dec. 1916, Pte. France. Wounded once.	
MORT, ALBERT H. G. (38, Parchment Street)	Pte.	D.L.I., Dec. 1915, Pte. France.	
MORT, CHARLES E. (4, Chesil Street)	Pte.	Lab. C., May 1917, Pte. Home.	
MORT, ERNEST A. (5, Upper Wolvesey Terrace)	Corpl.	Hants, Jan. 2, 1915, Pte. France. Wounded twice.	
MORT, GEORGE (38, Parchment Street)	Pte.	Hants, 1914, Pte. Salonica.	
MORTON, NATHAN E. C. (6, King Alfred Terrace)	Pte.	R.A.O.C., Jan. 1916, Pte. France.	
MOSS, EDWIN J. (20A, St. Thomas Street)	Pte.	D.L.I., 1899, Pte. Home.	
MOSS, WILLIAM (22, Hyde Abbey Road)	Corpl.	Worc., June 1917, Pte. R.E. France.	
MOTT, GEORGE (39, Upper Brook Street)	Spr.	Hants, Nov. 1915, Pte. R.E. Mesopotamia, India.	
MOTT, JOHN D. (9, St. Paul's Hill)	L.-Corpl.	Lond., Apl. 1915, Pte. R.F. France.	
MOULD, ALBERT J. (41, Upper Brook Street)	Pte.	D.C.L.I., Apl. 1916, Pte. France. Wounded, Sept. 3, 1916, and Oct. 4, 1917.	
MOULD, ARTHUR (32, Tower Street)		R.N., May 1917. Home.	
MOULD, CHARLES H. (32, Tower Street)	Drummer	Canadians, Feb. 1916, Drummer. France. Wounded, 1917.	
MOULD, GEORGE A. (1, Chesil Terrace)	Dr.	R.F.A., May 25, 1916, Dr. R.G.A., R.A.S.C. (M.T.). Home.	

WINCHESTER WAR SERVICE REGISTER

MOULD, JAMES (32, Tower Street)	...	Pte. ...	Hants, Aug. 1914, Pte. France.
✠ MOULD, JOHN A. S. (15, St. John's Road)	...	Pte. ...	Hants, Aug. 1914, Pte. Home. *Died, Sept. 20, 1916.*
MOULD, JOHN S. (3, Richmond Terrace)	...	Pte. ...	R.A.M.C., Oct. 1915, Pte. Italy, France, Belgium. M.M.
MOULD, PERCY L. (3, Richmond Terrace)	...	Pte. ...	R.A.M.C., Oct. 1915, Pte. France.
MOULD, SEYMOUR H. (26, Elm Road)	...	Pte. ...	Dorset, June 1916, Pte. Essex. India.
MOULD, WALTER F. (3, Richmond Terrace)	...	Sergt. ...	Hants, Sept. 1914, Pte. Egypt, India.
MOWER, ALBERT E. (3, Nuns Road)	...	Sergt. ...	Devon, Nov. 1916, Pte. Lab. C. Home.
MUDDIMAN, BERTIE (61, Canon Street)	...	L.-Corpl.	Hussars, 1897, Tpr. Coldstream Gds. France. Wounded, Dec. 5, 1915.
MUDDIMAN, ERNEST (61, Canon Street)	...	Gun. ...	R.H.A., 1910, Gun. France.
✠ MUDDIMAN, OLIVER (61, Canon Street)	...	Corpl.	Coldstream Gds., 1898, Pte. France. *Missing (believed Killed), Sept. 22, 1914.*
MUDDIMAN, STEPHEN (61, Canon Street)	...	A.B. ...	Merc. Mar., 1907, A.B. H.M.A.S. *Panama.*
MUDDIMAN, WILLIAM (61, Canon Street)	...	Lt. and Q.M.	Hussars, 1905, Tpr. France.
MUGFORD, GEORGE R. (23, Elm Road)	...	Corpl.	Arg. and Suth. H., Oct. 1915, Pte. R.A.F. France.
✠ MULDOWNEY, JOHN (15A, Greenhill Road)	...	Pte. ...	American Legion, June 1916, Pte. France. Wounded, July 15, 1917. *Killed in Action, Aug. 8, 1918.*
MULDOWNEY, THOMAS (15A, Greenhill Road)	...	Gun. ...	R.M.A., Aug. 1914, Gun. France.
MULLETT, EDGAR J. (71, Greenhill Road)	...	Gun. ...	R.G.A., Aug. 1916, Gun. France. Wounded twice.
MULVEAHY, THOMAS (71, Wales Street)	...	Rfn. ...	Hants, Sept. 1914, Pte. K.R.R.C. Dardanelles. Wounded, Apl. 26, 1915.
MULVEY, WILLIAM F. (8, St. Catherine's Road)	...	Bug. ...	R.B., 1902, Rfn. France.
MUNDAY, CHARLES (67, Chesil Street)	...	...	R.F.A., Nov. 1916, Gun. Agric. Coy. Home.
MUNDEN, HENRY C. (4, Eastgate Street)	...	Pte. ...	Somerset L.I., Feb. 1916, Pte. R.A.O.C. France.
✠ MUNDY, ALFRED (14, Granville Place)	...	Pte. ...	Hants, Nov. 11, 1915, Pte. France. *Killed in Action, Sept. 9, 1916.*
MUNDY, ALFRED G. (4, St. George's Street)	...	Pte. ...	Hants, Aug. 31, 1914, Pte. Home.
MUNDY, ARTHUR R. (17, Andover Road)	...	Spr. ...	Hants, June 1916, Pte. R.E. France.

WINCHESTER WAR SERVICE REGISTER

MUNDY, ERNEST ... 2nd Lieut. R.A.S.C., Aug. 1914, Corpl. Egyptian Lab. C.
(35, Hyde Close) Egypt. Despatches.

✠ MUNDY, GEORGE ... Pte. ... Dorset, Aug. 1914, Pte. France. *Killed in Action,*
(14, Granville Place) *Apl. 12, 1915.*

MUNDY, WILLIAM C. ... Dr. ... R.A.S.C., Apl. 1915, Dr. Salonica.
(24, Middle Brook Street)

MUNN, CHARLES W. W. ... C.S.M. ... R.F., 1896, Pte. Hants. India, Mesopotamia,
(7, Sussex Street) Salonica. Wounded, Jan. 21, 1916.

MUNSON, ARTHUR G. E. ... Lieut. ... R.E., Sept. 1914, Spr. Con. Ran. Palestine,
(3, Edgar Road) Egypt, Macedonia.

MUNT, ALBERT A. ... ... S.A. Force. E. Africa.
(13, King Alfred Place)

MUNT, CYRIL F. ... Tpr. ... Hants Y., Nov. 1915, Tpr. Hussars, Staffs Y.
(13, King Alfred Place) Egypt, Palestine, Syria.

MUNT, STANLEY T. A. ... Q.M.S. ... R.A.S.C., 1914, Dr. Gallipoli, Mesopotamia, Egypt,
(19, Sussex Street) India, Russia.

✠ MUNT, THOMAS W. ... Sig. ... Hants, 1911, Pte. R.E. India, Mesopotamia, Kut.
(13, King Alfred Place) Taken Prisoner by Turks, Apl. 26, 1916.
Died, Sept. 30, 1916, Afion-Kara-Hissan.

MURRAY, CHARLES ... 2nd A.M. R.F.C., Sept. 1917, 2nd A.M. R.A.F. Home.
(3, City Road)

MURRAY, CHARLES G. ... Corpl. ... R.F.C., Nov. 1917, Cadet. R.A.F. Home.
(3, City Road)

MURTAUGH, ALBERT G. ... Sergt. ... Worc., June 1916, Pte. Somerset L.I., R. Sussex.
(17, North View) Palestine, France.

NAISH, WALTER ... C.F. Hants, 1891, C.F. India.
(Trafalgar House, Trafalgar St.) (Lt.-Col.)

NAISH, WALTER V. J. ... Capt. ... Hants, 1912, 2nd Lieut. India, Mesopotamia,
(Trafalgar House, Trafalgar St.) France.

NASH, GEORGE E. ... Stoker ... R.N., 1911, Stoker. North Sea, Russia.
(73, Wales Street)

NASH, GEORGE H. ... L.-Corpl. R.B., 1899, Rfn. France. Taken Prisoner by
(33, Colebrook Street) Germans, Aug. 26, 1914, Mons.

NASH, HENRY E. P. ... Lt.-Col. ... R. Scots, 1891, 2nd Lieut. France, Belgium,
(34, Edgar Road) Germany. D.S.O. and Bar 1918, Despatches 1917, 1918, 1919.

NEALE, FREDERICK ... Pte. ... R.A.S.C., May 1917, Pte. Suffolk. France.
(31, Fairfield Road)

NEALE, WALTER ... Pte. ... Essex, Oct. 1916, Pte. Home.
(31, Fairfield Road)

NEALE, WILLIAM ... P.O. ... R.N., 1901, Boy. North Sea. Taken Prisoner
(31, Fairfield Road) by Germans, May 7, 1915. D.S.M. 1915.

NEATE, THOMAS A. ... Pnr. ... R.E., Sept. 1917, Pnr. France.
(5, Boscobel Road)

WINCHESTER WAR SERVICE REGISTER

NEEDLE, WILLIE R. (138, Stockbridge Road)	Rfn.	Worc., Apl. 16, 1918, Pte. K.R.R.C. France. Wounded, Sept. 5, 1918.	
NELSON, ALEXANDER T. (2, Tower Street)	Sergt.	Sherwood For., Oct. 1915, Pte. Yorks, R. Sussex, Suffolk. France.	
NEW, CHARLES (20, North View)		Worc., Oct. 1916. France. Wounded, Sept. 29, 1918.	
NEWBERY, ERIC A. (Christ Church Vicarage)	Lieut.	Indian Army, Feb. 5, 1918, 2nd Lieut. India, Palestine.	
✠ NEWBY, WILLIAM E. (1, Ashley Terrace)	Stoker	R.N., 1912, Stoker. North Sea; H.M.S. *Queen Mary*. *Killed in Action, May 31, 1916, Jutland.*	
NEWHAM, HUBERT F. (23, Highcliffe Road)	Corpl.	Hants, Sept. 1914, Pte. Lab. C., A.P.C. France.	
NEWMAN, ALBERT (10, Back Street, St. Cross)	Spr.	Hants, Sept. 1914, Pte. R.E. France, Belgium.	
NEWMAN, ARTHUR J. (32, Colebrook Street)	Sergt.	Dragoon Gds., 1905, Tpr. A.V.C. France, Italy.	
✠ NEWMAN, ARTHUR W. (29, Colson Road)	L.-Corpl.	Hants, 1906, Band Boy. Egypt, France. Wounded, Apl. 1918. *Died of Wounds, Apl. 1918.*	
NEWMAN, CHARLES F. (19, Jewry Street)	A.B.	R.N., 1911, A.B. North Sea, China.	
NEWMAN, EDWIN (7, St. Paul's Hill)		R.A.S.C., 1912. N. Fus. France, Italy. Gassed, 1917.	
NEWMAN, FREDERICK (10, Back Street, St. Cross)	Corpl.	Hants, Sept. 1914, Pte. R.E. India, Mesopotamia.	
NEWMAN, FREDERICK (1, Greenhill Road)	Sergt.	R.A.S.C., Nov. 1916, Dr. Home.	
NEWMAN, GEORGE (7, St. Paul's Hill)	Pte.	Hants, 1917, Pte. Germany.	
NEWMAN, GEORGE A. (32, Wales Street)	Dr.	R.A.S.C., July 1914, Dr. Palestine, Dardanelles, Mesopotamia. Wounded, 1915 and 1917.	
NEWMAN, GEORGE H. (32, Colebrook Street)	Sergt.	Hants, 1907, Pte. France. Wounded, 1914, 1915, 1917, 1918. Gassed three times.	
NEWMAN, HENRY J. (32, Colebrook Street)	Pte.	R.A.S.C. (M.T.), 1916, Pte. France.	
NEWMAN, JAMES (29, St. Paul's Hill)		R.G.A., Nov. 27, 1915. France.	
✠ NEWMAN, REGINALD W. (29, Colson Road)	Pte.	Hants, Nov. 1911, Boy. France. Wounded, Apl. 9 and July 22, 1917. *Killed in Action, Sept. 3, 1918.*	
NEWMAN, THOMAS E. (32, Wales Street)	Pte.	Dorset, Jan. 1917, Pte. Home.	
NEWSAM, BENJAMIN R. (8, Middle Brook Street)	L.-Corpl.	R.M.L.I., 1913, Pte. North Sea, Ostend, Jutland.	
✠ NEWTON, ALAN H. (Morn Dale, Bereweeke Road)	2nd Lieut.	Middlesex, May 1915, 2nd Lieut. France. Wounded, Apl. 7, 1916. *Died of Wounds, Apl. 7, 1916, Albert.*	

WINCHESTER WAR SERVICE REGISTER

Name (Address)	Rank	Service
NEWTON, THOMAS M. B. (Morn Dale, Bereweeke Road)	Capt.	Hants, 1914, Pte. Shropshire L.I., R. Berks, R.A.F. France.
NIBLETT, EDWIN (19, Southgate Street)		R.M.A., 1915. France.
NICHOLLS, HERBERT A. (3, Alexandra Terrace)		R.A.S.C., Apl. 8, 1915, Barrack Warden. Home.
NICHOLLS, SIDNEY A. (17, Milverton Road)	C.S.M.	R.B., 1894, Rfn. France.
NOICE, GEORGE (6, Cathedral View)	Pte.	Glos., 1914, Pte. France. Wounded once.
NOICE, JESSE (11, Colebrook Street)	Spr.	R.E., Apl. 1917, Pnr. France. Gassed once.
NOOKES, HORACE H. (49, Fairfield Road)	Steward	R.N., Mch. 7, 1917, Steward. North Sea.
✠ NORGATE, PERCY D. (4, Brassey Road)	Sig.	R.G.A., Apl. 1917, Sig. France. Taken Prisoner by Germans, Mch. 21, 1918. *Died, Aug. 10, 1918, Valenciennes.*
NORRIS, CHARLES T. (41, Eastgate Street)	Dr.	R.A.S.C., Apl. 1915, Dr. Salonica.
NORRIS, FRANK (8, Staple Garden)	L.-Corpl.	R.B., 1914, Rfn. France.
NORRIS, PERCY H. (42B, Eastgate Street)	1st A.M.	R.N.A.S., Jan. 1916, 2nd A.M. R.A.F. Gallipoli.
NORTH, WILLIAM (Nelson Road)	Pte.	Bedford, Sept. 1914, Pte. France. Gassed, May 5, 1915.
NORTH, WILLIAM C. (112, Stockbridge Road)		R.F.A., Oct. 1915. R.G.A. France.
NOYCE, FRANK (2, Westgate Lane)	L.-Corpl.	R.A.S.C., Pte. R. Scots. France. Wounded, Aug. 1918.
NOYCE, HAROLD J. (10, Crowder Terrace)	Pte.	R.A.S.C. (M.T.), Dec. 1915, Pte. Egypt. Palestine.
NOYCE, HARRY W. (10, Crowder Terrace)	Pte.	R.A.M.C., Oct. 1915, Pte. Home.
NUNN, ERNEST E. (38, Upper Brook Street)	Stoker	R.N., 1913, Stoker. North Sea; H.M.S. *Fearless.*
NUNN, WILLIAM A. (38, Upper Brook Street)	2nd Lieut.	Hants, Aug. 1914, Pte. France. Wounded, 1915, 1916, and 1917.
NUNN, WILLIAM A. C. (1, St. George's Terrace)	2nd Lieut.	Hants, Aug. 1914, Pte. Gallipoli, Egypt, France. Wounded, Aug. 11, 1915, May 1, 1916, Nov. 30, 1917.
NUTBEAM, ALBERT (19, Alresford Road)	Pte.	Dorset, 1905, Pte. India, France, Dardanelles.
NUTBEAM, ALFRED (12, Colebrook Street)	Cook's Mate	R.N., July 1918, Cook's Mate. Home, H.M.S. *Pembroke.*
NUTBEAM, CHARLES (12, Colebrook Street)	Pte.	Hants, May 1916, Pte. R.A.S.C. (M.T.). France.
NUTT, EDWARD M. (4, Step Terrace)		R.A.M.C., Aug. 1914. France.

WINCHESTER WAR SERVICE REGISTER

OAKES, EDWARD (11, St. Giles' Hill Hutments)	Rfn.	K.R.R.C., Oct. 1914, Rfn. R.B. Home.
OAKSHOTT, ALBERT (1, Castle Terrace)	Pte.	Hants, July 1916, Pte. Mesopotamia, Persia.
OAKSHOTT, CHARLES (1, Castle Terrace)	Pte.	Hants, Dec. 1915, Pte. Wilts. Egypt, Palestine.
✠ OFFER, ALBERT (2, Abbey Passage)	Pte.	Hants, June 1916, Pte. France, Salonica. Wounded, Sept. 1, 1918. *Died of Wounds, Sept.* 17, 1918.
OFFER, ALFRED J. (5, Cheriton Road)	Corpl.	R.B., Oct. 1916, Rfn. A.P.C. Home.
OFFER, BENJAMIN (13, St. John's Road)	Pte.	Hants, Oct. 1914, Pte. India.
✠ OFFER, CECIL H. (2, Abbey Passage)	Sergt.	Hants, 1911, Pte. India, Persian Gulf. *Killed in Action, Jan.* 21, 1916.
OFFER, EDWIN T. (26, Sussex Street)	Pte.	R.A.F., 1917, Pte. Home.
OFFER, FRANK H. (65, Chesil Street)	Gun.	R.G.A., Nov. 1916, Gun. E. Africa.
OFFER, FREDERICK (18, St. John's Road)	Bdr.	R.G.A., Aug. 1915, Gun. France.
OFFER, FREDERICK G. ... (105, Colebrook Street)	Pte.	Hants, Aug. 1914, Pte. India, Mesopotamia, Persian Gulf, Russia.
✠ OFFER, JOHN A. (105, Colebrook Street)	A.B.	R.N., 1911, Boy. English Channel, North Sea; H.M.S. *Impregnable, Colossus, Bulwark,* and *Black Prince. Killed in Action, May* 31, 1916, *Jutland.*
OFFER, LESLIE F. (18, Fairfield Road)	Sig.	Hants, Jan. 1917, Sig. France, Turkey.
OFFER, WILLIAM (63, Canon Street)	Dr.	R.F.A., 1902, Dr. France. Wounded, Aug. 18, 1915.
✠ OFFER, WILLIAM J. (77, Lower Brook Street)	Pte.	Hants, Sept. 1914, Pte. Gallipoli, France. Wounded, Apl. 1, 1916. *Killed in Action, Apl.* 23, 1917, *Mouchez.*
OLIVER, ALFRED T. (9, Edgar Road)	Sergt.	R.A.S.C. (M.T.), May 1916, Pte. Salonica, Egypt.
OLIVER, ARTHUR A. (20, St. John's Street)	Pte.	Lab. C., Feb. 1917, Pte. France.
OLIVER, CHARLES J. (13, Princes Buildings)		R.N.A.S., July 1917. Home.
OLIVER, ERNEST G. (20, St. John's Street)	Gun.	R.F.C., Sept. 1914, Gun. R.A.F. Mesopotamia, India, France.
OLIVER, FRANK C. V. (20, St. John's Street)	Boy	R.N., Mch. 1917, Boy. Mediterranean.
O'NEILL, ALFRED C. W. (4, St. John's Park Terrace)		T.R., June 1917, Pte. Somerset. Home.
OPENSHAW, FRANCIS R. (Fairlawn, Sleepers Hill)	Lt.-Comdr.	R.N., 1902, Mid. Grand Fleet, Mediterranean; H.M.S. *Devonshire* and *Téméraire.*

WINCHESTER WAR SERVICE REGISTER

✠ OPENSHAW, HAROLD M. ... Lieut. ... Norfolk, 1900, 2nd Lieut. France. Wounded,
   (Fairlawn, Sleepers Hill)   Aug. 24, 1914. Taken Prisoner by Germans.
                                                      Died in Hospital, Thulin.

ORSBORN, CHARLES H. ... Sig. ... Hants, Nov. 1915, Pte. India, Egypt, Palestine,
   (3, Monks Road)   France, Germany. Wounded once.

ORSBORN, JOHN F. ... ... A.M. ... R.A.F., 1916, A.M. Home.
   (3, Monks Road)

ORSBORN, WILLIAM J. ... Dr. ... R.A.S.C., Sept. 1914, Dr. France, Germany.
   (3, Monks Road)

ORWELL, HECTOR W. ... Pte. ... Essex, Oct. 1916, Pte. Home.
   (44, Hyde Abbey Road)

OSBORNE, ALFRED ... ... Tpr. ... Dragoon Gds., Tpr. France. Wounded, 1916.
   (5, The Weirs)

✠ OSBORNE, PERCY ... ... Tpr. ... R. Dragoons, Tpr. France. *Killed in Action, Nov.*
   (5, The Weirs)   *13, 1914.*

OSMOND, EDWIN P. ... ... Staff S.M. R.A.S.C., Nov. 1915, Pte. Home.
   (17, Hyde Street)

OSMOND, ERNEST ... ... L.-Corpl. Hants, Nov. 1917, Pte. R.I.F. France. Wounded,
   (7, St. Swithun Street)   1918.

OSMOND, FRANK ... ... Pte. ... Hants, Nov. 1915, Pte. Bedford. India.
   (7, St. Swithun Street)

OTTER, EDWARD J. ... ... Gun. ... R.M.A., Apl. 1917, Gun. France, H.M.S. *Canopus.*
   (16, Prison Quarters)

OWEN, ARTHUR A. ... ... C.Q.M.S. K.R.R.C., 1897, Rfn. France. Wounded, Sept.
   (30, Romsey Road)   14, 1914. M.S.M. 1919.

OXFORD, WILLIAM H. ... Sergt. ... Wilts, Jan. 1916, Pte. Home.
   (6, St. Leonard's Road)

PACEY, ALFRED C. ... ...   R.A.F., Apl. 1918. Home.
   (57, Sussex Street)

PACK, ALBERT ... ... Pte. ... Hants, 1918, Pte. Warwick. Germany.
   (2, Gordon Avenue)

PACK, ALBERT E. ... ... Pte. ... Hants, Nov. 1915, Pte. India, Egypt, Palestine,
   (44, Upper Brook Street)   France. Wounded, Aug. 28, 1918.

PACK, ALBERT H. ... ...   R.G.A., Apl. 1917. Home.
   (2, Gordon Avenue)

PACK, EDWARD G. ... ... Pte. ... Hants, Nov. 1915, Pte. India, Egypt, Palestine,
   (44, Upper Brook Street)   France. Wounded, Aug. 26, 1918.

PACK, FREDERICK A. ... ... A.B. ... R.N., 1915, O.S. Mediterranean; H.M.S. *Monitor,*
   (Down View, Highcliffe Park)   22.

✠ PACK, JOHN T. ... ...   R.N., 1895. *Killed in Action, Jan. 12, 1918,*
   (44, Upper Brook Street)   H.M.S. *Opal.*

PACK, WILLIAM ... ...   R.M.L.I., rejoined Aug. 1914. Persian Gulf;
   (44, Upper Brook Street)   H.M.S. *Minerva* and *Proserpine.*

WINCHESTER WAR SERVICE REGISTER

PACKHAM, FREDERICK M. (9, St. Giles' Hill Hutments)	Sergt.	R. Sussex, Feb. 1914, Pte. France. Wounded, Sept. 10, 1914.
PADDINGTON, EDWARD C. (75, Wales Street)	Corpl.	Wilts, June 1915, Pte. France, Belgium, Germany. Wounded, July 8, 1916.
PADDINGTON, RODNEY A. E. (Chilcomb)	Spr.	R.E., Mch. 1915, Spr. Salonica.
PADWICK, CHARLES H. (12, St. Cross Road)	Sergt.	Hussars, rejoined Oct. 1916, Corpl. Home.
PADWICK, HERBERT (4, Clausentum Road)	Gun.	R.F.A., Jan. 1917, Gun. R.G.A. Home.
PAGE, ALFRED E. (54, Sussex Street)	Sergt.	Nat. Res., 1914, Pte. R.D.C. Home.
PAGE, CHARLES (39, Andover Road)	Sergt.	Hants, 1915, Pte. France. Wounded, 1916 and 1917. Gassed, 1916. M.M. 1917.
PAGE, ERNEST (48, Sussex Street)		R.F.C., May 1917. R.A.F. Home.
PAGE, ERNEST F. (27, Stockbridge Road)	Sergt.	Hants (T.F.), 1889, Pte. Hants, R.D.C. Home.
PAGE, FRANK (15, Upper High Street)	Pte.	Hants, Oct. 1916, Pte. France, Belgium. Wounded, Mch. 1918.
PAGE, FRANK, jun. (15, Upper High Street)	Stoker	R.N., 1917, Boy. North Sea; H.M.S. *Glorious*.
✠ PAGE, HENRY C. (3, St. George's Terrace)	Spr.	Hants, Dec. 1915, Pte. R.E. France. *Killed in Action*, Aug. 21, 1916.
PAGE, HENRY R. (29, Wharf Hill)	Pte.	Hants, Feb. 28, 1916, Pte. Dorset. France.
PAGE, HERBERT B. (18, Upper High Street)	Spr.	Devon, July 1916, Pte. R.E. Home.
PAGE, JOHN D. (12, Monks Road)		Devon, Nov. 1916. R. Berks. France.
PAGE, LEONARD (15, Upper High Street)	Pte.	Hants, June 1914, Pte. Home.
PAGE, PERCY G. (30, Upper High Street)	Spr.	R.E., June 1916, Spr. France.
PAGE, REGINALD (54, Sussex Street)	Bdr.	R.G.A., 1910, Gun. France. Gassed once.
PAGE, RICHARD G. (Pond Cottage, Weeke)	Gun.	R.F.A., Aug. 1914, Gun. France, Mesopotamia. Wounded, Mch. 8, 1916.
PAGE, RICHARD N. (17, Gladstone Street)		R.N., 1906, Boy. North Sea; H.M.S. *Boscawen*.
✠ PAGE, THOMAS (11, Monks Road)	C.S.M.	K.R.R.C., Pte. Home. *Died*.
PAGE, WILLIAM (48, Sussex Street)		Hants Y., May 1915. Hants. France, Belgium, Italy.
PAGE, WILLIAM H. (4, Rene Villas)	Bdr.	R.G.A., 1917, Bdr. France.

WINCHESTER WAR SERVICE REGISTER

Name (Address)	Rank	Service
PAGE, WILLIAM J. (27, Stockbridge Road)		R.N., 1913. Dover Patrol, Russia, H.M.S. *Syren* and *Winchester*.
PAIN, CHARLES (29, Trinity Terrace)	Pte.	Middlesex, Apl. 1916, Pte. Hants. Home.
PAIN, GEORGE (6, Lower Wolvesey Terrace)	Dr.	R.A.S.C., Jan. 1915, Dr. Egypt, Gallipoli.
PAIN, JAMES F. (49, Parchment Street)	Spr.	R.E., Aug. 1916, Spr. Mesopotamia.
PAIN, JESSE T. (6, Lower Wolvesey Terrace)	A.-Corpl.	R.M.L.I., Sept. 1916, Pte. Dover Patrol, North Sea, Zeebrugge, Russia, H.M.S. *Broke*.
PAIN, REGINALD E. (6, Lower Wolvesey Terrace)	2nd A.M.	D.C.L.I., 1910, Pte. Oxf. and Bucks L.I., R.A.F. China, France, India. Wounded, Jan. 1915.
PAIN, WILLIAM A. (6, Lower Wolvesey Terrace)	Pte.	Hants Y., Mch. 1917, Tpr. R.N.Devon Hus., Glos., Hants, E. Surrey. France. Gassed, May, 1918.
PAINTER, WILLIAM (6, Nuns Road)	Bandsman	Hants (T.F.), Oct. 1914, Bandsman. Home.
PALMER, ALFRED (11, North View)		Nat. Res., Sept. 1914, Pte. R.D.C. Home.
PALMER, CECIL T. M. (42, Hyde Abbey Road)	L.-Corpl.	Hants Y., Apl. 1916, Tpr. Hants. Mesopotamia.
PALMER, WILLOUGHBY S. (27, Monks Road)	Cadet	R.A.F., May 1918, Cadet. Hants. Home.
PARIS, JOHN (5, South View)	Gun.	R.F.A., rejoined Aug. 1916, Gun. France. Wounded, Sept. 5, 1917.
PARIS, REGINALD J. (Chilcomb)	Sergt.	R.F.A., Aug. 1914, Pte. France. Gassed once.
PARIS, SIDNEY C. C. (16, Water Lane)	Gun.	R.F.A., 1913, Gun. France, Italy. Wounded once.
PARIS, WILLIAM G. (Chilcomb)	Sergt.	Worc., 1907. France. Wounded, Aug. 24, 1916.
PARKER, ALBERT (Ross House, Station Hill)	Gun.	R.G.A., 1916, Gun. France. Wounded, 1917.
PARKER, CHARLES (18, Wales Street)	Spr.	R.E., rejoined 1916, Spr. France.
PARKER, JOHN (9, Greenhill Terrace)		R.A.S.C. (M.T.), May 1915, Pte. France.
PARKER, JOHN B. (55, Kingsgate Street)	S.B.A.	R.N., June 1915, S.B.A. Malta.
PARKER, THOMAS (14, Water Lane)	Pte.	Hants, Sept. 1914, Pte. India, Mesopotamia.
PARKER, THOMAS S. (Upper Chilcomb)		K.R.R.C., Sept. 1916, Rfn. Lab. C. Home.
PARMITER, FRANK (10, St. Swithun Street)	Corpl.	Hants, Nov. 1915, Pte. India.
PARMITER, WALTER L. (10, St. Swithun Street)	Pte.	Hants, Sept. 1914, Pte. Mesopotamia, India. Wounded, Feb. 1917.

WINCHESTER WAR SERVICE REGISTER

PARMITER, WILFRED E. B. (10, St. Swithun Street)	L.-Corpl.	R.A.S.C., Jan. 1915, Dr. Hants. Egypt.
✠ PARR, BENJAMIN (7, Alresford Road)	L.S.	R.N., 1897, Boy. Grand Fleet, Mediterranean. *Died of Pneumonia, Oct. 5, 1915.*
✠ PARRACK, RICHARD R. (13, Chester Road)	Pte.	Hants, rejoined Aug. 4, 1914, Pte. Dardanelles, Egypt, France. Wounded once. *Wounded and Missing, Oct. 16, 1916.*
PARROTT, THOMAS (14, North Walls)	Corpl.	A.P.C., Nov. 1914, Pte. Hants. Home.
PATES, RICHARD R. (10, City Road)	Dr.	R.A.S.C. (M.T.), 1917, Dr. France.
PATIENCE, HERBERT H. (2, Hyde Church Lane)	A.M.	R.F.C., Dec. 11, 1915, A.M. R.A.F. France, Italy.
✠ PATTERSON, CECIL J. (47, St. Catherine's Road)	O.S.	R.N., 1902, O.S. H.M.S. *Good Hope*. *Killed in Action, Nov. 1, 1914, Chilian Coast.*
PATTERSON, ERNEST C. (44, St. Catherine's Road)	Pte.	Nat. Res., Jan. 1915, Pte. Glos. Home.
PATTERSON, HARRY (47, St. Catherine's Road)	A.B.	R.N., 1900, O.S. North Sea.
PATTERSON, SYDNEY A. (47, St. Catherine's Road)	Dr.	R.F.A., Jan. 1916, Dr. France.
PAUL, WILLIAM H. (43, Lower Brook Street)	Pte.	A.V.C., Apl. 11, 1915, Pte. Hants. Home.
✠ PAYNE, HENRY J. (68, Brassey Road)	Pte.	T.R., Dec. 1916, Pte. M.G.C. France. *Killed in Action, Aug. 5, 1917.*
PEARCE, A. V. D. C. (17, Little Minster Street)	Gun.	R.G.A., Gun. Salonica, Palestine. Despatches, 1917.
PEARCE, CHARLES E. (22, Staple Garden)	Corpl.	R.G.A. (Anti-Aircraft), Nov. 1916, Gun. Home.
PEARCE, CHARLES H. (28, Highcliffe Road)	Pte.	R.A.M.C., Oct. 1915, Pte. Hospital Ships.
PEARCE, CHARLES R. (35, Hyde Street)	L.-Corpl.	Devon, June 1916, Pte. Home.
PEARCE, EDWARD W. (14, Back Street, St. Cross)	Sergt.	A.P.C., Nov. 1914, Pte. Somerset L.I. Home.
PEARCE, ERNEST F. (39, Brassey Road)	A.-Sergt.	Hants, Mch. 1914, Pte. Mesopotamia. M.S.M.
PEARCE, FREDERICK (8, North View)	2nd A.M.	R.F.C., rejoined Nov. 1916, 2nd A.M. R.A.F. France.
PEARCE, FREDERICK J. (4, Lower Brook Street)	Pte.	Hants, Aug. 1914, Pte. France, Dardanelles. Gassed, 1915.
PEARCE, GEORGE H. (12, Water Lane)	Dr.	R.A.S.C., Sept. 1914, Dr. France.
PEARCE, GEORGE W. (4, Lower Brook Street)	Gun.	R.F.A., Aug. 1914, Gun. France.
PEARCE, LEONARD (39, Brassey Road)	Pte.	R. Warwick, Apl. 1918, Pte. Home.

WINCHESTER WAR SERVICE REGISTER

Pearce, Percy S. (69, Wales Street)	...	Pte.	Hants, July 1915, Pte. M.G.C. France.
Pearce, William (2, Nelson Road)	...	L.-Corpl.	Hants, 1914, Pte. R. Warwick, M.F.P. France.
Pearce, William (22, Water Lane)	...	Corpl.	Hants, Apl. 1916, Pte. Somerset L.I. France. Wounded, May 6, 1917.
Pearce, William E. (22, Staple Garden)	...	Pte.	Lond. P.O. Rif., 1916, Pte. France. Wounded, Sept. 10, 1917.
Pearman, Alfred (13, Staple Garden)	...	C.Q.M.S.	Middlesex, Dec. 1915, Pte. M.G.C. France, Salonica, Palestine.
Pearman, George (13, Staple Garden)	...	Corpl.	R.A.S.C., Mch. 1916, Pte. Home.
✠ Pearman, Thomas B. (20, Victoria Road)	...	Rfn.	R.B., 1900, Rfn. France. *Killed in Action, May 4, 1915.*
✠ Pearman, William H. (13, Staple Garden)	...	Pte.	Northants, Aug. 1914, Pte. France. Wounded, 1915. *Killed in Action, Oct. 1916.*
Pearson, Alfred W. (85, Lower Brook Street)	...	2nd Lieut.	Canadians, June 1915, Pte. R.A.F. France.
✠ Pearson, George A. (85, Lower Brook Street)	...	Pte.	Canadians, Aug. 1914, Pte. France. *Killed in Action, July 25, 1916.*
Peates, William G. (90, Brassey Road)	...	Stoker	R.N., 1898, Stoker. Falkland Islands.
Peckham, Cecil (15, Cross Street)	...	Pte.	Hants, June 1916, Pte. France, Belgium, Palestine, Germany. Wounded, Feb. 26 and June 12, 1917, July 20, 1918.
Peckham, Henry S. (7, Connaught Terrace)	...	Corpl.	Hants Y., Dec. 6, 1915, Tpr. Hussars, Dragoon Gds., Northants Y. France, Italy.
Pedley, Kenneth F. (8, Southgate Street)	...	2nd Lieut.	R.A.F., Apl. 1918, Cadet. France.
Penney, Arthur C. (114, Stockbridge Road)	...	Pte.	R.A.S.C., July 1915, Pte. France.
Penney, Frederick C. (114, Stockbridge Road)	...	Pte.	R.A.S.C., Sept. 1915, Pte. R. Innis. Fus. Dardanelles, Egypt, France. Wounded, Oct. 14, 1918.
Penney, Roland G. (114, Stockbridge Road)	...	Pte.	T.R., May 1917, Pte. Northants. France. Taken Prisoner by Germans, May 27, 1918.
Penny, Edmund C. (39, St. John's Street)	...	Pte.	Scots Gds., rejoined 1914, Pte. Belgium, France. Wounded, Oct. 1914.
Penny, William F. (4, Step Terrace)	...		R.N.V.R. Belgian Coast. Gassed, 1917 and 1918. Despatches 1919.
✠ Penson, Lionel R.	...	C.Q.M.S.	R.F., Aug. 1915, Pte. France. Wounded. *Died of Wounds,* Aug. 6, 1917, *Etaples.*
Penton, Albert C. (50, Eastgate Street)	...	1st A.M.	R.N.A.S., Aug. 1917, 1st A.M. Home.
Perkins, Walter W. (8, Riflemen's Cottages)	...	Sergt.	K.R.R.C., rejoined 1914, Sergt. France. Wounded, Sept. 14, 1914.
✠ Perrin, Alfred J. (34, Water Lane)	...	Sergt.	R.B., 1905, Rfn. Belgium, France. *Killed in Action, May 8, 1915, Ypres.*

WINCHESTER WAR SERVICE REGISTER

PERRIN, ARCHIBALD H. (64, Stockbridge Road)	Pte.	Hants, Sept. 1916, Pte. Glos. France.
PERRY, ALBIN (21, Victoria Road)	Spr.	Hants, Nov. 1914, Pte. R.E. Mesopotamia, India.
PERRY, ARCHIBALD J. (60, Lansdowne Terrace)	2nd Lieut.	R.G.A., Aug. 1914, Gun. Anti-Aircraft. Home.
PERRY, ARTHUR W. (4, Colebrook Place)	Stoker	R.N., 1904. Mediterranean, North Sea; H.M.S. Nelson, Princess Royal, Lupin and T.B. 90.
PERRY, FRANK (21, Victoria Road)	Pte.	Leicester, Sept. 1914, Pte. R.A.F. France.
✠ PERRY, PERCY (21, Victoria Road)	Pte.	Lancers, rejoined Aug. 1914, Tpr. A.V.C., R.F. France. Killed in Action, May 9, 1918.
PERRY, WILFRED J. (2, St. Leonard's Road)	Pte.	R.M.A., 1917, Gun. M.F.P. Home.
PERRY, WILFRED L. (5, Eastgate Street)	Pte.	Hants, 1910, Pte. India.
PERRY, WILLIAM (7, Cathedral View)	A.B.	R.N., Feb. 1917, O.S. North Sea.
PERRY, WILLIAM J. (37, Tower Street)	Rfn.	K.R.R.C., rejoined Aug. 1914, Rfn. Home.
PERRY, WILLIAM R. (69, North Walls)	Sergt.	R.A.S.C., 1909, Pte. Dardanelles, Salonica.
PETTY, ARTHUR (34, Upper Brook Street)	Pte.	Hants, Aug. 1914, Pte. Salonica, Dardanelles, Malta, France.
PETTY, WILLIAM C. (109, Colebrook Street)	Stoker	R.N., Dec. 1916. Stoker. North Sea; H.M.S. Gossamer.
PEYTON, LUMLEY S. (Rosslyn, Park Road)	Col.	Recruiting Officer, 1915. Home.
PHILIS, WALTER T. (16, St. John's Park Terrace)	Pte.	Hants, June 1918, Pte. Home.
PHILLIPS, ALFRED (1, Hyde Close)	Pte.	Hants, Nov. 1914, Pte. India, Egypt.
✠ PHILLIPS, ARTHUR (1, Hyde Close)	L.-Corpl.	Hants, Aug. 1914, Pte. Dardanelles. Killed in Action, Aug. 10, 1915, Gallipoli.
PHILLIPS, DAVID T. (Manor Cottages, Weeke)	Pte.	Hants, July 1916, Pte. R. Warwick. France.
PHILLIPS, GEORGE C. (131, Upper Brook Street)	Spr.	R.E., Oct. 1915, Spr. Egypt, Turkey.
PHILLIPS, GEORGE F. (1, Alresford Road)	Spr.	Can. Ry.C.C., Mch. 1915, Spr. France.
PHILLIPS, PHILIP J. (16, Clausentum Road)	Sergt.	R.B., Oct. 1914, Rfn. France. Wounded, Sept. 6, 1915, and Sept. 15, 1916.
PHILLIPS, THOMAS H. (13, Hedges Buildings)	Sergt.	Hants, Nov. 1914, Pte. S. Lancs. India, Mesopotamia. Wounded, Feb. 3, 1917.
✠ PHILLIPS, WALTER (1, Hyde Close)	Pte.	Hants, May 1916, Pte. France. Killed in Action, Dec. 3, 1917.

WINCHESTER WAR SERVICE REGISTER

PHILLIPS, WILLIAM A. ... (Scarsdale, Stockbridge Road)	C.Q.M.S.	Hants, 1912, Sergt. Home.
PHILLIPS, WILLIAM H. (1, Alresford Road)	Pte.	Can. Inf., Aug. 1916, Pte. P.P.C.L.I. France. Wounded, Oct. 30, 1917.
PHILLIPS, WILLIAM J. ... (23, Hyde Close)	Pte.	Hants, May 1916, Pte. India, Egypt. Gassed once.
PHILLIS, ARTHUR (40, Upper Brook Street)	Tpr.	Hants Y., Nov. 1915, Tpr. Home.
✠ PHILLIS, CHARLES (15, Monks Road)	Pte.	Hants, Sept. 1914, Pte. India. Wounded, Feb. 7, 1917. *Died of Wounds, Feb.* 13, 1917.
PHILLIS, CHARLES (5, Percy Terrace)	Pte.	Hants, Dec. 1915, Pte. Home.
PHILLIS, HENRY (16, St. John's Park Terrace)	Pte.	R.A.M.C., July 1917, Pte. Home.
PHILLIS, JAMES E. (16, St. John's Park Terrace)	Pte.	Lab. C., Nov. 1917, Pte. Home.
PHILLIS, LEONARD (15, Monks Road)	L.-Corpl.	Glos., Mch. 1916, Pte. France. Wounded once.
PHILLIS, ROBERT J. (16, St. John's Park Terrace)	Pte.	E. Surrey, Feb. 1915, Pte. Monmouth, Suffolk, R.W.S. Home.
✠ PHILPOT, CHARLES J. ... (Bar End)	Pte.	Can. Gds., 1916, Pte. France. *Killed in Action, Sept.* 23, 1916.
PICK, VICTOR G. (22, Brassey Road)	Corpl.	R.F.A., Feb. 1915, Gun. Lab. C. France. Gassed, Mch. 1916.
PICKETT, ATHOL F. B. (2, East Cliffe)	Observer	R.F.C., Dec. 1916, 2nd A.M. R.A.F. France. Gassed, Nov. 1918.
PICKNELL, ERNEST A. (82A, Chesil Street)		R.N. North Sea; H.M.S. *Orford*.
PICKNELL, LEONARD (16, Canon Street)	Pte.	Worc., June 1915, Pte. Hants, Worc. France, Egypt. Wounded, Aug. and Sept. 1917.
PIKE, FREDERICK (6, Queen's Terrace)	Pte.	R.A.M.C., Mch. 1916, Pte. Home.
PIKE, FREDERICK H. (6, Princes Buildings)	Pte.	Hants, Apl. 7, 1916, Pte. Home.
PIKE, JOHN (6, Princes Buildings)	...	R.A.F., Aug. 1918. Home.
PINK, CYRIL V. ... (Neatham, Sleepers Hill)	Capt.	Ind. M.C., Oct. 1915. R.A.M.C. Mesopotamia.
PINK, HENRY C. (3, Ashley Terrace)	1st A.M.	R.F.C., Jan. 1917, 3rd A.M. R.A.F. France. Belgium.
PINNICK, CECIL Y. (2, St. Swithun Street)	Lieut.	R.G.A., May 1916, Gun. Home.
PINNICK, HENRY J. (2, St. Swithun Street)	Sergt.	Hants, Sept. 1914, Pte. India, Siberia.
PINNICK, LOUIS W. (2, St. Swithun Street)	Lieut.	Lond., 1913, Pte. E. Surrey. France, India. Wounded, Apl. 24, 1915, and Nov. 27, 1916. Taken Prisoner by Germans, Apl. 9, 1918.

WINCHESTER WAR SERVICE REGISTER

PINNICK, WILLIAM G. (1, Cross Street)	...	Pnr.	R.E., May 1917, Pnr. Home.
PIPER, A. CECIL (57, Hatherley Road)	...	Sergt.	R.B., June 1, 1916, Rfn. France, Belgium.
✠ PIPER, ALFRED G. (16, St. Clement Street)	...	Corpl.	Hants, 1912, Pte. M.G.C. France. Wounded four times, 1914, 1915, and 1916. *Killed in Action, Aug. 21, 1918.*
PIPER, ARTHUR F. (12, Upper Brook Street)	...	Pte.	Hants, Sept. 1914, Pte. India, Egypt, France. M.M.
✠ PIPER, CHARLES S. (72, Hyde Street)	...	L.-Corpl.	Hants, Aug. 1916, Pte. R.A.S.C. France. *Died, Jan. 4, 1919.*
PITTS, BERNARD T. (2, St. James' Terrace)	...	C.F.	C.F., 4th Class, June 10, 1918. France, Mediterranean, Black Sea.
PLATNAUER, MAURICE (7, Kingsgate Street)	...	A.-Capt.	R.G.A., Aug. 1915, 2nd Lieut. France.
PLEYDELL-BOUVERIE, CHARLES W. (Dirleton Lodge, Bereweeke Rd.)		Capt.	R.N., rejoined Aug. 1915, Comdr. Home.
POMEROY, ALBERT (140, Stockbridge Road)	...	Pte.	Dub. Fus., Sept. 2, 1914, Pte. Gallipoli, Serbia, Bulgaria. Wounded twice, 1916.
POOLE, ALBERT E. F. (29, Sussex Street)	...	A.B.	R.N., 1912, Boy. North Sea.
POOLE, CECIL (55, Middle Brook Street)	...	A.B.	R.N., 1915, A.B. North Sea.
POOLE, DOUGLAS (65, Middle Brook Street)	...	Sig.	R.N., 1913. North Sea.
POOLE, ERNEST R. J. (29, Sussex Street)	...		R.M.L.I., 1913, Pte. South Africa, Pacific; H.M.S. *Kent*.
POOLE, HARRY T. (24, Fairfield Road)	...	Corpl.	R.A.O.C., May 1917, Pte. France.
POOLE, WALTER G. (34, Colson Road)	...	Gun.	R.M.A., May 1917, Gun. Salonica, Russia.
✠ POPE, SAMUEL H. (12, Lawn Street)	...	L.-Corpl.	Hants, Aug. 1914, Pte. Mesopotamia, India. *Died, Apl. 10, 1918.*
PORCAS, LEONARD H. (65, Sussex Street)	...	Pte.	R.A.S.C. (M.T.), Jan. 1915, Pte. Egypt, Salonica.
PORTER, JOHN E. L. (1, Christ Church Road)	...	Capt.	Artists' Rif., Aug. 1914. R.M.A. France, Flanders, North Sea.
PORTER, RICHARD J. (11, St. James' Villas)	...	2nd Lieut.	R.F., July 1917, Pte. H.A.C., E. Kent. France.
PORTSMOUTH, CYRIL A. V. (76, Parchment Street)	...	W.T.	Merc. Mar., W.T., 1918. Batoum, Theodosia.
POSTANS, HENRY H. (26, Stockbridge Road)	...	Pte.	R.A.M.C., rejoined Aug. 1914, Pte. France. Wounded, Nov. 17, 1916, and July 31, 1917.
✠ POTTER, THOMAS (82, Lower Brook Street)	...		K.R.R.C. Salonica, France. *Killed in Action, Jan. 17, 1917.*

WINCHESTER WAR SERVICE REGISTER

Povey, Bertram (1, Lower Wolvesey Terrace)	Dr.	R.A.S.C., Feb. 1915, Dr. Salonica, Egypt, Dardanelles.
✠ Povey, George O. (1, Lower Wolvesey Terrace)	Corpl.	R.M.L.I., Pte. R.N.D. At Sea, France. *Killed in Action, Apl. 23, 1917.*
✠ Povey, Percy (1, Lower Wolvesey Terrace)	Pte.	Hants, Sept. 1914, Pte. Dardanelles. *Killed in Action, Aug. 10, 1915, Suvla Bay.*
Powell, Albert (20, St. John's Road)	Pte.	Worc., Oct. 1916, Pte. Glos. France, Egypt, Italy. Wounded, July 1918.
Powell, Archie (21, North View Terrace)	Pte.	Hants, Aug. 1914, Pte. Suffolk. Home.
Powell, Frederick (68, Chesil Street)		Hants, Oct. 1916. Devon. Home.
Powell, Walter (20, St. John's Road)	Pte.	Hants Y., Nov. 1915, Tpr. R.A.S.C. (M.T.). E. Africa.
Powers, Frederick W. (50, Greenhill Road)	Bug.	K.R.R.C., 1898, Bug. France. Wounded Aug. 27, 1917.
✠ Powney, William B. (76, Stockbridge Road)	L.-Corpl.	R. Berks, 1899, Pte. France. *Killed in Action, May 16, 1915, Richebourg.*
Poynter, Ernest F. (35, Parchment Street)		R.A.F., 1918. France, Gibraltar.
✠ Prangle, Albert (13, Water Lane)	Pte.	Hants Y., 1914, Tpr. Hants. France. *Killed in Action, Mch. 23, 1918, Bapaume.*
Prangle, Cecil G. (16, Victoria Road)	Pte.	Hants, Nov. 1915, Pte. Home.
Prangle, Charles H. (16, Victoria Road)	Sergt.	I. of W. Militia, 1898. Hussars. France.
Prangle, Colin A. (12, Greenhill Avenue)	Pte.	Worc., Oct. 1916, Pte. Home.
Prangle, Walter H. (15, St. Paul's Hill)	A.B.	R.F.R., Aug. 1914, A.B. North Sea.
Prangle, William G. (16, Victoria Road)	Corpl.	Hants Militia, 1900, Pte. R.B. France. M.M.
Prangnell, Charles R. (3, Eastgate Street)		R.N.A.S., June 1917. Home.
Prangnell, John C. (28, Hatherley Road)	Gun.	R.G.A., May 1916, Gun. Home.
Prall, William J. (80, Parchment Street)	Pte.	Hants, Pte. India, Mesopotamia. Wounded, 1916.
Preece, William (93, Colebrook Street)	Pte.	Hants, Oct. 1916, Pte. France.
✠ Presslee, Albert (2, St. Clement Street)	Pte.	Hants, 1914, Pte. Dardanelles. *Killed in Action, Aug. 10, 1915.*
Presslee, Laban (2, St. Clement Street)	Pte.	Hants, 1916, Pte. India, Mesopotamia, France.

WINCHESTER WAR SERVICE REGISTER

Presslee, William (2, St. Clement Street)	Pte.	R. Marines, 1906, Pte. North Sea.
Pretty, Allen C. W. (130, High Street)	Tpr.	Hants Y., Mch. 1916, Tpr. Cav. Res. Home.
Pretty, Harry P. (15, Tower Street)	Pte.	R.A.S.C., May 1917, Pte. France.
Pretty, Jack H. (130, High Street)	Corpl.	Hants Y., Oct. 1915, Tpr. Hants. France, Italy, Germany. Wounded once.
Price, Alfred J. G. (17, St. Thomas Street)	Sergt.	R.A.S.C., June 1915, Wheeler. France.
Price, Charles J. (3, Leckford Cottages)	Q.M.S.	R.A.M.C., 1913, Pte. France.
Price, William J. (3, Leckford Cottages)	Sergt.	R.A.M.C., 1908, Pte. Hussars. France. D.C.M., Médaille Militaire 1915.
Prichard, Arthur E. (7, Boundary Street)		Devon, Sept. 1914. France. Wounded, May 1918.
✠ Prichard, William C. (7, Boundary Street)		Devon, Nov. 1914. France. *Killed in Action, Sept. 25, 1915.*
Prideaux, Charles W. (3, Domum Road)	Pnr.	R.E., Sept. 1915, Pnr. France.
Prideaux, Edmund (23, Owens Road)		Hants, Feb. 1917, Pte. France. Wounded, Aug. 3, 1917.
Prideaux, Harold (3, Domum Road)	Steward	R.N., July 27, 1918, Steward. Home, H.M.S. *Excellent.*
Prideaux, Herbert H. (3, Domum Road)	Pte.	Worc., June 1918, Pte. Home.
✠ Prideaux, John T. (3, Domum Road)	Pte.	Hants, Sept. 1914, Pte. Dardanelles, Balkans. Wounded, Sept. 19, 1915. *Missing, believed Killed, Dec. 7, 1915.*
Prideaux, Philip M. (89, Colebrook Street)	A.-Capt.	R.G.A., 1906, Gun. France. D.C.M. 1916, Despatches 1917, Croix de Guerre 1915.
Prince, Arthur T. (15, Lawn Street)	Drummer	Hants, 1913, Drummer. Home. Wounded twice (accidentally)
Prince, Ernest A. (2, Domum Cottages)	Stoker	R.N., 1911, Stoker. North Sea, Jutland, Russia, T.B. 98, H.M.S. *Cardiff.*
✠ Prince, George H. A. (45, Colebrook Street)	Pte.	Hants, Aug. 1914, Pte. Dardanelles, France. *Killed in Action, July* 1, 1916, *Somme.*
Prince, Hubert (7, Cross Street)	A.M.	R.A.F., July 1918, A.M. France, Belgium, Germany.
Prince, John M. (45, Colebrook Street)	Pte.	R.A.S.C., Apl. 1917, Pte. Home.
Prince, Ralph J. J. (39, Colebrook Street)	Pte.	Hants, July 1916, Pte. Devon, Lab. C. France, Salonica. Wounded and Gassed, Aug. 2, 1917.
Prince, William J. (16, Hyde Church Path)	Staff Sergt.	Hants, Sept. 4, 1914, Pte. A.G.S. Home.
✠ Prior, George (21, Cranworth Road)	Pte.	Canadians, Pte. France. *Killed in Action, Apl.* 9, 1917, *Vimy Ridge.*

I

WINCHESTER WAR SERVICE REGISTER

PRITCHARD, BERTIE (18, Eastgate Street)	...	Corpl.	R.A.S.C., Aug. 1914, Pte. Gallipoli, France.
PRITCHARD, CECIL (44, Lansdowne Terrace)	...	A.B.	R.N., Mch. 1917. North Sea.
PRITCHARD, GEORGE H. (18, Eastgate Street)	...	Sergt.	Innis. D., 1911, Tpr. France, Egypt, Salonica.
PRITCHARD, JOHN K. (11, Jewry Street)	...	A.-Paymstr.	R.B., Sept. 1916, Rfn. A.P.C. Home.
✠ PRITCHARD, REGINALD (44, Lansdowne Terrace)	...		Hants, Nov. 1914. Home. *Died, Nov. 28, 1916.*
PRITCHARD, WALTER J. (44, Lansdowne Terrace)	...	P.O.	R.N., Oct. 1915, Carpenter. North Sea, Russia.
PRITCHARD, WILLIAM F. (18, Eastagte Street)	...	Pte.	Hants, Aug. 1914, Pte. India, Persian Gulf, Mesopotamia. Taken Prisoner by Turks, Kut.
PRIVETT, EDWARD J. (9, Boundary Street)	...		R.G.A., 1904. Hants. France.
PRIVETT, GEORGE H. (36, Colebrook Street)	...	Pte.	Guards, Oct. 1916, Tpr. R.W.S., Lab. C. France.
PRIVETT, GEORGE R. (1, Abbey Passage)	...	Pte.	R.A.S.C. (M.T.), Aug. 1914, Pte. France. Gassed, Oct. 1916.
PRIVETT, WILLIAM J. (26, St. John's Road)	...	Gun.	R.M.A., 1895, Gun. Grand Fleet, H.M.S. *Tiger* and *Crescent.*
PROWTING, FREDERICK W. (7, Culver Road)	...	Spr.	R.E., June 1918, Spr. Home.
PROWTING, JOHN H. (16, St. Thomas Street)	...	Corpl.	A.P.C., Apl. 1915, Pte. Home.
PRYOR, FRANK H. (9, Clausentum Road)	...	Capt.	R.B., 1897, Rfn. France. Despatches 1916.
✠ PULLINGER, WILLIAM (3, Staple Garden)	...	Corpl.	R. Berks., 1914, Pte. France. *Killed in Action, July* 1, 1916, *Somme.*
PUNTER, ERNEST (79, Lower Brook Street)	...		Hants, Jan. 1916. M.G.C. India, Russia.
PURKISS, WILLIAM J. (43, St. John's Street)	...	Pte.	Hants, Aug. 1914, Pte. France, Gallipoli. Wounded, Oct. 2, 1915.
PYKE, GEORGE E. (1, Saxon Road)	...	Pte.	Hants Y., Oct. 1914, Tpr. Hants. France. Wounded, 1916 (twice), July 31 and Nov. 30, 1917.
PYKE, HERBERT A. (23, Fairfield Road)	...	L.-Corpl.	T.R., Feb. 1917, Pte. Glos., M.G.C. France. Gassed once.
QUINTON, RICHARD F. (Westbourne, Barnes Close)	...	Surg.-Lieut.	R.N., Aug. 1914, Surg.-Lieut. Dardanelles, Mesopotamia, China; H.M.S. *Scarab.*
QUIRK, ROBERT (Southgate House, St. Cross Rd.)	...	C.F.	C.F., Jan. 1917. France, Belgium.

WINCHESTER WAR SERVICE REGISTER

RABBITTS, GEORGE F. A. (32, Middle Brook Street)	1st A.M.	R.A.O.C., Oct. 1915, Pte. R.A.F. Home.
RADFORD, REGINALD H. (Park House, Park Road)	A.-Lt.-Col.	Leicester, 1901, 2nd Lieut. France. Despatches 1918.
RADWELL, FREDERICK J. (38, Monks Road)	Bug.	K.R.R.C., 1890, Bug. Home.
RAMSAY, ALLAN A. (35, Owens Road)	...	R.N., Mch. 7, 1917. Home, H.M.S. *Hermione*.
RANDALL, GEORGE H. (3, Newburgh Street)	Pte.	Hants, Feb. 1916, Pte. India, Mesopotamia.
RANDALL, HARRY (2, Alresford Road)	Sergt.	Lancers, 1910, Tpr. France.
RANDALL, THOMAS R. (21, Clausentum Road)	Gun.	A.V.C., Dec. 1915, Pte. R.F.A. France.
RANSLEY, WILLIAM G. (13, St. James' Villas)		Army Scripture Reader, Dec. 1914. France.
RATTEY, ARTHUR C. (22, Fairfield Road)	Gun.	R.G.A., Apl. 1917, Gun. France.
RATTEY, CHARLES (9, Water Lane)	Pte.	Hants, 1915, Pte. Egypt.
RATTEY, FREDERICK H. (22, Fairfield Road)	Pte.	Hants, Mch. 1915, Pte. Bedford. India.
RATTEY, GEORGE (9, Water Lane)	...	Nat. Res., May 1915. R.D.C. Home.
RATTEY, WILLIAM (9, Water Lane)	Rfn.	Hants, 1915, Pte. K.R.R.C. France.
RAWLINGS, WILLIAM H. (55, Hatherley Road)	L.-Corpl.	R.E. (Sigs.), Jan. 1916, Spr. Mesopotamia.
RAYMONT, ALBERT E. (18, Western Road)	2nd A.M.	R.F.C., Sept. 1917, Boy. R.A.F. India.
RAYMONT, DANIEL W. (18, Western Road)	Sergt.	Hants, Oct. 1914, Pte. India, Egypt, France, Germany. M.M. 1918.
READ, EWART G. (13, Tower Street)	A.B.	R.N., 1900, O.S. Grand Fleet. Wounded, May 1915.
READ, KEMPTON C. (13, Tower Street)	Spr.	R.E., Nov. 1915, Pnr. France.
READ, LEONARD C. (21, Western Road)	A.-Staff Sergt.	R.A.S.C., May 10, 1916, Pte. R.A.F. Home.
✠ READ, LEONARD S. (13, Tower Street)	Pte.	Hants, Sept. 1914, Pte. India, Persian Gulf, Mesopotamia. *Killed in Action, July* 24, 1915, *Nasariyeh.*
READ, WILFRED E. (30, Fairfield Road)	Corpl.	R.G.A., Oct. 1915, Gun. R.E. France.
READINGS, ALFRED (10, Staple Garden)	Cook's Mate	R.N., 1913, Cook's Mate. Dardanelles, English Channel Patrol; H.M.S. *Cornwallis*, and P. 37.
READINGS, HUGH (42, Sussex Street)	Bandsman	R. Marines, 1905, Bandsman. Grand Fleet, Mediterranean, Black Sea; H.M.S. *Téméraire*.

WINCHESTER WAR SERVICE REGISTER

✠ READINGS, WILLIAM (10, Staple Garden) ... Corpl. ... E. Lancs., 1894, Pte. France. Wounded, 1917. *Killed in Action.*

REDMAN, FREDERICK E. (16, City Road) ... Pte. ... R.A.S.C., 1917, Pte. France, Belgium.

REDMAN, RALPH (23, City Road) ... Pte. ... R.A.S.C., Apl. 1917, Pte. E. Africa.

REED, FRANK (13, Southgate Street) ... 2nd A.M. ... R.F.C., Oct. 1, 1916, 3rd A.M. R.A.F. Home.

✠ REEVES, JOHN H. (40, Sussex Street) ... Sergt. ... R.B., 1915, Rfn. Home. *Died, July 15, 1918.*

REX, EDWIN G. (8, Brassey Road) ... A.B. ... R.N., A.B. Home.

REX, SYDNEY A. (8, Brassey Road) ... Gun. ... Can. Arty., Sept. 1914, Gun. France. Gassed, May, 1915.

REYNISH, WILLIAM (13, Eastgate Street) ... Lieut. ... Wilts Y., Aug. 1914, Tpr. Dragoons. France.

✠ REYNOLDS, EDWARD C. (19, Clausentum Road) ... Pte. ... Lond., Mch. 1917, Pte. France. Wounded and taken Prisoner by Germans, Nov. 24, 1917. *Died of Wounds, Dec. 21, 1917, Seigsburg.*

REYNOLDS, JOHN F. (52, St. Catherine's Road) ... Spr. ... R.E., Mch. 1915, Spr. Gallipoli, Mesopotamia.

RIBBICK, ARTHUR (37, Wharf Hill) ... Pte. ... Hants, 1904, Pte. France. Wounded, Aug. 26, 1914. Taken Prisoner by Germans, Aug. 27, 1914.

RIBBICK, JOHN (4, Mants Lane) ... L.-Corpl. ... Hants, Aug. 1914, Pte. Essex, D.L.I. Salonica.

RICHARDS, ALBERT G. (33, Hyde Close) ... Corpl. ... R.A.S.C. (M.T.), Jan. 1915, Pte. France.

RICHARDS, ALFRED (33, Hyde Close) ... L.-Corpl. ... Hants, Aug. 1914, Pte. Mesopotamia, India.

RICHARDS, ALFRED (21, Western Road) ... L.-Sergt. ... Hants, Nov. 1915, Pte. Home.

RICHARDS, CHARLES A. (67, Upper Brook Street) ... Corpl. ... R.A.O.C., Sept. 1915. Home.

RICHARDS, CYRIL A. (67, Upper Brook Street) ... Corpl. ... R.G.A., 1912, Gun. Anti-Aircraft. Home.

RICHARDS, EDWIN E. (33, Hyde Close) ... Corpl. ... Hants, Oct. 1915, Pte. France. Wounded, Feb. 1, 1917.

RICHARDS, FRANK A. (67, Upper Brook Street) ... Spr. ... R.G.A., 1912, Gun. R.E. France.

✠ RICHARDS, FREDERICK C. (29, Western Road) ... Pte ... Hants, 1912, Pte. India, Mesopotamia. Wounded, Dec. 11, 1915. Taken Prisoner by Turks, Apl. 29, 1916, Kut. *Died, June 17, 1916, Nesibin.*

RICHARDS, GEORGE (7, Arthur Road) ... Q.M. ... K.R.R.C., Rfn. M.G.C. France. M.C.

RICHARDS, HARRY C. (33, Hyde Close) ... Pte. ... Hants, Oct. 1915, Pte. France, Italy. Wounded, July, 1918.

WINCHESTER WAR SERVICE REGISTER

RICHARDS, PERCY B. ... Pte. ... R. Warwick, Dec. 1917, Pte. France, Belgium.
(33, Hyde Close)

RICHARDSON, ARTHUR E. ... R.S.M. ... R.B., 1898, Rfn. France, Flanders. Wounded, 1917 and 1918. Gassed once. M.C. 1918, Despatches 1917, 1918.
(8, North Walls)

RICHARDSON, BASIL ... C.Q.M.S. R.B., Rfn. France. Wounded, Sept. 1914.
(41, Monks Road)

RICHARDSON, CHARLES H. ... Sergt. ... Hants, Sept. 1915, Pte. France, Germany. M.M. 1918.
(49, Milverton Road)

✠ RICHARDSON, EDWARD M. ... Pte. ... Hants, Oct. 1915, Pte. France. *Killed in Action, Sept. 3, 1916, Glanchy.*
(31, Middle Brook Street)

RICHARDSON, FRANK A. ... R.M.L.I., Jan. 1914. E. Africa, Russia.
(31, Middle Brook Street)

RICHARDSON, WILLIAM P. ... Pte. ... Hants, Oct. 1915, Pte. M.G.C. France.
(31, Middle Brook Street)

RICKETTS, WILFRED E. ... L.-Corpl. Hants, Apl. 1916, Pte. Somerset L.I. France. Wounded, May 4, 1917.
(30, St. John's Park Road)

RICKMAN, CHARLES ... Pte. ... Hants, rejoined Sept. 1914, Pte. D.C.L.I. Home.
(65, Colebrook Street)

✠ RICKMAN, FREDERICK ... Drummer Hants, 1906, Drummer. Dardanelles. Wounded, 1915. *Killed in Action*, 1915.
(65, Colebrook Street)

RICKMAN, GEORGE ... Gun. ... R.G.A., June 1916, Gun. Salonica.
(65, Colebrook Street)

✠ RICKMAN, TOM ... Sergt. ... Scots Gds., Aug. 1914, Tpr. France. Wounded, Oct. 1915. D.C.M. 1915. *Killed in Action, Sept.* 1916.
(65, Colebrook Street)

ROBERTS, ARTHUR L. ... Lieut. ... R.G.A., May 1916, Gun. Hants. Home.
(5, Newburgh Street)

ROBERTS, DAVID A. F. ... Pte. ... Hants, Sept. 1914, Pte. Mesopotamia. Taken Prisoner by Turks, Apl. 29, 1916, Kut.
(2, Cromwell Terrace)

✠ ROBERTS, FRANK A. ... Pte. ... Hants, Nov. 1914, Pte. India, Mesopotamia. *Killed in Action, Jan. 21, 1916, Arab.*
(1, Queen's Terrace)

✠ ROBERTS, HERBERT R. ... Pte. ... Worc., 1916, Pte. M.G.C. France. *Killed in Action, May 27, 1918.*
(5, St. John's North)

✠ ROBERTS, LESLIE W. ... Pte. ... Dorset, Jan. 1917, Pte. R.A.S.C. (M.T.), Yorks. France, Belgium. Wounded, July 17, 1917. *Killed in Action, Sept. 20, 1917.*
(1, Queen's Terrace)

ROBERTS, REGINALD ... Corpl. ... R.N.D., June 1916. Devon, Lab. C. France.
(5, St. John's North)

ROBERTSON, JOHN L. ... L.-Corpl. R.B., 1912, Bandsman. Salonica, France.
(2, Back St., St. Cross)

ROBERTSON, MALCOLM ... Major ... D. of W. Regt., Sept. 16, 1914, Capt. France, Flanders. M.C. 1917, O.B.E. 1919, Despatches twice.
(10, College Street)

ROBINSON, ALFRED W. ... Pte. ... R.M.L.I., 1913, Pte. France, Egypt, Dardanelles.
(34, Lower Brook Street)

ROBINSON, BENJAMIN ... Corpl. ... R.G.A., May 1915, Gun. France. Wounded once.
(3, Nelson Road)

WINCHESTER WAR SERVICE REGISTER

ROBINSON, EDWARD A. G. ... Lieut. ... R.N.A.S., Feb. 1917, Prob. Flight Off. R.A.F.
(8, The Close) At Sea.

ROBINSON, HERBERT C. ... A.B. ... R.N., Oct. 1914, O.S.
(34, Lower Brook Street)

ROBINSON, JAMES H. ... ... Stoker ... R.N., 1912, O.S.
(34, Lower Brook Street)

ROBINSON, JOHN R. ... ... Lond., May 1916, Pte. Egypt.
(1, Nuns Road)

ROBINSON, STEPHEN G. ... Lieut. ... R.N.A.S., June 1917, Prob. Flight Off. R.A.F.
(8, The Close) France, At Sea.

ROBINSON, THOMAS A. ... Bdr. ... R.H.A., 1911, Gun. France. Wounded, Sept.
(3, Nelson Road) 14, 1914.

ROBINSON, WALTER ... ... Corpl. ... Hants, rejoined Aug. 1914, Pte. India, Persian
(34, Lower Brook Street) Gulf.

ROBINSON, WALTER F. ... A.B. ... R.N., 1911, O.S. Grand Fleet.
(34, Lower Brook Street)

ROBINSON, WILLIAM ... ... Pte. ... R.E., June 1916, Spr. Tank C. France. Wounded,
(2, Highland Terrace) Aug. 21, 1918.

ROE, HERBERT C. G. ... C.S.M. ... R.A.S.C. (M.T.), 1908, Pte. France, Belgium.
(52, Parchment Street) Despatches, 1919.

ROE, WILLIAM A. ... ... C.Q.M.S. ... R.A.S.C. (M.T.), 1905, Pte. France, Belgium.
(52, Parchment Street) M.S.M. 1916.

ROGERS, ALFRED ... ... Pte. ... Hants, 1910, Pte. France.
(7, Queensland Terrace)

✠ ROGERS, ARTHUR W. ... ... Corpl. ... Hants, Dec. 1914, Pte. R.E. (Sigs.). India,
(8, Crowder Terrace) Mesopotamia. *Died*, *Sept. 27, 1918, Poona.*

ROGERS, CHARLES E. ... ... Pte. ... Hants, July 1916, Pte. Wilts. France. Wounded
(3, King Alfred Terrace) twice.

ROGERS, HARRY M. ... ... Pte. ... Devon, May 1916, Pte. France.
(3, Maidstone Terrace)

ROGERS, HORACE ... ... Sergt. ... R.B., 1909, Rfn. Lab. C. France.
(4, Westgate Lane)

ROGERS, WILLIAM A. ... ... Spr. ... R.E., May 1917, Spr. Home.
(3, King Alfred Terrace)

ROGERS, WILLIAM D. ... L.-Corpl. ... Hants Y., Oct. 1915, Tpr. Hants. France, Italy.
(19, St. Peter's Street) M.M. 1918.

ROGERS, WILLIAM G. ... ... 2nd A.M. ... R.F.C., Nov. 1917, Storeman. R.A.F. Home.
(12A, Water Lane)

ROLFE, ALEXANDER L. ... Sergt. ... S.A. Lab. C., rejoined 1917. France.
(18, Colebrook Street)

ROLFE, ALFRED C. ... ... Corpl. ... Worc., Apl. 1918, Pte. Home.
(86, Wales Street)

ROLFE, GEORGE J. ... ... Pte. ... Devon, Oct. 1916, Pte. Lab. C. Home.
(86, Wales Street)

ROSE, ALFRED ... ... Pte. ... R.F., Feb. 1916, Pte. France. Gassed once.
(5, Greyfriars Terrace)

WINCHESTER WAR SERVICE REGISTER

Rose, D'Arcy L. (6, Ranelagh Road)	...	Major ...	Hants, 1914, Capt. India, Mesopotamia.
Rose, Frederick (5, Greyfriars Terrace)	...	...	R.A.S.C., Aug. 1915. France.
✠ Rose, James (5, Greyfriars Terrace)	...	...	Hants, Sept. 1914. France. Wounded twice. *Killed in Action, Sept.* 13, 1918.
Rose, Thomas (44, St. John's Street)	...	Bandsman	Hants, July 1914, Bandsman. India.
Rose, William (5, Greyfriars Terrace)	...	...	R.A.S.C., June 1916. France.
Ross, George (69, Hyde Street)	...	Capt. ...	Hants Y., Lieut. Sea. H. France. Wounded, Sept. 1917.
Ross, Henry (35, Clifton Road)	...	Sergt. ...	Hants, 1889, Pte. Dorset, Devon. France, India, Mesopotamia.
Rowe, Bertie (13, Cheriton Road)	...	Pte. ...	R.A.S.C. (M.T.), June 1916, Pte. France.
Rowe, Cecil (16, Staple Garden)	...	Pte. ...	Hants, Nov. 1915, Pte. Home.
Rowe, Horace (25, Union Street)	...	Dr. ...	R.A.S.C., Apl. 1917, Dr. Home.
✠ Rowell, William G. (8, Cross Street)	...	Stoker ...	R.N., 1912, Stoker. North Sea; H.M.S. *Hampshire. Drowned, June* 5, 1916.
Rowland, Henry T. (70, Sussex Street)	...	1st A.M. ...	R.N.A.S., Mch. 1917, 1st A.M. R.A.F. France.
Rowland, William G. (10, Saxon Road)	...	2nd Corpl.	R.A.O.C., Oct. 1915, Pte. Home.
✠ Rowlands, John H. (5, Hyde Close)	...	L.-Corpl.	R. Berks, Pte. Devon. Egypt. Wounded once. *Died, June* 25, 1918.
Rowlands, William C. (21, North Walls)	...	Pte. ...	Hants, June 1917, Pte. Worc., Hants Cyc. France. Gassed, 1918.
Ruffell, Edwin H. (3, Tangier Terrace)	...	Sergt. ...	R.E., rejoined Aug. 1914, Dr. Egypt, Dardanelles, Mesopotamia.
Ruffell, James W. (21, King Alfred Place)	...	C.P.O. ...	R.N., 1875. Grand Fleet, H.M.S. *Kent* and *Dolphin*.
Ruffell, William S. (27, St. Catherine's Road)	...	Sergt. ...	R.G.A., 1910, Gun. W. Africa, France. Gassed, Nov. 1917.
Ruffels, Albert E. (5, Highland Terrace)	...	Dr. ...	R.G.A., Nov. 1915, Dr. France.
Ruffels, Harry (5, Highland Terrace)	...	C.S.M. ...	Lond., May 1915, Pte. Home.
Ruffels, John J. (5, Highland Terrace)	...	...	R.N., rejoined Aug. 1916. Mining School. Home.
Ruffels, Philip H. (5, Highland Terrace)	...	Sergt. ...	R. Berks, June 1916, Pte. France. M.S.M. 1918. Despatches 1918.
Rumbold, Alfred (4, St. George's Terrace)	...	...	R.A.M.C., 1915. R.I.R. Home.

WINCHESTER WAR SERVICE REGISTER

☩ RUMBOLD, ARTHUR ... ...   Dorset. Gallipoli, France, Belgium. *Killed in*
(4, St. George's Terrace)   *Action, Dec. 1918, near Ypres.*

RUMBOLD, CHARLES J. ... Gun. ... R.H.A., 1913, Gun. France.
(11, Colebrook Place)

RUMBOLD, FRANK ... ... Pte. ... Black Watch, Sept. 1914, Pte. Arg. and Suth. H.,
(4, St. George's Terrace)   Lab. C., Bedford. France. Wounded, Sept. 25, 1915, July 16 and Oct. 25, 1916.

RUMBOLD, GEORGE A. ... ... L.-Corpl. Hants, Oct. 1916, Pte. Home.
(9, Parchment Street)

RUMBOLD, HARRY ... ... L.-Corpl. Devon, Aug. 1916, Pte. Lab. C. France.
(5, St. Leonard's Road)

☩ RUMBOLD, PERCY B. ... ... Corpl. ... Hants, June 1915, Pte. France. *Killed in Action,*
(2, St. James' Villas)   *July 1, 1916, Beaumont Hamel.*

RUMMEY, JOHN W. ... ... R.A.S.C. (M.T.), Nov. 15, 1915. France.
(38, Brassey Road)

RUMSEY, PERCY G. ... ... L.-Corpl. Hants, Aug. 8, 1914, Pte. Mesopotamia, India,
(15, Hyde Church Path)   Russia, Persia.

RUSSELL, ALBERT E. ... ... S.M. ... R.A.S.C. (M.T.), June 1916, Pte. Home.
(1, Highland Terrace)

RUSSELL, ALFRED J. ... ... P.O. R.N., rejoined Aug. 1914, P.O. (Class 1). Home.
(12, Queen's Road)   (Class 1)

RUSSELL, ARTHUR A. S. ... A.B. ... R.N., 1912, Boy. S. Africa, E. Africa, North
(45, Hyde Abbey Road)   Sea; H.M.S. *Impregnable, Hyacinth,* and T.B.D. *Observer.*

RUSSELL, B. ... ... Pte. ... R.A.M.C., Nov. 1914, Pte. France. Gassed, 1918.

RUSSELL, CHARLES H. ... Sergt. ... Hants, 1905, Pte. Oxf. and Bucks L.I. India,
(76, Lower Brook Street)   Mesopotamia. Taken Prisoner by Turks, 1916.

RUSSELL, JOHN E. ... ... Pte. ... R.A.S.C. July 1917, Pte. E. Africa.
(14, Fairfield Road)

☩ RUSSELL, LEONARD C. B. ... Capt. ... R.B., Aug. 1914, 2nd Lieut. France. *Killed in*
(St. Cross Mede, St. Cross Rd.)   *Action, Oct. 7, 1916, Gaudecourt.*

RUSSELL, LEONARD G. ... Major ... R.B., 1878, 2nd Lieut. Home.
(St. Cross Mede, St. Cross Rd.)

RUSSELL, SYDNEY H. ... ... L.-Corpl. Nat. Res., Sept. 1914, Pte. Hants. Home.
(45, Hyde Abbey Road)

RUSSELL, WALTER   Staff S.M. R.A.S.C., Aug. 1914, Pte. France.
(74, Fairfield Road)

RUSSELL, WILLIAM A. ... Pte. ... Hants, Nov. 1914, Pte. India, Egypt, France.
(76, Lower Brook Street)

RUSTELL, FREDERICK   R.N.A.S., Aug. 1917, R.A.F. Home.
(94, Brassey Road)

RYALL, WILLIAM J. ... ... Gun. ... R.G.A., July 1916, Gun. France, Belgium.
(Fircroft, East Hill)

WINCHESTER WAR SERVICE REGISTER

SACREE, ALFRED G. ... (4, Nuns Road)	...	Dr.	R.F.A., Sept. 1914, Dr. France.
SACREE, ARTHUR L. ... (4, Nuns Road)	...		R.A.S.C., Aug. 1916. R.F.A. Home.
SACREE, CHARLES W. (4, Nuns Road)		P.O.	R.N., 1909, Boy. H.M.S. *Iron Duke*.
SACREE, ERNEST J. ... (4, Nuns Road)		Pte.	Hants, Mch. 1917, Pte. Cambridge, Staffs. France. Wounded once.
SAINSBURY, JOHN W. ... (118, Stockbridge Road)		Pte.	R.A.S.C. (M.T.), June 6, 1915, Pte. Home.
SAINT, WILLIAM H. N.... (6, Greenhill Road)	...		R.N. 1916. High Seas.
SAIT, ALBERT E. (60, Tower Street)		Pte.	R.F., Sept. 1914, Pte. Middlesex. France. Wounded, July 7, 1915.
SAIT, HENRY J. (60, Tower Street)		Pte.	Hants, Nov. 1915, Pte. India, Egypt, France. Wounded, April 1918.
SALMON, GILBERT H. ... (77, High Street)		Capt.	Hants, Sept. 1914, Pte. R. Warwick. France, Italy. Despatches 1919.
SALMON, JAMES H. (46, Tower Street)		Pte.	Hants, Dec. 1915, Pte. Mesopotamia.
SALMON, RONALD D. ... (46, Tower Street)		Tpr.	Lord Strathcona's Horse, Oct. 1916, Tpr. France. Wounded, Mch. 23, 1918.
SALTER, ALFRED J. (9, Middle Brook Street)		Pte.	Hants, Aug. 1914, Pte. Dardanelles. Wounded twice, Aug. 9, 1915.
SALTER, CHARLES (9, Middle Brook Street)		Pte.	Hants, Sept. 1914, Pte. Devon, Lab. C. Italy, France.
SALTER, FREDERICK C. (85, Chesil Street)		Spr.	R.A.M.C., Nov. 1915, Pte. R.E. France.
SALTER, THOMAS W. ... (9, Middle Brook Street)		Spr.	Hants, Nov. 1915, Pte. R.E. France. Wounded once.
SALTER, WALTER W. ... (45, Parchment Street)		Sergt.	Hants, 1914, Pte. Home.
SANDELL, RAYMOND J.... (15, City Road)		Capt.	Dragoon Gds., 1886, Tpr. Hants Y. Home.
SANDOM, HARRY J. (15, Greenhill Road)		Bandsman	Hants, July 1914, Bandsman. Devon, Wilts, Lab. C. Home.
SANKEY, ALBERT (96, Lower Brook Street)		Pte.	Hants, 1911, Pte. Mesopotamia. M.M. 1917.
SANKEY, FRANK (95, Lower Brook Street)		P.O.	R.N., 1909. North Sea; H.M.S. *Invincible*.
SAUNDERS, ALBERT W. (38, Lower Brook Street)		Pte.	R.A.S.C., Aug. 1916, Pte. France.
SAUNDERS, ARTHUR (35, Western Road)		C.Q.M.S.	Nat. Res., Aug. 5, 1914, Pte. Hants. India, Persia, Mesopotamia. M.S.M.
SAUNDERS, ARTHUR C. (35, Western Road)		L.-Corpl.	Hants, Apl. 1914, Bug. India, Mesopotamia.

WINCHESTER WAR SERVICE REGISTER

SAUNDERS, EVELYN G. ... Rfn. ... K.R.R.C., Jan. 1915, Rfn. France.
(19, Egbert Road)

SAUNDERS, FRANCIS P.... ... L.-Corpl. Hants, Jan. 1917, Pte. Devon, Hants. Home.
(29, Greenhill Road)

SAUNDERS, FREDERICK W. J. 2nd Lieut. R.F.C., May 1918, Cadet. Egypt.
(20, West End Terrace)

SAUNDERS, HARRY W. W. ... S.M. ... Can. Fus., 1914, Pte. Home.
(58, Sussex Street)

SAUNDERS, JACK G. ... ... A.M. ... R.N.A.S., June 1916, A.M. Home.
(62, Stockbridge Road)

SAUNDERS, WILLIAM C. ... L.-Corpl. Devon, Mch. 1918, Pte. France. Gassed, 1918.
(29, Greenhill Road)

SAUNDERS, WILLIAM H. ... Gun. ... R.G.A., Mch. 13, 1916, Gun. Egypt. Palestine.
(6, Gladstone Street)

SAUNDERS, WILLIAM J. ... Capt. ... Hants, Sept. 1914, Lieut. and Q.M. Gallipoli, Salonica, Black Sea. M.C. 1915, Despatches.
(20, West End Terrace)

SAVAGE, GEORGE W. ... ... Corpl. ... T.R., Aug. 1917, Pte. R. Sussex. Home.
(4, Elm Road)

SAVAGE, HAROLD F. ... ... Sergt. ... Hants, Sept. 1914, Pte. India, Mesopotamia.
(4, Elm Road)

SAVAGE, JOHN F. ... ... Lieut. ... Hants Cyc., Jan. 1915, Pte. R.E. France. M.C.
(7, Sparkford Road)

SAWLE, GEORGE ... ... Merc. Mar. Hospital Ships, 1914. France, Dardanelles, Salonica, Alexandria.
(35, Nuns Road)

✠ SAWLE, WALTER... ... ... Boy ... R.N., Nov. 1918, Boy. H.M.S. *Impregnable*. Died of pneumonia, Feb. 25, 1919.
(35, Nuns Road)

SAWYER, JOHN A. ... ... Sergt. ... Hants Y., 1898, Tpr. Home.
(Shortacre, Park Road)

✠ SCADDAN, ALFRED ... ... Pte. ... Kent Cyc., Oct. 1915, Pte. Buffs. France. *Missing, believed Killed*, Oct. 5, 1916.
(10, Andover Road)

SCADDAN, CHARLES H. ... Cook ... R.N., Aug. 1915, Cook. Egypt, Dardanelles Salonica, France, H.M.S. *Arcadian* and *Norman*.
(5, Avenue Road)

SCADDAN, FREDERICK ... ... Pte. ... Kent Cyc., July 1915, Pte. Home.
(10, Andover Road)

✠ SCOTT, CYRIL ... ... Pte. ... Wilts, Jan. 1916, Pte. France. *Killed in Action, June 14, 1917.*
(32, Nuns Road)

✠ SCOTT, EDWARD C. ... ... Lieut. ... R.A., 1912, Lieut. France. *Killed in Action, Nov. 21, 1914, Armentières.*
(The Garth, Lankhills Road)

SCOTT, ERNEST W. ... ... Bdr. ... R.F.A., Aug. 4, 1914, Wheeler. Wounded once. Gassed three times.
(32, Nuns Road)

SCOTT, RICHARD B. ... ... Corpl. ... R.E., Aug. 17, 1914, Spr. France.
(1, Queensland Terrace)

SCUTT, EDWARD ... ... Capt. ... K.R.R.C., Lieut. Home. Despatches, 1919.
(Benhilton, Arthur Road)

SEALEY, ARTHUR ... ... 2nd Corpl. R.E. (Sigs.), Jan. 1916, Spr. France.
(55, Hatherley Road)

WINCHESTER WAR SERVICE REGISTER

SEALEY, HARRY (60, Western Road)	Sergt.	Hants (T.F.), July 1914, Bandsman. R.G.A. Home.	
SEALEY, LEONARD (72, Fairfield Road)	Sergt.	R.E. (Sigs.), Jan., 1916, Spr. France.	
SEARGENT, WILLIAM H. (23, Upper High Street)	Sergt.	Hants, rejoined Aug. 1914, Pte. India.	
SEARLE, CHARLES E. (18, The Weirs)	Pte.	Hants, Oct. 1915, Pte. M.G.C., Hants. France, Mesopotamia.	
SELWAY, WILLIAM (16, Colson Road)		Hants, rejoined May 1917, Pte. Home.	
SERGEANT, GEOFFREY O. H. (36, Christ Church Road)	Lieut.	Hants, June 1916, 2nd Lieut. France. Wounded, Sept. 20, 1917. M.C. 1917.	
SERGEANT, THOMAS W. (36, Christ Church Road)	2nd Lieut.	O.C.B., May 1918. K.R.R.C. Home.	
SEWARD, CHARLES S. (16, Stockbridge Road)	Pte.	Hants, Oct. 1915, Pte. N. Fus. Mesopotamia. Wounded once.	
SEWARD, GEORGE (16, Stockbridge Road)	Pte.	Hants, Aug. 1915, Pte. R.A.F. Home.	
✠ SEWARD, JOHN W. (16, Stockbridge Road)	Sergt.	R.B., 1904, Rfn. India, France. Wounded four times. *Killed in Action, Aug. 26, 1917.*	
SHARP, ARTHUR C. (40, St. Catherine's Road)		Worc., June 1916, Pte. Hants. Home.	
SHARP, ARTHUR S. (4, Bar End)	Pte.	Somerset L.I., Apl. 1916, Pte. Shropshire L.I. Home.	
SHARP, FRANCIS G. (2, Station Hill)	Lieut.	Hants Y., 1914, Tpr. Hants. France. Wounded, Apl. 1918.	
SHARP, WILLIAM (30, Western Road)	Sergt.	A.P.C., Nov. 1914, Pte. Oxf. and Bucks L.I., D.C.L.I. France, Italy, Belgium.	
SHARP, WILLIAM A. (5, Clausentum Road)	Pte.	R.A.F., Oct. 1918, Pte. Home.	
✠ SHARPE, ALFRED (2, Granville Place)	Pte.	Hants, Mch. 1916, Pte. India, Egypt, France. Wounded once. *Killed in Action, July 28, 1918.*	
SHARPE, FREDERICK (2, Granville Place)	Gun.	R.G.A., July 4, 1916, Gun. France. Wounded, Mch. 22, 1918.	
SHARPE, WILLIAM R. (2, Granville Place)		Lab. C., Nov. 1918, Pte. Home.	
SHAW, JAMES W. (49, Nuns Road)	Lieut. and Q.M.	R.B., Aug. 1914, R.Q.M.S. R.F. France. M.B.E.	
SHAWYER, ALBERT J. (Bank Chambers, High Street)	Pte.	Hants, Oct. 1915, Pte. India, Mesopotamia, Salonica.	
SHAWYER, GEORGE (55, Greenhill Road)	Rfn.	Hants, Mch. 1917, Pte. Dorset, R.B. Egypt, Mesopotamia. Wounded once. Taken Prisoner by Turks, Dec. 1917.	
SHAWYER, GEORGE (16, Water Lane)		S.A. Transport, 1914. E. Africa.	

WINCHESTER WAR SERVICE REGISTER

SHAWYER, HENRY V. (55, Greenhill Road)	...	Sergt. ...	R.B., 1911, Rfn. France, Mesopotamia. Wounded, Dec. 8, 1914, and Oct. 4, 1917.
SHAWYER, WILLIAM T. (55, Greenhill Road)	...		R.E., Aug. 1917. Home.
SHEARMAN, CHARLES E. G. (Byrnelmscote, Park Road)	...	Lieut.-Col.	Bedford and Herts, 1909, 2nd Lieut. Belgium, France. Wounded, Aug. 24, 1914, and Oct. 23, 1918. Chev. Légion d'Honneur 1914, M.C. 1915, D.S.O. 1918.
SHEARMAN, ROBERT C. (3, Culverwell Gardens)	...	Pte. ...	R. Warwick, Oct. 18, 1918, Pte. Home.
✠ SHEARS, SAMUEL (12, Ashley Terrace)	...	...	Hants, Aug. 1914. Home. *Died, Feb. 5, 1919.*
SHEARS, SAMUEL G. (12, Ashley Terrace)	...	Corpl. ...	Hants Y., June 1915, Tpr. Worc. France, Belgium.
SHEARS, WILLIAM E. (13, Durngate Place)	...	Pte. ...	Hants, May 20, 1918, Pte. Home.
✠ SHEFFERD, CECIL (94, Fairfield Road)	...	L.-Corpl.	Hants, 1914, Pte. India, Mesopotamia. Wounded, Mch. and July, 1915. Taken Prisoner by Turks. *Died as P.O.W.*
SHEFFERD, CHARLES D. (94, Fairfield Road)	...	Sergt. ...	R.E., 1917, Spr. Mesopotamia.
SHEFFERD, GEORGE (94, Fairfield Road)	...	Pte. ...	T.R., Aug. 8, 1917, Pte. Hants. France.
SHEFFERD, RONALD (94, Fairfield Road)	...	...	R.A.M.C., 1917. France.
SHELDON, EDWARD (6, East Cliffe)	...	Corpl. ...	Hants, Sept. 1914, Pte. R. Warwick. France.
SHELDON, LEONARD (6, East Cliffe)	...	Corpl. ...	Hants, Sept. 15, 1914, Pte. R. Warwick, Lab. C., Devon. France. Wounded, June 27, 1916.
SHEPHERD, ARTHUR W. L. (8, St. John's Street)	...	L.-Corpl.	T.R., May 1917, Pte. France.
SHEPPARD, WALLACE G. (3, De Lunn Buildings)	...		M.M.G.C., Mch. 1915, Gun. Tank C. France.
✠ SHEPPARD, WILLIAM J. (13, Lawn Street)	...		Hants, Oct. 1916, Pte. France. *Killed in Action, Feb. 1, 1917.*
SHERGOLD, ALFRED (86, Chesil Street)	...	Corpl. ...	Hussars, 1892, Tpr. Home.
SHERGOLD, ALFRED J. (81, Wales Street)	...	L.-Corpl.	Hants, 1914, Pte. Salonica.
SHERGOLD, ALFRED L. (86, Chesil Street)	...	L.-Corpl.	R.E., Feb. 1917, Spr. E. Surrey, R.F. France. Wounded, Oct. 11, 1918.
SHERGOLD, EDWIN F. (103, Upper Brook Street)	...	Sergt. ...	Hants (T.F.), 1894, Bandsman. Lab. C. France, Belgium.
SHERGOLD, ERNEST H. (5, Hyde Abbey Road)	...	L.-Corpl.	Hants, Aug. 1916, Pte. Lab. C. France, Belgium. Wounded, Apl. 21, 1918.
SHERGOLD, FREDERICK W. (30A, Hyde Street)	...		Devon, July 1916. Home.

WINCHESTER WAR SERVICE REGISTER

Shergold, Henry (30A, Hyde Street)		R.F.A., Nov. 1916. R.A.O.C. Home.
Shergold, James F. (86, Chesil Street)	Corpl.	Hussars, Aug. 1915, Tpr. France. Wounded, Mch. 23, 1918.
Shergold, John H. (Wilton, St. Leonard's Road)	C.P.O.	R.N., 1893, Boy. Persian Gulf, Grand Fleet. D.S.M. 1917.
Shergold, Sydney (14, Elm Road)		Hants, Oct. 1915. R. Berks. France.
Sherren, Percy G. (2, Queen's Road)	Pte.	R.A.S.C. (M.T.), Feb. 1917, Pte. Home.
Sherren, William R. (2, Queen's Road)	Corpl.	Hants, June 1916, Pte. France, Belgium.
Sherriff, Alexander (28, Christ Church Road)		R.A.O.C., Aug. 1917, Pte. France.
Sherriff, Bristow (Drayton Lodge, St. Cross Road)	Gun.	R.G.A., May 1916, Gun. Home.
Sherry, Herbert M. (31, Stockbridge Road)	S.Q.M.S.	Hants Y., Oct. 1914, Tpr. Home.
Sherwood, Charles A. (3, East Cliffe)	P.O. (Class 1)	R.N., 1902. North Sea, Mediterranean; H.M.S. *Invincible* and *Alarm*.
✠ Sherwood, Frank E. (Highcliffe Park Farm)		Hants, Aug. 1914. Dardanelles. *Killed in Action*, Aug. 10, 1915.
✠ Sherwood, George (Highcliffe Park Farm)	Pte.	Hants, rejoined Aug. 1914, Pte. France. *Killed in Action*, Nov. 30, 1914.
Sherwood, Harry (23, Lower Brook Street)		M.M.G.C. Tank C. Egypt, France.
Shilling, Reginald F. (46, Hatherley Road)		R.N., Sept. 1, 1917. R.A.F. Home.
Shilton, Edwin D. (Conservative Club, Jewry Street)	Spr.	R.E., Feb. 1917, Pnr. France.
Shiner, George (15, Upper Wolvesey Terrace)	Pte.	Devon, Oct. 1916, Pte. Home.
Shiner, Reginald W. (15, Upper Wolvesey Terrace)	1st A.M.	R.N.A.S., 1913. R.A.F. Italy.
Ship, John R. (10, Prison Quarters)	Pte.	R.B., rejoined Aug. 1914, Rfn. Lab. C. France. Wounded, May 1915.
Ship, William V. (10, Prison Quarters)	Pte.	Hants, Sept. 1914, Pte. Devon. France. Despatches 1917.
Shipton, Thomas (1, Lawn Street)	Pte.	Devon, Dec. 11, 1915, Pte. Lab. C. France, Belgium.
Shore, Alfred E. (Little Minster Street)	C.S.M.	Hants (T.F.), 1905, Pte. Hants. India, Mesopotamia.
✠ Shore, Alfred G. (Little Minster Street)	A.-C.Q.M.S.	Hants (T.F.), Pte. Hants. India, Mesopotamia. Wounded once. Taken Prisoner by Turks, Kut. *Died, as P.O.W.*
Shore, William V. (Little Minster Street)	Sergt.	Hants (T.F.), Pte. Hants. India, Mesopotamia.

WINCHESTER WAR SERVICE REGISTER

SHORT, WILLIAM ... ... Pte. ... Hants, July 1916, Pte. India, Palestine, France.
(82, Colebrook Street) Wounded, Nov. 1917.
SHORT, WILLIAM E. ... ... R.N., M.B.R., May 13, 1918. H.M.S. *Hermione*.
(67, Parchment Street)
SHRIMPTON, ARTHUR O. ... Gun. ... R.G.A., June 1916, Gun. France.
(12, Fairfield Road)
SHRIMPTON, SIDNEY C. ... Pte. ... R.A.S.C. (M.T.), Jan. 1917, Pte. France.
(9, Saxon Road)
SILCOX, ALEXANDER J. ... Sergt. ... R.B., 1914, Rfn. Wounded, May 1915.
(16, Nuns Road)
SILLENCE, WILLIAM F. ... Stoker ... R.N., 1913, Stoker. North Sea, Mediterranean.
(15, Upper Brook Street)
SILVER, BERTIE C. ... ... Gun. ... Hants, Dec. 1915, Pte. R.G.A. India.
(5, St. Thomas Street)
✠ SIMMONDS, ALBERT W. ... Pte. ... Hants, 1913, Pte. France. Wounded, Oct. 15,
(Railway Cottages, St. Cross) 1914. *Killed in Action, May* 13, 1915.
SIMMONDS, CHARLES H. ... Pte. ... Hants, Mch. 1917, Pte. Home.
(28, Lower Brook Street)
SIMMONDS, ERNEST F. ... ... A.V.C., 1914. R.F.A. France.
(3, Ilex Terrace)
SIMMONDS, F. ... ... Pte. ... R.A.O.C., Oct. 1915, Pte. Home.
(12, High Street)
SIMMONDS, FREDERICK J. ... Corpl. ... Hants, 1916, Pte. India, Mesopotamia, Persia.
(3, Ilex Terrace)
SIMMONDS, H. B. ... ... Bdr. ... R.G.A., 1915, Gun. Egypt, Palestine.
SIMMONDS, WALTER ... ... Pte. ... R.F.C., Pte. R.A.F. Home.
(111, Upper Brook Street)
✠ SIMMONS, JOHN ... ... 2nd Lieut. R.W.S., 1888, Band Boy. R.B. France. *Killed*
(4, Greenhill Road) (*accidentally*), *Aug.* 21, 1916, *Aldershot.*
SIMMONS, JOHN G. ... ... Boy ... R.F.C., Oct. 1917, Boy. R.A.F. Germany.
(4, Greenhill Road)
SIMONDS, J. BARROW ... *See* BARROW SIMONDS.
SIMPKINS, MARTYN ... ... 1st A.M. ... R.F.C., July 1916, A.M. R.A.F. France.
(70, Stockbridge Road)
SIMPKINS, ROBERT A. ... ... C.S.M. ... Devon, rejoined 1916, Pte. R.A.S.C. Home.
(36, Andover Road)
SIMS, WILLIAM ... ... L.-Corpl. Hants, Sept. 1914, Pte. R.D.C. Home.
(25, Clifton Road)
SIMS, WILLIAM J. ... ... L.-Corpl. Hants, Sept. 1914, Pte. Mesopotamia, Palestine.
(25, Clifton Road)
SINFIELD, JOHN ... ... Sergt. ... Hants, Aug. 26, 1914, Corpl. Dardanelles, Egypt.
(47, Chesil Street) Wounded, Sept. 1915.
✠ SINGLE, ALBERT E. ... ... Rfn. ... R.B., 1905, Rfn. Home. *Died*, 1916, *Winchester*.
(11, St. John's Street)
SINGLETON, HARRY ... ... Corpl. ... Hants, Aug. 1914, Pte. R.D.C., Bedford. Home.
(6, Crowder Terrace)

WINCHESTER WAR SERVICE REGISTER

✠ Sippetts, Jack ... (12, High Street)	Pte.	Hants, Sept. 1914, Pte. Mesopotamia. *Killed in Action.*
Skelcher, Thomas (55, Sussex Street)	Sergt.	K.O.S.B., Sept. 1914, Pte. Lab. C. France.
Skinner, Hugh C. (High Croft, Romsey Road)	Sub-Lieut.	R.N., Aug. 1914, Cadet. North Sea; H.M.S. *Laurel, Gorgon,* and *St. Vincent.*
Skinner, John E. M. ... (High Croft, Romsey Road)	Lieut.	K.R.R.C., Aug. 1914, 2nd Lieut. Flanders, France. Wounded, Sept. 25, 1915, July 27, 1916, and April 13, 1917.
Skipton, Thomas (2, Lawn Street)	Pte.	D.C.L.I., Mch. 1916, Pte. Lab. C. France, Belgium.
✠ Slater, Harry F. (55, Upper Brook Street)		R.F.A., Sept. 7, 1914. Gallipoli. *Killed in Action,* Aug. 9, 1915.
Slaymaker, Alfred J. (3, Granville Place)	L.-Corpl.	R.E., Dec. 29, 1917, Spr. Home.
Small, Albert V. (8, Hyde Abbey Road)	Gun.	R.G.A., Dec. 1915, Gun. Palestine, Egypt, France.
Small, Charles H. (85, Fairfield Road)	L.-Sergt.	R.B., Oct. 1916, Rfn. A.P.C. Home.
Small, William J. (58, Stockbridge Road)		R.G.A., May 1916. France.
✠ Smart, Edward T. (9, Freelands Buildings)	Dr.	R.H.A., Aug. 1914, Dr. France. Wounded once. *Died of Tuberculosis,* Mch. 2, 1916.
Smart, Lewis F. (8, Mants Lane)	Corpl.	A.V.C., Jan. 1916, Pte. Egypt.
Smart, Reginald A. (23, Canon Street)	L.-Corpl.	Hants, 1912, Pte. D.C.L.I. India, Mesopotamia, France. Wounded, 1918.
Smeed, John W. (39, Bar End Road)	Sergt.	Leicester Y., rejoined 1914, Sergt. Home.
Smith, Albert (53, Winnall)	Pte.	Hants, July 1914, Pte. India, Egypt.
✠ Smith, Albert E. (5, Staple Garden)	Stoker	R.N., 1904, Stoker. Pacific Ocean. *Killed in Action,* 1914, H.M.S. *Good Hope.*
Smith, Albert W. (11, Clifton Terrace)	Gun.	R.G.A., Apl. 1917, Gun. Egypt, Salonica.
Smith, Alfred (3, East Cliffe)		Hants, Apl. 18, 1917, Pte. France. Wounded, Oct. 2, 1918.
✠ Smith, Alfred C. (30, Monks Road)	Pte.	Somerset L.I., May 1916, Pte. Surrey Rif. France. *Killed in Action,* Oct. 8, 1916, *Somme.*
✠ Smith, Alfred J. (44, Water Lane)	Pte.	Hants, Aug. 1914, Pte. Dardanelles. Wounded, Aug. 1915. *Died of Wounds,* July 1917.
✠ Smith, Archibald C. (13, Cheriton Road)	Pte.	Hants, Dec. 1916, Pte. Mesopotamia. *Died,* July 13, 1917, *Baghdad.*
Smith, Arthur (8, Colebrook Place)	Pte.	Hants, 1913, Bandsman. R.D.C., R.F. India, France.
Smith, Augustus L. (62, Fairfield Road)	S.M.	R.N.A.S., 1914, C.P.O. R.A.F. Home.

WINCHESTER WAR SERVICE REGISTER

SMITH, CECIL C. (Jewry Street)	Pte.	Hants Y., Aug. 1915, Tpr. Hants. France.
SMITH, CECIL F. (30, St. Faith's Road)	Corpl.	R.A.M.C., rejoined Aug. 1914, Pte. France. Wounded, June 3 and Nov. 30, 1917. D.C.M. 1918.
SMITH, CHARLES (13, Upper Brook Street)	Cook	R.N., 1915, Cook. Cape of Good Hope, Dardanelles; H.M.S. *Empress of Britain*.
SMITH, CHARLES DANIEL (6, Hyde Street)		R.F.A., Aug. 1914. R.A.S.C. France. Wounded once. Gassed twice.
SMITH, CHARLES DAVID (79, Colebrook Street)	Pte.	Wilts, Jan. 1916, Pte. Hants. Mesopotamia.
✠ SMITH, CHARLES F. (Southall Cottage, Alresford Rd.)	Pte.	Hants, rejoined Aug. 1914, Pte. India, Persian Gulf. *Killed in Action, June 12, 1915, Basra.*
SMITH, CLARENCE I. H. (34, Sussex Street)	Capt.	Lond., Mch. 1916, Pte. Middlesex. France. Wounded, Oct. 1, 1916.
SMITH, CLEMENT O. (11, Fairfield Road)	Corpl.	T.R., Feb. 1917, Pte. R. Warwick. France.
SMITH, EDWARD (8, Colebrook Place)	Sergt.	Dorset, 1906, Pte. R.F.A. France, Germany, Russia. M.M.
SMITH, EDWARD (1, St. Cross Road)	2nd Lieut.	R.F.C., Oct. 1917, Cadet. R.A.F. France.
SMITH, EDWARD G. (44, Water Lane)	Dr.	R.F.A., Aug. 1914, Dr. France. Taken Prisoner by Germans, Mch. 21, 1918.
SMITH, EDWARD J. (53, Winnall)	Stoker	R.N., 1908, Stoker. North Sea.
✠ SMITH, EDWIN A. (11, Fairfield Road)	Pte.	Hants, Sept. 1914, Pte. India, Persia, Mesopotamia. *Killed in Action, Feb. 23, 1917.*
SMITH, EDWIN C. (11, Canute Road)	Sergt.	Hants, Aug. 1914, Pte. France. Despatches 1918.
SMITH, EMANUEL (51, Canon Street)	Pte.	R. Berks, Dec. 1915, Pte. Lab. C. France.
SMITH, ERNEST (62, Fairfield Road)	Corpl.	K.R.R.C., Sept. 1914, Rfn. Home.
SMITH, ERNEST G. (13, Union Street)	Rfn.	R.B., Oct. 1915, Rfn. Home.
SMITH, ERNEST R. (77, Sussex Street)	L.-Corpl.	Hants, Aug. 1914, Pte. Egypt.
SMITH, ERNEST W. (101, Colebrook Street)	Pte.	Dorset, Feb. 1917, Pte. Home.
SMITH, FRANCIS H. T. (98, High Street)	Pte.	Hants, 1911, Pte. Mesopotamia.
SMITH, FRANK H. (49, St. John's Street)	Spr.	R.E., Apl. 1916, Spr. France.
SMITH, FREDERICK (10, Granville Place)	Pte.	Hants Y., Nov. 1915, Tpr. Berks Y., M.G.C. Egypt, France. Wounded, Nov. 15, 1916.
SMITH, FREDERICK (62, Lansdowne Terrace)	Stoker	R.N., Mch. 1917, Stoker. North Sea; H.M.S. *Minotaur.*

WINCHESTER WAR SERVICE REGISTER

SMITH, FREDERICK (13, Upper Brook Street)	Sergt.	Hants, 1902, Pte. M.F.P. Egypt.
✠ SMITH, FREDERICK C. (4, Hedges Buildings)	Corpl.	Hants, June 1916, Pte. France. *Killed in Action, Aug. 24, 1917, Ypres.*
SMITH, FREDERICK J. (2, Stockbridge Road)	Corpl.	R.G.A. (T.F.), Nov. 1915, Gun. France, Belgium.
SMITH, FREDERICK W. (76, Parchment Street)	Sergt.	R.M.L.I., 1904, Pte. North Sea.
SMITH, FREDERICK W. (5, Avenue Road)		A.I.F., Dec. 25, 1915. Egypt, France, Belgium.
SMITH, FREDERICK W. (2, Boundary Street)	Sergt.	R.G.A., Aug. 1914, Gun. France. Wounded, June 4, 1917.
SMITH, FREDERICK W. (30, Monks Road)	L.-Corpl.	Hants, Jan. 1914, Pte. R. Warwick. France.
SMITH, GEOFFREY (9, Clausentum Road)	Lieut.	Hants, Sept. 1914, Pte. India, France.
SMITH, GEORGE H. (8, Colebrook Street)	Bdr.	R.G.A., 1906, Gun. India, France. Gassed, June 1916.
SMITH, GEORGE J. (51, Canon Street)	Pte.	Wilts, Sept. 1915, Pte. T.R., Lab. C. Home.
SMITH, HAROLD R. (3, Greyfriars Villas)	Dr.	R.A.S.C. (M.T.), Mch. 1916, Dr. France.
SMITH, HARRY A. (66, Chesil Street)	Corpl.	T.R., Feb. 1917, Pte. Somerset L.I. France. Gassed, Aug. 1918.
SMITH, HARRY A. C. (16, St. Clement Street)	Dr.	R.B., Sept. 5, 1914, Rfn. R.A.S.C. Salonica.
SMITH, HENRY F. (14, Gladstone Street)	Tpr.	Dragoon Gds., 1905, Tpr. France, Belgium. Wounded 1916.
SMITH, HENRY J. (5, Avenue Road)	Pte.	Hants, 1899, Pte. Belgium, Dardanelles.
SMITH, HENRY W. (1, St. Cross Road)	Sig.	R.G.A., July 1917, Gun. Home.
✠ SMITH, HORACE (14, Gladstone Street)	Tpr.	D.C.L.I., 1907, Pte. Dragoon Gds. France, Belgium. Wounded three times, 1914 and 1918. *Died, Mch. 1918.*
SMITH, ISAAC J. (5, Staple Garden)	Stoker	R.N., 1896, Stoker. H.M.S. *Cardiff.*
SMITH, JAMES (3, St. Giles' Hill Hutments)	C.S.M.	R.E., 1896, Spr. China.
SMITH, JOHN W. H. (6, Chesil Street)	Pte.	Hants, June 26, 1916, Pte. India, Palestine, France, Belgium, Germany.
SMITH, LAWRENCE (39, Lower Brook Street)	Spr.	R.E. Sig. Coy., Mch. 1917, Spr. France.
SMITH, LEONARD T. (32, Hatherley Road)	Cadet	R.N.A.S., Sept. 1914, A.M. R.A.F. Flanders, France, Dardanelles.
SMITH, MAURICE T. (98, High Street)	Pte.	T.R., May 1917, Pte. M.G.C. Belgium, France.

WINCHESTER WAR SERVICE REGISTER

SMITH, REGINALD (29, Union Street)	...	Corpl.	R.B., Sept. 1914, Rfn. France. Wounded, June 1917. M.M.
SMITH, RICHARD G. (Southall Cottage, Alresford Road)	...	A.B.	R.N., 1906. H.M.S. *Malaya*.
SMITH, ROBERT H. J. (25, St. John's Street)	...	Pte.	R.E., Feb. 1917, Spr. Hants Cyc. France.
✠ SMITH, ROBERT W. (2, Westgate Lane)	...	Sergt.	R.B., 1898, Rfn. France. *Died, Aug. 6, 1916, Abbéville*.
SMITH, SAMUEL J. (5, St. Catherine's Road)	...	Dr.	R.A.S.C., Oct. 1914, Dr. Dardanelles, Salonica, Egypt, Palestine, Serbia.
✠ SMITH, SYDNEY E. (13, Union Street)	...	Pte.	R.M.L.I., 1913, Pte. North Sea, Dardanelles, Salonica, France. *Killed in Action, Apl. 1, 1918.*
SMITH, SYDNEY H. (8, Queen's Road)	...	Lieut.	R.A.S.C., 1908, Pte. Bedford. France, Belgium. M.C. 1918.
SMITH, THOMAS (47, Hyde Street)	...	Sergt.	Hants, 1901, Pte. France. Wounded four times.
SMITH, WALTER H. (11, Fairfield Road)	...	Corpl.	Hants, Oct. 1915, Pte. Egypt, Palestine. Wounded, Dec. 15, 1917.
SMITH, WALTER H. M. (3, Fairfield Road)	...	2nd A.M.	R.N.A.S., Nov. 1916, 2nd A.M. France.
SMITH, WILFRED J. (12, King Alfred Place)	...	Pte.	T.R., Feb. 1917, Pte. R. Warwick. Home.
✠ SMITH, WILFRID S. (66, Kingsgate Street)	...		R.G.A., Nov. 1, 1916. Home. *Accidentally Drowned, Nov. 4, 1916, Plymouth.*
SMITH, WILLIAM (8, Colebrook Place)	...	Corpl.	Devon, Mch. 1915, Pte. R.F., Lab. C. France. Wounded, Feb. 1916.
SMITH, WILLIAM (55, Milverton Road)	...	Pte.	Hants, Aug. 1916, Pte. Dorset, Devon. Home.
SMITH, WILLIAM (49, Wharf Hill)	...	Sergt.	Hants, Sept. 1914, Pte. Egypt, France.
SMITH, WILLIAM E. (10, King Alfred Place)	...		R.A.S.C., 1910. R.I.R. Gallipoli, Salonica, Egypt, France.
SMITH, WILLIAM G. (36, Clifton Road)	...	Pte.	D.C.L.I., Apl. 1917, Pte. R. Warwick. Home.
SMITH, WILLIAM JAMES (78, High Street)	...	Pte.	Hants (T.F.), 1895, Pte. Hants. Home.
SMITH, WILLIAM JOHN (24, Hyde Close)	...	C.Q.M.S.	Worc. 1897, Pte. E. Lancs. France.
SMITH, WILLIAM P. (79, Colebrook Street)	...	Pte.	R.M.L.I., Oct. 1915, Pte. Salonica, France. Wounded, 1918.
SMITHER, WALTER F. (70, Hyde Street)	...	O.S.	R.N., Nov. 1916, O.S.
SMITHER, WALTER H. (70, Hyde Street)	...	Sergt.	Hants, 1902, Pte. Home.
SMITHERS, ALBERT E. (36, Fairfield Road)	...	S.B.A.	R.N., Jan. 1916, S.B.A. Ægean; H.M.S. *Valhalla II*.

WINCHESTER WAR SERVICE REGISTER

Name (Address)	Rank	Service
SMITHERS, FREDERICK (36, Fairfield Road)	C.Q.M.S.	Hants Y., Apl. 1916, Tpr. Dragoons, R. Warwick. France. Wounded, Sept. 13, 1918.
SMITHERS, HARRY J. (8, Great Minster Street)	L.-Corpl.	R.A.O.C., June 1917, Pte. Home.
SMITHERS, REGINALD W. (65, Greenhill Road)	Pte.	Nat. Res., Aug. 1914, Pte. Hants, Worc. France. Wounded once.
SNELL, ALFRED J. (9, Victoria Road)	Spr.	R.E., Mch. 1917, Spr.
SNELSON, WILLIAM (51, North Walls)	Sergt.	R.A.S.C., Aug. 1914, Pte. Egypt, Palestine, Dardanelles, France.
SNOOK, ALFRED M. (150, High Street)	Cook's Mate	R.N., Oct. 1917, Cook's Mate. Home.
✠ SNOOK, CYRIL A. (53, St. Catherine's Road)	Sergt.	R.G.A., 1913, Gun. France. Wounded and Gassed, Sept. 25, 1917. M.M. 1917. *Died of Wounds*, 1918.
SNOW, DOUGLAS G. (41, Fairfield Road)	2nd Lieut.	Hants, Nov. 1914, Pte. R.E., Lond. India, Mesopotamia. Despatches.
SNOW, ERNEST H. (41, Fairfield Road)	Capt.	R.G.A., 1899, Gun. France.
SNOW, HERBERT J. (41, Fairfield Road)	Sergt.	Hants, Pte. Ind. Ord. Dept. India, Mesopotamia.
SNOW, PERCY (41, Fairfield Road)	S.M.	R.A.M.C., 1900, Pte. France. Despatches, three times.
SNOW, RALPH (41, Fairfield Road)	Sergt.	Hants, Pte. Ind. Ord. Dept. India, Afghanistan, Mesopotamia. Wounded, July 24, 1915. D.C.M. 1915, Despatches.
SNOW, RICHARD S. (41, Fairfield Road)	Sergt.	R.G.A., 1913, Gun. France. Gassed, Apl. 10, 1918.
SOFFE, ARTHUR J. (17, St. Paul's Hill)	Gun.	R.M.A., 1902, Gun. Home.
SOFFE, ERNEST T. (17, St. Paul's Hill)	Corpl.	Hants, Aug. 1915, Pte. M.G.C. Salonica.
SOFFE, FREDERICK (22, North View)	Corpl.	R.G.A., July 1916, Gun. France, Salonica, Constantinople.
✠ SOFFE, GEORGE (17, St. Paul's Hill)	Pte.	Hants, Aug. 1914, Pte. India, Mesopotamia. Taken Prisoner by Turks, Apl. 29, 1916, Kut. *Died, June 26, 1916, Mosul.*
✠ SOFFE, HENRY J. (17, St. Paul's Hill)	Pte.	Hants, 1915, Pte. France. *Killed in Action*, Oct. 20, 1916, *Goudecourt*.
SOLE, BASIL J. B. (14, Clifton Road)	2nd Lieut.	Middlesex, Sept. 1914, Pte. Home.
SOLOMON, EDGAR E. (8, Grafton Road)	Capt.	R.G.A., 1911, 2nd Lieut. France.
SOTHCOTT, PHILIP W. (64, Lower Brook Street)	Sergt.	Hants, Pte. D.C.L.I. India.
SOUTH, WILLIAM S. (19, King Alfred Place)	Writer	R.N., Sept. 7, 1914, Writer. Egypt, Red Sea, Persian Gulf, India.

WINCHESTER WAR SERVICE REGISTER

✠ SOUTHCOTT, CHARLES F. ... Sergt. ... Hants (T.F.), Pte. Persian Gulf. Wounded once. *Died, Dec. 16, 1917.*
(5, Ilex Terrace)

✠ SOUTHCOTT, HERBERT ... Pte. ... R.A.F., June 1918, Pte. Home. *Died, July 1, 1918, Blandford.*
(77, Canon Street)

SOUTHCOTT, REGINALD C. ... Band Boy ... Hants, Dec. 1916, Band Boy. Home.
(5, Ilex Terrace)

SOUTHWELL, ARTHUR T. ... Sergt. ... R.G.A., 1910, Gun. Egypt.
(84, Chesil Street)

SOUTHWELL, FRANK ... Pte. ... Hussars, Sept. 1914, Tpr. Yorks L.I., Lancs. Fus., R.A.M.C. Egypt, France. Wounded, Apl. 1, 1917.
(44, Eastgate Street)

SOUTHWELL, THOMAS A. ... Pte. ... Hants, Dec. 1914, Pte. India, Mesopotamia.
(44, Eastgate Street)

SOUTHWELL, WALTER J. ... Saddler ... R.F.A., Mch. 1915, Saddler. France.
(44, Eastgate Street)

SPARKS, EDWARD C. ... Corpl. ... R.F.A., 1910, Boy. France. Wounded, Aug. 1914. Taken Prisoner by Germans, Aug. 1914.
(21, Colebrook Street)

SPARKS, ERNEST J. ... Pte. ... Hants, Sept. 1914, Pte. India, Mesopotamia.
(21, Colebrook Street)

SPARKS, LEONARD A. ... 2nd A.M. ... R.N.A.S., Oct. 1917, A.M. R.A.F. France, India, Germany.
(21, Colebrook Street)

SPARKS, VICTOR R. ... Sergt. ... Hants, Sept. 1914, Pte. India, Mesopotamia.
(21, Colebrook Street)

SPEARING, HENRY G. ... C.S.M. ... R.B., 1896, Rfn. France, Belgium. Wounded once.
(7, Saxon Road)

✠ SPENCER, ALBERT ... Pte. ... Hants, Feb. 1916, Pte. Egypt. *Missing, believed Killed.*
(6, Percy Terrace)

SPENCER, EDWARD J. ... P.O. ... R.N., 1897, Stoker. North Sea.
(6, Percy Terrace)

SPENCER, JOHN ... ... Hants, 1914. Glos. France.
(12, Cathedral View)

✠ SPENCER, JOSEPH ... L.-Corpl. ... Hants, 1911, Pte. India, Mesopotamia. *Killed in Action, Feb. 17, 1916, Kut.*
(2, St. John's Park Terrace)

SPILLER, ROBERT W. ... Corpl. ... R.F.C., Apl. 1914, 3rd A.M. R.A.F. Home.
(11, St. John's North)

SPINNEY, CHARLES H. ... L.-Corpl. ... R.B., Sept. 1915, Rfn. Middlesex. China, Russia.
(33, Eastgate Street)

SPREADBURY, GEORGE H. ... ... R.N., Aug. 4, 1914. Home.
(53, Wharf Hill)

✠ STACEY, FRANK ... Corpl. ... Lond. (Civil Service Rif.), 1916, Rfn. Mesopotamia, Egypt. *Killed in Action, Dec. 14, 1917.*
(12, Westgate Lane)

✠ STACEY, FREDERICK ... Corpl. ... Glos., Mch. 1916, Pte. Hants. France. Wounded, Apl. 23, 1918. *Died of Wounds, Apl. 24, 1918.*
(12, Westgate Lane)

STACEY, WILLIAM G. ... Rfn. ... R.B., 1899, Rfn. France. Wounded and taken Prisoner by Germans, Aug. 26, 1914.
(111, Colebrook Street)

STAGG, ARTHUR G. ... Corpl. ... Hants, June 6, 1916, Pte. Belgium. Wounded, Oct. 22, 1918.
(3, Princes Buildings)

WINCHESTER WAR SERVICE REGISTER

✠ STAGG, CHARLES T. ... Rfn. ... K.R.R.C., rejoined Aug. 1914, Rfn. France.
(85, Chesil Street) *Killed in Action, July 10, 1917.*

STAGG, FRANK E. ... Pte. ... Innis. Dragoons, 1907, Tpr. Worc. France.
(85, Chesil Street) Wounded, Apl. 1, 1918.

STAGG, FREDERICK W. ... Pte. ... Devon, Nov. 19, 1916, Pte. France.
(18, Wharf Hill)

✠ STAGG, HENRY ... Pte. ... Hants, Mch. 1916, Pte. India, Mesopotamia.
(7, Upper Brook Street) *Died of Fever, Sept. 3, 1918, Basra.*

STAGG, WILLIAM ... Pte. ... Devon, Sept. 1916, Pte. Home.
(85, Chesil Street)

STAINER, SYDNEY ... Pte. ... R.M.L.I., Sept. 1914, Pte. H.M.S. *Armadale*
(38, Eastgate Street) *Castle.*

✠ STAINER, TOM ... ... R.A.S.C., 1917. France. *Died, Dec. 4, 1918.*
(38, Eastgate Street)

STANBROOK, CHARLES ... R.A.S.C., 1914. France, India, Salonica, Palestine.
(36, Upper Brook Street)

STANBROOK, HARRY ... Pte. ... R.H.G., rejoined Nov. 1914, Tpr. R.A.M.C.
(17, St. John's South) France, Dardanelles, Egypt. Wounded three times.

STANBROOK, HENRY ... Lancers. Canadians. France.
(36, Upper Brook Street)

✠ STANLEY, JOHN H. ... A.B. ... R.N., 1913. North Sea; H.M.S. *Negro*. *Drowned,*
(57, Water Lane) *Dec. 20, 1915.*

STANNARD, WALTER J. ... Sergt. ... R.B., 1908, Rfn. France. Wounded, Oct. 22,
(17, Wharf Hill) 1914.

STAPLES, CHARLES F. ... Band Boy ... Hants, June 1914, Band Boy. France, Belgium.
(8, Cross Street)

✠ STEEL, FRANK ... Pte. ... Glos., Mch. 1916, Pte. R.W.K. France. Wounded,
(21, Eastgate Street) Apl. 3, 1917, and Aug. 27, 1918. *Died of Wounds, Aug. 27, 1918.*

STEEL, W. HENRY ... R.G.A., Mch. 1917. France.
(28, Western Road)

STEELE, HARRY ... Bdr. ... R.F.A., Aug. 1914, Gun. France. Gassed, Oct.
(5, St. Giles' Hill Hutments) 1917.

✠ STEELE, WALTER C. ... Pte. ... Hants, 1910, Pte. India, Mesopotamia, Egypt.
(47, Wales Street) Wounded, Apl. 1915 and Nov. 1917. *Killed in Action, Oct. 10, 1918.*

STEELE, WILLIAM G. ... Pte. ... Hants, rejoined Dec. 30, 1914, Pte. R.A.S.C. (M.T.).
(3, Colson Road) France, Mesopotamia.

STEELE, WILLIAM J. ... A.B. ... R.N., 1912, O.S. North Sea.
(8, Hedges Buildings)

STEPHENS, GEORGE T. ... Pte. ... R.M.L.I., Dec. 1917, Pte. N. Russia.
(28, Hyde Abbey Road)

STEPHENS, W. ... S.S.A. ... R.N., Sept. 1914, S.S.A.

STEVENS, CECIL T. ... L.-Corpl. ... T.R., Feb. 1917, Pte. Somerset L.I. France.
(22, Egbert Road) Wounded, Oct. 5, 1917.

✠ STEVENS, ERNEST ... 2nd Lieut. ... Sea. H., 1900, R.Q.M.S. France. Wounded, Feb. 2,
(11, Western Road) 1915. *Died of Wounds, Feb. 2, 1915.*

WINCHESTER WAR SERVICE REGISTER

STEVENS, SAMUEL (11, Western Road)	Lieut.	Hants (T.F.), Sept. 1914, Pte. Home.
STEVENSON, GEORGE J. H. (Glencairn, Park Road)	Major	Hants, rejoined Dec. 1914, Major. Recruiting Officer. Home.
STEWART, GEORGE (8, Poulsome Place)		R.D.C. Home.
✠ STICKLAN, CHARLES H. (14, Little Minster Street)	Bug.	Hants, 1893, Bug. France. *Killed in Action, May 3, 1915*.
STICKLAND, ARTHUR W. (43, Middle Brook Street)	Pte.	Hants, Aug. 1914, Pte. Home.
STICKLAND, FRANK (4, St. Leonard's Road)	Pte.	Hants, Feb. 1915, Pte. France, India, Palestine, Egypt. Wounded, July 20, 1918.
STICKLAND, JOHN (4, St. Leonard's Road)	Pte.	R. Warwick, 1918, Pte. Germany.
STICKLEY, ALFRED P. (11, Lawn Street)	Corpl.	Hants, Nov. 1915, Pte. S. Staffs. India, Malay States.
STICKLEY, CHARLES F. (11, Lawn Street)		Lond. Irish, Mch. 1915. Con. Ran. France, Salonica, Egypt, India.
STILLMAN, FRANK G. (33, Cranworth Road)	L.-Corpl.	Lond. (Civil Service Rif.), Dec. 1917, Rfn. France.
STOCKWELL, CHARLES J. (14, St. Clement Street)	L.-Corpl.	Hants, Oct. 1914, Pte. M.F.P. France.
STOKER, CHARLES (80, Canon Street)	L.-Corpl.	Lond., July 1915, Pte. R.E. France.
STONARD, ALFRED (12, South View)	Corpl.	R.F.C., Feb. 1917, 2nd A.M. R.A.F. Home.
STONE, ALBERT V. (4, Highcliffe Road)	Sergt.	Hants, 1905, Pte. India, Palestine.
✠ STONE, ARCHIBALD (22, Bar End)		Somerset L.I., Jan. 1916. R. Berks. France. *Killed in Action, May 8, 1917, Henninel*.
STONE, CHARLES (24, Tower Street)	Dr.	R.A.S.C. (M.T.), Feb. 1915, Dr. France.
STONE, CHARLES E. (Lancing, Worthy Road)	Eng.-Comdr.	R.N., 1895. Engineer. North Sea, Baltic Sea.
STONE, CHARLES P. (48, Nuns Road)	S.S.A.	R.N., Nov. 1914, S.S.A. North Sea.
STONE, EDWARD (26, Staple Garden)	Sergt.	Lond. Fus., 1914, Pte. Malta, France. M.M. and Bar, 1917-18.
STONE, ERNEST (26, Staple Garden)	Sergt.	R.F.C., Nov. 1914, A.M. Hants. India, Egypt, France, Germany. M.M. 1918.
STONE, FREDERICK G. (26, Staple Garden)	Pte.	E. Kent, Sept. 1914, Pte. Lab. C. Home.
STONE, JOHN D. (47, Egbert Road)	Spr.	R.E., May 1915, Spr. France.
STONE, PHILIP C. (4, Highcliffe Road)		Hants, 1911. R.F.A. France, Salonica.

WINCHESTER WAR SERVICE REGISTER

STONE, SYDNEY M. ... A.M. ... R.F.C., Sept. 1917, A.M. R.A.F. Home.
(48, Nuns Road)

STONE, WILLIAM J. ... Spr. ... R.E., 1915, Spr. France. Wounded, 1916.
(26, Staple Garden) Gassed, 1917.

STONEHILL, THOMAS H. ... Gun. ... A.V.C., Jan. 1916, Pte. R.F.A. Egypt. Wounded
(2, Mant's Lane) once.

STRANGE, VERNON C. ... Capt. ... Devon, Sept. 1914, 2nd Lieut. France, Italy.
(Denham Court, Park Road)

STRATTON, FREDERIC ... ... Rfn. ... R.B., 1899, Rfn. Innis., R.B. Salonica, France.
(7, St. John's Park Terrace)

STRATTON, JAMES P. ... ... Capt. ... R.A.S.C., Nov. 1914, 2nd Lieut. Palestine. M.B.E.
(Chilcomb House)

STRATTON, RICHARD I. ... Capt. ... Hants Y., Sept. 1914, Tpr. R.G.A. France.
(Chilcomb House)

STREET, FRANK W. ... ... R.A.S.C., Oct. 1918. Home.
(5, Alexandra Terrace)

STREET, JOHN W. ... ... Lt. and Q.M. K.R.R.C., 1894, Rfn. France, Germany.
(9, Southgate Street)

✠ STRIPP, ALFRED ... ... Pte. ... Hants, Nov. 1915, Pte. India, Egypt, Palestine.
(46, Water Lane) *Killed in Action, Apl. 9, 1918.*

STRIPP, ARTHUR ... ... L.-Corpl. R.B., 1905, Rfn. Lab. C. France. Wounded once.
(46, Water Lane)

STRIPP, FRANCIS ... ... Pte. ... Devon, May 1917, Pte. Lab. C. France.
(14, Durngate Place)

STRIPP, HARRY ... ... Sergt. ... R.E., Sept. 1916, Spr. Home.
(62, Water Lane)

STRIPP, HARRY W. ... ... Hants, Sept. 1914, Pte. India, Mesopotamia,
(62, Water Lane) Persia. Wounded, Feb. 1917.

STRIPP, WALTER C. ... ... Pte. ... Devon, Oct. 1916, Pte. Home.
(40, St. John's Road)

STROUD, ALBERT F. ... ... R.A.F., Oct. 1, 1918. Home.
(12, St. Clement Street)

STROUD, GEORGE S. ... ... Hants Y., Oct. 1916. Surrey Y. Salonica.
(3, St. Clement Street)

STROUD, PERCY ... ... Tpr. ... R. Dragoons, Tpr. France. Wounded, Nov. 22,
(5, The Weirs) 1914.

STUBBINGTON, HENRY W. ... Sergt. ... Hants, Apl. 1916, Pte. India, Egypt, France,
(60, Fairfield Road) Germany.

STUBBINGTON, WILLIAM H. ... Sergt. ... Canadians, 1914, Pte. Can. R.G.A. France.
(17, North Walls)

SUMMERBEE, CHARLES E. ... Art. ... R.A.S.C. (M.T.), Dec. 1916, Pte. Tank C. France.
(8, St. Giles' Hill Hutments) Wounded, 1917.

SUMMERBEE, WILLIAM ... ... R.N., 1901. H.M.S. *Tiger*. Wounded once.
(3, Cossack Lane)

✠ SUMMERBELL, CHARLES ... Pte. ... Hants, Pte. Dardanelles, Salonica. Wounded
(25, Hyde Close) once. *Died.*

WINCHESTER WAR SERVICE REGISTER

SUMMERBELL, JAMES (51, North Walls)			Hants, June 1916. France. Wounded, July 31, 1917.
✠ SUMMERBELL, WILLIAM (25, Hyde Close)		Dr.	R.E., 1905, Dr. Salonica, Serbia, Dardanelles. *Died.*
SUTTON, ARTHUR (Down View, Highcliffe Park)		P.O. (1st Class)	R.N., 1894, Boy. Grand Fleet; H.M.S. *Neptune.*
SUTTON, GEORGE (4, Culverwell Gardens)		Sergt.	Hants, 1896, Pte. R.D.C. Home.
SUTTON, HENRY (3, Canute Road)		Pte.	T.R., Feb. 1917, Pte. N. Staffs. France.
SUTTON, REGINALD (13, North Walls)		Pte.	Hants (T.F.), 1911, Pte. India, Mesopotamia, Salonica.
SWAFFIELD, WILLIAM G. (67, Lower Brook Street)		Pte.	T.R., Aug. 1917, Pte. Hants. France. Gassed once.
SWAIN, THOMAS E. (14, Newburgh Street)		R.S.M.	K.R.R.C., Aug. 1914, Corpl. France, Belgium. Wounded, July 31, 1915; Sept. 25, 1917; Apl. 20, 1918. Despatches 1917, Belgian Croix de Guerre 1917.
SWATHERIDGE, WILLIAM (20, Granville Place)		Pte.	Hants, July 1915, Pte. Lab. C. Home.
SWATTON, ALFRED W. (27, Western Road)		Pte.	Essex, Oct. 1916, Pte. R.A.M.C. Home.
✠ SWAYNE, DENNIS (19, St. John's Road)		Pte.	R. Sussex, Aug. 1914, Pte. France. Wounded, July 10, 1916. *Died of Wounds, July 11, 1916.*
SWORN, ROBERT C. (2, Tower Road)		Pte.	Glos., Pte. France. Gassed once.
SYMES, WILLIAM G. (The Nook, Sussex Street)		Sergt.	Hants, 1914, Sergt. Home.
TALBOT, ALBERT G. (28, Stockbridge Road)		Pte.	Glos., May 1915, Pte. France, Italy, Egypt.
TALBOT, ROBERT (9, Silver Hill)		Pte.	Glos., May 1916, Pte. France. Wounded, May 27, 1918. Taken Prisoner by Germans and Escaped.
TANNER, ERNEST G. (1, Middle Road)		Tpr.	Hants Y., May 1915, Tpr. Home.
TANNER, FREDERICK G. (11, Upper High Street)			R.A.S.C., 1912, Dr. France.
TANNER, HERBERT (29, Staple Garden)		1st A.M.	R.F.C., Mch. 5, 1917, 2nd A.M. R.A.F. Home.
TANNER, HORACE A. (69, High Street)		Gun.	R.M.A., Nov. 1916, Gun. Mudros, Mediterranean.
TANNER, HUGH N. (69, High Street)		2nd Lieut.	Hants Y., Sept. 1914, Tpr. Hants, Middlesex. France.
TANNER, WILLIAM A. (Rowanhurst, St. Giles' Hill)		Corpl.	Hants Y., Sept. 1914, Tpr. Home.

WINCHESTER WAR SERVICE REGISTER

TARGETT, THOMAS A. (48, Fairfield Road)	...	1st A.M. ...	R.A.F., Dec. 1915, 1st A.M. France.
TARRANT, FREDERICK J. (38, Wharf Hill)	...	Pte. ...	Devon, Apl. 13, 1916, Pte. Home.
TARRANT, LEONARD J. (41, Hyde Abbey Road)	...	Spr. ...	R.E., Aug. 1916, Spr. Mesopotamia.
TAYLOR, ALBERT W. (5, Westgate Lane)	...	Pte. ...	R. Berks, June 1916, Pte. Lab. C. France.
✠ TAYLOR, CHARLES W. (5, Westgate Lane)	...	Sergt. ...	Hants, Pte. Indian Supply Corps. India. Taken Prisoner by Turks, Apl. 29, 1916, Kut. *Died, Dec. 29, 1916.*
TAYLOR, EDWARD M. (10, Greenhill Avenue)	...	1st A.M. ...	R.N.A.S., Feb. 1917, 2nd A.M. R.N.V.R. France.
TAYLOR, FRANCIS H. (St. Breoke, Barnes Close)	...	Major ...	Recruiting Staff, Sept. 1, 1915, Major. Home.
TAYLOR, HENRY (72, Fairfield Road)	...	Pte. ...	Middlesex, May 1918, Pte. France.
TAYLOR, HERBERT (9, Brassey Road)	...	...	R.M.A., Aug. 1914. Dardanelles, France.
TAYLOR, SYDNEY J. (6, Kingsgate Street)	...	...	R. Berks, Mch. 1915. Belgium.
TEASDALE, GEORGE E. (73, Eastgate Street)	...	Corpl. ...	R.A.S.C., Oct. 1915, Pte. Mesopotamia.
TEASDALE, PERCY F. (73, Eastgate Street)	...	Pte. ...	R. Warwick, Dec. 1917, Pte. France.
TEASDALE, WILLIAM A. (73, Eastgate Street)	...	Pte. ...	Lond., Dec. 1915, Pte. Egypt.
TEE, GEORGE W. (1, Gordon Avenue)	...	Pte. ...	Glos., June 1918, Pte. R.A.O.C. Home.
TEE, HERBERT H. (21, Eastgate Street)	...	...	Hants, June 1916. India, Egypt, France.
TEE, KENNETH J. (1, Gordon Avenue)	...	Boy ...	R.N., June 1918, Boy. Russia.
✠ TEE, THOMAS V. (5, Lower Brook Street)	...	Stoker ...	R.N., Nov. 1915, Stoker. Grand Fleet. *Died, Feb. 22, 1915, R.N. Hospital, Gosport.*
✠ TEE, WALTER F. (5, Lower Brook Street)	...	Pte. ...	Hants Y., Nov. 1915, Tpr. Hants. France. *Killed in Action, June 7, 1917.*
TEE, WILLIAM (5, Lower Brook Street)	...	Dr. ...	R.A.S.C., Feb. 1914, Dr. France.
TEMPLE, ALFRED W. (47, St. John's Street)	...	2nd Corpl. ...	Somerset L.I., 1907, Pte. R.E. (Sigs.). India, Afghanistan.
✠ TEMPLE, HENRY J. (26, Wharf Hill)	...	Pte. ...	Hants, Sept. 1914, Pte. France. *Killed in Action, Apl. 9, 1916, Loos.*
TEMPLE, HENRY J., jun. (26, Wharf Hill)	...	...	R.A.F., Aug. 1918. Home.
TETLEY, WAUD	...	...	*See* WAUD TETLEY.

WINCHESTER WAR SERVICE REGISTER

TEUSH, FRANCIS E.	A.-C.-Sergt.	R.M.L.I., rejoined Aug. 1914, Sergt. France.
THATCHER, ALLAN (51, Wales Street)	...	Hants, Aug. 1914. India, Egypt.
THATCHER, WILLIAM (51, Wales Street)	...	Hants, Aug. 1914. Mesopotamia.
THOMPSETT, HERBERT B. (7, Bridge Street)	Pte.	Hants, June 1916, Pte. M.G.C. Egypt.
THOMPSON, ERNEST (15, Granville Place)	Tpr.	W. Somerset Y., Aug. 1917, Tpr. Home.
✠ THOMPSON, RICHARD J. (41, Sussex Street)	Sergt.	R.F.A., 1906, Gun. France. M.M. 1916. *Killed in Action, July 21, 1916, Festubert.*
THOMPSON, WILLIAM V. (15, Granville Place)	Bandsman	R.W. Fus., 1894, Bandsman. R.G.A., K.R.R.C. Home.
THORPE, ABNA T. M. (13, Sussex Street)	Corpl.	Hants (T.F.), 1914, Pte. India, Mesopotamia.
THORPE, FRANCIS W. (52, Upper Brook Street)	Pte.	Army Remounts, Mch. 1915, Pte. Home.
THORPE, JOHN (5, Greenhill Avenue)	Sergt.	R.B., 1915, Rfn. France. Wounded once.
THORPE, JOSEPH S. (90, Brassey Road)	Stoker	R.N., 1901, Stoker. North Sea, Baltic; H.M.S. *Neptune*, P. 47, and *Chelmsford*.
TIBBLE, WALTER J. (Abbotts Barton Lodge, Worthy Road)	Dr.	R.F.A., Aug. 1914, Dr. France, Belgium.
TIBBLE, WILLIAM H. (Abbotts Barton Lodge, Worthy Road)	Corpl.	Northants, Sept. 1914, Pte. France, Belgium.
TICKNER, THOMAS (12, Romsey Road)	Rfn.	R.B., Sept. 20, 1915, Rfn. Home.
TIDRIDGE, FREDERICK A. (8, Step Terrace)	Sergt.	Devon, Mch. 5, 1918, Pte. Germany.
TILBURY, A.	A.M.	R.A.F., 1917, A.M.
✠ TILL, HARRY (119, High Street)	2nd Lieut.	Hants, Pte. Glos. France, Belgium. *Killed in Action, Oct. 4, 1917, Ypres.*
TILLEY, HARRY H. (31, St. Faith's Road)	Gun.	Arg. and Suth. H., Jan. 5, 1915. Pte. R.G.A. Belgium, France.
TITHERIDGE, FREDERICK J. (17, St. Giles' Hill Hutments)	L.-Corpl.	R.A.S.C. (T.F.), 1909, Pte. Lab. C. Home.
TOLES, DUDLEY (31, Clifton Road)	Pte.	Hants, Nov. 1916, Pte. Lab. C. Home.
✠ TOLLMAN, CHARLES V. (32, Water Lane)	A.B.	R.N., 1913, O.S. North Sea; H.M.S. *Queen Mary*. *Killed in Action, May 31, 1916, Jutland.*
✠ TOLLMAN, THOMAS J. (32, Water Lane)	Pte.	Middlesex, July 1915, Pte. France. *Killed in Action, July 1, 1916, Somme.*
TOMBS, REGINALD A. C. (2, Ilex Terrace)	Corpl.	Worc. Y., 1915, Tpr. Tank C. France. Wounded, Mch. 1918.

WINCHESTER WAR SERVICE REGISTER

TOMBS, REGINALD J. ... (67, Wales Street)	Gun.	R.F.A., Nov. 1916, Gun. Home.	
TOMPSON, HEW W. (Cheriton Road)	Col.	Hants, 1892. Remount Dept. France. C.M.G. 1918, Despatches three times.	
TONG, ARTHUR E. (12, Elm Road)	L.-Sergt.	A.P.C., 1914, Pte. Oxf. and Bucks L.I., Wilts. France. Wounded, Oct. 23, 1918.	
TONG, AUGUSTINE H. ... (11, Stockbridge Road)	P.O.	R.N.A.S., 1916. Home.	
✠ TONG, HERBERT L. ... (11, Stockbridge Road)	L.-Corpl.	Wilts, 1916, Pte. France. *Killed in Action, Apl. 12, 1917, Somme.*	
TONG, STEPHEN G. ... (23, Greenhill Road)	Corpl.	R.E., 1914, Spr. Home.	
TONG, SYDNEY J. ... (11, Stockbridge Road)		R.N.A.S., 1917. R.A.F. Italy.	
TONGE, LEONARD ... (35, St. John's Street)	Spr.	Hants, 1912, Pte. R.E. Salonica, Constantinople.	
TOPPLE, HERBERT ... (40, Clifton Road)	Dr.	R.A.S.C., Oct. 1914, Dr. France.	
TOPPLE, LEONARD ... (40, Clifton Road)	Pte.	R.A.M.C., Feb. 1915, Pte. Mesopotamia, Egypt.	
TOPPLE, WILLIAM J. ... (40, Clifton Road)	Pte.	Lab. C., Aug. 1915, Pte. France.	
TORMEY, JAMES ... (43, Milverton Road)	C.S.M.	Hants, 1893, Pte. Glos. France, Italy.	
TOWNEND, ERNEST C. (30, High Street)	Sergt.	Lond., Mch. 1916, Pte. France, Salonica, Palestine.	
TRAVERS, WALTER G. ... (9, Upper Wolvesey Terrace)	Pte.	Hants, Sept. 1914, Pte. Home.	
TREMLETT, HENRY F. ... (42, Brassey Road)	L.-Corpl.	R.A.S.C. (M.T.), Nov. 11, 1914, Pte. France.	
TREVETT, THOMAS G. (Marlfield Cottage, St. James' Lane)	Pte.	R.A.F., June 1918, Pte. Home.	
✠ TRIMBLE, WILLIAM C. ... (18, Chesil Street)	Pte.	R.W. Fus., Aug. 1914, Pte. France. Wounded once. *Died of Wounds, Givenchy.*	
TRUEMAN, FRANK ... (26, Stockbridge Road)		Hants, Aug. 1914, Pte. Home.	
TRUEMAN, GEORGE A. (4, St. Catherine's Road)	Gun.	R.G.A., May 1915, Gun. Mesopotamia.	
TRUEMAN, SIDNEY C. (15, Stockbridge Road)	Pte.	Hants, Sept. 1914, Pte. Salonica. Wounded, Aug. 1915.	
TRUEMAN, THOMAS ... (39, St. John's Street)	Pte.	Hants, Feb. 1916, Pte. Devon, Lab. C. Home.	
TRUEMAN, WILLIAM H. (4, St. Catherine's Road)	A.B.	Remount Depot, Aug. 1914, Pte. Merc. Mar., R.N. Home.	
TRUMAN, WILLIAM E. ... (43, Sussex Street)	Corpl.	K.R.R.C., 1906, Rfn. Crete, Malta, India, France. Wounded, May 9, 1915.	

WINCHESTER WAR SERVICE REGISTER

✠ TUCKER, ALFRED E. ... ... Stoker ... R.M.L.I., 1899. R.N. North Sea, Jutland. *Died.*
(73, Middle Brook Street)

TUCKER, ERNEST ... ... Steward R.N., Oct. 1915, Steward. North Sea.
(73, Middle Brook Street)

TUCKER, JAMES J. ... ... R.N.A.S., June 1917. R.A.F. Home.
(39, High Street)

TUCKER, LEONARD ... ... Pte. ... R. Berks, June 1916, Pte. France.
(5, Staple Garden)

TUCKER, STANLEY R. ... ... A.M. ... R.N.A.S., Mch. 1917, Steward. R.A.F. Home.
(73, Middle Brook Street)

TUCKETT, FRANCIS J. ... ... Capt. ... Hants, Sept. 2, 1914, Pte. Attd. R.A.M.C. India, Mesopotamia. Despatches 1919.
(13, Kingsgate Street)

TUERSLEY, FRANK E. ... ... Capt. ... R.F.A., 1895, Tptr. France.
(2, Highland Terrace)

TUFFIN, ALBERT ... ... Pte. ... A.V.C., Feb. 1916, Pte. France.
(86, Wales Street)

✠ TUFFIN, J. ARNOLD ... ... Gun. ... R.G.A., May 1917, Gun. France. Wounded once. *Died of Wounds,* May 29, 1918.
(32, Christ Church Road)

TUFFNELL, CHARLES ... ... R.F.A., Sept. 1914. R.G.A. France, Italy.
(36c, Clifton Road)

TUFFNELL, CHRISTOPHER ... R.A.S.C., Aug. 1914. Salonica, Gallipoli, Egypt, Russia.
(36c, Clifton Road)

TUFFNELL, ERNEST ... ... C.P.O. ... R.N.A.S., 1906. R.A.F. Mediterranean, Belgium, France.
(36c, Clifton Road)

TUFFNELL, WALTER ... ... R.N., Aug. 1917. Atlantic; H.M.S. *Terrible* and *Porpoise.*
(36c, Clifton Road)

TUKER, HENRY E. ... ... Pte. ... N. Fus., rejoined, Pte. France. Wounded once.
(25, Hyde Close)

TULL, ERNEST F. ... ... Pte. ... A.V.C., Apl. 1917, Pte. Mesopotamia.
(32, St. John's Road)

TULL, GEORGE W. ... ... Pte. ... A.V.C., July 15, 1915, Pte. France.
(20, Hyde Church Path)

TULL, JOHN ... ... Clerk ... R.A.F., July 1918, Clerk. Home.
(31, Greenhill Road)

TULLIS, GEORGE D. E. ... Capt. ... R.A.M.C., Dec. 1915, Lieut. France.
(Denstone, Christ Church Road)

TUNGATE, G. S. ... ... Sergt. ... R.E., Oct. 1914, Corpl. France.
(37, Upper High Street)

TUNKS, CYRIL ... ... R.N.A.S., 1916. R.A.F. Home.
(Rippledene, Sussex Street)

✠ TUNKS, EDWARD J. A. ... 2nd Lieut. Arg. and Suth. H., 1915, Pte. France. *Killed in Action,* 1918.
(Rippledene, Sussex Street)

TUNKS, JOSEPH J. ... ... Sergt. ... Hants, 1914, Pte. India. Wounded once.
(Rippledene, Sussex Street)

TURNER, ARNOLD G. ... ... Major ... R.E., 1900, 2nd Lieut. France, Salonica, Egypt. Wounded, Aug. 1915. D.S.O. 1915, Croix de Guerre 1916.
(Holm Lodge, St. James' Lane)

WINCHESTER WAR SERVICE REGISTER

TURNER, ARTHUR R. ... (8, St. James' Street)	Pte.	R.A.S.C. (M.T.), Mch. 1915, Pte. France, Belgium, Italy.
TURNER, ERNEST V. ... (Holm Lodge, St. James' Lane)	Col.	R.E., 1893, 2nd Lieut. France. D.S.O. 1917, C.M.G. 1919, Cavalier de Savoie 1917.
✠ TURNER, FREDERICK J. (10, Little Minster Street)		Hants, Sept. 1914, Pte. Dardanelles. Wounded, Aug. 1915. *Killed in Action, 1915.*
TURNER, HAROLD W. ... (22, Cranworth Road)	2nd Lieut.	R.F., May 1916, Pte. France. Wounded, July 24, 1917.
TURNER, RALPH B. ... (Holm Lodge, St. James' Lane)	Lt.-Col.	S.A. Force, 1915. E. Africa. D.S.O. 1917, C.M.G. 1919.
TURNER, WALTER T. ... (8, St. James' Street)	L.-Corpl.	R.B., Mch. 1915, Rfn. Home.
✠ TURNER, WILLIAM G. ... (10, Little Minster Street)		Hants, Sept. 1914. Persian Gulf. Taken Prisoner by Turks, May 1916. *Died, 1916, Nesblin.*
✠ TYLER, FREDERICK C. (16, King Alfred Place)	Corpl.	Hants Y., Nov. 1915, Pte. Hants. France. Wounded, May 26, 1917. *Died of Wounds, June 13, 1917.*
✠ TYLER, WILLIAM C. ... (16, King Alfred Place)	Corpl.	Hants, Aug. 1914, Pte. India, Mesopotamia. *Killed in Action, Feb. 1917.*
TYNDALE, HENRY E. G. (58, Kingsgate Street)	Lieut.	K.R.R.C., Lieut. France. Wounded once. M.B.E., Despatches.
TYRRELL, GEORGE A. ... (7, St. John's Park Terrace)	Boy	R.F.C., Sept. 1917, Boy. R.A.F. Home.
UNDERWOOD, JAMES ... (2, Mews Hill, St. James' Terrace)	Pte.	R. Berks, Jan. 1916, Pte. Devon. France, Belgium.
UPHAM, ALFRED ... (2, St. Clement Street)	Corpl.	R.A.S.C. (M.T.), May 1916, Pte. E. Africa.
UPTON, ALBERT E. ... (74, Canon Street)	2nd Corpl.	R.E., June 1916, Spr. Home.
UTTERTON, EDWIN E. S. ... (Ledrede, Christ Church Road)	C.F.	C.F. France.
UTTERTON, FRANK LE C. ... (Ledrede, Christ Church Road)	Lieut.	Inns of Court O.T.C., Pte. York and Lancs. France. Wounded once.
✠ VACHER, GEORGE H. ... (36, Edgar Road)	2nd Lieut.	R. Warwick, Aug. 1914, 2nd Lieut. France. *Killed in Action, Oct. 1914, Zandvoorde.*
VACHER, WILLIAM E. (36, Edgar Road)	Capt.	Wilts, Sept. 1914, 2nd Lieut. Worc., T.M.B. France. Taken Prisoner by Germans, 1918.
✠ VANDELEUR, JOHN B. ... (1, Romsey Road)		Leicester. Belgium. *Killed in Action, Nov. 7, 1914, Ploegstraat.*
VARLEY, JOHN T. ... (Abbottsacre Lodge, Abbot's Rd.)	2nd Lieut.	R.F.A., Jan. 1918, 2nd Lieut. France.

WINCHESTER WAR SERVICE REGISTER

Name (Address)	Rank	Service
VAUGHAN, CHARLES (Hilldrop Villa, Fordington Rd.)		R.A.S.C. (M.T.), Dec. 1916. Salonica, France.
VEALE, HARRY (35, Canon Street)		Hants, Sept. 1914, Pte. India, Mesopotamia.
VECK, GEORGE (7, New Road, Bar End)	Staff Q.M.S.	R.B., Mch. 1915, Rfn. Home.
VENEER, ALFRED (40, Colson Road)	C.S.M.	R.B., 1897, Rfn. France. D.C.M., Italian Bronze Medal.
VENTHAM, HERBERT C. (15, Andover Road)		Hants, Aug. 1915, Pte. R.W.K., R.A.S.C. France, Germany. Gassed three times.
VERRALL, EGBERT (27, Egbert Road)	Gun.	R.G.A., July 1914, Gun. France. Gassed once.
VERRALL, WILLIAM G. (27, Egbert Road)	L.-Corpl.	Warwick Y., Feb. 1915, Tpr. France.
VESEY, LAWRENCE F. (2, Staple Garden)	Pte.	Hants, 1906, Pte. R.A.S.C., R.A.F. France.
VICARY, ALFRED E. (10, Nelson Road)		R.B., 1899. France. Taken Prisoner by Germans, Aug. 26, 1914.
VICK, JOHN (41, St. John's Road)	Bdr.	R.G.A., Nov. 1915, Gun. France.
VICKERS, ERNEST (40, Blue Ball Hill)	C.S.M.	Hants, 1914, Pte. France. Wounded, Sept. 1917 and 1918.
VICKERS, FREDERICK (40, Blue Ball Hill)	Pte.	Hants, Oct. 1914, Pte. Mesopotamia, India.
VICKERS, HARRY (40, Blue Ball Hill)	Stoker	R. Marines, Oct. 24, 1918. R.N. Russia.
VICKERS, WILLIAM H. (40, Blue Ball Hill)	Pte.	Hants, 1914, Pte. India, Mesopotamia. Wounded, Oct. 24, 1917.
VIDLER, WILLIAM H. (76, Canon Street)	Drummer	Hants, Apl. 1914, Drummer. India, Palestine, Egypt, France, Belgium, Germany. Wounded, 1918.
VINCENT, THOMAS (20, Parchment Street)	A.B.	R.N., Jan. 1914, Boy. France, H.M.S. *Attentive* and *Dido*.
VOKES, ALLEN W. (11, West End Terrace)	Pte.	Hants, Nov. 1914, Pte. R.D.C. Home.
VOKES, CHARLES B. (54, Hyde Abbey Road)	Pte.	Leicester, Sept. 1916, Pte. N. Fus. France.
WADDINGTON, THOMAS (5, Egbert Road)		R.N.A.S., Jan. 1915. R.A.S.C. (M.T.). France.
✠ WADE, WILLIAM (1A, Newburgh Street)	Pte.	Hants Y., May 1916, Tpr. Hants. France. Wounded, Feb. 1, 1917. *Killed in Action, June 3, 1917, Ypres.*
WADHAM, ALBERT H. (12, Staple Garden)	C.Q.M.S.	R.A.S.C. (M.T.), June 1915, Dr. France, Belgium. M.S.M. 1919.

WINCHESTER WAR SERVICE REGISTER

WAGHORN, ARTHUR J. ... (32, Brassey Road)		R.F.C., May 1917. R.A.F. Home.
WAINWRIGHT, ERNEST G. (Training College)	Capt.	Hants, 1912, Capt. T.F. Depot, No. 184. Home.
✠ WAKE, FREDERICK W. (64, Fairfield Road)	A.-Sergt.	Hants, Mch. 1916, Pte. Mesopotamia. *Died, Aug. 29, 1919, Basra.*
WAKE, THOMAS J. ... (17, Little Minster Street)	Corpl.	R.A.S.C. (M.T.), June 1916, Pte. Salonica, Constantinople.
WALDEN, FRANCIS A. ... (91, Upper Brook Street)	Pte.	Devon, Aug. 1916, Pte. Home.
WALDEN, GEORGE A. ... (91, Upper Brook Street)	Boy	R.N., Aug. 1917, Boy. North Sea, Black Sea.
WALKER, ALBERT E. ... (18, The Weirs)	Pte.	Devon Y., Mch. 1917, Tpr. R.A.M.C. Home.
WALKER, CHRISTOPHER G. (37, Brassey Road)	L.-Corpl.	Lond., Sept. 1914, Pte. France. Wounded, July 18, 1915, and Sept. 1918.
WALKER, FREDERICK J. (2, Magdalen Hill)	Pte.	R.A.S.C., Aug. 1914, Pte. Dardanelles, Salonica, Egypt. Wounded, 1915.
WALKER, WILLIAM ... (1, North View)	C.S.M.	R.A.S.C., 1911, Pte. Camel T.C. Gallipoli, Egypt, Palestine.
WALSH, EDWARD V. ... (3, Highland Terrace)	Sergt.	R.B., Oct. 1914, Rfn. R.A.F. Egypt. Palestine.
WALSH, GEORGE F. ... (3, Highland Terrace)	A.M.	R.H.A., 1910, Tptr. R.A.F. France.
WALSH, HENRY W. ... (23, Tower Street)	Bdr.	R.G.A., Sept. 1, 1914, Gun. France.
WALSH, JOHN ... (14, Egbert Road)		American Army, Sept. 1917. France.
WALSH, THOMAS R. ... (14, Egbert Road)	Corpl.	R.A.S.C. (M.T.), June 1915, Pte. France.
WALSH, WILLIAM J. ... (3, Highland Terrace)	L.-Corpl.	R.B., Nov. 1914, Rfn. Manch., R.A.S.C. (M.T.). France.
WARBURTON, HUGH N. ... (The Chestnuts, St. Cross Road)	Lieut.	R.N.V.R., Aug. 1915, Lieut. R.N.A.S., R.A.F. Home.
WARD, CHARLES H. ... (10, Percy Terrace)	Corpl.	Devon, Dec. 31, 1917. Worc. Belgium, France. Gassed once.
✠ WARD, DONALD H. C. ... (51, Chesil Street)	L.-Corpl.	Devon Cyc., Sept. 1916, Pte. France. *Killed in Action, Oct. 7, 1917, Hooge.*
WARD, EDWARD D. ... (32, Arbour Terrace)		Essex, Oct. 1916. R.A.S.C., R. Scots Greys. France.
WARD, FREDERICK ... (34, St. John's Street)	Pte.	Welsh, June 1916, Pte. Lincoln, Dub. Fus. Salonica, France.
WARD, GEORGE ... (59, Eastgate Street)		Wilts, Feb. 1915. France, Belgium. Wounded, Nov. 1916, Apl. 1918.
WARD, GEORGE E. ... (17, Upper High Street)	Pte.	Hants, Aug. 1916, Pte. R.E., Middlesex, Border, Lab. C. Home.

WINCHESTER WAR SERVICE REGISTER

✠ WARD, GEORGE W. (2, Water Lane)	... ...		Hants, Sept. 1914, Pte. France, Gallipoli. *Killed in Action, Apl.* 29, 1916.
WARD, HENRY J. (2, Water Lane)	...	Dr.	R.A.S.C., Sept. 1914, Dr. Egypt, Gallipoli. Wounded once.
WARD, HENRY T. (32, Arbour Terrace)	...		Devon, Aug. 1916. R.E. France.
WARD, JESSE R. (38, Wharf Hill)	... ...		R.N., 1895. At Sea.
WARD, REGINALD W. ... (17, Upper High Street)		Sergt.	Hants, Feb. 1915, Pte. France, Mesopotamia. Wounded, Apl. 16, 1916.
WARD, SIDNEY A. A. ... (30, St. John's Terrace)		Corpl.	R. Berks, 1910, Pte. France. Wounded three times. M.M.
WARD, STANLEY E. ... (17, Upper High Street)			Hants, June 1917. Home.
✠ WARD, THOMAS ... (2, Water Lane)		Pte.	Dorset, 1905, Pte. France. *Killed in Action,* Oct. 13, 1914.
WARD, TOM ... ... (17, Upper High Street)		Pte.	Hants, Aug. 1914, Pte. Bucks, Oxf. and Bucks L.I., Innis. Fus. Gallipoli, France, Salonica, Egypt. Wounded, Aug. 9, 1915.
WARD, WILLIAM GEOFFREY (17, Upper High Street)	...	Bdr.	R.G.A., Dec. 1915, Gun. France.
✠ WARD, WILLIAM GEORGE (30, St. John's Terrace)		Pte.	Devon, Apl. 1916, Pte. France. *Killed in Action, Sept.* 22, 1916.
WARE, FRANCIS C. ... (2, Castle Terrace)		A.-Corpl.	R.A.S.C. (M.T.), Feb. 1915, Pte. Gallipoli, Egypt.
WARE, GEOFFREY T. L. ... (29, City Road)		Lieut.	Wilts, Sept. 1914, Pte. R.F. France. Wounded, Mch. 3, 1915, and Oct. 9, 1917.
WARE, HARRY ... ... (18, Upper Brook Street)		Pte.	R.A.S.C. (M.T.), Pte. France.
WARREN, FRANK ... (Danesacre, Worthy Road)		Lieut.	K.R.R.C., May 1916, Rfn. France, Flanders. Wounded, Mch. 30 and Nov. 4, 1918.
WARREN, HENRY R. ... (33, Southgate Street)		2nd Lieut.	Hants, Nov. 1914, Pte. Mesopotamia, India, Persia.
WARREN, RICHARD C. ... (Courtenay House, Courtenay Rd.)		Lieut.	Oxf. and Bucks L.I., Dec. 1916, 2nd Lieut. France. Wounded, Dec. 1917, and July 1918. M.C. and Bar, 1917–18.
WARREN, WALLIS L. ... (Courtenay House, Courtenay Rd.)	...	Mid.	R.N., Oct. 1918, Mid. Home, H.M.S. *Resolution.*
WARWICK, HAROLD H. ... (20, Water Lane)		Corpl.	Aus. Cyc. C., 1915, Pte. France, Egypt. Wounded, Apl. and June 1918.
WARWICK, HENRY J. E. ... (8, Canute Road)		Corpl.	Can. Inf., Aug. 1914, Pte. Can. M.P. France. Wounded, Aug. 4, 1917.
WATERER, GEORGE W. ... (9, King Alfred Place)		Pte.	Derby Y. (Cyc.), Oct. 1918, Pte. Home.
WATERMAN, THOMAS ... (5, Chester Road)		Pte.	R.N. Lancs., 1914, Pte. Hants. India, Egypt.

WINCHESTER WAR SERVICE REGISTER

WATERS, ARTHUR T. ... (39, Middle Brook Street)	Pte.	Hussars, Sept. 1914, Tpr. D.L.I., R.A.S.C. France.
WATFORD, HERBERT ... (78, Stockbridge Road)	L.-Corpl.	R. Berks, May 1916, Pte. Home.
WATLEY, JESSE ... (36, Lower Brook Street)	Pte.	R.D.C., 1914, Pte. Home.
✠ WATSON, ARTHUR F. ... (3, St. Peter Street)	Sig.	Hants, Mch. 1916, Sig. India, Palestine. *Killed in Action, Apl. 9, 1918.*
WATSON, DONALD E. ... (3, St. Peter Street)	Cadet	R.N., Oct. 1918, Cadet. Home.
WATSON, JOHN G. ... (3, St. Peter Street)	Sergt.	Hants, Mch. 1916, Pte. Ind. Ord. Dept. India.
WATSON, ROBERT C. ... (Ross House, Hyde Street)	Lieut.	R.N.R., 1914, Lieut. Vice-Consul, Denmark. Atlantic, Denmark.
WATSON, VICTOR G. ... (3, St. Peter Street)	Sergt.	Hants, Dec. 1915, Pte. M.G.C. France.
WATTS, CHARLES W. ... (3, North View)	Pte.	Hants, Aug. 1914, Pte. Home.
WATTS, CHRISTOPHER ... (3, North View)	Pte.	Nat. Res., Sept. 1914, Pte. R.D.C., Lab. C. Home.
WATTS, ERNEST C. ... (39, Eastgate Street)		Hants, June 1916, Pte. France. Taken Prisoner by Germans, Apl. 23, 1917.
WATTS, FRANK W. ... (33, Parchment Street)	Corpl.	R.A.S.C., 1912, Dr. Gallipoli, Palestine, Egypt.
WATTS, HENRY E. ... (56, Wales Street)		Hants, Aug. 1914, Pte. Persian Gulf, Palestine.
WATTS, JOHN ... (3, North View)	L.-Corpl.	R.A.S.C. (M.T.), Oct. 1916, Pte. France, Germany.
WATTS, JOHN R. ... (34, Brassey Road)	L.-Corpl.	Hants, Sept. 1914, Pte. R.E. Mesopotamia, India.
✠ WAUD TETLEY, CLARENCE E. (The Lodge, Bereweeke Road)	Lieut.	Lancs. Fus., Aug. 1914, 2nd Lieut. Gallipoli. Despatches 1915. *Missing, believed Killed, Aug. 21, 1915, Suvla Bay.*
WAUD TETLEY, JOSEPH ... (The Lodge, Bereweeke Road)	Lieut.	Northants, 1916, 2nd Lieut. France. Wounded, Oct. 1918. M.C. 1918.
WAUD TETLEY, THOMAS H. ... (The Lodge, Bereweeke Road)	Capt.	Wilts, 1910, 2nd Lieut. France, Belgium. Wounded and Taken Prisoner by Germans, Oct. 27, 1914. Despatches 1914, 1918, 1920.
WAYGOOD, GEORGE ... (2, Step Terrace)		R.A.M.C., 1918. France.
WEALE, JAMES L. ... (44, Monks Road)	C.S.M.	Hants, 1901, Pte. Salonica. Despatches.
WEAVER, WILLIAM T. ... (35, Wharf Hill)	A.-Sergt.	A.P.C., Sept. 1914, Pte. Glos., R. Warwick.
✠ WEBB, ALFRED ... (33, St. John's Terrace)	Pte.	Dorset, Apl. 1917, Pte. India, Mesopotamia. *Killed in Action,* 1918.

L

WINCHESTER WAR SERVICE REGISTER

WEBB, ALFRED M. (10, Silver Hill)	...	Stoker	R.N., 1912, Stoker. Malta, North Sea.
WEBB, CHARLES H. (156, Stockbridge Road)	...	L.T.	R.N., 1912. North Sea; H.M.S. *Queen Mary*, *Petard*, and *Indefatigable*.
WEBB, FELIX F. (23, Eastgate Street)	...	L.-Corpl.	Hants, Sept. 1914, Pte. India, Mesopotamia.
WEBB, FRANK G. (156, Stockbridge Road)	...	Boy	R.N., 1915, Boy. North Sea; H.M.S. *Foxglove*, *Renown*, and *Marlborough*.
WEBB, JOHN C. (20, King Alfred Place)	...	Pte.	Somerset L.I., Mch. 1916, Pte. Lincoln. India.
✠ WEBB, ROBERT A. (43, St. Catherine's Road)	...	Corpl.	Hants, Sept. 1914, Pte. Egypt, India, France. *Killed in Action*, 1918.
✠ WEBB, WILLIAM F. (53, Southgate Street)	...	Rfn.	Lond. P.O. Rif., Feb. 1917, Rfn. France. *Killed in Action, Sept.* 20, 1917, *St. Julien*.
WEBB, WILLIAM C. (13, Wales Street)	...	Pte.	Hants, 1916, Pte. France. Wounded, Sept. 26, 1917.
WEBSTER, PERCY (17, Parchment Street)	...	Corpl.	Hants Y., Jan. 1917, Tpr. Wilts Y. Home.
WEDGE, ALFRED E. (28, Hyde Close)	...	Sergt.	Hants, 1906, Boy. France, Belgium. Wounded, July 1, 1916.
✠ WEDGE, CHARLES (6, Andover Road)	...	Pte.	Wilts, 1911, Pte. France. Wounded, 1914. *Killed in Action, Mch.* 11, 1915.
WEDGE, EDWARD L. (27, Hyde Close)	...	Pte.	R.A.S.C. (M.T.), Pte. India.
✠ WEDGE, JAMES C. T. (6, Andover Road)	...	C. Gun. Instr.	R.N., 1894. Belgian Coast, Dardanelles, Dover Patrol. *Killed, Oct.* 21, 1918, *mine explosion*.
WEDGE, WALTER C. (28, Hyde Close)	...	L.-Corpl.	Hants Y., Oct. 1914, Tpr. Hants. France, Italy. Wounded once. Gassed once.
WEDGE, WILLIAM P. (28, Hyde Close)	...	Sergt.	Hants, 1906, Pte. Essex, Hants. Dardanelles, France. Wounded, July 1915.
WEEKS, ALBERT A. (26, Tower Street)	...	Spr.	R.E., Sept. 1916, Spr. Mesopotamia.
WEEKS, EDWARD W. J. (26, Tower Street)	...	Corpl.	Hants, 1895, Pte. M.F.P. Home.
WEEKS, HARRY (Pinehurst Cottage, Bereweeke Rd.)	...	Pte.	Hants Y., May 1916, Tpr. Hants. France.
WEEKS, HENRY G. (26, Tower Street)	...	Corpl.	Canadians, 1914, Pte. France.
WELCH, HENRY C. (19, Stockbridge Road)	...	Pte.	Hants Y., Mch. 1916, Tpr. Hants, M.F.P. France.
WELLARD, EDWIN A. J. (9, Lawn Street)	...	Dr.	R.A.S.C., Aug. 1914, Dr. Salonica.
WELLARD, JAMES C. (47, Lower Brook Street)	...	Pte.	Wilts, Sept. 1915, Pte. M.G.C. France. Wounded, Aug. 3, 1916, and Nov. 22, 1917.
WELLER, KENNETH C. H. (52, Stockbridge Road)	...	L.-Corpl.	Winnipeg Rif., Aug. 1914, Pte. P.P.C.L.I. France, Flanders. Wounded, May 4, 1915.

WINCHESTER WAR SERVICE REGISTER

WELLER, WILLIAM A. (25, St. Thomas Street)	Lieut.	Hants Y., Aug. 4, 1914, Tpr. France, Italy. Wounded, Mch. 22, 1918.
WELLER, WILLIAM J. (52, Stockbridge Road)	Corpl.	R.E., 1912, Spr. Mauritius.
WELLS, JOHN (11, College Street)	Major	H.A.C., June 1914, Pte. Devon, Sherwood For. France. Wounded, July 1916 and May 1917. M.C. and Bar 1917.
WELLS, PHILIP (11, College Street)	Lieut.	Hants Y., 1907, Tpr. R.F.A. France. Wounded, June 1917. M.C. 1918.
WELLS, SYDNEY W. (2, Connaught Terrace)		R.B., 1914. Worc. Home.
WENTWORTH, FRANK (68, Hyde Street)	Gun.	R.G.A., Gun. France.
WESLEY, HARRY (15, Colebrook Street)	Pte.	Hants Y., May 1916, Tpr. Hants. France, Salonica. Wounded, Apl. 26, 1916.
WESLEY, HERBERT (26, Upper Brook Street)	Pte.	Hants Y., Oct. 1915, Tpr. Hants. France. Wounded, June 7, 1917.
WEST, GEORGE E. (26, Western Road)	Corpl.	R.N.A.S., Aug. 1916, 2nd A.M. R.A.F. France, Egypt.
WESTBROOK, ALBERT E. (78, Wales Street)	Pte.	Hants, Oct. 1915, Pte. India, Egypt, Palestine. Wounded, Apl. 10, 1918.
WESTBROOK, HENRY W. (12, Cranworth Road)	Spr.	R.E., Mch. 1916, Spr. Salonica.
WESTMORLAND, HERBERT C. (Dalkeith, Park Road)	T.-Lt.-Col.	Hants, 1913, 2nd Lieut. Entrenching Bn., Hants, Devon, Hants. France, Belgium, Germany. Wounded, Sept. 15, 1914; Apl. 30, 1916; Aug. 24, 1918. D.S.O. and Bar 1918; Despatches 1917, 1918, 1919; Croix de Guerre.
WESTMORLAND, HERBERT G. (Dalkeith, Park Road)	Lt.-Col.	Hants, 1881, 2nd Lieut. Home.
WETTON, PERCY J. (35, Egbert Road)	Pte.	Worc., Jan. 1917, Pte. Hants. Home.
WHATMORE, WALTER F. (11, St. Catherine's Road)	L.-Corpl.	Hants, Nov. 1915, Pte. Bedford. India.
WHEBLE, RANDOLPH J. (74, Sussex Street)	1st A.M.	R.A.F., 1917, 1st A.M. France, Germany.
WHEELER, CHARLES (50, Hatherley Road)	Spr.	R.E., rejoined Aug. 1914, Spr. France, Salonica. Wounded, Nov. 1915.
WHEELER, FRANK (11, Upper Wolvesey Terrace)	Sergt.	R.B., rejoined Aug. 1914, Rfn. Lab. C. France. Wounded, Oct. 22, 1914, and Sept. 3, 1916.
WHEELER, FREDERICK T. (18, North Walls)	Sergt.	Hants, Nov. 1915, Pte. R.E. India.
WHEELER, HAROLD V. (Elderfield, Hatherley Road)	Pte.	Hants, 1913, Pte. India, Persian Gulf. Taken Prisoner by Turks, Apl. 29, 1916.
WHEELER, HENRY J. (20, Water Lane)	Pte.	Hants, Sept. 1914, Pte. France, Gallipoli.
WHEELER, JOHN A. (4, St. Faith's Road)	Sig.	R.N., June 1917, Sig. Atlantic.

WINCHESTER WAR SERVICE REGISTER

WHEELER, WALTER H. (35, Hyde Abbey Road)	Spr.	R.E., Dec. 1915, Spr. France.
WHEELER, WILLIAM (4, Water Lane)	Pte.	Wilts, Dec. 9, 1915, Pte. France.
✠ WHICHER, EDWIN W. (2, Avenue Road)	Tpr.	Derby Y., Sept. 1, 1918, Tpr. Home. *Died, Sept.* 24, 1918, *Canterbury.*
WHISTLER, ARTHUR J. (53, Hatherley Road)	Capt.	Hants (T.F.), May 1916, Capt. R.D.C. Home.
WHITCHER, ARTHUR H. (12, St. Catherine's Road)	Gun.	R.G.A., Jan. 1916, Gun. Egypt.
WHITCHER, DAVID (6, Andover Road)	C.S.M.	Hants, 1899, Drummer. India, Aden, Egypt, Gallipoli. Wounded, Aug. 10, 1915.
WHITCHER, FREDERICK (10, Hillside Terrace)	Pte.	Hants, Nov. 1915, Pte. R.A.S.C. (M.T.). France. Wounded, Aug. 1917.
WHITCHER, WILLIAM A. (8, Westgate Lane)	Pte.	Hants, Sept. 1914, Pte. India; Mesopotamia.
WHITE, ALBERT J. (21, Greenhill Road)	Pte.	Dorset, June 24, 1918, Pte. Manch. Mesopotamia.
WHITE, ALFRED A. (44, Western Road)	...	Hants, Mch. 14, 1916. Wilts. India, Egypt, Palestine.
WHITE, FRANCIS R. (West Highlands, Romsey Road)	L.-Corpl.	R.A.O.C., 1913, Pte. Egypt.
✠ WHITE, FREDERICK A. (36, Stockbridge Road)	L.-Corpl.	Grenadier Gds. France. *Killed in Action, Apl.* 13, 1918.
WHITE, FREDERICK D. (28, Arbour Terrace)	Pte.	Monmouth, May 1917, Rfn. Lab. C. France.
WHITE, FREDERICK J. (18, Victoria Road)	Corpl.	R.A.S.C., Sept. 1914, Pte. France.
WHITE, GEORGE A. (22, Hyde Close)	Pte.	R.A.M.C., 1915, Pte. France. Wounded once.
WHITE, GEORGE J. (28, Arbour Terrace)	Pte.	K.R.R.C., Aug. 1914, Rfn. Hants, Lab. C. France, Belgium. Wounded, 1917.
✠ WHITE, HAROLD W. (3, Connaught Terrace)	Pte.	Inns of Court O.T.C., June 1915, Pte. Home. *Died, Dec.* 1916, *Winchester.*
✠ WHITE, HAVILAND (3A, King Alfred Place)	Stoker	R.N., Aug. 1914, Stoker. China; H.M.S. *Venus. Died, Sept.* 19, 1918.
WHITE, HENRY R. (4, Cathedral View)	Corpl.	R.B., Dec. 1914, Rfn. Home.
WHITE, HERBERT C. (32, Fairfield Road)	...	R.G.A., Oct. 1916, Gun. France.
✠ WHITE, LEONARD F. (West Highlands, Romsey Road)	Pte.	R.F.C., Feb. 1917, 2nd A.M. R.I. Fus. France. Wounded, Apl. 11, 1918. *Died of Wounds, Apl.* 12, 1918, *Ypres.*
WHITE, LESLIE (9, Gordon Avenue)	...	Hants, 1917. France.

WINCHESTER WAR SERVICE REGISTER

WHITE, LOUIS ... (19, Hyde Close)	Corpl.	Hants, rejoined Jan. 1915, Pte. Home.	
WHITE, SAMUEL J. ... (81, Greenhill Road)	Sergt.	Hants, 1902, Bandsman. R.A.F. France.	
WHITE, SIDNEY J. ... (39, Middle Brook Street)	Pte.	Essex, Oct. 1916, Pte. R.W.S., R.F. France. Wounded, Dec. 28, 1917, and June 15, 1918.	
WHITE, WALTER J. ... (36, Stockbridge Road)	L.-Corpl.	R.E., Jan. 1917, Spr. France, Belgium.	
WHITE, WILLIAM A. ... (9, Cathedral View)	Staff Sergt.	R.A.S.C., Sept. 1914, Pte. Gallipoli, Egypt, France, Salonica.	
✠ WHITE, WILLIAM E. ... (32, Fairfield Road)	Pte.	Hants, Aug. 1914, Pte. Mesopotamia. Taken Prisoner by Turks, Apl. 29, 1916, Kut. *Died, July 22, 1916.*	
WHITE, WILLIAM G. ... (4, Middle Brook Street)	Rfn.	R.B., May 1915, Rfn. France, Belgium. Wounded, Aug. 2, 1916.	
WHITEAR, ALBERT E. ... (29, Kingsgate Street)	Pte.	Hants, Oct. 1916, Pte. D.C.L.I., R.D.C. France. Wounded, Aug. 22, 1917.	
WHITEAR, ARTHUR W. ... (52, Greenhill Road)	Corpl.	Hants, July 1914, Pte. India, Egypt, France, Belgium, Germany.	
WHITEAR, CHARLES H. G. ... (4, Freelands Buildings)		Hants, Aug. 1914. M.G.C. Salonica. Wounded, Oct. 13, 1916.	
WHITEAR, EDWARD C. ... (29, Kingsgate Street)	Dr.	R.H.A., Aug. 1915, Dr. France, Belgium. Wounded, Oct. 5, 1917.	
WHITEAR, FREDERICK J. ... (19, North View)	Pte.	K.R.R.C., June 1916, Rfn. W. Yorks, Lab. C., E. Yorks, R.F. France.	
WHITEAR, LEONARD W. ... (36, Kingsgate Street)	Pte.	Hants, Aug. 1914, Pte. Persian Gulf. Wounded, July 24, 1915.	
WHITEAR, ROBERT ... (3, Boundary Street)	Gun.	R.G.A., May 1916, Gun. France, Germany.	
WHITING, JAMES W. ... (6, Sussex Street)	L.-Corpl.	R.B., 1897, Rfn. Home.	
WHITLOCK, CHARLES ... (8, Crowder Terrace)	Pte.	Devon, Apl. 1915, Pte. R.F. France.	
WHITTAKER, CECIL G. ... (2, Jubilee Villas)	Sergt.	Hants, Nov. 1914, Pte. Mesopotamia.	
WHITTAKER, WILLIAM A. P. ... (2, Jubilee Villas)	L.-Corpl.	Hants, Aug. 1914, Pte. Mesopotamia.	
WHITWAM, JABEZ E. ... (70, High Street)	Corpl.	R.N.A.S., Oct. 1917, 1st A.M. R.A.F. Home.	
WICKENS, GEORGE H. ... (28, North Walls)	Pte.	R.A.S.C. (M.T.), May 1915, Pte. France.	
WICKHAM, WILLIAM ... (42, Greenhill Road)	C.S.M.	K.R.R.C., 1901, Rfn. France. Wounded, May 1915 and July 1916.	
WIELD, FRANCIS H. ... (23, The Square)	Corpl.	Hants Y., 1915, Tpr. Egypt.	

WINCHESTER WAR SERVICE REGISTER

WILCOCK, THOMAS E. ... (14, Clausentum Road) ... C.S.M. ... K.R.R.C., 1900, Rfn. Lab. C. France.

WILCOCKS, JOHN (3, Staple Garden) ... L.-Corpl. ... M.G.C. France, Italy.

WILD, GEORGE J. (77, Middle Brook Street) ... R.N., Jan. 1916. North Sea.

WILD, WILLIAM T. (6, Avenue Terrace) ... Sergt. ... K.R.R.C., 1899, Rfn. R.A.F. France. Wounded, Aug. 6, 1917.

WILDE, LEONARD G. (19, Union Street) ... Dr. ... R.A.S.C., July 1914, Dr. R.F.A. France, Salonica. Gassed once.

WILKIN, ALBERT E. (1, St. Catherine's Road) ... Spr. ... R.E., Apl. 1918, Spr. France.

WILKINS, EDWARD J. (16, Cross Street) ... Sergt. ... Hants, Feb. 1915, Pte. Home.

WILKINS, EDWARD P. (16, Cross Street) ... Pte. ... Hants, 1912, Pte. India, Mesopotamia, Persia.

WILKINS, FREDERIC (42, Nuns Road) ... C.Q.M.S. ... Hants, rejoined 1914, Sergt. R. Berks. Home.

WILKINS, FREDERICK (19, Hyde Street) ... Sergt. ... Hants, Jan. 1915, Sergt. R. Berks. Home.

WILKINS, HAROLD J. (16, Cross Street) ... Bug. ... Hants, Apl. 1914, Bug. India, Mesopotamia, Egypt, France, Germany.

WILKINS, WILLIAM F. (Hants Constabulary, Romsey Road) ... M.M.P. 1915. E. Africa.

WILKINSON, EDWARD A. G. (Kingshot, St. Cross) ... Surg.-Comdr. ... R.N., 1903, Surgeon. North Sea; H.M.S. *Iron Duke*, *Revenge*, and *Egmont*. O.B.E.

WILKINSON, JAMES V. S. (Kingshot, St. Cross) ... Lieut. ... Indian Army, 1916, 2nd Lieut. Kashmir Rif. Palestine.

WILKINSON, LESLIE G. (10, Eastgate Street) ... R.F.C., Oct. 1915. R.A.F. France.

WILKINSON, NORMAN C. T. (10, Eastgate Street) ... 1st A.M. ... R.F.C., June 1914, 2nd A.M. France.

WILKINSON, THOMAS (10, Eastgate Street) ... Sergt. ... R.B., Sept. 1914, Rfn. Home.

WILKINSON, WALTER H. J. (Kingshot, St. Cross) ... Staff Capt. ... Ind. Cav., Interpreter, 2nd Lieut. Intelligence Corps. France. C.I.E. 1919, Despatches four times, Chev. Légion d'Honneur, Order Leopold I, Belgian Croix de Guerre.

WILLIAMS, DONOVAN N. (63, Kingsgate Street) ... Gun. ... H.A.C., 1917, Gun. France.

WILLIAMS, HENRY (17, Granville Place) ... Pte. ... 1906, Pte. France. Wounded twice.

WILLIAMS, KENNETH E. N. (63, Kingsgate Street) ... 2nd Lieut. ... Hants Y., 1908, Tpr. R. Dragoons. France.

WINCHESTER WAR SERVICE REGISTER

WILLIAMS, LIONEL G. N. (63, Kingsgate Street)	... Tpr.	...	Hants Y., 1914, Tpr. France, Germany.
WILLIAMS, LOFTUS (15, Gladstone Street)	... C.Q.M.S.		R.B., 1896, Rfn. France, Belgium. Gassed once.
WILLIAMSON, SAMUEL A. (160, High Street)	... Pte.	...	R.A.O.C., Sept. 1917, Pte. Home.
WILLIAMSON, WILLIAM W. (39, Wharf Hill)	... Bandsman		R. Sussex, Dec. 1915, Bandsman. Home.
WILLIS, ALFRED G. (50, Monks Road)	... Sergt.	...	R.B., Aug. 1914, Bug. France.
✠ WILLIS, EDWIN G. (5, Percy Terrace)	... A.B.	...	R.N., 1883. North Sea. *Killed in Action, May 31, 1916, Jutland.*
WILLIS, FREDERICK (23, Parchment Street)	... Rfn.	...	Lond. P.O. Rif., Sept. 1916, Pte. R.I.R. France. Wounded, Oct. 1918.
WILLS, ALBERT (8, Clausentum Road)	... Staff Sergt.		Grenadier Gds., 1902, Pte. A.P.C. France.
WILSON, ALBERT H. (55, Western Road)	... Pte.	...	Hants, Aug. 1914, Pte. R.A.F. India, Mesopotamia, Egypt.
WILSON, EDWARD H. J. (48, Kingsgate Street)	... Pte.	...	Hants, July 1917, Pte. R. Warwick. Germany.
WILSON, EVELYN R. (16, St. James' Lane)	... A.-Capt.	...	R.B., May 1, 1916, 2nd Lieut. G.H.Q. Palestine, Syria.
WILSON, GEORGE (2, St. Thomas Street)	... Dr.	...	R.A.S.C., Mch. 1916, Dr. Salonica.
WILSON, HENRY E. (77, Colebrook Street)	... Pte.	...	Hants Y., Dec. 9, 1915, Tpr. Northants, Lab. C. France. Wounded, Sept. 30, 1917 (accidentally). Gassed, Aug. 19, 1918.
WILSON, HERBERT J. (56, Parchment Street)	... L.-Corpl.		Hants, Oct. 1914, Pte. R. Warwick. France. Gassed, Dec. 8, 1917.
WIMHURST, WILLIAM F. (2, St. Catherine's Road)	... Corpl.	...	Hants, Sept. 1914, Pte. India.
WINCHCOMB, ERNEST E. (34, Wharf Hill)	... L.S.	...	R.N., 1912, Boy. North Sea, Baltic; H.M.S. *Vivien.*
✠ WINCHCOMB, FREDERICK J. (34, Wharf Hill)	... Stoker	...	R.N., 1912, Stoker. North Sea; Submarine G. 8. *Killed in Action, Dec.* 1917.
WINDSOR, WILLIAM R. (18, Nuns Road)	... Sergt.	...	R.B., Aug. 1914, Rfn. Home.
WINKWORTH, ALBERT J. (7, Freelands Buildings)	... Pte.	...	Lab. C., 1917, Pte. France.
WINKWORTH, ARTHUR (17, St. Clement Street)	... Pte.	...	Hants, Oct. 1915, Pte. R. Berks, Lab. C. France.
WINKWORTH, CHARLES H. (11, Westgate Lane)	... Pte.	...	Hants, Aug. 1914, Pte. India, Mesopotamia. Wounded twice, 1918.
✠ WINKWORTH, HARRY (17, St. Clement Street)	... Chief Cook		R.N., 1893, Cook's Mate. North Sea. *Drowned, Oct.* 15, 1914.

WINKWORTH, LEONARD G. (14, Chester Road)	...		R.A.S.C., Sept. 1914, Pte. Gallipoli, Egypt, France.
✠ WINKWORTH, WILLIAM (20, Parchment Street)	...	Rfn.	R.B., 1903, Rfn. France. Wounded, 1914. *Killed in Action, May* 10, 1915, *Ypres.*
WINKWORTH, WILLIAM J. (18, Stockbridge Road)	...	Pte.	Hants, 1915, Pte. India, Mesopotamia. Wounded, Feb. 24, 1917.
✠ WINTER, CHARLES J. ... (Pond Cottage, Weeke)	...	Stoker	R.N., Stoker. North Sea, Jutland; H.M.S. *Queen Mary. Killed in Action, May* 31, 1915, *Jutland.*
WINZAR, PERCY (31, Colson Road)	...	Pte.	Hants, 1915, Pte. Home.
WISE, JOHN F. T. (12, Cross Street)	...	...	R.N., 1911, Boy. H.M.S. *Saracen.*
WISE, THOMAS W. (12, Cross Street)	...	Pte.	Hants, Mch. 1914, Pte. Mesopotamia, India.
WISEMAN, ALBERT (3, Cheriton Road)	...	L.-Corpl.	Devon, June 1916, Pte. Home.
WISEMAN, ALFRED (13, Cheriton Road)	...	L.-Corpl.	Hants, Nov. 1915, Pte. Lab. C., Hants. Mesopotamia, Persia. Wounded, Feb. 27, 1917.
WITCHER, CHRISTOPHER H. (16, Upper High Street)	...	Pte.	Hants, rejoined Aug. 1914, Pte. R. Marines, Lab. C. France.
WITCHER, ERNEST J. ... (13, Stockbridge Road)	...	Pte.	Can. Field Amb., Mch. 1916, Pte. France.
WITCHER, REGINALD W. (16, Upper High Street)	...	Pte.	R. Warwick, Jan. 1918, Pte. France. Wounded, Oct. 24, 1918.
WITHERINGTON, BERT ... (36, Water Lane)	...	Pte.	Hants, 1915, Pte. France, Serbia.
WITHERS, CHARLES R. J. (64, Water Lane)	...	Pte.	Hants (T.F.), Nov. 1915, Pte. R.E., Dorset. Home.
WITNEY, ALFRED G. ... (25, Fairfield Road)	...	Pte.	Hants, May 1917, Pte. Home.
WITTS, FRANK (47, Wharf Hill)	...	Stoker	R.N., 1913, Stoker. North Sea.
WITTS, HENRY ... (44, Water Lane)	...	L.-Corpl.	Hants, 1910, Pte. France.
WOLFREYS, CHARLES F. (30, Elm Road)	...	1st A.M.	R.N.A.S., July 18, 1917, 2nd A.M. R.A.F. France.
WOOD, EDWARD P. D. (10, South View)	...	A.B.	R.N., June 1906. North Sea; H.M.S. *Malaya* and *Parker.*
WOOD, HARRY C. (66, Hyde Street)	...	...	R.E. (Sigs.). France, Macedonia.
WOOD, JOHN P. (10, South View)	...	C.S.M.	R.B., 1899, Rfn. France, Salonica, Russia.
WOOD, NORMAN F. (66, Hyde Street)	...	...	Hussars. R.A.F. Home.

WINCHESTER WAR SERVICE REGISTER

✠ Wood, Robert C. ... Rfn. ... K.R.R.C., 1906, Rfn. France, Belgium. *Killed in Action, Nov. 14, 1914, Ypres.*
(10, Gordon Avenue)

Wood, Victor R. ... ... R.A.M.C., Mch. 1915. France.
(66, Hyde Street)

Woodcock, Frederick J. ... Corpl. ... R.G.A., 1912, Gun. Aden.
(8, St. James' Terrace)

Woodcock, Harry ... ... Gun. ... R.G.A., May 1916, Gun. France.
(8, St. James' Terrace)

Woodcock, William C. ... Corpl. ... R.A.S.C., 1907, Dr. R.F. France. Wounded, June 17, 1916.
(8, St. James' Terrace)

Woodgate, Frank ... Corpl. ... Hants Y., Nov. 1914, Tpr. Lancers, Yorks, R.W.F., S. Lancs. France. Wounded and Gassed twice.
(12, High Street)

Woodman, William ... ... Rfn. ... K.R.R.C., 1898, Rfn. France.
(25, Colson Road)

Woodmore, John ... ... Pte. ... Hants Y., June 1915, Tpr. Hants. France. Wounded, Sept. 4, 1918.
(41, North Walls)

✠ Woods, Frederic G. ... ... Pte. ... Hants, Dec. 1914, Pte. India. *Died of Malaria.*
(26, Nuns Road)

Woods, John T. ... ... Pte. ... Hants, Aug. 8, 1914, Pte. Mesopotamia. Wounded, July 1915.
(26, Nuns Road)

Woods, William C. ... L.-Corpl. ... R. Innis. Fus., Aug. 1914, Bandsman. France. Wounded, May 1915.
(26, Nuns Road)

Woods, William H. ... ... Bandmaster Hants, Aug. 1914, Bandmaster. Mesopotamia, India.
(26, Nuns Road)

Wooldridge, Charles D. ... A.-Capt. ... Ceylon Planters Rif. C., 1909, Rfn. Egypt, France. Wounded, Aug. 1917.
(Ellerslie, St. Cross Road)

Woolf, Philip ... ... R.B., 1898. Lab. C. France, Salonica. Wounded, May 9, 1915.
(4, East Cliffe)

Woolford, William ... Corpl. ... R.E., Sept. 1916, Spr. Mesopotamia.
(48, St. John's Street)

Worsam, George J. ... ... Dr. ... R.F.A., Nov. 1915, Dr. Mesopotamia, Aden.
(33, St. Catherine's Road)

✠ Worsam, John E. ... ... Pte. ... T.R., Mch. 1917, Pte. Hants, R. Berks. France. *Killed in Action, Mch. 29, 1918, Arras.*
(33, St. Catherine's Road)

Wort, William A. ... ... Sergt. ... Hants Cyc., Aug. 1915, Pte. India, Russia.
(51, Western Road)

Worthington, Charles ... Pte. ... Hants, 1914, Pte. Home.
(6, Brassey Road)

Worthington, Charles ... Pte. ... Hants, July 1915, Pte. Home.
(54, Wharf Hill)

Wright, Arthur ... ... Spr. ... R.E., June 1916, Spr. Mesopotamia.
(32, Upper High Street)

Wright, Charles ... ... Pte. ... K. Liverp., Feb. 1917, Pte. France, Germany.
(29, Hyde Abbey Road)

WINCHESTER WAR SERVICE REGISTER

WRIGHT, CHARLES G. (16, High Street)	... 2nd A.M.	...	R.N.A.S., Dec. 1917. R.A.F. Home.
WRIGHT, FRANK (29, Hyde Abbey Road)	... Pte.	...	R.A.M.C., Feb. 1916, Pte. R.A.F. France, India.
WRIGHT, GEORGE V. (13, West End Terrace)	... Corpl.	...	Hants, June 1916, Pte. France.
WRIGHT, JAMES H. (4, Granville Place)	... Pte.	...	Dorset, Aug. 4, 1914, Pte. France. Wounded and taken Prisoner by Germans, Oct. 22, 1914.
WRIGHT, JOSEPH (29, Hyde Abbey Road)	... Pte.	...	D.C.L.I., Feb. 1916, Pte. Devon. France, Palestine, Germany.
✠ WRIGHT, WILLIAM C. (19, Wales Street)	... Pte.	...	Hants, Aug. 1914, Pte. Egypt, Dardanelles. *Killed (accidentally), Aug. 10, 1915.*
✠ WROE, HAROLD B. (11, Alswitha Terrace)	... Pte.	...	Hants, 1913, Pte. India, Mesopotamia. *Killed in Action, July 1915, Nasireyah.*
WROE, HARRY (11, Alswitha Terrace)	... Sergt.	...	Hants, 1909, Pte. R. Sussex. Gallipoli. Wounded, Aug. 15, 1915.
WROE, JAMES H. (18, Cranworth Road)	... C.S.M.	...	K.R.R.C., 1895, Rfn. Nigerian Regt. E. Africa. Wounded and taken Prisoner by Germans, Jan. 24, 1917.
WROE, WILLIAM G. (11, Alswitha Terrace)	... Staff Q.M.S.		K.R.R.C., Mch. 1915, C.-Sergt. Home.
✠ WYATT, ALFRED H. (67, Hyde Street)	... A.B.	...	R.N., 1894, O.S. North Sea. *Killed in Action, May 31, 1916, Jutland.*
WYATT, CECIL B. (11, Owens Road)	... P.O.	...	Hants Y., Sept. 1914, Tpr. R.N.A.S., R.A.F. Home.
✠ WYATT, ERNEST W. (67, Hyde Street)	... C.S.M.	...	R.B., 1894, Rfn. France. Wounded, Sept. 1915. *Died of Wounds, Sept. 11, 1915, Ypres.*
WYETH, RAYMOND A. (10, Victoria Road)	...		K.R.R.C., Aug. 1914, Rfn. Hants Y., R.N.A.S., R.A.F. Home.
WYLIE, FREDERICK W. (6, Alswitha Terrace)	... C. Engr.		R.N. (Motor Boat Res.), Nov. 1917, C. Engr.
YALDREN, ERNEST P. (15, Staple Garden)	... Pte.	...	Hants, Nov. 1916, Pte. R.A.S.C. France.
YALDREN, ERNEST R. (15, Staple Garden)	... Pte.	...	Devon, Mch. 1918, Pte. R. Berks. France.
YALDREN, LEONARD G. (30, Hyde Street)	... 2nd A.M.		R.F.C., Dec. 1916, 2nd A.M. Home.
YALDREN, WILFRED (14, Staple Garden)	... Sergt.	...	Hants, Aug. 1914, Pte. India, Mesopotamia.
YARNEY, HERBERT F. (6, Greenhill Avenue)	... Sig.	...	R.G.A., Jan. 1915, Gun. France, Egypt.
YARNEY, WILLIAM (6, Greenhill Avenue)	... Corpl.	...	Hants, Sept. 1914, Pte. M.F.P. Home.

WINCHESTER WAR SERVICE REGISTER

YARNEY, WILLIAM L. ... ... Pte. ... Devon, 1915, Pte. Home.
(6, Greenhill Avenue)

YARROW, WILLIAM C. ... ... Wireman... R.N., Nov. 1916, Wireman. North Sea.
(38, North Walls)

YATES, CHARLES J. E. ... ... Gun. ... R.G.A., Oct. 1916, Gun. Palestine, Egypt.
(Upper House, Symonds Street)

YATES, PHILIP E. ... ... C. Steward H.M. Hosp. S. *Braemar Castle*, 1914, C. Steward.
(Upper House, Symonds Street)   Salonica, Malta, Russia, Egypt.

YELLAND, ALFRED H. ... Sig. ... R.G.A., Sig. Home.
(5, Queen's Road)

YORK, EDWARD J. ... ... Pte. ... Hants, Apl. 1918, Pte. Home.
(1, Newburgh Street)

YOUNG, ALBERT H. ... ... R.N.A.S., Oct. 1917. R.A.F. North Sea.
(12, Greyfriars Terrace)

YOUNG, ARCHIBALD J. ... Pte. ... Hants, Nov. 1915, Pte. Wilts. Egypt, India,
(12, Greyfriars Terrace)   Palestine.

YOUNG, EDWARD A. ... ... Rfn. ... R.B., Aug. 1914, Rfn. Home.
(1, Andover Road)

YOUNG, ROBERT... ... ... Pte. ... Somerset L.I., 1915, Pte. R. Berks. France.
(15A, City Road)   Wounded twice.

APPENDIX TWO

THE STRUCTURE OF THE HAMPSHIRE REGIMENT IN THE FIRST WORLD WAR[1]

Background

In the First World War, The Hampshire Regiment consisted of four elements:

The Regular Battalions
The Special Reserve Battalion
The Territorial Force Battalions
The Service Battalions

The Regular Battalions

The 1st and 2nd Battalions were made up of regular (professional) soldiers and was formed from the old 37th (North Hampshire) Regiment and the 67th (South Hampshire) Regiment. At the start of the War, the 1st Battalion was in England and deployed to France in August 1914, the 2nd Battalion was in India and only returned to England in the winter of 1914, once relieved by the Territorial Battalions.

The Special Reserve

The 3rd Battalion (known as the Special Reserve Battalion) was made up of volunteers and was a direct descendant of the Hampshire Militia; as such it did not deploy. Its soldiers enlisted for a 6 year period, accepting the risk of being called up in the event of a general mobilisation. Their period as a Special Reservist started with 6 months full time training and they had 3-4 weeks training per year thereafter. The job of the 3rd Bn was to provide reinforcements for the active service battalions.

The Territorial Force

The Territorial Force had originally been raised for home service only and

[1] Supplied by Colin Bulleid and Rachel Holmes, The Royal Hampshire Regiment Museum

was made up of volunteers who trained on a part-time basis (much like the Territorial Army of today called the Reserves). The Territorial Force Battalions of the Hampshire Regiment recruited extensively across the County from the following areas:

Winchester	4th Battalion
Southampton	5th Battalion
Portsmouth	6th Battalion (Duke of Connaught's Own)
Bournemouth	7th Battalion
Isle of Wight	8th Battalion (Princess Beatrice's Isle of Wight Rifles)
Southampton	9th (Cyclists) Battalion

As with other Territorial Force Battalions, their task at the start of the War, was to relieve Regular Battalions who were stationed overseas. By this time recruitment was well under way and all of the Territorial Battalions had split, thus forming another battalion; hence the 4th Battalion became the First Fourth and the Second Fourth (always written as: 1/4th and 2/4th) etc. [RH notes that all territorial soldiers were renumbered early in 1917 see D.G. and E.H. Alexander etc]

They rendered valuable service to the War effort and ended up serving all over the world, as listed below:

1/4th Bn	India, Mesopotamia, Persia
2/4th Bn	India, Palestine, Western Front
1/5th Bn	India, Burma, North West Frontier Afghanistan 1919
2/5th Bn	India, Palestine
1/6th Bn	India, Mesopotamia
2/6th Bn	UK
1/7th Bn	India, Aden
2/7th Bn	India, Mesopotamia
1/8th Bn	Gallipoli, Palestine
1/9th Bn	India, Siberia
2/9th Bn	UK

The Service Battalions

With the introduction of Lord Kitchener's great recruiting drive, The Hampshire Regiment also raised 5 Service Battalions. These were in existence only for the duration of the War and served in the following theatres of war:

10th (Service) Bn	Gallipoli, Salonika
11th (Service) Bn (Pioneers)	Western Front
12th (Service) Bn	Western Front, Salonika, Bulgaria
14th (Service) Bn	Western Front
15th (Service) Bn	Western Front, Italy

In addition, The Hampshire Regiment also raised a number of other battalions for duties in the rear areas of France, the Home Service Battalions which provided for the defence of the UK mainland and other training organisations, including:[1]

A Garrison Battalion
A Reserve Battalion
A Young Soldiers' Battalion
A Graduated Battalion
The Depot

The Hampshire Carabiniers Yeomanry

The Hampshire Carabiniers Yeomanry (HCY) was a Territorial Force cavalry unit independent of the Hampshire Regiment for most of its history.

At the beginning of the First World War the unit was split into two. The first line or 1/1st Hampshire Carabiniers Yeomanry went to serve on the Western Front and the 2/1st Hampshire Carabiniers Yeomanry became Cyclists and remained in the UK and Ireland.

In August 1917 while serving on the Western Front, the 1/1st HCY received orders that they were to be dismounted and converted to Infantry. They were to become part of the Hampshire Regiment and were posted to the 15th Battalion who also adopted their title becoming, 15th (Hampshire Carabiniers) Battalion, Hampshire Regiment.

This unit was converted to Royal Artillery in 1922.

---

[1] Charles Forbes Southcott (391) returned home in 1916 with malaria and was posted to the 17th Hampshires. He died at Herne Bay in 1918.
17th Battalion: Formed at Herne Bay on 1 January 1917 from what had previously been the 84th Provisional Battalion of the TF. It had been formed in June 1915 from "Home Service only" personnel. Moved to Whitstable in October 1917 and on in February 1918 to Southwold. We are grateful to Alan Bungey for this information.

APPENDIX THREE

SIX MEN IN ADDITION TO 'WINCHESTER'S 459'

Alan Bungey

✠**BRAMBLE, George, (7 Poulsom Place, Middle Brook Street)**
Son of John Bramble & Eliza Bramble (nee Arnold), of 7, Poulsom Place, Middle Brook Street, Winchester; husband of Kate Bramble, of 73, Cadogan Terrace, Victoria Park, London. 31587 Private 15th (Service) Battalion (2nd Portsmouth) Hampshire Regiment. Bramble had previously served for 12 years with the Hampshire Regiment between 1896 and 1908. On 7 December 1915 he re-enlisted under the terms of the Group Scheme (also known as the Derby Scheme). He was mobilised on 14 September 1916 and joined his old regiment. During the war, he served with 2nd, 11th and 15th Battalions of The Hampshire Regiment. He died of wounds on 28 October 1917 age 39. Wounds received on 20 September at the Battle of Menin Road Bridge, part of the Passchendaele campaign. Buried at Zuydcoote Military Cemetery, France. As a member of the '2nd Pompey Pals', George Bramble was remembered on the Portsmouth Football Club shirt for the 2014/2015 season.

✠**EDMONDS, Harry, (67 Lower Brook Street)**
Step-brother of Rose Swaffield, of 67, Lower Brook St, Winchester. Born St. Maurice Ward, Winchester, later living St. Denys and enlisted Southampton. He married Margaret Mary Kelly in Winchester in 1908. His number 3/4734 shows that he was a member of the Special Reserve, and as such, was mobilised at the outbreak of war in August 1914. He was a Sergeant in 2nd Battalion Hampshire Regt. when he was posted overseas in a draft of reinforcements destined for the Gallipoli campaign, on board His Majesty's Troop ship 'Royal Edward'. On 28 July 1915 HMT Royal Edward set sail from Avonmouth with 1,387 officers and men with reinforcements for the British 29th Infantry Division. Having stopped at Alexandria on 10 August, Royal Edward was heading for Moudros on the island of Lemnos when on the morning of 13 August German U-Boat UB-14 launched two torpedoes into the stern of 'Royal Edward', sinking it within 6 minutes in the Aegean Sea. Edmonds was reported missing believed drowned by the Admiralty along with 863 other men. His body was never recovered and he is remembered on the Helles Memorial.

✠ ILLINGWORTH, William Thomas, (86 Brassey Road)

Born in Romford, Essex in 1891. On 3 August 1913, listed as a dentist, he married Constance Edith Long at St. James's Church, Hackney. He was mobilised as number 36708 Private 10th (Service) Battalion, Gloucestershire Regiment 12 May 1916 having probably enlisted at Winchester under the short lived Group Scheme (also known as the Derby Scheme) sometime between October and December 1915 whilst living in the city. Served in France. Wounded 18 Nov 1916 and Died of Wounds the same day. High Wood, Somme. Buried Becourt Military Cemetery, Becordel-Becourt. Military records show his name as Thomas William and some census records name him as Thomas.

✠ MARTIN, Thomas George, (47 St. Johns Street)

Thomas Martin was born in St Pancras, London in 1880. In April 1911 he was boarding in Winchester at 58 St Johns Street with married couple, James and Katherine Jones. James Jones was employed as a Newspaper Machine Printer and Thomas Martin a Printer's Reader. On 3 June 1911 Martin was married to Beatrice Alice Temple, a shirt and collar machinist (b. 1886 Winchester) of 47 St Johns Street by the Revd Dickins, Vicar of St Johns Church, Winchester. Following their marriage Thomas and Beatrice lived at the family home, 47 St Johns Street, living with Beatrice's sister, mother and grandmother. They had two daughters, Doris Martin born 23 Oct. 1912 and Emily Jane Martin born 2 Jan. 1915. On 7 December 1914, Just before the birth of his second child, he travelled back to his birth place and enlisted into the 19th Battalion London Regiment as Private 3341 of D. Company. He embarked with his battalion at Southampton on 9 March 1915 and landed at Le Harve, France the next day. He was Killed in Action on 20 May 1915, north of Lens, France and is buried at Guards Cemetery, Windy Corner, Cuinchy and named on the Roll of Honour in St Johns Church, Winchester. His widow, Beatrice continued to live at 47 St Johns Street into the 1920s.

✠ RUSSELL, Charles Henry, (76 Lower Brook Street)

Sergeant 200016 1st/4th Hampshire Regt. Died 17 November 1918 age 31. Son of Charles and Emma Russell, 76 Lower Brook Street, Winchester. Although Russell is listed in the original Winchester War Service Register, there is no mention of him being a casualty and is not counted among the 459 Winchester men said to have died. Charles Henry Russell had joined the 4th Battalion Hampshire Regiment, Territorial Force, before the war, attaining the rank of sergeant. He was mobilised with the battalion in August 1914. The 1st/4th Battalion sailed for India on 9 October 1914 in order to replace regular troops, allowing them to return to fight in Western Europe. Early in 1915 the 1st/4th Battalion were sent to Mesopotamia as part of the 33rd Indian Brigade, landing at Basra on 15 March 1915.

Russell was taken prisoner by Turkish Forces on 29 April 1916 at Kut-el-Amara when the British Garrison led by Major General Charles Townshend

was forced to surrender following a four month siege. Like his father, also named Charles, Charles Henry Russell was a bell ringer in Winchester Cathedral and is named on the Cathedral's memorial to all Hampshire bell ringers who died in the Great War. In the Cathedral, there hangs a portrait of Sergeant Russell[1] with the following inscription "Charles Henry Russell, Sergeant 1/4 Hampshire Regiment, born 24th September 1887, Died in Turkey 17th November 1918 after being a prisoner of war for 2½ years. For 10 years a Ringer in this Cathedral."
Russell is buried at the Haidar Pasha Cemetery, Istanbul, Turkey.

✠YALDREN, Albert Cecil, (70 Lower Brook Street)
Son of William Henry and Edith Maude Yaldren, of 70, Lower Brook St., Winchester. Born in Winchester December 1899, he would have been conscripted upon his 18th birthday under the terms of the Military Service Act 1916. Posted to The Hampshire Regiment Dec. 1917 following a medical examination at Southampton, he was later transferred to 2nd Battalion Devonshire Regt. as Private 32224 before going overseas. Served in France. Killed in Action 14 September 1918 Arras, age 18. CWGC gives his death as 15 Sept. Buried at La Targette British Cemetery, Nueville-St Vaast. Military records show his name spelt YAULDREN, civil records show YALDREN which is most likely to be correct.

Alan Bungey
14 October 2018

---

1   See front cover for an image of Sergeant Russell.

APPENDIX FOUR

DEATHS BY STREET

The *WWSR* is not comprehensive as shown in the Introduction. However it undoubtedly contains the majority of names and addresses of those who died in the Great War.

In the discussions outlined above about the memorial townsfolk argued that they mainly entered the cathedral Close from the north as their main residential area lay north of High Street in The Brooks area and the northern and north-eastern suburbs. Jen Best's counting of the dead by street reinforces this point. The greatest loss in any area was in The Brooks (Lower, Middle and Upper Brook streets) where over 30 people gave their lives to which may be added a further three from that area identified in Appendix 3. The greatest loss of life from one street was from Wales Street, 15 (towards NE margin maps 2 and 3 below). Many also died from the northern suburb of St Bartholomew's Hyde. These numbers alone support the claim that the proposed – and indeed the memorial as erected to the west of the cathedral – was not sited where the majority of townspeople entered the Close as they came from the north. Suggestions that the memorial should be sited near Morley College almshouses, south of High Street, was mooted, but was not realised. The area south of High Street was largely occupied by the cathedral and its Close and the castle (barracks), with Winchester College and some of its possessions dominating the southern suburb with Wolvesey, the bishop's palace, and St Cross Hospital.

The plans of Winchester, and the enlargement of the Brooks area, on the following pages, are reproduced from Ordnance Survey mapping published in 1910.

Deaths according to street addresses in the *WWSR*

Airlie Road	1	City Road	1
Arthur Road	1	Colebrook Place	1
Barnes Close	1	Colebrook Road	1
Bridge Street	1	Connaught Terrace	1
Butts Close	1	Cossack Lane	1
Canute Road	1	Cross Keys Passage	1
Chesil Terrace	1	Crowder Terrace	1
Chilcomb Manor	1	Culver's Close	1

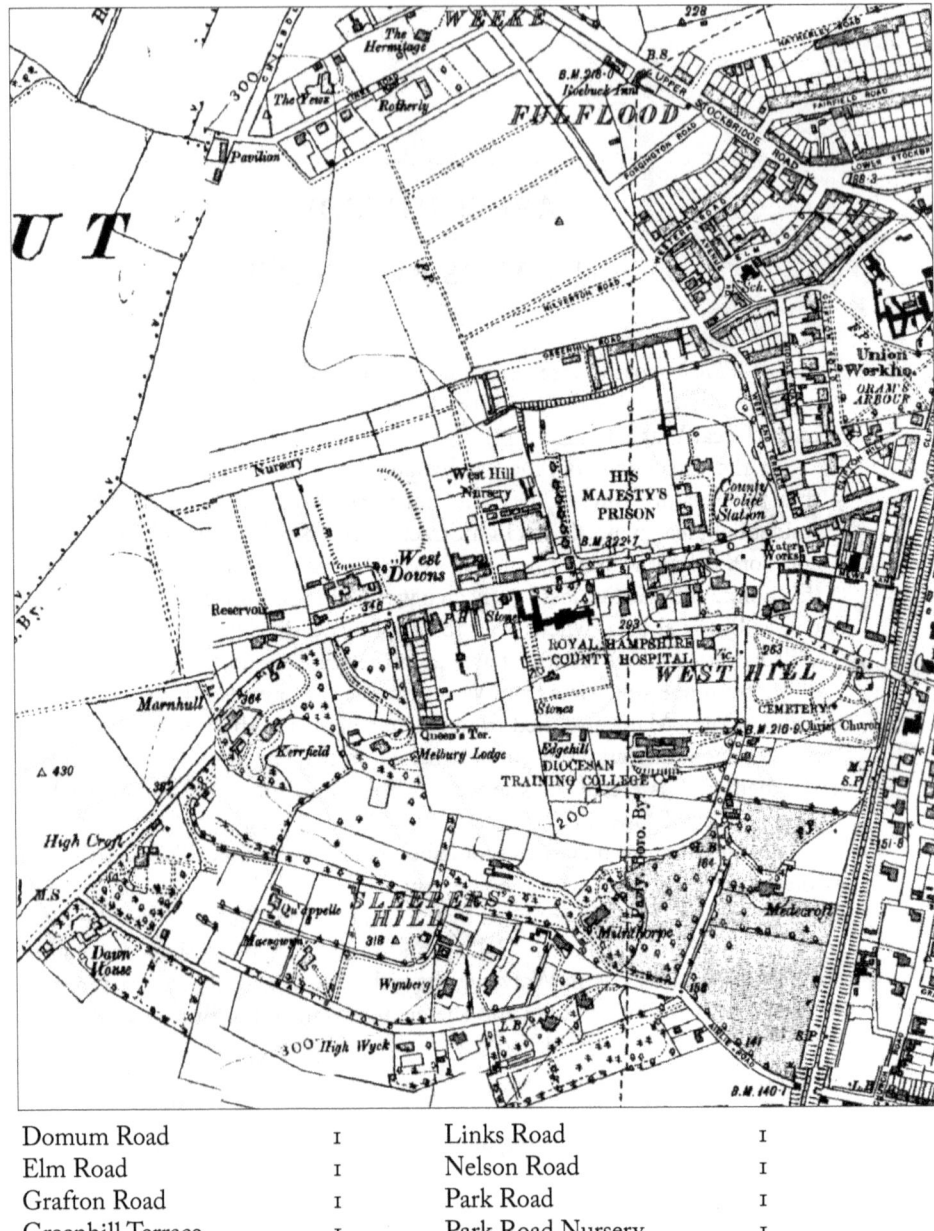

Domum Road	1	Links Road	1
Elm Road	1	Nelson Road	1
Grafton Road	1	Park Road	1
Greenhill Terrace	1	Park Road Nursery	1
Hillside Terrace	1	St Faith's Road	1
Hyde Church Path	1	St James's Villas	
Jewry Street	1	(?St James's Lane)	1
King Alfred Terrace	1	St Swithun Street	1
Kingsgate Road	1	The Square	1
Lankhills Road	1	The Weirs	1

Birinus Road	2	Mants Lane	2
Boundary Street	2	Milverton Road	2
Chester Road	2	Newburgh Street	2
Chilbolton Avenue	2	North View	2
Christ Church Road	2	Percy Terrace	2
Clifton Road	2	Queen's Road	2
College Street	2	Queen's Terrace	2
Cranworth Road	2	Queensland Terrace	2
Gladstone Street	2	Silver Hill	2
Highcliffe Park Farm	2	St Cross Road	2

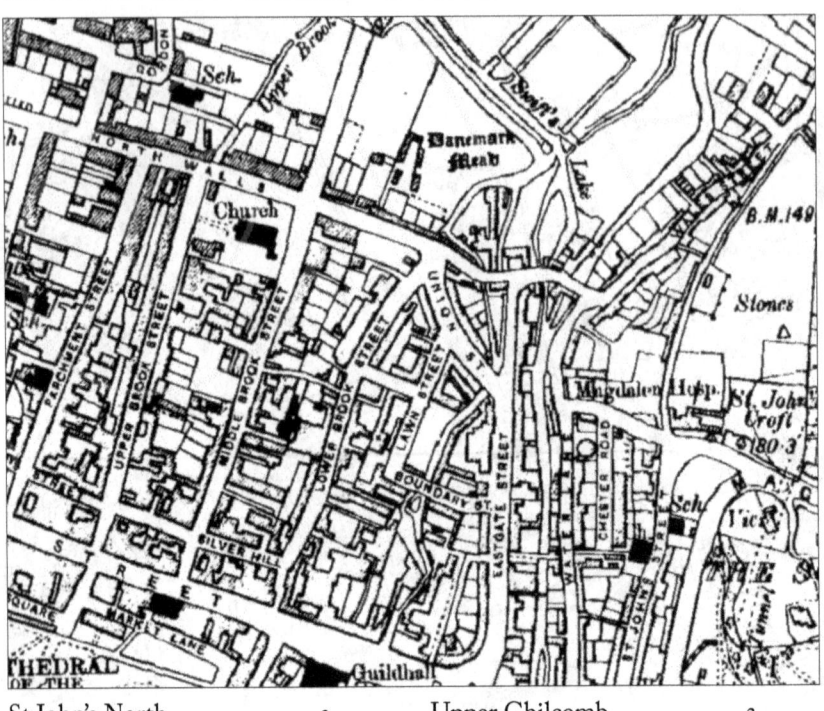

St John's North	2	Upper Chilcomb	3
St John's Park Terrace	2	Victoria Road	3
St John's Road	2	Bereweeke Road	4
St John's South	2	Brassey Road	4
The Close	2	Cross Street	4
Upper High Street	2	King Alfred Place	4
Abbey Passage	3	Kingsgate Street	4
Alswitha Terrace	3	St Thomas Street	4
Ashley Terrace	3	including Penarth Place (1)	
Avenue Road	3	Union Street	4
Clausentum Road	3	Weeke	4
Gordon Avenue	3	Western Road	4
Lawn Street	3	Cheriton Road	5
Ranelagh Road	3	Granville Place	5
Romsey Road	3	High Street	5
including Ilex Terrace (1)	3	Hyde Abbey Road	5
Sleeper's Hill	3	Little Minster Street	5
Southgate Street	3	Monks Road	5
St George's Street	3	St Clement Street	5
(St George's Terrace 3)	3	St Cross	5
St Leonard's Road	3	Bar End including	5
St Paul's Hill	3	Prinstead Terrace (1)	6
St Peter Street	3	Chesil Street	6

Colson Road	6	Stockbridge Road area including Osmond's Passage (Fulflood Wyke/Stockbridge Road)	9
Greenhill Road	6		
North Walls including Trinity Terrace (1)	6 6		
Nuns Road	6	Bar End including Prinstead Terrace (1)	9
St Catherine's Road	6		
Staple Garden	6	Canon Street	9
Culver Road including Maidstone Terrace (3)	7 7	Colebrook Street	9
		Eastgate Street	9
Fairfield Road	7	St John's Street, including St John's Terrace (3)	9
Hyde Street	7		
Sussex Street	7	Hyde Close	11
Tower Street	7	Lower Brook Street including Greyfriars Terrace (3), Greyfriars Villas (1)[1]	12
Upper Brook Street	7		
Westgate Lane	7		
Wharf Hill including Upper Wolvesey Terrace (1) and Lower Wolvesey Terrace (3)	7		
		Middle Brook Street including Freelands Buildings (4) Poulsome Place (1), Lansdowne Terrace (1)	12
Andover Road	8		
Egbert Road	8		
Parchment Street	8		
Alresford Road including Hedges Buildings (4)	9	Wales Street	15

[1] See Appendix 3 for further deaths from Lower Brook Street.

APPENDIX FIVE

CASUALTIES BY RANK ETC

Jen Best has counted the following numbers from the *WWSR* to provide information on deaths by service (Navy, Army, RFC/RAF etc); by age; by enlistment; by year of the war; cause and places of death; by rank; by theatre of war. These figures are of course indicative. However they show how important the Western Front was during the war, also reminding us of the significance, especially for The Hampshire Regiment who were also embroiled in the disaster at Kut and elsewhere in the Middle East as well as serving in India. The loss of nearly three dozen sailors indicates the importance of the Navy.

There remains much work to be done, but we hope that what we have achieved to date will be of value.

Services
How many Navy? 35
How many Army? 421
How many RFC/RAF? 3

Age
How many aged under 25? 153
How many aged under 19? 15
How many 25 and over? 229
77 unknown age at date of death

Pre-war Enlisted
How many pre-war who enlisted died?
115 who enlisted in 1913 or before
11 who rejoined in August 1914
1 who rejoined in March 1915
1 who rejoined date unknown

How many pre-war who enlisted survived?
548 who enlisted in 1913 or before

83 who re-enlisted after 1914

Years
How many died for each year of the war?
1914   35
1915   66
1916   123
1917   111
1918   102
1919   16
unknown   6

How many died in Britain? 34, mainly based on cemetery information and where they were at time of death
How many died of disease/exposure? 20 definitely, some simply stated as died so possibly more.
How many died as POWs? 33
How many killed in action?
293 Killed, Killed in action, drowned but this does not include any of the

Died of Wounds. This may be a misleading statistic.
19 died of wounds, but different sources say KIA and DOW so uncertain. This does not include those who are stated as simply died.
How many missing presumed dead? 23

Ranks and Designations
Which ranks and designations died (both officers and men)?

In the following list ranks from which fewer than 15 died are followed by their surnames alphabetically.

Private 175

Lance-Corporal 33

No known rank 29

Corporal 26

Sergeant 26

Rifleman 21

Stoker 17

Captain 14
Bosanquet, Braithwaite, Bunbury, Causton, Dyer, Elgee, Gale, Gifford, Gudgeon, Gye, Hill, Lewis, Mayo, Russell

Lieutenant 14
Bligh, Cancellor, Clowes, Dennistoun, Fielder, Germain, Gudgeon, Lewis, Loveland, Mathews, Mayo, Openshaw, Scott, Waud Tetley

2nd Lieutenant 11
Bartlett, Cook, Cowan, Gould, Hall, Newton, Simmons, Stevens, Till, Tunks, Vacher

Gunner 11
Andrews, Brewer, Bugg, Burrows, Godsell, Hawkins, Kibble, Kilford, Martin, Mathews, Tuffin

Trooper 9
Cobb, Dobson, Drake, Groves, Jupe, Maslin, Osborne, Smith, Whicher

Company Sergeant Major 8
Brown, Churcher, Coles, Fielder, Lloyd, Lund, Page, Wyatt

Able Seaman 7
Andrews, Loader, Offer, Stanley, Tollman, Willis, Wyatt

Major 5
Bell, Brown, Clark, Forster, Morrah

Signaller 5
Carter, Dowse, Fraser, Norgate, Watson

Company Quartermaster Sergeant 4
Beckingham, Bogie, Bosworth, Penson

Bombardier 4
Andrews, Dunmill, Lawrence, Long

Leading Seaman 3
Adams, Groves, Parr

Petty Officer 3
Axe, Head, Johnson

Regimental Sergeant Major 3
Adams, Head, Leach

Acting Sergeant 2
Bright, Wake

Boy 2
Cassidy, Sawle

Driver 2
Smart, Summerbell

Drummer 2
Eade, Rickman

Lieutenant and Quartermaster 2
Bartlett, Kemish

Lieutenant-Colonel 2
Baring, Hamilton

Sergeant Major 2
Hedge, Laverty

1st Air Mechanic Dickinson,
2nd Air Mechanic Hawkins,
Acting Company Quartermaster Sergeant Shore
Artificer Jupe
Blacksmith's Mate Alexander

Brigadier-General Maclachlan
Bugler Sticklan
Cadet Alexander
Chief Cook Winkworth
Chief Gunnery instructor Wedge
Conductor Bellinger
Ordinary Seaman Patterson
Sapper Page
Staff Captain Bishop
Staff Sergeant Facey
Sub-Lieutenant Briggs
Yeoman of Signals Dowse

Theatres of War statistics
Gibraltar 1
East Africa 2
Germany 3
Balkans 5
Unknown 10
Home 25
Sea 33
Dardanelles 34
Middle East 85
Western Front 261

SELECT BIBLIOGRAPHY

Primary Sources
The National Achive, Public Record Office (TNA PRO)
ADM 188 Royal Naval Ratings Records (Online including Service and Awards).
WO 95 Battalion Diaries.
WO 97 Army Service Record.
WO 100/231 Boer War Register (see C Kemish, W Laverty).
WO 339 Service Papers (see William Mathews)
WO 372 Soldiers' Medal Index Cards (Online)
1911 Census. RG 14 etc. Online transcription used. Original checked in apparently problem cases.
CWGC Commonwealth War Graves Commission (online) contains details of places of burial/commemoration, also on occasion names and addresses of parents, wives etc.
England and Wales Birth Transcriptions 1837-2007.
IWM Indexes. E.g. Private Papers for Captain Alexander Mayo's two Flying Log Books.
Hampshire Archives and Local Studies Centre (HALS)
HRO W/B5/40/1 War Memorial Committee minutes etc

Printed works
9th Marquis de Ruvigny et al., n.d. *The Roll of Honour: A Biographical Record of All members of His Majesty's Naval and Military Forces who have Fallen in the War*. 5 Volumes. References here to de Ruvigny all online. [1]
C. T. Atkinson, *The Royal Hampshire Regiment to 1914*. Vol 1 (The Regiment: 1950)
C. T. Atkinson (ed), *The Royal Hampshire Regiment 1914-18*. Vol 2 (Glasgow: Glasgow University Press, 1952)
BMD [Births, Marriages, Deaths]. Online.. Various: Civil Registration Events: [Births, Marriages, Deaths]; Armed Forces [Births, Marriages and Deaths, General Register Office, War Deaths Other Ranks etc]
Vera Brittain, 1933. *Testamant of Youth* (London: Victor Gollancz)

---

[1] Not a complete record. Covers some 25,000 people and contains some 7.000 photographs. A mixture of official records and contributions from families etc from personal knowledge. See below Albert Gibson, for example: *WWSR* states 'Killed in Action' de Ruvigny states died of wounds. Better for the early part of the war. Large number of casualties made the project unviable.

Creagh, O'Moore and E. M. Humphris, n.d. *The V.C. and D.S.O. A complete record of all those officers, non-commissioned officers and men of His Majesty's naval, military and air forces who have been awarded these decorations from the time of their institution, with descriptions of the deeds and services which won the distinctions and with many biographical and other details.* (3 vols, London: The Standard Art Book Co. Ltd.).

A. S. Evans, 1986. *Beneath the Waves: a History of HM Submarine Losses 1904-71.* (London: William Kimber).

David Hepper, 2006. *British Warship Losses in the Ironclad Era 1860-1919* (London: Chatham Publishing).

Mark Hichens, 1992. *West Downs: a portrait of and English Prep* School (Pentland Press); also A4 information sheet by JEA/RNA 11 November 2012 for memorial.

The Monthly Army List, September 1918. (HMSO).

V. Hope, 1933. *St Peter's College, Radley Register 1847-1933.* (Oxford: OUP for The Radleian Society).

The Oxford and Buckinghamshire Light Infantry Chronicle. (References courtesy of K. Gray).

A. Cecil Piper (ed), 1921. *Winchester War Service Register. A Record of the Service of Winchester Men in the Great War 1914-1918* (Winchester: Warren and Co.).

M. J. Rendall (ed.), 1921. *Wykehamists who Died in the Great War,* four volumes (Winchester).

Andrew Renshaw, 2014. *Wisden on The Great War: the Lives of Cricket's Fallen 1914-1918* (London: Wisden).

The Rifle Brigade Chronicle. 1923 (Reference courtesy of K. Gray).

Hew Strachan, rp. 2014. *The First World War* (Simon & Schuster).

Kate Tiller, 2014. *Remembrance and Community: War Memorials and Local History* (British Association for Local History).

Samuel Walls, 2013. 'The changing Memories and Meanings of the First World War Expressed through Commemorations in Exeter, Devon' in *Historical Archaeologies of Cognition*, ed. James Symonds, Anna Badcock and Jeff Oliver (Equinox, Sheffield) pp. 176-190.

The Wykehamist October 19th 1917 (No 567).

Unpublished Dissertations

Claire Atkins, 1999 'A study of military monuments and service in First World War Winchester'. BA Undergraduate Dissertation Archaeology and Computing, King Alfred's College Winchester.

Derek Whitfield, 2015, 'To what extent and why did voluntaryism characterise Winchester's response to the War in 1914 and 1915.' University of Birmingham MA.

Many Web Sources have been consulted and are found in notes above referring to sources and individuals.

THE AUTHORS

JEN BEST writes:
I've always had an interest in history, inspired by my father who talked history instead of bedtime stories. In 2002 I began an archaeology degree at Winchester and also visted Flanders, staying at Talbot House with my mother. I became fascinated with the First World War. Professor Tom James gave us a tour of Winchester, starting with St Giles Hill. I was distracted by the Commonwealth War Graves, which got us talking. I took on the research of 458 of the men who died and have spent several years creating biographies for each man. Meanwhile I have established and run Beaker Button Fibre Craft Shop at Weyhill, Hampshire from which I travel widely to teach and encourage craft on which I have published a number of books.

TOM BEAUMONT JAMES, MBE, PhD, FSA lived in Winchester on and off for some 50 years. His publications on the city include *Winchester: a pictorial history* (1993 including an image of a tank driving into the city) and *Winchester: from Prehistory to the Present* (rp 2010). In Paris in 1916 his father completed *The Story of France 1814-1914* for the troops, In filial piety *The Story of England* (rp. 2013) followed almost a century later. Retired from the University of Winchester on which he published a 175th anniversary account in 2015 he now works on the Winchester Project, to establish property histories in the city 1550 to the present. An expert on medieval palaces he travels to and volunteers at Clarendon Palace, Wiltshire whenever he can.

www.ingramcontent.com/pod-product-compliance
Lightning Source LLC
Chambersburg PA
CBHW070949160426
43193CB00012B/1815